LEADING CASES ON THE LAW OF THE EUROPE

EUROPA INSTITUTE
UNIVERSITY OF AMSTERDAM

LEADING CASES ON THE LAW OF THE EUROPEAN COMMUNITIES

FIFTH EDITION

Edited by

M. van Empel, H.G. Schermers,
E.L.M. Völker, J.A. Winter

KLUWER LAW AND TAXATION PUBLISHERS
Deventer • Boston

Kluwer Law and Taxation Publishers
P.O. Box 23   Tel: 31-5700-47261
7400 GA Deventer   Telex: 49295
The Netherlands   Fax: 31-5700-22244

Library of Congress Cataloging-in-Publication Data

Leading cases on the law of the European communities. – 5th Ed.
edited by M. van Empel ... [et al.]
   p. cm.
   At head of title: Europa Institute, University of Amsterdam.
   Includes bibliographical references.
   ISBN 9065442359
   1. Law–European Economic Community countries–Cases.   I. Empel,
M. van.   II. European Economic Community.   III. Universiteit van
Amsterdam. Europa Instituut.
KJE947.L4   1990
341.24′22–dc20   89–39501
                                                                  CIP

ISBN 90 6544 235 9

© 1990, Kluwer Law and Taxation Publishers, Deventer/The Netherlands

All rights reserved. No part of this publication may be reproduced, stored in a retrieval system, or transmitted in any form or by any means, electronic, mechanical, photocopying, recording or otherwise, without the prior written permission of the publisher.

Introduction to the fifth edition

It has taken rather more time to prepare the fifth edition than the previous ones. Most of this delay has been caused by a change in the editors team and a change in the reproduction technics.

To prevent any confusion on the side of the readers the editors have stayed as closely as possible to the original outline of the book.

This edition has been updated upto 1 January 1989.

We would like to thank professor R.H. Lauwaars for arranging Chapter One on the Institutions of the European Communities. Chapter Two, concerning the Court of Justice of the EC was arranged by Professor H.G. Schermers, while Professor J.A. Winter dealt with Chapter Three on the relationship between Community law and national law. Professor M. van Empel was in charge of most of Chapter Four and Five on the Foundations and the Policy of the Community. E.L.M. Völker finally, was responsible for the remainder of Chapters Four and Five and for Chapter Six on the external competence of the EC and on the Common Commercial Policy.

We like to thank Geert W. van der Klis for his valuable editorial and research assistance in preparing this edition.

Amsterdam, June 1989

M. van Empel, H.G. Schermers, E.L.M. Völker, J.A. Winter

Abbreviations

CDE	–	Cahiers de Droit Européen
CMLR	–	Common Market Law Reports
CMLRev.	–	Common Market Law Review
Competition Law	–	D.J. Gijlstra ed. Competition Law in Western Europe and the United States, Kluwer, Deventer
EAEC	–	European Atomic Energy Community
EC	–	European Communities
ECR	–	European Court Reports
ECSC	–	European Coal and Steel Community
EEC	–	European Economic Community
ELRev.	–	European Law Review
EUR	–	Europarecht
FIDE	–	Féderation Internationale pour le droit Européen
GATT	–	General Agreement on Tariffs and Trade
G and O	–	Government and Opposition
Gen. Rep.	–	General Report on the Activities of the European Communities
ICLQ	–	International and Comparative Law Quarterly
JCMS	–	Journal of Common Market Studies
JCP	–	Juris Classeur Periodique
JO	–	Journal Officiel de Communautés Européennes
JT	–	Journal des Tribunaux
Jud. Rem.	–	Judicial Remedies in the European Communities, a case book (Brinkhorst and Schermers, 2^d ed. Deventer 1977)
JWTL	–	Journal of World Trade Law

LIEI	–	Legal Issues of European Integration
LQR	–	Law Quarterly Review
NLJ	–	New Law Journal
OJ	–	Official Journal of the European Communities
Rec. D	–	Receuil Dalloz
RIW	–	Recht der Internationalen Wirtschaft
RMC	–	Revue du Marché Commun
RTDE	–	Revue Trimesterielle de Droit Européen
SEW	–	Sociaal Economische Wetgeving
YEL	–	Yearbook of European Law

Contents

Introduction to the fifth edition v
Abbreviations vii

CHAPTER ONE
LANGUAGES, TERRITORIAL APPLICATION AND INSTITUTIONS
OF THE EUROPEAN COMMUNITIES 1

I. Languages 1

II. Territorial application 1

III. Institutions 1
   A. Cases 1
      (1) *Netherlands – High Authority Case* (66/63) 1
      (2) *Reynier and Erba Cases* (79, 82/63) 2
      (3) *Mills Case* (110/75) 4
   B. Materials 5

IV. Powers of the Council and the Commission of the
    European Communities 5
   A. Powers of attribution 5
     1. Introduction 5
     2. Literature 6
   B. Article 235 EEC 6
     1. Introduction 6
     2. Cases 6
       (1) *ERTA Case* (22/70) 6
       (2) *Lead and Zinc Case* (38/69) 10
       (3) *Massey-Ferguson Case* (8/73) 12
     3. Literature 13
   C. Implied Powers 13
     1. Introduction 13
     2. Cases 14
       (1) *Publication of Transport Tariffs Case I* (25/59) 14
     3. Literature 17
   D. Powers of delegation 17

1. Introduction	17
2. Cases	18
(1) *Meroni Case I* (9/56)	18
(2) *Netherlands – High Authority Case* (66/63)	18
(3) *Köster Case* (25/70)	18
(4) *Tedeschi Case* (5/77)	21
(5) *Opinion of the Court* (1/76)	23
(6) *Akzo Chemie Case* (5/85)	29
3. Literature	32

V. The legally binding acts of the Council and the Commission 32
   A. General character 33
      1. Introduction 33
      2. Cases 33
         (1) *Lead and Zinc Case* (38/69) 33
      3. Literature 33
   B. Is the enumeration of Community acts in Article 189
     EEC exhaustive? 33
      1. Introduction 33
      2. Cases 34
         (1) *Dairy Products Case* (90, 91/63) 34
   C. The binding acts of Article 189 EEC 36
      1. Regulations 36
        a. Introduction 36
        b. Cases 36
           (1) *Zuckerfabrik Watenstedt Case* (6/68) 36
           (2) *Turkey Tail Case* (40/69) 38
           (3) *Slaughtered Cow Case II* (39/72) 40
      2. Directives 41
        a. Introduction 41
        b. Cases 42
           (1) *Marketing of vegetable seed Case* (52/75) 42
           (2) *Enka Case* (38/77) 43
        c. Literature 44
      3. Decisions 44
        a. Introduction 44
        b. Cases 45
           (1) *Cement Convention Case* (8–11/66) 45

VI. Acts of the representatives of the Governments of the Member
    States meeting within the Council of Ministers 45
   A. Introduction 45
      1. Literature 45

CHAPTER TWO
THE COURT OF JUSTICE OF THE EUROPEAN COMMUNITIES 47

I. Introduction 47
   A. Review of the legality of Community acts 47
      1. Action for annulment 47
      2. Action against failure to act 48
      3. Plea of illegality 48
      4. Interim measures 48
   B. Unlimited jurisdiction 48
   C. The role of national courts 49
   D. Actions against Member States 49
   E. Procedures 50
   F. Literature 50

II. Judicial review of Community acts 50
    A. Action for annulment 50
       1. Acts susceptible of judicial review 50
          a. Cases 51
             (1) *Geitling Case I* (2/56) 51
             (2) *ERTA Case* (22/70) 51
             (3) *IBM Case* (60/81) 53
       2. Capacity to bring an action 55
          a. There must be a legal act 55
             i. Cases 55
                (1) *Cement Convention Case* (8–11/66) 55
          b. The act must be a decision 57
             i. Cases 57
                (1) *CAM Case* (100/74) 57
                (2) *Scholten-Honig Case I* (101/76) 59
                (3) *Giuffrida Case II* (64/80) 60
          c. Direct and individual concern 61
             i. Cases 61
                (1) *Plaumann Case* (25/62) 61
                (2) *Toepfer Case* (106–107/63) 63
                (3) *International Fruit Company Case I* (41–44/70) .. 65
                (4) *Chinese Mushrooms Case* (62/70) 67
                (5) *COFAZ Case* (169/84) 69
       3. Grounds of illegality 72
          a. Competence 73
             i. Cases 73
                (1) *Meroni Case I* (9/56) 73
          b. Misuse of powers 76
             i. Cases 76
                (1) *Giuffrida Case I* (105/75) 76

			c. Essential procedural requirements	77
			i. Cases	77
			(1) *Brennwein Case* (24/62)	77
			(2) *Beus Case* (5/67)	79
			(3) *Maizena Case* (139/79)	79
			(4) *ICI Case* (48/69)	81
			d. Infringement of the Treaty or of any rule of law relating to its application	82
			i. Cases	82
			(1) *Handelsgesellschaft Case* (11/70)	82
			(2) *International Fruit Company Case III* (21–24/72)	84
			(3) *Nold Case II* (4/73)	85
		B.	Action against failure to act	87
			1. Cases	87
			(1) *Eridania Case I* (10, 18/68)	87
			(2) *Chevalley Case* (15/70)	88
			(3) *Steel subsidies Case* (59/70)	89
		C.	Plea of illegality	91
			1. Cases	91
			(1) *Meroni Case I* (9/56)	91
			(2) *Wöhrmann Case* (33/62)	93
			(3) *Belgian Railway subsidies Case* (156/77)	94
		D.	Interim measures	94
			1. Cases	94
			(1) *Ilford Order* (1/84 R)	94
		E.	Effect of annulment	96
III.	Unlimited jurisdiction			97
	A.	Non-contractual liability		97
		1. Introduction		97
		2. Cases		97
		(1) *Kampffmeyer Case I* (5, 7, 13–24/66)		97
		(2) *Lütticke Case III* (4/69)		100
		(3) *CNTA Case* (74/74)		102
		(4) *Krohn Case II* (175/84)		105
	B.	Action against penalties		107
		1. Cases		108
		(1) *Boehringer Case I* (45/69)		108
IV.	Preliminary rulings			109
	A.	Introduction		109
	B.	Competence of the Court of Justice		110
		1. Cases		110
		(1) *Van Gend en Loos Case* (26/62)		110
		(2) *Costa-ENEL Case* (6/64)		114

		(3) *Schwarze Case* (15/65)	115
		(4) *Foglia Novello Case II* (244/80)	116
	C.	The request for a preliminary ruling appealed	117
		1. Introduction	117
		2. Cases	118
		(1) *Bosch Case* (13/61)	118
		(2) *Chanel Case* (31/68)	119
		(3) *Rheinmühlen Case* (166/73)	120
	D.	The obligation to request preliminary rulings	121
		1. Cases	121
		(1) *Costa-ENEL Case* (6/64)	121
		(2) *Hoffmann-La Roche Case I* (107/76)	122
		(3) *Da Costa-Schaake Case* (28–30/62)	123
		(4) *CILFIT Case I* (238/81)	124
		(5) *FOTO-FROST Case* (314/85)	126
	E.	Competence to request preliminary rulings	128
		1. Cases	128
		(1) *Widow Vaassen Case* (61/65)	128
		(2) *Nordsee Case II* (102/81)	129
	F.	Effect of preliminary rulings on the validity	131
		1. Cases	131
		(1) *International Chemical Corporation Case* (66/80)	131
		(2) *Roquette Case IV* (145/79)	133
V.	Action against Member States		134
	A. Introduction		134
	B. Cases		135
		(1) *Tax Refund in Italy Case* (45/64)	135
		(2) *Wool imports Case* (7/69)	137
		(3) *Wood Case* (77/69)	138
		(4) *Lütticke Case I* (48/65)	139
		(5) *Art Treasures Case II* (48/71)	140
		(6) *Kohlegesetz Case* (70/72)	142
		(7) *Public insurance Case* (226/87)	143
		(8) *Wine Case* (42/82 R)	144
VI.	Procedure		146
	A. Sources		146
	B. Languages		146
	C. Proceedings		146
	D. Time Limits		148
	E. Effects of proceedings		148
	F. Costs		148
	G. Special proceedings		149
		1. Preliminary rulings	149

```
        2. Intervention .......................................... 149
    H. Court of First Instance ................................. 150

VII. Questions to be discussed ................................. 156


CHAPTER THREE
THE RELATIONSHIP BETWEEN COMMUNITY LAW AND
NATIONAL LAW .............................................. 159

I.   Introduction ............................................. 159

II.  The development of Community law as an autonomous system ... 160
     A. The Community's New Legal Order ....................... 160
        1. Cases ............................................. 160
           (1) Van Gend en Loos Case (26/62) .................. 160
           (2) Costa-ENEL Case (6/64) ........................ 161
     B. Division of competences, obligations of the Member States ... 163
        1. Introduction ...................................... 163
        2. Cases ............................................. 165
           (1) Reliable Importers Case (39/70) ................ 165
           (2) Walt Wilhelm Case (14/68) ..................... 167
           (3) ERTA Case (22/70) ............................ 169
     C. Autonomy of Community law vis-à-vis national law
        (fundamental rights) .................................. 172
        1. Introduction ...................................... 172
        2. Cases ............................................. 174
           (1) Stauder Case (26/69) .......................... 174
           (2) Handelsgesellschaft Case (11/70) ................ 174
           (3) Nold Case II (4/73) ........................... 174
           (4) Hauer Case (44/79) ........................... 175
        3. Literature ........................................ 176

III. Legal effect of Community law in the municipal legal order –
     the concept of direct applicability .......................... 176
     A. Introduction .......................................... 176
        1. General .......................................... 176
        2. Literature ........................................ 177
     B. Conditions for direct applicability ...................... 177
        1. Development of the concept with regard to provisions
           of the Treaty ..................................... 177
        2. Direct effect of secondary Community law ............. 180
           a. Regulations .................................... 180
           b. Decision and directives ......................... 180
        3. Cases ............................................. 181
           (1) Grad Case (9/70) ............................. 181
```

	(2) *Tax deduction Case* (51/76)	184
	(3) *Ratti Case* (148/78)	186
	(4) *Becker Case* (8/81)	188
	(5) *Marshall Case* (152/84)	189
	(6) *Kolpinghuis Case* (80/86)	193
	4. Direct effect of international agreements	194
C.	Some implications of direct effect	195
	1. Cases	195
	(1) *Slaughtered Cow Case I* (93/71)	195
	(2) *Slaughtered Cow Case II* (39/72)	197
	(3) *Comet Case* (45/76)	198
	(4) *Simmenthal Case II* (106/77)	200

IV. Conflicts between legal systems: the supremacy question – national constitutions and the attitude of municipal courts 203
  A. Introduction 203
  B. Constitutions of the original Member States containing an explicit recognition of the supremacy of Treaty Law 205
    1. The Netherlands 205
    2. France 206
      a. Introduction 206
      b. Cases 206
        (1) *French Ramel Case* 206
        (2) *French Vabres Case* 208
  C. Constitutions of the original Member States not containing an explicit recognition of the supremacy of Treaty Law 210
    1. Belgium 210
      a. Introduction 210
      b. Cases 210
        (1) *Belgian Fromagerie Le Ski Case* 210
    2. Germany 212
      a. Introduction 212
      b. Cases 214
        (1) *German Handelsgesellschaft Case* 214
    3. Italy 221
      a. Introduction 221
      b. Cases 221
        (1) *Italian Costa ENEL Case* 221
        (2) *Italian Frontini Case* 223
        (3) *Italian ICIC Case* 225
        (4) *Italian Granital Case* 226
  D. Constitutional rules of the 'new' Member States 228
    1. Ireland 228
      a. Constitutional provisions 228
      b. Commentary 230
    2. Denmark 231

   a. Constitutional provisions 231
   b. Commentary 231
  3. United Kingdom 232
   a. The constitutional position 232
   b. The European Communities Act 1972 234
   c. The supremacy of Community Law 235
  4. Greece 237
   a. Constitutional provisions 237
   b. Commentary 237
  5. Spain 238
  6. Portugal 239

CHAPTER FOUR
FOUNDATIONS OF THE COMMUNITY 241

I. Introduction 241

II. General Principles 242
  A. Objectives of the EEC 242
   1. Cases 242
    (1) *French Maritime Labour Code Case* (167/73) 242
  B. Member States' obligations 244
   1. Cases 244
    (1) *Deutsche Grammophon Case* (78/70) 244
    (2) *ERTA Case* (22/70) 245
    (3) *International Fruit Company Case II* (51–54/71) 246
    (4) *Rewe Case* (33/76) 246
  C. Non discrimination 249
   1. Cases 249
    (1) *Refrigerators Case* (13/63) 249
    (2) *Hochstrass Case* (147/79) 250
    (3) *Oebel Case* (155/80) 252
  D. Literature 254

III. The four freedoms 254
  A. Free movement of goods 254
   1. The Customs Union: all trade in goods 254
    a. Cases 254
     (1) *Art treasures Case I* (7/68) 254
   2. Elimination of customs duties between the Member States
    and the setting up of the Common Customs Tariff 255
    a. Customs duties 255
     i. Cases 255
     (1) *Van Gend en Loos Case* (26/62) 255
    b. Charges having an equivalent effect as customs duties .. 256

		i. Cases	256
		(1) *Statistical Levy Case* (24/68)	256
		(2) *Capolongo Case* (47/72)	260
		(3) *Bauhuis Case* (46/76)	262
	c.	Internal taxation	264
		i. Cases	264
		(1) *Lütticke Case II* (57/65)	264
		(2) *Statens Kontrol Case* (142/77)	267
		(3) *Taxation of Alcohol in Ireland Case* (55/79)	272
		(4) *Taxation of Alcohol in Denmark Case* (171/78) ...	274
		(5) *Vinal Case* (46/80)	283
		(6) *Schul Case I* (15/81)	285
	d.	Customs legislation	292
		i. Cases	292
		(1) *Turkey tail Case* (40/69)	292
		(2) *Deutsche Bakels Case* (14/70)	294
		(3) *Überseehandel Case* (49/76)	296

3. Elimination of quantitative restrictions between Member States and measures having equivalent effect 299
   a. Cases 299
      (1) *Salgoil Case* (13/68) 299
      (2) *Dassonville Case* (8/74) 302
      (3) *Van Tiggele Case* (82/77) 304
      (4) *Cassis de Dijon Case* (120/78) 306
      (4a) *Sequel*: Communication Commission concerning Cassis de Dijon 309
      (5) *Groenveld Case* (15/79) 312
      (6) *Fietje Case* (27/80) 313
      (7) *Oebel Case* (155/80) 316
      (8) *Buy Irish Case* (249/81) 318
      (9) *Cinéthèque Case* (60–61/84) 320
4. Public morality, public policy, public security, protection of health, national treasures, industrial policy 323
   a. Cases 323
      (1) *Art Treasures Case I* (7/68) 323
      (2) *Centrafarm-Sterling Drug Case* (15/74) 324
      (3) *De Peijper Case* (104/75) 329
      (4) *EMI-CBS Case* (51/75) 334
      (5) *Terrapin-Terranova Case* (119/75) 336
      (6) *Ratti Case* (148/78) 339
      (7) *Obscene articles Case* (34/79) 339
      (8) *Eyssen Case* (53/80) 345
      (9) *Commission-Italy Case* (95/81) 348
      (10) *Campus Oil Case* (72/83) 348
5. Literature 352
B. Workers 353

1. Free movement of workers 353
   a. General 353
   b. Direct applicability of Article 48 and
      Regulation 1612/68 356
      i. Cases 356
         (1) *French Maritime Labour Code Case* (167/73) 356
         (2) *Van Duyn Case* (41/74) 357
   c. Article 48(2): abolition of discrimination 358
      i. Cases 358
         (1) *Ugliola Case* (15/69) 358
         (2) *Sotgiu Case* (152/73) 360
         (3) *Casagrande Case* (9/74) 361
         (4) *Choquet in re driving licence Case* (16/78) 363
         (5) *Saunders Case* (175/78) 364
   d. Article 48(3): limitations on grounds of public policy,
      public security or public health 366
      i. Cases 366
         (1) *Van Duyn Case* (41/74) 366
         (2) *Bonsignore Case* (67/74) 370
         (3) *Rutili Case* (36/75) 372
         (4) *German Aliens Act Case* (8/77) 374
         (5) *Bouchereau Case* (30/77) 378
         (6) *Pecastaing Case* (98/79) 382
   e. Article 48(4): employment in public service 383
      i. Cases 383
         (1) *Sotgiu Case* (152/73) 383
         (2) *Belgian employment in public service Case*
             (149/79) 383
2. Social Security 387
   a. General 387
   b. Cases 393
      (1) *Hoekstra-Unger Case* (75/63) 393
      (2) *Hessische Knapschaft Case* (44/65) 395
      (3) *Costa Case* (39/74) 396
      (4) *Janssen Case* (23/71) 397
      (5) *Massonet Case* (50/75) 399
      (6) *Petroni Case* (24/75) 401
      (7) *Pinna Case* (41/84) 404
3. Literature 406
C. Right of establishment and the freedom to provide services ... 406
1. Right of establishment 406
   a. Cases 406
      (1) *Costa-ENEL Case* (6/64) 406
      (2) *Reyners Case* (2/74) 407
      (3) *Royer Case* (48/75) 411
      (4) *Thieffry Case* (71/76) 414

            (5) *Patrick Case* (11/77) 417
            (6) *Auer Case* (136/78) 420
            (7) *Knoors Case* (115/78) 423
            (8) *Broekmeulen Case* (246/80) 428
            (9) *Klopp Case* (107/83) 428
            (10) *Daily Mail Case* (81/87) 431
      2. Freedom to provide services 434
         a. Cases 434
            (1) *Van Binsbergen Case* (33/74) 434
            (2) *Walrave-Koch Case* (36/74) 438
            (3) *Van Wesemael Case* (110–111/78) 441
            (4) *Debauve Case* (52/79) 443
            (5) *Webb Case* (279/80) 446
            (6) *Coditel Case I* (62/79) 448
            (7) *Coditel Case II* (262/81) 449
            (8) *Luisi and Carbone Case* (286/82–26/83) 450
            (9) *Gravier Case* (293/83) 454
            (10) *German insurance Case* (205/84) 454
      3. Literature 467
   D. Capital 467
      1. Cases 467
         (1) *Thompson Case* (7/78) 467
         (2) *Casati Case* (203/80) 469
         (3) *Luisi and Carbone Case* (286/82–26/83) 474
         (4) *Brugnoni Case* (157/85) 478
      2. Literature 481

CHAPTER FIVE
POLICY OF THE COMMUNITY 483

I.   Introduction 483

II. Competition policy 484
     A. Rules applying to undertakings 484
        1. Principles common to Articles 85 and 86 484
           a. Scope of application of Articles 85 and 86 484
              i. Ratione territorii 484
                  aa. Cases 484
                      (1) *Woodpulp Case* (89, 104, 114, 116–117,
                          125–129/85) 484
              ii. Ratione materiae 487
                  aa. Cases 487
                      (1) *Züchner Case* (172/80) 487
                      (2) *Asjes (Nouvelles Frontières) Case*
                          (209–213/84) 491

   iii. Ratione temporis 491
    aa. Cases 491
     (1) *Sirena Case* (40/70) 491
 b. The concept of trade between Member States 492
  i. Cases 492
   (1) *Grundig Case* (56, 58/64) 492
   (2) *LTM-MBU Case* (56/65) 494
   (3) *VCH Case* (8/72) 496
   (4) *Windsurfing Case* (193/83) 497
 c. The notion of undertaking 499
  i. Decisions 499
   (1) *Reuter-BASF Decision* 499
   (2) *Christiani and Nielsen Decision* 500
2. Article 85 502
 a. Agreements 502
  i. Cases 502
   (1) *LTM-MBU Case* (56/65) 502
 b. Decisions by associations of undertakings 503
  i. Cases 503
   (1) *Fedetab Case* (209–215, 218/78) 503
 c. Concerted practices 504
  i. Cases 504
   (1) *Züchner Case* (172/80) 504
 d. Object or effect 505
  i. Cases 505
   (1) *Grundig Case* (56, 58/64) 505
 e. Competition 506
  i. Cases 506
   (1) *Metro Case I* (26/76) 506
   (2) *Remia Case* (42/84) 508
   (3) *Philip Morris-Rothmans Case* (142, 156/84) 510
 f. De minimis 514
  i. Cases 514
   (1) *Völk-Vervaecke Case* (5/69) 514
 g. Nullity 516
  i. Cases 516
   (1) *Haecht Case II* (48/73) 516
   (2) *LTM-MBU Case* (56/65) 517
 h. Article 85(3) 518
  i. Cases 518
   (1) *Grundig Case* (56, 58/64) 518
   (2) *VBVB-VBBB Case* (43, 63/82) 520
3. Article 86 522
 a. Relevant market 522
  i. Cases 522
   (1) *United Brands Case* (27/76) 522

		b. Dominant position	526
		i. Cases	526
		(1) *Hoffmann-La Roche (vitamins) Case (85/76)*	526
		c. Abuse	531
		i. Cases	531
		(1) *Hoffmann-La Roche (vitamins) Case (85/76)*	531
		d. Concentration	532
		i. Cases	532
		(1) *Continental Can Case (6/72)*	532
		4. Member States and Articles 85 and 86	537
		a. Cases	537
		(1) *Leclerc Case (229/83)*	537
	B.	Public enterprise	541
		1. Cases	541
		(1) *Port de Mertert Case (10/71)*	541
		(2) *Sacchi Case (155/73)*	542
		(3) *British Telecom Case (41/83)*	544
	C.	State aid	547
		1. Cases	547
		(1) *French rediscount Case (6–11/69)*	547
		(2) *French textile industry Case (47/69)*	547
		(3) *Italian textile industry Case (173/73)*	550
		(4) *Steinike Case (78/76)*	553
		(5) *Philip Morris Case (730/79)*	558
		(6) *Intermills Case (323/82)*	563
		(7) *COFAZ Case (169/84)*	564
	D.	Literature	571
III.	Approximation of Laws		571
	A.	Article 100	571
		1. Cases	571
		(1) *Enka Case (38/77)*	571
		(2) *Denkavit Case II (251/78)*	572
		(3) *Hormones Case (68/86)*	573
	B.	Article 102	573
		1. Cases	573
		(1) *Costa-ENEL Case (6/64)*	573
	C.	Literature	574
IV.	Economic, social and environment policies		574
	A.	Economic policies	574
		1. Cases	574
		(1) *French rediscount Case (6–11/69)*	574
		(2) *Balkan Import-Export Case (5/73)*	578
		(3) *Luisi and Carbone Case (286/82–26/83)*	582
	B.	Social policy	582

  1. Cases 582
   (1) *Defrenne Case II* (43/75) 582
   (2) *Defrenne Case III* (149/77) 589
   (3) *Macarthys-Smith Case* (129/79) 592
   (4) *Jenkins Case* (96/80) 594
   (5) *Garland Case* (12/81) 597
   (6) *Burton Case* (19/81) 599
   (7) *Marshall Case* (152/84) 601
   (8) *Gravier Case* (293/83) 601
 C. Environment 605
  1. Cases 605
   (1) *Italian sulphur Case* (92/79) 605
   (2) *Waste oil Case* (240/83) 606
   (3) *Danish bottle Case* (302/86) 608
 D. Literature 609
V. Sectorial policy 610
 A. Agriculture 610
  1. Objectives 610
   a. Cases 610
    (1) *Balkan Import-Export Case* (5/73) 610
    (2) *Eridana Case II* (250/84) 611
  2. Field of application 614
   a. Cases 614
    (1) *König Case* (185/73) 614
    (2) *Santa Anna Case* (85/77) 616
    (3) *CILFIT Case II* (77/83) 617
  3. The Common Agricultural Policy and the general rules
   on the free movement of goods 619
   a. Cases 619
    (1) *Charmasson Case* (48/74) 619
    (2) *Commissionaires Réunies-Ramel Case* (80–81/77) .. 620
  4. The rules of competition 622
   a. Cases 622
    (1) *Frubo Case* (71/74) 622
  5. The Common Agricultural Policy 624
   a. The market organization 624
    i. Cases 624
     (1) *Deutsche Getreide Case* (31/70) 624
     (2) *Handelsgesellschaft Case* (11/70) 625
     (3) *South African maize Case* (58/86) 627
   b. The procedures, Management Committee 629
    i. Cases 629
     (1) *Köster Case* (25/70) 629
     (2) *Rey Soda Case* (23/75) 629
   c. Monetary complications 633
    i. Cases 633

			(1) *Malt Case* (236/84)	633
	6.	The C.A.P. and national law		637
		a.	Execution by national authorities – execution and subdelegation	637
			i. Cases	637
			(1) *Beauport Case* (103–109/78)	637
		b.	The necessity of uniform application; force majeure	639
			i. Cases	639
			(1) *Kampffmeyer Case III* (158/73)	639
		c.	The competence of national legislation	641
			i. Limits of national competence	641
			aa. Cases	641
			(1) *Amsterdam Bulb Case* (50/76)	641
			(2) *Pigs Marketing Board-Redmond Case* (83/78)	642
			ii. Restrictions of production	644
			aa. Cases	644
			(1) *Van den Hazel Case* (111/76)	644
			iii. Regulation of prices	646
			aa. Cases	646
			(1) *Galli Case* (31/74)	646
			(2) *Russo Case* (60/75)	649
			(3) *Irish excise duty Case* (36, 71/80)	651
			iv. Harmonization of national legislation	654
			aa. Cases	654
			(1) *Hormones Case* (68/86)	654
	7.	Market Organization and individuals		657
		a.	Protection of price level	657
			i. Cases	657
			(1) *Russo Case* (60/75)	657
		b.	Non-discrimination	658
			i. Cases	658
			(1) *The Lion Case* (292–293/81)	658
			(2) *Balkan Import-Export Case* (5/73)	659
			(3) *Eridania Case II* (250/84)	659
		c.	The right freely to pursue a trade or profession and the right to property	660
			i. Cases	660
			(1) *Hauer Case* (44/79)	660
		d.	Legitimate expectations	665
			i. Cases	665
			(1) *CNTA Case* (74/74)	665
	8.	Literature		665
B.	Transport			666
	1.	Cases		666
		(1) *ERTA Case* (22/70)		666

(2) *French maritime labour code Case* (167/73) 666
(3) *Opinion of the Court* (1/76) 666
(4) *Belgian Railway subsidies Case* (156/77) 666
(5) *Failing transport policy Case* (13/83) 670
(6) *Asjes (Nouvelles Frontières) Case* (209/213/84) 672
2. Literature 674

CHAPTER SIX
EXTERNAL RELATIONS 675

I. The external competences of the EEC 675
   A. Introduction 675
   B. Cases 676
      (1) *ERTA Case* (22/70) 676
      (2) *Opinion of the Court* (1/76) 676
   C. Literature 676

II. The relationship between Community law and international law: the question of direct effect 677
   A. Introduction 677
   B. Cases 677
      (1) *Küpferberg Case* (104/81) 677
      (2) *International Fruit Company Case III* (21–24/72) 682
   C. Literature 685

III. The Common Commercial Policy 685
   A. Introduction 685
   B. The Common Commercial Policy Powers of the EC 686
      1. Introduction 686
      2. Cases 686
         (1) *Opinion of the Court* (1/75) 686
         (2) *Opinion of the Court* (1/78) 690
      3. Literature 695
   C. Dumping 696
      1. Introduction 696
      2. Cases 696
         (1) *FEDIOL Case* (191/82) 696
         (2) *Allied Corporation Case* (239, 275/82) 699
      3. Literature 701
   D. Article 115 EEC 701
      1. Introduction 701
      2. Cases 702
         (1) *Donckerwolcke Case* (41/76) 702
      3. Literature 704

xxiv

IV. The Common Fisheries Policy 704
   A. Introduction 704
   B. Cases 705
      (1) *Commission-United Kingdom Case* (804/79) 705
      (2) *Ireland-Commission Case* (325/85) 709
   C. Literature 710

Table of extracted Cases and Opinions – by number 711
Tables of extracted Cases, Decisions and Opinions – alphabetical 721

Chapter One

Languages, territorial application and institutions of the European Communities

I. Languages

See Materials on the Law of the European Communities, Chapter One.

1. Council Regulation No 1 of 15 April 1958.
2. Rules of Procedure of the Court of Justice Article 29.

II. Territorial application

See Article 227 of the EEC Treaty as amended by the 1972, 1979 and 1986 Acts of Accession.
See Materials on the Law of the European Communities, Chapter One.

1. Answer to written question No 489/73 by Lord O'Hagan.

III. Institutions

A. CASES

(1) Netherlands – High Authority Case

The Netherlands v. *High Authority*; Case 66/63; Judgment of 15 July 1964; (1964) ECR 546; (1964) CMLR 522.

Facts:

The Netherlands opposed a Decision of the High Authority by which the mining companies of the Ruhr received permission to sell their products jointly through two selling agencies.

The Court held:

On the other hand, in Article 15 (3) of the contested Decision the departments of the High Authority were wrongly referred to as distinct from the Authority itself. The departments of the High Authority have no separate capacity and may act only under its responsibility. The contested Decisions were thus required to reserve the power of decision to the High Authority alone which must arrange for such power to be exercised on its own responsibility and with due regard to the rules of the Treaty. Since the reference to the departments as separate entities is without legal foundation, it cannot properly appear in the contested Decision. The said reference is separable from the rest of the contested Decisions with the result that their Articles 15 (3) may be annulled to the extent that they contain the words 'of its departments'.

. . . . .

Sequel:

The above point was the only one accepted by the Court in favour of the applicants. Both their claims that the Treaty and an essential procedural requirement had been infringed and their contentions that lack of competence and misuse of powers should lead to annulment of the Decisions concerned were rejected by the Court.

The application was thus dimissed as unfounded save for the point mentioned above. The words 'or its departments' were annulled from the Decisions.

Note:

However, for an apparently accepted form of internal delegation within the Commission organization see the *Cement Convention Case* in Chapter Two where a letter of the Director General for Competition was found to be a decision (of the Commission). See also the *Akzo Chemie Case*, Chapter One at p. 29.

(2) Reynier and Erba Cases

Reynier and Erba v. *Commission*; Joined cases 79 and 82/63; Judgement of 9 June 1964; (1964) ECR 266.

Facts:

Reynier and Erba dsagreed with the Commission about their position within the administration of the Commission.

The Court held:

The applicants have named as defendants in their applications the European Economic Community or, alternatively, the Commission.

Article 179 of the EEC Treaty provides that: 'The Court of Justice shall have jurisdiction in any dispute between the Community and its servants within the limits and under the conditions laid down in the Staff Regulations or the Conditions of Employment'. The phrase 'the conditions laid down in the Staff Regulations' applicable to officials and other servants necessarily implies that the appointing authority, which exercises in fact the powers of an employer with regard to officials, has the capacity to be a party to legal proceedings. In this instance the appointing authority is the Commission itself. The wording of the Regulations confirms this reasoning.

Under Title VIII, headed 'Appeals' Article 91 of the Staff Regulations of officials of the European Economic Community is a continuation of Article 90 which describes the procedure through official channels, which it is both logical and desirable to follow before proceedings are instituted before the Court. Any official may submit his case to the appointing authority of his institution by means of this procedure. Consequently the appeal to the Court provided for in Article 91 ought, in the absence of any provision to the contrary, to obey similar rules and thus be directed against that same authority.

The applicants further claim that it is necessary to compel the Community to appear because it comprises several institutions and because of the distribution of budgetary and financial powers among these institutions.

The Regulations were adopted in accordance with the procedure laid down by Article 212 of the Treaty by the authorities designated for the purpose, and the institutions are bound by their provisions; therefore the Court's interpretation of the Regulations applies equally to all the institutions of the Community.

Moreover, the force of res judicata prevents rights confirmed by a judgment of the Court from being disputed anew. Since the Community is a single entity, it is inconceivable that judgment of the Court which has the force of res judicata with regard to an institution – in this case the Commission – should not have the same force with regard to the Community as a whole.

For these reasons the applications must be regarded as being made against the Commission and there is, moreover, no reason to hold them to be inadmissible.

(3) Mills Case

J. Mills v. *European Investment Bank*; Case 110/75; Interlocutory Judgment of 15 June 1976; (1976) ECR 955.

Facts:

The applicant brought an appeal for annulment against the decision of the EIB. about the termination of his employment and required that he would be reinstated.

The Court held:

The jurisdiction of the Court:

According to Article 179 of the Treaty establishing the European Economic Community: 'The Court of Justice shall have jurisdiction in any dispute between the Community and its servants within the limits and under the conditions laid down in the Staff Regulations or the Conditions of Employment'.

It is accordingly necessary to ascertain whether the defendant must for the purposes of this article be considered as forming part of the Community.

Title IV of Part Three of the Treaty on the policy of the Community is devoted to the European Investment Bank.

8. Article 129 thereof provides: 'A European Investment Bank is hereby established; it shall have legal personality'.
9. The Statute of the Bank forms the subject-matter of a Protocol annexed to the Treaty.
10. According to Article 13 (7) of that Statute: 'The officials and other employees of the Bank shall be under the authority of the President. They shall be engaged and discharged by him'.
11. Article 21 of the Protocol on the Privileges and Immunities of the European Economic Community provided that it should also apply to the Bank, to the members of its organs and to its staff.
12. That Protocol was replaced by the Protocol on the Privileges and Immunities of the European Communities of which Article 22 is identical to the provision cited.
13. The staff of the Bank are thereby placed in a special legal situation identical to that of the staff of the institutions of the Community.
14. It must thus be concluded that by the words 'any dispute between the Community and its servants' Article 179 is not restricted exclusively to the institutions of the Community and their staff but also includes the Bank as a Community institution established and with a legal personality conferred by the Treaty.
15. This conclusion is not invalidated by the fact that Article 180 of the

Treaty contains a special provision relating to certain disputes of the Bank.
16. This provision merely confers upon the Board of Directors of the Bank powers analogous to those conferred upon the Commission by Article 169 and renders measures adopted by the Board of Governors and those adopted by the Board of Directors subject to the same jurisdiction of the Court of Justice as that conferred by Article 173 with regard to the measures of the Council and of the Commission.
17. This complementary nature of Article 180 thus confirms the conclusion that when in Article 179 mention is made of the Community this does not exclude the Bank.
18. Under this article the Court thus has jurisdiction in any dispute between the Bank and its servants.

. . . . .

Sequel:

Subsequently the First Chamber of the Court dismissed the application in a judgment of 17 November 1976, (1976) ECR 1613. See in respect of disputes between officials and the Economic and Social Committee and the Court of Auditors Regulation (EEC, Euratom, ECSC) No 1376/77, OJ 1977, L 157/1.

B. MATERIALS

See Materials on the law of the European Communities, Chapter One.

No 4. The Rules of Procedure of the Council.
No 5. The Rules of Procedure of the Commission.
No 6. Excerpt of the 1966 Luxembourg Agreement.

IV. Powers of the Council and the Commission of the European Communities

A. POWERS OF ATTRIBUTION

1. Introduction

The powers by which the Council and Commission of the EC are authorized to legally bind the subjects of the Communities are not of a general nature:

such powers are particularly attributed to or conferred upon the institutions in the various fields of application designated by the Treaties.

2. Literature

Lasok & Bridge, *Law & Institutions of the European Communities*, Fourth ed., London 1987, pp. 99–104.
Lauwaars, *Lawfulness and legal Force of Community Decisions*, Leiden 1973, pp. 56–59.
Pescatore, *The Law of Integration*, Leiden 1974. Especially p. 37 e.f. and p. 63.

B. ARTICLE 235 EEC

1. Introduction

In order to achieve the objectives of the Communities, the Council and Commission have been granted particular powers in many fields (supra A). Where it appears that Community action is necessary to achieve a Treaty objective, and the necessary competences have not been provided by the Treaty, Article 235 EEC (Article 203 EAEC, Article 95, para 1, ECSC) provides the legal basis for additional decision making powers.

2. Cases

(1) ERTA Case

Commission of the EC v. *Council of the EC*; Case 22/70; Judgment of 31 March 1971; (1971) ECR. 273; (1971) CMLR 335.

Facts:

On 19 January 1962, under the auspices of the United Nations Economic Commission for Europe, the European Agreement concerning the work of crews of vehicles engaged in International Road Transport (ERTA) was signed in Geneva by five of the six Member States of the EEC and by a certain number of other European States. This Agreement never came into force for lack of a sufficient number of ratifications. In 1967, negotiations began for the revision of the Agreement, under the auspices of the European Conference of Ministers of Transport, and subsequently of the Economic Commission for Europe (ECE). Meanwhile work had been going on within the EEC with regard to the harmonization of driving and rest periods of drivers of road transport vehicles. These activities resulted in the adoption of Council Regulation No 543/69 of 25 March 1969 (OJ 1969, L 66/49) concerning the harmonization of certain social provisions in the field of road transport.

In view of the forthcoming meeting of the road transport subcommittee of the ECE due to be held 1–3 April 1970 in Geneva, the Council of the European Communities, in its meeting of 20 March 1970, discussed the attitude to be adopted by the six Member States in the negotiations for the revised European Road Transport Agreement. In the negotiations the six Member States took up the common position agreed on during discussions in the Council of 20 March 1970. The revised ERTA was declared to be open for signature by States as from 1 July 1970.

The Commission disagreed with the procedure followed by the Council and the Member States in respect of the revised ERTA. Claiming that the negotiation and conclusion were no longer a matter of State authority but should have been carried out by the Community, the Commission started the present proceedings on 19 May 1970, seeking annulment of the Council's discussion of 20 March 1970, regarding the negotiation and conclusion of the ERTA by the Member States.

The Court held:

. . . . .

2. As a preliminary objection, the Council has submitted that the application is inadmissible on the ground that the proceedings in question are not an act the legality of which is open to review under the first paragraph of Article 173 of the Treaty.
3. To decide this point, it is first necessary to determine which authority was, at the relevant date, empowered to negotiate and conclude the AETR.
4. The legal effect of the proceedings differs according to whether they are regarded as constituting the exercise of powers conferred on the Community, or as acknowledging a coordination by the Member States of the exercise of powers which remain vested in them.
5. To decide on the objection of inadmissibility, therefore, it is necessary to determine first of all whether, at the date of the proceedings in question, power to negotiate and conclude the AETR was vested in the Community or in the Member States.

I – The initial question

6. The Commission takes the view that Article 75 of the Treaty, which conferred on the Community powers defined in wide terms with a view

to implementing the common transport policy, must apply to external relations just as much as to domestic measures in the sphere envisaged.
7. It believes that the full effect of this provision would be jeopardized if the powers which it confers, particularly that of laying down 'any appropriate provisions', within the meaning of subparagraph (1) (c) of the article cited, did not extend to the conclusion of agreements with third countries.
8. Even if, it is argued, this power did not originally embrace the whole sphere of transport, it would tend to become general and exclusive as and where the common policy in this field came to be implemented.
9. The Council, on the other hand, contends that since the Community only has such powers as have been conferred on it, authority to enter into agreements with third countries cannot be assumed in the absence of an express provision in the Treaty.
11. More particularly, Article 75 relates only to measures internal to the Community, and cannot be interpreted as authorizing the conclusion of international agreements.
12. In the absence of specific provisions of the Treaty relating to the negotiation and conclusion of international agreements in the sphere of transport policy – a category into which, essentially, the AETR falls – one must turn to the general system of Community law in the sphere of relations with third countries.
13. Article 210 provides that 'The Community shall have legal personality'.
14. This provision, placed at the head of Part Six of the Treaty, devoted to 'General and Final Provisions', means that in its external relations the Community enjoys the capacity to establish contractual links with third countries over the whole field of objectives defined in Part One of the Treaty, which Part Six supplements.
15. To determine in a particular case the Community's authority to enter into international agreements, regard must be had to the whole scheme of the Treaty no less than to its substantive provisions.
16. Such authority arises not only from an express conferment by the Treaty – as is the case with Articles 113 and 114 for tariff and trade agreements and with Article 238 for association agreements – but may equally flow from other provisions of the Treaty and from measures adopted, within the framework of those provisions, by the Community institutions.
17. In particular, each time the Community, with a view to implementing a common policy envisaged by the Treaty, adopts provisions laying down common rules, whatever form these may take, the Member States no longer have the right, acting individually or even collectively, to undertake obligations with third countries which affect those rules.
18. As and when such common rules come into being, the Community alone is in a position to assume and carry out contractual obligations toward third countries affecting the whole sphere of application of the Community legal system.
19. With regard to the implementation of the provisions of the Treaty the

system of internal Community measures may not therefore be separated from that of external relations.
20. Under Article 3 (e), the adoption of a common policy in the sphere of transport is specially mentioned amongst the objectives of the Community.
21. Under Article 5, the Member States are required on the one hand to take all appropriate measures to ensure fulfilment of the obligations arising out of the Treaty or resulting from action taken by the institutions and, on the other hand, to abstain from any measure which might jeopardize the attainment of the objectives of the Treaty.
22. If these two provisions are read in conjunction, it follows that to the extent to which Community rules are promulgated for the attainment of the objectives of the Treaty, the Member States cannot, outside the framework of the Community Institutions, assume obligations which might affect those rules or alter their scope.
23. According to Article 74, the objectives of the Treaty in matters of transport are to be pursued within the framework of a common policy.
24. With this in view, Article 75 (1) directs the Council to lay down common rules and, in addition, 'any other appropriate provisions'.
25. By the terms of subparagraph (a) of the same provision, those common rules are applicable 'to international transport to or from the territory of a Member State or passing across the territory of one or more Member States'.
26. This provision is equally concerned with transport from or to third countries, as regards that part of the journey which takes place on Community territory.
27. It thus assumes that the powers of the Community extend to relationships arising from international law, and hence involve the need in the sphere in question for agreements with the third countries concerned.
28. Although it is true that Articles 74 and 75 do not expressly confer on the Community authority to enter into international agreements, nevertheless the bringing into force, on 25 March 1969, of Regulation No 543/69 of the Council on the harmonization of certain social legislation relating to road transport (OJ L 77, p. 40) necessarily vested in the Community power to enter into any agreements with third countries relating to the subject-matter governed by that regulation.
29. This grant of power is moreover expressly recognized by Article 3 of the said regulation which prescribes that: 'The Community shall enter into any negotiations with third countries which may prove necessary for the purpose of implementing this regulation'.
30. Since the subject-matter of the AETR falls within the scope of Regulation No 543/69, the Community has been empowered to negotiate and conclude the agreement in question since the entry into force of the said regulation.
31. These Community powers exclude the possibility of concurrent powers on the part of Member States, since any steps taken outside the framework of the Community institutions would be incompatible with the unity

of the Common Market and the uniform application of Community law.
32. This is the legal position in the light of which the question of admissibility has to be resolved.

. . . . .

Sequel:

The Council raised various further points as regards the admissibility of the case, which were not accepted.

The Commission lost the case on the merits. Both its claims of breach of Articles 75, 228 and 235 EEC and of non-fulfilment of the requirement regarding the reasoning of the Council's decision were rejected by the Court.

As the Article 235 the Court held:

Although Article 235 empowers the Council to take any 'appropriate measures' equally in the sphere of external relations, it does not create an obligation, but confers on the Council an option, failure to exercise which cannot affect the validity of proceedings.

(2) Lead and Zinc Case

The Commission v. *Italian Republic*; Case 38/69; Judgment of 18 February 1970; (1970) ECR 56; (1970) CMLR 77.

Facts:

The Italian Government had been authorized under Article 226 EEC to take special protective measures until 31 December 1967 resulting in the isolation of the Italian market in lead and zinc. After this date Italy was required to charge duties on lead and zinc imports at the reduced rate resulting from the 1966 decision of the Council of Ministers accelerating the realisation of the Common Market. (Acceleration Decision). Considering that Italy had failed to fulfil its obligations both under the Treaty and under the Council's decision, the Commission set in motion the procedure of Article 169 EEC subsequently referring the matter to the Court of Justice.

The Italian government did not challenge the fact, as alleged by the Commission, but sought to justify its action i.a. by questioning the legal nature of the Council decision of 1966 and the reservations made by themselves before the decision was laid down.

The Court held:

. . . . .

According to the defendant, the Acceleration Decision was the result of 'negotiations during which the contracting parties retained the independance which they enjoyed by virtue of their sovereignty' and therefore, in spite of its form, the nature of this decision is that of an international agreement having the same value as the Treaty itself, to which it has made certain additions, in accordance with the principles of both international law and community law, statements made by a contracting party at the conclusion of such negotiations form an integral part of the agreement reached. In these circumstances, according to the defendant, the reservations expressed by the Italian delegation must be interpreted as a refusal to accept the Acceleration Decision as regards the products in question.

The Acceleration Decision was taken by virue of Article 235 which provides that 'if action by the Community should prove necessary to attain, in the course of the operation of the Common Market, one of the objectives of the Community and this Treaty has not provided the necessary powers, the Council shall, acting unanimously on a proposal from the Commission and after consulting the Assembly, take the appropriate measures'. The power to take the measures envisaged by this article is conferred, not on the Member States acting together, but on the Council acting in its capacity as a Community institution. Under Article 235 the Council acts on a proposal from the Commission and after consulting the Assembly. Although the effect of the measures taken in this manner by the Council is in some respects to supplement the Treaty, they are adopted within the context of the objectives of the Community.

In these circumstances, a measure which is in the nature of a Community decision on the basis of its objective and of the institutional framework within which it has been drawn up cannot be described as an 'international agreement'.

Sequel:

From the fact that the Acceleration Decision was not of an international law character but that it conditioned or prepared the implementation of Article 23 lc EEC and Regulation No 950/68 concerning the Common Customs Tariff, the Court deduced that the protective measures isolating the Italian market in lead and zinc could have been justified only by recourse to Article 226 under which a Commission authorization was required. However, the Italian Government had not instituted proceedings against the last Commission decision refusing a further extension to the Italian measures. Subsequently the Court found that the Italian government had failed to fulfil certain obligations under the Treaty.

(3) Massey – Ferguson Case

Hauptzollamt Bremerhaven v. *Massey-Ferguson GmbH*; Case 8/73; Judgment of 12 July 1973; (1973) ECR 897.

Facts:

In a dispute about the amount of customs duties which had been fixed by the customs authorities without taking account of a discount, a question arose as to the validity of Regulation No 803/68 of the Council of 27 June 1968 on the valuation of goods for customs purposes (OJ 1968, L 148/6). This Regulation cites as its legal basis 'the Treaty establishing the E.E.C. and in particular Article 235'. The national court involved (the *Bundesfinanzhof*) asked for a preliminary ruling about *i.a.* the question whether the reference to this Article was sufficient.

The Court held:

. . . . .

The first question

2. By the first question it is asked whether the necessary authority for the validity of the Regulation is to be found in Article 235 of the Treaty, on which it is based, or in any other provision of the Treaty.
3. The first recital in the Preamble to the Regulation declares that it is adopted by virtue of 'the Treaty establishing the European Economic Community, and in particular Article 235 thereof'.

Thus it is proper to examine first of all whether this Article constitutes a sufficient legal basis.

Article 235 authorizes the Council to take the appropriate measures if action by the Community should prove necessary to attain, in the course of the operation of the Common Market, one of the objectives of the Community and if the Treaty has not provided the necessary powers.

The establishment of a customs union between the Member States is one of the objectives of the Community under Article 3 (a) and (b) of the Treaty.

The functioning of a customs union requires of necessity the uniform determination of the valuation for customs purposes of goods imported from third countries so that the level of protection effected by the Common Customs Tariff is the same throughout the whole Community.

Such a uniform determination does not follow to the extent necessary from the fact that the Member States are all adherents of the Brussels Convention on the valuation of goods for customs purposes signed on 15 December 1950. This is because the provisions of this convention have to give the signatory States the power to amend certain specific matters.

As the procedure prescribed by Article 100 for the approximation of legislation by means of directives does not provide a really adequate solution one must examine if the provisions on the implementation of the customs-union and the common commercial policy could have possibly furnished the Council with an adequate basis for action.

4. If it is true that the proper functioning of the customs union justifies a wide interpretation of Articles 9, 27, 28, 111 and 113 of the Treaty and of the powers which these provisions confer on the institutions to allow them thoroughly to control external trade by measures taken both independently and by agreement, there is no reason why the Council could not legitimately consider that recourse to the procedure of Article 235 was justified in the interest of legal certainty. This is the more so as the Regulation in question was adopted during the transitional period.

By reason of the specific requirements of Article 235 this course of action cannot be criticized since, under the circumstances, the rules of the Treaty on the forming of the Council's decisions or on the division of powers between the institutions are not to be disregarded.

5. No one has disputed the fact that on the adoption of Regulation No 803/68 the procedure prescribed by Article 235 was carried out in the proper manner.
6. Consequently, as the authority for this Regulation is to be found in Article 235 of the Treaty, examination of the question raised has exposed no factor which is capable of affecting its validity.

3. Literature

Lauwaars, *Lawfulness and Legal Force of Community Decisions*, Leiden 1973, 81–93;
Schwartz, I.E., 'Article 235 and Law-Making Powers in the European Community', 27 ICLQ 1978, 614 and ff.
Tizzano, A., 'The Powers of the Community', in: Commission of the E.C., *Thirty years of Community Law*, Luxemburg 1981.

C. IMPLIED POWERS

1. Introduction

The theoretical difference between an additional power and an implied power is mainly one of degree. An additional power supplements powers already granted in order to achieve a stated objective. An implied power, on the other hand, serves to complete an existing power in the specification of which certain elements are evidently lacking.

2. Cases

(1) Publication of Transport Tariffs Case I

Government of the Kingdom of the Netherlands v. *High Authority*; Case 25/59; Judgment of 15 July 1960; (1960) ECR 355.

Facts:

It is recognized in the ECSC Treaty that the establishment of the common market in coal and steel requires the application of such transport rates for coal and steel as will make possible comparable price conditions for consumers in comparable circumstances. (Art. 70, 1 ECSC).

By the Treaty, all inter-State transport contracts which involve discrimination in transport rates or conditions of any kind based upon the country of origin or of destination of the products being transported are declared illegal, and in order that the High Authority might be able to keep watch over the tariffs actually being charged, it was further provided that:

The rates, prices and tariff provisions of all kinds, applied to the transport of coal and steel within each Member State and between Member States shall be published or brought to the knowledge of the High Authority. (Article 70 (3) ECSC).

By a letter dated 12 August 1958, the High Authority asked Member States to take one of three sets of measures in order to achieve that objective of ECSC Article 70, para 3. The High Authority left each government to choose between the following solutions:

(a) Publication by the authorities of a tariff on transport rates, coupled with a duty to impose such tariffs on transport enterprises.
(b) . . . .
(c) In the absence of the latter tariffs, or should such tariffs comprise maximum or minimum prices, the prices and conditions of transport to be brought to the notice of the High Authority immediately after the conclusion of each transport contract. The High Authority added that should the application of choice (c) not achieve the Treaty objectives in a satisfactory manner, it reserved the right after a trial period to consider other measures.

In a letter dated 29 November 1958, the Netherlands government stated that it had taken measures to conform to (c) and asked the High Authority to keep secret the information supplied to it. On 18 February 1959, the High Authority adopted Decision 18/59 which stated that the Netherlands government had failed to comply with its Treaty obligations, as it had neither satisfactory complied with (c), as interpreted by the High Authority, nor with one of the other two alternatives set out in the letter of 12 August 1958. The Dutch government was given until 30 June 1959 to adopt either alternative (a) or alternative (b).

The Netherlands government brought an appeal for annulment against this Decision, denying the right of the High Authority to enforce by means of a Decision the obligations of Member States under Article 70, para 3, since no power to do so was conferred by the Treaty.

The Court held:

. . . . .

With regard to such implementing measures it is necessary to inquire whether the Treaty gives the High Authority power to make regulations either (1) expressly or (2) by implication.

1. The third paragraph of Article 70 provides that 'The scales, rates and all other tariff rules of every kind applied to the carriage of coal and steel within each Member State and between Member States shall be published or brought to the knowledge of the High Authority'.

    It must be observed that these provisions are silent with regard to the conditions of their application and the implementation measures which they assume and certainly they do not give the High Authority any power to take decisions in this respect.

    Moreover, a comparison between the third paragraph of Article 70 and the provisions of Article 60 (2) (a) shows that in a similar matter the Treaty has made the obligations to publish provided for in Article 60 subject to the power of the High Authority to provide for its application by providing that this publication must take place 'to the extent and in the manner prescribed by the High Authority after consulting the Consultative Committee'.

    The fact that for the publication of the price-lists and conditions of sale applied within the Common Market the Treaty has expressly given the High Authority a legislative power, providing even for review by the Consultative Committee, shows the importance which it attributes in this matter to its regulation by the High Authority.

    The absence of any provision in this respect in Article 70 shows on the other hand that in the transport sector the wording of the Treaty denies the High Authority any power to take implementing decisions.

2. Having regard to the different atttitude adopted by the Treaty in respect of two similar situations it is proper to inquire whether a legislative power on the part of the High Authority does not arise by implication from (a) other provisions of the Treaty or (b) its general structure.

Writers and case-law agree in recognizing that the rules established by a treaty imply the principles without which these rules cannot effectively or reasonably be applied.

(a) In the present case the High Authority maintains first that since the provisions of Article 60 (2) (a) require the publication of the price-lists and conditions of products coming within the European Coal and Steel Community, they require by implication the publication of the scales, rates and other tariff rules applied to the carriage of the same products.

According to the High Authority if the latter are not published the publication of the prices would lose their purpose and be of no use to those concerned.

In order for those concerned to be able to align their prices and maintain healthy competition they cannot remain ignorant of the important factor constituted by the transport rates in the formation of their quotations on the Common Market.

According to this argument, the corollary of the obligation to publish prices is the publication of transport tariffs and this obligation follows by implication from the concepts of 'price lists' and 'conditions of sale' referred to in Article 60.

It is wrong both in law and in fact to say that the expressions 'price lists' and 'conditions of sale' cover both those in respect of goods and those in respect of transport.

The seller can be required to publish only his own prices and not the rates applied by a transport undertaking.

In so far as the seller is required to pay the carrier's charges they represent an element of the seller's cost price.

The seller is not required to publish the details of his cost price.

The High Authority's argument that it is necessary to publish the transport rates in order to know the prices is contradicted by its own attitude with regard to Article 60 (2) (a).

If the view which it is now advocating were correct, that is to say, if the sale prices included transport rates, on laying down the rules for the scope and forms for the publication of the price-lists and conditions of sale it could have provided in the relevant decisions (No 3/53, 30/53, 31/53 and 1 to 3/54) for the transport costs as a price factor.

It did not, however, do so.

Although it is true that in the 'Information' which it sent out after certain of the abovementioned decisions on the publication of prices the High Authority refers to transport costs, it does so however only to align the steel prices on the delivery price of another undertaking and even in this case it takes into account the price actually paid which does not require any previous publication but is subject only to checking afterwards.

(b) From another point of view it is not possible to infer a structural and functional correlation between the obligation to publish the prices of products and the obligation to publish transport costs from the basic principle of the Treaty which although guaranteeing economic freedom in the sphere of competition is nevertheless aimed at restraining abuse by prohibiting any discrimination, the checking of which is for the High Authority.

Although it is true that by virtue of the general principle, applied to transport by Article 70, checking discrimination and taking action against it is for the High Authority, it is not however possible to infer from this principle a power for the High Authority to take decisions concerned with prior control by laying down the publication of scales or rates, since such a power is exceptional and subject to renunciation by the Member States which in the present case the Treaty does not provide for either expressly or by implication. The High Authority thus has no power to implement the provisions of the third paragraph of Article 70 by means of decisions.

Sequel:

The Netherlands Government further challenged Decision 18/59 on the ground that Article 88, chosen by the High Authority to justify its powers could not legally be used for these purposes and if it could so be used, then it had not been applied in accordance with the prescribed rules. Consequently it was found by the Court that Article 88 could not be used to prescribe regulatory provisions, and that Decision 18/59 was void because of the violation of a substantial procedural requirement. Thus the Decision was annulled.

3. Literature

Mann, *The function of Judicial Decision in European Economic Integration*, The Hague 1972, 288–299.
Schermers, *Judicial Protection in the European Communities*, Fourth Edition, Deventer 1987, para 264–267.

D. Powers of delegation

1. Introduction

In the following part a number of cases have been grouped together which have in common that they deal with the exercise of transferred competence, and the conditions under which such a transfer can be effected. A number of different forms may be distinguished.

A first form is the handing over of the mere exercise of executive powers by an organ of an organization to another organ of the same organization.

Examples are the management committee procedure, *Case 25/70, infra* sub (3) and the 'Standing Committee for Feeding-Stuffs' *Case 5/77, infra* sub (4).

A second form comprises the exercise of executive powers transferred by an official institution to a body newly formed by that institution. The conditions whereunder such a transfer can be effected have been established by the Court in the *Meroni Case, 9/56 infra* sub (1).

A third form that can be distinguished is the attribution of competences of an international organization to its Member States. Limitations on this form have been set by the Court in *Case 23/75, Rey Soda*, Judgment of 30 October 1975, (1975) ECR 1300, see Ch. Five A.5.b.i (2), at p. 629.

Again a different form of the exercise of powers by an entity different from the original recipient is the case where the former is established by means of an international agreement with a third state. This form is reviewed by the Court in its *Opinion 1/76, infra* sub (5).

It is at least doubtful whether in all of these forms one can properly speak of delegation. Also the Court does not make use of this terminology in all cases. The differences on points like revocation of the authority concerned, the exercise of supervision, the right to give directions and the form of judicial protection are such that not all forms should come within the scope of a single term on the risk of defining the meaning of such a concept in legal terms becoming quite meaningless.

2. Cases

(1) Meroni Case I

See at pages 73, 91.

(2) Netherlands v. High Authority Case

For facts and references see page 1.

Note:

However, for an apparently accepted form of internal delegation within the Commission organisation refer to the *Cement Convention Case*, see Chapter 2 below where a letter of the Director General for Competition was found to be a decision (of the Commission), and to the *Akzo Chemie Case, infra* sub (6).

(3) Köster Case

Einfuhr- und Vorratsstelle für Getreide und Futtermittel v. *Fa. Köster, Berodt & Co.*; Case 25/70; Preliminary ruling of 17 December 1970; (1970) ECR 1170; (1972) CMLR 255.

Facts:

The firm Köster, Berodt & Co. obtained on 2 June 1965 an export licence for 1,200 tons of maize groats. This certificate had been accompanied by the lodging of a deposit at the rate of 0,5 units of account per ton to enforce completion of the exportation under Article 7 (1) of Regulation No 102/64. Since no exports were made during the period of validity of the licence the Einfuhrund Vorratsstelle für Getreide und Futtermittel forfeited 2,400 DM. The exporter brought an action in the Verwaltungsgericht, Frankfurt am Main, for the return of the estreated deposit and that court, by judgment of 12 December 1966, held for the plaintiff. The defendant agency appealed, and the Hessischer Verwaltungsgerichtshof by judgment of 21 April 1970 stayed proceedings and referred the following questions to the Court of Justice under Article 177:

1. Should the procedure laid down in Article 26 of Council Regulation No 19 of 4 April 1962 on the gradual establishment of a common organization of the market in cereals, in application of which Regulation No 102/64 was enacted, be regarded as contrary to the EEC Treaty?

    In particular, is this procedure compatible with Articles ..., 155, ... of the EEC Treaty? ...

The Court held:

. . . . .

4. This question concerns the legality of the so-called Management Committee procedure introduced by Articles 25 and 26 of Regulation No 19 and re-enacted by numerous other agricultural regulations. The above-mentioned provisions of the Treaty reveal that the question put concerns more particularly the compatibility of the Management Committee procedure with the Community structure and the institutional balance as regards the relationship between institutions and the exercise of their respective powers.
5. It is alleged in the first place that the power to adopt the system in dispute belonged to the Council which, under the terms of the third subparagraph of Article 43 (2) of the Treaty, should have acted on a proposal from the Commission and after consulting the Assembly and that therefore the procedure followed derogated from the procedures and powers fixed by this provision of the Treaty.
6. Both the legislative scheme of the Treaty, reflected particularly by the last indent of Article 155, and the consistent practice of the Community institutions establish a distinction, according to the legal concepts recognised in all Member States, between the measures directly based on

the Treaty itself and derived law intended to ensure their implementation. It cannot therefore be a requirement that all the details of the regulations concerning the common agricultural policy be drawn up by the Council according to the procedure in Article 43. It is sufficient for the purposes of that provision that the basic elements of the matter to be dealt with have been adopted in accordance with the procedure laid down by that provision. On the other hand, the provisions implementing the basic regulations may be adopted according to a procedure different from that in Article 43, either by the Council itself or by the Commission by virtue of an authorisation complying with Article 155.

7. The measures dealt with by implementing Regulation No 102/64 of the Commission do not go beyond the limits of the principles of basic Regulation No 19. The Commission was thus validly authorised by Regulation No 19 to adopt the implementing measures in question, the validity of which cannot therefore be disputed within the context of the requirements of Article 43 (2) of the Treaty.

8. Secondly, the respondent in the main action criticizes the Management Committee procedure in that it constitutes an interference in the Commission's rights of decision, to such an extent as to put in issue the independence of that institution. Further, the interposition between the Council and the Commission of a body which is not provided for by the Treaty is alleged to have the effect of distorting the relationships between the institutions and the exercise of the right of decision.

9. Article 155 provides that the Commission shall exercise the powers conferred on it by the Council for the implementation of the rules laid down by the latter. This provision, the use of which is optional, enables the Council to determine any detailed rules to which the Commission is subject in exercising the power conferred on it. The so-called Management Committee procedure forms part of the detailed rules to which the Council may legitimately subject a delegation of power to the Commission. It follows from an analysis of the machinery set up by Articles 25 and 26 of Regulation No 19 that the task of the Management Committee is to give opinions on draft measures proposed by the Commission, which may adopt immediately applicable measures whatever the opinion of the Management Committee. Where the Committee issues a contrary opinion, the only obligation on the Commission is to communicate to the Council the measures taken. The function of the Management Committee is to ensure permanent consultation to guide the Commission in the exercise of the powers conferred on it by the Council and to enable the latter to substitute its own action for that of the Commission. The Management Committee does not therefore have the power to take a decision in place of the Commission or the Council. Consequently, without distorting the Community structure and the institutional balance, the Management Committee machinery enables the Council to delegate to the Commission an implementing power of appreciable scope, subject to its power to take the decision itself if necessary.

10. The legality of the so-called Management Committee procedure, as established by Articles 25 and 26 of Regulation No 19, cannot therefore be disputed in the context of the institutional structure of the Community.

Sequel:

Further questions by the Hessischer Verwaltungsgerichtshof concerned the legality of the provisions of Regulation 102/64 containing the duty to export, the necessity to lodge a deposit and the possibility of forfeiture thereof. It was found by the Court that the Commission had the power to include the above provisions in the Regulation concerned, and that the measures used were appropriate for ensuring the normal functioning of the market organization for cereals in the general insterest as defined in Article 39 of the Treaty.

(4) Tedeschi Case

Carlo Tedeschi v. *Denkavit Commerciale s.r.l.*; Case 5/77; Preliminary ruling of 5 October 1977; (1977) ECR 1579; (1978) 1 CMLR 1.

Facts:

Several Community directives which aim at harmonizing national provisions intended to ensure that feeding-stuffs do not endanger animal and human health have been adopted, inter alia on the fixing of maximum permitted levels for undesirable substances and products in feeding-stuffs.

Under Article 3 of this Directive Member States must prescribe that the undesirable substances and products listed in the annex shall be tolerated in feeding-stuffs only under the conditions and up to the maximum content therein set out.... Article 5 however provides a safeguard clause which reads as follows:
'1. Where a Member State considers that a maximum content fixed in the annex presents a danger to animal or human health, that Member State may provisionally reduce this content....
2. In accordance with the procedure laid down in Article 10, an immediate decision shall be made as to whether the annex should be modified. So long as no decision has been made by either the Council or the Commission the Member State may maintain the measures it has implemented.'

The Pretura di Lodi posed four questions to the Court.

The Court held:

. . . . .

The fourth question.
48. If the Court replies in the affirmative to the first three questions, the next question asks whether Article 5 of Directive No 74/63 must be considered as valid to the extent to which it extends the powers of the Member States beyond the limits justified by Article 36 and permits them, by means of the last sentence of Article 10, to escape, without any limitation as to time, the directly applicable provisions of Article 30 of the Treaty and those concerning the common organization of the agricultural markets.
49. The Directive, whilst obliging the Member States to adopt common provisions in relation to the presence of harmful or undesirable substances in feeding-stuffs leaves those Member States, by means of Article 5, a discretionary power to implement provisional supplementary measures relating to other substances or to the level of the substances listed in the annex to the directive.

. . . . .

51. The defendant in the main action alleges in support of its statement that Article 5 of the directive is invalid that the procedure laid down in Article 10 might in certain cases lead to an indefinite extension of the provisional measures by virtue of the last sentence of that article.
52. Article 10 (4) provides that a decision on the modification of the annex must be adopted either by the Commission in accordance with the opinion of the Standing Committee for Feeding-stuffs or, if the Commission is not in accordance with that opinion or if the Committee does not deliver an opinion, by the Council at the proposal of the Commission.
53. Article 10 (4) continues by specifying that: 'If the Council has not adopted any measures within fifteen days of the proposal being submitted to it, the Commission shall adopte the proposed measures and implement them forthwith, except where the Council has voted by a simple majority against such measures'.
54. It is true that the last sentence of Article 10 prevents the Commission from implementing the proposal rejected by the Council where its proposal has been rejected by the Council and even where, in that case, the latter does not put forward an alternative solution.
55. However the Commission still has jurisdiction to issue, in accordance with the procedure laid down in the first subparagraph of Article 10 (4),

any other measure which it considers appropriate.
56. The final paragraph of Article 10 therefore does not have the effect of paralysing the Commission or of enabling the national measure adopted provisionally to be prolonged indefinitely.
57. It is therefore necessary to conclude that consideration of the fourth question has disclosed no factor of such a kind as to affect the validity of Article 5 of the directive.

(5) Opinion of the Court

Opinion of the Court given pursuant to Article 228 of the EEC Treaty; Opinion 1/76 of 26 April 1977 (European Laying-up Fund for Inland Waterway Vessels); (1977) ECR 754; (1977) CMLR 279.

Facts:

In this request the Commission has asked for the opinion of the Court as to whether a draft Agreement establishing a 'European laying-up fund for inland waterway vessels' is compatible with the provisions of the Treaty.

The draft agreement was the subject of negotiations between the Commission, acting on behalf of the Community in accordance with a decision of the Council, and Switzerland, with the participation of delegations from the six Member States (Belgium, the Federal Republic of Germany, France Luxembourg, the Netherlands and the United Kingdom) who are parties either to the revised Convention for the Navigation of the Rhine of 17 October 1868 (hereinafter referred to as 'the Mannheim Convention') or to the Convention for the Canalization of the Moselle of 27 October 1956.

The objective of the Agreement is to introduce a system intended to eliminate the disturbances arising from the surplus carrying capacity for goods by inland waterway in the Rhine and Moselle basins and by all the Netherlands inland waterways and the German inland waterways linked to the Rhine basin. The system consists in formulating an arrangement for the temporary laying-up of a part of the available carrying capacity in return for financial compensation to carriers who voluntarily withdraw vessels from the market for a certain period. A fund (called the 'laying-up fund for inland waterway vessels') is responsible for compensation and is financed by contributions imposed on all vessels using the inland waterways which are subject to the system.

The Court held:

1. The object of the system laid down by the draft Agreement and expressed in the Statute annexed thereto is to rationalize the economic situation of

the inland waterway transport industry in a geographical region in which transport by inland waterway is of special importance within the whole network of international transport. Such a system is doubtless an important factor in the common transport policy, the establishment of which is included in the activities of the Community laid down in Article 3 of the EEC Treaty. In order to implement this policy, Article 75 of the Treaty instructs the Council to lay down according to the prescribed procedure common rules applicable to international transport to or from the territory of one or more member States. This article also supplies, as regards the Community, the necessary legal basis to establish the system concerned.

2. In this case, however it is impossible fully to attain the objective pursued by means of the establishment of common rules pursuant to Article 75 of the Treaty, because of the traditional participation of vessels from a third State, Switzerland, in navigation by the principal waterways in question, which are subject to the system of freedom of navigation established by international agreements of long standing.

It has thus been necessary to bring Switzerland into the scheme in question by means of an international agreement with this third State.

3. The power of the Community to conclude such an agreement is not expressly laid down in the Treaty. However, the Court has already had occasion to state, most recently in its judgment of 14 July 1976 in Joined Cases 3, 4 and 6/76, Cornelis Kramer and others, (1976) ECR 1279, that authority to enter into international commitments may not only arise from an express attribution by the Treaty, but equally may flow implicitly from its provisions. The Court has concluded inter alia that whenever Community law has created for the institutions of the Community powers within its internal system for the purpose of attaining a specific objective, the Community has authority to enter into the international commitments necessary for the attainment of that objective even in the absence of an express provision in that connection.

4. This is particularly so in all cases in which internal power has already been used in order to adopt measures which come within the attainment of common policies. It is, however, not limited to that eventuality. Although the internal Community measures are only adopted when the international agreement is concluded and made enforceable, as is envisaged in the present case by the proposal for a regulation to be submitted to the Council by the Commission, the power to bind the Community vis-à-vis third countries nevertheless flows by implication from the provisions of the Treaty creating the internal power and in so far as the participation of the Community in the international agreement is, as here, necessary for the attainment of one of the objectives of the Community.

5. In order to attain the common transport policy, the contents of which are defined in Articles 74 and 75 of the Treaty, the Council is empowered to lay down any other appropriate provisions, as expressly provided in Article 75 (1) (c). The Community is therefore not only entitled to enter into contractual relations with a third country in this connection but also

has the power, while observing the provisions of the Treaty, to cooperate with that country in setting up an appropriate organism such as the public international institution which it is proposed to establish under the name of the 'European Laying-up Fund for Inland Waterway Vessels'. The Community may also in this connection, cooperate with a third country for the purpose of giving the organs of such an institution appropriate powers of decision and for the purpose of defining, in a manner appropriate to the objectives pursued, the nature, elaboration, implementation and effects of the provisions to be adopted within such a framework.

6. A special problem arises because the draft Agreement provides for the participation as contracting parties not only of the Community and Switzerland but also of certain of the Member States. There are the six states which are party either to the revised Convention of Mannheim for the Navigation of the Rhine of 17 October 1868 or the Convention of Luxembourg of 27 October 1956 on the Canalization of the Moselle, having regard to the relationship of the latter to the Rhine Convention. Under Article 3 of the Agreement, these States undertake to make the amendments of the two abovementioned conventions necessitated by the implementation of the Statute annexed to the Agreement.

7. This particular undertaking, given in view of the second paragraph of Article 234 of the Treaty, explains and justifies the participation in the Agreement, together with the Community, of the six abovementioned States. Precisely because of that undertaking the obstacle presented by the existence of certain provisions of the Mannheim and Luxembourg Conventions to the attainment of the scheme laid down by the Agreement will be removed. The participation of these States in the Agreement must be considered as being solely for this purpose and not as necessary for the attainment of other features of the system. In fact, under Article 4 of the Agreement, the enforceability of this measure and of the Statute extends to the territories of all the Member States including those who are not party to the agreement; it may therefore be said that, except for the special undertaking mentioned above, the legal effects of the agreement with regard to the Member States result, in accordance with Article 228 (2) of the Treaty, exclusively from the conclusion of the latter by the Community. In these circumstances, the participation of the six Member States as contracting parties to the Agreement is not such as to encroach on the external power of the Community. There is therefore no occasion to conclude that this aspect of the draft Agreement is incompatible with the Treaty.

8. The participation of these Member States in the negotiations, though justified for the abovementioned purpose, has however produced results extending beyond that objective which are incompatible with the requirements implied by the very concepts of the Community and its common policy. In fact, this situation seems to be at the root of an ambiguity concerning the field of application of the Agreement and the Statute. Thus, under Article 4, the Agreement and the Statute are enforceable on the

territory of the nine Member States and Switzerland whilst the general obligations laid down in Article 6 concern the 'Contracting Parties', that is, the Community as such and the seven contracting States.

9. In the Statute itself there are various grouping of those who are either given rights or placed under duties; sometimes all the Member States of the Community and Switzerland (as in Articles 39, 43, 45 and 46) sometimes the Member States with one exception, and Switzerland (which is the scheme of the provision laid down in Article 27 on the composition of the Supervisory Board), sometimes the Community as such and Switzerland (in Article 40, concerning the publication of the measures adopted by the Fund) and sometimes five States to which a special functon is reserved in the decision-making process (Article 27 (5) of the Statute). On the whole, the part played by the institutions of the Community is extremely limited: the Commission provides the chairman and the secretarial services for the Supervisory Board but without exercising a right to vote therein. The determinative functions in the operation of the Fund are performed by the States. In fact, under Article 27 (1) the supervisory Board consists of 'representatives' who receive their powers and authority from the States concerned.

10. The Court considers that these provisions, and more particularly those on the organization and the deliberations of the Supervisory Board, the controlling organ of the Fund, call in question the power of the institutions of the Community and, moreover, alter in a manner inconsistent with the Treaty the relationship between Member States within the context of the Community as it was in the beginning and when the Community was enlarged.

11. More particularly, it is necessary to point out two factors in this connection.
    (a) The substitution in the structure of the organs of the Funds, of several Member States in place of the Community and its institutions in a field which comes within a common policy which Article 3 of the Treaty has expressly reserved to the activities of the Community;
    (b) The alteration, as a result of this substitution, of the relationships between Member States, contrary to a requirement laid down right from the second paragraph of the recitals of the preamble to the Treaty, according to which the objectives of the Community must be attained by 'common action', given that under Article 4 that action must be carried out by the institutions of the Community each one acting within the limits of its powers. More precisely, the following appears to be incompatible with the concept of such common action:
       – the complete exclusion, even voluntary, of a specific Member State from and participation in the activity of the Fund,
       – the power reserved to certain Member States under the third sub-paragraph of Article 27 (1) of the Statute to take no part in a matter which comes within a common policy, and finally,
       – the fact that, in the decision-making procedure of the Fund, special

prerogatives are reserved to certain States by derogation from the concepts which, within the Community, obtain with regard to the adoption of decisions within the field of the common policy involved in this case.
12. Thus it appears that the Statute, far from restricting itself to the solution of problems resulting from requirements inherent in the external relations of the Community constitutes both a surrender of the independence of action of the Community in its external relations and a change in the internal constitution of the Community by the alteration of essential elements of the Community structure as regards both the prerogatives of the institutions and the position of the Member States vis-à-vis one another. The Court is of the opinion that the structure thereby given to the Supervisory Board and the arrangement of the decision-making procedure within that organ are not compatible with the requirements of unity and solidarity which it has already had occasion to emphasize in its judgment of 31 March 1971 in Case 22/70, Commission v. Council (ERTA), (1971) ECR 263 and, at greater length, in its opinion 1/75 of 11 November 1975, (1975) ECR 1355 and OJ C 268, p. 18.
13. The attempt belatedly to introduce into the functioning of the Supervisory Board by means of Article 5 of the draft regulation concepts which are closer to the requirements of the Treaty is no proper way to correct faults which are inherent in the structure of the Fund as set out in the text negotiated by the Commission.
14. The Court has examined all aspects of this question and it has duly considered the difficulties which may arise in the search for a practical solution to the problems posed by the organization of a public international institution managed by the Community and a single third country while maintaining the mutual independence of the two partners. Doubtless the specific nature of the interests involved may explain the desire, within the context of organs of management, to have recourse to administrative bodies more directly concerned with the problems of inland navigation. Does this objective justify the creation of a mixed organization in which the presence of national representatives on the Supervisory Board together with the chairman and the Swiss representative would ensure the defence of the interests of the Community? After considering the arguments for and against, the Court has reached the conclusion that it is no doubt possible to attain an appropriate balance in the composition of the organs of the Fund but that this must not result in weakening the institutions of the Community and surrendering the bases of common policy even for a specific and limited objective. The possibility that the Agreement and the Statute, according to the statements of the Commission, might constitute the model for future arrangements in other fields has confirmed the Court in its critical attitude: the repetition of such procedures is in fact likely progressively to undo the work of the Community irreversibly, in view of the fact that each time the undertakings involved will be entered into with third countries. It was for these

reasons that an adverse decision finally prevailed within the Court as regards this aspect of the proposal.
15. As regards the powers of decision given to the organs of the Fund, Article 39 of the Statute provides that decisions of the organs of the Fund having general application shall be binding in their entirety and directly applicable in all Member States of the Community and in Switzerland. The question has been raised whether the grant of such powers extending to all the territory of the Community to a public international organ separate from the Community comes within the powers of the institutions. More particularly, there arises the problem whether the institutions may freely transfer to non-Community organisms powers or part of the powers granted by the Treaty and thus create for the Member States the obligation to apply directly in their legal systems rules of law which are not of Community origin adopted in forms and under conditions which are not subject to the provisions and guarantees contained in the Treaty.
16. However it is unnecessary in this opinion to solve the problem thus posed. In fact the provisions of the Statute define and limit the powers which the latter grants to the organs of the Funds so clearly and precisely that in this case they are only executive powers. Thus the field in which the organs may take action is limited to the sphere of the voluntary laying-up of the excess carrying capacity subject to the condition that financial compensation is paid by a Fund financed by contributions levied on the vessels using the inland waterways covered by the Fund. Here a further point arises out of the third paragraph of Article 1 of the Agreement according to which the Fund may not be used with the aim of fixing a permanent minimum level for freight rates during all periods of slack demand or of remedying structural imbalance. More particularly, the rate of contributions, that is, the basic rate and the adjustment coefficients, for the first year of the operation of the system is laid down in the actual terms of the Statute and subsequent amendments by decision of the Supervisory Board must either remain within certain limits or result from a unanimous decision.

. . . . .

In conclusion,

The Court

gives the following opinion:
The draft Agreement on the establishment of a European Laying-up Fund for Inland Waterway Vessels is incompatible with the EEC Treaty.

(6) Akzo Chemie Case

Akzo Chemie B.V. and *Akzo Chemie (UK) Ltd* v. *Commission*; Case 5/85; Judgment of 23 September 1986; (1986) ECR 2585.

Facts:

In order to complete its examination of Akzo Chemie's pricing behaviour in the flour additives sector, which had already been the subject of preliminary measures (see Decision of 22 July 1983, L 252/13), the Commission announced in October 1984 that it would also carry out an investigation regarding the firm's behaviour in the plastics sector. When Akzo Chemie refused to submit to this investigation, the Commission ordered it by a decision of 6 November 1984 adopted by virtue of Article 14, para. 3 of Regulation No 17. Akzo Chemie brought an action for annulment against this decision. It based its appeal on four grounds. In its reply it presented three further grounds for annulment.

The Court declared the three supplementary grounds to be inadmissible. The four original grounds were rejected. The judgment of the Court about the fourth ground (misuse of powers of delegation) reads as follows:

The Court

. . . . .

28. In their fourth submission, the applicants first challenge the delegation of authority under which the contested decision was adopted inasmuch as it is not in accordance with the principle of collegiate responsibility laid down in Article 17 of the Treaty of 8 April 1965 establishing a Single Council and a Single Commission of the European Communities (hereinafter referred to as 'the Merger Treaty'). Such a system does not provide parties to proceedings with the same guarantees. Thus, the failure to publish the decision delegating authority to certain members of the Commission makes it impossible to review the legality of that delegation. Furthermore, the decision is, according to the applicants, the result of a misuse of the authority delegated inasmuch as the delicate circumstances surrounding the investigations should have led the member of the Commission responsible for competition matters to have the decision adopted by the full Commission.
29. For its part, the Commission emphasizes first that the system of delegation of authority which it has established guarantees respect for the principle of collegiate responsibility because machinery is provided which

ensures that important decisions are adopted by the full Commission. Moreover, it points out that a decision ordering an undertaking to submit to investigation is a straightforward measure of management and there was therefore no need in this case to refer it to the full Commission.

30. With regard to the first part of the fourth submission concerning the compatibility of the system of delegations of authority with the principle of collegiate responsibility, it must first be pointed out that that principle is to be traced to Article 17 of the Merger Treaty according to which 'the Commission shall act by a majority of the number of members provided for in Article 10. A meeting of the Commission shall be valid only if the number of members laid down in its rules of procedure is present'. The principle of collegiate responsibility thus laid down is founded on the equal participation of the members of the Commission in the adoption of decisions and it follows from that principle, in particular, that decisions should be the subject of a collective deliberation and that all the members of the college of Commissioners bear collective responsibility on the political level for all decisions adopted.

31. It is also necessary to describe, particularly from the point of view of the system of delegations of authority, the measures adopted by the Commission in order to prevent the rule requiring collective deliberation from having a paralysing effect on the full Commission.

32. In the first place, on 23 July 1975, the Commission introduced into its Provisional Rules of Procedure a new Article 27 according to which 'subject to the principle of collegiate responsibility being respected in full the Commission may empower its members to take, in its name and subject to its control, clearly defined measures of management or administration' (Official Journal, L 199, p. 43).

33. In the second place, on the same date, the Commission adopted an internal decision laying down the principles and conditions on which delegations of authority would be granted. According to the information supplied by the Commission in reply to a question put to it by the Court, that decision established certain procedural guarantees in order to ensure that the decisions adopted pursuant to a delegation of authority complied with the principle of collegiate responsibility. Thus, decisions delegating authority must be adopted at meetings of the Commission and such delegations may only be made to designated persons for designated categories of everyday measures of management or administration. Furthermore, the person to whom authority has been delegated may adopt a decision only if all the departments concerned are in agreement and only if he is satisfied that the decision does not need, for whatever reason, to be considered by the full Commission. Finally, all decisions adopted under a delegation of authority are transmitted on the day following their adoption to all the members of the Commission and to all departments.

34. In the third place, in the particular sphere of competition law, the member of the Commission responsible for competition matters was granted, by decision of 5 November 1980, the power to adopt in the name of the

Commission certain procedural measures provided for in Regulation No 17. He may decide alone to initiate the procedure, on his own, to seek information from undertakings and to order an undertaking to submit to an investigation under Article 14 (3) of Regulation No 17.

35. With regard to the compatibility of that system with the principle of collegiate responsibility, it should be pointed out that in its judgment of 17 January 1984 (Joined Cases 43 and 63/82, *VBCB and VBBB* v. *Commission*, [1984] ECR 19), the most recent decision on that point, the Court decided that the Commission could, within certain limits and subject to certain conditions, authorize its members to adopt certain decisions in its name without the principle of collegiate responsibility which governed its functioning being impaired by such authorization. Two considerations underlie that settled case-law.

36. On the one hand, such a system of delegation of authority does not have the effect of divesting the Commission of powers by conferring on the member to whom authority is delegated powers to act his own right. Decisions adopted under a delegation of authority are adopted in the name of the Commission, which is fully responsible for them, and may be the subject of an application for annulment under the same conditions as if they had been considered by the full Commission. Moreover, the Commission has set up machinery making it possible to reserve for the full Commission certain measures which could be adopted under a delegation of authority. Finally, it has retained the right to reconsider the decisions granting delegations of authority.

37. On the other hand, limited to specific categories of measures of management or administration, and thus excluding by definition decisions of principle, such a system of delegations of authority appears necessary, having regard to the considerable increase in the number of decisions which the Commission is required to adopt, to enable it to perform its duties. The need to ensure that the decision-making body is able to function corresponds to a principle inherent in all institutional systems and which is set out in particular in Article 16 of the Merger Treaty, according to which 'the Commission shall adopt its rules of procedure so as to ensure that both it and its departments operate ...'.

38. Contrary to what the applicants maintain, a decision ordering an undertaking to submit to an investigation is a form of preparatory inquiry and as such, must be regarded as a straightforward measure of management. That is true even if the undertakings are opposed to the investigation. The power conferred on the Commission by Article 14 (3) of Regulation No 17 is exercised precisely and above all when the Commission expects that the undertakings will not submit voluntarily to an investigation.

39. With regard to the argument based on the failure to publish the decision granting the delegation of authority, it is true that the principle of legal certainty and the need for administrative decisions to be transparent require that the Commission should publish decisions granting delegations of authority as if they were rules of procedure, such as those contained in

the decision of 23 July 1975, which lays down the general framework in which such decisions are adopted. However, the failure to publish the decision delegating authority to the member of the Commission responsible for competition matters did not deprive the applicants of the opportunity of contesting that decision or the decision adopted under the delegation of authority on the ground that they were defective.
40. In those circumstances, it must be held that the decision of 5 November 1980 authorizing the member of the Commission responsible for competition matters to adopt in the name of the Commission and subject to its control a decision under Article 14 (3) of Regulation No 17 ordering undertakings to submit to investigations does not breach the principle of collegiate responsibility laid down in Article 17 of the Merger Treaty.
41. With regard to the second part of the submission concerning misuse in this case of the authority delegated, it must be pointed out that the failure of the undertakings concerned to agree to the scheduled investigations is not a ground which ought to have led the member of the Commission responsible for competition matters to have the measure considered by the full Commission. As has already been remarked, decisions ordering investigations under Article 14 (3) of Regulation No 17 are, by definition, adopted in cases in which the Commission expects that the undertakings will not submit voluntarily, for whatever reasons, to investigation.
42. The member of the Commission responsible for competition matters was therefore entitled to adopt the contested decision in the name of the Commission.

. . . . .

3. Literature

Bertram, 'Decision-Making in the EEC: Management Committee Procedure', (1967/8) CMLRev 246.
Schermers, *Judicial Protection in the European Communities*, Deventer, Fourth Edition. 1987, para 257–263.
Schindler, "The Problems of Decision-Making by way of the Management Committee Procedure in the European Economic Community", (1971) CML Rev. 184–205.
Wainwright, 'The execution of Community Food Aid to Developing Countries', (1976) CMLRev, 367–374.

V. The legally binding acts of the Council and the Commission

Whether an act of the Council or the Commission entails legal consequences for one or more subjects of the Communities is a question ultimately to be decided by the Court of Justice. In this respect neither the form nor the designation of the act appears to be conclusive; the nature and content of the act should also be considered.

The difference between the legal instruments mentioned in Article 189 EEC (Article 161 EAEC) and those mentioned in Articles 14, 15 (2) and 33 (2) ECSC are more apparent than real. Generally speaking, the characteristics of Regulations, Directives and Decisions in the EEC and Euratom systems are similar to those of general decisions, recommendations and individual decisions, respectively, in the ECSC system.

A. GENERAL CHARACTER

1. Introduction

The direct applicability of the legally binding acts of the Community institutions within the legal systems of the Member States – a particularly important aspect of Community law – is dealt with separately in Chapters two and three. Chapters two and three also include an examination of the general aspects of Community law.

2. Cases

(1) Lead and Zinc Case

For the facts and the ruling of the Court see page 10.

3. Literature

Lasok & Bridge, *Law & Institutions of the European Communities*, Fourth ed., London 1987, 111–135.
Lauwaars, *Lawfulness and Legal Force of Community Decisions*, Leiden 1973.
Pescatore, *The Law of Integration*, Leiden 1974, 65–71.

B. IS THE ENUMERATION OF COMMUNITY ACTS IN ARTICLE 189 EEC EXHAUSTIVE?

1. Introduction

If an act is found to entail legally binding consequences it does not immediately follow that it must be categorised as one of the acts mentioned in Article 189 EEC (Article 161 EAEC, Articles 14 and 33 para 2 ECSC); however, by far the greater part of Community law does consist of the Article 189 – type acts.

2. Cases

(1) Dairy Products Case

Commission of the EEC v. *Grand Duchy of Luxembourg and the Kingdom of Belgium*; Joined cases 90 and 91/63, Judgment of 13 November 1964; (1964) ECR 631; (1965) CMLR 58.

Facts:

By a Belgian Royal Decree of 3 November 1958, and a Grand Ducal Decree of 17 November 1958, the Belgium and Luxembourg governments introduced a tax payable on the delivery of import licences for various dairy products (evaporated milk, condensed milk, cheese).

In a letter dated 8 November 1961, the Commission of the EEC expressed the view that such charges were contrary to Article 12 of the Treaty and disapproved of their continuance. They invited the Governments concerned to give their observations. On receipt of these observations, the Commission, on 3 April 1963, issued a reasoned opinion under Article 169 of the Treaty. The two Governments declared themselves prepared to abolish the levies as soon as agreement was reached with the Commission on a suitable substitute, but stated that in the meantime the levies would remain in force. The Commission thereupon instituted proceedings in the Court on 15 October 1963.

The Commission asked the Court to find that the introduction and levying of a special duty on the issue of import licences for certain dairy products, such introduction and application having taken place after 1 January 1958, was in conflict with the Treaty, and in particular with Article 12.

The two Governments concerned contested the admissibility of the complaint. They argued that the Council of Ministers resolved on 4 April 1962, to issue a regulation relating to the setting-up of a common organization of markets for dairy produce, under Article 43 of the Treaty, before 31 July 1962. This Council Resolution was, however, not effected in proper time. The Commission, it was asserted, consequently lacked the right to bring proceedings in the Court for a finding which would require the two Governments to repeal measures which would have already existed in another form for some considerable time had the Community institutions complied with the obligations they had assumed.

The Court held:

As to the admissibility

The defendants, arguing that the application is inadmissible, complain that the Community failed to comply with the obligations falling on it by reason of the Resolution of the Council of 4 April 1962, and was thus responsible for the continuance of the alleged infringement of the Treaty, which should have ceased before the issue of the reasoned opinion under Article 169. In their view, since international law allows a party, injured by the failure of another party to perform its obligations, to withhold performance of its own, the Commission has lost the right to plead infringement of the Treaty. However, this relationship between the obligations of parties cannot be recognized under Community law.

In fact the Treaty is not limited to creating reciprocal obligations between the different natural and legal persons to whom it is applicable, but establishes a new legal order which governs the powers, rights and obligations of the said persons, as well as the necessary procedures for taking cognizance of and penalizing any breach of it. Therefore, except where otherwise expressly provided, the basic concept of the Treaty requires that the Member States shall not take the law into their own hands. Therefore the fact that the Council failed to carry out its obligations cannot relieve the defendants from carrying out theirs.

Moreover, the Resolution of the Council to take a decision under Article 43 by 31 July 1962 at the latest, so that the rules for milk products should enter into force by 1 November 1962 at the latest, does not create time-limits having the same effect as those laid down in the Treaty. The intention of the authors of the measures is clear from the fact that they adopted it under a style and form which are not those of the binding measures of the Council within the meaning of Article 189 of the Treaty. Therefore the Council did not infringe the Treaty when it failed to observe the time-limits which it had set itself in its Resolution of 4 April 1962.

. . . . .

Sequel:

Regarding the substantive part of the case the defendants advanced the argument that the introduction of new customs duties on agricultural products was not caught by the prohibition contained in Article 12 EEC because of the provisions of Article 39 – 46 EEC.

The Court rejected this argument on the grounds that Article 44 decreed the progressive abolition of customs duties for agricultural products and that it contained nothing from which any sort of exception to the principle laid down in Article 12 EEC could be inferred.

The argument that the Member States were given the right to maintain the national market organizations and thus also the means necessary to preserve their effectiveness (including the disputed one) was also refused by the Court. Thus Belgium and Luxembourg were found to have failed to comply with the obligation laid down in Article 12 EEC.

C. THE BINDING ACTS OF ARTICLE 189 EEC

The distinction between the various acts mentioned in Article 189 EEC (Article 161 EAEC, Article 14 ECSC) is important for a number of reasons e.g.:
- The extent of the right of appeal of private parties against Community acts varies according to the type of act used.
- In certain areas of Community competence the institutions are obliged to exercise their powers by the adoption of a particular type of act.

1. Regulations

a. Introduction

More use is made of the Regulation than any other legal instrument provided by the Treaties. The principal characteristics of the regulation, i.e. general and direct applications, facilitate the uniform application of Community law, a factor indispensible to the proper functioning of the Communities.

b. Cases

(1) Zuckerfabrik Watenstedt Case

Zuckerfabrik Watenstedt GmbH v. *Council of the EC*; Case 6/68; Judgment of 11 July 1968; (1968) ECR 413; (1969) CMLR 26.

Facts:

In December 1967 the EC Council issued Regulation No 1009/67 on the common organization of the market in sugar. The regulation provided for guaranteed sales and guaranteed prices for the various kinds of sugar products produced in the Community at different stages of processing. Article 9 (3) of the regulation provided that the scheme of guarantees should cease to have effect in relation to raw beet sugar from 1 January 1969. The applicant, a producer of raw beet sugar in the Federal German Republic, asked the European Court to annul Article 9 (3) on the ground that it was an unlawful decision in the form of a regulation prejudicing the applicant's special interests. The Council (the respondent) raised a preliminary objection to the applicant on the ground of inadmissibility.

The Court held:

The applicant seeks the annulment of Article 9 (3) of Regulation No 1009/67 of the Council of 18 December 1967 on the common organization of the market in sugar. By virtue of the contested provision the obligation, laid down by Article 9 (1), on the part of the intervention agencies designated by the Member States to buy in, subject to certain conditions, at the intervention price the quantities of raw or white beet or cane sugar offered to them, terminates on 31 December 1969. The defendant has raised an objection of inadmissibility under Article 91 of the Rules of Procedure, arguing that there is at issue no decision which is of direct and individual concern to the applicant.

In order to determine whether the application is admissible, it is necessary to examine whether the contested measure is a regulation or a decision within the meaning of Articles 173 and 189 of the Treaty. By virtue of the second paragraph of Article 189 of the Treaty the criterion for distinguishing between a regulation and a decision is whether the measure at issue is of 'general application' or not. The nature of the contested provision must therefore be studied and in particular the legal effect which it is intended to or does actually produce.

Having observed that this provision is addressed to various classes of persons, namely the intervention agencies, the other buyers and the sellers, including those producers who manufacture exclusively raw beet sugar, the applicant says that in the present case, in order to decide whether the measure at issue is in the nature of a regulation or an individual decision, it is necessary to examine specifically what significance the measure has for the applicant or for the class of persons to which it belongs. According to the applicant the effects of the contested measure are of direct and individual concern to 'a specific class of persons: the producers of raw beet sugar' because the contested measure produces for them specific effects which are different from and more burdensome than those which it produces on the other persons to which it applies.

The common organization of the market in sugar, established by Regulation No 1009/67, is essentially governed by means of price. In order to ensure that the necessary guarantees in respect of employment and standards of living are maintained for Community growers of sugar beet and sugar cane this regulation makes provision for measures to stabilize the sugar market by providing for the fixing of a target price for white sugar, as well as derived intervention prices which take account both of differences between regional prices and of the stage of processing of the products. The obligation on the part of the intervention agencies to buy the quantities offered to them is an essential condition for maintaining a level of prices corresponding to the intervention prices. Thus, by requiring these agencies to buy in raw sugar beet until 31 December 1969, Article 9 (3) of Regulation No 1009/67 in fact stipulates that measures relating to the common organization of the market in sugar shall only apply to raw beet sugar until the said date.

This provision therefore regulates the prices of a product and, as a result, the rights and duties of buyers and sellers, including producers. Such a measure is of general application within the meaning of Article 189 of the Treaty, for it is applicable to objectively determined situations and involves legal consequences for categories of persons viewed in a general and abstract manner. It affects the applicant solely by virtue of its capacity as a seller of raw beet sugar, and not by reason of any more narrowly defined characteristic. Furthermore, a provision which, like Article 9 (3), abrogates a provision of general application or places a time-limit on its applicability, partakes of the general nature of the latter provision.

Moreover, a measure does not lose its character as a regulation simply because it may be possible to ascertain with a greater or lesser degree the number or even the identity of the persons to which it applies at any given time as long as there is no doubt that the measure is applicable as the result of an objective situation of law or of fact which it specifies and which is in harmony with its ultimate objective. Furthermore, the fact that a legal provision may have different practical effects on the different persons to whom it applies in no way contradicts its nature as a regulation provided that the situation to which it refers is objectively determined.

The defendant has not contravened these requirements in not regulating the system of prices for one product in the same way as for other products. If one were to refuse to recognize a measure regulating prices as being in the nature of a regulation simply because it concerns a particular product and affects the producers thereof by reason of circumstances in which they are differentiated from all other persons, the concept of a decision would thereby be expanded to such an extent as to emperil the system of the Treaty which only allows individuals to bring application for annulment against individual decisions addressed to them or against measures which affect them in a similar manner.

The application must therefore be dismissed as inadmissible.

(2) Turkey Tail Case

Hauptzollamt Hamburg-Oberelbe v. *Forma Paul G. Bollmann*; Case 40/69; Preliminary ruling of 18 February 1970; (1970) ECR 79; (1970) CMLR 141.

Facts:

Defendant Bollmann had imported into Germany goods from the USA described as 'turkey tails'. The German Customs Office originally classified these turkey tails under the tariff heading for 'edible turkey offal' and imposed the appropriate levy for this heading.

A few months later, however, a new decision was taken, classifying turkey tails under the heading 'poultry parts' and requesting Bollmann to pay an additional levy. Bollmann appealed against this decision to the Finanzgericht (Court of Finance) Hamburg which annulled the decision. The appellant Chief Customs Office lodged an appeal with the Bundesfinanzhof against the judgment of the Finanzgericht. The Bundesfinanzhof requested the Court of Justice to give a preliminary ruling, not only whether 'turkey tails' should be considered to come under the one or the other heading of the Common

Customs Tariff, but also whether the relevant Community Regulation No 22, establishing the Common Market organization for poultry allowed the national legislation to interpret these definitions autonomously or not. The latter point raised some questions of principle.

The Court held:

The first question

2. In its first question the Bundesfinanzhof asks the Court whether the correct interpretation of Article 14 of Regulation No 22/62 is that Member States are entitled and obliged to take internal legislative measures to specify which products are subject to the levy by virtue of Article 1 of that regulation and to differentiate between them.
3. According to Article 14 of Regulation No 22/62 'Member States shall take all steps to adapt their laws, regulations, and administrative provisions in such a way that the provisions of the present regulation, unless hereby otherwise provided, may be effectively implemented as from 1 July 1962'.
4. Since Regulation No 22/62, in conformity with the second paragraph of Article 189 of the Treaty, is directly applicable in all Member States, the latter, unless otherwise expressly provided, are precluded from taking steps, for the purpose of applying the regulation, which are intended to alter its scope or supplement its provisions. To the extent to which member States have transferred legislative powers in tariff matters with the object of ensuring the satisfactory operation of a common market in agriculture they no longer have the powers to adopt legislative provisions in this field.

. . . . .

6. Therefore the answer to the first question must be in the negative.

The second question

7. In the event of the first question's being answered in the negative the Budesfinanzhof asks the Court whether 'Article 1 of Regulation No 22/62 which mentions some of the goods included in the Common Customs Tariff is to be construed as meaning that national legislatures may interpret the terms by which these goods are described, since the terms by which goods in a customs tariff are described of necessity require interpretation'.
8. As the description of the goods referred to in the regulations establishing a common organization of a market is part of Community law its inter-

pretation can only be settled in accordance with Community procedures. Moreover the common organization of the markets in agriculture, such as the one which it is the aim of Regulation No 22/62 to establish progressively, can only achieve their objectives if the provisions adopted for their realization are applied in a uniform manner in all Member States. The descriptions of goods covered by these organizations must therefore have exactly the same range in all Member States.

9. Such a requirement would be placed in jeopardy if, whenever there was a difficulty in the classification of any goods for tariff purposes, each Member State could determine the range covered by the descriptions in question by way of interpretation. Although it is true that in the event of any difficulty in the classification of any goods the national administration may be led to take implementing measures and clarify in the particular case the doubts raised by the description of the goods, it can only do so if it complies with the provisions of Community law and subject to the reservation that the national authorities cannot issue binding rules of interpretation.

10. The second question must therefore be answered in the negative.

Sequel:

In its third question the Federal Finance Court asked for the classification of the turkey parts in question. The Community Court replied that 'edible offals' included 'products having similar commercial value as the disputed products'.

(3) Slaughtered Cow Case II

EEC Commission v. *Italy*; Case 39/72; Judgment of 7 February 1973; (1973) ECR 101.

Facts:

To combat the substantial and growing surpluses in the sector of milk and milk products in the Community the Council by Regulation No 1975/69 of 6 October 1969 instituted a system of premiums for slaughtering cows and for withholding milk and milk products from the market. The methods of implementing this system were established by Regulation No 2195/69 of the Commission of 4 November 1969.

As Italy did not adopt the required implementing legislation, the Commission by letter of 21 June 1971 commenced the procedure provided for by Article 169 of the EEC Treaty. This letter was followed by a reasoned opinion of 21 February 1972. On 3 July 1972 the Commission, under Article 169, para 2, brought the failure of the Italian Republic before the Court of

Justice. One of the Commission's complaints was that the Italian Government, in its interministerial decree of 22 March 1972, had only reproduced the provisions of the Regulation.

The Court held:

. . . . .

17. By following this procedure, the Italian Government has brought into doubt both the legal nature of the applicable provisions and the date of their coming into force.

    According to the terms of Article 189 and 191 of the Treaty, Regulations are, as such, directly applicable in all Member States and come into force solely by virtue of their publication in the Official Journal of the Communities, as from the date specified in them, or in the absence thereof, as from the date provided in the Treaty.

    Consequently, all methods of implementation are contrary to the Treaty which would have the result of creating an obstacle to the direct effect of Community Regulations and of jeopardizing their simultaneous and uniform application in the whole of the Community.

. . . . .

Sequel:

The Court declared that the Italian Republic, in not taking the necessary implementing measures, had failed to fulfil its obligations under the said Regulations.

2 Directives

a. Introduction

As opposed to the use of the Regulation, the use of the Directive is not intended to achieve complete uniformity in the area with which it deals. The Directive is binding as to the result to be achieved, the choice of the method of implementation being left to the addressee. However, it is doubtful whether the difference between the end to be achieved and the method of implementation is as clearcut as would appear from the wording of Article

189 EEC. In many cases the result to be achieved is so dependent on the method of implementation that the choice of the latter is severely restricted.
The following cases deal with:
1. The binding effect of the time-limit for implementation which a directive normally contains;
2. The question whether a directive about the harmonization of legislation may contain very detailed provisions and may even require the adoption of uniform rules.

b. Cases

(1) **Marketing of vegetable seed Case**

Commission of the EC v. *Italian Republic*; Case 52/75; Judgment of the Court of 26 February 1976; (1976) ECR 284; (1976) 2 CMLR 320.

Facts:

By an application lodged by the Court Registry on 10 June 1975, the Commission brought before the Court, under Article 169 of the EEC Treaty, an action for a declaration that by failing to bring into force within the time-limit laid down by Article 43 of Council Directive No 70/458 on the marketing of vegetable seed, all the laws, regulations and administrative provisions necessary to comply with the provisions of the said directive, the Italian Republic has failed in its obligations under the Treaty.

The Court held:

. . . . .

10. The correct application of a directive is particularly important since the implementing measures are left to the discretion of the Member States and would be ineffective if the desired aims are not achieved within the prescribed time-limits. Although the provisions of a directive are no less binding on the Member States to which they are addressed than the provisions of any other rule of Community law, such an effect attaches a fortiori to the provisions relating to the periods allowed for implementing the measures prescribed, in particular since the existence of differences in

the rules applied in the Member States after these periods have expired might result in discrimination.

. . . . .

Sequel:

The Court ruled:

That by not adopting within the time prescribed all the laws, regulations and administrative provisions necessary to comply with Council Directive No 70/458, the Italian Republic had failed in one of its obligations under the Treaty.

(2) Enka Case

Enka B.V. v. *Inspecteur Invoerrechten en Accijnzen Arnhem*; Case 38/77; Preliminary ruling of 23 November 1977; (1977) ECR 2203.

Facts:

According to Article 1 (1) Regulation No 803/68 on the valuation of goods for customs purposes (OJ 1968, L 148/6) the value for customs purposes is the 'normal price', i.e. the price which a buyer and a seller, who are independent of each other, would fetch on a sale in the open market. Article 9 of the Regulation provides, however, that this 'normal price' may be 'the price paid or payable' if, in particular, that price is adjusted, if necessary, to take account of circumstances of the sale which differ from those on which the normal price is based.

This provision has, as regards in particular determination of the value for customs purposes of goods placed in a customs warehouse, been implemented by Article 10 of Council Directive No 69/74 EEC of 4 March 1969 on the harmonization of provisions laid down by law, regulation or *administrative action relating to customs warehousing procedure* (OJ 1969, L 58/7). Article 10, para. 2 (d) of this Directive provides that as regards the price paid or payable 'the costs of warehousing and of preserving the goods while in warehouses borne by a purchaser shall not be included in the value for customs purposes where the price paid or payable by that purchaser is taken as the basis for valuation'.

When in the present case the Inspector of Customs and Excise refused to accept the deduction of costs of storage from the actual invoice price and Enka had brought an action against this decision before the Tariefcommissie (the Dutch administrative court of last instance in customs matters), the latter asked the Court to give a preliminary ruling on (1) the direct effect of Article 10.2 (d) of the Directive, and (2) the meaning of this provision.

The Court held:

. . . . .

11. It emerges from the third paragraph of Article 189 of the Treaty that the choice left to the Member States as regards the form of the measures and the methods used in their adoption by the national authorities depends upon the result which the Council or the Commission wishes to see achieved.
12. As regards the harmonization of the provisions relating to customs matters laid down in the Member States by law, regulation or administrative action, in order to bring about the uniform application of the Common Customs Tariff it may prove necessary to ensure the absolute identity of those provisions which govern the treatment of goods imported into the Community, whatever the Member State across whose frontier they are imported.

. . . . .

Sequel:

Subsequently the Court confirmed the direct effect of Article 10, para. 2(d) of the Directive. As to the meaning of this provision it held that the costs of warehousing and of preserving the goods whilst in warehouses within the territory of the Community should indeed have been deducted.

c. Literature

Easson, 'EEC Directives for the Harmonization of Laws: Some Problems of Validity, Implementation and Legal Effects', 1 Yb. Eur. Law 1984, 1–44.
Timmermans, 'Directives: their Effect within the National Legal Systems', (1978) CMLRev., 533–555.

3. *Decisions*

a. Introduction

The characterization of a legal act as a Decision within the meaning of Article 189 EEC is important primarily because of the extended judicial remedy available to the addressee. Thus, the Court of Justice has often been asked to pronounce on the distinction between a Decision and a Regulation on the one hand and a Decision and a non-binding act on the other hand.

b. Cases

(1) Cement Convention Case

See below page 55.

VI. Acts of the representatives of the Governments of the Member States meeting within the Council of Ministers

A. INTRODUCTION

Some decisions dealing with the functioning of the Communities are made by the Representatives of the Governments of the Member States meeting within the framework of the Council of Ministers. These decisions should not be confused with acts adopted by the Council of Ministers as such. The legal nature and effect of these decisions of the Representatives of the Member States remain unclear, but the general view is that they are agreements under international law.

1. Literature

Bebr, 'Acts of representatives of the Governments of the Member States taken within the Council of Ministers of the European Communities', SEW 1966, 529–545.
Lauwaars, 'The European Council', (1977) CMLRev., 25–44.
Mortelmans, 'The extramural meetings of the Ministers of the Member States of the Community', (1974) CMLRev., 62–91.
Schwartz, 'Article 235 and Law-Making Powers in the European community', 27 ICLQ 1978, 614–628.
Toth, 'The legal status of the declarations annexed to the Single European Act', (1986) CMLRev., 803–812.

Chapter Two

The Court of Justice of the European Communities

I. Introduction

(Survey of the functions attributed to the
Court of Justice of the European Communities)

A. Review of the legality of Community acts

1. Action for annulment

The Community Treaties allow community legislation in specific fields only and under several restrictions. Regulations, directives and decisions need an explicit legal basis in the treaties, they must be reasoned, they can only be taken by particular institutions, etc.

The Court of Justice is charged with the legal review of such provisions. Whenever an act of a Community organ does not fulfil the necessary conditions it can be annulled by the Court (EEC Article 173).

The right to bring an action for annulment has been restricted. The treaty-makers feared too much dispute of the legality of community acts and therefore restricted this right to the Member States, the Commission, the Council and those persons most directly affected by the act concerned.

To illustrate the action for annulment – (and in particular the questions against what, by whom and on what grounds it can be brought) – we present some extracts of case-law in sub-chapter II A.

The action for annulment in the European Coal and Steel Community differs to some extent from that in the other Communities. In particular it is easier to challenge decisions addressed to other persons. In order not to extend this case-book beyond the essentials the cases under ECSC Article 33 have been omitted.

2. Action against failure to act

Sometimes Community institutions are obliged to take action for the benefit of particular persons. If in such cases no action is taken the interested person may bring an action against failure to act (EEC Article 175). This action is very similar to the action for annulment, but for the fact that there is no act which can be annulled. This is illustrated in sub-chapter II B.

3. Plea of illegality

An individual may not bring an action against regulations. He may be affected, however, by a decision addressed to him which is based on an irregular regulation. In such a case he would have no judicial remedy as the decision is not irregular and the underlying regulation not challengeable. To remedy that situation the individual may then invoke the illegality of the underlying regulation when attacking the decision. To illustrate this plea of illegality (EEC Article 184) we shall give some extracts of cases in sub-chapter II C.

4. Interim measures

In urgent matters the President of the Court of Justice may issue interim measures. We shall give an example under IID.

B. UNLIMITED JURISDICTION

The power of the Court of Justice to ensure the legality of Community acts is limited. It can annul the acts concerned on specific grounds only, and has no third choice other than to annul such acts in whole or in part or to uphold them. In most Community countries such supervision is the task of special administrative courts.

But, in addition to action against administrative acts, the administration can be sued for contractual or non-contractual liability. In most countries such proceedings fall under the jurisdiction of the ordinary civil courts, and are not basically different from proceedings between private persons. Under Community law cases of contractual liability are brought before the ordinary civil court of the Member State concerned. Cases of non-contractual liability often concern official acts of the communities which should not be judged by national courts. The treaties therefore provide that they must be brought before the Court of Justice (EEC Articles 178 and 215, para 2).

In particular circumstances the Communities have a right to levy fines. The Court of Justice has jurisdiction in respect of actions against such fines (EEC Article 172, ECSC Article 36).

The Court of Justice also operates as administrative tribunal for the civil service of the Communities (EEC Article 179).

In the above mentioned cases the task of the court is not limited to checking the legality of administrative acts on the basis of specific grounds of illegality, nor is it limited in the scope of its jurisdiction to either upholding or annulling an administrative act: it is completely free to pronounce upon the existence and ambit of the rights of the parties involved and replace the opinions of the administration by its own judgment. Consequently, this jurisdiction is called 'unlimited jurisdiction'. Some cases of unlimited jurisdiction have been extracted in sub-chapter III.

C. The role of national courts

The Court of Justice only controls the *legality* of community law, its *application* has been attributed to the national courts. These courts must apply community law, as part of their national legal system, between individuals and their States as well as between individuals mutually.

In the next chapter the role of national courts will be discussed and it will be seen, that when applying Community law national courts may meet questions of interpretation of community law or of validity of acts of community institutions. For such questions they may (or in highes instance: must) obtain the official interpretation by the Court of Justice, called 'preliminary ruling' (EEC Article 177). The procedure of preliminary ruling promotes uniform interpretation of community law within all Member States. The possibility of obtaining a ruling on the validity of Community acts also widens the scope of judicial review. The individual, unable to bring an action against regulations, may request his national court to ask a preliminary ruling on the validity of a regulation and in this manner ensure that incorrect regulations will not be applied.

In sub-chapter IV some extracts of preliminary rulings of the Court of Justice have been reproduced.

D. Actions against Member States

When the Commission or another Member State alleges that a Member State has violated the Community Treaties, the Court of Justice may have to decide whether the allegation is well founded. The Court thus reviews the application of the Treaties by the Members (EEC Article 169).

According to Article 171 of the EEC Treaty Member States are required to take the necessary measures to comply with the judgment whenever the Court of Justice finds that they have failed to fulfil any of their obligations. The EEC Treaty does not provide for further sanctions.

Of particular interest is the question whether interested persons may claim damages from States which have violated the EEC Treaty.

Extracts of cases on the action against Member States are included in subchapter V.

The action against Member States under the ECSC Treaty differs from that under the other treaties, but have been omitted for the sake of brevity.

E. PROCEDURES

A final chapter on procedure has been added, mainly for reference purpose.

F. LITERATURE

For a detailed description of the actions mentioned, see:

Gerhard Bebr, *Development of Judicial control of the European Communities*, The Hague 1982.

L. Neville Brown and F.G. Jacobs, *The Court of Justice of the European Communities*, London.

T.C. Hartley, *The Foundations of European Community Law*, Oxford 1981.

Henry G. Schermers, *Judicial Protection in the European Communities*, Deventer 1987, fourth edition.

A.G. Toth, *Legal Protection of Individuals in the European Communities*, Amsterdam, 1978.

II. Judicial review of Community acts

A. ACTION FOR ANNULMENT

(EEC Article 173)

1. Acts susceptible of judicial review

The action for annulment can be brought against binding acts of the Communities during two months after the acts have been published. The issue of which acts are susceptible of review has been discussed in Chapter One. See the *Cement Convention Case*. In several cases (not quoted) the Court has decided that one action is possible against a number of decisions. In the *Geitling Case I* (quoted below) the question is discussed whether an action can be brought against part of a decision. In the *ERTA Case* the question was whether an action is possible against acts other than those enumerated in Article 189. In the *IBM Case* the Court had to decide the possibility to bring an action against acts which are not necessarily final.

a. Cases

(1) Geitling Case I

Geitling GmbH and Associated Coalmines v. *High Authority*; Case 2/56; Judgment of 20 March 1957; [1957] ECR 14.

Facts:

By decision No 5/56 the High Authority had approved a sales agreement between 19 mining enterprises united in the sales agency 'Geitling'. A number of sales conditions in Article 8 of this Decision were unacceptable to Geitling. It did not, however, want to question the authorization, as such, contained in the Decision and brought an action only against Article 8. The High Authority objected that an action against only one provision in a decision was inadmissible.

The Court held:

. . . . .

During the oral procedure it has been argued that an application cannot be admissible if it contests an isolated provision of a decision as a whole, since a partial annulment automatically transforms the remainder of the decision into a new decision, and that this is contrary to Article 34 of the Treaty, which provides that where a decision is annulled, the matter shall be referred back to the High Authority.

This objection is unfounded because under Article 34 the judgment cannot anticipate the measures which the High Authority may be required to adopt in order to amend its decision, having regard to the annulment.

Sequel:

The Court subsequently annulled Article 8 of the Decision.
Note: Under the EEC Treaty a similar decision was given in the *Transocean Marine Paint Case* (17/74), 23 October 1974, [1974] ECR 1082.

(2) ERTA Case

Commission of the EC v. *Council of the EC*; Case 22/70; Judgment of 31 March 1971; [1971] ECR 273; [1971] CMLR 335.

Facts:

19 January 1962, under the auspices of the United Nations Economic Commission for Europe (ECE), the European Road Transport Agreement (ERTA: concerning the work of crews of vehicles engaged in international transport) was signed in Geneva by five of the six Member States of the EEC and by a certain number of other European States. This Agreement never came into force for lack of a sufficient number of ratifications.

In 1967, negotiations began for the revision of the Agreement, under the auspices of the European Conference of Ministers of Transport, and subsequently of the Economic Commission for Europe (ECE). Meanwhile work had been going on within the EEC with regard to the harmonization of driving and rest periods of drivers of road transport vehicles. These activities resulted in the adoption of Council Regulation No 543/69 of 25 March 1969 (JO 1969, L 77/49) concerning the harmonization of certain social provisions in the field of road transport.

In view of the forthcoming meeting of the road transport subcommittee of the EEC due to be held 1–3 April 1970 in Geneva, the Council of the European Communities, in its meeting of 20 March 1970, discussed the attitude to be adopted by the six Member States in the negotiations for the revised European Road Transport Agreement. In the negotiations the six Member States took up the common position agreed on during discussions in the Council of 20 March 1970. The revised ERTA was declared to be open for signature by States as from 1 July 1970.

The Commission disagreed with the procedure followed by the Council and the Member States in respect of the revised ERTA. Claiming that the negotiation and conclusion were no longer a matter of State authority but should have been carried out by the Community, the Commission started the present proceedings on 19 May 1970, seeking annulment of the Council's discussion of 20 March 1970, regarding the negotiation and conclusion of the ERTA by the Member States. The questions arose whether the discussion in the Council was susceptible of judicial review.

The Court held:

. . . . .

34. The Council considers that the proceedings of 20 March 1970 do not constitute an act, within the meaning of the first sentence of the first paragraph of Article 173, the legality of which is open to review.
35. Neither by their form nor by their subject-matter or content, it is argued, were these proceedings a regulation, a decision or a directive within the meaning of Article 189.

36. They were really nothing more than a coordination of policies amongst Member States within the framework of the Council, and as such created no rights, imposed no obligations and did not modify any legal position.
37. This is said to be the case more particularly because in the event of a dispute between the institutions admissibility has to be appraised with particular rigour.
38. Under Article 173, the Court has a duty to review the legality 'of acts of the Council ... other than recommendations or opinions'.
39. Since the only matters excluded from the scope of the action for annulment open to the Member States and the institutions are 'recommendations or opinions' – which by the final paragraph of Article 189 are declared to have no binding force – Article 173 treats as acts open to review by the Court all measures adopted by the institutions which are intended to have legal force.
40. The objective of this review is to ensure, as required by Article 164, observance of the law in the interpretation and application of the Treaty.
41. It would be inconsistent with this objective to interpret the conditions under which the action is admissible so restrictively as to limit the availability of this procedure merely to the categories of measures referred to by Article 189.
42. An action for annulment must therefore be available in the case of all measures adopted by the institutions, whatever their nature of form, which are intended to have legal effects.

. . . . .

(3) IBM Case

International Business Machines Corporation (IBM) v. *Commission*; Case 60/81; Judgment of 11 November 1981; [1981] ECR 2651; [1981] 3 CMLR 7.

Facts:

By a letter of 19 December 1980 the Commission informed IBM that it was of the opinion that IBM had infringed Article 86 of the EEC Treaty by abusing its dominant position on the Common Market. The Commission considered imposing a fine on IBM but before taking a decision it wished to take account of any observations which IBM might want to take. With the letter the Commission enclosed a Statement of Objections.

IBM brought an action for annulment against this letter. The question was whether this letter was an act susceptible of appeal.

The Court held:

. . . . .

8. According to Article 173 of the Treaty proceedings may be brought for a declaration that acts of the Council and the Commission other than recommendations or opinions are void. That remedy is available in order to ensure, as required by Article 164, that in the interpretation and application of the Treaty the law is observed, and it would be inconsistent with that objective to interpret restrictively the conditions under which the action is admissible by limiting its scope merely to the categories of measures referred to in Article 189.
9. In order to ascertain whether the measures in question are acts within the meaning of Article 173 it is necessary, therefore, to look to their substance. According to the consistent case-law of the Court any measure the legal effect of which are are binding on, and capable of affecting the interests of, the applicant by bringing about a distinct change in his legal position is an act or decision which may be the subject of an action under Article 173 for a declaration that it is void. However, the form in which such acts or decisions are cast is, in principle, immaterial as regards the question whether they are open to challenge under that article.
10. In the case of acts or decisions adopted by a procedure involving several stages, in particular where they are the culmination of an internal procedure, it is clear from the case law that in principle an act is open to review only if it is a measure definitively laying down the position of the Commission or the Council on the conclusion of that procedure, and not a provisional measure intended to pave the way for the final decision.

. . . . .

20. An application for a declaration that the initiation of a procedure and a statement of objections are void might make it necessary for the Court to arrive at a decision on questions on which the Commission has not yet had an opportunity to state its position and would as a result anticipate the arguments on the substance of the case, confusing different procedural stages both administrative and judicial. It would thus be incompatible with the system of the division of powers between the Commission and the Court and of the remedies laid down by the Treaty, as well as the requirements of the sound administration of justice and the proper course of the administrative procedure to be followed in the Commission.
21. It follows from the foregoing that neither the initiation of a procedure nor

a statement of objections may be considered, on the basis of their nature and the legal effects they produce, as being decisions within the meaning of Article 173 of the EEC Treaty which may be challenged in an action for a declaration that they are void. In the context of the administrative procedure as laid down by Regulations No 17 and No 99/63, they are procedural measures adopted preparatory to the decision which represents their culmination.

The Court declared the case inadmissible.

2. Capacity to bring an action

N.B.: Read carefully Article 173, para 2. The paragraph demonstrates that an individual may bring an action against a decision addressed to himself, but that actions against regulations are impossible and actions against decisions addressed to others extremely difficult. An individual who wants to challenge an act other than a decision addressed to himself has to overcome two hurdles: (a) he must demonstrate that the act is in fact not a regulation, but a decision and (b) he must show that the act is of direct and individual concern to him. Our first question is whether the second hurdle includes the first: if an act is of direct and individual concern to a person is it then not by definition a decision? We shall see in the *CAM Case* that this question can be answered in the affirmative if an entire act is disputed. The *Scholten Honig Case I* demonstrates that an act cannot be challenged by an individual if it is part of a regulation or of a system of regulations even in the case where the individual could be directly and individually concerned. In that case the regulatory nature of the act remains to be a separate and preceding hurdle.

a. There must be a legal act

i. CASES

(1) Cement Convention Case

CBR et al. v. *Commission*; Cases 8–11/66; Judgment of 15 March 1967; [1967] ECR 91; [1967] ECR 91; [1967] CMLR 77.

Facts:

On 6 July 1956, seventy-four enterprises concluded the so-called 'Noordwijks Cement Accoord' (NAC). On 31 October 1962, the EEC was notified of the agreement, in pursuance of Regulation No. 17, on Competition (OJ 204/62). Under Article 15, para 2a of Regulation No. 17, enterprises which participate in a cartel contrary to the EEC Treaty are liable to heavy fines. The fine cannot, however, be imposed in respect of cartels which have been notified to the Commission so long as the Commission has not pronounced on their validity and on the possibility of exempting it from the prohibition of cartels (Article 15, para 5). There is, however, an exception to this temporary safeguard for notified cartels. If after a provisional enquiry the Commission is of the opinion that the cartel in question is incompatible with the EEC rules and that there are no grounds for exemption, it can communicate this to the parties concerned. This then removes the protection against fines for the period between notification and the final Decision of the Commission (Article 15, para 6).

On 14 December 1965, the Commission decided to address to the enterprises in question such a communication, as provided for in Article 15, para 6, of Regulation No. 17. This communication was transmitted by a registered letter of 3 January 1966, by the Director-General of the 'Competition' division, a Member of the staff of the Commission, who had been duly authorized for that purpose by the Commission. The letter stated:

'The Commission has submitted the agreement to a provisional examination. It has arrived at the conclusion that the conditions for Article 85, para 1 of the Treaty are fulfilled and that it is not justified in applying Article 85, para 3 to the agreement as notified.

The Commission calls your attention to the fact that the provisions of Article 15 para 5 of the Regulation, no longer apply to the aforesaid agreement from the day of receipt of this communication ...'.

Against this communication the plaintiffs lodged an appeal. The plaintiffs argued that the communication had to be considered as a Decision because of its legal effects. The legal position of the enterprises had been modified by the communication insofar as the latter had now become subject to the penalties provided for in Article 15 para 2. The plaintiffs asked for the annulment of the Decision, in particular for infringement of the procedural rule requiring that all Community acts are fully reasoned.

The Commission argued that the appeal should not be allowed, as a communication under Article 15, para 6 was in no sense a Decision within the meaning of Article 189 and 173, para 2, of the Treaty, but merely an 'opinion'. Neither the form nor the content of the communication, which was an act devoid of definite legal effect and not the result of an internal administrative procedure, allowed any doubt on that point.

The Court held:

The effect of the measure of 14 December 1965 and 3 January 1966 was that the undertakings ceased to be protected by Article 15 (5) which exempted them from fines, and came under the contrary rules of Article 15 (2) which thenforth exposed them to the risk of fines. This posed them to a grave financial risk. Thus the said measure affected the interests of the undertakings by bringing about a distinct change in their legal position. It is unequivocally a measure which produces legal effects touching the interests of the undertakings concerned and which is binding on them. It thus constitutes not a mere opinion but a decision. Any doubt which might be raised by the question whether the notification of the said decision was made in proper form in no way alters the nature of that decision and cannot affect the admissibility of the application.

Sequel:

The grounds on which the Commission contested the admissibility of the case were not accepted by the Court. The applicants won the application for annulment of the decision in question as it was found that the Commission had failed to state the reasons on which it was based.

b. The act must be a decision

i. CASES

(1) CAM Case

Société CAM S.A. v. *Commission*; Case 100/74; 18 November 1975; [1975] ECR 1402.

Facts:

Having regard to the difficulties in the agricultural sector caused, during the summer of 1974, in particular by the increase in costs of production aggravating the effects of inflation on agriculture, the Council by regulation No. 2496/74 (OJ L 268 of 3 October 1974), by way of derogation from the principle of the annual fixing of prices, made an increase of 5% in the common prices of numerous agricultural products with effect from 7 October 1974. Article 4 of that regulation provided that the detailed rules for its application, any transitional measures and the alterations to be made to prices as a result of this regulation, should be adopted by the Commission.

On that basis the Commission adopted Regulation (EEC) No 2546/74 which provided that exports of cereals in respect of which the advance-fixing certificate was dated prior to 7 October 1974, should not benefit from the exceptional increase in the threshold price because it was reasonable to believe that the exporters concerned had already covered themselves by purchasing before the increase laid down by the Council on 2 October 1974.

CAM had on 19 July 1974 obtained an export licence for 10.000 metric tons of barley, valid until 16 October 1974 with advance fixing of the refund at nil.

It was refused the increase provided for by the Council and it brought an action for the annulment of Regulation No 2346/74 of the Commission.

CAM considered its application to be admissible because Regulation No 2546/74 of the Commission did not amount to a provision having general application within the meaning of the second paragraph of Article 189 of the Treaty, but constituted a group of individual decisions in the form of a regulation, directly and individually concerning a limited number of addresses, including the applicant.

According to the Commission, the contested measure being a regulation, the application must, since it came from a private person, be rejected as admissible as Article 173 of the Treaty did not entitle natural or legal persons other than the Member States, the Council or the Commission to seek the annulment of such measures.

The Court held:

. . . . .

14. The contested measure, by denying to a class of traders the benefit of an increase in the amount of refunds for specific exports which was on the contrary granted to those whose applications for advance fixing were made at a later date, directly concerns the said traders.
15. On the other hand it applies to a fixed and known number of cereal exporters as well as, in respect of each of them, to the amount of the transactions for which advance fixing had been requested.
16. This is all the more so because, as refunds were abolished as from 26 July, the category of traders affected is reduced to those who, having had advance fixing before 26 July 1974, still had current export licences on 7 October.
17. It appears from the above-mentioned recital that the distinction drawn in respect of them is based on the presumption that they were already previously covered in respect of exports not yet effected on 7 October at prices not yet affected by the increase which was to take effect on that date.
18. By adopting these distinguishing criteria the contested measure affects a fixed number of traders indentified by reason of the individual course of action which they pursued or are regarded as having pursued during a particular period.
19. Such a measure, even if it is one of a number of provisions having a legislative function, individually concerns the persons to whom it applies in that it affects their legal position because of a factual situation which differentiates them from all other persons and distinguishes them individually just as in the case of the person addressed.

20. The application is admissible.

(after the Court had studied the merits of the case, the application was dismissed as unfounded).

(2) Scholten-Honig Case I

Koninklijke Scholten-Honig N.V. v. *Council*; Case 101/76; Judgment of 5 May 1977; [1977] ECR 806; [1980] 2 CMLR 669.

Facts:

By Regulations of 27 July 1976 and of 31 August 1976 the Council and the Commission had reduced the amount of the subsidy on starch used in the manufacture of a particular sort of glucose for the year 1976/1977 and had provided for the complete abolition of the subsidy for 1977/78.
Scholten-Honig, the most important manufacturer of that sort of glucose, lodged an application for the annulment of the Regulations. It submitted that only a limited number of manufacturers were affected and that no others could be added because the necessary investments would take longer than the period during which the Regulations were applicable. The Regulations, or at least part of them, should, therefore be seen as bundles of Decisions, which were of direct and individual concern to Scholten-Honig.

The Court held:

. . . . .

8. In order to make a decision as to the admissibility of the application it is therefore necessary to examine whether the contested measures are regulations or decisions within the meaning of Article 173 of the Treaty.
9. By virtue of the second paragraph of Article 189 of the Treaty the criterion for distinguishing between a regulation and a decision is whether the measure at issue is of general application or not.
10. The nature of the contested measures must therefore be studied and in particular the legal effects which it is intended to or does actually produce.
11. It is necessary in this connection to consider the provisions in question in the context of the rules on production refunds for starches.

. . . . .

20. A regulation which provides for the reduction of a production refund for a whole marketing year with regard to a certain product processed from cereals and rice and for its complete abolition from the following marketing year is by its nature a measure of general application within the meaning of Article 189 of the Treaty.
21. It in fact applies to objectively determined situations and produces legal effects with regard to categories of persons regarded generally and in the abstract.
22. It only affects the applicant by virtue of its capacity as a producer of glucose having high fructose content without any other specification.
23. Moreover the nature of a measure as a regulation is not called in question by the possibility of determining more or less precisely the number of even the identity of the persons to whom it applies at a given moment as long as it is established that it is applied by virtue of an objective legal or factual situation defined by the measure in relation to the objective of the latter.
24. Moreover the fact that a legal provision may have different actual effects for the various persons to whom it applies is not inconsistent with its nature as a regulation when that situation is objectively defined.
25. To refuse to acknowledge that rules on production refunds amounted to a regulation only because they concerned a specific product and to take the view that such rules affected the manufacturers of that product by virtue of circumstances which differentiated them from all other persons would enlarge the concept of a decision to such an extent as to jeopardize the system of the Treaty which only permits an application for annulment to be brought by any person against an individual decision which affects him as the person to whom it is addressed or against a measure which affects him as in the case of such a person.
26. For the same reason it is necessary to sustain the objection raised by the Commission.
27. It follows that the application must be dismissed as inadmissible.

(3) Giuffrida Case II

F. Giuffrida and G. Campogrande v. *the Council*; Case 64/80; Judgment of 26 February 1981; [1981] ECR 693.

Facts:

By Regulation No 160/80 of 21 January 1980 the Council amended the tables of monthly basic salaries of a particular group of staff members. According to the applicants this regulation was of individual concern to them because the addresses of the regulation were identifiable. In the Council's view the regulation had a general and abstract, legislative nature and could, therefore, not be challenged by individuals.

The Court held:

. . . . .

3. Under the second paragraph of Article 189 of the Treaty the test for distinguishing between a regulation and a decision is to ascertain whether the measure in question has general application or not.

. . . . .

6. It follows that the contested regulation applies to objectively determined situations and involves legal effects in respect of categories of persons regarded generally and in the abstract. It does therefore have the characteristics of a regulation.
7. These characteristics are not called in question by the fact that it is possible to determine more or less exactly the number or even the identify of the persons to whom it applies at any given time as long as it is established that such application takes effect as in this case, by virtue of an objective legal or factual situation defined by the instrument in question in relation to its purpose.
8. The action must therefore be declared inadmissible.

c. Direct and individual concern

i. CASES

(1) Plaumann Case

Plaumann v. *EEC Commission*; Case 25/62; Judgment of 15 July 1963; [1963] ECR 106; [1964] CMLR 29.

Facts:

Action by one of thirty German importers against a refusal by the Commission, in a Decision under EEC Article 25 (3), to grant a request by the Federal Republic for permission partially to suspend the customs-duties on the import of fresh mandarines and clementines from non-EEC countries. The Commission contested the admissibility of the action in terms of EEC Article 173, para 2, on two grounds:

1. The Decision addressed to a Member Government was one of a special nature, and therefore not susceptible to appeals by private persons.
2. Plaumann was not directly and individually concerned.

The Court held:

I – On the application for annulment

Admissibility

Under the second paragraph of Article 173 of the EEC Treaty any natural or legal person may ... institute proceedings against a decision ... which, although in the form of ... a decision addressed to another person, is of direct and individual concern to the former, the defendant contends that the words 'other persons' in this paragraph do not refer the Member States in their capacity as sovereign authorities and that individuals may not therefore bring an action for annulment against the decisions of the Commission or of the Council addressed to Member States.

However the second paragraph of Article 173 does allow an individual to bring an action against decisions addressed to 'another person' which are of direct and individual concern to the former, but this Article neither defines nor limits the scope of these words. The words and the natural meaning of this provision justify the broadest interpretation. Moreover, provisions of the Treaty regarding the right of interested parties to bring an action must not be interpreted restrictively. Therefore, the Treaty being silent on the point, a limitation in this respect may not be presumed.

It follows that the defendant's argument cannot be regarded as well-founded.

The defendant further contends that the contested decision is by its very nature a regulation in the form of an individual decision and therefore action against it is no more available to individuals than in the case of legislative measures of general application.

It follows however from Articles 189 and 191 of the EEC Treaty that decisions are characterized by the limited number of persons to whom they are addressed. In order to determine whether or not a measure constitutes a decision one must enquire whether that measure concerns specific persons. The contested Decision was addressed to the government of the Federal Republic of Germany and refuses to grant it authorization for the partial suspension of customs duties on certain products imported from third countries. Therefore the contested measure must be regarded as a decision referring to a particular person and binding that person alone.

Under the second paragraph of Article 173 of the Treaty private individuals may institute proceedings for annulment against decisions which, although addressed to another person, are of direct and individual concern to them, but in the present case the defendant denies that the contested decision is of direct and individual concern to the applicant.

It is appropriate in the first place to examine whether the second requirement of admissibility is fulfilled because, if the applicant is not individually concerned by the decision, it becomes unnecessary to enquire whether he is directly concerned.

Persons other than those to whom a decision is addressed may only claim to be individually concerned if that decision affects them by reason of certain attributes which are peculiar to them or by reason of circumstances in which they are differentiated from all other persons and by virtue of these factors distinguishes them individually just as in the case if the person addressed. In the present case the applicant is affected by the disputed Decision as an importer of clementines, that is to say, by reason of a commercial activity which may at any time be practised by any person and is not therefore such as to distinguish the applicant in relation to the contested Decision as in the case of the addressee.

For these reasons the present action for annulment must be decided inadmissible.

(2) Toepfer Case

Toepfer K.G. and Getreide-Import-Gesellschaft v. *EEC Commission*; Case 106–107/63; Judgment of 1 July 1965; [1965] ECR 410; [1966] CMLR 111.

Facts:

The plaintiffs were engaged in the import of and wholesale trading in cereals. They were among the largest such firms in Germany. Some of the maize imported into Germany came from France. Regulation No 19 subjected maize imports under certain circumstances to a levy resulting from the difference between the treshold price (set by the importing Member State annually) and the free-at-frontier price fixed weekly by the Commission for the exporting State. The levy was calculated and charged by the competent national customs authorities, in this case the German 'Einfuhr- und Vorratstelle für Getreide und Futtermittel' (EVST). The EVST had in this way calculated the levy for 1 October 1963, at zero. That day applications by plaintiffs and 25 other importing companies were received to import 126,000 tons in January 1964. The plaintiffs applied that day for import licences (24,000 and 21,000 tons, forming part of the said 126,000 tons) with a levy fixed in advance at the 1 October levy, i.e. zero. The EVST refused the licences on account of the prospective measures taken by the German Government on the same date under Article 22 of Regulation No 19. By a decision of 1 October the Commission fixed a new (and much higher) free-at-frontier price for maize imported into Germany, to come into force on 2 October. By a Decision of 3 October, the Commission authorized Germany with retroactive effect to maintain the protective measures up to 4 October inclusive. The plaintiffs brought an action against the last mentioned Decision. The questions was again whether the claim of plaintiffs was admissible in terms of EEC Article 173, para 2.

The Court held:

Admissibility of the applications

As the contested decision was not addressed to the applicants the defendant argues that it was not of direct and individual concern to them within the meaning of Article 173 of the Treaty; it only concerns the applicants through the effect of the protective measure in question, and thus indirectly.

The defendant further argues that, since the protective measure was drawn up in general terms applicable to all importers in a position to ask for an import licence during the period between 1 and 4 October 1963, neither this measure nor the decision which upheld it is of individual concern to the applicants.

The expression 'of direct ... concern'

According to the terms of Article 22 of Regulation No 19, when a Member State has given notice of the protective measures provided for in paragraph (1) of the said Article, the Commission shall decide within four working days of the notification whether the measures are to be retained, amended or abolished.

The last sentence of the second paragraph of Article 22 provides that the Commission's decision shall come into force immediately. Therefore a decision of the Commission amending or abolishing protective measures is directly applicable and concerns interested parties subject to it as directly as the measures which it replaces.

It would be illogical to say that a decision to retain protective measures had a different effect, as the latter type of decision does not merely give approval to such measures, but renders them valid.

Therefore a decision made under the third and fourth subparagraphs of Article 22 (2) are of direct concern to the interested parties.

The expression 'of ... individual concern'

It is clear from the fact that on 1 October 1963 the Commission took a decision fixing new free-at-frontier prices for maize imported into the Federal

Republic as from 2 October, that the danger which the protective measures retained by the Commission were to guard against no longer existed as from this latter date.

Therefore the only persons concerned by the said measure were importers who had applied for an import licence during the course of the day of 1 October 1963. The number and identity of these importers had already become fixed and ascertainable before 4 October, when the contested decision was made. The Commission was in a position to know that its decision affected the interests and the position of the said importers alone.

The factual situation thus created differentiates the said importers including the applicants, from all other persons and distinguishes them individually just as in the case of the person addressed.

Therefore the objection of inadmissibility which has been raised is unfounded and the applicants are admissible.

The Court subsequently annulled the Decision of the Commission.

(3) International Fruit Company Case I

N.V. International Fruit Company and others v. *Commission*; joined cases 41–44/70; Judgment of 13 May 1971; [1971] ECR 421.

Facts:

By Council Regulations No 2513/69 and 2514/69 protective measures were taken with the object of limiting the import of dessert apples from third countries into the Community in the period from 1 April 1970 to 30 June 1970. These Regulations provided for a system of import licences which permitted apples from third countries to the extent the Community market could absorb them without detrimental effect on the prices.

Under this system the Member States had to communicate each week to the Commission the quantities for which import licences had been requested during the preceding week. On the basis of those communications the Commission decided on the issue of the licences.

By Regulation 565/70 of 25 March 1970 the Commission provided that the applications lodged up to 20 March 1970 should be granted only up to 80%. By Regulation 983/70 of 28 May 1970 the same was decided for the week ending 22 May 1970. The question arose whether the International Fruit Company could bring an action against this Regulation.

The Court held:

14. Hence, the issue of admissibility in the present cases must be determined in the light of the lastmentioned regulation.

15. For this purpose, it is necessary to consider whether the provisions of that regulation – in so far as they make the system established by Article 1 of Regulation No 565/70 applicable – are of direct and individual concern to the applicants within the meaning of the second paragraph of Article 173 of the Treaty.
16. It is indisputable that Regulation No 983/70 was adopted with a view on the one hand to the state of the market and on the other to the quantities of dessert apples for which applications for import licences had been made in the week ending on 22 May 1970.
17. It follows that when the said regulation was adopted, the number of applications which could be affected by it was fixed.
18. No new application could be added.
19. To what extent, in percentage terms, the applications could be granted, depended on the total quantity in respect of which applications had been submitted.
20. Accordingly, by providing that the system introduced by Article 1 of Regulation No 565/70 should be maintained for the relevant period, the Commission decided, even though it took account only of the quantities requested, on the subsequent fate of each application which had been lodged.
21. Consequently, Article 1 of Regulation No 983/70 is not a provision of general application within the meaning of the second paragraph of Article 189 of the Treaty, but must be regarded as a conglomeration of individual decisions taken by the Commission under the guise of a regulation pursuant to Article 2 (2) of Regulation No 459/70, each of which decisions affects the legal position of each author of an application for a licence.
22. Thus, the decisions are of individual concern to the applicants.
23. Moreover, it is clear from the system introduced by Regulation No 459/70, and particularly from Article 2 (2) thereof, that the decision on the grant of import licences is a matter for the Commission.
24. According to this provision, the Commission alone is competent to assess the economic situation in the light of which the grant of import licences must be justified.
25. Article 1 (2) of Regulation No 459/70, by providing that 'the Member States shall in accordance with the conditions laid down in Article 2, issue the licence to any interested party applying for it', makes it clear that the national authorities do not enjoy any discretion in the matter of the issue of licences and the conditions on which applications by the parties concerned should be granted.
26. The duty of such authorities is merely to collect the data necessary in order that the Commission may take its decision in accordance with Article 2 (2) of that regulation and subsequently adopt the national measures needed to give effect to that decision.
27. In these circumstances as far as the interested parties are concerned, the issue of or refusal to issue the import licences must be bound up with this decision.

28. The measure whereby the Commission decides on the issue of the import licences thus directly affects the legal position of the parties concerned.
29. The applications thus fulfil the requirements of the second paragraph of Article 173 of the Treaty, and are therefore admissible.

(4) Chinese Mushrooms Case

Werner A. Bock v. *Commission*; Case 62/70; Judgment of 23 November 1971; [1971] ECR 897; [1972] CMLR 160.

Facts:

In 1970, the German Federal Republic, for various reasons, prohibited imports of mushrooms into its territory from the People's Republic of China.

This prohibition was easy to enforce when the German importer intended to import directly from China or a non-member country into Germany.

On the other hand, the problem was much more complex when the importer wanted to buy Chinese mushrooms put into free circulation in one of the countries of the Community.

In fact, since the adoption of Regulation 865/68 of 28 June 1968, the German authorities had been obliged normally to issue the permit requested automatically and within a very short period because the goods were in free circulation in a Member State. They could only refuse the permit if they had already received from the Commission the authorization mentioned in Article 115 (1) of the Treaty – an authorization which in exceptional cases, and particularly in a case of deflection of trade, permits a Member State to exclude from Community treatment certain products originating in non-Member countries but already in free circulation in one or more of the other Member States.

However, such authorization in respect of mushrooms from China was not requested by Germany until 15 September 1970.

On 4 September 1970 the firm Werner A. Bock applied for an import permit for a consignment of Chinese mushrooms with a value of DM 150,000 for which it had a firm offer and which according to its declaration, was in free circulation in Holland.

On 9 September 1970 it reminded the appropriate German authority, the Federal Office for Food and Forestry, of this application.

Finally, on 11 September it repeated its request by telex. This telex launched a brisk activity on the part of the German authorities. In fact on the same day: (1) the German delegation at Brussels, alerted by the German Ministry of Agriculture, informed the Commission by telex that the German authorities had received an application for an import permit for a consignment of Chinese mushrooms to a value of DM 150,000 and that the German Government was asking the Commission urgently to authorize Germany to exclude

from Community treatment such imports 'including the import envisaged' in the application mentioned above;
(2) The German authority informed Bock that it had decided to reject their application for a permit as soon as 'the Commission has given its authorization under Article 115 of the Treaty'.

Bock took further measures which remained unsuccessful. On 15 September the Commission adopted the decision requested, authorizing Germany to exclude from Community treatment mushrooms originating in China in free circulation in the Benelux States. This decision included a sentence which concerned applications for permits 'at present and duly pending before the German authorities'.

On 12 November 1970 Bock brought an action against this Decision. The Commission claimed that the action was inadmissible as the Decision was not of direct and individual concern to the plaintiff.

The Court held:

. . . . .

4. In the present case it is sufficient to note that the Federal Government, which had justified its initiative by reference to an application submitted to it at the time, might have assumed that the provision at issue was precisely intended to cover applications which had already been submitted. On 15 September 1970, the date when the contested decision was taken, the defendant was aware that the authorization was to extend, in accordance with the wishes of the Federal Government, to applications for licences which were already pending before the German authorities before 11 September 1970, the date on which the German Government applied to the defendant. Therefore, if the defendant intended to exclude these applications from the protective measure it should have expressed this clearly, instead of using the words 'the present authorization likewise covers', with which, by implication, it extended the scope of the first sentence of Article 1 of the Decision.
5. Accordingly, since the second sentence of that article must be interpreted as applying to the applicant's case, the provision the annulment of which is sought is of concern to the applicant.
6. The defendant contends that in any event an authorization granted to the Federal Republic is not of direct concern to the applicant since the Federal Republic remained free to make use of it.
7. The appropriate German authorities had nevertheless already informed the applicant that they would reject its application as soon as the Commission had granted them the requisite authorization. They had requested that authorization with particular reference to the applications already before them at that time.

8. It follows therefore that the matter was of direct concern to the applicant.
9. The defendant claims that the contested decision is not of individual concern to the applicant but covers in abstract all traders wishing to import the products in question into Germany while the decision is in force.
10. However, the applicant has challenged the decision only to the extent to which it also covers imports for which applications for import licences were already pending at the date of its entry into force. The number and identity of importers concerned in this way was already fixed and ascertainable before that date. The defendant was in a position to know that the contested provision in its decision would affect the interests and situation of those importers alone. The factual situation thus created differentiates the latter from all other persons and distinguishes them individually just as in the case of the person addressed.

Sequel:

The Court, declaring the action admissible and well founded, annulled the Decision in as far as it concerned products for which requests for licences were pending on the date the Decision was made.

(5) COFAZ Case

Compagnie Française de L'Azote (COFAZ) S.A. and others v. Commission; Case 169/84; Judgment of 28 January 1986, [1986] ECR 391.

Facts:

The raw material from which nitrate fertilizers are manufactured in ammonia. In order to produce ammonia an immense amount of energy is needed. This means that the price for nitrate fertilizers is largely dependent on the price of energy. In the Netherlands a main source of energy is natural gaz, which is produced by Gasunie (the Gaz Board), a government owned company. Gasunie granted special rebates for Dutch ammonia producers. The cheap ammonia enabled the Dutch nitrate industry to produce their fertilizers considerably cheaper than their competitors.

In June 1983 the French association of producers of nitrate fertilizers submitted a complaint to the Commission. Also the Belgian and French Governments, together with a German undertaking raised objections to the preferential tariff system applied in the Netherlands.

In October 1983 the Commission decided to initiate the procedure under Article 93 (2) of the EEC Treaty against the Dutch tariff system. The Commission invited all parties concerned to submit their comments. The French association, which also represents COFAZ, gave its comment early 1984.

In April 1984 Gasunie amended its tariff structure with retroactive effect from 1 November 1983. Subsequently, by a decision of 17 April 1984, the Commission terminated the procedure initiated under Article 93 (2). The Netherlands government and the French association were informed of this decision. The French association, however, was of the opinion that the new tariff structure of Gasunie was still discriminatory and it wanted to have the Commission's Decision of 17 April 1987 annulled. The question arose whether the French association, or its member Cofaz could bring an action against the Commission's Decision terminating its procedure under Article 93. The Commission considered that the contested decision was not of individual concern to the applicants, inter alia on the ground that the applicants were not the only producers of nitrate fertilizers.

The Court held:

. . . . .

22. It is clear from a consistent line of decisions of the Court that persons other than those to whom a decision is addressed may claim to be concerned within the meaning of the second paragraph of Article 173 only if that decision affects them by reason of certain attributes which are peculiar to them, or by reason of circumstances in which they are differentiated from all other persons, and by virtue of these factors distinguishes them individually just as in the case of the person addressed (judgment of 15 July 1963 in Case 25/62 *Plaumann* v. *Commission* [1963] ECR 95).
23. More particularly, as regards the circumstances referred to in that judgment, the Court has repeatedly held that where a regulation accords applicant undertakings procedural guarantees entitling them to request the Commission to find an infringement of Community rules, those undertakings should be able to institute proceedings in order to protect their legitimate interests (judgments of 25 October 1977 in Case 26/76 *Metro* v. *Commission* [1977] ECR 1875, 5 October 1983 in Case 191/82 *Fediol* v. *Commission* [1983] ECR 2913, and 11 October 1983 in Case 210/81 *Demo-Studio Schmidt* v. *Commission* [1983] ECR 3045).
24. In its judgment of 20 March 1985 in Case 264/82 (*Timex Corporation* v. *Council and Commission* [1985] ECR 849) the Court pointed out that it was necessary to examine in that regard the part played by the undertaking in the administrative proceedings. The Court accepted as evidence that the measure in question was of concern to the undertaking, within the meaning of the second paragraph of Article 173 of the EEC Treaty,

the fact that the undertaking was at the origin of the complaint which led to the opening of the investigation procedure, the fact that its views were heard during that procedure and the fact that the conduct of the procedure was largely determined by its observations.
25. The same conclusions apply to undertakings which have played a comparable role in the procedure referred to in Article 93 of the EEC Treaty provided, however, that their position on the market is significantly affected by the aid which is the subject of the contested decision. Article 93 (2) recognizes in general terms that the undertakings concerned are entitled to submit their comments to the Commission but does not provide any further details.
26. With regard to the position of the applicants whilst the Commission's investigation concerning the aid in question was in progress, it should be noted that on 1 June 1983 they lodged a complaint with the Commission concerning the preferential tariff system in favour of Netherlands producers of nitrate fertilizers. In their complaint, they laid particular emphasis on their competitive position in relation to the three Netherlands producers and on the adverse efferts of the aid. Moreover, the applicants complied with the Commission's request to submit their comments under Article 93 (2).
27. With regard to the impact of economic factors as a whole on the market in nitrate fertilizers, the applicants have pointed out that, according to their calculations, the preferential tariff system represents an annual transfer of approximately *HfL* 165 million to the three Netherlands producers of ammonia. According to the applicants in France the cost of natural gas represents approximately 80% of the ex-works cost price of ammonia which, in its turn, is the raw material from which nitrate fertilizers are manufactured. They have also argued that they compete directly with the three Netherlands producers of nitrate fertilizers who, between 1978 and 1982, more than tripled their volume of exports of nitrate fertilizers to France and whose share of the French market rose between 1980 and 1982 from 9% to 21.7%.
28. It is not for the Court, at this stage of the procedure, when it is considering whether the application is admissible, to make a definitive finding on the competitive relationship between the applicants and the Netherlands undertakings. It is sufficient to note that the applicants have adduced pertinent reasons to show that the Commission's decision may adversely affect their legitimate interests by seriously jeopardizing their position on the market in question.
29. In those circumstances, the fact that, according to the Commission, a fourth undertaking which is not in competition with the applicants also qualifies for tariff F is immaterial. Again on the assumption that the aid in question falls within the scope of Article 92, the advantage gained from a tariff system by an outside undertaking not in competition with the applicants does not detract from the validity of the argument that a system of that kind may distort or threaten to distort competition between the other

undertakings and does not affect the substantive nature of the damage allegedly sustained by the applicants.
30. As regards the question whether the Commission's decision to terminate the procedure is of direct concern to the applicants, it is sufficient to observe that the decision has left intact all the effects of the tariff system set up, whilst the procedure sought by the applicants would lead to the adoption of a decision to abolish or amend that system. In those circumstances, it must be held that the contested decision is of direct concern to the applicants.
31. It follows that the contested measure is a decision of direct and individual concern to the applicants, within the meaning of the second paragraph of Article 173 of the Treaty.
32. For all those reasons, the application must be declared admissible and the proceedings must take their course.

3. Grounds of illegality

Article 173, para 1, mentions five grounds of illegality. The ground 'lack of competence' has only rarely been invoked. Two cases may further illustrate this ground: the *Fédéchar Case* on implied powers and the *Meroni Case I* on delegation of powers.

On the ground of 'infringement of an essential procedural requirement', community acts may be annulled in three cases:
a) when there is no sufficient reasoning
b) when the organs which should be consulted according to the Treaty, have not been consulted
c) when the act has not been properly published or notified.

On the reasoning see the *Brennwein* and *Beus Cases*; on the consultation of other institutions, the *Maizena Case* and on notification the *ICI Case*.

The fourth ground, 'infringement of this Treaty' is by far the most important one. It is alleged in almost all cases.

The fifth ground, 'infringement of any rule of law relating to the application of the Treaty' had opened a way for the Court to annul Community acts which violate general international law or basic principles of law, such a human rights. See thereon the *Stauder, Handelsgesellschaft* and *International Fruit Company III Cases*.

The Court reviews the legality of Community acts not only under Article 173. The legality can also be reviewed under Article 177 when national courts ask for preliminary rulings (see below sub-chapter IV).

In most of the cases quoted below the question of legality reached the Court in procedures under Article 177. These decisions of the Court illustrate equally well as the direct actions on what grounds the Court will declare Community acts to be illegal.

a. Competence

i. CASES

(1) Meroni Case I

Meroni et al. v. *High Authority*; Case 9/56; Judgment of 13 June 1958; [1957 and 1958] ECR 133.

Facts:

The plaintiffs were a steel producing enterprise who used scrap in the production of their steel. As such they became liable to pay a prescribed levy to the Subsidy Fund. By letter dated 4 March 1954 the Fund requested from the plaintiffs the figures of all scrap bought by them so that it could determined the amount of the levy. Following a series of discussions between the two parties, the Fund requested the High Authority to take de Decision demanding the money which itself had assessed unilaterally. This Decision was passed on 24 October 1956 and appealed by the plaintiffs in December of the same year, i.a. on the grounds that the entire system for the assessment and collection of the levy as set up by the High Authority Decision 14/55 and the structures and working of the organizations involved (known as the Brussels organizations) were unlawful . . .

The Court held:

. . . . .

The High Authority could have argued that the power of its representative, pursuant to Article 9 of Decision No 14/55 to 'subordinate the decision to the approval of the High Authority' meant that it remained responsible for any decision of the Brussels agencies. However the above quotation from the statement of defence renders it necessary to take the view that the High Authority does not take over as its own the deliberations of the Brussels agencies leading to the fixing of the equalization rate.

Therefore Decision No 14/55 brings about a true delegation of powers, and the question whether such delegation accords with the requirements of the Treaty must be examined.

Details of the application of Decision No 14/55

If the High Authority had itself exercised the powers the exercise of which is conferred by Decision No 14/55 on the Brussels agencies, those powers would have been subject to the rules laid down by the Treaty and in particular those which impose upon the High Authority:

The duty to state reasons for its decisions and to refer to any opinions which were required to be obtained (Article 15);

The duty to publish annually a general report on its activities and its administrative expenses (Article 17);

The duty to publish wuch data as could be useful to governments or to any other parties concerned (Article 47).

On the same supposition, its decisions and recommendations would have been subject to review by the Court of Justice on the conditions laid down by Article 33.

Decision No 14/55 did not make the exercise of the powers which it conferred upon the Brussels agencies subject to any of the conditions to which it would have been subject if the High Authority had exercised them directly. Even if the delegation resulting from Decision No 14/55 appeared as legal from the point of view of the Treaty, it could not confer upon the authority receiving the delegation powers different from those which the delegating authority itself received under the Treaty.

The fact that it is possible for the Brussels agencies to take decisions which are exempt from the conditions to which they would have been subject if they had been adopted by the High Authority in reality gives the Brussels agencies more extensive powers than those which the High Authority holds from the Treaty.

In not making the decisions of the Brussels agencies subject to the rules to which the decisions of the High Authority are subject under the Treaty, the delegation resulting from Decision No 14/55 infringes the Treaty.

. . . . .

...the power of the High Authority to authorize or itself to make the financial arrangements mentioned in Article 53 of the Treaty gives it the right to entrust certain powers to such bodies subject to conditions to be determined by it and subject to its supervision.

However, in the light of Article 53, such delegations of powers are only legitimate if the High Authority recognizes them 'to be necessary for the performance of the tasks set out in Article 3 and compatible with this Treaty, and in particular with Article 65'.

Article 3 lays down no fewer than eight distinct, very general objectives, and it is not certain that they can all be simultaneously pursued in their entirety in all circumstances.

In pursuit of the objectives laid down in Article 3 of the Treaty, the High

Authority must permanently reconcile any conflict which may be implied by these objectives when considered individually, and when such conflict arises must grant such priority to one or other of the objectives laid down in Article 3 as appears necessary having regard to the economic facts or circumstances in the light of which it adopts its decisions.

Reconciling the various objectives laid down in Article 3 implies a real discretion involving difficult choices, based on a consideration of the economic facts and circumstances in the light of which those choices are made.

The consequences resulting from a delegation of powers are very different depending on whether it involves clearly defined executive powers the exercise of which can, therefore, be subject to strict review in the light of objective criteria determined by the delegating authority, or whether it involves a discretionary power, implying a wide margin of discretion which may, according to the use which is made of it, make possible the execution of actual economic policy.

A delegation of the first kind cannot appreciably alter the consequences involved in the exercise of the powers concerned, whereas a delegation of the second kind, since it replaces the choices of the delegator by the choices of the delegate, brings about an actual transfer of responsibility.

In any event under Article 53 as regards the execution of the financial arrangements mentioned therein, it is only the delegation of those powers 'necessary for the performance of the tasks set out in Article 3' are binding not only on the High Authority, but on the 'institutions of the Community ... within the limits of their respective powers, in the common interest'.

From that provision there can be seen in the balance of powers which is characteristic of the institutional structure of the Community a fundamental guarantee granted by the Treaty in particular to the undertakings and associations of undertakings to which it applies.

To delegate a discretionary power, by entrusting it to bodies other than those which the Treaty has established to effect and supervise the exercise of such power each within the limits of its own authority, wound render that guarantee ineffective.

In the light of the criteria set out above, it is appropriate to examine whether the delegation of powers granted by the High Authority to the Brussels agencies by virtue of Decision No 14/55 satisfies the requirements of the Treaty.

. . . . .

Since objective criteria whereby their decisions may be formulated are lacking, the Brussels agencies must exercise a wide margin of discretion in carrying out the tasks entrusted to them by Decision No 14/55.

However on two occasions, by Decisions Nos 9/56 and 34/56, the High

Authority has itself adopted, in the plae and instead of the Brussels agencies, decisions which imply the exercise of a discretionary power.

. . . . .

Article 9 of Decision No 14/55 of the High Authority gives its permanent representative on the Brussels agencies the power to make any decision subject to the approval of the High Authority.

In reserving to itself the power to refuse its approval, the High Authority has not retained sufficient powers for the delegation resulting from Decision No 14/55 to be contained within the limits defined above.

In the paragraph of the statement of defence set out above the High Authority has made it clear that it 'adopts the data furnished by the Brussels agencies without being able to add anything thereto'.

In those circumstances the delegation of powers granted to the Brussels agencies by Decision No 14/55 gives those agencies a degree of latitude which implies a wide margin of discretion and cannot be considered as compatible with the requirements of the Treaty.

The decision of 24 October 1956 is based on a general decision which is unlawful from the point of view of the Treaty and it must, for this reason also, be annulled.

b. Misuse of powers

i. CASES

(1) Giuffrida Case I

Franco Giuffrida v. *the Council*; Case 105/75; Judgment of 29 September 1976; [1976] ECR 1403.

Facts:

For a vacant post of principal administrative a competition was held in which Mr. Giuffrida participated. The authorities, however, appointed Mr. Martino. Mr. Giuffrida sought annulment of this appointment, i.a. on the ground of misuse of powers. He submitted that there had been no free competition, but that the post had been reserved for Mr. Martino which was demonstrated by the conditions for admission to the competition which contained the provision that the candidate must have held the secretariat for meetings of Council working parties or Committees for at least four years, a requirement fulfilled by Mr. Martino.

The Court held:

. . . . .

10. It is clear from the above-mentioned note and from the forgoing statements that Internal Competition No A/108 was organized by the appointing authority for the sole purpose of remedying the anomalous administrative status of a specific official and of appointing that same official to the post declared vacant.
11. The pursuit of a specific objective is contrary to the aims of any recruitment procedure, including the internal competition procedure, and thus constitutes a misuse of powers.
12. The existence of misuse of powers in this instance is moreover confirmed by the fact that one of the conditions for admission to the competition was that the successful candidate must have held the secretariat for meetings of Council working parties or committees on regional policy for at least four years.
13. It is not disputed that such a restrictive condition corresponds exactly to the duties performed by Emilio Martino in his previous post.
14. Furthermore, none of the information provided by the defendant shows why it was necessary in the interests of the service to lay down such a specific condition as regards the duration of the duties referred to.

. . . . .

18. On these grounds it must be concluded that the decision to make the appointment in question involves a misuse of powers and must therefore be annulled.

c. Essential procedural requirements

i. CASES

(1) Brennwein Case

Federal Republic of Germany v. *Commission*; Case 24/62; Judgment of 4 July 1963; [1963] ECR 69; [1963] CMLR 347.

Facts:

Before the establishment of the Common Market, Germany used to import cheap wines for the production of 'Brennwein'. In 1961 it asked the Commission for a tariff quota of 450,000 hectolitres of wine for this purpose. The Commission granted a quota of only 100,000 hectolitres. The question arose of how specific the reasoning for such a Decision should be.

The Court held:

In imposing upon the Commission the obligation to state reasons for its Decisions, Article 190 is not taking mere formal considerations into account but seeks to give an opportunity to the parties of defending their rights, to the Court of exercising its supervisory functions and to Member States and to all interested nationals of ascertaining the circumstances in which the Commission has applied the Treaty. To attain these objectives, it is sufficient for the Decision to set out, in a concise but clear and relevant manner, the principal issues of law and of facts upon which it is based and which are necessary in order that the reasoning which has led the Commission to its decision may be understood. Apart from general considerations, which apply without distinction to other cases, or which are confined to repeating the wording of the Treaty, the Commission has been content to rely upon 'the information collected' without specifying any of it, in order to reach a conclusion 'that the production of the wines in question is amply sufficient'.

This elliptical reasoning is all the more objectionable because the Commission gave no indication, as it did belatedly before the Court, of the evolution and size of the surpluses, but only repeated, without expanding the reasons for it, the same statement 'that there was no indication that the existing market situation within the Community did not allow these branches of the industry in the German Federal Republic a supply which is adequate in quantity'. On the other hand, although it maintained that the production of the Community was sufficient, the Commission restricted itself to 'deducing from this' that 'the grant of a tariff quota of the volume requested might therefore lead to serious disturbances of the market in the products in question, but these disturbances were not specified. Thus it neither described the risk involved in this case, nor did it disclose what it considered to be the necessary and sufficient connection in the present case between the two concepts which it links one with the other by a simple deduction. However, by granting a restricted quota notwithstanding its description of production as 'amply sifficient', and thereby admitting that Article 25 (3) applied, the Commission thus conceded that this factor was not enough to make it possible 'to deduce from it' the risk of serious disturbance.

Thus the statement of reasons expressed appears in this point to be contradictory, since in spite of its statement with regard to an adequate supply and of the automatic conclusion to be drawn therefrom, the Commission grants a quota and thereby implies that it would not cause any serious disturbances. Moreover, several of the recitals in the German text, which is authentic, lack the necessary clarity.

It follows from these factors that the inadequacy, the vagueness and the inconsistency of the statement of reasons for the Decision, both in respect of the refusal of the quota requested and of the concession of the quota granted, do not satisfy the requirements of Article 190.

Those parts of the Decision which have been submitted to the Court must therefore be annulled.

(2) Beus Case

Beus GmbH v. *Hauptzollamt München – Landsbergerstrasse*; Case 5/67; Preliminary ruling of 31 March 1968 on the request of Finanzgericht München; [1968] ECR 95; [1968] CMLR 145.

Facts:

Beus, on importing grapes from Bulgaria, had to pay a levy of 8 DM per 100 kg according to Regulation No 144/65 of the EEC Commission. It argued that inadequate reasons had been given for the regulation; the more individual an act, the more detailed the reasoning should be. Regulation 144/65 was meant to counteract a particular disturbance of the market. It should therefore show in verifiable form that such a disturbance existed. That had not been done. The regulation, therefore, had to be considered null and void.

The Court held:

'The extent of the requirement laid down by Article 190 of the Treaty to state the reasons on which measures are based, depends on the nature of the measure in question.

It is a question in the present case of a regulation, that is to say a measure intended to have general application, the preamble to which may be confined to indicating the general situation which led to its adoption, on the one hand, and the general objectives which it is intended to achieve on the other.

Consequently, it is not possible to require that it should set out the various facts, which are often very numerous and complex, on the basis of which the regulation was adopted, or a fortiori that it should provide a more or less complete evaluation of those facts'.

(3) Maizena Case

Maizena GmbH v. *Council*; Case 139/79; Judgment of 29 October 1980; [1980] ECR 3424.

Facts:

Maizena challenged certain provisions of a Council Regulations which were of direct and individual concern to it. The Regulation was based on Article 43 of the EEC Treaty which requires consultation of the European Parliament. Maizina claimed that this consultation had been insufficient. It was supported by the European Parliament which had been permitted to intervene.

The Council had consulted the Parliament to some extent. On 19 March 1979 it sent the Commission's proposal to the European Parliament requesting it to discuss the proposal in its April-session as the Regulation had to enter into force on 1 July 1979. The Parliament could not discuss the proposal in April as it had to be commented on first by the competent committees of the Parliament. In May the competent committees proposed to approve the regulation but the European Parliament rejected this proposal. On the basis of the Parliament's remarks the Agricultural Committee had to draft a new report. Because of the elections for the European Parliament in July there was no session of the European Parliament between May and August, but the bureau of the Parliament announced that an extra session could be convened whenever the Council, the Commission or a majority of the members of the Parliament requested. The Council did not request an extra session and adopted the regulation on 25 June 1979.

Was the Parliament sufficiently consulted?

The Court held:

. . . . .

34. The consultation provided for in the third subparagraph of Article 43 (2) as in other similar provisions of the Treaty, is the means which allows the Parliament to play an actual part in the legislative process of the Community. Such power represents an essential factor in the institutional balance intended by the Treaty. Although limited, it reflects at Community level the fundamental democratic principle that the peoples should take part in the exercise of power through the intermediary of a representative assembly. Due consultation of the Parliament in the cases provided for by the Treaty therefore constitutes an essential formality disregard of which means that the measure concerned is void.
35. In that respect it is pertinent to point out that observance of that requirement implies that the Parliament has expressed its opinion. It is impossible to take the view that the requirement is satisfied by the Council's simply asking for the opinion. The Council is, therefore, wrong to include in the reference in the preamble to Regulation No 1293/79 a statement to the effect that the Parliament has been consulted.

36. The Council has not denied that consultation of the Parliament was in the nature of an essential procedural requirement. It maintains however that in the circumstances of the present case the Parliament, by its own conduct, made observance of that requirement impossible and that it is therefore not proper to rely on the infringement thereof.
37. Without prejudice to the questions of principle raised by that argument of the Council it suffices to observe that in the present case on 25 June 1979 when the Council adopted Regulation No 1293/79 amending Regulation No 1111/77 without the opinion of the Assembly the Council had not exhausted all the possibilities of obtaining the preliminary opinion of the Parliament. In the first place the Council did not request the application of the emergency procedure provided for by the internal regulation of the Parliament although in other sectors and as regards other draft regulations it availed itself of that power at the same time. Further the Council could have made use of the possibility it had under Article 139 of the Treaty to ask for an extraordinary session of the Assembly especially as the Bureau of the Parliament on 1 March and 10 May 1979 drew its attention to that possibility.
38. It follows that in the absence of the opinion of the Parliament required by Article 43 of the Treaty Regulation No 1293/79 amending Council Regulation No 1111/77 must be declared void without prejudice to the Council's power following the present judgment to take all appropriate measures pursuant to the first paragraph of Article 176 of the Treaty.

. . . . .

Note:

The *Roquette Case V* (138/79) of the same date contains the same ruling.

(4) ICI Case

Imperial Chemical Industries Ltd. v. *Commission*; Case 48/69; Judgment of 14 July 1972; [1972] ECR 652; [1972] CMLR 557.

Facts:

Before Britain became a Member of the Communities the Commission addressed a Decision to the English company Imperial Chemical Industries Ltd. (decision of 24 July 1969). As it could not notify this decision in Britain, the Commission notified it to the registered office of a subsidiary established within the Common Market. The question arose whether by so notifying the Commission had infringed an essential procedural requirement.

The Court held:

. . . . .

39. Irregularities in the procedure for notification of a decision are extraneous to that measure and cannot therefore invalidate it.
40. In certain circumstances such irregularities may prevent the period within which an application must be lodged from starting to run.
41. The last paragraph of Article 173 of the Treaty provides that the period for instituting proceedings for the annulment of individual measures of the Commission starts to run from the date of notification of the decision to the applicant or, in the absence thereof, from the day on which it came to the knowledge of the latter.
42. In the present case it is established that the applicant has had full knowledge of the text of the decision and that it has exercised its right to institute proceedings within the prescribed period.
43. In these circumstances the question of possible irregularities concerning notification ceases to be relevant.
44. Therefore the abovementioned submissions are inadmissible for want of relevance.

. . . . .

d. Infringement of the Treaty or of any rule of law relating to its application

i. Cases

(1) Handelsgesellschaft Case

International Handelsgesellschaft GmbH. v. *Einfuhr- und Vorratstelle für Getreide und Futtermittel*; Case 11/70; Preliminary ruling of 17 December 1970; [1970] ECR 1133; [1972] CMLR 255.

Facts:

The Handelsgeseuschaft obtained an export licence for 20,000 tons of cornflour, valid until 31 December 1967, on the ground of Article 12 para 1 (3) of

Council Regulation 120/67/EEC of 13 July 1967 (OJ 1967, p. 2269). The granting of the licence depended on a deposit of 0.50 Units of account per ton, as a guarantee that the export would be realised. When the Handelsgesellschaft did not export the full amount of corn-flour, a notice was served upon it for forfeiture of the deposit of 17,026.47 DM. Before the national court (Administrative Court Frankfurt) the Handelsgesellschaft maintained that such forfeiture was a violation of its basic human rights and therefore unconstitutional. In previous cases the Administrative Court had accepted that defence and declared similar regulations invalid. In the present case the Administrative Court had asked the Court of Justice whether the disputed regulation was valid.

The Court of Justice held:

. . . . .

2. It appears from the grounds of the order referring the matter that the Verwaltungsgericht has until now refused to accept the validity of the provisions in question and that for this reason it considers it to be essential to put an end to the existing legal uncertainty. According to the evaluation of the Verwaltungsgericht, the system of deposits is contrary to certain structural principles of national constitutional law which must be protected within the framework of Community law, with the result that the primacy of supranational law must yield before the principles of the German Basic Law. More particularly, the system of deposits runs counter to the principles of freedom of action and of disposition, of economic liberty and of proportionally arising in particular from Articles 2 (1) and 14 of the Basic Law. The obligation to import or export resulting from the issue of the licence, together with the deposit attaching thereto, constitutes an excessive intervention in the freedom of disposition in trade, as the objective of the regulations could have been attained by methods of intervention having less serious consequences.

The protection of fundamental rights in the Community legal system

3. Recourse to the legal rules or concepts of national law in order to judge the validity of measures adopted by the institutions of the Community would have an adverse effect on the uniformity and efficiency of Community law. The validity of such measures can only be judged in the light of Community law. In fact, the law stemming from the Treaty, an independent source of law, cannot because of its very nature be overridden by rules of national law, however framed, without being deprived of its character as Community law and without the legal basis of the Com-

munity itself being called in question. Therefore the validity of a Community measure or its effect within a Member State cannot be affected by allegations that it runs counter to either fundamental rights as formulated by the constitution of that State or the principles of a national constitutional structure.

4. However, an examination should be made as to whether or not any analogous guarantee inherent in Community law has been disregarded. In fact, respect for fundamental rights forms an integral part of the general principles of law protected by the Court of Justice. The protection of such rights, whilst inspired by the constitutional traditions common to the Member States, must be ensured within the framework of the structure and objectives of the Community. It must therefore be ascertained, in the light of the doubts expressed by the Verwaltungsgericht, whether the system of deposits has infringed rights of a fundamental nature, respect for which must be ensured in the Community legal system.

. . . . .

20. It follows from all these considerations that the fact that the system of licences involving an undertaking, by those who apply for them, to import or export, guaranteed by a deposit, does not violate any right of a fundamental nature. The machinery of deposits constitutes an appropriate method, for the purposes of Article 40 (3) of the Treaty, for carrying out the common organization of the agricultural markets and also conforms to the requirements of Article 43.

(2) International Fruit Company Case III

International Fruit Company v. *Produktschap voor Groenten en Fruit*; Case 21–24/72; Preliminary ruling of 12 December 1972; [1972] ECR 1225; [1975] 2 CMLR 1.

Facts:

The International Fruit Company claimed that certain regulations of the Commission should be considered void as they violated Article XI of the General Agreement on Tariffs and Trade (GATT).

The Court held:

1. By decision of 5 May 1972, received at the Court Registry on 8 May 1972, the College van Beroep voor het Bedrijfsleven referred to the Court,

under Article 177 of the EEC Treaty, two questions relating to the interpretation of that article and to the validity of certain regulations adopted by the Commission.
2. The first question invites the Court to rule whether the validity of measures adopted by the institutions of the Community also refers, within the meaning of Article 177 of the EEC Treaty, to their validity under international law.
3. The second question, which is raised should the reply to the first question be in the affirmative, asks, whether Regulations No's 459/70, 565/70, 686/70 of the Commission – which laid down, by way of protective measures, restrictions on the importation of apples from third countries – are invalid as being contrary to Article XI of the General Agreement on Tariffs and Trade (GATT)', hereafter called 'the General Agreement'.
4. According to the first paragraph of Article 177 of the EEC Treaty 'the Court of Justice shall have jurisdiction to give preliminary rulings concerning ... the validity ... of acts of the institutions of the Community'.
5. Under that information, the jurisdiction of the Court cannot be limited by the grounds on which the validity of those measures may be contested.
6. Since jurisdiction extends to all grounds capable of invalidating those measures, the Court is obliged to examine whether their validity may be affected by reason of the fact that they are contrary to a rule of international law.
7. Before the incompatibility of a Community measure with a provision of international law can affect the validity of that measure, the Community must first of all be bound by that provision.
8. Before invalidity can be relied upon before a national court, that provision of international law must also be capable of conferring rights on citizens of the Community which they can incoke before the courts.

It is therefore necessary to examine whether the General Agreement satisfies these two conditions.

Sequel:

The Court subsequently held that the Community was bound by the GATT agreement, but that this agreement was not capable of conferring rights on citizens of the Community which they could invoke before the courts. The GATT agreement could, therefore, not affect the validity of the regulations concerned.

(3) Nold Case II

J. Nold v. *Commission*; Case 4/73; Judgment of 14 May 1974; [1974] ECR 507; [1974] 2 CMLR 354.

Facts:

By a Decision of 21 December 1972 (OJ 1973, L 120, p. 14) the Commission authorized new trading rules which would have the effect that Nold, a trader in coal, no longer qualified as a wholesaler. Nold brought an action before the Court of Justice, submitting, inter alia, that the Decision should be annulled as it infringed rules of law relating to the application of the Treaty, namely fundamental rights.

The Court held:

12. The applicant asserts finally that certain of its fundamental rights have been violated, in that the restrictions introduced by the new trading rules authorized by the Commission have the effect, by depriving it of direct supplies, of jeopardizing both the profitability of the undertaking and the free development of its business activity, to the point of endangering its very existence.

    In this way, the Decision is said to violate, in respect of the applicant, a right akin to a proprietary right, as well as its right to the free pursuit of business activity, as protected by the Grundgesetz of the Federal Republic of Germany and by the Constitutions of other Member States and various international treaties, including in particular the Convention for the Protection of Human Rights and Fundamental Freedoms of 4 November 1950 and the Protocol to that Convention of 20 March 1952.

13. As the Court has already stated, fundamental rights form an integral part of the general principles of law, the observance of which it ensures.

    In safeguarding these rights, the Court is bound to draw inspiration from constitutional traditions common to the Member States, and it cannot therefore uphold measures which are incompatible with fundamental rights recognized and protected by the Constitution of those States.

    Similarly, international treaties for the protection of human rights on which the Member States have collaborated or of which they are signatories, can supply guidelines which should be followed within the framework of Community law.

    The submissions of the applicant must be examined in the light of these principles.

. . . . .

15. The disadvantages claimed by the applicant are in fact the result of economic change and not of the contested Decision.

    It was for the applicant, confronted by the economic changes brought

about by the recession in coal production, to acknowledge the situation and itself carry out the necessary adaptations.
16. This submission must be dismissed for all the reasons outlined above.
17. The action must accordingly be dismissed.

B. ACTION AGAINST FAILURE TO ACT

(EEC Article 175)

1. Cases

(1) Eridania Case I

Societa 'Eridania' Zuccherifici Nazionale et al. v. *Commission*; Case 10, 18/68; Judgment of 10 December 1969; [1969] ECR 483.

Facts:

Eridania wanted the annulment of certain Decisions addressed to other sugar refineries, but as it was not directly and individually concerned by these Decisions, its action was unsuccessful. At the same time Eridania requested the Commission to rescind the said Decisions, and when the Commission did not reply to this respect, it brought an action against failure to act under Article 175.

The Court held:

. . . . .

16. Without stating under which provisions of Community law the Commission was required to annul or to revoke the said decisions, the applicants have confined themselves to alleging that those decisions were adopted in infringement of the Treaty and that this fact alone would suffice to make the Commission's failure to act subject to the provisions of Article 175.
17. The Treaty provides, however, particularly in Article 173, other methods of recourse by which an allegedly illegal Community measure may be disputed and if necessary annulled on the application of a duly qualified party.

To admit, as the applicants wish to do, that the parties concerned could ask the institution from which the measure came to revoke it and, in the event of the Commission's failing to act, refer such failure to the Court as an illegal omission to deal with the matter would amount to providing them with a method of recourse parallel to that of Article 173, which would not be subject to the conditions laid down by the Treaty.

18. This application does not therefore satisfy the requirements of Article 175 of the Treaty and must thus be held to be inadmissible.

. . . . .

(2) Chevalley Case

Amadeo Chevalley v. *Commission*; Case 15/70; Judgment of 18 November 1970, [1970] ECR 979.

Facts:

Chevalley was the owner of agricultural land in Italy. In December 1969 the Italian Senate approved a draft law on the rents for agricultural lands which would lead to discrepancies between the Member States. Chevalley was of the opinion that the Commission should act under EEC Articles 101 and 102 and organize consultation with the Member States. By letter of 9 December 1969 he officially requested the Commission to do so.

By letter of 16 February 1970 the President of the Commission informed the applicant's lawyer that the Commission 'is not obliged in this case to adopt any measure whatever with regard to your client' and that by virtue of the third paragraph of Article 175 of the Treaty 'it will not be possible for your client to bring an action for failure to act based on the request submitted by you'.

On 13 April 1970 the applicant introduced the present application under EEC Article 175.

In a document of 22 June 1970 the applicant alternatively submitted an action under EEC Article 173 against the letter of 16 February. One of the questions was whether either action was possible. Under Article 175 no action can be brought when the institution concerned had defined its position, which was done by the letter of 16 February (though belatedly). Under Article 173 individuals may institute proceedings only against a decision, which the letter of 16 February was not, at least not in the formal sense. This would mean that no action should be brought at all.

The Court held:

. . . . .

The designation of the application

5. The preliminary objection of inadmissibility is based essentially on the ground that no measure exists capable of forming the subject-matter of an action under Article 175.
6. The concept of a measure capable of giving rise to an action is identical in Articles 173 and 175, as both provisions merely prescribe one and the same method of recourse.
7. It appears unnecessary therefore, for the purpose of a decision on the preliminary objection of inadmissibility, to designate the application in relation to the two provisions cited by the applicant.

Sequel:

The application was declared inadmissible on the ground that the measure sought was an opinion or advice which is not susceptible of annulment. The case was confirmed by the *Camera Case* (792/79 R), of 17 January 1980, [1980] ECR 129.

(3) Steel subsidies Case

Netherlands v. *Commission*; Case 59/70; Judgment of 6 July 1971, [1971] ECR 652.

Facts:

In the framework of its Fifth Economic and Social Development Plan, the French Government granted the French steel industry some low interest loans in order to enable this industry to improve its competitive position vis-a-vis foreign steel companies. The High Authority was informed of these measures in September 1966 and concluded provisionally in June 1967, that these loans were not prohibited under Article 4 (c) ECSE nor entailed the need to issue a recommendation pursuant to Article 67 ECSC.

The newly formed Commission of the EC definitely confirmed this opinion in a letter of 4 December 1968 to the French Government, of which the Dutch Government was informed on 9 December 1968.

The latter Government, not content with this reply, requested the Commission on 24 June 1970 to issue a decision pursuant to Article 88 ECSC, declaring that France had violated its obligations under Article 4 (c) ECSC, and subsidiarily, to issue a recommendation under Article 67 ECSC. When the Commission did not take the requested measures, the Dutch Government, on 2 October 1970, lodged an appeal under Article 35 against the implicit refusal of the Commission to act.

The Commission asked the Court to declare the appeal inadmissible on the grounds that the prescribed time had elapsed.

The Court held:

. . . . .

12. Article 35, which is intended to extend the power to review the legality of the conduct of the Commission to those cases where this institution refrains from taking a decision or from making a recommendation, affords an opportunity to institute proceedings before the Court on the basis of the fiction of an implied decision of refusal arising on the expiry of a period of two months in cases where the Commission is required or empowered by a provision of the Treaty to take a decision or make a recommendation but refrains from doing so.
13. On the expiry of this period of inaction, the interested party has a further period of one month to institute proceedings before the Court.
14. However, the Treaty does not provide for any specific period for the exercise of the right to raise the matter with the Commission under the first and second paragraphs of Article 35.
15. It follows, however, from the common purpose of Articles 33 and 35 that the requirements of legal certainty and of the continuity of Community action underlying the time-limits laid down for bringing proceedings under Article 33 must be taken into account – having regard to the special difficulties which the silence of the competent authorities may involve for the interested parties – in the exercise of the rights conferred by Article 35.
16. These requirements may not lead to such contradictory consequences as the duty to act within a short period in the first case and the absence of any limitation in the second.
17. This view finds support in the system of time-limits in Article 35, which allows the Commission two months in which to define its position, and the interested party one month in which to institute proceedings before the Court.
18. Thus it is implicit in the system of Articles 33 and 35 that the exercise of the right to raise the matter with the Commission may not be delayed indefinitely.

19. If the interested parties are thus bound to observe a reasonable time-limit where the Commission remains silent, this is so a fortiori once it is clear that the Commission has decided to take no action.
20. In the present case the communication to the Netherlands Government on the 4th of December 1968 could leave no doubt as to the Commission's attitude on the substance of the problem raised, especially since, at the applicant's request, it had been discussed by the Council and the Netherland's Minister for Economic Affairs had against brough his Government's anxiety to the notice of the Commission in a letter dated 5 April 1968.
21. Furthermore, the duty of cooperation imposed on Member States by Article 86 must prompt a Member State which considers a system of aids to be contrary to the Treaty to resort to the procedures of means of legal action placed at its disposal by the Treaty in sufficient time to ensure that effective intervention is still possible and that the position of third parties is not needlessly called in issue.
22. In view of these circumstances, a period of eighteen months between the communication of 9 December 1968 and the request addressed to the Commission on 24 June 1970 in order to initiate the procedure provided for in Article 35 cannot be regarded as reasonable and was all the more unjustifiable in that the character of the communication of 9 December 1968 was in no way new or unexpected.
23. Therefore on 24 June 1970 the Netherlands Government was no longer in a position to take advantage of Article 35 of the Treaty.
24. The application must be dismissed as inadmissible.

C. PLEA OF ILLEGALITY

(EEC Article 184)

1. Cases

(1) Meroni Case I

Meroni et al. v. *High Authority*; Case 9/56; Judgment of 13 June 1958; [1957 and 1958] ECR 133.

Facts:

The *Meroni Case I*, quoted in Chapter One for its importance for delegation of powers, is also relevant for the exception of illegality. Meroni's principle objections were against general Decisions Nos 22/54 and 14/55 in which powers were delegated to some private institutions in Brussels.

General Decisions under the ECSC Treaty are similar to regulations in the EEC and, as in the EEC, they cannot be brought before the Court of Justice by private parties. In the ECSC Treaty the equivalent of Article 184 EEC (Article 36) provides for a plea of illegality only when pecuniary penalties have been imposed. In the *Meroni Case* there was no question of penalties and therefore the High Authority submitted that the plea of illegality did not exist.

The Court held:

As the Advocate General says in his opinion, an illegal general decision ought not to be applied to an undertaking and no obligations affecting the said undertaking must be deemed to arise therefrom.

Article 36 of the Treaty provides that in support of an application against a decision of the High Authority imposing pecuniary sanctions or periodic penalty payments 'a party may, under the same conditions as in the first paragraph of Article 33 ... contest the legality of the decision or recommendation which that party is alleged not to have observed'.

That provision of Article 36 should not be regarded as a special rule, applicable only in the case of pecuniary sanctions and periodic penalty payments, but as the application of a general principle, applied by Article 36 to the particular case of an action in which the Court has unlimited jurisdiction.

No argument can be based on the express statement in Article 36 to the effect that a contrario the application of the rule laid down is excluded in cases in which it has not been expressly stated. For the Court has decided, in its judgment in Case 8/55, that an argument in reverse is only admissible when no other interpretation appears appropriate and compatible with the provision and its context and with the purpose of the same.

Any other decision would render it difficult, if not impossible, for the undertakings and associations mentioned in Article 48 to exercise their right to bring actions, because it would oblige them to scrutinize every general decision upon publication thereof for provisions which might later adversely affect them or be considered as involving a misuse of powers affecting them.

It would encourage them to let themselves be ordered to pay the pecuniary sanctions or periodic penalty payments for which the Treaty makes provision so as to be able, by virtue of Article 36, to plead the illegality of the general decisions and recommendations which they were alleged not to have observed.

An applicant's right, after the expiration of the period prescribed in the last paragraph of Article 33, to take advantage of the irregularity of general decisions or recommendations in support of proceedings against decisions or recommendations which are individual in character cannot lead to the annulment of the general decision, but only to the annulment of the individual decision which is based on it.

Article 84 of the Treaty establishing the European Economic Community expressly adopts a similar point of view and provides that: ...;

The fact that the position adopted is the same does not constitute a decisive argument but confirms the reasoning set out above by showing that the authors of the new Treaties regarded it as compelling.

The annulment of an individual decision based on the irregularity of the general decisions on which it is based only affects the effects of the general decision in so far as those effects take concrete shape in the annulled individual decision. To contest an individual decision concerning him, any applicant is entitled to put forward the four grounds of annulment set out in the first paragraph of Article 33. In the circumstances, there is no reason why an application who is contesting an individual decision should not be entitled to put forward the four grounds of annulment set out in the first paragraph of Article 33 so as to question the legality of the general decisions and recommendations on which the individual decision is based.

(2) Wöhrmann Case

Milchwerke Wöhrmann et al. v. *EEC Commission*; Case 33/62; Judgment of 14 December 1962; [1962] ECR 506; [1963] CMLR 152.

Facts:

The plaintiffs brought an action in a German court against the levy of an import duty based on Decisions by the EEC Commission taken on 15 March and 13 December 1961, under EEC Article 46. While this action was pending, plaintiff, on 4 October 1962, lodged a complaint with the Court of Justice pursuant to EEC Article 184, or, in the alternative, EEC Article 173, against the 'regulations issued in the form of decisions of the EEC Commission'. The question arose whether the inapplicability of a regulation could be invoked before the Court of Justice under EEC Article 184 if the proceedings in which the regulation was in issue, were pending before a *municipal* Court.

The Court held:

. . . . .

The applicants base their proceedings on Article 184 of the EEC Treaty from which they infer the existence of a right, so far as jurisdiction is concerned, to refer to the Court, for the purpose of having them declared void or inapplicable, Article 3 of the Decision of the Commission of 15 March 1961 and the whole of the Decision of the Commission of 13 December 1961.

Before examining the question whether the contested measures are by their nature decisions or regulations, it is necessary to examine whether Article 184 empowers the Court to adjudicate upon the inapplicability of a regulation when this is invoked in proceedings – as in the present case – before a national court or tribunal.

Article 184 enables any party, notwithstanding the expiry of the period laid down in the third paragraph of Article 173, to invoke before the Court of Justice, for the purpose of making an application for annulment, the inapplicability of a regulation in proceedings in which it is at issue and to plead the grounds specified in the first paragraph of Article 173.

Because Article 184 does not specify before which court of tribunal the proceedings in which the regulations is at issue must be brought, the applicants conclude that the inapplicability of that regulation may in any event be invoked before the Court of Justice. This would mean that there would exist a method of recourse rerunning concurrently with that available under Article 173.

This is however not the meaning of Article 184. It is clear from the wording and the general scheme of this Article that a declaration of the inapplicability of a regulation is only contemplated in proceedings brought before the Court of Justice itself under some other provision of the Treaty, and then only incidentally and with limited effect.

More particularly, it is clear from the reference to the time limit laid down in Article 173 that Article 184 is applicable only in the context of proceedings brought before the Court of Justice and that it does not permit the said time limit to be avoided.

The sole object of Article 184 is thus to protect an interested party against the application of an illegal regulation, without thereby in any way calling in issue the regulation itself, which can no longer be challenged because of the expiry of the time limit laid down in Article 173.

(3) Belgian Railway subsidies Case

See page 666.

D. INTERIM MEASURES

(EEC Articles 185, 186)

1. Cases

(1) Ilford Order

Ilford SpA v. *Commission*; Case 1/84 R; Order of the President of the Court of 1 February 1984; [1984] ECR 423.

Facts:

By decision of 20 October 1983 addressed to the Italian Republic the Commission authorized Member States, as from 5 October 1983 and until 5 March 1984, not to apply Community treatment to films in rolls, sensitized, unexposed, perforated or not, for colour photographs originating in Japan and put into the free circulation in the other Member States, for which applications for import permits had been lodged after 4 October 1983.

By application registered at the Court on 3 January 1984 Ilford SpA, a company registered under Italian law, brought proceedings for a declaration that the Commission Decision of 20 October 1983 is void. In a separate document registered at the Court on the same day, the applicant applied, pursuant to Article 185 of the EEC Treaty and Article 83 of the Rules of Procedure, for the operation of the decision at issue to be suspended.

The Commission submitted that the application for suspension or for other interim measures should be dismissed since it was both inadmissible and unfounded. The Commission disputed the admissibility on the ground that the decision, addressed to the Italian Republic was not of individual concern to Ilford.

The President of the Court held:

Admissibility

6. In the course of the oral procedure it was revealed that the applicant had duly submitted applications for import permits on 13 October 1983, that is, before the date on which the contested decision was adopted (20 October 1983) but after the date on which it took effect (9 October 1983). As the Court pointed out in its judgment of 23 November 1981 (Case 62/70, *Bock* v. *Commission*, [1971] ECR 897), that fact is sufficient to differentiate importers in such a situation from others and to distinguish them individually just as in the case of the person addressed.
7. Without prejudice to the Court's decision concerning the admissibility of the main application, these findings are sufficient for a conclusion that the application for suspension or for interim measures is admissible.
11. At this stage in the proceedings the Commission has not, either in the statement of the reasons on which the decision is based or in the course of these interlocutory proceedings, succeeded in showing satisfactorily that the conditions for the execution of the protective measures referred to in Article 115 are met in this case, and in particular has not shown the existence of any Italian domestic measure of commercial policy taken in accordance with the Treaty.
20. It follows from the above considerations that the question of the conformity with Article 115 of the Treaty of the decision contested in the main proceedings raises serious problems, so that in any event the first

condition to which the suspension of its operation or the granting of interim measures is subject has been met.
23. In the light of all the circumstances referred to above, the operation of the contested decision should be suspended to the extent set out below.

On those grounds,

THE PRESIDENT

by way of interim decision

hereby orders as follows:

1. The operation of the Commission's decision of 20 October 1983 authorizing the Italian Republic not to apply Community treatment to films in rolls, sensitized, unexposed, perforated or not, for colour photographs (subheadings 37.02 ex A II and EX B IV of the Common Customs Tariff) originating in Japan and in free circulation in the other Member States (Official Journal, C 285 of 22 October 1983, p. 6) shall be suspended in respect of the applications for import permits submitted by Ilford between 5 and 20 October 1983, to the extent necessary in order to ensure normal supplies to the applicant during the period from 5 October 1983 to 31 March 1984. Those needs shall be assessed in consideration of the stocks of the products in question held by Ilford on 5 October 1983 and of its sales figures for those products over the previous 12 months. The Commission and Ilford will come to an agreement before 29 February 1984 on the number of units which it must thus be possible to import for release into free circulation. Should they be unable to agree they will inform the President of the Court, by 1 March 1984, of their respective proposals, giving the reasons for their failure to agree.
2. The costs are reserved.

Sequel:

The case was subsequently withdrawn.

E. EFFECT OF ANNULMENT

The Court's annulment of Community acts is *ab initio*. The annulled act will have no legal effect (Article 173 (1)). However, in the case of a regulation the Court may state that some effects may be considered as definitive, or it may rule that the annulment will be *ex nunc* (Article 173 (2)).

III. Unlimited jurisdiction

A. NON-CONTRACTUAL LIABILITY (EEC ARTICLE 215)

1. Introduction

The Communities may be used for their wrongful acts. The *Kampffmeyer Case* demonstrates what sort of damages may be obtained. Of particular interest is the question whether or not damages may be asked for normative acts causing injury. We have seen above that individuals usually have not action against regulations, nor against decisions addressed to others. Can they sue the Communities for damages caused by such acts? We may conclude that this is possible in principle, but difficult in practice.

2. Cases

(1) Kampffmeyer Case I

Kampffmeyer et al. v. *EEC Commission*; Cases 5, 7 and 13–24/66; Judgment of 14 July 1967; [1967] ECR 262.

Facts:

As a result of the *Toepfer Case* (Case 106, 107/73), in which a Commission Decision authorizing the German Government to apply certain safeguard measures concerning the importation of maize was set aside, plaintiffs brought action against the EEC Commission for damages under Article 178, and EEC Article 215, para 2.

Plaintiffs argued that the EEC Commission was liable because it had wrongfully authorized the German Government to take such safeguard measures, as a result of which importers were unable at a certain time to obtain licences to import maize from France. This action by the Commission was alleged to constitute a wrongful act for which the Community was liable.

In its defence, the Commission denied that the annulment of the decision by the Court's Judgment in cases Nos 106 and 107/63 automatically meant liability on the part of the Community to pay damages. It further denied that the provisions of Regulation No 19, which were declared by the Court in that judgment to be violated, were provisions on which a private party might rely (Schutznormen): they were, it contended, laid down solely in the interests of free trade within the Community.

Finally the Commission argued that one of the conditions for a successful claim for damages was lacking, namely, negligence on its part. Plaintiffs had also brought suit for damages in the competent German courts against the

German Federal Republic, which they argued was jointly liable with the Commission. With regard to the quantum of damage, plaintiffs claimed:
(I) (a) damages on account of having had to purchase maize at higher prices than would have been possible had the measures in question not been taken by the Commission, and (b) damages as a result of the compensation some firms had to pay for the cancellation of contracts (datum emergens);
(II) damages as a result of loss of profits through not being able to import maize at low prices (lucrum cessans).

The Court of Justice had to decide whether the annulment of a Decision authorizing Germany to take certain measures constituted sufficient grounds for an action for damages.

The Court held:

. . . . .

On 3 October 1963 the Commission applied Article 22 (2) of Regulation No 19 in circumstances which did not justify protective measures in order to restore the situation resulting from the fixing by it of a zero levy. As it was aware of the existence of applications for licences, it caused damage to the interests of importers who had acted in reliance on the information provided in accordance with Community rules. The Commission's conduct constituted a wrongful act or omission capable of giving rise to liability on the part of the Community.

In trying to justify itself by the assertion that in view of the economic data at its disposal on 3 October 1963 a threat of serious disturbance was not to be excluded and that consequently its mistaken evaluation of the said data is excusable, the defendant misjudges the nature of the wrongful act or omission attributed to it, which is not to be found in a mistaken evaluation of the facts but in its general conduct which is shown clearly by the improper use made of Article 22, certain provisions of which, of a crucial nature, were ignored.

The Commission's assertion that supervisory organizations cannot, under a general principle common to the laws of the Member States, be made liable, except in the case of gross malfeasance is equally irrelevant. In fact, however, the powers which Article 22 of Regulation No 19 confers on the Commission are described, the latter is required in respect of each protective measure notified to it to conduct as exhaustive an examination as that required to be made by the Governments of the Member States and bears independent responsibility for the retention of a protective measure.

With regard to the argument that the rule of law which is infringed is not intended to protect the interests of the applicants, the said Article 22, together with the other provisions of Regulation No 19, is directed, according to the wording of the fourth recital in the preamble to the regulation, to ensuring appropriate support for agricultural markets during the transitional period on the one hand, and to allowing the progressive establishment of a single market by making possible the development of the free movement of goods on the other. Furthermore, the interests of the producers in the Member States and of free trade between these States are expressly mentioned in the preamble to the said regulation. It appears in particular from Article 18 that the exercise of freedom of trade between States is subject only to the general requirements laid down by its own provisions and those of subsequent regulations. Article 22 constitutes an exception to these general rules and consequently an infringement of that article must be regarded as an infringement of those rules and of the interests which they are intended to protect. The fact that these interests are of a general nature does not prevent their including the interests of individual undertakings such as the applicants which as cereal importers are parties engaged in intra-Community trade. Although the application of the rules of law in question is not in general capable of being of direct and individual concern to the said undertakings, that does not prevent the possibility that the protection of their interests may be – as in the present case it is in fact – intended by those rules of law. The defendant's argument that the rule of law contained in Article 22 of Regulation No 19 is not directed towards the protection of the interests of the applicants cannot therefore be accepted.

Since the liability of the Community has been recognized in principle, it is necessary to establish the facts of the alleged injury to which that liability relates.

. . . . .

The alleged injury in respect of the loss of profit is based on facts of an essentially speculative nature. In fact, it should be said first of all that the hasty lodging of an abnormally large number of applications for import licences on 1 October provides an indication that the persons concerned know that the decisions in force on 1 October 1963 offered unusual advantages. Furthermore, as the applicants for licences knew the French market and the actual level of prices ruling there, they were able to perceive the error committed by the Commission in the decision of 27 September 1963, fixing the free-at-frontier prices. Thus the applicants may be regarded as having been aware of the abnormal speculative nature of the transaction involved in their purchases of maize. By cancelling the transactions concerned, they avoided any commercial risk to themselves inherent in importation into the Federal Republic. Consequently it is not justifiable to acknowledge their rights to recover the whole profit that they would have been able to obtain if the transaction which had been started had been performed. Taking this into account, the injury resulting from loss of profit for which the Community must be regarded as being liable cannot equitably be evaluated at a sum exceeding 10% of that which the applicants would have paid by way of levy, if they had carried out the purchases made but cancelled.

However, with regard to any injury suffered by the applicants belonging to te first and second categories above-mentioned, those applicants have informed the Court that the injury alleged is the subject of two actions for damages, one against the Federal Republic of Germany before a German Court and the other against the Community before the Court of Justice. It is necessary to avoid the applicants being insufficiently or excessively compensated for the same damage by the different assessment of two different courts applying different rules of law. Before determining the damage for which the Community should be held liable, it is necessary for the national court to have the opportunity to give judgment on any liability on the part of the Federal Republic of Germany.

(2) Lütticke Case III

Lütticke v. *Commission of the EC*; Case 4/69; Judgment of 28 April 1971; [1971] ECR 336.

Facts:

Lütticke imported dairy products into Germany. Until January 1968 the Federal Republic levied a compensatory turnover tax on such imports. Lütticke had informed the Commission that this tax had become illegal after the end of the first stage of the transitional period (1 January 1962). He had asked the Commission to take action against Germany; when the Commission refused to do so he appealed to the Court. His appeal was declared inadmissible. Before the German courts Lütticke brought an action against the tax. This action, finally, led to a request for a preliminary ruling by the Finanzgericht Saarland. The preliminary ruling given by the Court of Justice clearly demonstrated that the German taxes were no longer valid. Lütticke had suffered considerable damages for which he blamed the Commission, submitting that it should have followed a more active policy against Germany. In the present case he sued the Commission for these damages.

The Court held:

On the admissibility

. . . . .

5. Secondly, the defendant contests the admissibility of the action by reason of the fact that, although introduced on the basis of Article 178 and the

second paragraph of Article 215, it seeks in reality to establish a failure to act on the part of the Commission and to constrain it indirectly to initiate against the Federal Republic of Germany the procedure under the second paragraph of Article 97 and, possibly, that under Article 169. It is claimed that this manner of proceeding has the effect of distorting the conditions to which Article 175 has subjected actions for failure to act.

6. The action for damages provided for by Article 178 and the second paragraph of Article 215 was established by the Treaty as an independent form of action with a particular purpose to fulfill within the system of actions and subject to conditions for its use, conceived with a view to its specific purpose. It would be contrary to the independent nature of this action as well as to the general system of forms of action created by the Treaty to regard as a ground of inadmissibility the fact that, in certain circumstances, an action for damages might lead to a result similar to that of an action for failure to act under Article 175.

7. This objection of inadmissibility must therefore be dismissed.

. . . . .

The substance of the case

. . . . .

10. By virtue of the second paragraph of Article 215 and the general principles to which this provision refers, the liability of the Community presupposes the existence of a set of circumstances comprising actual damage, a causal link between the damage claimed and the conduct alleged against the institution, and the illegality of such conduct.

11. In this case, it is appropriate to examine first the question whether the Commission, acting as it did, failed to fulfil the obligations imposed on it by the second paragraph of Article 97.

. . . . .

17. It is established that as early as 1962 the Commission began, with experts from the Member States, an examination of the average rates provided for by national laws with a view to checking their conformity with the requirements of Article 95 and the first paragraph of Article 97. During this examination it discussed with the German authorities and with those of the other Member States concerned in the powdered milk trade the

rate applicable to this product. Having studied the arguments put forward by the German Government it informed it that the average rate of 4% in force for imports of milk powder into the Federal Republic seemed to it to be too high. Since the Federal Republic, following this intervention, reduced the rate of the tax at issue from 4% to 3% with effect from 1 April 1965 – a date subsequently brought forward to 1 January 1962 – the Commission considered that there was no longer any need to adopt a directive or a decision under Article 97 in order to obtain an even greater reduction. Furthermore, there were no complaints of any sort made by Member States whose exports could have been adversely affected by the tax system criticized by the applicant. It follows from the above that in the circumstances the Commission had not failed to perform its task of supervision.

18. In addition, although the expert's report produced by the applicant reaches the conclusion that for powdered milk the average rate should be lower, it is capable of confirming that the calculation of the indirect taxes imposed on this product include a whole series of uncertain factors which may give rise to very different assessments, with the result that it is in general possible only to establish certain minimum and maximum limits between which several solutions appear equally justifiable.

19. The applicant has not proved that for the product in question an average rate of 3% exceeds the limits authorized by Articles 95 and 97 the observance of which the Commission must ensure. Consequently, the application must be dismissed.

. . . . .

(3) CNTA Case

Comptoir National Technique Agricole (CNTA) S.A. v. Commission; Case 74/74; Judgment of 14 May 1975; [1975] ECR 549; [1977] 1 CMLR 171.

Facts:

The regime in force in January 1972 for the marketing of colza contained rules for 'refunds' to be granted to exports to third countries in order to compensate for the lower prices prevailing on the world market. These 'refunds' were paid on actual sales but could be fixed in advance. Apart from these 'refunds' the Member States were also authorized to grant 'compensatory amounts' when fluctuations in exchange rate of national currencies led to disturbances to trade. For France this compensatory amount was established by the Commission at FF 3.95 per 100 kgs from 3 January 1972, and increased to FF 4.75 per 100 kgs, as from 24 January 1972. The compensatory amounts were granted on exports, they could not be fixed in advance.

On 6 January 1972 Comptoir National Technique Agricole (CNTA) had the refunds fixed for the export of a specific amount of colza. In setting its price it took into account the refunds and the FF 3.95 per 100 kgs. 'compensatory amount', then in force. But on 26 January the Commission adopted a regulation, published on 28 January by which all 'compensatory amounts' applicable to oils and fats were rescinded with effect from 1 February 1972, because the Commission considered that 'the present situation on the market is such that the application of these compensatory amounts no longer proves to be essential for avoiding disturbance to trade.'

CNTA performed its exports after 1 February 1972 and therefore received no compensatory amounts. It considered that the abolition of the compensatory amounts disturbed the performance of current delivery contracts and claimed damages.

The Court held:

. . . . .

16. Since the disputed measure is of a legislative nature and constitutes a measure taken in the sphere of economic policy, the Community cannot be liable for any damage suffered by individuals as a consequence of that measure under the provisions of the second paragraph of Article 215 of the Treaty, unless a sufficiently flagrant violation of a superior rule of law for the protection of the individual has occurred.

. . . . .

40. It follows that the system of compensatory amounts cannot be considered to be tantamount to a guarantee for traders against the risks of alteration of exchange rates.
41. Nevertheless the application of the compensatory amounts in practice avoids the exchange risk, so that a trader, even a prudent one, might be induced to omit to cover himself against such risk.
42. In these circumstances, a trader may legitimately expect that for transactions irrevocably undertaken by him because he has obtained, subject to a deposit, export licences fixing the amount of the refund in advance, no unforeseeable alteration will occur which could have the effect of causing him inevitable loss, by re-exposing him to the exchange risk.
43. The Community is therefore liable if, in the absence of an overriding matter of public interest, the Commission abolished with immediate effect and without warning the application of compensatory amounts in a specific sector without adopting transitional measures which would at least permit traders either to avoid the loss which would have been suffered in the performance of export contracts, the existence and irrevo-

cability of which are established by the advance fixing of the refunds, or to be compensated for such loss.
44. In the absence of an overriding matter of public interest, the Commission has violated a superior rule of law, thus rendering the Community liable, by failing to include in Regulation No 189/72 transitional measures for the protection of the confidence which a trader might legitimately have had in the Community rules.
45. With regard to the extent of the loss to be compensated, it is necessary to take into consideration the fact that the maintenance of the compensatory amounts was in no way guaranteed to the applicant and that it could not therefore legitimately expect under all circumstances to make the profits which would have accrued to it from the contract under the system of compensatory amounts.
46. The protection which it may claim by reason of its legitimate expectation is merely that of not suffering loss by reason of the withdrawal of these amounts.
47. As the amount of the compensation due to the applicant cannot be determined at the present stage of the proceedings, it must be held by interlocutory judgment that the Community is obliged to compensate the applicant for the loss which it has suffered, by reason of the withdrawal of the compensatory amounts, in the execution of export transactions for which the refunds had been fixed by the certificates of 6 January 1972, while reserving the fixing of the amount of compensation either by agreement between the parties or by the Court in the absence of such agreement.

On those grounds,

THE COURT

By interlocutory judgment

1. Rules that the Commission of the European Communities must compensate the Comptoir National Technique Agricole for the loss suffered, by reason of Regulation No 189/72 of 26 January 1972 in the execution of export transactions for which the refunds had been fixed by the certificates of 6 January 1972;
2. Orders the parties to produce to the Court within six months of the date of this judgment figures of the amount of the compensation arrived at by agreement between the parties;
3. In the absence of agreement, orders the parties to produce to the Court within the same period their conclusions with detailed figures;
4. Reserves the costs.

Sequel:

The action of CNTA finally failed as no damage could be proven, see decision of the Court of 15 June 1976, [1976] ECR 797.

(4) Krohn Case II

Krohn & Co Import-Export GmbH v. *Commission of the EC*; Case 175/84; Judgment of 26 February 1986; [1986] ECR 753.

Facts:

On 16 November 1982 Krohn had requested the Bundesanstalt für landwirtschaftliche Marktordnung (German Federal Office for the Organization of Agricultural Markets) to issue it with some licenses for importation of manioc from Thailand. On the instruction of the Commission the Bundesanstalt refused the requested license. Relying on the illegality of the Commission's instruction Krohn brought an action against the Commission under EEC Article 215. In response to doubts which the Commission had expressed as to the admissibility of the action, the Court of Justice decided on its own motion to rule separately upon the following arguments against admissibility:
(a) The refusal to issue the requested import licences was the decision of the Bundesanstalt. Consequently, only that national body can incur liability and these proceedings fall outside the jurisdiction of the Court.
(b) Even if the Commission is potentially liable, the applicant must have previously exhausted the remedies available to it before the national courts for the purposes of obtaining the annulment of the Bundesanstalt's decision.
(c) Finally, in any event, upholding the admissibility of the action would amount to nullifying the legal effects of the Commission's individual decisions with regard to the applicant (telex messages of 23 November and 21 December 1982), which were not challenged in due time and have become definitive.

The Court held:

The first argument against admissibility

. . . . .

18. The Court, wishes to point out that the combined provisions of Articles 178 and 215 of the Treaty only give jurisdiction to the Court to award compensation for damage caused by the Community institutions or by their servants in the performance of their duties, or in other words for damage capable of giving rise to non-contractual liability on the part of the Community. Damage caused by national institutions, on the other hand, can only give rise to liability on the part of those institutions, and the national courts retain sole jurisdiction to order compensation for such damage.

19. Where, as in this case, the decision adversely affecting the applicant was adopted by a national body acting in order to ensure the implementation of Community rules, it is necessary, in order to establish the jurisdiction of the Court, to determine whether the unlawful conduct alleged in support of the application for compensation is in fact the responsibility of a Community institution and cannot be attributed to the national body.

. . . . .

21. With regard to that point, it is clear from the very wording of Article 7 (1) of Regulation No 2029/82 that its provisions do not merely confer upon the Commission the right to give an opinion on the decision to be adopted in the context of the cooperation between itself and the national bodies responsible for applying the Community rules, but actually empower it to insist that such national bodies refuse requests for import licences where the conditions laid down in the Cooperation Agreement have not been fulfilled.
22. Moreover, the information submitted by the parties and their arguments before the Court make it clear that the Commission's telex messages of 23 November and 21 December 1982 were intended as an effective exercise of the power conferred upon it by the provisions and that their effect was to instruct the Bundesanstalt to refuse the import licences at issue if no satisfactory reply was given to the requests for information made to Krohn.
23. It follows from the foregoing that the unlawful conduct alleged by the applicant in order to establish its claim for compensation is to be attributed not to the Bundesanstalt, which was bound to comply with the Commission's instructions, but to the Commission itself. The Court therefore has jurisdiction to entertain the action brought by Krohn, and the first argument against admissibility must be rejected.

. . . . .

The second argument against admissibility

. . . . .

26. According to an established body of decisions of the Court, the application for compensation provided for by Article 178 and the second paragraph of Article 215 of the Treaty was introduced as an autonomous form of action with a particular purpose to fulfil within the system of actions and subject to conditions on its use dictated by its specific nature.
27. Nonetheless, it is true that such actions must be examined in the light of the whole system of legal protection for the individual established by the

Treaty and that the admissibility of such an action may in certain cases be dependent on the exhaustion of a national rights of action available to obtain the annulment of a national authority's decision. In order for that to be the case, however, it is necessary that those national rights of action should provide an effective means of protection for the individual concerned and be capable of resulting in compensation for the damage alleged.

28. That is not the case here. There is nothing to suggest that the annulment of the Bundesanstalt's decision and the issue, after a lapse of several years, of the import licenses claimed in 1982 would compensate Krohn for the damage suffered by it at that time; such an annulment would therefore not remove the need for the applicant, if it is to obtain compensation, to bring an action before the Court under Article 178 and the second paragraph of Article 215 of the Treaty.

29. In those circumstances, the admissibility of this action cannot be made dependent on the exhaustion of the national rights of action available against the Bundesanstalt's decision, and the second argument against admissibility must also be rejected.

. . . . .

The third argument against admissibility

. . . . .

32. As the Court has pointed out above, the action provided for by Article 178 and the second paragraph of Article 215 of the Treaty was introduced as an autonomous form of action with a particular purpose to fulfil. It differs from an action for annulment in particular in that its purpose in not to set aside a specific measure but to repair the damage caused by an institution. It follows that the existence of an individual decision which has become definitive cannot act as a bar to the admissibility of such an action.

33. The decision cited by the Commission relates solely to the exceptional case where an application for compensation is brought for the payment of an amount precisely equal to the duty which the applicant was required to pay under an individual decision, so that the application seeks in fact the withdrawal of that individual decision. At all events, such considerations are foreign to this case.

34. It follows that the third argument against admissibility must also be rejected.

B. ACTION AGAINST PENALTIES
(EEC Article 172)

Some regulations (e.g. Regulation No 17/62 on competition) permit the Commission to levy fines. Some considerable fines have been imposed for dividing markets and fixing prices. All fines may be challenged before the Court.

1. Cases

(1) Boehringer Case I

Boehringer Mannheim GmbH v. *Commission*; Case 45/69; Judgment of 15 July 1970; [1970] ECR 769; Competition Law CM/M/111/18.

Facts:

Plaintiff, a German manufacturer of chemical and pharmaceutical products, brought an action against the Decision of the Commission of the EC of 16 July 1969 (OJ 1969, L 192/5) by which a fine of 190,000 Units of Account was imposed upon him for having been a party to an international gentlemen's agreement dividing the markets for, and fixing the prices of, quinine. It objected to this fine on a number of grounds.

The Court held:

. . . . .

52. The applicant complains that the Commission imposed on it a fine for an infringement which had come to an end and that by omitting to take this fact into consideration, at least for the purposes of fixing the amount of the fine, the defendant was guilty of an abuse of powers.
53. The penalties provided for in Article 15 of Regulation No 17 are not in the nature of periodic penalty payments. Their object is to suppress illegal activities and to prevent any recurrence. This object could not be adequately attained if the imposition of a penalty were to be restricted to current infringements alone. The Commission's power to impose penalties is in no way affected by the fact that the conduct constituting the infringement has ceased and that it can no longer have detrimental effects. For the purpose of fixing the amount of the fine, the gravity of the infringement is to be appraised by taking into account in particular the nature of the restrictions on competition, the number and size of the undertakings concerned, the respective proportions of the market controlled by them within the Community and the situation of the market when the infringement was committed.
54. The applicant complains that the Commission first of all fixed an aggre-

gate amount for the fine on the cartel and then divided it amongst the undertakings. This procedure is incompatible with the requirement of fixing the fine individually. Furthermore, the applicant subject to discriminates as compared with the other undertakings, by reason of the disproportionate amount of the fine imposed upon it.
55. The prior fixing of a maximum aggregate amount for the fine, fixed in relation to the seriousness of the danger which the agreement represented to competition and trade in the Common Market, is not incompatible with the individual fixing of the penalty. Consideration of the situation and of the individual conduct of each undertaking and of the importance of the rôle which it played in the agreement of the fine.
56. In the present case the contested decision, particularly paragraphs (2) and (4) of No 40, expressly considered the situation and rôle of the applicant within the framework of the cartel.

. . . . .

58. It appears lastly from the minutes of the joint meetings which the members of the cartel held on 25 September and 29 October 1962 that they were aware of the incompatibility of their actions with the prohibitions in Community law. The serious and conscious nature of the infringements therefore justified a large fine.
59. The findings in the contested decision relating to the infringements alleged against the applicant are thus well founded in their essentials. Since excluding the fixing of sales quotas for the period from November 1962 to February 1965 does not appreciably diminish the gravity of the restrictions of competition arising from the agreement, it justifies only a slight reduction in the fine. It is appropriate to reduce the fine to 180,000 units of account.
60. The applicant maintains that the fine of 80,000 dollars which was imposed upon it by a court in the USA, arising out of the same facts, and which was already paid before the contested decision, should be deduced from the amount of the disputed fine.
61. These penalties were imposed in respect of restrictions on competitions which occurred outside the Community.

Consequently there is no reason to take them into account in these proceedings.

IV. Preliminary rulings

A. Introduction

In subchapter II we discussed remedies against invalid acts of the Community (EEC Article 173). It need not be illustrated that such acts are rare. Usually

Community acts are valid and must be applied within the legal orders of the Member States. Their application has been left to the national courts, which proved to be wise as rules of Community law are so interwoven with national rules that it would be very difficult to bring their application before a separate Community Court.

The general rule that national courts apply Community law could lead to divergent application in different Member States or even to application contrary to the principles of Community law. Article 177 EEC has been introduced primarily to guarantee uniform interpretation within all Member States. Therefore, the highest national courts, whose cases usually set the important precedents, are obliged to refer questions of Community law to the Court of Justice.

Several questions brought to the Court of Justice under Article 177 enabled that Court to decide important principles of Community law, such as the principles of priority of Community law over national law. In many preliminary rulings the Court of Justice decided whether particular articles in the Treaty or in regulations could be invoked by individuals before their national courts or whether they needed further legislation before they could be applied.

Under Article 177 national courts may also ask a preliminary ruling on the *validity* of community acts.

Under II above, we noticed that individuals may not usually bring an action before the Court of Justice for the annulment of regulations or decisions addressed to others. This omission in legal protection is partly restored by the possibility to invoke the illegality of such acts before a national court. If that court is willing to request a preliminary ruling and if the Court of Justice subsequently rules that the act is invalid, it will then not be applied by the national court, which actually means that the act obtains no force of law.

B. Competence of the Court of Justice

1. Cases

(1) Van Gend en Loos Case

Van Gend en Loos v. *Netherlands Fiscal Administration*; Case 26/62; Preliminary ruling of 5 February 1963; [1963] ECR 10; [1963] CMLR 128.

Facts:

By transferring ureaformaldehyde from one tariff class to another the Netherlands' Government actually increased import duties. Van Gend en Loos – importers of ureaformaldehyde – claimed that such a transfer was contrary to Article 12 of the Treaty. The Dutch Court handling the case requested a preliminary ruling, first on the question whether Article 12 could be invoked by an individual before a national court and, second, on the question whether the transfer to another tariff class constituted a violation of Article 12.

The Belgian Government submitted that the transfer was consequent to a Benelux-protocol which would have priority over the EEC Treaty. An interpretation of the EEC Treaty would therefore be irrelevant and the Court of Justice would have no jurisdiction.

The Court held:

. . . . .

II – The first question

The Government of the Netherlands and the Belgian Government challenge the jurisdiction of the Court of Justice on the ground that the reference relates not to the interpretation but to the application of the Treaty in the context of the constitutional law of the Netherlands, and that in particular the Court has no jurisdiction to decide, should the occasion arise, whether the provisions of the EEC Treaty prevail over Netherlands legislative or over other agreements entered into by the Netherlands and incorporated into Dutch national law. The solution of such a problem, it is claimed, falls within the exclusive jurisdiction of the national courts, subject to an application in accordance with the provisions laid down by Articles 169 and 170 of the Treaty.

However in this case the Court is not asked to adjudicate upon the application of the Treaty according to the principles of the national law of the Netherlands, which remains the concern of the national courts, but is asked, in conformity with subparagraph (a) of the first paragraph of Article 177 of the Treaty, only to interpret the scope of Article 12 of the said Treaty within the context of Community law and with reference to its effect on individuals. This argument has therefore no legal foundation.

The Belgian Government further argues that the Court has no jurisdiction on the ground that no answer which the Court could give to the first question of the Tariefcommissie would have any bearing on the result of the proceedings brought in that court.

However, in order to confer jurisdiction on the Court in the present case it is necessary only that the question raised should clearly be concerned with the interpretation of the Treaty. The considerations which may have led a national court or tribunal to its choice of questions as well as the relevance which it attributes to such questions in the context of a case before it are excluded from review by the Court of Justice.

It appears from the wording of the questions referred that they relate to the interpretation of the Treaty. The Court therefore has the jurisdiction to answer them.

This argument, too, is therefore unfounded.

B – On the substance of the Case

The first question of the Tariefcommissie is whether Article 12 of the Treaty has direct application in national law in the sense that nationals of Member States may on the basis of this Article lay claim to rights which the national courts must protect.

To ascertain whether the provisions of an international treaty extend so far in their effects it is necessary to consider the spirit, the general scheme and the wording of those provisions.

The objective of the EEC Treaty, which is to establish a Common Market, the functioning of which is of direct concern to interested parties in the Community, implies that this Treaty is more than an agreement which merely creates mutual obligations between the contracting states. This view is confirmed by the preamble to the Treaty which refers not only to governments but to peoples. It is also confirmed more specifically by the establishment of instructions endowed with sovereign rights, the exercise of which effects Member States and also their citizens. Furthermore, it must be noted that the nationals of the states brought together in the Community are called upon to cooperate in the functioning of this Community through the intermediary of the European Parliament and the Economic and Social Committee.

In addition the task assigned to the Court of Justice under Article 177, the object of which is to secure uniform interpretation of the Treaty by national courts and tribunals, confirms that the states have acknowledged that Community law has an authority which can be invoked by their nationals before those courts and tribunals.

The conclusion to be drawn from this is that the Community constitutes a new legal order of international law for the benefit of which the states have limited their sovereign rights, albeit within limited fields, and the subjects of which comprise not only Member States but also their nationals. Independently of the legislation of Member States, Community law therefore not only imposes obligations on individuals but is also intended to confer upon them rights which become part of their legal heritage. These rights arise not only where they are expressly granted by the Treaty, but also by reason of obligations which the Treaty imposes in a clearly defined way upon individuals as well as upon the Member States and upon the institutions of the Community.

With regard to the general scheme of the Treaty as it relates to customs duties and charges having equivalent effect it must be emphasized that Article 9, which based the Community upon a customs union, includes as an essential provision the prohibition of these customs duties and charges. This provision is found at the beginning of the part of the Treaty which defined the 'Foundations of the Community'. It is applied and explained by Article 12.

The wording of Article 12 contains a clear and unconditional prohibition which is not a positive but a negative obligation. This obligation, moreover, is not qualified by any reservation on the part of states which would make its implementation conditional upon a positive legislative measure enacted under national law. The very nature of this prohibition makes it ideally adapted to produce direct effects in the legal relationship between Member States and their subjects.

The implementation of Article 12 does not require any legislative intervention on the part of the States. The fact that under this Article it is the Member States who are made the subject of the negative obligation does not imply that their nationals cannot benefit from this obligation.

In addition the argument based on Articles 169 and 170 of the Treaty put forward by the three Governments which have submitted observations to the Court in their statement of case is misconceived. The fact that these Articles of the Treaty enable the Commission and the Member States to bring before the Court a State which has not fulfilled its obligations, should the occasion arise, before a national court, any more than the fact that the Treaty places at the disposal of the Commission ways of ensuring that obligations imposed upon those subject to the Treaty are observed, precludes the possibility, in actions between individuals before a national court, of pleading infringements of these obligations.

A restriction of the guarantees against an infringement of Article 12 by Member States to the procedures under Articles 169 and 170 would remove all direct legal protection of the individual rights of their nationals. There is the risk that recourse to the procedure under these articles would be ineffective if it were to occur after the implementation of a national decision taken contrary to the provisions of the Treaty.

The vigilance of individuals concerned to protect their rights amounts to an effective supervision in addition to the supervision entrusted by Articles 160 and 170 to the diligence of the Commission and of the Member States. It follows from the foregoing considerations that, according to the spirit, the general scheme and the wording of the Treaty, Article 12 must be interpreted as producing direct effects and creating individual rights which national courts must protect.

III – The second question

A – The jurisdiction of the Court

According to the observations of the Belgian and Netherlands Governments, the wording of this question appears to require, before it can be answered, an examination by the Court of the tariff classification of ureaformaldehyde imported into the Netherlands, a classification on which Van Gend en Loos and the Inspector of Customs and Excise at Zaandam hold different opinions with regard to the 'Tariefbesluit' of 1974. The question clearly does not call for an interpretation of the Treaty but concerns the application of Netherlands customs legislation to the classification of aminoplasts, which is outside the jurisdiction conferred upon the Court of Justice of the European Communities by subparagraph (a) of the first paragraph of Article 177.

The Court has therefore no jurisdiction to consider the reference made by the Tariefcommissie.

However, the real meaning of the question put by the Tariefcommissie is whether, in law, an effective increase in customs duties charged on a given product as a result not of an increase in the rate but of a new classification of the product arising from a change of its tariff description contravenes the prohibition in Article 12 of the Treaty.

Viewed in this way the question put is concerned with an interpretation of this provision of the Treaty and more particularly of the meaning which should be given to the concept of duties applied before the Treaty entered into force.

Therefore the Court has jurisdiction to give a ruling on this question.

B – On the substance

It follows from the wording and the general scheme of Article 12 of the Treaty that, in order to ascertain whether customs duties or charges having equivalent effect have been increased contrary to the prohibition contained in the said Article, regard must be had to the customs duties charges actually applied at the date of the entry into force of the Treaty.

(2) Costa – ENEL Case

Costa v. *ENEL*; Case 6/64; Preliminary ruling of 15 July 1964; [1964] ECR 592; [1964] CMLR 425.

Facts:

In a case before the Justice of the Peace in Milano, Mr. Costa denied the validity of the Italian nationalization law which led to the establishment of the ENEL Company. One of the submissions was that this law violated the EEC Treaty. The Justice of the Peace asked a preliminary ruling on the compatibility of the nationalization law with the Treaty. The Italian Government was of the opinion that the request for a preliminary ruling was inadmissible.

The Court held:

On the application of Article 177

On the submission regarding the wording of the question

The complaint is made that the intention behind the question posed was to obtain, by means of Article 177, a ruling on the compatibility of a national law with the Treaty.

By the terms of this Article, however, national courts against whose decisions, as in the present case, there is no judicial remedy, must refer the matter to the Court of Justice so that the preliminary ruling may be given upon the 'interpretation of the Treaty' whenever a question of interpretation is raised before them. This provision gives the Court no jurisdiction either to apply the Treaty to a specific case or to decide upon the validity of a provision of domestic law in relation to the Treaty, as it would be possible for it to do under Article 169.

Nevertheless, the Court has power to extract from a question imperfectly formulated by the national court those questions which alone pertain to the interpretation of the Treaty. Consequently a decision should be given by the Court not upon the validity of an Italian law in relation to the Treaty, but only upon the interpretation of the abovementioned Articles in the context of the points of law stated by the Giudice Conciliatore.

On the submission that an interpretation is not necessary

The complaint is made that the Milan court has requested an interpretation of the Treaty which was not necessary for the solution of the dispute before it.

Since, however, Article 177 is based upon a clear separation of functions between national courts and the Court of Justice, it cannot empower the latter either to investigate the facts of the case or to criticize the grounds and purposes of the request for interpretation.

(3) Schwarze Case

Schwarze v. *Einfuhr- und Vorratstelle*; Case 16/65; Preliminary ruling of 1 December 1965; [1965] ECR 886; [1966] CMLR 172.

Facts:

The question was raised before the Finanzgericht whether sufficient reasons had been given for the relevant EEC Decision. The Finanzgericht referred several questions on the interpretation of the Community law concerned to the Court of Justice and the French government argued that a number of these questions went beyond interpretation and concerned the actual validity of the Decision.

The Court had to decide whether, when approached under Article 177 (1)b for an interpretation of Community law, it could pass upon the validity of an act of a Community institution.

The Court held:

If it appears that the real purpose of the questions submitted by a national court is concerned rather with the validity of community measures than with their interpretation, it is appropriate for the Court to inform the national court at once of its view without compelling the national court to comply with purely formal requirements which would uselessly prolong the procedure under Article 177 and would be contrary to its very nature. Although this type of strict adherence to formal requirements may be defined in the case of litigation between two parties whose mutual rights must be subject to strict rules, it would be inappropriate to the special field of judicial cooperation under Article 177 which requires the national court and the Court of Justice, both keeping within their respective jurisdiction, and with the aim of ensuring that Community law is applied in a unified manner, to make direct and complementary contributions to the working out of a decision.

(4) Foglia Novello Case II

Pasquale Foglia v. *Mariella Novello*; Case 244/80; Preliminary ruling of 16 December 1981; [1981] ECR 3045.

Facts:

The Italian trader in wine, Foglia, sold wine to another Italian, Novello. The wine was to be delivered in France. Novello was to pay all costs of delivery. When Foglia sent him the bill, Novello refused to pay some charges which France had levied at the importation of the wine. Novello's argument was that these charges were illegally paid. Foglia sued Novello before the Pretura in Bra. The Pretura requested a preliminary ruling which in fact concerned the legality of the French charges. Obviously, Foglia and Novello agreed that the French charges were illegal and their only purpose was to obtain a decision of the Court of Justice implicitly condemning France.

In *Foglia Novello Case I* (104/79, [1980] ECR 745) the Court of Justice replied to the Pretura in Bra that it had no jurisdiction to give a ruling on the questions submitted by the Pretura.

In its judgment the Court found that the parties to the main action were concerned 'to obtain a ruling that the French tax system is invalid for liqueur wines by the expedient of proceedings before an Italian court between two private individuals who are in agreement as to the result to be attained and who have inserted a clause in their contract in order to induce the Italian court to give a ruling on the point', and concluded that:

'The duty of the Court of Justice under Article 177 of the EEC Treaty is to supply all courts in the Community with the information on the interpretation of Community law which is necessary to enable them to settle genuine disputes which are brought before them. A situation in which the Court was obliged by the expedient of arrangements like those described above to give rulings would jeopardize the whole system of legal remedies available to private individuals to enable them to protect themselves against tax provisions which are contrary to the Treaty.'

The Pretura in Bra considered this preliminary ruling insufficient and applied for a new preliminary ruling in November 1980. It asked some further questions on the division of competence between the Court of Justice and the national judiciary.

The Court held:

1. According to the intended role of Article 177, an assessment of the need to obtain an answer to the questions of interpretation raised, regard being had to the circumstances of fact and of law involved in the main action, is a matter for the national court; it is nevertheless for the Court of Justice, in order to confirm its own jurisdiction, to examine, where necessary, the conditions in which the case has been referred to it by the national court.
2. In the absence of provisions of Community law, the possibility of taking proceedings before a national court against a Member State other than that in which that court is situated depends both on the procedural law of the latter and on the principles of international law.
3. In the case of questions intended to permit the national court to determine whether provisions laid down by law or regulation in another Member State are in accordance with Community law. The degree of legal protection may not differ according to whether such questions are raised in proceedings between individuals or in an action to which the State whose legislation is called in question is a party, but in the first case the Court of Justice must take special care to ensure that the procedure under Article 177 is not employed for purposes which were not intended by the Treaty.
4. The circumstance referred to by the Pretore, Bra, in his second order for reference does not appear to constitute a new fact which would justify the Court of Justice in making a fresh appraisal of its jurisdiction and it is therefore for the Pretore, within the framework of the collaboration between a national court and the Court of Justice, to ascertain in the light of the foregoing considerations whether there is any need to obtain an answer from the Court of Justice to the fifth question and, if so, to indicate to the Court any new factor which might justify it in taking a different view of its jurisdiction.

C. THE REQUEST FOR A PRELIMINARY RULING APPEALED

1. Introduction

When a party appeals to a higher national court against the decision by which a lower court has asked for a preliminary ruling most Dutch and German lower courts nevertheless forward their request for a preliminary ruling to the

Court of Justice. Belgian and French courts wait until their decisions have become final. For British courts Order 114 provides:

'Transmission of order to the European Court

5. When an order has been made, the Senior Master shall send a copy thereof to the Registrer of the European Court; but in the case of an order made by the High Court, he shall not do so, unless the Court otherwise orders, until the time for appealing against the order has expired or, if an appeal is entered within that time, until the appeal has been determined or otherwise disposed of.

Appeals from orders made by the High Court

6. An order by the High Court shall be deemed to be a final decision, and accordingly an appeal against it shall lie to the Court of Appeal without leave; but the period within which a notice of appeal must be served under Order 59, rule 4 (1), shall be 14 days.'

2. Cases

(1) Bosch Case

De Geus en Uitenbogerd v. *Bosch en Van Rijn*; Case 13/61; Preliminary ruling of 6 April 1962; [1962] ECR 49; [1962] CMLR 1.

Facts:

The Court of Appeal of the Hague, in an interlocutory judgment suspended the proceedings before it, in order to ask for a preliminary ruling of the Court of Justice concerning the interpretation of EEC Article 85 para 1. Defendants had appealed to the Hoge Raad (Supreme Court) for annulment of this interlocutory order, but the Hoge Raad had not yet taken a decision when the case came before the Court of Justice.

The Court held:

Both plaintiffs in the proceedings in the Netherlands, Bosch and Van Rijn, as well as the Government of the French Republic, cast doubt on the question whether a preliminary ruling may be given at the request of the Court of Appeal of The Hague, in view of the fact that a petition in cassation has been lodged against the judgment in which the request was made.
    This doubt has resulted from an interpretation of Article 177 of the Treaty. The argument is that a request to this Court under Article 177 cannot be

made unless the judgment of the ruling of the national court containing the reference to this Court has the force of res judicata. This interpretation of Article 177 is not only *not* suggested by the literal meaning of the wording, but rests also on a failure to appreciate that the municipal law of any Member State, whose courts request a preliminary ruling from this court, and Community law constitute two separate and distinct legal orders.

Just as the Treaty does not prevent the national Court of Cassation from making cognizance of the petition but leaves the determination of its admissibility to the national law and the decision of the national judge, so that the Treaty makes the jurisdiction of this Court dependant solely on the existence of a request for a preliminary ruling within the meaning of Article 177. And it does so without requiring this Court to discover whether the decision of the national court has acquired the force of res judicata under the national law.

(2) Chanel Case

SA Chanel v. Cepeha Handelsmaatschappij NV; Case 31/68; Preliminary ruling of 16 June 1970; [1970] ECR 404; [1971] CMLR 403.

Facts:

The Rotterdam District Court, by its judgment of 3 December 1968 had asked for a preliminary ruling on Article 85 of the EEC Treaty. On 29 January 1969 the registrar of the Rotterdam Court notified the Court of Justice that an appeal had been lodged against the judgment of 3 December 1968. Nevertheless the Court of Justice decided on 23 March 1969 that the oral proceedings would be held on 29 April 1969. The Advocat-General concluded on 20 May 1969 that no valid request for a preliminary ruling had been made as long as the decision of the Rotterdam court was not final. He proposed that the Court of Justice should stay the proceedings until the outcome of the appeal before the Dutch court was known.

The Court held: (3 June 1969)

. . . . .

Judgment in the present case is suspended pending notification to the Court that the appeal has been decided.

. . . . .

Further facts:

On 6 May 1970 the Court of Appeal in The Hague annulled the decision of the Rotterdam Court by which the preliminary ruling had been requested.

The Court held: (16 June 1970)

. . . . .

By a letter received at the Registry on 12 June 1970, the Registrar of the Arrondissementsrechtbank informed the Court that a judgment of 6 May 1970 of the Gerechtshof, The Hague, had amended the judgment of 3 December 1968.
Accordingly the reference for interpretation has lost its purpose.

(3) Rheinmühlen Case

Rheinmühlen-Düsseldorf v. *Einfuhr- und Vorratstelle für Getreide und Futtermittel*; Case 166/73; Preliminary ruling of 16 January 1974; [1974] ECR 33; [1974] 1 CMLR 523.

Facts:

The dispute between the parties had been decided by the Hessische Finanzgericht (lower court). Rheinmühlen appealed to the Bundesfinanzhof (supreme court), which annulled the decision and referred the matter back to the Hessische Finanzgericht. According to German law (Finanzgerichtordnung 6 October 1965, para 126) the lower court is bound to the legal consideration of the supreme court in case of such a back reference. The lower court, however, considered that the legal considerations of the supreme court violated some provisions of Community law and requested a preliminary ruling on those provisions (Case 146/73). Rheinmühlen considered that this was in violation with German legislation and appealed to the Bundesfinanzhof against the Order of Reference by which the preliminary ruling was requested. The Bundesfinanzhof then requested a preliminary ruling on the question whether under Article 177 a lower court has a completely unfettered right to refer questions to the Court of Justice or whether that Article leaves unaffected rules of national law to the contrary, under which a Court is bound on points of law by the judgments of the Courts superior to it in the hierarchy (Case 166/73). The Court of Justice had to decide inter alia:
a) In relation to the questions asked by the lower court whether it could

answer these questions while the appeal against the Order of Reference was pending;

b) In answer to the questions asked by the supreme court what rights lower courts have.

The Court held:

(A) in case 146/73 (reply to lower court):

3. However, in the case of a court against whose decisions there is a judicial remedy under national law, Article 177 does not preclude a decision of such a court referring a question to this Court for a preliminary ruling from remaining subject to the remedies normally available under national law.

Nevertheless, in the interests of clarity and legal certainty, this Court must abide by the decision to refer, which must have its full effect so long as it has not been revoked.

(B) in Case 166/73 (reply to the supreme court)

. . . . .

4. On the other hand the inferior court must be free, if it considers that the ruling on law made by the superior court could lead it to give a judgment contrary to Community law, to refer to the Court questions which concern it.

If inferior courts were bound without being able to refer matters to the Court, the jurisdiction of the latter to given preliminary rulings and the application of Community law at all levels of the judicial systems of the Member States would be comprised.

The reply must therefore be that the existence of a rule of domestic law whereby a court is bound on point of law by the rulings of the court superior to it cannot of itself take away the power provided for by Article 177 of referring cases to the Court.

D. The obligation to request preliminary rulings

1. Cases

(1) Costa-ENEL Case

For facts and references see p. 114, 161, 406, 573. The preliminary ruling was asked by the lowest Italian Court, but due to the small interest involved there

121

was no appeal possible. Was under Article 177 the Justice of Peace *obliged* to request a preliminary ruling?

The Court held:

. . . . .

By the terms of this Article, however, national courts against whose decisions, as in the present case, there is no judicial remedy, must refer the matter to the Court of Justice so that a preliminary ruling may be given upon the 'interpretation of the Treaty' whenever a question of interpretation is raised before them.

. . . . .

(2) Hoffmann-La Roche Case I

Hoffmann-La Roche v. *Centrafarm*; Case 107/76; Preliminary ruling of 24 May 1977; [1977] ECR 974; [1977] 2 CMLR 334.

Facts:

Under German law interim orders can be given in urgent cases. Against such interim orders appeal can be lodged before again in interim proceedings. Subsequently, normal proceedings may follow. In the present case, questions of community law were raised in the last instance of the interim proceedings and the Oberlandesgericht Karlsruhe requested a preliminary ruling on the question whether a court against whose decisions there is no judicial remedy is under the obligation to request a preliminary ruling in interim proceedings.

The Court ruled:

The third paragraph of Article 177 of the EEC Treaty must be interpreted as meaning that a national court or tribunal is not required to refer to the Court a question of interpretation or of validity mentioned in that article when the question is raised in interlocutory proceedings for an interim order (einstweilige Verfügung), even where no judicial remedy is available against the decision to be taken in the context of those proceedings, provided that each of the parties is entitled to institute proceedings or to require proceedings to be instituted on the substance of the case and that during such proceedings the question provisionally decided in the summary proceedings may be re-examined and may be the subject of a reference to the Court under Article 177.

(3) Da Costa-Schaake Case

Da Costa and Schaake v. *Netherlands Fiscal Administration*; Case 28–30/62; Preliminary ruling of 27 March 1963; [1963] ECR 37–39; [1963] CMLR 224.

Facts:

The facts of these cases are the same as in the *Van Gend en Loos Case* (Case 26/62). The national court (Tariff Commission) had asked identical questions.

The Court held:

. . . . .

The Commission, appearing by virtue of the provisions of Article 20 of the Statute of the Court of Justice of the EEC, urges that the request should be dismissed for lack of substance, since the questions on which an interpretation is requested from the Court in the present cases have already been decided by the judgment of 5 February 1963 in Case 26/62, which covered identical questions raised in a similar case.

This contention is not justified. A distinction should be made between the obligation imposed by the third paragraph of Article 177 upon national courts or tribunals of last instance and the power granted by the second paragraph of Article 177 to every national court or tribunal to refer to the Court of the Communities a question on the interpretation of the Treaty. Although the third paragraph of Article 177 unreservedly requires courts or tribunals of a Member States against whose decisions there is no judicial remedy under national law – like the Tariefcommissie – to refer to the Court every question of interpretation raised before them, the authority of an interpretation under Article 177 already given by the Court may deprive the obligation of its purpose and thus empty it of its substance. Such is the case especially when the question raised is materially identical with a question which has already been the subject of a preliminary ruling in a similar case.

When it gives an interpretation of the Treaty in a specific action pending before a national court, the Court limits itself to deducing the meaning of the Community rules from the wording and spirit of the Treaty, it being left to the national court to apply in the particular case the rules which are thus interpreted. Such an attitude conforms with the function assigned to the Court by Article 177 of ensuring unity of interpretation of Community law within the six Member States. If Article 177 had not such a scope, the procedural requirements of Article 20 of the Statute of the Court of Justice, which provides for the participation in the hearing of the Member States and the Community institutions, and of the third paragraph of Article 165 of the Treaty, which requires the Court to sit in plenary session, would not be justified. This aspect of the activity of the Court within the framework of Article 177 is confirmed by the absence of parties, in the proper sense of the word, which is characteristic of this procedure.

It is no less true that Article 177 always allows a national court, if it considers it desirable, to refer questions of interpretation to the Court again. This follows from Article 20 of the Statute of the Court of Justice, under which the procedure laid down for the settlement of preliminary questions is automatically set in motion as soon as such a question is referred by a national court.

The Court must, therefore, give a judgment on the present application.

The interpretation of Article 12 of the EEC Treaty, which is here requested, was given in the Court's judgment of 5 February 1963 in Case 26/62. This ruled that: ...

. . . . .

The questions of interpretation posed in this case are identical with those settled as above and no new factor has been presented to the Court.

In these circumstances the Tariefcommissie must be referred to the previous judgment.

(4) CILFIT Case I

Srl CILFIT v. *Italian Ministry of Health*; Case 283/81; Preliminary ruling of 6 October 1982; [1982] ECR 3415.

Facts:

CILFIT contested the legality of an Italian regulation on wool on the ground that it conflicted with EEC regulation 827/68. As regulation 827/68 does not apply to wool, the lower Italian courts had rejected CILFIT's argument. The Italian Court of Cassation was in doubt whether, as the highest court, it was obliged to refer this question to the Court of Justice under EEC Article 177 (3). It asked the following question of the Court of Justice:

'Does the third paragraph of Article 177 of the EEC Treaty, which provides that where any question of the same kind as those listed in the first paragraph of that article is raised in a case pending before a national court or tribunal against whose decisions there is no judicial remedy under national law that court or tribunal must bring the matter before the Court of Justice, lay down an obligation so to submit the case which precludes the national court from determining whether the question raised is justified or does it, and if so within what limits make that obligation conditional on the prior finding of a reasonable interpretative doubt?'

The Court held:

. . . . .

13. It must be remembered in this connection that in its judgment of 27 March 1963 in Joined Cases 25 to 30/62 (*Da Costa* v. *Nederlandse Belasting administratie* [1963] ECR 31) the Court ruled that: 'Although the third paragraph of Article 177 unreservedly requires courts or tribunals of a Member State against whose decisions there is no judicial remedy under national law ... to refer to the Court every question of interpretation raised before them, the authority of an interpretation under Article 177 already given by the Court may deprive the obligation of its purpose and thus empty it of its substance. Such is the case especially when the question raised is materially identical with a question which has already been the subject of a preliminary ruling in a similar case.'
14. The same effect, as regards the limits set to the obligation laid down by the third paragraph of Article 177, may be produced where previous decisions of the Court have already dealt with the point of law in question, irrespective of the nature of the proceedings which led to those decisions, even though the questions at issue are not strictly identical.
15. However, it must not be forgotten that in all such circumstances national courts and tribunals, including those referred to in the third paragraph of Article 177, remain entirely at liberty to bring a matter before the Court of Justice if they consider it appropriate to do so.
16. Finally, the correct application of Community law may be so obvious as to leave no scope for any reasonable doubt as to the manner in which the question raised is to be resolved. Before it comes to the conclusion that such is the case, the national court or tribunal must be convinced that the matter is equally obvious to the courts of the other Member States and to the Court of Justice. Only if those conditions are satisfied, may the national court or tribunal refrain from submitting the question to the Court of Justice and take upon itself the responsibility for resolving it.
17. However, the existence of such a possibility must be assessed on the basis of the characteristic features of Community law and the particular difficulties to which its interpretation gives rise.

18. To begin with, it must be borne in mind that Community legislation is drafted in several languages and that the different language versions are all equally authentic. An interpretation of a provision of Community law thus involves a comparison of the different language versions.
19. It must also be borne in mind, even where the different language versions are entirely in accord with one another, that Community law uses terminology which is peculiar to it. Furthermore, it must be emphasized that legal concepts do not necessarily have the same meaning in Community law and in the law of the various Member States.
20. Finally, every provision of Community law must be placed in its context and interpreted in the light of the provisions of Community law as a whole, regard being had to the objectives thereof and to its share of evolution at the date on which the provision in question is to be applied.
21. In the light of all those considerations, the answer to the question submitted by the Corte Suprema di Cassazione must be that the third paragraph of Article 177 of the EEC Treaty is to be interpreted as meaning that a court or tribunal against whose decisions there is no judicial remedy under national law is required, where a question of Community law is raised before it, to comply with its obligation to bring the matter before the Court of Justice, unless it has established that the question raised is irrelevant or that the Community provision in question has already been interpreted by the Court or that the correct application of Community law is so obvious as to leave no scope for any reasonable doubt. The existence of such a possibility must be assessed in the light of the specific characteristics of Community law, the particular difficulties to which its interpretation gives rise and the risk of divergences in judicial decisions within the Community.

(5) FOTO-FROST Case

Firma Foto-Frost v. *Hauptzollamt Lübeck-Ost*; Case 314/85; Preliminary ruling of 22 October 1987 (not yet published).

Facts:

Article 177 provides that lower courts *may* request a preliminary ruling on the validity and interpretation of Community acts. They are not obliged to do so. Only in last instance is there an obligation to request preliminary rulings. During the nineteensixties a lower German court (the *Verwaltungsgericht Frankfurt*) concluded from this provision that it could ignore rules of EEC law which it considered invalid, without requesting a preliminary ruling thereon. This view was severely criticized as being contrary to the spirit of Community law but it did not conflict with the text of Article 177. In practice the Frankfurt court was not followed by others. Lower courts either applied

Community acts or requested a preliminary ruling on their validity. Still the question remained unsolved until in 1985 the finance court in Hamburg was faced with a decision of the Commission which it considered invalid. It then expressly asked a preliminary ruling on the question whether it was entitled to review the validity itself or whether it was under an obligation to request a preliminary ruling on the validity.

The Court held:

. . . . .

13. In enabling national courts against whose decisions there is a judicial remedy under national law to refer to the Court for a preliminary ruling questions on interpretation or validity. Article 177 did not settle the question whether those courts themselves may declare that acts of Community institutions are invalid.
14. Those courts may consider the validity of a Community act and, if they consider that the grounds put forward before them by the parties in support of invalidity are unfounded, they may reject them, concluding that the measure is completely valid. By taking that action they are not calling the existence of the Community measure in question.
15. On the other hand, those courts do not have the power to declare acts of the Community institutions invalid. As the Court emphasized in the judgment of 13 May 1981 (Case 66/80, *International Chemical Corporation* v. *Amministrazione delle Finanze*, [1981] ECR 1191), the main purpose of the powers accorded to the Court by Article 177 is to ensure that Community law is applied uniformly by national courts. That requirement of uniformity is particularly imperative when the validity of a Community act is in question. Divergences between courts in the Member States as to the validity of Community acts would be liable to place in jeopardy the very unity of the Community legal order and detract from the fundamental requirement of legal certainty.
16. The same conclusion is dictated by consideration of the necessary coherence of the system of judicial protection established by the Treaty. In that regard it must be observed that requests for preliminary rulings, like actions for annulment, constitute means for reviewing the legality of acts of the Community institutions. As the Court pointed out in its judgment of 23 April 1986 (Case 294/83, *Parti Ecologiste 'Les Verts'* v. *European Parliament*, [1986] ECR 1339), 'in Articles 173 and 184, on the one hand, and in Article 177, on the other, the Treaty established a complete system of legal remedies and procedures designed to permit the Court of Justice to review the legality of measures adopted by the institutions'.
17. Since Article 173 gives the Court exclusive jurisdiction to declare void an

act of a Community institution, the coherence of the system requires that where the validity of a Community act is challenged before a national court the power to declare the act invalid must also be reserved to the Court of Justice.

18. It must also be emphasized that the Court of Justice is in the best position to decide on the validity of Community acts. Under Article 20 of the Procotol on the Statute of the Court of Justice of the EEC, Community institutions whose acts are challenged are entitled to participate in the proceedings in order to defend the validity of the acts in question. Furthermore, under the second paragraph of Article 21 of that Protocol the Court may require the Member States and institutions which are not participating in the proceedings to supply all information which it considers necessary for the purposes of the case before it.

19. It should be added that the rule that national courts may not themselves declare Community acts invalid may have to be qualified in certain circumstances in the case of proceedings relating to an application for interim measures; however, that case is not referred to in the national court's question.

20. The answer to the first question must therefore be that the national courts have no jurisdiction themselves to declare that acts of Community institutions are invalid.

E. COMPETENCE TO REQUEST PRELIMINARY RULINGS

Article 177, paragraph 2 provides that any court or tribunal of a Member State may request a preliminary ruling. Sometimes the question was raised whether particular tribunals were covered by this provision.

1. Cases

(1) Widow Vaassen Case

Widow Vaassen-Göbbels v. *Beambtenfonds voor het Mijnbedrijf*; Case 61/65; Judgment of 30 June 1966; [1966] ECR 272; [1966] CMLR 508.

Facts:

According to the legal provisions involved, a dispute between the widow Vaassen and the Beambtenfonds voor het Mijnbedrijf had to be brought before the 'Scheidsgerecht' (arbitral tribunal) of the staffund for the miners. The question arose whether that arbitral tribunal was competent to request preliminary rulings.

The Court held:

The Scheidsgerecht is properly instituted under Netherlands law, and is provided for by the 'Reglement van het Beambtenfonds voor het Mijnbedrijf' (RBFM) which governs the relationship between the Beambtenfonds and those insured by it.

According to the terms of the Netherlands Invalidity Law, the compulsory insurance provided for by that law does not apply to persons whose invalidity or old-age pension is provided for under the terms of another scheme which is intended to replace the general scheme. Such substitution will occur when the competent authorities declare that the substituted scheme satisfies the legal requirements and offers sufficient guarantees for the provision of pensions. Analogous provisions exist for other branches of social security. It follows that the Rules and any subsequent amendments of them must be approved not only by the Netherlands Minister responsible for the mining industry, but also by the Minister for Social Affairs and Public Health.

It is the duty of the Minister responsible for the mining industry to appoint the members of the Scheidsgerecht, to designate its charman and to lay down its rules of procedure.

The Scheidsgerecht is a permanent body charged with the settlement of the disputes defined in general terms in Article 89 of the RBFM, and it is bound by rules of adversary procedure similar to those used by the ordinary courts of law.

Finally, the persons referred to in the RBFM are compulsory members of the Beambtenfonds by virtue of a regulation laid down by the Mijnindustrieraad (Council of the Mining industry), a body established under public law. They are bound to take any diputes between themselves and their insurer to the Scheidsgerecht as the proper judicial body. The Scheidsgerecht is bound to apply rules of law.

In this case the question whether rules such as the RBFM are covered by Regulation No 3 of the Council of the EEC concerns the interpretation of this regulation, and it must be examined in the context of the first question put by the Scheidsgerecht.

It follows from the above that the Scheidsgerecht should be considered a court or tribunal within the meaning of Article 177. Therefore the request for interpretation is admissible.

(2) Nordsee Case II

Nordsee Deutsche Hochseefischerei GmbH v. *Reederei Mond Hochseefischerei Nordstern*; Case 102/81; Preliminary ruling of 23 March 1982; [1982] ECR 1095.

Facts:

Some German shipping groups had a dispute about pooling the aid which the Community had granted them under the European Agricultural Guidance and Guarantee Fund. The dispute was submitted to arbitration and the arbitration court considered that it needed the interpretation of some EEC regulations. It was not sure whether it was entitled to ask for a preliminary ruling under Article 177 and it expressly requested the Court to rule on its competence.

The Court held:

. . . . .

9. It must be noted that, as the question indicates, the jurisdiction of the Court to rule on questions referred to it depends on the nature of the arbitration in question.
10. It is true, as the arbitrator noted in his question, that there are certain similarities between the activities of the arbitration tribunal in question and those of an ordinary court or tribunal inasmuch as the arbitration is provided for within the framework of the law, the arbitrator must decide according to law and his award has, as between the parties, the force of *res judicata*, and may be enforceable if leave to issue execution is obtained. However, those characteristics are not sufficient to give the arbitrator the status of a 'court or tribunal of a Member State' within the meaning of Article 177 of the Treaty.
11. The first important point to note is that when the contract was entered into in 1973 the parties were free to leave their disputes to be resolved by the ordinary courts or to opt for arbitration by inserting a clause to that effect in the contract. From the facts of the case it appears that the parties were under no obligation, whether in law or in fact, to refer their disputes to arbitration.
12. The second point to be noted is that the German public authorities are not involved in the decision to opt for arbitration nor are they called upon to intervene automatically in the proceedings before the arbitrator. The Federal Republic of Germany, as a Member State of the Community responsible for the performance of obligations arising from Community law within its territory pursuant to Article 5 and Articles 169 to 171 of the Treaty, has not entrusted or left to private individuals the duty of ensuring that such obligations are compiled with in the sphere in question in this case.

13. It follows from these considerations that the link between the arbitration procedure in this instance and the organization of legal remedies through the courts in the Member State in question is not sufficiently close for the arbitrator to be considered as a 'court or tribunal of a Member State' within the meaning of Article 177.
14. As the Court has confirmed in its judgment of 6 October 1981 *Broekmeulen*, Case 246/80 [1981] ECR 2311), Community law must be observed in its entirety throughout the territory of all the Member States; parties to a contract are not, therefore, free to create exceptions to it. In that context attention must be drawn to the fact that if questions of Community law are raised in an arbitration resorted to by agreement the ordinary courts may be called upon to examine them either in the context of their collaboration with arbitration tribunals, in particular in order to assist them in certain procedural matters or to interpret the law applicable, or in the course of a review of an arbitration award – which may be more or less extensive depending on the circumstances – and which they may be required to effect in case of an appeal or objection, in proceedings for leave to issue execution or by any other method of recourse available under the relevant national legislation.
15. It is for those national courts and tribunals to ascertain whether it is necessary for them to make a reference to the Court under Article 177 of the Treaty in order to obtain the interpretation or assessment of the validity of provisions of Community law which they may need to apply when exercising such auxiliary or supervisory functions.
16. It follows that in this instance the Court has no jurisdiction to give a ruling.

F. EFFECT OF PRELIMINARY RULINGS ON THE VALIDITY

1. Cases

(1) International Chemical Corporation Case

SpA International Chemical Corporation v. *Amministrazione Finanze*; Case 66/80; Preliminary ruling of 13 May 1981; [1981] ECR 1191.

Facts:

The dispute concerned a regulation which had been considered invalid by the Court of Justice in a previous preliminary ruling. The question was raised whether this previous preliminary ruling had effect *erga omnes* or whether it was binding only on the court which had requested the ruling.

The Court held:

. . . . .

10. The scope of judgments given under this head should be viewed in the light of the aims of Article 177 and the place it occupies in the entire system of judicial protection established by the Treaties.
11. The main purpose of the power accorded to the Court by Article 177 is to ensure that Community law is imperative not only when a national court is faced with a rule of Community law the meaning and scope of which need to be defined; it is just as imperative when the Court is confronted by a dispute as to the validity of an act of the institutions.
12. When the Court is moved under Article 177 to declare an act of one of the institutions to be void there are particularly imperative requirements concerning legal certainty in addition to those concerning the uniform application of Community law. It follows from the very nature of such a declaration that a national court may not apply the act declared to be void without once more creating serious uncertainty as to the Community law applicable.
13. It follows therefrom that although a judgment of the Court given under Article 177 of the Treaty declaring an act of an institution, in particular a Council or Commission regulation, to be void is directly addressed only to the national court which brought the matter before the Court, it is sufficient reason for any other national court to regard that act as void for the purposes of a judgment which it has to give.
14. That assertion does not however mean that national courts are deprived of the power given to them by Article 177 of the Treaty and it rests with those courts to decide whether there is a need to raise once again a question which has already been settled by the Court where the Court has previously declared an act of a Community institution to be void. There may be such a need in particular if questions arise as to the grounds, the scope and possibly the consequence of the invalidity established earlier.
15. If that is not the case national courts are entirely justified in determining the effect on the cases brought before them of a judgment declaring an act void given by the Court in an action between other parties.
16. It should further be observed, as the Court acknowledged in its judgments of 19 October 1977 in Joined Cases 117/76 and 16/77, *Ruckdeschel and Diamalt* and Joined Cases 124/76 and 20/77, *Moulins de Pont-à-Mousson and Providence Agricole* (1977) ECR 1753 and 1795, that as those responsible for drafting regulations declared to be void the Council or the Commission are bound to determine from the Court's judgment the effects of that judgment.
17. In the light of the foregoing considerations and in view of the fact that by its second question the national court has asked, as it was free to do,

whether Regulation No 563/76 was void, the answer should be that that is in fact the case for the reasons already stated in the judgments of 5 July 1977.

(2) Roquette Case IV

SA Roquette Frères v. *French Customs Administration*; Case 145/79; Preliminary ruling of 15 October 1980; [1980] ECR 2917.

Facts:

The dispute concerned a regulation on monetary compensatory amounts which was considered invalid.

The Court held:

. . . . .

50. Since this declaration of invalidity is made within the framework of a preliminary ruling under Article 177 of the Treaty, it is necessary to specify its consequences.
51. Although the Treaty does not expressly lay down the consequences which flow from a declaration of invalidity within the framework of a reference to the Court for a preliminary ruling, Articles 174 and 176 contain clear rules as to the effects of the annulment of a regulation within the framework of a direct action. Thus Article 176 provides that the institution whose act has been declared void shall be required to take the necessary measures to comply with the judgment of the Court of Justice. In its judgments of 19 October 1977 in the Joined Cases 117/76 and 16/77 (*Albert Ruckdeschel & Co. and Hansa-Lagerhaus Stroh & Co.* [1977] ECR 1753) and in Joined Cases 124/76 and 20/77 (*Moulins et Huileries de Pont-à-Mousson and Providence Agricole de la Campagne*, [1977] ECR 1795) the Court has already referred to that rule within the context of a reference to it for a preliminary ruling.
52. In this case it is necessary to apply by analogy the second paragraph of Article 174 of the Treaty, whereby the Court of Justice may state which of the effects of the regulation which it has declared void shall be considered as definitive, for the same reasons of legal certainty as those which form the basis of that provision. On the one hand the invalidity of the regulation in this case might give rise to the recovery of sums paid but not owed by the undertakings concerned in countries with hard cur-

rencies and by the undertakings concerned in countries with depreciated currencies and by the national authorities in question in countries with hard currencies which, in view of the lack of uniformity of the relevant national legislation, would be capable of causing considerable differences in treatment, thereby causing further distortion in competition. On the other hand, it is impossible to appraise the economic disadvantages resulting from the invalidity of the provisions of the regulations in question without making assessments which the Commission alone is required to make under Regulation No 974/71, having regard to other relevant factors, for example the application of the 'green rate' to the production refund.

53. For these reasons it must be held that the fact that the provisions of the regulations in question have been found invalid does not enable the charging or the payment of monetary compensatory amounts by the national authorities on the basis of those provisions to be challenged as regards the period prior to the date of this judgment.

V. Actions against Member States

(Article 169)

A. INTRODUCTION

Until 31 December 1987 the Commission brought 561 cases before the Court in which Member States were accused of Treaty violations (either under EEC Article 169, or under EEC Article 93).

In the *Dairy Products Case* (see at page 34) the Court held that Treaty violations may not be justified by the failure of others (in that case the Council) to comply with their obligations. In the first two cases mentioned below Italy was sued for having a law contrary to its Treaty obligations. It changed that law during the proceedings. Must the Commission start its action anew?

Treaty violations may be committed by national institutions independent of the national government, such as the parliament or the judiciary. Is the Member State responsible for such violations?

A supreme national court would commit a Treaty violation by refusing to request a preliminary ruling under Article 177 para 3, when a question of Community law was raised. Such a violation has never been brought before the Court of Justice, but when in 1968 the French Conseil d'Etat had applied a municipal act irrespective of French obligations under Community law, a member of the European Parliament asked the Commission whether it could take action. The Commission replied that it was of the opinion that the Conseil d'Etat had violated the EEC Treaty, that it could initiate the procedure of Article 169 and that it was considering what action would be appropriate (OJ 1968, C 71/1). When after a year no action was taken another member of the European Parliament asked the Commission what it intended to do (OJ 1970, C 20/3), the Commission replied:

'As the Commission has observed ... before, it is certainly not excluded to engage the procedure under Article 169 EEC in the cases mentioned ... However, the Legal Commission of the Parliament is of the opinion that the application of such a procedure would undoubtedly go against the independence of the judiciary vis-à-vis the executive. On these grounds the Commission's view is that the procedure referred to in Article 169 EEC ought not be engaged in all cases in which a decision of a municipal court violates the object of the law of the Community.'

The Court of Justice met with a similar problem in the Wood Case, quoted below, where the violation had been committed by the Belgian parliament.

In the *Lütticke Case I* the question whether individuals may initiate the proceedings of Article 169 is discussed. In former cases the Court of Justice had accepted individual actions against failure to act under the ECSC Treaty when the Commission (High Authority) had been negligent in acting against treaty violations by Member States. However both the action against failure to act and the action against Member States of the ECSC Treaty are different from those under the EEC Treaty.

The *Art Treasure Case II*, finally, offers us the only example of a State not complying with a judgment of the Court of Justice rendered under Article 169.

B. CASES

(1) **Tax refund in Italy Case**

EEC Commission v. *Italy*; Case 45/64; Judgment of 1 December 1965; [1965] ECR 864; [1966] CMLR 97.

Facts:

The Republic of Italy, in pursuance of Law No 103 of 10 March 1955, which was extended to 31 December 1963, by Law No 284 of 18 March 1958, granted on the export of certain machine products, a refund of the specific customs duty and of other customs imposed on steel products used in the manufacture of the exported products.

The EEC Commission was convinced that in fact other taxes, such as those imposed on raw materials or on semi-finished products used in Italian machine products, even those levied on an entirely different basis, were also being refunded. This matter formed the subject of negotiations between the Commission of the EEC and the Italian government. Following these negotiations the Italian Government reduced the amount refunded on products exported to other Member States of the Community. After further negotiations, the Commission, on 11 December 1963, issued a reasoned opinion, as provided for in Article 169, para 1. In this reasoned opinion, the Commission explained its finding that the Republic of Italy had failed in the obligations incumbent upon it under Article 96, and requested the Italian government to end, no later than 31 December 1963, the drawbacks of internal charges granted for exported machine products.

In a note dated 18 December 1963, Italy's Representative conveyed to the Commission the text of a bill which had been approved by the Italian Council of Ministers and submitted to Parliament, and which was intended to replace Law No 103.

The Commission, considering the bill to be identical in content to Law No 103, informed the Italian government, in a letter dated 28 January 1964, that it considered that the introduction of rules designed to provide for the continued granting of drawbacks which it had found to be incompatible with the Treaty constituted a failure to comply with the reasoned opinion.

The bill in question was nevertheless approved by both houses of the Italian Parliament and a new Law No 639 was substituted for Law No 103 on 5 July 1964. This new Law came into force with effect retroactive to 1 January 1964.

The Italian government pleaded that the action was inadmissible because the subject of the case before the Court was different from the subject of the administrative proceedings. It alleged that the subject of the administrative proceedings was Law No 103 of 1955, whereas the suit before the Court concerned Law No 639 of 1964. With respect of Law No 639, it was alleged that there was a violation of Article 169 of the Treaty, since the Italian government had not submitted comments on it and the Commission had not offered a reasoned opinion on it.

The Court held:

As to the admissibility

It emerges from the documents in the file that in both the administrative stage of the proceedings and that before the Court the Commission criticized the actual application by the Italian government of the system of repayments on exports, without limiting the complaints which it thought itself entitled to make to the legislative measures capable of constituting the legal basis of the said system.

Moreover, in its reasoned opinion issued on 11 December and conveyed to the defendant on 16 December 1963, the Commission invited the Italian Republic to terminate by 31 December 1963 at the latest the grant of a repayment which, for the reasons set out therein, contravened Article 96 of the Treaty.

The purpose of the reasoned opinion was therefore, first, to establish that the Italian Government had failed to fulfil an obligation under the Treaty and, secondly, to warn the defendant not to continue such alleged infringement beyond the date indicated, either by a measure continuing the existing legislation or by similar future legislation.

This objection must therefore be rejected.

(2) Wool imports Case

Commission of the EC v. *Italian Republic*; Case 7/69; Judgment of 10 March 1970; [1970] ECR 117; [1970] CMLR 97.

Facts:

In 1969 Italy had not yet introduced the system of value added tax. It levied a turnover tax on all sales of goods based on their total value. On imported wool a tax was levied to compensate the taxes on national wools when they were transferred between different stages of production.

In practice, however, Italian wool was not transferred between stages of production since virtually all wool remained with the same owner during the entire process. The Commission considered that the compensatory taxes (which did not compensate anything) were protective taxes in violation of Article 95 of the EEC Treaty.

By letter of 12 July 1966 the Commission instituted proceedings under Article 169. The Italian Government remedied the situation to a large extent, but not entirely.

On 16 July 1968 the Commission issued a reasoned opinion (as provided for by Article 169, para 1). The Italian government did not comply with the opinion. On 4 February the Commission brought the matter before the Court of Justice. On 2 July 1969 the Italian Government issued a new law which in their view fully redressed the situation.

The Commission considered in the first place that the law of 2 July 1969 did not entirely terminate the violation. Both parties discussed in detail whether this submission was correct. The Commission furthermore considered that the Court should in any case declare that Italy was in violation of its obligations until 2 July 1969.

The Court held:

. . . . .

3. However, the parties have devoted since then the major part of their argument to the effects and the burden of the tax system brought into operation

by the said Decree-Law. The Commission does not, moreover, refer to any objective other than that of putting an effective end to the specific violation alleged against the Italian Republic, so that its only aim appears to be to terminate any violation which may still exist.
4. It follows from the foregoing that, although the parties still disagree about the effects of the above-mentioned Decree-Law, they have nevertheless taken the view that this measure substantially affects the outcome of the present dispute and they have accordingly requested the Court to consider the resulting situation as a whole. In so doing the applicant has thus amended the subject-matter of its application so that it is no longer concerned only with the question whether at the time when the application was lodged there was a failure on the part of the Italian Republic to fulfil its obligations under Article 95, but principally with the question whether this failure still continues after the coming into force of the Decree-Law.
5. In the present action it is not possible for the Court to decide whether the situation created by Decree-Law No 319 is incompatible with the obligations imposed upon Member States under Article 95 of the Treaty. Because of the importance which the Treaty attaches to the action available to the Community against Member States for failure to fulfil obligations, this procedure in Article 169 is surrounded by guarantees which must not be ignored, particularly in view of the consequence of this action the necessary measures to comply with the judgment of the Court. Accordingly the Court cannot give judgment in the present case on the failure to fulfil an obligation occurring after legislation has been amended during the course of the proceedings without thereby adversely affecting the rights of the Member State to put forward its arguments in defence based on complaints formulated according to the procedure laid down by Article 169.
6. In such circumstances it is for the Commission to commence new proceedings under Article 169 with regard to the effects of Decree-Law No 319, and if necessary to refer to the Court the specific shortcoming upon which it desires the Court to pronounce. In view of the change in the subject-matter of the dispute, the request as originally formulated in the application must therefore be dismissed.

(3) Wood Case

Commission of the EC v. *Belgium*; Case 77/69; Judgment of 5 May 1970; [1970] ECR 243.

Facts:

Belgium levied a tax on imported wood, which, according to the Commission, violated Community law. The Belgian government thereupon presented to the Belgian parliament a draft law lapsed however when a new Parliament had to be elected on 2 March 1968.

On 28 November 1968, the Commission again started the procedure of Article 169, which caused the new Government again to present a draft-law to the Parliament. When this new law had not been adopted by 30 June 1969, the Commission instituted proceedings before the Court on 22 December 1969. The Belgian Government submitted that it had used its best efforts in order to obtain a change in the legislation. Under the circumstances it could, therefore, not be held responsible for the negligence of the Belgian Parliament. The question before the Court was, whether Article 169 is only intended to be used against governments which violated the Treaty or whether the action would also be possible in cases where the Treaty is alleged to have been violated by other independent institutions of the Member States.

The Court held:

. . . . .

15. The obligations arising from Article 95 of the Treaty devolve upon States as such and the liability of a Member State under Article 169 arises whatever the agency of the State whose action or inaction is the cause of the failure to fulfil its obligations, even in the case of a constitutionally independent institution.
16. The object raised by the defendant cannot therefore be sustained.
17. In these circumstances, by applying a duty at the same rate, as laid down by Article 31-14 of the Royal Decree of 3 March 1927 as amended, to home-grown wood calculated on its value at the time of the declaration of entry for home use, the Kingdom of Belgium has failed to fulfil its obligations under Article 95 of the Treaty.

(4) Lütticke Case I

Lütticke v. *EEC Commission*; Case 48/65; Judgment of 1 March 1966; [1966] ECR 27; [1966] CMLR 378.

Facts:

From January 1962, Germany had levied a compensatory turnover tax on imported dairy products. Plaintiffs claimed that this was incompatible with EEC Article 95. On 15 March 1965, they asked the Commission to start Article 169 proceedings against Germany. The Director-General for Competition replied that the Commission did not agree that Germany had violated the Treaty and that Lütticke had no right to ask for such action. Lütticke brought an action under Article 173 against this letter. They also brought proceedings against the Commission under Article 175 for not acting against Germany as requested in their letter of 15 March. The question was whether this action was admissible under Article 175.

The Court held:

The object of the request of 15 March is to ensure the initiation of the procedure laid down in Article 169 against a Member State and to compel the Commission to take the measures implied by that Article.

The object of the procedure under Article 169 is to prevent Member States from failing in their obligations under the Treaty.

For this purpose, the said Article empowers the Commission to set in motion a procedure which may lead to an action before the Court of Justice to determine the existence of such a failure by a Member State: under the terms of Article 171 of the Treaty the State concerned would then be required to take the necessary measures to comply with the judgment of the Court.

The part of the procedure which precedes reference of the matter to the Court constitutes an administrative stage intended to give the Member State concerned the opportunity of comforming with the Treaty. During this stage, the Commission makes known its view by way of an opinion only after giving the Member State concerned the opportunity to submit its observations.

No measure taken by the Commission during this stage has any binding force. Consequently, an application for the annulment of the measure by which the Commission arrived at a decision on the application is inadmissible.

. . . . .

Under the terms of the second paragraph of Article 175, proceedings for failure to act may only be brought if at the end of a period of two months from being called upon to act the institution has not defined its position.

It is established that the Commission has defined its position and has notified this position to the applicants within the prescribed period.

The plea of inadmissibility is therefore well founded.

(5) Art Treasures Case II

Commission of the EC v. *Italian republic*; Case 48/71; Judgment of 13 July 1972; [1972] ECR 532; [1972] CMLR 699.

Facts:

In the first Art Treasures Case the Court of Justice had held that Italy had failed to fulfill its obligations under Article 16 of the EEC Treaty by continuing after 1 January 1962 to impose a tax on the exportation of art treasures to other Member States of the Community pursuant to an Italian law of 1 June 1939. When, more than two years later, the Italian law had still not been repealed and continued to be enforced by the Italian customs authorities, the Commission on 23 July 1971 brought a new action against Italy before the Court of Justice for failure to fulfil its obligations. This time a violation of Article 171 EEC was argued, which requires Member States 'to take the necessary measures to comply with the judgment of the Court of Justice'.

The Italian Government objected that the tax could only be withdrawn by law and that it had introduced a draft-law for the repeal of the 1939 law; however, the Italian Parliament had not yet occasion to approve it because of its early dissolution on 28 February 1972.

In the meantime the non-applicability of the Italian tax had been invoked by a private party before a municipal court. Upon a request for a preliminary ruling by the president of the Tribunal of Turin the Court of Justice had held that Article 16 EEC had direct effect in the relation between Member States and their subjects since 1 January 1962 and created rights in favour of private persons, which municipal courts must safeguard (*Eunomia Case*).

After the conclusions of the advocate-general and just before the judgment was to be rendered, the Italian Government on 4 July 1972 informed the Court of Justice that it had formally repealed the tax (by a decree) with retroactive effect as of 1 January 1962.

The Court held:

. . . . .

5. Without having to examine the validity of such agreements, it suffices for the Court to observe that by judgment of 10 December 1968 it answers in the affirmative the question in dispute between the Italian Government and the Commission: whether or not the tax in question was to be regarded as a tax having an effect equivalent to a customs duty on exports within the meaning of Article 16 of the Treaty.

    Further by another judgment of 26 October 1971 given in Case 18/71, *Eunomia* v. *Italian Republic*, the Court expressly found that the prohibition contained in Article 16 produces direct effects in the national law of all Member States.

6. Since it is a question of a directly applicable Community rule, the argument that the infringement can be terminated only by the adoption of

measures constitutionally appropriate to repeal the provision establishing the tax would amount to saying that the application of the Community rule is subject to the law of each Member State and more precisely that this application is impossible where it is contrary to a national law.
7. In the present case the effect of Community law, declared as 'res judicata' in respect of the Italian Republic, is a prohibition having the full force of law on the competent national authorities against applying a national rule recognized as incompatible with the Treaty and, if the circumstances so require, an obligation on them to take all appropriate measures to enable Community law to be fully applied.
8. The attainment of the objectives of the Community requires that the rules of Community law established by the Treaty itself or arising from procedures which it has instituted are fully applicable at the same time and with identical effects over the whole territory of the Community without the Member States being able to place any obstacles in the way.
9. The grant made by Member States to the Community of rights and powers in accordance with the provisions of the Treaty involves a definitively limitation on their sovereign rights and no provisions whatsoever of national law may be invoked to override this limitation.
10. It is therefore necessary to find that in not complying with the judgment of the Court of 10 December 1968 in Case 7/68 the Italian Republic has failed to fulfil the obligation imposed on it by Article 171 of the Treaty.

.....

On those grounds,

.....

THE COURT

hereby

1. Takes note that the failure of the Italian Republic to fulfil the obligations imposed on it by Article 171 of the EEC Treaty has ceased with effect from 1 January 1962.
2. Orders the defendant to bear the costs.

(6) Kohlegesetz Case

Commission of the EC v. *Federal Republic of Germany*; Case 70/72; Judgment of 12 July 1973; [1973] ECR 826.

From this case we may conclude that the Commission may require Member States to claim back illegally paid subsidies.

(7) Public insurance Case

Commission of the EC v. *Hellenic Republic*; Case 226/87; Judgment of 30 June 1988 (not yet published).

Facts:

Greece had failed to take the measures necessary to comply with Commission decision 85/276, adopted in the basis of Article 93 (3) EEC, in which the Commission had declared that some Greek legal provisions were incompatible with Articles 90, 52, 53, 5 and 3 of the EEC Treaty.

The Greek Government contended that the decision must be regarded as a mere opinion and it contested its lawfulness.

*The Court held:**

Under those conditions, the Commission decision of 24 April 1985 was, by virtue of the provisions of Article 189, 'binding in its entirety' on the Hellenic Republic, to which it was addressed. The latter was therefore required to comply with its terms until it obtained from the Court of Justice either suspension of the operation of the decision or a declaration that it was void. It is common ground that in this case, the Greek Government neither applied to the Court for any such order nor obtained it subsequently.

In any event, the Greek Government cannot plead the unlawfulness of the decision of 24 April 1985 in answer to the complaint that it has failed to fulfil its obligations.

The system of remedies established by the Treaty distinguishes the actions of Articles 169 and 170 on the failure of a Member State to fulfil its obligations from the actions of Articles 173 and 175 on the control of legality of Community acts or Community in action. These actions intend to achieve distinct objectives and operate in different ways. In the absence of a specific provision of the Treaty expressly so authorizing, a Member State cannot therefore rely on the unlawfulness of a decision addressed to it as a defense in an action for failure to fulfil obligations arising out of the failure to implement that decision.

At the hearing, the Hellenic Republic argued that, nonetheless, the Court should make an exception and exercise judicial review of the decision of 24 April 1985. It argued that that decision was contrary to the fundamental principle of the division of powers between the Community and the Member States and therefore lacked a legal basis in Community law.

As the Court has already decided, such an objection can be accepted only if

---

* Unofficial translation. No English text yet available.

the measure at issue was vitiated by particularly serious and obvious defects allowing it to be regarded as non-existent (decision of 26 February 1987, *Consorzio Cooperative d'Abruzzo* 15/85, not yet published). The arguments put forward by the Hellenic Republic contain no precise factor of such a nature as to permit the Commission's decision to be so regarded. Furthermore, it itself considered that the decision of 24 April 1985 was not non-existent inasmuch as it announced all through the prelitigation procedure that it intended to comply therewith.

(8) Wine Case

Commission of the EC v. *French Republic*; Case 42/82 R; Order of 4 March 1982; [1982] ECR 841.

Facts:

On 4 February 1982 the Commission brought an action against the French Republic under Article 169 of the EEC Treaty, because of unacceptable delays in the customs clearance of wine imported from Italy. The Commission considered the matter of such importance that it requested interim measures under EEC Article 186 to ensure the free movement of wine products pending the outcome of the main action.

The Court held:

. . . . .

5. Article 83 (2) of the Rules of Procedure provides that an order for interim measures is to be conditional upon there being circumstances giving rise to urgency and factual and legal grounds establishing a prima facie case for the interim measures applied for.

. . . . .

14. It follows that having regard to the submissions of fact and law made in support of the main action the grant of interim measures appears prima facie to be justified.
15. The next question which must be considered in accordance with Article 186 of the Treaty, is whether interim measures are necessary, that is to

say, whether there is urgency in ordering such measures with a view to avoiding serious and irreparable damage resulting, in the absence of interim measures, from the continuance of the practices at issue during the main proceedings.

. . . . .

21. It follows from the foregoing that the conditions to which the grant of interim measures is subject are fulfilled in this case and that pending the delivery of the judgment in the main action it is necessary, under Article 186 of the EEC Treaty, to suspend the practices at issue which are being applied by the French authorities.

. . . . .

Subsequently, the Court ordered:

1. Pending the judgment in the main action the French Republic is required to observe the limitations hereinafter specified regarding the practices relating to the release to the market in France of wines imported from Italy;
    (a) Apart from special cases in which specific evidence may justify a suspicion of fraud the frequency of analyses before the release to the market of the consignments in question must not exceed 15% of the consignments presented at the frontier;
    (b) The duration of analyses made before the release to the market of the consignments in question must not exceed 21 days from presentation of the consignments and the documents at the frontier unless there are special grounds which justify specific analyses in exceptional cases;
    (c) The release to the market of consignments of wine may not be refused on grounds of irregularity of the accompanying documents unless the irregularities are substantial;
    (d) When substantial irregularities are found by the French authorities they must without delay inform the Italian authorities of such irregularities and supply them with the necessary documents. Where the accompanying document in respect of any consignment has been regularized by the Italian authorities that consignment must immediately be released to the market.
2. When the release to the market of quantities of wine from Italy in excess of 50,000 hectolitres is refused for more than 21 days on grounds either of analyses or irregularities in accompanying documents the French authorities must inform the Commission of the reasons for such refusal.
3. The costs are reserved.

VI. Procedure

A. Sources

The basic rules on the procedure before the Court of Justice are to be found in the protocols on the Statute of the Court annexed to each of the Community Treaties. The EEC and Euratom provisions are almost identical, whilst the ECSC Statute contains a few materially different provisions (*e.g.* on intervention). Detailed procedural regulations are contained in the Rules of Procedure (OJ 1982, C 39). See Materials on the Law of the European Communities, Chapter Two.

B. Language

According to Article 29, para 1 of the Rules of procedure, proceedings before the Court must be in one of the official languages of the Communities (i.e. Danish, Dutch, English, French, Greek, German, Irish, Italian, Portuguese and Spanish). In cases against the Communities a plaintiff may select the language of the proceedings from among these. In cases against a Member State or a natural person of a Member State's nationality, the language of the proceedings shall be the official language of that State; should this Member States have more than one official language, as in the case of Belgium and Ireland, the plaintiff may choose between them. The use of another official language may be authorized either upon the joint application of the parties, or upon the application of one party under special circumstances, provided that such party is not an institution of the Communities (Rules Article 29, para 2). In cases involving preliminary rulings, the language of the proceedings is that of the municipal court concerned.

Publications of the Court are issued in six of the languages which may be used for proceedings. In conformity with the other institutions the Court issues no publications in Irish (Rule 30 and Annex I to the Act of Accession, Chapter XIV). The text in the language of the proceedings is the authentic text (Rules, Article 31).

C. Proceedings

The procedure before the Court consists of two stages: one written and the other oral (EEC Statute Article 18), and is much the same as the civil procedures in Member States. The written procedure, consisting of application and defence, reply and rejoinder, is followed by oral arguments in court. Other procedural matters, such as the procedure for finding facts and making the award are also based on continental civil procedure.

A case is brought before the Court by means of an application addressed to the Registrar (EEC Statute Article 19). The Registrar notifies the defendant of the application (Rules, Articles 39 jo. 79), to which the latter must deliver his defence within one month (Rules, Article 40). At the end of the written proceedings the judge rapporteur appointed for each case delivers a preliminary report on whether measures of enquiry (i.e. personal appearance of the parties; requests for information; oral testimony; experts' reports; inspection of the place). The Court decides whether such measures are necessary after hearing the Advocate-General (Rules, Article 45).

In general – and especially in the case of an action for annulment – the written proceedings are the most important part of the procedure. It is then that the plaintiff has to formulate his claim (Rules, Article 38, para 1). New contentions may be raised during the case only when based upon matters of fact and law which have already been disclosed during the written proceedings (Rules, Article 42, para 2).

If the Court decides to make inquiries the oral proceedings are commenced as soon as the preparatory inquiry has been completed (Rules Article 54), otherwise on whatever date is fixed by the Court (Rules, Article 28). Parties may participate in the proceedings only through their agents, advisors or lawyers (Rules, Article 58). The President of the Court, Judges or the Advocate-General may, during the oral proceedings, put questions to these agents, advisors or lawyers (EEC Statute Article 29; Rules Article 57). After the Advocate-General has delivered his opinion the oral proceedings are closed (Rules Article 59) and the Court deliberates on the case in private (EEC Statute Article 32).

Judgments are read in open Court. The parties are summoned to be present and after the reading a certified copy of the judgment is sent to each party (Rules Article 64).

Article 65 of the Rules provides that the judgment shall be binding from the day on which it is delivered. Steps can then be taken to enforce it in a Member State according to its national rules of civil procedure, which may vary from country to country (EEC Article 192); ECSC Article 92; EAEC Article 164). The Registrar is responsible for seeing to the publication of the official reports of Court judgments (Rules Article 68).

Interim proceedings are allowed in two instances:
(1) Application may be made for a stay of execution of an act of an institution if an action is brought against such act;
(2) Application may be made for any other interim order if the applicant is a party in the main proceedings before the Court and such application has a connection with the case.

Requests for interim measures are addressed to the Court, but the President may himself decide the matter or may refer it to the Court for decision. In the latter case the views of the Advocate-General must be heard. It follows from their provisional nature that these interim orders do not prejudice the decision by the Court on the substance of the case (Article 86, para 4 of the Rules).

On request by a party, the Court may make a separate order deciding a preliminary objection or other procedural issue without going into the merits of the case.

D. TIME LIMITS

There are certain time limits for bringing cases before the Court. In the case of an action for annulment proceedings must be instituted within one month (ECSC Article 33, para 3 and Article 38, para 2) or two months (EEC Article 173, para 3; EAEC Article 146, para 3) after the measure concerned has been published or has been notified to the addressee, or, if there has been no such publication or notification from the day on which the latter learnt of it. The same applies in the case of an action against failure to act. In this case time starts to run two months after the Community institution concerned has been asked to take action (ECSC Article 35, para 3; EEC Article 175, para 3; EAEC Article 148, para 3). Action by employees of the Communities may be brought within three months of publication or notification (Staff Regulation Article 91, para 2). If the competent authority of an institution has failed to act, however, the same period of two months applies in the case of an ordinary action against failure to act. Proceedings against the Community in tort are time-barred five years after the occurrence on which the action is based (EEC Statute Article 43).

By decision of the Court of Justice of 4 December 1974 (OJ 1974 L 350/28), all time-limits are extended if a party's customary residence is outside Luxembourg. The extension varies from two days (for Belgium) to 14 days (for European States not Members of the EEC) to one month (for all States outside Europe).

E. EFFECT OF PROCEEDINGS

Generally speaking, proceedings before the Court have no suspensive effect (ECSC Article 39; EEC Article 185; EAEC Article 157).

EAEC Article 83, para 2(2) and ECSC Article 66, para 5 provide for exceptions to this rule. Furthermore, the Court may order the suspension of a contested measure in special circumstances, e.g. if irrepairable harm may ensure for a plaintiff if no suspension is ordered (see the Court's order of 12 May 1959, Case 19/59. Jur. VI, p. 89, Rec. VI, p. 90) or if third party interests are at stake (order of the President of the Court of 4 May 1964, Case 12, 29/64, [1965] ECR 132).

F. COSTS

All costs of the Court itself are borne by the Communities. Proceedings before the Court are free of charge (Rules Article 72). In its final judgment the Court gives a decision regarding costs (Rules Article 69). As a rule, the losing party will have to bear its own costs and the costs of the winning party, but unnecessary or vexations costs will be ordered to be borne by the party which has caused them. The Court may also decide that each party shall bear its own costs, either wholly or in part 'where a party partly succeeds and partly looses'. Where a case does not proceed to judgment, the costs shall be at the discretion of the Court. Costs incurred by an institution as the result of proceedings instituted against it by an employee are not recoverable by the institution even if the official loses his case (Rules Article 70). Finally, Article 76 of the Rules provides for free legal aid under certain conditions.

The Court of Justice treats proceedings to obtain a preliminary ruling as incidental to the principal action before a municipal court. It therefore leaves the issue of costs to be decided by the municipal court concerned. (See the *Bosch Case* (13/61), Judgment of 6 April 1962, [1962] ECR 45). Costs incurred by Member States or institutions in submitting observations in pursuance of Article 20 of the EEC Statute are not recoverable.

The costs of intervening parties are – depending on the outcome of the case – sometimes borne by themselves, sometimes by the losing party. Occasionally an intervening party has been ordered to pay costs incurred by another party because of his intervention (*e.g.* in: *Chambre Syndicale de l'Est de la France* v. *High Authority*, Case 24, 34/58; Jud. Rem. pp. 47, 73, and *Fruit and Vegetables Case*, Case 16, 17/62, Jud. Rem. pp. 40, 57).

G. Special proceedings

Title Three of the Rules covers a number of special procedures, the most important of which will be briefly discussed below.

1. Preliminary rulings

The written procedure in preliminary rulings under EEC Article 177, which is regulated by Article 20 of the EEC Statute and Article 103 of the Rules differs from the contentious proceedings in that the Court has not to decide between two litigants, but to advise a national court. Strict rules are less necessary. A national court which wishes to seek a preliminary ruling suspends its proceedings and submits a request to the Court of Justice. The decision by the national court is forwarded to the Court of Justice together with such information as the requesting court may consider relevant. The request is notified by the Registrar of the Court of Justice to the parties, Member States, the Commission and, under certain circumstances, to the Council of Ministers, all of which may submit written and oral observations to the Court. Parties to the principal action are not, however, parties to the Court.

2. Intervention

Third parties may intervene in cases pending before the Court. Article 34 of the ECSC Statute and Article 37 of the EEC Statute differ in this respect, however. Under the EEC Regulations, a distinction is drawn between Member States and institutions on the one hand, and, on the other 'any person who shows that he has a valid interest'. This last category may not intervene in cases between Member States, between institutions or between Member States and institutions. There is no comparable limitation in the ECSC Treaty (*cf.* intervention in the *Publication of Transport Tariffs Case I*, Jud. Rem. p. 254). Article 37, para 2, of the EEC Statute (Article 34, para 2, of the ECSC Statute) provides that the submissions contained in an application to intervene must be confined to supporting the case of one of the parties.

H. COURT OF FIRST INSTANCE

Council Decision
of 24 October 1988
establishing a Court of First Instance of the European Communities
(88/591/ECSC, EEC, Euratom, 25/11/88, L 319/1)
The council of the European communities,

. . . . .

Has decided as follows:

Article 1

A Court, to be called the Court of First Instance of the European Communities, shall be attached to the Court of Justice of the European Communities. Its seats shall be at the Court of Justice.

Article 2

1. The Court of First Instance shall consist of 12 members.
2. The members shall elect the President of the Court of First Instance from among their number for a term of three years. He may be re-elected.
3. The members of the Court of First Instance may be called upon to perform the task of an Advocate-General.
   It shall be the duty of the Advocate-General, acting with complete impartiality and independance, to make, in open court, reasoned submissions on certain cases brought before the Court of First Instance in order to assist the Court of First Instance in the performance of its task.
   The criteria for selecting such cases, as well as the procedures for designating the Advocates-General, shall be laid down in the Rules of Procedure of the Court of First Instance.

A member called upon to perform the task of Advocate-General in a case may not take part in the judgment of the case.
4. The Court of First Instance shall sit in chambers of three or five judges. The composition of the chambers and the assignment of cases to them shall be governed by the Rules of Procedure. In certain cases governed by the Rules of Procedure the Court of First Instance may sit in plenary session.
5. Article 21 of the Protocol on Privileges and Immunities of the European Communities and Article 6 of the Treaty establishing a Single Council and a Single Commission of the European Communities shall apply to the members of the Court of First Instance and to its Registrar.

Article 3

1. The Court of First Instance shall exercise at first instance the jurisdiction conferred on the Court of Justice by the Treaties establishing the Communities and by the acts adopted in implementation thereof:
   (a) in disputes between the Communities and their servants referred to in Article 179 of the EEC Treaty and in Article 152 of the EAEC Treaty;
   (b) in actions brought against the Commission pursuant to the second paragraph of Article 33 and Article 35 of the ECSC Treaty by undertakings by associations of undertakings referred to in Article 48 of that Treaty, and which concern individual acts relating to the application of Article 50 and Articles 57 to 66 of the said Treaty;
   (c) in actions brought against an institution of the Communities by natural or legal persons pursuant to the second paragraph of Article 173 and the third paragraph of Article 175 of the EEC Treaty relating to the implementation of the competition rules applicable to undertakings.
2. Where the same natural or legal person brings an action which the Court of First Instance has jurisdiction to hear by virtue of paragraph 1 of this Article and an action referred to in the first and second paragraphs of Article 40 of the ECSC Treaty, Article 178 of the EEC Treaty, or Article 151 of the EAEC Treaty, for compensation for damage caused by a Community institution through the act or failure to act which is the subject of the first action, the Court of First Instance shall also have jurisdiction to hear and determine the action for compensation for that damage.
3. The Council will, in the light of experience, including the development of jurisprudence, and after two years of operation of the Court of First Instance, re-examine the proposal by the Court of Justice to give the Court of First Instance competence to exercise jurisdiction in actions brought against the Commission pursuant to the second paragraph of Article 33 and Article 35 of the ECSC Treaty by undertakings or by associations of undertakings referred to in Article 48 of that Treaty, and which concern acts relating to the application of Article 74 of the said Treaty as well as in actions brought against an institution of the Communities by natural of legal persons pursuant to the second paragraph of Article 173 and the third paragraph of Article 175 of the EEC Treaty and relating to measures to

protect trade within the meaning of Article 113 of that Treaty in the case of dumping and subsidies.

Article 4

Save as hereinafter provided, Articles 34, 36, 39, 44 and 92 of the ECSC Treaty, Articles 172, 174, 176, 184 to 187 and 192 of the EEC Treaty, and Articles 147, 149, 156 to 159 and 164 of the EAEC Treaty shall apply to the Court of First Instance.

Article 5; omitted

Article 6; omitted

Article 7

The following provisions shall be inserted after Article 43 of the Protocol on the Statute of the Court of Justice of the European Economic Community;

'Title IV:

The court of first instance on the European communities

Article 44

Articles 2 to 8, and 13 to 16 of this Statute shall apply to the Court of First Instance and its members. The oath referred to in Article 2 shall be taken before the Court of Justice and the decisions referred to in Articles 3, 4 and 6 shall be adopted by that Court after hearing the Court of First Instance.

Article 45

The Court of First Instance shall appoint its Registrar and lay down the rules governing his service. Articles 9, 10 and 13 of this Statute shall apply to the Registrar of the Court of First Instance *mutatis mutandis*.

The President of the Court of Justice and the President of the Court of First Instance shall determine, by common accord, the conditions under which officials and other servants attached to the Court of Justice shall render their services to the Court of First Instance to enable it to function. Certain officials or other servants shall be responsible to the Registrar of the Court of First Instance under the authority of the President of the Court of First Instance.

Article 46

The procedure before the Court of First Instance shall be governed by Title III of this Statute, with the exception of Article 20.

Such further and more detailed provisions as may be necessary shall be laid down in the Rules of Procedure established in accordance with Article 168a(4) of the Treaty.

Notwithstanding the fourth paragraph of Article 18 of this Statute, the Advocate-General may make his reasoned submissions in writing.

Article 47

Where an application or other procedural document addressed to the Court of First Instance is lodged by mistake with the Registrar of the Court of Justice it shall be transmitted immediately by that Registrar to the Registrar of the Court of First Instance; likewise, where an application or other procedural document addressed to the Court of Justice is lodged by mistake with the Registrar of the Court of First Instance, it shall be transmitted immediately by that Registrar to the Registrar of the Court of Justice.

Where the Court of First Instance finds that it does not have jurisdiction to hear and determine an action in respect of which the Court of Justice has jurisdiction, it shall refer that action to the Court of Justice; likewise, where the Court of Justice finds that an action falls within the jurisdiction of the Court of First Instance, it shall refer that action to the Court of First Instance, whereupon that Court may not decline jurisdiction.

Where Court of Justice and the Court of First Instance are seised of cases in which the same relief is sought, the same issue of interpretation is raised or the validity of the same act is called in question, the Court of First Instance may, after hearing the parties, stay the proceedings before it until such time as the Court of Justice shall have delivered judgment. Where applications are made for the same act to be declared void, the Court of First Instance may also decline jurisdiction in order that the Court of Justice may rule on such applications. In the cases referred to in this subparagraph, the Court of Justice may also decide to stay the proceedings before it; in that event, the proceedings before the Court of First Instance shall continue.

Article 48

Final decisions of the Court of First Instance, decisions disposing of the substantive issues in part only or disposing of a procedural issue concerning a plea of lack of competence or inadmissibility, shall be notified by the Registrar of the Court of First Instance to all parties as well as all Member States and the Community institutions even if they have not intervened in the case before the Court of First Instance.

Article 49

An appeal may be brought before the Court of Justice, within two months of the notification of the decision appealed against, against final decisions of the Court of First Instance and decisions of that Court disposing of the substantive issues in part only or disposing of a procedural issue concerning a plea of lack of competence or inadmissibility.

Such an appeal may be brought by any party which has been unsuccessful, in whole or in part, in its submissions. However, interveners other than the Member States and the Community institutions may bring such an appeal only where the decision of the Court of First Instance directly affects them.

With the exception of cases relating to disputes between the Communities and their servants, an appeal may also be brought by Member States and Community institutions which did not intervene in the proceedings before the Court of First Instance. Such Member States and institutions shall be in the same position as Member State or institutions which intervened at first instance.

Article 50

Any person whose application to intervene has been dismissed by the Court of First Instance may appeal to the Court of Justice within two weeks of the notification of the decision dismissing the application.

The parties to the proceedings may appeal to the Court of Justice against any decision of the Court of First Instance made pursuant to Article 185 or 186 or the fourth paragraph of Article 192 of the Treaty within two months from their notification.

The appeal referred to in the first two paragraphs of this Article shall be heard and determined under the procedure referred to in Article 36 of this Statute.

Article 51

An appeal to the Court of Justice shall be limited to points of law. It shall lie on the grounds of lack of competence of the Court of First Instance, a breach of procedure before it which adversely affects the interests of the appellant as well as the infringement of Community law by the Court of First Instance.

No appeal shall lie regarding only the amount of the costs or the party ordered to pay them.

Article 52

Where an appeal is brought against a decision of the Court of First Instance, the procedure before the Court of Justice shall consist of a written part and an oral part. In accordance with conditions laid down in the Rules of Procedure the Court of Justice, having heard the Advocate-General and the parties, may dispense with the oral procedure.

Article 53

Without prejudice to Articles 185 and 186 of the Treaty, an appeal shall not have suspensory effect.

By way of derogation from Article 187 of the Treaty, decisions of the Court of First Instance declaring a regulation to be void shall take effect only as from the date of expiry of the period referred to in the first paragraph of Article 49 of this Statute or, if an appeal shall have been brought within that period, as from the date of dismissal of the appeal, without prejudice, however, to the right of a party to apply to the Court of Justice, pursuant to Articles 185 and 186 of this Treaty, for the suspension of the effects of the regulation which has been declared void or for the prescription of any other interim measure.

Article 54

If the appeal is well founded, the Court of Justice shall quash the decision of the Court of First Instance. It may itself give final judgment in the matter, where the state of the proceedings so permits, or refer the case back to the Court of First Instance for judgment.

Where a case is referred back to the Court of First Instance, that Court shall be bound by the decision of the Court of Justice on points of law.

When an appeal brought by a Member State or a Community institution, which has not intervened in the proceedings before the Court of First Instance, is well founded Court of Justice may, if it considers this necessary, state which of the effects of the decision of the Court of First Instance which has been quashed shall be considered as definitive in respect of the parties to the litigation.'

Article 8

The former Articles 44, 45 and 46 of the Protocol on the Statute of the Court of Justice of the European Economic Community shall become Articles 55, 56 and 57 respectively.

Article 9; omitted

Article 10; omitted

Article 11

The first President of the Court of First Instance shall be appointed for three years in the same manner as its members. However, the Governments of the Member States may, by common accord, decide that the procedure laid down in Article 2 (2) shall be applied.

The Court of First Instance shall adopt its Rules of Procedure immediately upon its constitution.

Until the entry into force of the Rules of Procedure of the Court of First Instance, the Rules of Procedure of the Court of Justice shall apply *mutatis mutandis*.

Article 12

Immediately after all members of the Court of First Instance have taken oath, the President of the Council shall proceed to choose by lot the members of the Court of First Instance whose terms of office are to expire at the end of the first three years in accordance with Article 32d (3) of the ECSC Treaty, Article 168a (3) of the EEC Treaty, and Article 140a (3) of the EAEC Treaty.

Article 13

This Decision shall enter into force on the day following its publication in the *Official Journal of the European Communities*, with the exception of Article 3, which shall enter into force on the date of the publication in the *Official Journal of the European Communities* of the ruling by the President of the Court of Justice that the Court of First Instance has been constituted in accordance with law.

Article 14

Cases referred to in Article 3 of which the Court of Justice is seised on the date on which that Article enters into force but in which the preliminary report provided for in Article 44 (1) of the Rules of Procedure of the Court of Justice has not yet been presented shall be referred back to the Court of First Instance.

. . . . .

VII. Questions to be discussed

Action for annulment

1. In what way are the possibilities for actions by Member States greater than those by private parties?
2. The Commission addresses an identical decision to each of the three Benelux countries, ordering them to levy certain import duties on goods from Eastern Europe. Is such a decision an individual decision?
3. Is it possible to obtain the annulment of an act which is of legislative nature?
4. a. What was/were the decisive factor(s) for the admissibility of Toepfer's action?
   b. What were the decisive factors in the *Chinese Mushrooms Case*?
5. Do you think the Plaumann action would have been held admissible if Plaumann had been only importer of clementines

(a) in Germany
(b) in Europe?
6. Why does the Court insist upon sufficient reasons being given for a decision?
7. Why is the *Nold Case II* of general interest?
8. Do you agree with the Court of Justice in the *International Fruit-Company Case III*?

Action against failure to act

9. What are the differences between the action for annulment and the action against failure to act?

Plea of illegality

10. What is understood by the 'plea of illegality' in Community law and against what acts can it be used?
11. What is the effect of a successful plea of illegality? Is it unlimited in time?
12. Article 184 EEC speaks of 'proceedings placing in issue a regulation of the Council or of the Commission'. Are these necessarily proceedings before the Court of Justice, and why?

Non-contractual liability

14. Under which conditions can the Community be sued for damages?
15. To what extent can the Community be sued for damages for the effects of decisions against which no action or annulment has been brought?
16. What sorts of damages may be claimed?

Preliminary ruling

17. When is an arbitral tribunal entitled to request a preliminary ruling?
18. To what extent do municipal courts act as Community courts when exercising their duties under EEC Article 177?
19. Is it possible under the EEC Treaty for an individual to obtain a court decision that a Government has failed to fulfill its obligations under the EEC Treaty?
20. Can the Court of Justice set national laws aside as being contrary to EEC provisions?
21. Individuals have only a limited right to bring an action for annulment. To what extent is this right extended by Article 177? What is the consequence of shifting legal protection from the action for annulment to the preliminary ruling?
22. Could Governments advise lower national courts not to request preliminary rulings?
23. Would the highest national court be obliged to ask for a preliminary

ruling whenever one of the parties raises a question of Community law?
24. Does the *Chanel Case* conflict with the *Bosch* and *Rheinmühlen Cases*?

Actions against Member States

25. If Germany and Italy (in violation of EEC rules) restrict certain imports from the Netherlands, would that constitute a legal basis for Dutch restrictions (otherwise contrary to EEC rules) on comparable imports from Germany and Italy?
26. If the Commission refrains from ordering the Italian Government to rescind an import prohibition imposed on pork in contravention of the EEC Treaty, can a Dutch exporter of pork institute proceedings in the Court of Justice of the Communities?
27. Do you agree with the view of the Commission expressed in the introduction of sub-chapter V in its reply to the European Parliament?
28. Assume your State has been condemned under Article 169 for illegaly limiting the import of biffles. Can the importers sue for damages?

Chapter Three

The Relationship between Community Law and National Law

I. Introduction

The Treaties establishing the European Communities have created a new legal order which can neither be explained in terms of general international law nor be described as a particular type of national law. In a series of decisions the Court of Justice has ruled that the legal system set up by the Treaties is *autonomous* in its own sphere. As a legal order sui generis it should be distinguished from municipal law and from international law. However, this does not mean that there is no need for close contacts between the Community legal order and the legal systems of the Member States. For its proper functioning the Community legal order depends heavily on *co-operation* of the Member States; the Community legal order is said to be integrated with the municipal legal systems of the Member States. Thus, with regard to the enforcement of Community law, not only the Court of Justice but also municipal courts are obliged to apply Community law. Other national authorities are required to ensure the implementation of Community law by adopting laws, regulations or administrative measures.

The Treaties have in common with other international agreements that they have been incorporated in the legal order of the Member States through the usual incorporation devices. Each Member State has applied its own constitutional procedures to give the Treaties internal effectiveness. However, the Treaties have created a new legal order the subjects of which comprise not only the Community institutions and the Member States but also the nationals of these Member States. The Court of Justice, basing itself on the concept of the new legal order, has deprived the Member States of the power to determine unilaterally the scope of their commitments vis-à-vis the Community and vis-à-vis their nationals. It has clearly stated that dualist views which Member States may hold in respect of the relationship between international treaties and national law cannot be maintained with regard to Community law. The Treaties and the measures laid down for their implementation may not be regarded as provisions of international law 'transformed' into national law. The law flowing from a Community source retains its specific character.

It does not take its place in the hierarchy of nationally enacted provisions and national canons of statutory interpretation do not apply.

As a result, Community law is beyond the reach of national measures which are inconsistent with it. Under international law a State can validly adopt internal measures deviating from Treaty law. It then incurs international responsibility but at the domestic level of most States the national measures prevail and will be enforced if their contents cannot be squared with the Treaty. This rule does not obtain within the framework of Community law. This is especially important in view of the fact that a substantial number of provisions of Community law confers rights on private individuals. These rights are enforceable in the national courts, regardless of any national measures by which a State could attempt to vary or ignore these rights.

Summing up the terms for the admission of new Member States to the Community, the Commission in its opinion of 19 January 1972 emphasized that it is an essential feature of the legal system set up by the Treaties establishing the Communities that certain of their provisions and certain acts of the Community institutions are directly applicable, that Community law takes precedence over any national provision conflicting with it, and that procedures exist for ensuring the uniform interpretation of this law.

Section (i.e. subchapter) II of the present Chapter focuses on some important general aspects of the Community's autonomous legal order. Questions relating the direct applicability of Community law will be examined in Section III and the problems relating to the supremacy of Community law are treated in Section IV of this chapter. Details on the procedure designed to ensure the uniform interpretation of Community law have been given in Chapter Two.

II. The Development of Community Law as an autonomous system

A. THE COMMUNITY'S NEW LEGAL ORDER

1. Cases

(1) Van Gend en Loos Case

For references and facts, p. 110, 255.

The Court held:

'The first question of the Tariefcommissie is whether Article 12 of the Treaty has direct application in national law in the sense that nationals of Member

States may on the basis of this Article lay claim to rights which the national court must protect.

To ascertain whether the provisions of an international treaty extend so far in their effects it is necessary to consider the spirit, the general scheme and the wording of those provisions.

The objective of the EEC Treaty, which is to establish a Common Market, the functioning of which is of direct concern to interested parties in the Community, implies that this Treaty is more than an agreement which merely creates mutual obligations between the contracting states. This view is confirmed by the preamble to the Treaty which refers not only to governments but to peoples. It is also confirmed more specifically by the establishment of institutions endowed with sovereign rights, the exercise of which affects Member States and also their citizens. Furthermore, it must be noted that the nationals of the states brought together in the Community are called upon to co-operate in the functioning of the Community through the intermediary of the European Parliament and the Economic and Social Committee.

In addition the task assigned to the Court of Justice under Article 177, the object of which is to secure uniform interpretation of the Treaty by national courts and tribunals, confirms that the states have acknowledged that Community law has an authority which can be invoked by their nationals before those courts and tribunals.

The conclusion to be drawn from this is that the Community constitutes a new legal order of international law for the benefit of which the States have limited their sovereign rights, albeit within limited fields, and the subjects of which comprise not only Member States but also their nationals. Independently of the legislation of Member States Community law therefore not only imposes obligations on individuals but is also intended to confer upon them rights which become part of their legal heritage. These rights arise not only where they are expressly granted by the Treaty, but also by reason of obligations which the Treaty imposes in a clearly defined way upon individuals as well as upon the Member States and upon the institutions of the Community'.

(2) Costa-ENEL Case

For references and facts pages 114, 121, 406, 573.

After rejecting a preliminary objection regarding the wording of the questions referred to the Court and regarding the lack of relevance of a preliminary ruling for the solution of the dispute before the national court, the Court of Justice dealt with the submission that the national court could only apply the national law.

The Court held:

. . . . .

'The Italian Government submits that the request of the Giudice Conciliatore is "absolutely inadmissible", inasmuch as a national court which is obliged to apply a national law cannot avail itself of Article 177.

By contrast with ordinary international treaties, the EEC Treaty has created its own legal system which, on the entry into force of the Treaty, became an integral part of the legal systems of the Member States and which their courts are bound to apply.

By creating a Community of unlimited duration, having its own institutions, its own personality, its own legal capacity and capacity of representation on the international plane and, more particularly, real powers stemming from a limitation of sovereignty or a transfer of powers from the States to the Community, the Member States have limited their sovereign rights, albeit within limited fields, and have thus created a body of law which binds both their nationals and themselves.

The integration into the laws of each Member State of provisions which derive from the Community, and more generally the terms and the spirit of the Treaty, make it impossible for the States, as a corollary, to accord precedence to a unilateral and subsequent measure over a legal system accepted by them on a basis of reciprocity. Such a measure cannot therefore be inconsistent with that legal system. The executive force of Community law cannot vary from one state to another in deference of subsequent domestic laws, without jeopardizing the attainment of the objectives of the Treaty set out in Article 5 (2) and giving rise to the discrimination prohibited by Article 7.

The obligations undertaken under the Treaty establishing the Community would not be unconditional, but merely contingent, if they could be called in question by subsequent legislative acts of the signatories. Wherever the Treaty grants the States the right to act unilaterally, it does this by clear and precise provisions (for example Articles 15, 93 (3), 223, 224 and 225). Applications by Member States for authority to derogate from the Treaty are subject to a special authorization procedure (for example Article 8 (4), 17 (4), 25, 26, 73, the third paragraph of Article 93 (2), and 226), which would lose its purpose if the Member States could renounce their obligations by means of an ordinary law.

The precedence of Community law is confirmed by Article 189, whereby a regulation "shall be binding" and "directly applicable in all Member States". This provision, which is subject to no reservation, would be quite meaningless if a State could unilaterally nullify its effects by means of a legislative measure which could prevail over Community law.

It follows from all these observations that the law stemming from the Treaty, an independent source of law, could not because of its special and original nature, be overridden by domestic legal provisions, however framed, without being deprived of its character as Community law and without the legal basis of the Community itself being called into question.

The transfer by the States from their domestic legal systems to the Community legal system of the rights and obligations arising under the Treaty carries with it a permanent limitation of their sovereign rights, against which a subsequent unilateral act incompatible with the concept of the Community cannot prevail. Consequently Article 177 is to be applied regardless of any domestic law, whenever questions relating to the interpretation of the Treaty arise.'

B. DIVISION OF COMPETENCES, OBLIGATIONS OF THE MEMBER STATES

1. Introduction

The Member States by accepting to be bound by the Treaties have transferred certain powers to the Community institutions, thus suffering a more or less extensive *loss of national autonomy*.

Article 5 first paragraph of the EEC Treaty specifies that the Member States shall abstain from any measure which could jeopardize the attainment of the objectives of the Treaty and that they shall take all appropriate measures to ensure fulfilment of the obligations arising out of the Treaty or resulting from action taken by the institutions of the community. The Court has repeatedly emphasized that the fundamental principle of Article 5 implies an obligation for the Member States to implement Community law in such a way that it receives *uniform application* throughout the Community and that its *useful effect* is ensured. They must of course also respect the *division of competences* resulting from the Treaty or from secondary Community law. As it is impossible to describe all concrete manifestations of the problems raised in this connection, it may suffice to deal with the following aspects of the question only:

a. Member States may not resort to *methods of implementation* that may bring into doubt the legal nature of (directly applicable) provisions of Community law. In Case 34/73) (*Variola*), [1973] ECR 990, the Court held:
   10. 'The direct application of a Regulation means that its entry into force and its application in favour of or against those subject to it are independent of any measure of reception into national law.

   By virtue of the obligations arising from the Treaty and assumed on ratification, Member States are under a duty not to obstruct the direct applicability inherent in Regulations and other rules of Community law.

Strict compliance with this obligation is an indispensable condition of simultaneous and uniform application of Community Regulations throughout the Community.

11. More particularly, Member States are under an obligation not to introduce any measure which might affect the jurisdiction of the Court to pronounce on any questions involving the interpretation of Community law or the validity of an act of the institutions of the Community which means that no procedure is permissible whereby the Community nature of a legal rule is concealed from those subject to it.'

(See also Case 39/72 (*Slaughtered Cow II*), p. 40 and 197, and Case 50/76 (*Amsterdam Bulb*), see p. 641.)

b. Directly applicable provisions of Community law render *automatically inapplicable* any conflicting provisions of current national law and preclude the valid adoption of new legislative measures to the extent to which they would be incompatible with Community provisions. *Every* national court must give full effect to the Community provisions and, if necessary, refuse of its own motion to apply any conflicting national rules, even if adopted subsequently. The *effectiveness* of Community law would be impaired if ordinary courts lacked the power to solve such conflicts themselves and were to request or await the prior setting aside of national provisions by the legislature or by a constitutional court.

(See Case 106/77, *Simmenthal Case II*, p. 200.)

c. If national legislation is incompatible with Community law, it must be repealed, even if the Community provisions have direct effect and for that reason would take precedence over the national provisions anyway. See Case 167/73, *French Maritime Labour Code Case*, p. 242). Likewise the fact that under certain circumstances private individuals may rely in law on a directive as against a defaulting Member State does not absolve the Member State from taking in due time implementing measures sufficient to meet the purpose of the directive. See Case 102/79, *Commission* v. *Belgium*, [1980] ECR 1473.

d. Member States are no less obliged to *faithfully execute directives* than regulations or decisions. In Case 52/75 (*Marketing of vegetable seed Case*), [1976] ECR 284, the Court stated:

10. 'The correct application of a directive is particularly important since the implementing measures are left to the discretion of the Member States and would be ineffective if the desired aims were not achieved within the prescribed time-limits. Although the provisions of a directive are no less binding on the Member States to which they are addressed than the provisions of any other rule of Community law, such

an effect attaches a fortiori to the provisions relating to the periods allowed for implementing the measures prescribed, in particular since the existence of differences in the rules applied in the Member States after these periods have expired might result in discrimination.'
e. The Member States' obligation under a *directive* to achieve the result envisaged by that directive and their duty under Article 5 of the Treaty to take all appropriate measures to ensure the fulfillment of that obligation, is binding on *all* the authorities of Member States, including the Courts. It follows that national courts must interpret and apply their national law, and in particular the legislation adopted for the implementation of a directive, in the light of the wording and the purpose of the directive, in so far as they are given discretion to do so under national law (Case 14/83, *Colson and Kamann*, [1984] ECR 1981.
f. Member States are frequently required to adopt provisions for the *implementation of regulations*. In adopting such provisions they must in particular be aware of the need to respect the principle of the *division of competence*. Thus the Court held in Case 40/69 (*Turkey Tails*), [1970] ECR 80, that the Member States are not entitled to give binding definitions of headings of the customs nomenclature, since this might jeopardize the uniform application of the Common Customs Tariff. See p. 38 and 292.

The following case also shows that the residual powers of the Member States in respect of customs legislation are very limited.

2. Cases

(1) Reliable Importers Case

Norddeutsche Vieh- und Fleischkontor GmbH v. *Hauptzollamt Hamburg*; Case 39/70; Preliminary ruling of 11 February 1971; [1971] ECR 49; [1971] CMLR 281.

Facts:

According to EEC Regulations 805/68 and 1082/68, manufacturers exporting tinned meat were exempted from paying the import levy on the frozen meat needed for their exports under a number of rather detailed conditions. The German customs authorities required in addition that the importers of frozen meat had to be reliable (*vertrauenswürdig*). The Norddeutsche Vieh- und Fleischkontor was not considered sufficiently reliable and therefore had to pay import levies on the frozen meat which it used for making tinned meat for export. Before the *Finanzgericht* the question arose whether EEC Regulations permitted further national requirements or whether they were exhaustive. The *Finanzgericht* asked for a preliminary ruling.

The Court held:

4. Where national authorities are responsible for implementing a Community regulation it must be recognized that in principle this implementation takes place with due respect for the forms and procedures of national law.

    However, the uniform application of Community provisions allows no recourse to national rules except to the extent necessary to carry out the regulations.

    No such need has been established in the present instance, as the rules an interpretation of which has been requested lay down all the conditions which must be fulfilled for the levy to be suspended, as well as arrangements for security and the supervisions designed to prevent fraud.
5. Although the national authorities are free to use all the appropriate methods which their law provides to prevent the fraudulent evasion of Community rules, this cannot apply where the national law is based upon criteria which do not conform to the system of guarantees and proof introduced by the Community rules.

    In particular, such national rules must be regarded as incompatible with the Community rules when the national rules are based upon a criterion which leaves the national authorities too wide an area of discretion, such as the degree of trust to be accorded to an importer.

    The application of criteria of this nature may lead to differences of treatment between the importers of the various Member States and thus endanger the essential uniformity of application of Community provisions throughout the whole of the Common Market.

    It is, therefore, impossible to apply national provisions based upon criteria which are not in harmony with those adopted by the Community legislature.
6. For this reason it would be incompatible with Community rules for any customs authority to subject an importer's claim for suspension of the levy to internal legal requirements based upon subjective assessments.

Sequel to introduction

g. In later cases the Court, rather than relying on the *nature* of Community regulations (Article 189, para 2), emphasized the need to protect the functioning of *common organizations of agricultural markets* as such from unilateral interference by the Member States. Its decisions in *e.g.* Case 159/73 (*Hannoverische Zucker*). [1974] ECR, 121, Case 190/73 (*Van Haaster*), [1974] ECR 1123 [see p. 000) and Case 31/74 (*Galli*), [1975] ECR 47 (see p. 646), suggested that the existence of a common organization of agricultural markets virtually excludes any residual powers of the Member States in the same sector. However, in subsequent cases the Court has indicated that the Member States have retained rather substantial powers of intervention in areas covered by a common organization of the market. See e.g. Cases 65/75 (*Tasca*), [1976] ECR 201 and 88–90/75 (*SADAM*) [1976] ECR 323. In these cases the Court admitted the possibility that the unilateral fixing by a Member State of maximum prices for the sale of an agricultural commodity can be compatible with the market organization concerned if the State measures do not jeopardize the objectives and the functioning of this organization. (*Cfr.* also case 50/76 (*Amsterdam Bulb*), preliminary ruling of February 2, 1977, [1977] ECR 137, p. 641).

h. In other areas of Community competence the same principles apply. Even if there is room for *cumulative* application of Community legislation and national legislation covering the same field but seen from different perspectives, Member States must see to it that the useful effect of Community law and its uniform application are not compromised. A typical example of such a problem is the *competition law* of the Community – limited to agreements which may affect trade between Member States – which may coincide with the application of national legislation.

(2) Walt Wilhelm Case

Walt Wilhelm a.o. v. *Bundeskartellamt*; Case 14/68; Preliminary ruling of 13 February 1969; [1969] ECR 13; (1969) CMLR 100.

Facts:

Walt Wilhelm and others were fined by the *Bundeskartellamt* (Federal Cartel Office) for violation of the German Law on Restraint of Competition.

The EEC Commission had initiated proceedings against Walt Wilhelm and others under Article 85 of the EEC Treaty. In its appeal against the German fines, Walt Wilhelm submitted that the *Bundeskartellamt* could not maintain proceedings for an offence which was at the same time the subject of parallel proceedings by the EEC Commission. The German court (*Kammergericht Berlin*) asked for a preliminary ruling on the question of cumulation of proceedings.

The Court held:

3. Article 9 (3) of Regulation No 17 is concerned with the competence of the authorities of the Member States only in so far as they are authorized to apply Articles 85 (1) and 86 of the Treaty directly when the Commission has taken no action of its own. This provision does not apply where the said authorities are acting in pursuance not of the said articles but only of their internal law. Community and national law on cartels consider cartels from different points of view. Whereas Article 85 regards them in the light

of the obstacles which may result for trade between Member States, each body of national legislation proceeds on the basis of the considerations peculiar to it and considers cartels only in that context. It is true that as the economic phenomena and legal situations under consideration may in individual cases be interdependent, the distinction between Community and national aspects could not serve in all cases as the decisive criterion for the delimitation of jurisdiction. However, it implies that one and the same agreement may, in principle, be the object of two sets of parallel proceedings, one before the Community authorities under Article 85 of the EEC Treaty, the other before the national authorities under national law.

4. Moreover this interpretation is confirmed by the provision in Article 87 (2) (e), which authorizes the Council to determine the relationship between national laws and the Community rules on competition; it follows that in principle the national cartel authorities may take proceedings also with regard to situations likely to be the subject of a decision by the Commission. However, if the ultimate general aim of the Treaty is to be respected, this parallel application of the national system can only be allowed in so far as it does not prejudice the uniform application throughout the common Market of the Community rules on cartels and of the full effect of the measures adopted in implementation of those rules.

. . . . .

6. The EEC Treaty has established its own system of law, integrated into the legal systems of the Member States, and which must be applied by their courts. It would be contrary to the nature of such a system to allow Member States to introduce or to retain measures capable of prejudicing the practical effectiveness of the Treaty. The binding force of the Treaty and of measures taken in application of it must not differ from one state to another as a result of internal measures, lest the functioning of the Community system should be impeded and the achievement of the aims of the Treaty placed in peril. Consequently, conflicts between the rules of the Community and national rules in the matter of the law on cartels must be resolved by applying the principle that Community law takes precedence.

7. It follows from the foregoing that should it prove that a decision of a national authority regarding an agreement would be incompatible with a decision adopted by the Commission at the culmination of the procedure initiated by it, the national authority is required to take proper account of the effects of the latter decision.

8. Where, during national proceedings, it appears possible that the decision to be taken by the Commission at the culmination of a procedure still in progress concerning the same agreement may conflict with the effects of the decision of the national authorities, it is for the latter to take the appropriate measures.

9. Consequently, and so long as a regulation adopted pursuant to Article 87 (2) (e) of the Treaty has not provided otherwise, national authorities may take action against an agreement in accordance with their national law, even when an examination of the agreement from the point of view of its compatibility with Community law is pending before the Commission, subject however to the condition that the application of national law may not prejudice the full and uniform application of Community law or the effects of measures taken or to be taken to implement it.

Sequel to introduction

i. A dynamic interpretation of the scope of the powers explicitly or impliedly transferred by the Member States to the Community may entail a loss of national autonomy not contemplated or visualised when the Treaties were drafted. In Case 22/70 which concerned the powers of the Community in the field of *external relations*, the Court held that the ambit of the Community powers spreads with the growth of the various Community policies.

(3) ERTA Case

For references and facts see p. 6.

The parties held different views on the question of whether authority to negotiate and conclude the European Road Transport Agreement was a matter of Community authority, or was within the authority of the Member States.

The Court held:

12. In the absence of specific provisions of the Treaty relating to the negotiation and conclusion of international agreements in the sphere of transport policy – a category into which, essentially, the AETR falls – on must turn to the general system of Community law in the sphere of relations with third countries.
13. Article 210 provides that 'The Community shall have legal personality'.
14. This provision, placed at the head of Part Six of the Treaty, devoted to 'General and Final Provisions', means that in its external relations the Community enjoys the capacity to establish contractual links with third countries over the whole field of objectives defined in Part One of the Treaty, which Part Six supplements.
15. To determine in a particular case the Community's authority to enter into international agreements, regard must be had to the whole scheme of the Treaty no less than to its substantive provisions.
16. Such authority arises not only from an express conferment by the Treaty

- as is the case with Articles 113 and 114 for tariff and trade agreements and with Article 238 for association agreements – but may equally flow from other provisions of the Treaty and from measures adopted, within the framework of those provisions, by the Community institutions.
17. In particular, each time the Community, with a view to implementing a common policy envisaged by the Treaty, adopts provisions laying down common rules, whatever form these may take, the Member States no longer have the right, acting individually or even collectively, to undertake obligations with third countries which affect those rules.
18. As and when such common rules come into being, the Community alone is in a position to assume and carry out contractual obligations towards third countries affecting the whole sphere of application of the Community legal system.
19. With regard to the implementation of the provisions of the Treaty the system of internal Community measures may not therefore be separated from that of external relations.
20. Under Article 3 (e), the adoption of a common policy in the sphere of transport is specially mentioned amongst the objectives of the Community.
21. Under Article 5, the Member States are required on the one hand to take all appropriate measures to ensure fulfilment of the obligations arising out of the Treaty or resulting from action by the institutions and, on the other hand, to abstain from any measure which might jeopardize the attainment of the objectives of the Treaty.
22. If these two provisions are read in conjunction, it follows that to the extent to which Community rules are promulgated for the attainment of the objectives of the Treaty, the Member States cannot, outside the framework of the Community institutions, assume obligations which might affect those rules or alter their scope.

Under this heading mention should also be made of the Court's *opinions under Article 228*. In its opinion 1/75 of 11 November 1975, [1975] ECR 1355, concerning the compatibility with the EEC Treaty of a draft 'Understanding on Local Cost Standard' drawn up under the auspices of the OECD, the Court confirmed the exclusive nature of the Community's powers in respect of commercial policy. Whenever a certain subject-matter comes within the field of the common commercial policy, the Community has sole power to conclude agreements with third countries, even if no autonomous internal rules have come into being. The Court has thus specified its ruling in the *ERTA*-case and it has implicitly rejected the view of those who had argued that according to the ERTA-ruling an exclusive authority for the Community in the sphere of external commercial policy was contingent on the adopting of common internal measures in this area. 'A commercial policy', the Court held, 'is in fact made up by the combination and interaction of internal and external measures, without priority being taken by one over the other. Sometimes agreements are concluded in execution of a policy fixed in advance, sometimes that policy is defined by the agreements themselves'. In *opinion 1/76* of 26 April 1977, [1977] ECR 755, (see p. 666) concerning the compatibility with the EEC Treaty of a draft Agreement establishing a European laying-up fund for inland waterway vessels, the Court, recalling its earlier jurisprudence (notably cases 3, 4 and 6/76, (*Kramer*), [1976] ECR 1279 stated:

3. 'The Court has concluded inter alia that whenever Community law has created for the institutions of the Community powers within its internal system for the purpose of attaining a specific objective, the Community has authority to enter into the international commitments necessary for the attainment of the objective even in the absence of an express provision in that connection.
4. This is particularly so in all cases in which internal power has already been used in order to adopt measures which come within the attainment of common policies. It is, however, not limited to that eventuality. Although the internal Community measures are only adopted when the international agreement is concluded and made enforceable, as is envisaged in the present case by the proposal for a Regulation to be submitted by the Commission to the Council, the power to bind the Community vis-à-vis third countries nevertheless flows by implication from the provisions of the Treaty creating the internal power and in so far as the participation of the Community in the international agreement is, as here, necessary for the attainment of one of the objectives of the Community.'

See also for the question of the (exclusive) external powers of the Community, Reply of the Commission to written question No. 173/77 (Maigaard) OJ 1978, C 72/1 in **Materials on the Law of the European Communities** Chapter Six. See further Chapter Six below.

Sequel to introduction

j. Powers once conferred upon the Community can only be restored to the field of authority of the Member States by virtue of an express provision of the Treaty. In order to enhance the useful effect of the Community Treaties, a principle '*in dubio pro Communitate*' has evolved and there is never a presumption operating in favour of the Member States' retention of prerogatives and against the Community (See Case 7/71, [197] ECR 1015).
k. In the past decades the Court of Justice has taken an 'activist' stand with regard to the impact of Community law on the legal order of the Member States, mainly by its case law on the primacy of Community law and on the *direct applicability* of Community provisions. See Section III below.
l. The end of the *transitional period* has enabled the Court to extract from the Treaty very broad effects in respect of several of its provisions. See e.g. Case 2/74 (*Reyners*), p. 407 and Case 33/74 (*Van Binsbergen*), p. 434.
m. Derogations from the rules on the free movement of goods in respect of *agricultural* products (Article 38, para 2) have not survived the transitional period, which ended on 31 December 1969. In Case 48/74 (*Charmasson*), [1974] ECR 1383, (see p. 619) it was held that agricultural products for

which no common organization of the market has been established, are entirely subject to the rules on the free movement of goods. As of the end of the transitional period Member States could no longer claim that the existence of a national organization of the market under these circumstances precludes the application of Articles 30 *et seq.* of the Treaty (quotas etc.). See also Cases 80 and 81/77 (*Commissionaires Réunis*), [1978] ECR 927, p. 620.

n. Finally, mention should be made of the wide interpretation which the Court has placed on the scope of the prohibitions laid down in Articles 30 *et seq.* of the Treaty. See Case 8/74 (*Dassonville*), (1974) ECR 837. p. 302). The definition given in that ruling of measures having an effect equivalent to quantitative restrictions may in particular result in a loss of power for the Member States to use certain instruments of conjunctural policy such as *e.g.* maximum price regulations. (See Case 88–90/75 (*SADAM*), [1976] ECR 323; Case 82/77 (*Van Tiggele*), (1978) ECR 25, p. 304. For a more recent case see Case 181/82 (*Roussel Laboratories*), [1983] ECR 3869.

C. AUTONOMY OF COMMUNITY LAW VIS-À-VIS NATIONAL LAW (FUNDAMENTAL RIGHTS)

1. Introduction

a. 'The effect of Community Law cannot vary from one State to another in favour of later internal laws without endangering the realization of the aims envisaged by the Treaty'. It was in these terms that the Court of Justice rejected an attempt by the Italian Government to make a later law prevail over the EEC Treaty. For good measure it was added that the obligations undertaken under the EEC Treaty would not be unconditional but merely potential if they could be affected by subsequent legislative acts of the signatories of the Treaties. (*Costa – ENEL*, see p. 160).

b. The Court has meant the Community legal order to be impervious to any inroads into its autonomy by way of national laws. Thus even the claim that Community law must be in conformity with the constitutional law of a Member State cannot be accepted, because there is no fundamental reason why the argument for supremacy should run any different with regard to constitutional laws of the Member States than in regard to subordinate national legislation.

In the *San Michele Case* (9/65, [1966] ECR 1) which related to the alleged unconstitutionality of the Italian act for the ratification of the ECSC Treaty, the Court of Justice stated: 'It follows from these acts of ratification, by which the Member States have bound themselves in an identical way, that all the States adhered to the Treaty in the same circumstances, definitely and without any other reservations than those expressed in the additional Protocols and that therefore it would be contrary to the Community legal order for any citizen of any Member State to claim to put this adhesion in issue.'

c. Fundamental rules of the domestic laws of the Member States, especially of the Federal Republic, have been pleaded in several cases to set aside Community law that failed to respect these basic provisions. In a number of early cases the Court strongly emphasized the autonomy of the Community's legal system and hence rejected the introduction of all concepts drawn from national constitutional law (Case 1/58, *Stork* v. *High Authority*, [1959] ECR 25; Cases 36–38/59 and 40/59, *Ruhrkohlen Verkaufsgesellschaft* v. *High Authority*, [1960] ECR 438; Case 40/64, *Sgarlata a.o.* v. *EEC Commission*, [1965] ECR 227).

This defensive attitude, however, has developed into a more accomodating one: when a threat to basic rights is alleged, the Court will investigate whether any guarantee inherent in Community law has been disregarded, as respect for fundamental rights is an integral part of the general principles of law of which the Court ensures the observance. (See the *Stauder Case*, the *Internationale Handelsgesellschaft Case* and the *Nold Case II*.) In the words of Judge Pescatore: 'The Court recognizes that the Community should consider as its own the constitutional tradition of Member States, and that it thereby participates in the common concepts of values – democracy, liberty, respect for the individual – that underlie German courts have long been occupied with cases where infringements of constitutionally guaranteed basic rights by secondary Community law were alleged. See further Section IV, C. 2 and the Judgment of the *Bundesver-fassungsgericht* of 29 May 1974, p. 214.

e. In its report on European Union (Bull, suppl. 1975, no 5) the Commission through a jurisprudential development of a protective system of basic rights independent of any formalised catalogue of fundamental rights, the German courts have long been occupied with cases where infringements of constitutionally guaranteed basic rights by secondary Community law were alleged. See further Section IV, C.2 and the Judgment of the *Bundesver-fassungsgericht* of 29 May 1974, p. 214.

e. In its report on European Union Bull, suppl. 1975, no 5) the Commission suggested that a separate codification be made of the fundamental human rights which are binding on the Communities. (See also the Commission's special report on the protection of fundamental rights in Bull. Suppl. 1976, no 5). In April 1977, the European Parliament, the Council and the Commission adopted a Joint Declaration on the protection of fundamental rights. This Joint Declaration was published in OJ 1977, C 103/1, (see Materials on the Law of the European Communities, Chapter Three). The Heads of State and of Government meeting in Copenhagen on 7 and 8 April 1978, have confirmed and amplified the Joint Declaration by the European Parliament, the Council and the Commission (see Materials on the Law of the European Communities, Chapter Three). The Commission has further proposed that the Community as such accedes to the European Convention for the Protection of Human Rights and Fundamental Freedoms (see Bull Suppl. 1979, no 2). The Single European Act of 27 and 28 February 1986 in its Preamble specifically refers to the fundamental rights recognized in the constitutions and the laws of the Member States, in the European Convention for the Protection of Human Rights and Fundamental Freedoms and in the European Social Charter, and in particular to liberty, equality and social justice.

2. Cases

(1) Stauder Case

Erick Stauder v. *City of Ulm*; Case 29/69; Judgment of 12 November 1969; [1969] ECR 419; [1970] CMLR 112.

Facts:

The Commission decision of 12 February 1969, OJ No. L 52, 3 March 1969, authorizes the Member States to make butter available at reduced prices to certain groups of consumers receiving social assistance where their income does not permit the use of butter at normal prices.

The German text of this decision required that the beneficiaries of the measures should present a voucher issued in their name when buying butter. Mr. Stauder submitted that the obligation to disclose his name was a humiliation and therefore contrary to his basic human rights. On that ground he requested the annulment of the decision. The Court considered (on the basis of the text of other languages of the decision) that Mr. Stauder was not obliged to disclose his name and subsequently

The Court held:

. . . . .

7. Interpreted in this way the provision at issue contains nothing capable of prejudicing the fundamental human rights enshrined in the general principles of Community law *and protected by the Court.*

(2) Handelsgesellschaft Case

See p. 82.

(3) Nold Case II

Nold v. *Commission of the EC*; Case 4/73; Decision of 14 May 1974; [1974] ECR 503. See also p. 84.

Facts:

The plaintiff challenged the legality of a Commission Decision of 21 December 1972, authorizing new terms of business for *Ruhrkohle A.G.* on the basis of Article 66 of the ECSC Treaty. One of the grounds advanced by Nold was an alleged infringement by the Commission of the plaintiff's *fundamental rights*.

The Court held:

. . . . .

12. The applicant asserts finally that certain of its fundamental rights have been violated, in that the restrictions introduced by the new trading rules authorized by the Commission have the effect, by depriving it of direct supplies, of jeopardizing both the profitability of the undertaking and the free development of its business activity, to the point of endangering its very existence.

    In this way the Decision is said to violate, in respect of the applicant, a right akin to a proprietary right, as well as its right to the free pursuit of business activity, as protected by the Grundgesetz of the Federal Republic of Germany and by the Constitutions of other Member States and various international treaties, including in particular the Convention for the Protection of Human Rights and Fundamental Freedoms of 4 November 1950 and the Protocol to that Convention of 20 March 1952.

13. As the Court has already stated, fundamental rights form in integral part of the general principles of law, the observance of which it ensures.

    In safeguarding these rights, the Court is bound to draw inspiration from constitutional traditions common to the Member States, and it cannot therefore uphold measures which are incompatible with fundamental rights recognized and protected by the Constitutions of those States.

    Similarly, international treaties for the protection of human rights on which the Member States have collaborated or of which they are signatories, can supply guidelines which should be followed within the framework of Community law.

    The submission of the applicant must be examined in the light of these principles.

(4) Hauer Case

See p. 660.

See for cases in which the Court assessed the propriety of limitations imposed by Member States on the freedom of movement and residence of persons (Articles 48, para 3, and 56, para 1) in the light of the European

Convention of the Protection of Human Rights and Fundamental Freedoms, Case 36/75 *Rutili*, [1975] ECR 1219, p. 000; Case 63/83, *Kirk*, [1984] ECR 2690.

3. Literature

Dauses, 'The Protection of Fundamental Rights in the Community Legal Order', (1985) ELRev. 398.
Mendelson, 'The European Court of Justice and Human Rights', (1981) YEL 126.
Pescatore, 'The Protection of Human Rights in the European Communities', (1972) CMLRev. 73.
Schermers, *Judicial Protection in the European Communities*. Deventer 1987, Fourth Edition, para 161–165.
Weiler, 'Eurocracy and Distrust: Some Questions Concerning the Role of the European Court of Justice in the Protection of Fundamental Human Rights within the Legal Order of the European Communities', (1986) Washington Law Rev. 1103.
Zuleeg, 'Fundamental Rights in the Law of the European Communities', (1971) CMLRev. 441.

III. Legal effect of Community law in the municipal legal order – the concept of direct applicability

A. INTRODUCTION

1. General

Community law does not merely regulate the legal regulations between Member States. It also imposes obligations on private individuals independently of the legislation of the Member States and it gives rise to rights which private parties can make applicable on their own behalf. A provision of Community law which may be enforced by action before municipal courts is variously described as 'directly applicable', 'immediately applicable' of 'directly effective'. These terms indicate that such provisions are apt to affect the legal rights and duties of private individuals in the Member States without any need for the interposition of a domestic legislative act to give these provisions the force of law.

It is especially through the device of direct applicability that the supremacy of Community law is ensured. If municipal courts are called upon to apply provisions of Community law they can make a particularly important contribution to upholding the supremacy of the Community legal order over conflicting national legislation. Indeed, if private individuals were not entitled to ask the municipal courts to enforce Community law provisions, thereby setting aside domestic measures incompatible with the Treaties, the supremacy of Community law could only be maintained by less direct and less effective methods, such as action by the Commission under Article 169 to obtain a declaration that a State has failed to fulfill its obligations under the Treaty. In the landmark *Case Van Gend en Loos* the Court rejected the argument that the Commission's right to proceed against Treaty violations in the Community Court would make a right of private individuals to enforce the Treaty provisions in the national courts superfluous. It was held that the vigilance of individuals concerned to protect their rights, amounts to an effective supervision, in addition to the supervision entrusted by Articles 169 and 170 to the Commission and the Member States.

2. *Literature*

Easson, 'The Direct Effect of EEC Directives', (1979), ICLQ, pp. 319–353.
Bebr, 'Agreements Concluded by the Community and Their Possible Direct Effect: From International Fruit Company to Kupferberg', (1983) CMLRev. p. 35.
Collins, *European Community Law in the United Kingdom*, Butterworths, third edition 1984, Ch. 2 (pp. 34–92).
Dashwood, 'The Principle of Direct Effect in European Community Law', (1978), *Journal of Common Market Studies*, 229.
Hartley, *The Foundations of European Community Law*, Oxford 1988, second edition, pp. 181–218.
Pescatore, 'The Doctrine of "Direct Effect": An Infant Disease in Community Law', (1983) 8 ELRev. 155.
Schermers, *Judicial Protection in the European Communities*, Kluwer, Deventer, fourth edition, 1987, paragraphs 239–263.
Steiner, 'Direct Applicability in EEC Law – A Chamereon Concept', (1982) 98 LQR 229.
Timmermans, 'Directives: Their effect within the national legal system', (1979) CMLRev. pp. 533–555.
Winter, 'Direct Applicability and Direct Effect; Two Distinct and Different Concepts in Community Law', (1972) CMLRev. p. 425.
Wyatt, 'Direct Applicable Provisions of EEC Law', (1975) NLJ p. 458.

B. CONDITIONS FOR DIRECT APPLICABILITY

1. Development of the concept with regard to provisions of the Treaty

(a) A Treaty provision may be directly applicable – in spite of the fact that the Member States are designated as its addressees and that the private individuals are not referred to as such – if by its nature it lends itself to producing direct effects in legal relations between the Member States and persons under their jurisdiction and creates individual rights to be recognized by the Courts. Therefore, the basic question is whether the provision invoked by a private individual sets out a rule which is sufficiently clear and specific to enable the judiciary to enforce it without further legislative activity on the part of the Member States or the Community institutions. For this to be the case a provision must be complete and legally perfect'. In the ideal case, a directly applicable provision satisfies, the following requirements: (a) the provision imposes a clear and precise obligation; (b) the obligation is not qualified by a reservation or a condition; and (c) no further legislative intervention of the Member States or the Community institutions is needed for the obligation to come into operation.

See in particular Case 26/62 (*Van Gend en Loos*), p. 255; Case 6/64 (*Costa* v. *ENEL*), p. 114; Case 57/65 (*Lütticke II*), p. 264; Case 13/68 (*Salgoil*), p. 299.

(b) However, even if the above conditions (b) and (c) are not fully met, a Treaty provision may be found to be directly applicable if the Member States do not enjoy substantial discretion in executing or implementing it. The Court has stated repeatedly that in principle a certain measure of discretion precludes direct applicability. (See *e.g.* Case 13/68 (*Salgoil*), p. 299). But if, by its nature the obligation is very clear and specific and leaves the Member States practically no latitude of judgment in executing it, the Court is inclined to dispense with the 'positive' measures the Member States (or the Community institutions) should have taken. (See especially Case 57/65 (*Lütticke II*), p. 264). This means that, in certain circumstances, private individuals can ask the national judge to apply a Treaty provision instead of the national legislation that should have been repealed or adjusted in order to achieve the legal situation described in the provision in question. The matter assumes special importance in cases where the Member States must adopt national measures before the expiry of a certain deadline. If this deadline has not been met (for instance, Article 8, para 7, of the Treaty providing that the expiry of the transitional period shall constitute the final date for the coming into force of all the rules laid down ...) the Treaty rule may be substituted for domestic legislation in the relations between the Member State and private individuals, provided that it fulfills the conditions for direct applicability.

Thus, in case 2/74 (*Reyners*), p. 407, the Court held that, since the end of the transitional period, Article 52 of the Treaty is a directly applicable provision despite the absence of Community directives designed to implement the prohibition of discrimination laid down in that provision.

Other important cases in which a similar reasoning has led to the recognition that a Treaty provision is directly applicable are Case 59/75 (*Manghera*; [1976] ECR 91, (concerning Article 37, para 1); Case 33/74 (*Van Binsbergen*), p. 434 and Case 36/74 (*Walrave-Koch*), see p. 438 (concerning Articles 59 and 60) and Case 43/75 (*Defrenne II*), p. 582 (concerning Article 119).

(c) Is Article 48 a directly applicable provision in spite of the fact that the clear obligation to grant equality of treatment to workers from other Member States appears to be subject to the reservation laid down in para. 3. See Case 41/75 (*Van Duyn*), p. 366, in which the Court held (Recital 7): 'Paragraph 3, which defines the rights implied by the principle of freedom of movement for workers, subjects them to limitations; justified on grounds of public policy, public security or public health. The application of these limitations is, however, subject to judicial control, so that a Member State's right to invoke the limitations does not prevent the provision of Article 48, which enshrines the principle of freedom of movement for workers, from conferring on individuals rights which are enforceable by them and which the national courts must protect.'

(d) Certain rules of the Treaty (and provisions of regulations) impose obligations on private individuals which other individuals may enforce (*e.g.* Article 85. See Cases 56 and 58/64 (*Consten and Grundig*), (1966) ECR 299, page 492). In general, in their mutual relations private individuals are not allowed to invoke provisions of Community law which address themselves only to the Member States. However, *direct horizontal effect* has been attributed to prohibitions which are of essential importance for the achievement of the Treaty's fundamental objectives. Thus in Case 36/74 (*Walrave-Koch*), see p. 438, the Court of Justice held that the prohibition of discrimination on the ground of nationality, as laid down in Articles 7, 48 and 59 of the Treaty, does not only apply to the action of public authorities but extends likewise to associations of a private character. Consequently, these prohibitions of discrimination impose obligations on private individuals likewise. The Court ruled in Case 43/75 (*Defrenne II*) p. 582, that Article 119, which orders Member States to ensure that men and women receive equal pay for equal work, can be invoked against private employers as well as against public authorities.

(e) Whenever the Court rules that a particular provision of Community law has direct effect, such an interpretation applies to the past as well as to the future. It is only in exceptional situations that *restrictions* on the *retroactive effect* of an interpretation can be allowed. See Case 43/75 (*Defrenne II*) p. 582. The Court has further held that restrictions *ratione temporis* may only be made in the actual judgment ruling upon the interpretation and that the need for a uniform and general application of Community law implies that it is for the Court of Justice alone to decide upon temporal restriction as regards the effects of the interpretation which it gives. See Case 61/79, *Denkavit Italiana*, [1980] ECR 1224.

2. Direct effect of secondary Community Law

a. Regulations

Since Article 189 declares regulations to be binding in their entirety and directly applicable in all Member States, provisions of regulations are particularly suitable to produce direct effect for citizens in the sense that they can invoke these provisions against conflicting measures of municipal law before the national courts. The term 'directly applicable' in Article 189 in regard to regulations denotes that no act of national legislation is needed to give the regulation internal effect. This does not mean, however, that provisions of regulations are invariably 'complete and legally perfect' to such an extent that they can be applied and enforced in the national courts. Regulations frequently impose obligations on Member States for the implementation of which they possess a certain measure of discretion. This would seem to preclude the birth of a right enforceable by private individuals; though directly applicable, the regulations then could not have any direct effect for individuals. The Court of Justice does not always distinguish between direct applicability and direct effect in the sense of enforceability in the national courts. However, the distinction was clearly made in e.g. the Case 31/64 (*Prévoyance Sociale* v. *Bertholet*), [1965] ECR 81, where the court held Article 52 of Regulation No. 3 to be enforceable in the municipal courts but where it also suggested that it would not necessarily come to the same conclusion in respect of other provisions of the Regulation. The distinction is implicit in the formula frequently used by the Court that 'by virtue of Article 189 regulations are directly applicable and, consequently, may by their very nature have direct effect'. See *e.g.* Case 8/81 (*Becker*) p. 188.

See for Court decisions involving enforcement of provisions of regulations, Case 43/71, *Politi* v. *Italian Ministry of Finance*, [1973] ECR, 1049; Case 34/73, *Variola* v. *Italian Ministry of Finance*, [1973] ECR 990; Case 93/71, *Slaughtered Cow I*, p. 195; Case 67/75, *Tasca* [1976] ECR 308.

b. Decisions and directives

If the question whether a provision has direct effect is decided by the nature and contents of that provision and if it is irrelevant that formally it is only addressed to a Member State, would it then not be possible to attribute direct effect to provisions of *decisions* and *directives* which impose clear and unconditional obligations on the Member States? The matter was decided by the Court of Justice in the Case 9/70, *Grad*, Preliminary ruling of 6 October 1970, in respect of decisions, see p. 181 and in Case 33/70, *SACE* v. *Italian Ministry of Finance*, Preliminary ruling of 17 December 1970, 16 ECR 1970. p. 1213 (not reproduced), in respect of *directives*. These Decisions of 1970 were confirmed several times. See e.g. Case 41/74 (*Van Duyn*) p. 366 recitals 9–15, and Case 51/76 (*Tax Deduction*), p. 184.

The *Ratti Case* (below (3)) and the *Becker-Case* (below (4)) are concerned more specifically with situations where private individuals in proceedings before national courts rely on provisions of directives which have not been implemented by the Member State concerned. The *Marshall Case* (below (5)) *inter alia* gives a negative answer to the question whether directives which have not been properly implemented can have *horizontal effects*, *i.e.* can be relied upon by individuals against other individuals. Finally, the *Kolpinghuis Case* (below (6)) demonstrates that a Member State may not rely as against private individuals upon provisions of a directive in cases where that Member State has not ensured that the provisions in question have been timely implemented in its internal legal order.

3. Cases

(1) Grad Case

Grad v. *Finanzamt Traunstein*; Case 9/70; Preliminary ruling of 6 October 1970; [1970] ECR 838; [1971] CMLR 1.

Facts:

The EEC Council had issued directives on the harmonization of turnover taxes. The Member States were to issue national laws introducing a system of value added tax before 1 January 1972.

As from the date on which a Member State had introduced the required legislation it was no longer allowed to maintain or introduce any levies based on turnover tax on imports or exports between the Member States.

The Federal Republic introduced the required legislation on 1 January 1968. On 1 January 1969, it introduced a *Strassengüterverkehrsteuer*, a tax of 1 Pfennig per ton-kilometer for long distance transport on German roads.

Grad considered this tax to be contrary to the EEC Directive and refused to pay.

The German Court asked three preliminary questions:
1. Can individuals before national courts invoke the directive of the Council and the decisions by which it was provided that this directive would be applicable to transport?
2. Could the Federal Republic introduce new turnover taxes after it issued the national tax provided for in the directive, but before 1 January 1972?
3. Is the Strassengüterverkehrsteuer a turnover tax?

As to the first question the Commission (intervening in the case) made the following list of arguments pleading *against* direct applicability.
1. Under the terms of Article 189 of the EEC Treaty, decisions addressed to Member States are binding only for the States designated. They should therefore have only an indirect effect for the national citizen. Thus, the

citizen could derive direct rights and incur obligations only through an implementing act of national law. In support of this argument, one might also point to the fact that Treaty Article 189 attributes direct effect only to regulations.
2. With regard to secondary Community law, the Treaty clearly distinguishes between legal acts that are directly applicable – the regulations – and legal acts not having such character (directives and decisions addressed to Member States). This carefully established distinction would be negated if some provisions of a decision addressed to the Member States were given direct applicability. The result would be legal insecurity.
3. In certain sectors (such as agriculture, transport, and commercial policy), the Treaty leaves a choice of legal acts. In other sectors, the single permissible instrument is the directive (for example, in the right of establishment and services, and the harmonization of legislation). Thus one can conclude that the Member States did not wish to confer upon the Community any direct legislative powers in these sectors.
4. Finally, the Treaty does not require the publication of decisions. Thus, it is left more or less to chance or to the adroitness of the individual whether he can or cannot invoke provisions of Community law in the courts of his country that are favourable to him. This produces some inequality before the law because it cannot be assumed a priori that the judge is aware of legal acts that have not been published.

The Commission also submitted the following list of arguments pleading in *favour* of direct applicability.
1. According to decisions of the Court of Justice dealing with provisions of the Treaty that produce direct effects, the fact that the Member States are designated as addressees is not controlling. The only test is whether a provision is, by its nature, directly applicable. The considerations relied on by the Court with regard to provisions of the Treaty can be applied to the provisions of a decision addressed to Member States.
2. It is true that Treaty Article 189 gives only the regulation a direct effect in every Member State. However, the definition of a decision given in Article 189 does not exclude the possibility, under certain conditions, of giving this same effect to a decisions addressed to Member States. A distinction must be made between 'direct applicability' within the meaning of Treaty Article 189 and provisions designed to 'produce direct effects in the legal relations between the Member States and persons under their jurisdiction'. Within the meaning of Article 189, 'direct applicability' means that a positive act of internal law is not necessary to give validity to a given act of Community law. As to the determination of whether provisions are, within the meaning of the Court's interpretation, likely to produce 'direct effects' for persons, this involves – to the extent that there is a duty to act – a determination of whether, notwithstanding the absence of an internal implementing law, the person can derive direct rights.
3. The danger of legal uncertainty should not be exaggerated. Basically, problems can arise only if decisions require the Member States to act in a

certain way and if the deadline allowed expires without any action having been taken. The situation could be avoided only if the deadline given were long enough, and the Member States did everything they could to adopt the necessary implementing provisions within the time allowed. If we were to add, furthermore, that according to the Court of Justice the provisions involved must be clear and unconditional, it follows that the question of direct applicability should not arise except in a small number of decisions.
4. The fact that certain provisions contained in decisions addressed to the States admittedly have direct applicability does not mean that the system of legal acts of Community secondary law, as provided for in Treaty Article 189 is abandoned. The direct applicability of certain provisions – leaving the system of Treaty Article 189 intact – tends, on the contrary, to increase the legal protection of the personal rights of individuals.
5. It is customary, except in rare instances, for the Community institutions to publish in the Official Journal, for information purpose, the decisions addressed to Member States. The argument that the publication of decisions addressed to Member States is not mandatory thus carries little weight to the extent that the Community institutions go beyond the obligation to publish provided in Article 191 of the Treaty and generally also publish decisions addressed to the States.
6. Decisions of the Court of Justice appear to furnish reasons for rather than against the direct applicability of decisions. Thus in its judgment of February 18, 1970, in Case 38/69, the Court of Justice expressed itself as follows on the subject of the so-called acceleration decision of July 26, 1966 (Official Journal 1966, p. 2971): 'The decision, although in form addressed only to the Member States, is meant to have effects on the entire Common Market; it regulates the effectiveness in the Member States of provisions that are directly applicable which are contained in Article 9, paragraph 1, of the Treaty and, as far as relations with third countries are concerned in particular, in Council Regulation No 950/68/EEC of June 1968, relating to the common customs tariff' (Official Journal 1968, No L, 172, page 1). (1970) ECR, p. 58).

The Court held:

. . . . .

2. With its first question the Finanzgericht asks the Court for a decision as to whether Article 4 (2) of the Decision in conjunction with Article 1 of the Directive produces a direct effect on the legal relations between the Member States and individuals and whether these provisions create rights for individuals to which the national courts must give effect.
3. The question concerns the total effect of provisions contained in a decision

or a directive. According to Article 189 of the EEC Treaty a decision is binding in its entirety upon those whom it designates. Furthermore, according to this article a directive is binding, in respect of the aim to be achieved, on every Member State to which it is directed although it leaves the choice of forms and methods to the internal national authorities.
4. The German Government in its submission maintains that Article 189 by distinguishing between the effects of regulations on the one hand and of decisions and directives on the other hand thus precludes the possibility of decisions and directives producing the effects mentioned in the question; it claims that such effects are on the contrary reserved to regulations.
5. It is true that by Article 189 regulations are directly applicable and may therefore certainly produce direct effects by virtue of their nature as law. However, it does not follow from this that other categories of legal measures mentioned in that article could never produce similar effects. The provision that decisions are binding in their entirety on those to whom they are addressed especially enables the question to be put as to whether the obligation created by the decision can only be invoked by the organs of the Community as against the addressee or whether such a right in a given case is attributed to all those who have an interest in the fulfilment of this obligation. It would be incompatible with the binding effect attributed to decisions by Article 189 to exclude in principle the possibility that persons affected might invoke the obligation imposed by a decision.

. . . . .

Although the effects of a decision may be different from those of a provision contained in a regulation, this difference does not prevent the end-result, namely the right of the individual to invoke the measure in the courts, from being the same in a given case as that in the case of a directly applicable provision of a regulation.
6. Article 177, whereby the national courts are empowered to submit to the Court all questions regarding the validity and interpretation of all measures of the organs without distinction, also presupposes that individuals may invoke such measures in the national courts. Therefore, in each particular case, one must examine whether the provision in question, by its legal nature, background and wording, is capable of creating direct effects in the legal relationships between the addressee of the measure and third parties. . . .

(2) Tax deduction Case

Federation of Dutch Undertakings v. *Inspector of Customs and Excises*; Case

51/76; Preliminary ruling of 11 February 1977; [1977] ECR 113; [1977] 1 CMLR 413.

Facts:

The plaintiff in the main action contested a decision adopted by the Inspector of Customs and Excises which sought to limit the right to deduct turnover tax on certain objects acquired by the Federation and used by it as office supplies. Article 11 (1) of the Second Council Directive of April 1967 on the harmonization of legislation of Member States concerning turnover taxes (OJ English Special Edition 1967, p. 16) provides that a taxable person shall be authorized to deduct from the tax for which he is liable *i.a.* value-added tax invoiced to him in respect of goods supplied to him or in respect of services rendered to him. However, this rule is subject to exceptions. In particular, by virtue of Article 17, para 1 of the Directive, the Member States may exclude, during a certain transitional period, capital goods from the deduction system provided for in Article 11. In application of that relieving provision the Dutch VAT legislation provided that only 67% of the tax on goods intended to be used as *'business assets'* could be deducted. The plaintiff claimed that the latter expression has a wider meaning than the expression 'capital goods' used by the Directive. Therefore, the exception to the right to make a deduction had been extended too widely, with the result that the Federation had had to bear tax not authorized by the Directive. The Hoge Raad referred three questions to the Court of Justice, seeking to obtain clarification of the expression 'capital goods' and raising also, in its third question, the matter of the direct effect of Article 11 of the Directive. On the third question,

The Court held:

20. This (third) question raises the general problem of the legal nature of the provisions of a directive adopted under Article 189 of the Treaty.
21. On this, the Court has already said, most recently in its judgment of 4 December 1974 (in Case 41/71 [1974] ECR 1337 at p. 1348) that if, by virtue of the provisions of Article 189, regulations are directly applicable and, consequently, may by their very nature have direct effects, it does not follow from this that other categories of acts mentioned in that article can never have similar effects.
22. It would be incompatible with the binding effect attributed to a directive by Article 189 to exclude, in principle, the possibility that the obligation which it imposes may be invoked by those concerned.
23. In particular, where the Community authorities have, by directive, imposed on Member States the obligation to pursue a particular course of conduct, the useful effect of such an act would be weakened if individuals were prevented from relying on it before their national courts and if the

latter were prevented from taking it into consideration as an element of Community law.
24. This is especially so when the individual invokes a provision of a directive before a national court in order that the latter shall rule whether the competent national authorities, in exercising the choice which is left to them as to the form and the methods for implementing the directive, have kept within the limits as to their discretion set out in the directive.
25. Paragraph (1) of Article 11 of the Second Directive on value-added tax states in explicit and precise terms the principle of the deduction of sums invoiced as value-added tax in respect of goods supplied to the taxable person, in so far as those goods are used for the purposes of his undertaking.
26. That basic principle, however, is subject to certain derogations and exceptions which the Member States may determine by virtue of other provisions of the directive.
27. When the nature of the provisions concerned is taken into account, the fact of having or of not having exercised the power to make a derogation or an exception is a matter for the discretion of the legislative or administrative authorities of the Member States in question and cannot, therefore be subject to legal review on the basis of the provisions of the directive.
28. The position is the same if the matter in dispute depends on one of the provisions which, either in express terms, or through the indefinite nature of the concepts usd, leave the legislative or administrative authorities of the Member States a margin of discretion concerning the material contents of the exceptions or derogations authorized.
29. Conversely, it is the duty of the national court before which the directive is invoked to determine whether the disputed national measure falls outside the margin of the discretion of the Member States and cannot therefore be considered as a legitimate exception to or derogation from the principle of immediate deduction laid down by paragraph (1) of Article 11, and to take this into account in giving effect to the taxable person's claim.
30. Therefore the appropriate answer to the third question is that, in the case of goods purchased in 1972 and intended to be used for the purposes of the undertaking which do not belong to the category of capital goods within the meaning of Article 17 of the directive, it is the duty of the national court before which the rule as to immediate deduction set out in Article 11 of the Directive is invoked to take those facts into account in so far as a national implementing measure falls outside the limits of the margin of the discretion left to the Member States.

(3) Ratti Case

Publico Ministerio v. *Ratti*; Case 148/78; Preliminary ruling of 5 April 1979; [1979] ECR 1637; [1980] 1 CMLR 96.

Facts:

Ratti had affixed labels to certain dangerous substances in a manner which was in conformity with the provisions of a directive but which contravened the relevant Italian legislation. Italy had failed to implement the directive, which would have involved amending the internal legislation.

In the course of the ensuing criminal proceedings, the Italian court, finding that 'there was a manifest contradiction between the Community rules and internal Italian law', wondered 'which of the two sets of rules should take precedence in the case before the court' and referred to the Court the first question, asking as follows:
'Does Council Directive 73/173/EEc of 4 June 1973, in particular Article 8 thereof, constitute directly applicable legislation conferring upon individuals personal rights which the national courts must protect?'

The Court held:

. . . . .

18. This question raises the general problem of the legal nature of the provisions of a directive adopted under Article 189 of the Treaty.
19. In this regard the settled case-law of the Court, last affirmed by the judgment of 1 February 1977 in Case 51/76 (Nederlandse Ondernemingen) [1977] 1 ECR 126, lays down that, whilst under Article 189 regulations are directly applicable and, consequently, by their nature capable of producing direct effects, that does not mean that other categories of acts covered by that article can never produce similar effects.
20. It would be incompatible with the binding effect which Article 189 ascribes to directives to exclude on principle the possibility of the obligations imposed by them being relied on by persons concerned.
21. Particularly in cases in which the Community authorities have, by means of directive, placed Member States under a duty to adopt a certain course of action, the effectiveness of such an act would be weakened if persons were prevented from relying on it in legal proceedings and national courts prevented from taking it into consideration as an element of Community law.
22. Consequently a Member State which has not adopted the implementing measures required by the directive in the prescribed periods may not rely, as against individuals, on its own failure to perform the obligations which the directive entails.
23. It follows that a national court requested by a person who has complied with the provisions of a directive not to apply a national provision incompatible with the directive not incorporated into the internal legal order of

a defaulting Member State, must uphold that request if the obligation in question is unconditional and sufficiently precise.

24. Therefore the answer to the first question must be that after the expiration of the period fixed for the implementation of a directive a Member State may not apply its internal law – even if it is provided with penal sanctions – which has not yet been adapted in compliance with the directive, to a person who has complied with the requirements of the directive.

(4) Becker Case

Ursula Becker v. *Finanzamt Münster-Innenstadt*; Case 8/81; Preliminary ruling of 19 January 1982; [1982] ECR 69–71.

Facts:

The plaintiff, engaged in the business of a self-employed credit negotiator, applied for exemption from tax in respect of her transactions, claiming that Article 13B (d) 1 of the Sixth Council Directive 77/388/EEC of 17 May 1977 on the harmonization of the national VAT-laws (O.J. 1977, L145/1) compelled the Member States to exempt from VAT *inter alia* 'the granting and the negotiation of credit' and that this provision had been directly effective as of the date on which the relevant implementing provisions should have become operative (1 January 1979) and until the date on which the German measures of implementation came into force (1 January 1980). The Finanzgericht requested the Court of Justice to rule on the direct effect of the directive.

The Court held:

17. According to the third paragraph of Article 189 of the Treaty, 'a directive shall be binding, as to the result to be achieved, upon each Member State to which it is addressed, but shall leave to the national authorities the choice of form and methods.'
18. It is clear from that provision that States to which a directive is addressed are under an obligation to achieve a result, which must be fulfilled before the expiry of the period laid down by the directive itself.
19. It follows that wherever a directive is correctly implemented, its effects extend to individuals through the medium of the implementing measures adopted by the Member State concerned (judgment of 6 May 1980 in Case 102/79, *Commission* v. *Belgium* [1980] ECR 1473).
20. However, special problems arise where a Member State has failed to implement a directive correctly and, more particularly, where the provisions of the directive have not been implemented by the end of the period prescribed for that purpose.

21. It follows from well-established case-law of the Court and, most recently, from the judgment of 5 April 1979 in Case 148/78, *Pubblico Ministero* v. *Ratti* [1979] ECR 1629, that whilst under Article 189 regulations are directly applicalbe and, consequently, by their nature capable of producing direct effects, that does not mean that other categories of measures covered by that article can never produce similar effects.
22. It would be incompatible with the binding effect which Article 189 ascribes to directives to exclude in principle the possibility of the obligations imposed by them being relied on by persons concerned.
23. Particularly in cases in which the Community authorities have, by means of a directive, placed Member States under a duty to adopt a certain course of action, the effectiveness of such a measure would be diminished if persons were prevented from relying upon it in proceedings before a court and national courts were prevented from taking it into consideration as an element of Community law.
24. Consequently, a Member State which has not adopted the implementing measures required by the directive within the prescribed period may not plead, as against individuals, its own failure to perform the obligations which the directive entails.
25. Thus, wherever the provisions of a directive appear, as far as their subject-matter is concerned, to be unconditional and sufficiently precise, those provisions may, in the absence of implementing measures adopted within the prescribed period, be relied upon as against any national provision which is incompatible with the directive or in so far as the provisions define rights which individuals are able to assert against the State....

(5) Marshall Case

Marshall v. *Southampton and South East Hampshire Area Health Authority*: Case 152/84; Preliminary ruling of 26 February 1986, [1986] ECR 737.

Facts:

In accordance with its general retirement policy the respondent had dismissed the plaintiff. Some time after she reached the age at which social security pensions become payable in the UK for women (60 years) but long before she reached the retirement age applicable to male employees (65 years), she brought proceedings before the Industrial Tribunal and appealed from the latter's decision to the Employment Appeal Tribunal. When the Employment Tribunal denied her the right to rely on the principle of equality of treatment laid down in Directive 76/207 of 9 February 1986, OJ 1976, L39/40, she appealed against that decision to the Court of Appeal of England and Wales. That Court referred to the Court of Justice the following questions for a preliminary ruling:
(1) Whether the respondent's dismissal of the appellant after she had passed

her 60th birthday pursuant to the policy (followed by the respondent) and on the grounds only that she was a woman who had passed the normal retiring age applicable to women was an act of discrimination prohibited by the Equal Treatment Directive.

(2) If the answer to (1) above is in the affirmative, whether or not the Equal Treatment Directive can be relied upon by the appellant in the circumstances of the present case in national courts or tribunals notwithstanding the inconsistency (if any) between the directive and section 6(4) of the Sex Discrimination Act.'

The Court held:

The first question

38. The answer to the first question referred to the Court by the Court of Appeal must be that Article 5 (1) of Directive No 76/207 must be interpreted as meaning that a general policy concerning dismissal involving the dismissal of a woman solely because she has attained the qualifying age for a State pension, which age is different under national legislation for men and for women, constitutes discrimination on grounds of sex, contrary to that directive.

The second question

39. Since the first question has been answered in the affirmative, it is necessary to consider whether Article 5 (1) of Directive No 76/207 may be relied upon by an individual before national courts and tribunals.
40. The appellant and the Commission consider that that question must be answered in the affirmative. They contend in particular, with regard to Articles 2 (1) and 5 (1) of Directive No 76/207, that those provisions are sufficiently clear to enable national courts to apply them without legislative intervention by the Member States, at least so far as overt discrimination is concerned.
41. In support of that view, the appellant points out that directives are capable of conferring rights on individuals which may be relied upon directly before the courts of the Member States; national courts are obliged by virtue of the binding nature of a directive, in conjunction with Article 5 of the EEC Treaty, to give effect to the provisions of directives where possible, in particular when construing or applying relevant provisions of national law (judgment of 10 April 1984 in Case 14/83 *von Colson and Kamann* v. *Land Nordrhein-Westfalen* [1984] ECR 181). Where there is any inconsistency between national law and Community law which cannot be removed by means of such a construction, the appellant submits that a national court is obliged to declare that the provision of national law which is inconsistent with the directive is inapplicable.

42. The Commission is of the opinion that the provisions of Article 5 (1) of Directive No 76/207 are sufficiently clear and unconditional to be relied upon before a national court. They may therefore be set up against section 6 (4) of the Sex Discrimination Act, which, according to the decisions of the Court of Appeal, has been extended to the question of compulsory retirement and has therefore become ineffective to prevent dismissals based upon the difference in retirement ages for men and for women.
43. The respondent and the United Kingdom propose, conversely, that the second question should be answered in the negative. They admit that a directive may, in certain specific circumstances, have direct effect as against a Member State in so far as the latter may not rely on its failure to perform its obligations under the directive. However, they maintain that a directive can never impose obligations directly on individuals and that it can only have direct effect against a Member State *qua* public authority and not against a Member State *qua* employer. As an employer a State is no different from a private employer. It would not therefore be proper to put persons employed by the State in a better position than those who are employed by a private employer.
44. With regard to the legal position of the respondent's employees the United Kingdom states that they are in the same position as the employees of a private employer. Although according to United Kingdom constitutional law the health authorities, created by the National Health Service Act 1977, as amended by the Health Services Act 1980 and other legislation, are Crown bodies and their employees are Crown servants, nevertheless the administration of the National Health Service by the health authorities is regarded as being separate from the Government's central administration and its employees are not regarded as civil servants.
45. Finally, both the respondent and the United Kingdom take the view that the provisions of Directive No 76/207 are neither unconditional nor sufficiently clear and precise to give rise to direct effect. The directive provides for a number of possible exceptions, the details of which are to be laid down by the Member States. Furtheremore, the wording of Article 5 is quite imprecise and requires the adoption of measures for its implementation.
46. It is necessary to recall that, according to a long line of decisions of the Court (in particular its judgment of 19 January 1982 in Case 8/81 *Becker v. Finanzamt Münster-Innenstadt* [1982] ECR 53), wherever the provisions of a directive appear, as far as their subject-matter is concerned, to be unconditional and sufficiently precise, those provisions may be replied upon by an individual against the State where that State fails to implement the directive in national law by the end of the period prescribed or where it fails to implement the directive correctly.
47. That view is based on the consideration that it would be incompatible with the binding nature which Article 189 confers on the directive to hold as a matter of principle that the obligation imposed thereby cannot be relied on by those concerned. From that the Court deduced that a

Member State which has not adopted the implementing measures required by the directive within the prescribed period may not plead, as against individuals, its own failure to perform the obligations which the directive entails.
48. With regard to the argument that a directive may not be relied upon against an individual, it must be emphasized that according to Article 189 of the EEC Treaty the binding nature of a directive, which constitutes the basis for the possibility of relying on the directive before a national court, exists only in relation to 'each Member State to which it is addressed'. It follows that a directive may not of itself impose obligations on an individual and that a provision of a directive may not be relied upon as such against such a person. It must therefore be examined whether, in this case, the respondent must be regarded as having acted as an individual.
49. In that respect it must be pointed out that where a person involved in legal proceedings is able to rely on a directive as against the State he may do so regardless of the capacity in which the latter is acting, whether employer or public authority. In either case it is necessary to prevent the State from taking advantage of its own failure to comply with Community law.
50. It is for the national court to apply those considerations to the circumstances of each case; the Court of Appeal has, however, stated in the order for reference that the respondent, Southampton and South West Hampshire Area Health Authority (Teaching), is a public authority.
51. The argument submitted by the United Kingdom that the possibility of relying on provisions of the directive against the respondent *qua* organ of the State would give rise to an arbitrary and unfair distinction between the rights of State employees and those of private employees does not justify any other conclusion. Such a distinction may easily be avoided if the Member State concerned has correctly implemented the directive in national law.
52. Finally, with regard to the question whether the provision contained in Article 5 (1) of Directive No 76/207, which implements the principle of equality of treatment set out in Article 2 (1) of the directive, may be considered, as far as its contents are concerned, to be unconditional and sufficiently precise to be relied upon by an individual as against the State, it must be stated that the provision, taken by itself, prohibits any discrimination on grounds of sex with regard to working conditions, including the conditions governing dismissal, in a general manner and in unequivocal terms. The provision is therefore sufficiently precise to be relied on by an individual and to be applied by the national courts.
53. It is necessary to consider next whether the prohibition of discrimination laid down by the directive may be regarded as unconditional, in the light of the exceptions contained therein and of the fact that according to Article 5 (2) thereof the Member States are to take the measures necessary to ensure the application of the principle of equality of treatment in the context of national law.

54. With regard, in the first place, to the reservation contained in Article 1 (2) of Directive No 76/207 concerning the application of the principle of equality of treatment in matters of social security, it must be observed that, although the reservation limits the scope of the directive *ratione materiae*, it does not lay down any condition on the application of that principle in its field of operation and in particular in relation to Article 5 of the directive. Similarly, the exceptions to Directive No 76/207 provided for in Article 2 thereof are not relevant to this case.

55. It follows that Article 5 of Directive No 76/207 does not confer on the Member States the right to limit the application of the principle of equality of treatment in its field of operation or to subject it to conditions and that that provision is sufficiently precise and unconditional to be capable of being relied upon by an individual before a national court in order to avoid the application of any national provision which does not conform to Article 5 (1).

56. Consequently, the answer to the second question must be that Article 5 (1) of Council Directive No 76/207 of 9 February 1976, which probhibits any discrimination on grounds of sex with regard to working conditions, including the conditions governing dismissal, may be relied upon as against a State authority acting in its capacity as employer in order to avoid the application of any national provision which does not conform to Article 5 (1).

(6) Kolpinghuis Case

Officier van Justitie v. *Kolpinghuis*; Case 80/86, Preliminary ruling of 8 october 1987 (not yet published).

Facts:

Criminal proceedings were brought against Kolpinghuis, a restaurant owner, who was charged with having held in stock for the purposes of sale and supply a beverage which he called 'mineral water' whereas it was in fact composed of tap-water and carbonic acid. What Kolpinghuis was in fact accused of was a breach of Article 2 of an ordinance of the City of Nijmegen which prohibited the sale of foodstuffs which were 'unsuitable' for human consumption. The public prosecutor argued that the mixture of tap-water and carbonic acid produced an 'unsuitable' beverage within the meaning of the City ordinance and Council Directive 80/777/EEC of 17 July 1980 (OJ 1980, 229/1) which provides that the Member States are to take the measures necessary to ensure that only waters extracted from the ground of a Member State may be marketed as 'mineral water'. The Dutch legislation implementing the directive was not passed until 8 August 1985 whereas the facts alleged against the accused took place on 7 August 1984. The District Court Arnhem referred to the Court of Justice four questions relating to the effect of a directive which has not been implemented by a Member State.

The Court held*:

11. The third question seeks to ascertain the extent to which a national court should or may take a directive into account as a factor in the interpretations of a rule of the national law applicable to the case before him.
12. As the Court emphasized in its judgment of 10 April 1984 (Case 14/83), *Colson and Kamann*, [1984] ECR 1891, the Member States' obligation arising from a directive to achieve the result envisaged by the directive and their duty under Article 5 of the Treaty to take all appropriate measures, whether general or particular, to ensure the fulfilment of that obligation, is binding on all the authorities of Member States including, for matters within their jurisdiction, the courts. It follows that, in applying the national law and in particular the provisions of a national law specifically introduced in order to implement the directive, national courts are required to interpret their national law in the light of the wording and the purpose of the directive in order to achieve the result referred to in the third paragraph of Article 189.
13. However, this obligation (...) is limited by the general principles of law which are an integral part of Community law, and in particular by the principle of legal certainty and the prohibition of retroactive effect. In its judgment of 11 June 1987 (Case 14/86, *Public Prosecutor* v. *X*, not yet published) the Court therefore has stated that a directive cannot, of itself and independently of a law adopted by a Member State in order to implement the directive, have the effect of determining or increasing the criminal liability of those persons who infringe its provisions.
14. The answer to the third question must therefore be that in applying its national legislation, a court of a Member State is bound to interpret it in the light of the letter and purpose of the directive, in order to attain the result required by the third paragraph of Article 189 of the Treaty; but a directive cannot, in itself and independently of a law adopted in order to implement the directive, determine or increase the criminal liability of persons who infringe its provisions.

* Unofficial translation; English text not yet available.

4. *Direct effect of international agreements*

International agreements entered into by the Community are capable of direct effect even if the other Parties to such agreements are not prepared to grant the same effect to these agreements within their own legal order. As is shown by Case 104/81, *Kupferberg*, (see p. 677) the question whether the provisions of an agreement with a third State have direct effect should be decided by having regard to the spirit, the general scheme and the objectives of the Agreement. So far the Court of Justice has held that the general scheme of the GATT, being characterised by possibilities of derogation and flexibility, is such that no rights have been conferred on citizens of the Community which they can invoke before national courts. Thus, as a matter of Community law, the provisions of the GATT may not be invoked before a national court to challenge the validity of Community legislation. See Joined Cases 21–24/72, *International Fruit Company Case III*, see p. 84 and 682. See for further cases concerning the relationship between Community law and international agreements, below, Chapter Six.

C. SOME IMPLICATIONS OF DIRECT EFFECT

1. *Cases*

(1) Slaughtered Cow Case I

Orsolina Leonesio v. *Italian Ministry of Agriculture and Forestry*; Case 93/71; Preliminary ruling of 17 May 1972; [1972] ECR 293; [1973] CMLR 343.

Facts:

In Regulation No 1975/69 of 27 June 1968, the Council provided that farmers having at least two dairy-cows, qualified for a slaughter-premium, half of which would be paid by the European Agricultural Guidance and Guarantee Fund.

In a further Regulation, No 2195/69, the Commission established that the premium would be paid within two months of the delivery of the certificate of slaughter. The Member States were empowered to issue further rules.

The Italian Government issued directives but decided that their execution should be postponed until the necessary budgetary provisions had been adopted.

During 1970, Mrs. Leonesio slaughtered five dairy-cows and claimed a premium of 625.000 lire.

The Pretore requested a preliminary ruling on the question whether the Regulations No 1975/69 and No 2195/69 were directly applicable in the Italian legal order and, if so, whether they created a claim which individuals may enforce against the State and whether national legislation may postpone payment of that claim.

The Court held:

. . . . .

3. According to Article 189 (2) of the Treaty regulations have 'general application' and are 'directly applicable' in every State. They therefore have direct effect on account of their nature and of the function in the system of Community sources of law and as such can give rise to private rights which national courts are bound to safeguard. The present claims which can be enforced against the State arise when the conditions provided for in a regulation are fulfilled without a possibility to subject their execution at the national level to provisions regarding application other than those which may be laid down in the regulation itself. The questions put must be answered in the light of these considerations.

. . . . .

9. The Italian Government pleads that the regulations in question do not give rise to a right of payment of the premium so long as the national legislature has not granted the necessary credits for this.
10. According to Article 5, para (1) of the Treaty Member States shall take all appropriate measures, whether general or particular, to ensure fulfilment of the obligations arising out of this Treaty or resulting from action taken by the institutions of the Community. If the objective of the Italian Republic were to be recognized, the farmers of that State would be placed in a less favourable position than those in the other states; this would involve disregard of the basic rule that regulations must be uniformly applied throughout the whole Community. Furthermore, the Regulations No 1975/69 and 2195/69, enumerating exhaustively the conditions on which the creations of the individual rights concerned depend, do not mention considerations of a budgetary character.

    In order to have the same force for the nationals of *all* Member States Community regulations are integrated in the legal system applicable in the national territory, which must permit the direct operation provided for in Article 189 so that private individuals can invoke them without national provisions or procedures being used against them; the budgetary provisions of a Member State can neither stand in the way of the direct application of a Community provision nor, consequently, in the way of the realization of individual rights which are conferred on private individuals by such a provision.

(2) Slaughtered Cow Case II

Commission of the EC v. *Italian Republic*; Case 39/72; Decision of 7 February 1973; [1973] ECR 113.

Facts:

Regulations No 1975/69 and No 2195/69 introducing a system of premiums to encourage the slaughter of dairy cows and to dissuade farmers from marketing milk products were not effectively carried out by Italy (see First Slaughtered Cow Case, above). The Commission complained *inter alia* of the dilatory implementation of the Regulations and of the legal methods used by Italy to give effect to the system introduced by Regulations.

The Court held:

. . . . .

1. With regard to the premiums for slaughtering:

14. The Regulations of the Council and of the Commission have provided precise time limits for the carrying into effect of the system of premiums for slaughtering.

    The efficacy of the agreed measures depended upon the observation of these time limits, since the measures could only attain their object completely if they were carried out simultaneously in all the Member States at the time determined in consequence of the economic policy the Council was pursuing.

    Over and above this, as has been stated by the Court in its judgment of 17 May 1972, (Case 93/71 *Orsolina Leonesio* v. *Ministry of Agriculture of the Italian Republic*, request for a preliminary ruling made by the Pretore di Lonato), Regulations Nos 1975/69 and 2195/69 conferred on farmers a right to payment of the premium as from the time when all the conditions provided by the Regulations were fulfilled.

    It consequently appears that the delay on the part of the Italian Republic in performing the obligations imposed on it by the introduction of the system of premiums for slaughtering constituted by itself a default in its obligations.

15. Apart from this delay in implementation, the Commission has raised certain complaints with regard to the manner in which the Italian Government has given effect to the provisions of the system in question.

    This criticism concerns more especially the fact that the provisions of the Community have been distorted by the procedure giving effect to them as adopted by the Italian authorities and that these same authorities have not taken into consideration an extension of the time allowed for the slaughter.

16. Whilst the Italian Law No 935 is limited to making the necessary financial arrangements for carrying out the system of premiums for slaughtering and to enabling the Government to institute the appropriate administrative measures for giving effect to the Community Regulations, the decree of 22 March 1972 provides, in the first Article, that the provisions of the Regulations 'are deemed to be included in the present decree'.

   In substance the same decree, apart from some procedural provisions of a national character, confines itself to reproducing the provisions of the Community Regulations.

17. By following this procedure, the Italian Government has brought into doubt the legal nature of the applicable provisions and the date of their coming into force.

   According to the terms of Article 189 and 191 of the Treaty, Regulations are, as such, directly applicable in all Member States and come into force solely by virtue of their publication in the Official Journal of the Communities, as from the date specified in them, or in the absence thereof, as from the date provided in the Treaty.

   Consequently, all methods of implementation are contrary to the Treaty which would have the result of creating an obstacle to the direct effect of Community Regulations and jeopardizing their simultaneous and uniform application in the whole of the Community.

18. Moreover, the implementing measures provided both by Law No 935 and by the decree of 22 March 1972 do not take into account the extension of the time allowed for slaughter by Regulation No. 580/70, so that Italian farmers have been misled as regards the extension of the time allowed for the slaughter of cows which have calved between 1 April and 30 May 1970.

   The default of the Italian Republic has thus been established by reason not only of the delay in putting the system into effect but also the manner of giving effect to it provided by the decree.

(3) Comet Case

Comet v. *Produktschap voor Siergewassen* (Ornamental Plant Authority) Case 45/76, Preliminary ruling of 16 December 1976; [1976] ECR 2052.

Facts:

Before the Dutch *College van Beroep voor het Bedrijfsleven*, the question arose whether directly applicable provisions of the Treaty require the Member States to grant private individuals an independent right of action which is unaffected by limitations known in the national laws of procedure relating e.g. to the expiry of periods of limitations.

The Court held:

. . . . .

6. There can, therefore, be no doubt that the levies imposed on the plaintiff in the main action ... were in breach of the prohibition in Article 16 of the Treaty.

. . . . .

11. The prohibition laid down in Article 16 of the Treaty and that contained in Article 10 of Regulation No 234/68 have direct effect and confer on individuals rights which the national courts must protect.
12. Thus, in application of the principle of co-operation laid down in Article 5 of the Treaty, the national courts are entrusted with ensuring the legal protection conferred on individuals by the direct effect of the provisions of Community law.
13. Consequently, in the absence of any relevant Community rules, it is for the national legal order of each Member State to designate the competent courts and to lay down the procedural rules for proceedings designed to ensure the protection of the rights which individuals acquire through the direct effect of Community law, provided that such rules are not less favourable than those governing the same right of action on an internal matter.
14. Articles 100 to 102 and 235 of the Treaty enable the appropriate steps to be taken, as necessary, to eliminate differences between the provisions laid down in such matters by law, regulation or administrative action in Member States if these differences are found to be such as to cause distortion or to affect the functioning of the Common Market.
15. In default of such harmonization measures, the rights conferred by Community law must be exercised before the national courts in accordance with the rules of procedure laid down by national law.
16. The position would be different only if those rules and time-limits made it impossible in practice to exercise rights which the national courts have a duty to protect.
17. This does not apply to the fixing of a reasonable period of limitation within which an action must be brought.
18. The fixing, as regards fiscal proceedings, of such a period is in fact an

application of a fundamental principle of legal certainty which protects both the authority concerned and the party from whom payment is claimed.
19. The answer must therefore be that, in the case of a litigant who is challenging before the national courts a decision of a national body for incompatibility with Community law, that law, in its present state, does not prevent the expiry of the period within which proceedings must be brought under national law from being raised against him, provided that the procedural rules applicable to this case are not less favourable than those relating to the same right of action on a domestic matter.

Note:

See for other cases in which the Court repeated and elaborated the dual criterion put forward in the *Comet Case* (no impossibility in practice to exercise directly enforcable Community provisions, no national procedural rules less favourable for the enforcement of Community rights than for rights arising under domestic rules) *e.g.* Case 33/76, *Rewe I*, [1976] ECR 1997, p. 246; Case 158/80, *Rewe II*, [1980] ECR 1807, Case 61/79, *Denkavit Italiana*, [1980] ECR 1205; Case 130/79, *Express Dairy Foods*, [1980] ECR 1882; Case 199/82, *San Giorgio*, [1983] ECR 3595; Case 265/78, *Ferwerda*, [1980] ECR 617.

(4) Simmenthal Case II

Italian Minister for Finance v. *Simmenthal S.p.A.*; Case 106/77; Preliminary ruling of 9 March 1978; [1978] ECR 629; [1978] 3 CMLR 263.

Facts:

The Simmenthal Company had brought an action before the Pretore of Susa for repayment of certain veterinary and public health fees levied on imports of beef and veal. During these proceedings an application was made for a preliminary ruling (Case 35/76, *Simmenthal Case I*, [1976] ECR 1871). Having regard to the answers given by the Court of Justice in that judgment, the Pretore held that the levying of the fees in question was incompatible within the provisions of Community law and ordered the Italian Finance Administration to repay the fees unlawfully charged. The fiscal authorities appealed against this order. They pointed out that the basis for charging fees under Italian law was to be found in a law of 30 December 1970. The issue before the Pretore therefore involved a conflict between certain directly applicable provisions of Community law and subsequent national law. According to recently decided cases of the Italian Constitutional Court (see the

ICIC-Case, below p. 225), ordinary courts have no power to discard domestic provisions which are incompatible with Community law. On the contrary, as long as the legislature does not amend the national provisions, the national courts are required to bring the matter before the Constitutional Court which may then declare that the national law is unconstitutional under Article 11 of the Constitution.

In view of these arguments the Pretore requested the Court of Justice to give a preliminary ruling on i.a. the following question: (a) Since, in accordance with Article 189 of the EEC Treaty and the established case-law of the Court of Justice of the European Communities, directly applicable Community provisions must, notwithstanding any internal rule or practice whatsoever of the Member States, have full, complete and uniform effect in their legal system in order to protect subjective legal rights created in favour of individuals, is the scope of the said provisions to be interpreted to the effect that any subsequent national measures which conflict with those provisions must be forthwith disregarded without waiting until those measures have been eliminated by action on the part of the national legislature concerned (repeal) or of other constitutional authorities (declaration that they are unconstitutional) especially, in the case of the latter alternative, where, since the national law continues to be fully effective pending such declaration, it is impossible to apply the Community provisions and, in consequence, to ensure that they are fully, completely and uniformly applied and to protect the legal rights created in favour of individuals?

The Court held:

. . . . .

13. The main purpose of the first question is to ascertain what consequences flow from the direct applicability of a provision of Community law in the event of incompatibility with a subsequent legislative provision of a Member State.
14. Direct applicability in such circumstances means that rules of Community law must be fully and uniformly applied in all the Member States from the date of their entry into force and for so long as they continue in force.
15. These provisions are therefore a direct source of rights and duties for all those affected thereby, whether Member States or individuals who are parties to legal relationships under Community law.
16. This consequence also concerns any national court whose task it is as an organ of a Member State to protect, in a case within its jurisdiction, the rights conferred upon individuals by Community law.
17. Furthermore, in accordance with the principle of the precedence of Community law, the relationship between provisions of the Treaty and

directly applicable measures of the institutions on the one hand and the national law of the Member States on the other is such that those provisions and measures not only by their entry into force render automatically inapplicable any conflicting provision of current national law but – in so far as they are an integral part of, and take precedence in, the legal order applicable in the territory of each of the Member States – also preclude the valid adoption of new legislative measures to the extent to which they would be incompatible with Community provisions.
18. Indeed any recognition that national legislative measures which encroach upon the field within which the Community exercises its legislative power or which are otherwise incompatible with the provisions of Community law had any legal effect would amount to a corresponding denial of the effectiveness of obligations undertaken unconditionally and irrevocably by Member States pursuant to the Treaty and would thus imperil the very foundations of the Community.
19. The same conclusion emerges from the structure of Article 177 of the Treaty which provides that any court or tribunal of a Member State is entitled to make a reference to the Court whenever it considers that a preliminary ruling on a question of interpretation or validity relating to Community law is necessary to enable it to give judgment.
20. The effectiveness of that provision would be impaired if the national court were prevented from forthwith applying Community law in accordance with the decision or the case-law of the Court.
21. It follows from the foregoing that every national court must, in a case within its jurisdiction, apply Community law in its entirety and protect rights which the latter confers on individuals and must accordingly set aside any provision of national law which may conflict with it, whether prior or subsequent to the Community rule.
22. Accordingly any provision of a national legal system and any legislative, administrative or judicial practice which might impair the effectiveness of Community law by witholding from the national court having jurisdiction to apply such law the power to do everything necessary at the moment of its application to set aside national legislative provisions which might prevent Community rules from having full force and effect are incompatible with those requirements which are the very essence of Community law.
23. This would be the case in the event of a conflict between a provision of Community law and a subsequent national law if the solution of the conflict were to be reserved for an authority with a discretion of its own, other than the court called upon to apply Community law, even if such an impediment to the full effectiveness of Community law were only temporary.
24. The first question should therefore be answered to the effect that a national court which is called upon within the limits of its jurisdiction, to apply provisions of Community law is under a duty to give full effect to those provisions, if necessary refusing of its own motion to apply any con-

flicting provision of national legislation, even if adopted subsequently, and it is not necessary for the court to request or await the prior setting aside of such provision by legislative or other constitutional means.

Note:

In a Judgment of 8 June 1984 (*Granital Case*, see p. 226) the Italian Constitutional Court followed the indications given by the Court of Justice in the *Simmenthal II* Decision. It removed all obstacles which up till then had prevented Italian Courts from discarding national provisions if these proved to be inconsistent with directly applicable rules of Community law.

IV. Conflicts between legal systems: the supremacy question – national constitutions and the attitude of municipal courts

Together with direct applicability the supremacy of Community law over national law is one of the key concepts of the Community. Without it the Community legal order could hardly function effectively.

On numerous occasions the Court has confirmed the supremacy of Community law. In cases such as *Costa–ENEL*, *Walt Wilhelm Case*, (see p. 161, 167), the primacy of Community law was asserted explicitly. In cases where provisions of Community law were declared to be directly applicable the supremacy question was decided implicitly, supremacy being inherent in any provision directly applicable.

The absolute and unconditional supremacy of Community law does not entail an absolute effect within the national legal order in the sense that it would ipso jure repeal domestic law inconsistent with provisions of Community law. The Court of Justice cannot purport to apply Community law in the Member States. It can only declare that it is applicable and their courts must follow. (*Cf.* the *Salgoil Case*, (see p. 299 and *Lück-Hauptzollamt Köln* (Case 34/67, [1968] ECR 245).

The most important cases on supremacy in general are the *Costa-ENEL Case* (p. 161, the *Walt Wilhelm Case* (p. 167), the *Handelsgesellschaft Case* (p. 82), the *Art Treasures Case II* (p. 140), the *Politi Case* [1973] ECR 1049), and the *Simmenthal Case II* (p. 200).

A. INTRODUCTION

'... Seeking to recognize the supremacy of Community law the courts encounter obstacles and difficulties originating in the national legal order within which they operate. They apply Community law within the context of their respective constitutional structure and practice influenced and formed by principles, legal thoughts and tradition which differ from one Member State to another. To a certain extent these difficulties have preconditioned the various attitudes of municipal courts toward Community law and its relation to municipal law. They may also explain the hesistancy or even resistance of municipal courts to accept the supremacy of Community law. Particularly in the early years of the operation of the Community it is hardly surprising that municipal courts viewed this relation through biased glasses, coloured by their traditional constitutional experience and practice. This understandable position, however much it may be regretted, may help to explain the different impacts the Court's case law has had on municipal courts, and their divergent case law. A few selected examples may illustrate the national obstacles to the supremacy of Community law.

For evident reasons municipal courts are inclined to apply constitutional provisions governing the relation of municipal law to traditional treaties. If a constitution recognizes the higher legal status of international treaties, as compared with municipal law (*e.g.* French Constitution Article 55) or places them even above the Constitution (Dutch Constitution, Article 94) the courts may be more favourable to the supremacy of Community law – even though on misleading and inadequate grounds. This is, however, not more than an explanation as the reserved attitude of the French *Conseil d'Etat* towards Article 55 of the Constitution demonstrates.

The attitude of municipal courts is also influenced by the nature of the procedure required for introducing an international treaty in the municipal legal order. If this requires its ratification in the form of a law, it is likely that a municipal court will view an international treaty to have the force of an ordinary law only – thus precluding *a priori* any supremacy of Community law.

A strict respect for the principle of separation of powers delimiting the judicial and legislative function, may also restrain municipal courts from recognizing the supremacy of Community law. Within the framework of such a legal system courts apply municipal law without having any right to question its constitutionality. On the other hand, in a legal system with a constitutional review the will of the legislator is not sacrosanct. Under such a system municipal courts are aware that a law may be declared unconstitutional and the intent of the legislator, as reflected in the law, disregarded. This may make it easier for municipal courts to set aside the application of a law contrary to Community law. These courts may not feel restrained to disregard such a subsequent law as would, for example, the French Conseil d'Etat, rigidly adhering to the principle of separation of power, leaving the decision as to its compatibility with an international treaty to the legislator. For the *Conseil d'Etat* to rule on such a conflict would be an infringement of the prerogatives of the legislator. Under the French legal system, only the executive may interpret public international treaties. Such an interpretation may already implicitly predetermine the solution of the conflict between an international treaty and a municipal law. This practice may not be particularly conducive for French courts to develop a judicial policy ensuring the supremacy of international treaties. This may in turn have some effect on the attitude of French courts toward Community law.

The barriers and conditions which undoubtedly influence municipal courts must be kept in mind when examining national case law concerning the supremacy of Community law. A clash of traditional views with the Court's case law has been bound to occur in view of the novel legal nature of the Community. And yet the critical examination of the national case law reflects a gradual, sometimes slow, but nevertheless definite impact of the Court's case law. The reluctance and resistance of municipal courts are gradually making room to an acceptance of the progressive case law of the courts. (Bebr, 'How Supreme is Community Law in the National Court?', [1974], CMLRev. p. 3 *et seq.*)

B. Constitutions of the original Member States containing an explicit recognition of the supremacy of Treaty law

1. The Netherlands

Constitution Article 91
'1. The Kingdom shall not be bound by treaties, nor shall such treaties be denounced without the prior approval of the States General. The cases in which approval is not required shall be specified by Act of Parliament.
2. The manner in which approval shall be granted shall be laid down by Act of Parliament, which may provide for the possibility of tacit approval.
3. Any provisions of a treaty that conflict with the Constitution or which lead to conflicts with it may be approved by the Chambers of the States General only if at least two-thirds of the votes cast are in favour.'

Constitution Article 92
'Legislative, executive and judicial powers may be conferred on international institutions by or pursuant to a treaty, subject, where necessary, to the provisions of Article 91 paragraph 3.'

Constitution Article 93
'Provisions of treaties and of resolutions by international institutions, which may be binding on all persons by virtue of their contents shall become binding after they have been published.'

Constitution Article 94
'Statutory regulations in force within the Kingdom shall not be applicable if such application is in conflict with provisions of treaties that are binding on all persons or of resolutions by international institutions.'

2. France

a. Introduction

Constitution Article 54
'If the Constitutional Council, the matter having been referred to it by the President of the Republic, by the Premier, or by the President of one or the other assembly, shall declare that an international commitment contains a clause contrary to the Constitution, the authorization to ratify or approve this commitment may be given only after amendment of the Constitution.'

Constitution Article 55
'Treaties or agreements duly ratified or approved shall, upon their publication have an authority superior to that of laws, subject, for each agreement or treaty, to its application by the other party.'

The *Conseil Constitutionnel* is the only judicial body in France entrusted with the task of ensuring preventive control of the constitutionality of laws and treaties. It has refused to extend its jurisdiction to questions concerning the compatibility of a national law with a treaty. In a judgment of 5 January 1975 (*Dalloz* 1975, Jurispr. p. 528) the *Conseil Constitutionnel* held that a law which violates a treaty is not for that reason infringing upon the Constitution. This suggests that it is up to the judicial and administrative courts to solve conflicts between treaties and national laws. However, although French courts could base themselves on Article 55 of the Constitution in order to solve such conflicts and to uphold the treaties against inconsistent subsequent national legislation, they have shown themselves reluctant to choose this approach. The reason for this attitude is probably that the courts traditionally have not been entitled to exercise constitutional review over legislative acts, the legislature being regarded as the final judge of the conformity of national law with international agreements. The courts therefore had no right to enforce the supremacy of the Constitution against a subsequent law. By analogy it was doubtful whether they would enforce the primacy of Community law against subsequent domestic law. The *Semoules Case* (*Conseil d'Etat*, decision of 1 March 1968) illustrated this lack of temerity but the *Ramel Case* and the *Vabres Case* indicate a change of attitude on the part of the *Cour de Cassation*.

b. Cases

(1) French Ramel Case

Administration des Contributions indirectes et Comité Interprofessionel des vins doux naturels v. *P. Ramel*; *Cour de Cassation* (*Chambre Criminelle*) (Court of Cassation); Decision of 22 October 1970; *GP*, 9–11 December

1970, No. 334–336; RTDE 1970, p. 750; JT 1971, pp. 25–26; CDE 1971, p. 256; Rec. D. 1971, pp. 221–224; JCP 1971 II, p. 16671; [1971] CMLR pp. 315–324.

Facts:

The defendant, a French merchant and importer of wines, had imported a certain quantity of Italian wines in April and May 1966. Upon examination by the French tax authorities it appeared that these wines did not conform to the requirements of the internal French legislation on the matter, which fixed a certain alcohol – and sugar percentage for tax purposes (Article 4 of the Wine Code).

When prosecuted by the plaintiff for fraudulently selling wine of an excessive alcohol – and sugar percentage, the *Tribunal Correctionnel* at Bourg en Bresse declared the defendant Ramel not guilty. This judgment was confirmed by the *Cour d'Appel* of Lyon. The plaintiff asked for a review in cassation.

Before the *Cour de Cassation* the defendant objected that the French legislation was inapplicable as being contrary to the provisions of the Common Market Organization for Wines of the EEC Regulation No. 24 and a Council Decision implementing the Regulation, both of 4 April 1962. According to Article 2 of the Decision, France and Italy were to admit a quota of 150,000 hectolitres of quality wines to all Member States.

Article 3 adds that wines from Italy are admitted within this quota provided that they are accompanied by a valid certificate of origin. It was not disputed that the wines imported by Ramel satisfied the Italian legal requirements.

The Cour de Cassation had to determine whether the municipal or the Community law provisions had to be applied.

The Cour de Cassation held:

. . . . .

'Under Article 55 of the Constitution of 4 October 1958, treaties and agreements regularly ratified and approved have, as soon as they are published, a higher authority than municipal laws provided that the other party to the agreement or treaty also implements them.

Furthermore, under Article 520 et seq. of the General Taxation Code, and Article 2 of Decree 1001 of 4 October 1963, imported alcohol, wine, perry and mead are subject to all the provisions laid down by municipal law and must therefore comply with French regulations.

In view of these laws and regulations, it was in strict pursuance of Article 55 of the Constitution that the Appeal Judges considered that they could not apply to imported wines the provisions of Article 4 of the Wine Code, or inflict on Ramel the penalties laid down by Article 3 of the Law of 1 August, 1905 II and Articles 443, 444 and 445 of the General Taxation Code. The reason was that the principle of territoriality of taxation laws could not overrule international law whose authority must prevail by virtue of constitutional law.

The wines involved in the present case were imported from Italy within the quota opened by the decision of 4 April 1962 and of Regulation 24, which decision and regulation are published international instruments having acquired the force of international treaties'.

(2) French Vabres Case

Director General of Customs and Indirect Taxes v. *Société des Cafés Jaques Vabres and SARL J. Weigl Cie*; *Cour de Cassation*, Decision of 24 May 1975; [1975] CMLR 369; [1976] CMLRev. 128 with note by Bebr.

Facts:

As of January 1964, the defendant companies had imported large quantities of soluble coffee and chicory mixture from the Netherlands with a view to their resale on the French market. As soluble coffees manufactured in France were subject to a much lower internal consumption charge than that borne by the imported coffees, the defendants brought actions before the Paris *Tribunal d'Instance*, claiming that Article 95 of the EEC Treaty prohibits such discrimination.

This claim was upheld both by the Tribunal and by the Court of Appeal. Contesting the right of the French judiciary to enforce provisions of the EEC Treaty in the face of a municipal act of a later date, the Customs Administration brought the matter before the *Cour de Cassation*.

The Cour de Cassation held:

. . . . .

On the second ground

4. It is also complained against the judgment that it held illegal the internal consumption tax laid down by section 265 of the Customs Code as a con-

sequence of its incompatibility with the provisions of Article 95 of the Treaty of 25 March 1957 on the ground that by virtue of Article 55 of the Constitution the latter has an authority higher than that of an internal statute, even if the statute be later in time; whereas, according to the appeal, it is for the fiscal court to judge the legality of regulations laying down a tax which is challenged, but it could not without exceeding its powers discard the application of an internal statute on the pretext that it is unconstitutional. The provisions of section 265 of the Customs Code taken together were enacted by the Act of 14 December 1966 which conferred on them the absolute authority which belongs to legislative provisions and which are binding on all French courts.
5. But the Treaty of 25 March 1957, which by virtue of the abovementioned Article of the Constitution has an authority greater than that of statutes, institutes a separate legal order integrated with that of the Member States. Because of that separateness, the legal order which it has created is directly applicable to the nationals of those States and is binding on their courts. Therefore the Cour d'Appel was correct and did not exceed its powers in deciding that Article 95 of the Treaty was to be applied in the instant case, and not section 265 of the Customs Code, even though the latter was not section 265 of the Customs Code, even though the latter was later in date. Whence it follows that the ground must be dismissed.

On the third ground

6. It is also complained that the judgment applied Article 95 of the Treaty of 25 March 1957 when, according to the appeal, Article 55 of the Constitution expressly subjects the authority which it gives to treaties ratified by France to the condition that they should be applied by the other party. The judge at first instance was not therefore able validly to apply this constitutional provisions without investigating whether the State (Holland) from which the product in question was imported has met this condition of reciprocity.
7. But in the Community legal order the failing of a Member State of the European Economic Community to comply with the obligations falling on it by virtue of the Treaty of 25 March 1957 are subject to the procedure laid down by Article 170 of that Treaty and so the plea of lack of reciprocity cannot be made before the national courts. Whence it follows that this ground must be dismissed'.

In a judgment of 15 December 1975 (*Von Kempis Epoux Geldof*, [1976] 2 CMLR 152), the *Cour de Cassation* deduced the primacy of Community law from the very nature of the Community legal order. It no longer felt the need to refer to Article 55 of the French Constitution. See Tenth Gen. Rep. 1976, para 574.

C. CONSTITUTIONS OF THE ORIGINAL MEMBER STATES NOT CONTAINING AN EXPLICIT RECOGNITION OF THE SUPREMACY OF TREATY LAW

1. Belgium

a. Introduction

The Belgian Constitution has no provisions on the supremacy of international treaties. It was only in July 1970 that a new article 25 was added to the Constitution which provides that a treaty or a law may confer upon international organizations the exercise of specified powers. Despite the lack of constitutional provisions Belgian courts have taken in general a favourable stand toward Community law.

Constitution Article 25 bis:
'Either by treaty or by law specific powers may be attributed to institutions created under international law'.

b. Cases

(1) Belgian Fromagerie Le Ski Case (Final instance)

Belgian State (represented by the Minister of Economic Affairs) v. *S.A. Fromagerie Franco-Suisse 'Le Ski'*; *Cour de Cassation* (first chamber); Decision of 27 May 1971; JT 1971, pp. 460–474; RTDE 1971, pp. 494–501; [1972] CMLR, pp. 372–373.

Facts:

A Belgian Royal Decree of 3 November 1958 introduced a tax payable on the delivery of import licences for various dairy products. The Commission considering this tax contrary to EEC Article 12 proceeded against Belgium under Article 169. In its decision of 13 November 1964 the Court of Justice held that the Belgian tax was in violation of the Treaty. (*Dairy Products Case*, 90 and 91/63; [1964] ECR 1217). Subsequently the Royal Decree was withdrawn.

Belgian legislation requires parliamentary approval of decrees of the executive concerning import duties, even if they have been subsequently withdrawn. The defunct Royal Decree was approved by an Act of Parliament of 19 March 1968, which stipulated that the amounts paid in application of the Decree were definite, irrecoverable and could not give rise to any dispute before any national authority whatsoever. Disregarding this Act of Parliament the Brussels' Court of Appeal did declare that the S.A. Fromagerie Franco-Suisse 'Le Ski' was in principle entitled to claim restitution of the duties paid pursuant to the Royal Decrees of 3 November 1958. The Belgian State instituted an appeal for cassation with the Cour de Cassation. It contested the decision of the Court of Appeal on a number of grounds, claiming inter alia that under Belgian law only the legislature could test the conformity of law with the Constitution or with treaties binding the Belgian State. In its submission the Court of Appeal had therefore wrongly refused to apply the law of 19 March 1968 which was of a later date than the law ratifying the EEC Treaty. Furthermore by enacting the law of 19 March 1968 the Belgian legislature had clearly implied its intention that this law should be applied irrespective even of Article 12 EEC. In the submission of the government this provision did not preclude the Belgian legislature from deciding for internal purposes whether duties paid should be capable of restitution.

The Cour de Cassation held:

. . . . .

'According to Article 12 of the Treaty setting up the European Economic Community, the Member States must refrain from introducing, as between themselves, any new customs duties on imports or exports or any charge having equivalent effect, and from increasing those which they already apply in their trade with each other;

The special duties on imports, of which the defendant claims restitution, were levied by the appellant pursuant to Royal Decrees and departmental orders that are all of a later date than 1 January 1958, the day on which the Treaty entered into force;

These Royal Decrees were repealed by Article 13 of the Royal Decree of 28 December 1961 and by Article 1 of the Royal Decree of 23 October 1965;

The law of 19 March 1968 nevertheless approved, with retroactive effect, the orders subsequent to 1 January 1958, under which the special duties have been levied – duties of which the defendant claims restitution. The only Article of this law provides that the amounts paid pursuant to these orders constitute 'final payment', and that 'this payment is irrevocable and cannot give rise to dispute before any authority whatsoever';

The orders, which established, after 1 January 1958, special duties on imports of certain milk products, were contrary to Article 12 of the Treaty;

In as much as it consolidates the effects of these orders, the law of 19 March 1968 is also contrary to this provision;

Even if assent to a treaty, as required by Article 68(2) of the Constitution, is given in the form of a statute, the legislative power, by giving this assent, is not carrying out a normative function. The conflict which exists between a legal norm established by an international treaty and a norm established by a subsequent statute, is not a conflict between two statutes.

The rule that a statute repeals a previous statute in so far as there is a conflict between the two, does not apply in the case of a conflict between a treaty and a statute.

In the event of a conflict between a norm of domestic law and a norm of international law which produces direct effects in the internal legal system, the rule established by the treaty shall prevail. The primacy of the treaty results from the very nature of international treaty law.

This is *a fortiori* the case when a conflict exists, as in the present case, between a norm of internal law and a norm of Community law.

The reason is that the treaties which have created Community law have instituted a new legal system in whose favour the Member States have restricted the exercise of their sovereign powers in the areas determined by those treaties.

Article 12 of the Treaty establishing the European Economic Community produces direct effects and creates individual rights, which the national courts must safeguard;

It follows from the preceding consideration that the court had the duty to reject the application of the provisions of domestic law that are contrary to this provision of the Treaty;

Since it had noted that the rules of Community law and the rules of domestic law were incompatible in the case at issue, the judgment on appeal here could decide – without violation of the provisions of law indicated in the grounds for annulment – that the effects of the law of 19 March 1968, were 'stayed in as much as this law was in conflict with a directly applicable provision of international treaty law'.

In this respect the grounds of appeal fail for lack of a legal basis. The appeal is rejected'.

2. Germany

a. Introduction

Constitution Article 24
1. The Federation may, by legislation, transfer sovereign powers to intergovernmental institutions.
2. For the maintenance of peace, the Federation may enter a system of mutual collective security; in doing so it will consent to such limitation upon its rights of sovereignty as will bring about and secure a peaceful and lasting order in Europe and among the nations of the world.
3. For the settlement of disputes between states, the Federation will accede to agreements concerning a general, comprehensive and obligatory system of international arbitration'.

Constitution Article 25
The general rules of public international law are an integral part of federal law. They shall take precedence over the laws and shall directly create rights and duties for the inhabitants of the federal territory.

Constitution Article 79
3. An amendment of this Basic Law affecting the division of the Federation

into Länder, the participation in principle of the Länderin legislation, or the basic principles laid down in Articles 1 and 20 shall be inadmissible.

Constitution Article 80
1. The Federal Government, a Federal Minister or the Land Governments may be authorized by a law to issue ordinances having the force of law (Rechtsverordnungen). The content, purpose and scope of the powers conferred must be set forth in the law. The legal basis must be stated in the ordinance. If a law provides that a power may be further delegated, an ordinance having the force of law shall be necessary in order to delegate the power.
2. The consent of the Bundesrat shall be required, unless otherwise provided by federal legislation, for ordinances having the force of law issued by the Federal Government or a Federal Minister concerning basic rules for the use of facilities of the federal railroads and of postal and telecommunication services, or charges therefor, or concerning the construction and operation of railroads, as well as for ordinances having the force of law issued on the basis of federal laws that require the consent of the Bundesrat or that are executed by the Länder as agents of the Federation or as matters of their own concern.

Constitution Article 100
1. If a court considers unconstitutional a law the validity of which is relevant to its decision, the proceedings shall be stayed, and a decision shall be obtained from the Land court competent for constitutional disputes if the matter concerns the violation of the Constitution of a Land, or from the Federal Constitutional Court if the matter concerns a violation of this Basic Law. This shall also apply if the matter concerns the violation of this Basic Law by Land law or the incompatibility of a Land law with a federal law.
2. If, in the course of litigation, doubt exists whether a rule of public international law is an integral part of federal law and whether such rule directly creates rights and duties for the individual (Article 25), the court shall obtain the decision of the Federal Constitutional Court.
3. If the constitutional court of a Land, in interpreting this Basic Law, intends to deviate from a decision of the Federal Constitutional Court or of the constitutional court of another Land, it must obtain the decision of the Federal Constitutional Court; if interpreting other federal law, it intends to deviate from the decision of the Supreme Federal Court or a higher federal court, it must obtain the decision of the Supreme Federal Court.

In general the German courts have found no difficulties in admitting the supremacy of Community law over subsequent legislation in spite of the fact that an explicit rule of supremacy has only been laid down in Article 25 in regard of general rules of international law. However, the courts have placed an extensive interpretation on Article 24 of the Constitution, suggesting that the delegation of powers implies recognition of supremacy.

Basically German courts have had to face two main sets of problems. In the first place courts have been asked to pronounce the unconstitutionality of Article 1 of the Ratification Law on the grounds that Article 24 of the Constitution cannot legally authorize a transfer of legislative powers to the Council and the Commission of the EEC. Since the exercise of these powers was not subjected to the same limitations as those laid down with regard to the powers of German authorities (*i.e.* Article 80: scope of permissible delegation; Article 79 (3): principle of separation of powers), this ought to entail the nullity of Article 1 of the Ratification Law (see decision of 5 July 1967 and 18 October 1967 of the *Bundesverfassungsgericht* Jud. Rem. pp. 181–185).

In the second place, the courts have been faced with the question whether the Community institutions may be given powers in pursuance of Article 24, without there being a guarantee against the exercise of these powers in disregard of fundamental rights guaranteed by the Constitution. In the decision of the Constitutional Court of 18 October 1967 (not reproduced), this Court ruled out the possibility of a direct constitutional complaint against Community acts for alleged violation of fundamental rights. However, in its closing remarks the Court left open the question whether or not Community acts could be challenged if referred under Article 100 of the Constitution. Such a procedure has subsequently been instituted by the Administrative Court of Frankfurt (see below).

b. Cases

(1) **German Handelsgesellschaft Case**

Internationale Handelsgesellschaft mbH v. *Einfuhr- und Vorratstelle für Getreide und Futtermittel*; Decision of 29 May 1974 of the Bundesverfassungsgericht, requested by the Verwaltungsgericht Frankfurt, [1974] CMLR 540 *et seq.*

Facts:

The Verwaltungsgericht Frankfurt by order of 18 March 1970, had requested the Court of Justice to rule on the validity of the system of export deposits laid down in Council Regulation No 120/67 and Commission Regulation No 473/67. In its decision of 17 December 1970, (Case 11/70, p. 82) the Court of Justice had upheld the validity of the provisions in question. The Verwaltungsgericht was not satisfied with the decision of the Community Court. Considering that even after the preliminary ruling the opinion of the European Court could not be brought into harmony with its own, it decided to submit the case to the *Bundesverfassungsgericht* under Article 100 (1) of the Constitution (Decision of 24 November 1971).

Judgment:

. . . . .

The reference is admissible.

1. . . . . .
   The present case only requires the clarification of the relationship between the guarantees of fundamental rights in the Constitution and the rules of secondary EEC law, the execution of which has been entrusted to administrative authorities in the Federal Republic of Germany. For there is at the moment nothing to support the view that rules of the Treaty establishing the EEC, *i.e.* primary Community law could be in conflict with provisions of the Constitution of the Federal Republic of Germany. It can equally remain undecided whether the same considerations apply to the relationship between the law of the Constitution *outside* its catalogue of fundamental rights, and Community law, as apply, according to the following reasoning, to the relationship between the guarantees of fundamental rights in the Constitution and secondary Community law.
2. This Court – in this respect in agreement with the law developed by the European Court of Justice – adheres to its settled view that Community law is neither a component part of the national legal system nor international law, but forms an independent system of law flowing from an autonomous legal source; for the Community is not a State, in particular not a federal State, but '*a sui generis* Community in the process of progressive integration', an 'inter-State institution' within the meaning of Article 24 (1) of the Constitution.

   It follows from this that, in principle, the two legal spheres stand independent of and side by side one another in their validity, and that, in particular, the competent Community organs, including the European Court of Justice, have to rule on the binding force, interpretation and observance of Community law, and the competent national organs on the binding force, interpretation and observance of the constitutional law of the Federal Republic of Germany. The European Court of Justice cannot give a binding decision on whether a rule of Community law is compatible with the Constitution, nor can the Bundesverfassungsgericht rule on whether, and with what effects, a rule of secondary Community law is compatible with primary Community law. This does not lead to any difficulties as long as the two systems of law do not come into conflict with one another in their substance. From the special relationship which has come into being between the Community and its members by the establishment of the Community first and foremost a duty has arisen for the competent organs, in particular for the two courts charged with reviewing law – the European Court of Justice and the *Bundesverfassungsgericht* – to concern themselves in their decisions with the concordance of the two systems of law. Only in so far as this is unsuccessful can there arise the conflict which demands the drawing of conclusions from the relationship of principle between the two legal spheres set out above.

In this case, it is not enough simply to speak of the 'precedence' of Community law over national constitutional law, in order to justify the conclusion that Community law must always take precedence over national constitutional law because, otherwise, the Community would be put in question. Community law is just as little put in question when, exceptionally, Community law is not permitted to prevail over entrenched (*zwingende*) constitutional law, as international law is put in question by Article 25 of the Constituion when it provides that the general rules of international law only take precedence over simple federal law, and as another (foreign) system of law is put in question when it is set aside by the public policy of the Federal Republic of Germany. The binding of the Federal Republic of Germany (and of all Member States) by the Treaty is not, according to the meaning and spirit of the Treaties, one-sided, but they also bind the Community which they establish to carry out its part in order to resolve the conflict here assumed, that is, to seek a system which is compatible with an entrenched precept of the constitutional law of the Federal Republic of Germany. Invoking such a conflict is therefore not in itself a violation of the Treaty, but sets in motion inside the European organs the Treaty mechanism which resolves the conflict on a political level.

3. Article 24 of the Constitution deals with the transfer of sovereign rights to inter-State institutions. This cannot be taken literally. Like every constitutional provision of a similar fundamental nature, Article 24 of the Constitution must be understood and construed in the overall context of the whole Constitution. That is, it does not open the way to amending the basic structure of the Constitution, which forms the basis of its identity, without a formal amendment to the Constitution, that is, it does not open any such way through the legislation of the inter-State institution. Certainly, the competent Community organs can make law which the competent German constitutional organs could not make under the law of the Constitution and which is nonetheless valid and is to be applied directly in the Federal Republic of Germany. But Article 24 of the Constitution limits this possibility in that it nullifies any amendment of the Treaty which would destroy the identity of the valid constitution of the Federal Republic of Germany by encroaching on the structures which go to make it up. And the same would apply to rules of secondary Community law made on the basis of a corresponding interpretation of the valid Treaty and in the same way affecting the structures essential to the Constitution. Article 24 does not actually give authority to transfer sovereignty rights, but opens up the national legal system (within the limitations indicated) in such a way that the Federal Republic of Germany's exclusive claim to rule is taken back in the sphere of validity of the Constitution and room is given, within the

States' sphere of rule, to the direct effect and applicability of law from another source.
4. The part of the Constitution dealing with fundamental rights is an inalienable feature of the current Constitution of the Federal Republic of Germany and one which forms an essential part of its structure. Article 24 of the Constitution does not allow it to be subjected to qualifications without reservation. In this, the present state of integration of the Community is of vital importance. The Community still lacks a democratically legitimated parliament directly elected by general suffrage which possesses legislative powers and to which the Community organs empowered to legislate are fully responsible on a political level: it still lacks in particular a codified catalogue of fundamental rights, the substance of which is reliably and unambiguously fixed for the future in the same way as the substance of the Constitution and therefore allows a comparison and a decision as to whether, at the time in question, the Community law standard with regard to fundamental rights generally binding in the Community is adequate in the long term measured by the standard of the Constitution with regard to fundamental rights (without prejudice to possible amendments) in such a way that there is no exceeding the limitation indicated, set by Article 24 of the Constitution. As long as this legal certainty, which is not guaranteed merely by the decisions of the European Court of Justice, favourable though these have been to fundamental rights, is not achieved in the course of the further integration of the Community, the reservation derived from Article 24 of the Constitution applies. What is involved is, therefore, a legal difficulty arising exclusively from the Community's continuing integration process, which is still in flux and which will end with the present transitional phase.

Provisionally, therefore, in the hypothetical case of a conflict between Community law and a part of national constitutional law or, more precisely, of the guarantees of fundamental rights in the Constitution, there arises the question of which system of law takes precedence, that is, sets aside the other. In this conflict of norms, the guarantee of fundamental rights in the Constitution prevails as long as the competent organs of the Community have not removed the conflict of norms in accordance with the Treaty mechanism.
5. From the relationship between Constitution and Community law outlined above, the following conclusions emerge with regard to the jurisdiction of the European Court of Justice and of the Bundesverfassungsgericht.

(a) In accordance with the Treaty rules on jurisdiction, the European Court of Justice has jurisdiction to rule on the legal validity of the norms of Community law (including the unwritten norms of Community law which it considers exist) and on their construction. It does not, however decide incidental questions of national law of the Federal Republic of Germany (or in any other Member State) with binding force for this State. Statements in the reasoning of its judgment that a particular aspect of a Community norm accords or is compatible in its substance with a constitutional rule of national law – here, with a guarantee of fundamental rights in the Constitution – constitute non-binding obiter dicta.

In the framework of this jurisdiction, the European Court determines the content of Community law with binding effect for all the Member States. Accordingly, under the terms of Article 177 of the Treaty, the courts of the Federal Republic of Germany have to obtain the ruling of the European Court before they raise the question of the compatibility of the norm of Community law which is relevant to their decision with guarantees of fundamental rights in the Constitution.

(b) As emerges from the foregoing outline, the *Bundesverfassungsgericht* never rules on the validity or invalidity of a rule of Community law. At most, it can come to the conclusion that such a rule cannot be applied by the authorities or courts of the Federal Republic of Germany in so far as it conflicts with a rule of the Constitution relating to fundamental rights. It can (just like, *vice versa*, the European Court) itself decide incidental questions of Community law in so far as the requirements of Article 177 of the Treaty, which are also binding on the *Bundesverfassungsgericht*, are not present or a ruling of the European Court, binding under Community law on the *Bundesverfassungsgericht*, does not supervene.

6. Fundamental rights can be guaranteed by law in numerous ways and may accordingly enjoy numerous types of judicial protection. As its previous decisions show, the European Court also considers that it has jurisdiction by its decisions to protect fundamental rights in accordance with Community law. On the other hand only the Bundesverfassungsgericht is entitled, within the framework of the powers granted to it in the *Constitution*, to protect the fundamental rights guaranteed in the Constitution. No other court can deprive it of this duty imposed by constitutional law. Thus, accordingly, in so far as citizens of the Federal Republic of Germany have a claim to judicial protection of their fundamental rights guaranteed in the Constitution, their status cannot suffer any impairment because they are directly affected by legal acts of authorities or courts of the Federal Republic of Germany which are based on Community law. Otherwise, a perceptible gap in judicial protection might arise precisely for the most elementary status rights of the citizen. Moreover, no different constitutions apply to the constitution of a community of States with a constitution based on freedom and democracy which is called in question than apply to a federal State with a constitution based on freedom and democracy: it does not harm the Community and its constitution based on freedom (and democracy) if and in so far as its members in their constitutions give stronger guarantees of the liberties of their citizens than does the Community.

7. . . . . .

The result is: As long as the integration process has not progressed so far that Community law also receives a catalogue of fundamental rights decided on by a parliament and of settled validity, which is adequate in comparison with the catalogue of fundamental rights contained in the Constitution, a reference by a court in the Federal Republic of Germany to the *Bundesverfassungsgericht* in judicial review proceedings, following the obtaining of a ruling of the European Court under Article 177 of the Treaty, is admissible and necessary if the German court regards the rule of Community law which is relevant to its decision as inapplicable in the interpretation given by the European Court, because and in so far as it conflicts with one of the fundamental rights in the Constitution.

. . . . .

Dissenting opinion:

Three judges held the reference to be inadmissible. In their view there is enough case law of the European Court to permit the statement that fundamental rights are adequately protected at Community level. Moreover, since France has ratified the European Human Rights Convention and the Supplementary Protocol of 20 March 1952, all Member States are now contracting parties to the Convention. It is therefore to be reckoned that the Court will make use of the provisions of the Convention and the Protocol in order to establish what are the legal principles which are common to the legal systems of the Member States, as is already indicated in the Nold Judgment (Case 4/73, [1972] ECR, p. 491). The legal system of the Communities also has at its disposal a legal protection system calculated to enforce these fundamental rights.

The three dissenting judges held that on an objective interpretation of Article 24, para 1 of the Constitution this provision says not only that the transfer of sovereign rights to inter-State institutions is admissible, but also that the sovereign acts of the inter-State institutions are to be recognized by the Federal Republic of Germany. This precludes any subjection of these acts to national judicial review. However, it may be admitted that the interpretation of Article 24, para 1 of the Constitution on which its identity rests yields the conclusion that the relinquishing of the exercise of sovereign power in particular spheres and toleration of the exercise of sovereign power by organs of a supranational community is admissible if – and only if the public power of the supranational community is bound under its legal system by the same principles as emerge, for the sphere of national law, from the fundamental and inalienable principles of the Constitution; this includes in particular the protection of the central nucleus of fundamental rights. This requirement is met in the case of the European Economic Community. The protection of fundamental rights guaranteed inside the Community does not differ in essence and structure from the fundamental rights system of the national Constitution. It would be unreasonable for a Member State to demand a guarantee of fundamental rights at Community level in precisely the same form as is known to the national Constitution.

It is not obvious – as the majority of the court held – that the present state of integration of the Community should be relevant to the relationship between Community law and the Constitution. The argument that the fundamental rights of the Constitution must also prevail over secondary Community law because the Community still lacks a directly legitimated parliament is not in itself conclusive. The protection of fundamental rights and the democratic principle are not interchangeable inside a democratically constituted Community based on the idea of freedom: they complement one another. Moreover, the dissenting opinion pointed out that the views of the law adopted by the majority would lead to a situation where legal rules of the Community are applicable in some Member States, but not in others. Even if it is true that the majority does not claim jurisdiction to declare the invalidity of a Community rule, it has nevertheless stated that the *Bundesverfassungsgericht* can declare such a norm inapplicable in the sphere of the Federal Republic of Germany. However, in the opinion of the dissenting judges the distinction between invalidity and inapplicability of a norm exhausts itself in the use of different words. If a court holds a legal norm generally inapplicable because of violation of superior law, it is thereby stating on a common sense view, that the norm does not apply, *i.e.* that it is invalid. The Constitutional Court does not possess this power in respect of the legal rules of the Community institutions. The fact that the majority of the Court nonetheless claims this power is an inadmissible trespass on the jurisdiction reserved to the Community Court. This trespass exposes the Constitutional Court to the justified reproach of infringing the EEC Treaty and jeopardizing the legal system of the Community.

Since its decision of 1974 (the '*So Lange*' judgment) the German Constitutional Court has clarified its attitude and, so it seems, slightly withdrawn from its initial position. In a judgment of 25 July 1979 the Court held that it lacks the power to rule that provisions of *primary* Community law, as interpreted by the Court of Justice are incompatible with the German Constitution. However, the question whether the new political and legal developments which had taken place in the Community could induce it to change the view expressed by the Court in 1974 with regard to the position of *secondary* Community law, was not answered in the decision of 25 July 1979 (the '*Vielleicht*' judgment).

However, in a judgment of 22 October 1986 the *Bundesverfassungsgericht* reversed its previous rulings of 1974 and 1979. It held that in the meantime (*i.e.* since 1979) the process of integration had improved the protection of fundamental rights in the Community to such an extent that there no longer was a need for legal review of the compatibility of Community law with German constitutional provisions in the area of fundamental rights and freedoms (the '*Mittlerweile*' judgment). See for this case: J.A. Frowein, (1988) CMLRev. pp. 201–206.

3. Italy

a. Introduction

Constitution Article 10, para 1
'Italy condemns war as an instrument of aggression against the liberties of international law'.

Constitution Article 11
'Italy condemns war as an instrument of aggression against the liberties of other peoples and as a means for settling international controversies; it agrees, on conditions of equality with other states, to such limitation of sovereignty as may be necessary for a system calculated to ensure peace and justice between Nations: it promotes and encourages international organizations having such ends in view'.

Constitution Article 134
'The Constitutional Court decides:
On controversies concerning the constitutional legitimacy of laws and acts having the force of law, enacting from central and regional government;
on controversies arising over constitutional assignment of powers within the State, between the State and the Regions, and between Regions; (.....)'.

b. Cases

(1) Italian Costa-ENEL Case

Costa v. *ENEL*, Corte Costituzionale (Constitutional Court), Judgment of 7 March 1964; *Foro Italiano* 1964, I Col. 465; [1964] I Col. 465; [1964] CMLR 435–436, [1964] CMLRev. 225–234.

Facts:

Apart from making a reference for a preliminary ruling under Article 177 of the EEC Treaty (see p. 114) the Justice of the Peace of Milan, requested the Italian Constitutional Court to render an opinion on the constitutionality of the Nationalization law. One of the grounds invoked was that this law was incompatible with Article 11 of the Italian Constitution since it was alleged to violate Articles 37 para 2, 53, 93 and 3, and 102 of the EEC Treaty.

The Constitutional Court held:

'The last question relates to the alleged conflict between the law creating ENEL and Article 11 of the Constitution.

Article 11 is invoked, stating that Italy agrees, on conditions of equality with other States, to such limitations of sovereignty as are necessary for the establishment of an order that will ensure peace and justice amongst nations; and it will promote and favour international organizations for this purpose.

This means that, given certain circumstances, it is possible to stipulate treaties as a result of which we accept certain limitations to our sovereignty and it is quite lawful to give effect to such treaties by means of an ordinary law; but this does not result in any deviation from the existing rule relating to the efficacy, within national law, of the obligations undertaken by the State in connection with its relations with other States, since Article 11 did not confer a greater effect upon the ordinary law that gives effect to a treaty. Nor can we agree with the view according to which any law containing provisions differing from those of international treaties is unlawful . . . (under) Article 11 . . .

Quite often this Court has declared unlawful certain provisions of legislative decrees that did not correspond with the law that granted delegated powers to issue them, relating the cause of illegality to a violation of Article 76 of the Constitution.

But the situation is quite different as regards the part of Article 11 containing the provision under consideration here. Article 76 lays down certain rules regarding the exercise of a delegated legislative function and for this reason non-compliance with the principles of the delegation-law results in violation of Article 76. Article 11, on the other hand, inasmuch as it is considered as a permissive provision, ascribes no particular significance to a law giving execution to an international treaty as opposed to any other law.

Nor is there any validity in the other argument, according to which the State, once it has agreed to limitations to its own sovereignty, could not thereafter pass any law withdrawing such limitations and restoring its freedom of action without violating the Constitution. Against this can be set our foregoing remarks, that the violation of a treaty, even if it results in responsibility by the State at the international level, does not detract from the (internal) validity of any conflicting law.

There is no doubt that the State is bound to honour its obligations, just as there is no doubt that an international treaty is fully effective in so far as a law has given execution to it. But with regard to such law, there must remain inviolate the prevalence of subsequent laws in accordance with the principles governing the succession of laws in time; it follows that any conflict between the one and the other cannot give rise to any constitutional question.

From the foregoing we reach the conclusion that for present purposes there is no point in dealing with the character of the EEC and with the consequences that derive from the law giving effect to the Treaty creating the EEC; nor is it necessary to question whether the law that is being attacked before us has violated the obligations undertaken by virtue of the Treaty aforesaid. It follows from this that the question regarding the remission of the file to the Court of Justice of the European Community, and the relevant question of jurisdiction, do not even arise.

For all these reasons this Court declares that any question upon the constitutional legality of the Law of 6 December 1962 No 1643 (creating ENEL), raised by the order before it ... is unfounded'.

(2) Italian Frontini Case

Frontini v. *Ministry of Finance, Corte Costituzionale* (Constitutional Court), Judgment of 18 December 1973 (No 183/1973), [1974] CMLR p. 386.

See for facts, text and further references, Jud. Rem. pp. 213–217.

The Constitutional Court, upholding the supremacy of Community Law, stated:

'Fundamental requirements of equality and legal certainty demand that the Community norms, which cannot be characterized as a source of international law, nor of foreign law, nor of internal law of the individual States, ought to have full compulsory efficacy and direct application in all the Member States, without the necessity of reception and implementation statutes, as acts having the force and value of statutes in every country of the Community, to the extent of entering into force everywhere simultaneously and receiving equal and uniform application to all their addressees'.

The following exerpt is taken from a commentary by G. Bebr on this Judgment:

'The request of the tribunal of Turin and Genova as to the constitutionality of the Italian law ratifying the Treaty as far as its Article 189 is concerned, raises the fundamental question as to the possible extent of this delegation pursuant to Article 11 of the constitution.

Dealing with this request for a Constitutional review, the Constitutional Court rendered on 18 December 1973, a judgment of basic importance most likely to introduce a new judicial policy. This decision settles two fundamental issues which were, for some time, controversial in the Italian legal system. First, it firmly upholds the constitutionality of the Italian law ratifying the EEC in general and that of its Article 189 in particular. Secondly, it recognizes the absolute supremacy of Community regulations.

In the view of the High Court '... each Member State carried out a partial transfer of the exercise of legislative function to the Community institutions'. This transfer, necessarily implying a limitation of national sovereignty, may be executed by an ordinary law pursuant to Article 11 of the Constitution which provision would be deprived of its 'specific normative content', reasons the court, if the acceptance of such a limitation would require a constitutional law. The constitutional control of Article 134 applies, according to the court, to laws, and acts having their force, of the competent Italian authorities only, not however to Community acts subject to the EEC Treaty providing for its own constitutional guarantees and its own judicial system. In the light of these considerations the constitutional court confirms the constitutionality of Article 189 and consequently of the Community legislative powers as well.

This explicit confirmation of the constitutionality of the EEC Treaty is, from the point of view of Community Law, very reassuring indeed. But the decision is of even greater importance for the further development of the relation of Italian law to Community law. In the opinion of the High Court, it is:

'... consistent with the logic of the Community system if regulations, as an immediate source of rights and obligations of Member States as well as of individuals ... require no national measures which would reproduce, complete or execute them in the national legal order', and these measures may therefore '... in no way postpone the entry into force of the regulations or impose conditions on them or even less to replace them to derogate or to appeal them, not even in part'.

The supremacy of Community law is perhaps recognized somewhat inconspicuously and with regard to regulations only. Since, however, regulations are based on Article 189 of the Treaty, there may be little doubt, if any, that the High Court recognizes the supremacy of the Treaty as well.

The Court's statement has more far-reaching consequences than would appear at first sight. In fact, it is a real turning point in the jurisprudential development. In this decision, the High Court maintains that an ordinary law is, constitutionally, sufficient for the ratification of the EEC Treaty. But significantly enough the court draws no inferences from the nature of the ratification law for the legal status of the Treaty in the Italian legal order. On the contrary, it does not hesistate to uphold the supremacy of Community law. This is an extremely important development indeed. It means that the constitutional court has abandoned its unfortunate ENEL ruling considering the nature of the ratification law as predetermining the legal nature of the EEC Treaty, which a priori blocked any attempt to ensure the supremacy of Community law. This may well be the most important consequence of this decision.

The High Court, it seems, bases the supremacy primarily on the delegation of State powers to the Community, as provided for by Article 11 of the Constitution – a practice similar to that frequently followed by German courts utilising Article 24 of the basic law. The decision makes no explicit, specific reference to the case law of the Court. Yet it seems a fair presumption that while the High Court formally based its judgment on the constitutional provisions, it nevertheless took cognisance of the Court's case law. The preliminary rulings Politi, Marimex and Leonesio, to quote only a few, may well have played a considerable, if not decisive part in developing the reasoning of the High Court. This is a true landmark decision which, in the long run, is bound to change fundamentally the attitude of Italian courts towards Community law'. (Bebr, 'How supreme is Community law in the National Courts?', ([1974] CMLRev. p. 37.)

(3) Italian ICIC Case

Industrie Chimiche dell'Italia Centrale v. *Minister of Foreign Trade, Corte Costituzionale* (Constitutional Court), Judgment of 30 October 1975, (No 232/75), *Foro Italiano* 1975, 2661–2670, [1976] CMLRev. 530–536.

In Italy laws must be applied unless the Constitutional Court decides otherwise. In the Frontini Case the Constitutional Court had not indicated whether *all* Italian courts are entitled to refuse to apply a national law which conflicts with a Community provision (which is the solution adopted by the German Constitutional Court, see above), or whether in case of conflict a decision that the national law is inapplicable can only be made by the judicial organ shich, according to the Italian legal order, has the exclusive power to review laws, i.e. the Constitutional Court. The matter was decided in the ICIC Case.

A special feature of this case was that the national provisions complained of were not materially at variance with the Community Regulation in question; they reproduced it practically word for word. But the Tribunal and subsequently the Court of Appeal and the *Corte di Cassazione* considered that they must apply the national provisions exclusively since these constituted a *lex posterior* vis-à-vis the Community Regulation in question. The Constitutional Court declared the national provisions unconstitutional:

'In reality, the subsequent adoption of internal legal provisions, even if they contain the same subject-matter as Community regulations, involves not only the possibility of deferring, wholly or in part, their application, in plain contradiction to the second paragraph of Article 189 of the Treaty of Rome, but has an even more serious consequence, namely that the transformation of Community law into national law would permanently withdraw its interpretation from the Court of Justice of the Communities, clearly breaching the system laid down in Article 177 of the Treaty to provide a necessary and basic guarantee of uniform application in all Member States'. This 'entails an infringement of Article 11 of our constitution, whereby Italy acceded to the Community consenting ... to the requisite limitation of sovereignty ...'.

However, it was less satisfactory to note that the Constitutional Court considered that 'the rules in force do not empower Italian courts to refuse to apply subsequent internal provisions adopted by law or by instruments having the effect of general law'. The judge is, on the contrary 'required to raise the question of their constitutional legitimacy'. Obviously, the drawback of this approach was that in Italy the question whether laws are in accordance with prior Community law was subjected to a cumbersome review procedure.

In the meantime the Court of Justice has confirmed that limitations placed by the national legal system on the power of national courts to solve a conflict themselves, by setting aside national provisions which might prevent Community rules from having full force and effect, are incompatible with 'those requirements which are the very essence of Community law'. See Case 106/77, Simmenthal II, above p. 200. For its part, the Constitutional Court has substantially accepted the Community Court's *Simmenthal* judgment, as is shown in the *Granital Case* (below).

(4) Italian Granital Case

S.p.a. Granital v. *Amministratione delle Finanze dello Stato, Corte Costituzionele* (Constitutional Court), Judgment of 8 June 1984, No 170/84, [1984] CMLRev. 756.

Facts:

Granital refused payment to the Italian Customs Authorities of an agricultural levy, arguing that the collection of this duty was contrary to Community law. While the case was pending a new Presidential Decree (No 695 of 1978) introduced changes in the system of assessing the rate of agricultural duties. The decree incorporated the interpretation given by the Court of Justice of the Community provisions at issue (Case 113/75, *Frecassetti*, [1976] ECR 983), but its article 3 specified that the new system would only apply as of the date on which the Court's ruling had been published in the Official Journal, *i.e*, 11 September 1976. However, Community law requires that an interpretation given by the Court of Justice is applied even to legal relationships arising and established before the judgment ruling on the request for interpretation (Cases 66, 127–128/79, *Salumi*, [1980] ECR 1237). By an order given on 30 April 1979, the Court of Genoa referred to the Constitutional Court the question of the constitutionality of Article 3 of the Presidential Decree No 695 of 1978.

The Court held:

. . . . .

2. First of all, it is necessary to state that the question of constitutionality was raised on the assumption that – according to existing case-law – provisions in a statute which conflict with a Community regulation cannot be deemed void or inoperative, but are regarded as unconstitutional and must therefore be referred to this Court because they are in breach of Article 11 of the Constitution. In this Court's opinion, this aspect of the question referred must be considered first, given its preliminary nature. . . .

  On the basis of Article 11 of the Constitution, Community legal rules are directly applicable in Italy, but do not belong to the municipal law system of legal sources. This means that Community rules cannot logically be affected by the models provided for the solution of conflicts among rules pertaining to Italian law. The assertion, contained in decision No. 232 of 1975, that national rules do not defer to Community rules on the basis of their respective force of resistance, must be read accordingly. The principles stated by this Court with regard to Community law – in the case under review, Community regulations – must be viewed in the light of the premise that Community law and Italian law, while separate and independent, must necessarily be coordinated, as the Treaty of Rome requires. This coordination stems from the fact that the Law implementing the Treaty transferred to Community institutions – according to Article 11 of the Constitution – those powers that these institutions exert with regard to subject-matters reserved for them.

However, it is necesary to clarify further the way in which the relationship between the two legal systems works in respect of the problem under review. Rules contained in a regulation are immediately applicable in Italy on the basis of their own strength. They need not, and may not, be reproduced or transformed into corresponding provisions of municipal law. The separation of Italian law from Community law further means that the rules in question do not become part of municipal law, nor do they come under the principles applying to municipal statutes or other municipal legislative acts which are as binding as statutes. Therefore, what was said in the decision referred to above only means that Italian law – on the basis of its specific relationship with EEC law and the underlying restriction of State sovereignty – allows Community regulations to operate as such in Italy. Regulations are given the same binding force as statutes only in the sense that the binding force of regulations in their system of origin is recognized....

5. Conclusions reached in previous decisions must therefore be rewritten in accordance with the approach implicit in those decisions.

When an Italian court finds that a provision stemming from a Community legal source covers the case in issue, this provision is applied with reference only to the legal system applicable to the supranational organization – that is, only the system that governs the legislative act to be applied and specifies its effects. Conflicting provisions in a national statute cannot constitute an obstacle to the recognition of the binding force conferred by the Treaty on Community regulations as a source of directly applicable rules. With regard to the effects of regulations thus recognized, municipal legislation appears to apply to a legal system that does not seek to interfere with rules produced in the Community's system, which is a separate and independent one, although municipal law does guarantee compliance with those rules in Italy....

Nevertheless the consequence thus defined applies with regard to a source of municipal law only in so far as powers transferred to the Community are exercised in producing legal rules which are complete and immediately applicable by municipal courts. Beyond the substantive and temporal scope of this Community legislation, municipal provisions keep their value and produce their effects. It is hardly necessary to add that these provisions fall under the principles applying to ordinary statutes – including the principle concerning the control of their constitutionality.

6. Community regulations are therefore always to be applied, whether they follow or precede in time statutes that are inconsistent with them. National courts entrusted with the task of applying regulations may refer a question of interpretation under Article 177 of the Treaty. The fundamental requirement of legal certainty can only be satisfied in this way. This requirement, which has always been acknowledged in this Court's decisions, involves the need for equality and uniformity of criteria in the application of regulations throughout the European Community. . . .
7. However, the remarks hitherto made do not imply that the whole area of the relationship between Community law and municipal law falls outside this Court's competence. In its decision No 183 of 1973, this Court has already stated that the Law implementing the Treaty may come under this Court's control with regard to basic principles of the Italian legal system and the respect for fundamental human rights in the case envisaged – albeit as an unlikely possibility – in part 9 of the reasons given for the said decision. In the present decision a further specification may be usefully made. Provisions of municipal law which are assumed to be unconstitutional because they intend to prevent or impair the continuous respect of the Treaty – with regard to the Community system or the fundamental core of its principles – must be referred to this Court. This case clearly differs from municipal provisions which are inconsistent with some specific Community regulations. In the case now considered the Court would be requested to assess whether the municipal legislator has unjustifiably removed some of the restrictions put on State sovereignty by the same legislator through the Law which implemented the Treaty, thereby complying with Article 11 of the Constitution in a direct and specific way.
8. In conclusion, the question referred to this Court by the Court of Genoa must be held to be inadmissible. The referring Court should assess whether, and for what reason, regulations and principles of Community law invoked in the order allow the regime pertaining to agricultural levies – under the aspect considered in the present case – to be given retrospective effect only up to the date on which the Luxembourg Court's judgment on interpretation referred to above was published'.

D. CONSTITUTIONAL RULES OF THE 'NEW' MEMBER STATES

1. Ireland

a. Constitutional provisions

Constitution Article 6
'1. All powers of government, legislative, executive and judicial, derive, under God, from the people, whose right it is to designate the rules of the State, and, in final appeal, to decide all questions of national policy, according to the requirements of the common good.

2. These powers of government are exercisable only by or on the authority of the organs of State established by this Constitution'.

Constitution Article 15
'2. 1. The sole and exclusive power of making laws for the State is hereby vested in the Oireachtas: no other legislative authority has power to make laws for the State?.'

Constitution Article 29
'1. Ireland affirms its devotion to the ideal of peace and friendly co-operation amongst nations founded on international justice and morality.
2. Ireland affirms its adherence to the principle of the pacific settlement of international disputes by international arbitration or judicial determination.
3. Ireland accepts the generally recognized principles of international law as its rule of conduct in its relations with other States.
4. 1. The executive power of the State in or in connection with its external relations shall in accordance with Article 28 of this Constitution be exercised by or on the authority of the Government.
    2. For the purpose of the exercise of any executive function of the State in or in connection with its external relations, the Government may to such extent and subject to such conditions, if any, avail of or adopt any organ, instrument, or method of procedure used or adopted for the like purpose by the members of any group or league of nations with which the State is or becomes associated for the purpose of international co-operation in matters of common concern.
5. 1. Every international agreement to which the State becomes a party shall be laid before the Dáil Eireann.
    2. The State shall not be bound by any international agreement involving a charge upon public funds unless the terms of the agreement shall have been approved by Dáil Eireann.
    3. This section shall not apply to agreements or conventions of a technical and administrative character.
6. No international agreement shall be part of the domestic law of the State save as may be determined by the Oireachtas'.

An amendment in the form of the addition of a third sub-paragraph to paragraph to Article 29 of the Constitution was adopted by the legislature and approved by the People of the Republic of Ireland in a referendum on 12 May 1972 ('The Third Amendment'). It reads as follows:

'The State may become a member of the European Coal and Steel Community (established by Treaty signed at Paris on the 18th day of April, 1951), the European Economic Community (established by Treaty signed at Rome on the 25th day of March, 1957) and the European Atomic Energy Community (established by Treaty signed at Rome on the 25th day of March, 1957). No provision of this Constitution invalidates laws enacted, acts done or measures adopted by the State necessitated by the obligations of membership of the Communities or prevents laws enacted, acts done or measures adopted by the Communities, or institutions thereof, from having the force of law in the State'.

b. Commentary

'The amendment avoids listing the provisions of the Constitution which are inconsistent with the present powers of the Community institutions. This makes for brevity, and avoids including a fairly long list of clauses in the amendment. It ensures that no problem can arise as a result of the accidental omission of some clause in the Constitution which it had not been foreseen would be incompatible with some provision of Community Law. It ensures that no difficulty can arise if one of the existing Communities obtains powers, such as power to impose taxes, which would be inconsistent with provisions of the Irish Constitution which have not so far been relevant. Omission of any list of constitutional provisions affected also enabled the Irish Government to avoid having to argue whether the Community Treaties are inconsistent with Article 5 of the Constitution: 'Ireland is a sovereign, independent, democratic state'. The better legal view is that the Treaties are consistent with this Article, but the question is, obviously, politically controversial.

The all-embracing terms of the amendment go further than is necessary to confer on the Community institutions the legislative, executive and judicial powers which the Treaties enable them to exercise. The amendment probably unnecessarily ensures that any Community legislation which in its content (as distinct from its source) is incompatible with, *e.g.* the fundamental human rights provisions of the Irish Constitution (Articles 40–44), will nevertheless be beyond challenge on constitutional grounds in the Irish courts. On this interpretation, the only limitations under Irish law will be those laid down by the Treaties themselves. The Communities have no powers outside the economic, nuclear energy and coal-and-steel spheres governed by the three Treaties, except in so far as other powers may have been given by the Treaties, either directly in, *e.g.* the social sphere or indirectly under Article 235 of the EEC Treaty (which allows the Council to adopt unanimously any measure to further the objectives of the Treaty, even if there is no express power under the Treaty to adopt the measure in question). Of course, the Community institutions must not infringe Community law in such a way as to invalidate their own acts under Article 173 of the EEC Treaty, and apparently will be required by the Community Court to comply with principles of fundamental human rights which the court will take into consideration.

The amendment has therefore eliminated any chance of conflict between the Constitution of Ireland and Community law. The amendment did not attempt to deal with the question of inconsistency between other rules of Irish law and Community law ...' (J. Temple, 'Legal and constitutional problems for Ireland of adhesion to the EEC Treaty', [1972] CMLRev. 168–169).

2. Denmark

a. Constitutional provisions

Constitution Article 19

'1. The King shall act on behalf of the Realm in international affairs. Provided that without the consent of the Folketing the King shall not undertake any act whereby the territory of the Realm will be increased or decreased, nor shall he enter into any obligation which for fulfilment requires the concurrence of the Folketing, or which otherwise is of major importance; nor shall the King, except with the consent of the Folketing, terminate any international treaty entered into with the consent of the Folketing.

. . . . .

3. The Folketing shall appoint from among its Members a Foreign Affairs Committee, which the Government shall consult prior to the making of any decision of major importance to foreign policy. Rules applying to the Foreign Affairs Committee shall be laid down by Statute.

Constitution Article 20

'1. Powers vested in the authorities of the Realm under this Constitution Act may, to such extent as shall be provided by Statute, be delegated to international authorities set up by mutual agreement with other states for the promotion of international rules of law and co-operation.
2. For the passing of a Bill dealing with the above a majority of five-sixths of the Members of the Folketing shall be required. If this majority is not obtained, whereas the majority required for the passing of ordinary Bills is obtained, and if the Government maintains it, the Bill shall be submitted to the Electorate for approval or rejection in accordance with the rules for Referenda laid down in section 42'.

b. Commentary

'The Danish Constitution seems to presuppose that even where a treaty has been duly ratified, it does not, normally, automatically become a part of municipal Danish law.

Incorporating the particular rule of international law into Danish law may be achieved in different ways. As examples may be mentioned the adoption of an act by the Folketing, or the issuance of some other legal ordinance with a view to implementing the national rule of law required by the substance of the treaty. This involves, in other words, a transcription or transformation of the rule of international law. A treaty will, however, become part of Danish law, if Danish legislation contains a provision authorizing the Government to conclude a treaty and subsequently implement it as part of national law. In such cases no transcription is called for.

The Danish Constitution, however, views certain treaties as so significant and of such consequence for the structure of the Danish Constitution as to necessitate stricter requirements, in form as well as in substance, for the making of a treaty. The provision on this subject are incorporated in Article 20 of the Constitution which to a certain limited extent authorities the government to delegate powers vested in the authorities of the Realm to international rules of law and co-operation. The Constitution provides that a delegation of this kind shall be made by enactment. In this type of situation it has, however, been found appropriate to deviate from the normal legislative procedure, simply because the effects of an act of this nature upon the Danish community could be of far-reaching importance.

The procedure laid down by Article 20 of the Constitution has not previously been used in Denmark, this being the first time Denmark is faced with the problem of joining a supranational organization. Admittedly, Denmark has already joined other international organizations, such as EFTA, but although they are of a far-reaching nature they are, in the strict legal sense, merely organizations, whose decisions have no immediate and direct effect upon the Danish community. To join such international organizations all that is required is the consent of the *Folketing*, given by an ordinary majority, to the Government's ratification of the treaties at hand' (I, Foighel, *EFTA-Bulletin*, September–October 1971, 11).

3. United Kingdom

a. The constitutional position

'In the United Kingdom, because the conclusion and ratification of an international treaty is within the prerogative of the Crown, a constitutional doctrine has been evolved in consequence of which a treaty only forms part of English law if an enabling Act of Parliament is passed.

The basic rule that obligations do not directly per se affect the subjects of the Crown derives from historical circumstances in the seventeenth century and has no ideological roots. Its object has been, of course, to prevent the Crown from legislating without the consent of Parliament and the rule has been held to be applicable to all international treaties which affect private rights or liabilities, or which result in a charge on public funds, or require a modification of common law or of statute for their enforcement in the courts.

This dualist approach to conventional international legal obligations is supplemented by a doctrine of 'incorporation' or 'adoption' in regard to customary rules of international law; such customary rules are considered as part of the law of the land, and enforced as such, only in so far as is not inconsistent with Acts of Parliament or prior judicial decisions of final authority. Nevertheless the formal 'incorporation' of a Treaty by Act of Parliament does not of itself establish an hierarchical order as between treaty law and national law. This is because, in strict constitutional theory and under certain conditions, a statute may bind the courts even if it is in conflict with subsequent treaty law. In addition treaty law may have to give way, in the event of conflict, to decided precedents.

Normally, however, British practice recognizes that States have a duty to bring their national laws into conformity with their treaty obligations, and to maintain a consistent conformity at all times. British courts will, when called upon to ascertain the meaning of an Act of Parliament, presume that the intention of the legislature was not to violate treaty obligations or generally accepted principles of international law.

. . . . .

It is very important here to stress that the law of the Communities, deriving from the Treaty of Rome, the legal acts of Community institutions, and the jurisprudence of the European Court of Justice and of national courts, is essentially a *lex specialis*. It must be carefully distinguished from international law and will certainly pose problems as to its application and implementation within the United Kingdom that are quire unlike those deriving from traditional obligations. As Mr. Lecourt recently said, 'Qui participe à la Communauté épouse son droit'.

The law of the Communities breaks away from traditional ideas of reciprocal rights and duties as between contracting States parties to an international agreement. Instead, an autonomous, inherently supreme, legal order has been created for the implementation of the objectives of the Treaty of Rome – and this legal order is intended to penetrate very deeply into the national legal systems of Member States. It is not possible here to examine particular problems of penetration and of reconciliation that will arise in the United Kingdom, but I would agree with a leading commentator, Professor J.D.B. Mitchell, that Parliament should be able to transfer certain of its legislative powers to Community institutions as required by the Treaty of Rome and that British Courts ought to be able to rise to the responsibility that will be imposed upon them of understanding and accepting the implications, as well as the rules, of a thoroughly novel legal order'. (K.R. Simmonds, *EFTA Bulletin* 1971, December, pp. 11, 12).

b. The European Communities Act 1972

Part I – General Provisions

1. Short title and interpretation

1. This act may be cited as the European Communities Act 1972.

2. General implementation of Treaties.

1. All such rights, powers, liabilities, obligations and restrictions from time to time created or arising by or under the Treaties, and all such remedies and procedures from time to time provided for by or under the Treaties as in accordance with the Treaties are without further enactment to be given legal effect or used in the United Kingdom shall be recognized and available in law, and be enforced, allowed and followed accordingly; and the expression 'enforceable Community right' and similar expressions shall be read as referring to one to which this subsection applies.
2. Subject to schedule 2 to this Act, at any time after its passing Her Majesty may by Order in Council, and any designated Minister or Department may by regulations, make provision:
    (a) for the purpose of implementing any Community obligation of the United Kingdom, or enabling any such obligation to be implemented, or of enabling any rights enjoyed or to be enjoyed by the United Kingdom under or by virtue of the Treaties to be exercised; or
    (b) for the purpose of dealing with matters arising out of or related to any such obligation or rights or the coming into force, or the operation from time to time, of subsection (1) above; and in the exercise of any statutory power or duty, including any power to give directions or to legislate by means of orders, rules, regulations or other subordinate instrument, the person entrusted with the power or duty may have regard to the objects of the Communities and to any such obligation or rights as aforesaid.
    In this subsection 'designated Minister or department' means such Minister of the Crown or government department as may from time to time be designated by Order in Council in relation to any matter or for any purpose, but subject to such restrictions or conditions (if any) as may be specified by the Order in Council.

. . . . .

4. The provision that may be made under subsection (2) above includes, subject to Schedule 2 to this Act, any such provision (of any such extent) as might be made by Act of Parliament, and any enactment passed or to be passed, other than one contained in this Part of this Act, shall be construed and have effect subject to the foregoing provisions of this section;

but, except as may be provided by any Act passed after this Act, Schedule 2 shall have effect in connection with the powers conferred by this and the following sections of this Act to make Orders in Council and regulations.

3. Decisions on, and proof of, Treaties and Community instruments, etc.

1. For the purposes of all legal proceedings any question as to the meaning or effect of any of the Treaties, or as to the validity, meaning or effect of any Community instrument, shall be treated as a question of law (and, if not referred to the European Court, be for determination as such in accordance with the principles laid down by any relevant decision of the European Court).
2. Judicial notice shall be taken of the Treaties, of the Official Journal of the Communities and of any decision of, or expression of opinion by, the European Court on any such question as aforesaid; and the Official Journal shall be admissible as evidence of any instrument or other act thereby communicated of any of the Communities or of any Community institution'.

c. The supremacy of Community Law

'Direct effect is given to Community rules, both as that effect is now understood and as it may evolve. Properly understood, clause 3 (2), in combination with this direct effect, can overcome the supposed difficulties springing from the British doctrine of the sovereignty of Parliament and dualist views.

Yet, the question remains will they be so in practice. The dualist view presented technical problems of incorporation of Community law without transforming its character. This danger has been avoided. The specific nature of that law is emphasized by the words 'as in accordance with the Treaties' in clause 2 (1). This body of law is separated off from general international law. The Treaties themselves are not enacted by the Bill when it becomes law. Their principles are taken to have been approved by Parliament on 22 October 1971. All that the Bill, when enacted, will do is to derive necessary consequences. The traditional way of scheduling the Treaties to an Act has been avoided and would have been impracticable.

. . . . .

The problem of dealing with existing Community law, and of creating a satisfactory system of processing mediately effective Community law as we have demonstrated – found relatively easy solutions. The hard problem was that of installing the supremacy of Community law as against future British statutes.

. . . . .

Pursuing the lines of honesty and legal elegance which mark the drafting of the Bill, this problem is faced by clause 2 (4). There are three elements in this clause. The first ends with the word 'Parliament'. It expressly overcomes the problem of the repeal of amendment of Acts of Parliament, past or future, by delegated legislation made by the procedures described. It allows that process. The third element, which starts with the word 'but', ensures that the limitations on this power contained in Schedule 2 endure unless and until repealed by a future statute. Thus the limitations receive a degree of entrenchment. The second element connects the two. It reads 'and any enactment passed or to be passed other than one contained in this part of this Act, shall be construed to have effect subject to the foregoing provisions of this section'. This looks to the past and the future. The future is most important in the context of the sovereignty of Parliament. Harking back to section 4 of the Statute of Westminster, the binding effect of which even on the Westminster Parliament has (as will appear) now been accepted, it enjoins courts, in their behaviour, in their interpretation of future legislation to give full effect to the concept of 'enforceable Community right' which, as defined in clause 2 (1) contains that element of supremacy. It does not say that Parliament cannot enact legislation which is in conflict with Community obligations. It denies effectiveness to such legislation by controlling the way in which the institutions concerned with the application of legislation, i.e. the courts, must both construe and give effect to it. Equally, since all life is not litigation, the effect of such legislation is subjected equally to clause 2 (1). In their dealings any legal person is bound only to give effect to a statute consistently with that. The future statute is not invalidated, its consequences are limited.

. . . . .

For the reason just given, a frontal attack was excluded on the grounds that such an attack might well lack judicial efficacy and that it would open up all the false arguments that can be based upon that elusive word 'sovereignty'. Finally the argument is not about legal theory but about how to secure within the Community the smooth working of a system in order that the desired economic and social results can be achieved by individuals too.

. . . . .

Thus the combination of clauses 2 (1) and 2 (4) achieve the essential results and Part I of the Bill is excluded from any possibility of amendment under the procedures contained within it. To depart from the position there set out would, in effect, require renunciation of the Treaty'. (Mitchell, Kuipers and Gall, [1972] CMLRev. 141–144).

4. Greece

a. Constitutional provisions

Constitution Article 28
'1. The generally acknowledged rules of international law, as well as international conventions as of the time they are sanctioned by law and become operative according to the conditions therein, shall be an integral part of domestic Greek law and shall prevail over any contrary provision of the law. The rules of international law and of international conventions shall be applicable to aliens only under the condition of reciprocity.
2. In order to serve an important national interest and to promote international co-operation with other States, powers provided for in the Constitution may be recognized by treaty or agreement (as appertaining) to organs of international organizations. A majority of three-fifths of the total number of members of Parliament shall be required to approve the Act by which the treaty or agreement is sanctioned.
3. Greece may freely proceed, by virtue of an Act passed by the votes of the absolute majority of the total number of members of Parliament, to limitations on the exercise of national sovereignty, provided that this is dictated by an important national interest, does not affect human rights and the foundations of democratic government and is effected in conformity with the principles of equality, and on condition of reciprocity.'

b. Commentary

The above provisions were introduced into the Greek Constitution in 1975 and were adopted to clear the constitutional path for accession. On the question of supremacy, a leading commentator has summarized the position as follows:

'In any attempt to speculate on the possible national attitude towards the principle of supremacy of Community law, a number of factors can and should be taken into consideration. There are factors of positive law, such as the rule of supremacy of international conventional law over ordinary, non-constitutional enactments, contained in and guaranteed by the Constitution in paragraph 1 of Article 28. There are further rules establishing the obligation of the courts to take judicial notice of international as well as of foreign law and placing on an equal footing the grant of the same remedy against judicial decisions which contravene rules belonging irrespectively to domestic, international or foreign law. Finally, in the same order of ideas, it should be stressed that the use of the comparative method has been traditionally widespread in Greece, both in legislation and adjudication.

Such factors might seem disparate, yet taken together they prompt on the part of the national judge a certain approach to the state's international commitments. It should be no misstatement to affirm that the attitude of the

Greek courts towards international law and foreign legal conceptions has always been marked by a spirit of openness.

Placed against such a background, the problem of implementing the principle of supremacy of Community law should in the normal course receive in Greece a solution favourable to the concept of the Communities. No major difficulties are likely to emerge as far as concerns the relationship of primary and secondary Community law to ordinary national law. But the determination of the rank of such Community law in relation to national rules of constitutional level, which in Greece prevail over other rules of law, might cause some embarrassment for the courts, as indeed it did and still does in many Member States. Greek judges of any rank feel proud of their ancient and deep-rooted prerogative of constitutional review of the law, reaffirmed in Article 93, paragraph 4, of the Constitution of 1975. The challenge of a new, non-national law capable of taking precedence over constitutional provisions risks upsetting established habits of legal thinking. It is symptomatic that the supremacy of Community law over constitutional law was cited both within and outside Parliament by the major opposition party as one of the main reasons underlying its anti-membership policy.

It is nevertheless to be expected that having regard to the Communities' respect of the basic constitutional traditions of Member States, enforcement of Community law against possible contrary rules of national law of whatever kind will, in principle, be accepted by the courts as a necessary corollary of the substantial legal implications of membership permitted by the Constitution itself on the strength of paragraphs 2 and 3 of Article 28'. (D. Evrigenis, 'Legal and constitutional implications of Greek accession to the European Communities', [1980] CMLRev., 166–167).

5. Spain

Constitution Article 92
'By means of an organic law, authorization may be established for the conclusion of treaties which attribute to an international organization or institution the exercise of competences derived from the Constitution. It is the responsibility of the Cortes Generales or the Government, depending on the cases, to guarantee compliance with these treaties and the resolutions emanating from the international or supranational organizations who have been entitled by this cession.'

Constitution Article 94
'1. The giving of the consent of the State to obligate itself to something by means of treaties or agreements shall require prior authorization of the Cortes Generales in the following cases:
  (a) Treaties of a political nature.
  (b) Treaties or agreements of a military nature.
  (c) Treaties or agreements which affect the territorial integrity of the

State or the fundamental rights and duties established in Title I.
- (d) Treaties or agreements which imply important obligations for the public treasury.
- (e) Treaties or agreements which involve modification or repeal of some law or require legislative measures for their execution.
2. The Congress and the Senate shall be immediately informed of the conclusion of the treaties or agreements.'

Constitution Article 95
'1. The conclusion of an international treaty which contains stipulations contrary to the Constitution shall require a prior constitutional revision.
2. The Government or either of the Chambers may request the Constitutional Court to declare whether or not such a contradiction exists.'

Constitution Article 96
1. 'International Treaties validly concluded and officially published in Spain shall be an integral part of the domestic legal order. Their provisions may only be repealed, amended or suspended in the manner provided for in the treaties themselves or in accordance with general norms of international law.
2. To denounce international treaties and agreements, the same procedure established for their approval in Article 94 shall be used'.

See for a commentary on the constitutional position in Spain: F. Santaolalla Gadea and S. Martinez Lage, 'Spanish accession to the European Communities: Legal and constitutional implications', (1986) CMLRev., 11–37.

6. Portugal

Constitution Article 8

'International Law
1. The rules and principles of general or ordinary international law shall be an integral part of Portuguese law.
2. Rules derived from international conventions duly ratified or approved shall, following their official publication, become operative in the domestic legal order in so far as they are internationally binding on the Portuguese State.
3. Measures adopted by the competent organs of international organizations to which Portugal belongs, automatically form part of the domestic legal order in accordance with the treaties establishing such organizations'.

Chapter Four

Foundations of the Community

I. Introduction

In Part One of the Treaty which comprises the Articles 1 to 8C included are set out the Principles on which the EEC is based. Those Principles are further elaborated in the remaining parts of the Tready, but set the framework within which those more specific provisions of the Treaty should be interpreted. Having stated in Article 1 that a 'EUROPEAN ECONOMIC COMMUNITY' is established the Treaty in Article 2 lays down that this Community shall be based on a 'common market' on the one hand and on the progressive approximation the economic policies of Member States on the other. These two elements are elaborated further in the more detailed program set forth in Article 3, of which items a), b), c), f) and h) relate to the 'common market', whereas the other items except k) indicate areas where 'approximation of policies' is called for.

The difference between what sometimes has been called 'negative integration' (Common Market) and 'positive integration' (approximation of policies) has proved to be an important one, both in principle and in practice. Indeed, provisions relating to the creation of a common market through the elimination of national barriers between Member States tend to be spelled out more categorically in the Treaty as such and by that some token could form the basis for the development of the Court's case law of direct effect, which put private interests in the vanguard of the progress towards the realisation of the objectives set out in Articles 2 and 3 of the Treaty. On the contrary, the approximation of national policies inevitably has to rely largely on the positive cooperation of Member States and has to leave much more room for discretion as to what the actual content of the common policy in the area concerned will eventually be. It is not surprising that this has proved to be a more arduous task than the former.

Article 4 introduces the various Institutions of the Community and insists that each of them 'shall act within the limits of the powers conferred upon it by this Treaty'.

Articles 5 and 6 underline the spirit of co-operation between the Member States and the Institutions of the Community. The way in which Article 5 (2), which imposes on the Member States the obligation to 'abstain from any measure which could jeopardise the attainment of the objectives of this

Treaty', has proved to be a basis for further elaboration of the Court's case law is an apt illustration of the importance of these 'Principles' as laid down in the first few articles of the Treaty.

In effect the same can be said of Article 7 which in general terms prohibits 'any discrimination on grounds of nationality'.

Article 8, which provides the time schedule for the setting up of the Common Market, is becoming ever more confined to a provision of largely historical interest only. On the contrary, the provisions of Articles 8A, 8B and 8C, which have been inserted into the Treaty by the Single European Act are of great importance. Indeed, it is Article 8A in which the by now famous '1992 Program' has been enshrined in the EEC Treaty. According to this provision by the end of 1992 an 'Internal Market' should be established which is defined as 'an area without internal frontiers in which the free movement of goods, persons, services and capital is ensured in accordance with the provisions of this Treaty'. Whilst Article 8B elaborates somewhat further on the practical arrangements for this '1992 Program', Article 8C is of considerable political importance in that it explicitly recognises the fact that the concept of an 'Internal Market' might well create difficulties for certain Member States whose economies are less developed than others' and that accordingly proposals made by the Commission in this regard should take those differences into account.

II. General Principles

A. OBJECTIVES OF THE EEC (EEC TREATY ARTICLES 2 AND 3)

1. Cases

(1) French Maritime Labour Code Case

Commission of the EC v. France
Case 167/73; Judgment of 4 April 1974; [1974] ECR 369; [1974] 2 CMLR.

Facts:

Article 3 (2) of the French Code du Travail Maritime of 13 December 1926 provides that 'such proportion of the crew of a ship as is laid down by order of the Minister for the Merchant Fleet must be French nationals'.

The Ministerial Order of 21 November 1960 (JORF of 1-12-1960, p. 10770), as amended by the Ministerial Order of 12 June 1969 (JORF of 13-6-1969, p. 5923) issued in implementation of this provision, reserves, subject to special exemptions, employments on the bridge, in the engine room and in the wireless room on French vessels to persons of French nationality, and general employment on board is limited in the ratio of three French to one non-French.

In the view of the Commission this Article contravenes the provisions of Articles 1, 4 and 7 of Regulation No. 1612/68/EEC of the Council of 15 October 1968 (OJ L 257, 19. 10. 1968, p. 2) and at the end of an exchange of correspondence it invited the French Government on 8 October 1971, in accordance with Article 169 of the Treaty, to amend its legislation on the subject to comply with the Community provisions.

The French Government took some steps to amend its legislation but the Commission considered that the French Government had not honoured its obligations and started an action under Article 169 EEC.

The Court held:

. . . . .

'17. To determine whether, in the sphere of transport, Member States are bound by the obligations provided in Articles 48 to 51 of the Treaty, it is proper to consider the place of Title IV of Part Two of the Treaty, relating to transport, in the general system of the Treaty, and the place of Article 84 (2) within Title IV.
18. Under Article 2 of the Treaty, which is placed at the head of the general principles which govern it, the Community has as its task to promote throughout the Community a harmonious development of economic activities by establishing a common market and progressively approximating the economic policies of Member States.
19. The establishment of the common market thus refers to the whole of the economic activities in the Community.
20. The basic object of Part Two of the Treaty, devoted to foundations of the Community, is to establish the basis of the common market, i.e. free movement of goods (Title I) and free movement of persons, services and capital (Title III).
21. Conceived as being applicable to the whole complex of economic activities, these basic rules can be rendered inapplicable only as a result of express provision in the Treaty.
22. Such exemption is provided, in particular by Article 38 (2) under which the rules laid down for the establishment of the common market shall apply to agricultural products save as provided in Title II of this part of the Treaty.
23. As regards transport, which is the subject of Title IV of this part, it is proper to enquire, viewing Article 84 (2) in the framework of this Title, whether the provisions of the Title contain a similar exemption.
24. When Article 74 refers to the objectives of the Treaty, it means the provisions of Articles 2 and 3, for the attainment of which the fundamental provisions applicable to the whole complex of economic activity are of prime importance.

25. Far from involving a departure from these fundamental rules, therefore, the object of the rules relating to the common transport policy is to implement and complement them by means of common action.
26. Consequently the said general rules must be applied insofar as they can achieve these objectives.
27. Since transport is basically a service, it has been found necessary to provide a special system for it, taking into account the special aspects of this branch of activity.
28. With this object, a special exemption has been provided by Article 61 (1), under which freedom to provide services in the field of transport 'shall be governed by the provisions of the Title relating to transport', thus confirming that the general rules of the Treaty must be applied insofar as they are not excluded.
29. Article 84 (1) provides that the provisions of the Title relating to transport shall apply to transport by rail, road and inland waterway.
30. Article 84 (2) provides that as regards sea transport, the Council may decide whether, to what extent and by what procedure appropriate provisions may be laid down.
31. Far from excluding the applications of the Treaty to these matters, it provides only that the special provisions of the Title relating to transport shall not automatically apply to them.
32. Whilst under Article 84 (2), therefore, sea and air transport, so long as the Council has not decided otherwise, is excluded from the rules of Title IV of Part Two of the Treaty relating to the common transport policy, it remains, on the same basis as the other modes of transport, subject to the general rules of the Treaty.
33. It thus follows that the application of Articles 48 to 51 to the sphere of sea transport is not optional but obligatory for Member States.

B. MEMBER STATES' OBLIGATIONS (EEC TREATY ARTICLES 5 AND 6)

1. *Cases*

(1) Deutsche Grammophon Case

Deutsche Grammophon GmbH v. *Metro-SB-Grossmärkte GmbH & Co. KG*; Case 78/70; Preliminary Ruling of 8 July 1971; (1971) ECR 498; [1971] CMLR 631.

Facts:

The national court (Hanseatisches Oberlandesgericht) submitted the following questions:

1. Does an interpretation of Sections 97 and 85 of the Statute concerning Copyright and similar Protection Rights of 9 September 1965 (I BGBI, 1273), whereby a German manufacturer of sound recordings by virtue of its distribution rights, can prohibit the marketing in the German Federal Republic of recordings which it has itself supplied to its subsidiary in France which is legally separate but economically completely dependent, conflict with Article 5 (2) of Article 85 (1) of the EEC Treaty?
2. Can the exercise of the distribution rights by the manufacturer of recordings be regarded as abusive if the tied selling price of the records is higher than the price of the same product reimported from another Member State and at the same time the performers in question are bound by exclusive contracts to the manufacturer of the recordings (Article 86 of the EEC Treaty)?

The Court held:

. . . . .

4. It is clear from the facts recorded by the Hanseatische Oberlandesgericht, that what it asks may be reduced in essentials to the question whether the exclusive right of distributing the protected articles which is conferred by a national law on the manufacturer of sound recordings may, without infringing Community provisions, prevent the marketing on national territory of products lawfully distributed by such manufacturer or with his consent on the territory of another Member State. The Court of Justice is asked to define the tenor and the scope of the relevant Community provisions, with particular reference to the second paragraph of Article 5 or Article 85 (1).
5. According to the second paragraph of Article 5 of the Treaty, Member States 'shall abstain from any measure which could jeopardize the attainment of the objective of this Treaty'. This provision lays down a general duty for the Member States, the actual tenor of which depends in each individual case on the provisions of the Treaty or on the rules derived from its general scheme.

(2) ERTA Case

See at pages 6, 51, 169, 666, 676.

(3) International Fruit Company Case II

International Fruit Company N.V. and others v. *Produktschap voor Groenten en Fruit*; Joined cases 51 to 54/71; Preliminary ruling of 15 December 1971; [1971] ECR 1115.

Facts:

This case is concerned with the same facts as the *International Fruit Company Case I* (see at p. 65), the present case being brought before the national court ("College van Beroep voor het Bedrijfsleven"), which referred two questions to the Court of Justice for a preliminary ruling under Article 177 of the EEC Treaty.

The national court submitted the following question:
'1. Does the fact that the provisions of the Treaty establishing the European Economic Community together with those of the regulations based thereon conferring powers or imposing obligations "upon the Member States" with regard to the implementation of the Treaty or of regulations imply, on a correct interpretation of those provisions, that the Member States may only transfer such powers or obligations to their authorities by means of an express provision?'

The Court held:
The first question

2. The Court is first of all asked whether the fact that various provisions of the Treaty and of regulations confer powers or impose obligations upon the Member States implies that the latter may only transfer those powers or obligations to national authorities by express provision.
3. Although under Article 5 of the Treaty the Member States are obliged to take all appropriate measures, whether general or particular, to ensure fulfilment of the obligations arising out of the Treaty, it is for them to determine which institutions within the national system shall be empowered to adopt the said measures.
4. The answer to the first question must therefore be that when provisions of the Treaty or of regulations confer power or impose obligations upon the States for the purposes of the implementation of Community law the question of how the exercise of such powers and the fulfilment of such obligations may be entrusted by Member States to specific national bodies is solely a matter for the constitutional system of each State.

(4) Rewe Case

Rewe – Zentralfinanz and Rewe – Zentral v. *Landwirtschaftskammer für das*

Saarland; Case 33/76; Preliminary ruling of 16 December 1976; [1976] ECR 1997; [1977] 1 CMLR 533.

Facts:

In 1968 the German companies Rewe-Zentralfinanz A.G. and Rewe-Zentral A.G. paid in respect of the import of French apples charges for phytosanitary inspection which were found by the judgment of the Court of 11 October 1973 in Case 39/73 (1973) ECR 1039 to be equivalent to customs duties.

In 1973 the said companies applied to the Landwirtschaftskammer für das Saarland to annul the decision imposing the charges and to refund the amounts paid including interest. This claim was dismissed as inadmissible on the ground that it was out of time under Article 58 of the Verwaltungsgerichtsordnung (Code of Procedure before the Administrative Court). The actions brought by the two companies before the Verwaltungsgericht für das Saarland (Saarland Administrative Court) were dismissed as was the appeal made by them to the Oberverwaltungsgericht (Higher Administrative Court).

Rewe-Zentralfinanz and Rewe-Zentral then appealed to the Bundesverwaltungsgericht (Federal Administrative Court). The latter took the view that the question whether it is possible to rely on an infringement of Community law irrespective of the expiry of time-limits in general national procedural provisions required the interpretation of the EEC Treaty and by order dated 23 January 1976 stayed the appeal and referred the following questions to the Court for a preliminary ruling under Article 177 of the EEC Treaty:
1. Where an administrative body in one State has infringed the prohibition on charges having an effect equivalent to customs duties (Articles 5, 9 and 13 (2) of the EEC Treaty) has the Community citizen concerned a right under Community law to
   (a) the annulment or revocation of the administrative measure;
   (b) and/or to a refund of the amount paid even if under the rules of procedure of the national law the time-limit for contesting the validity of the administrative measure is past?
2. Is this the case at least if the European Court of Justice has already ruled that there does exist an infringement of the prohibition contained in Community law?
3. If a right to a refund is held to exist under Community law, is interest to be paid on the amount and if so, from what date and at what rate?

The Court held:
The first question

4. Both the respondent and the national court accept that the charges in question had been unlawfully exacted.

Although it was been possible to rely on the direct effect of Article 13 (2) of the EEC Treaty only as from 1 January 1970, the end of the transitional period, it should be stated however, that the levying of the said charges was already previously unlawful by virue of Article 13 (1) of Regulation No 159/66/EEC of the Council of 25 October 1966 (JO No 192 of 27 October 1966) which abolished them in respect of fruit and vegetables as from 1 January 1967.

5. The prohibition laid down in Article 13 of the Treaty and that laid down in Article 13 of Regulation No 159/66/EEC have a direct effect and confer on citizens rights which the national courts are required to protect.

 Applying the principle of co-operation laid down in Article 5 of the Treaty, it is the national courts which are entrusted with ensuring the legal protection which citizens derive from the direct effect of the provisions of Community law.

 Accordingly, in the absence of Community rules on this subject, it is for the domestic legal system of each Member State to designate the courts having jurisdiction and to determine the procedural conditions governing actions at law intended to ensure the protection of the rights which citizens have from the direct effect of Community law, it being understood that such conditions cannot be less favourable than those relating to similar actions of a domestic nature.

 Where necessary, Articles 100 to 102 and 235 of the Treaty enable appropriate measures to be taken to remedy differences between the provisions laid down by law, regulation or administrative action in Member States if they are likely to distort or harm the functioning of the Common Market.

 In the absence of such measures of harmonisation the right conferred by Community law must be exercised before the national courts in accordance with the conditions laid down by national rules.

 The position would be different only if the conditions and time-limits made it impossible in practice to exercise the rights which the national courts are obliged to protect.

 This is not the case where reasonable periods of limitation of actions are fixed.

 The laying down of such time-limits with regard to actions of a fiscal nature is an application of the fundamental principle of legal certainty protecting both the tax-payer and the administration concerned.

6. The answer to be given to the first question is therefore that in the present state of Community law there is nothing to prevent a citizen who contests before a national court a decision of a national authority on the ground that it is incompatible with Community law from being confronted with the defence that limitation periods laid down by national law have expired, it being understood that the procedural conditions governing the action may not be less favourable than those relating to similar actions of a domestic nature.

The second question

7. The fact that the Court has given a ruling on the question of infringement of the Treaty does not affect the reply given to the first question.

The third question

8. In view of the reply given to the first question the third question does not arise.

C. Non discrimination (EEC Treaty Article 7)

1. Cases

(1) Refrigerators Case

Italian Republic v. *Commission of the EEC*; Case 13/63; Judgment of 17 July 1963; [1963] ECR, p. 177; [1963] CMLR p. 289.

Facts:

Until 1961 the import of refrigerators into France was subject to licensing control. The freeing of trade between Member States of the Common Market led to considerable imports from Italy into France, imports which increased between 1961 and 1962. As a result, on 19 December 1962, the French Government asked the Commission for authority to adopt protective measures in accordance with Article 226 of the EEC Treaty.

By its decision of 17 January 1963, the Commission acceded to the request and authorised the French Republic to impose a special tax on the import from Italy of electric domestic refrigerators, as well as of hermetically sealed motor compressor sets for electric domestic refrigerators and other accessories, 'unless the Italian Republic should itself apply this tax on the export of the goods'. The amount of the tax was staggered over a period of time, and determined according to the particular product; these protective measures came to an end on 31 July 1963.

The Italian Government brought an application against the decision of the EEC Commission.

The Court held:

. . . . .

4. As to discrimination
   (a) Complaint is made that the Decision improperly infringed the principle of non-discrimination by authorising the French Government to impose a special tax on Italian products only, excluding the same products coming either from other States of the Community or from third countries.

   The different treatment of non-comparable situations does not lead automatically to the conclusion that there is discrimination. An appearance of formal discrimination may therefore correspond in fact to an absence of material discrimination. Material discrimination would consist in treatment either similar situations differently or different situations identically.

(2) Hochstrass Case

René Hochstrass v. Court of Justice of the European Communities; Case 147/79; Judgment of 16 October 1980; [1980] ECR, p. 3018; [1981] 2 CMLR, p. 586.

For the facts see the judgment below.

The Court held:

1. By an application lodged at the Court Registry on 21 September 1979 the applicant brought an action for a declaration that Article 4 (2) of Annex VII to the Staff Regulations, as amended by Article 21 (2) of Council Regulation No 912/78 of 2 May 1978 (OJ L 119, p. 1), is invalid. The provision in question is worded as follows: "An official who is not and never has been a national of the State in whose territory he is employed and who does not fulfil the conditions laid down in paragraph (1) shall be entitled to a foreign residence allowance equal to one quarter of the expatriation allowance". According to Article 4 (1) to which the above provision refers, the expatriation allowance is to be paid to officials, as referred to above, who "during the five years ending six months before they entered the service did not habitually reside or carry on their main occupation within the European territory of that State. For the purposes of this provision, circumstances arising from work done for another State or for an international organization shall not be taken into account". The applicant further asked the Court to annul the decision of the administration of the Court of Justice dated 22 June 1979 rejecting the applicant's complaint relating to the memorandum from the Registrar of the Court of 16 January 1979 refusing to pay him the foreign residence allowance referred to in the above mentioned provision.

. . . . .

6. The applicant maintains that the provision in question, which refers solely and exclusively to the criterion of nationality for granting or refusing the foreign residence allowance, is a breach of the general prohibition on discrimination on grounds of nationality which is derived from the Community legal order and which finds expression, in particular, in Article 7 of the EEC Treaty and in the provisions of the Staff Regulations. The criterion which has been adopted for granting the foreign residence allowance, it is alleged, is not an objective one from two aspects: on the one hand, nationality does not constitute an objective basis for differentiation directly related to the purpose of the rules in question, and on the other hand the situation of recipients of the said allowance is not objectively different from those who do not receive it. That argument shows that the alleged discrimination does not lie in the unequal treatment of recipients of the expatriation allowance and recipients of the foreign residence allowance, but in the unequality between the latter category of officials and the category of those who do not receive either of the two allowances.
7. According to the consistent case-law of the Court the general principle of equality, of which the prohibition of discrimination on grounds of nationality is merely a specific expression, is one of the fundamental principles of Community law. That principle requires that comparable situations should not be treated differently unless such differentiation is objectively justified. Clearly it requires that employees who are in identical situations should be governed by the same rules, but it does not prevent the Community legislature from taking into account objective differences in the conditions or situations in which those concerned are placed.
8. In order to test the validity of the contested provision in Regulation No. 912/78 it is therefore necessary to consider whether the situation of officials who are not and have never been nationals of the State in whose territory the place where they are employed is situated has objective features which justify treatment different from that of officials who are or have been nationals of that State.
9. It must therefore be ascertained whether the features of the system introduced by Regulation No 912/78 have the effect of restoring the equality which there must be among officials or, on the contrary, give rise to inequality between them.

. . . . .

12 The applicant's arguments must be rejected. It cannot be denied that an official who has not and has never had the nationality of the State in whose territory has place of employment is situated may be subject, by reason of his status as an alien, to a number of inconveniences both in law and in fact, of a civic, family, educational, cultural and political nature, which

251

the nationals of the country do not experience. As the foreign residence allowance is intended to compensate for the disadvantages which officials undergo as a result of their status as aliens, the Community legislature was entitled, in applying its discretionary judgment to that situation, to rely on the single criterion of nationality, whereas in the case of the expatriation allowance, the object of which is 'to compensate officials for the extra expense and inconvenience of taking up employment with the Communities and being thereby obliged to change their residence' (Case 21/74 *Airola*, Paragraph 8 of the decision of 20 February 1975, (1975) ECR 221 at p. 228), the Community legislature adopted as the principal criterion that of the official's usual place of residence, considering nationality as of only secondary importance.
13. Whilst it is true that officials may experience the inconveniences of living abroad to varying degrees, the criterion of nationality has the merit of being: uniform, applying in an identical manner to all officials irrespective of the place in which they work, objective in nature and in its universality having regard to the average effect of the inconveniences arising from residence abroad on the personal situation of those concerned, and directly related to the purpose of the rules, namely to compensate for the difficulties and disadvantages arising from the status of an alien in the host country.
14. Although in border-line cases fortuitous problems must arise from the introduction of any general and abstract system of rules, there are no grounds for taking exception to the fact that the legislature has resorted to categorization, provided that it is not in essence discriminatory having regard to the objective which it pursues.
15. It follows from all those considerations that no factor has been disclosed of such a kind as to affect the validity of the provision in Point 2 of Article 21 (2) of Council Regulation No 912/78; consequently there is no ground for annulling the decision of the administration of the Court of Justice of the European Communities rejecting the applicant's complaint. In the circumstances it is not necessary to examine the objection of inadmissibility on the ground of lack of interest in taking proceedings.

. . . . .

(3) Oebel Case

Criminal proceedings against *S. Oebel*: Case 155/80; Preliminary ruling of 14 July 1981; [1981] ECR 2005.

Facts:

In the main proceedings concerning a contravention Sergius Oebel, a business manager, is charged with infringing Article 5 of the Law on working hours in bakeries. The defendant is alleged to have permitted 15 workers to be engaged in the production of bakers' wares at about 2.00 a.m. on 21 July 1978 on the business premises of the undertaking Bockenheimer Brot GmbH in Wiesbaden.

In the belief that Article 5 of the Law on working hours in bakeries and confectionery shops might be incompatible with Articles 7, 30 and 34 of the EEC Treaty because it creates distortion in competition within the Community owing to the fact that the Federal Republic of Germany is the only Member State of the Community which maintains the prohibition on nightwork in the sector under consideration, and as that law in practice excludes the delivery of fresh products in other Member States adjacent to Germany in time for them to be sold early in the morning, the Amtsgericht Wiesbaden stayed the proceedings and referred the following questions to the Court of Justice pursuant to Article 177 of the EEC Treaty:

'1. Must Article 7 of the EEC Treaty be interpreted as meaning that there is a breach of the prohibition of discrimination if by means of a statutory provision a Member State of the Community creates a situation which considerably impairs the competitiveness of its own nationals in relation to comparable nationals of other Member States?
2. Must Articles 30 and 34 of the EEC Treaty be interpreted as meaning that the effects of Article 5 of the Gesetz über die Arbeitszeit in Bäckereien (Law on working hours in bakeries) in regard to the export and import of fresh bakers' wares are to be regarded as measures equivalent to quantitative restrictions on imports or quantitative restrictions on exports?'

The Court held:

First question

6. It is clear from the grounds set out in the order making the reference that the purpose of the first question is to ascertain whether rules of one Member State which, in certain areas bordering other Member States in which there are no such rules, lead to distortion of competition to the detriment of traders established in the territory of the first State, are to be considered as discriminatory under Article 7 of the Treaty.
7. As the Court has repeatedly stated, most recently it its judgment of 30 November 1978 (Case 31/78 *Bussone* [1978] ERC 2429, at p. 2446), the principle of non-discrimination contained in Article 7 is not infringed by rules which are applicable not on the basis of the nationality of traders, but on the basis of their location.
8. It follows that national rules which make no distinction, directly or indirectly, on the ground of the nationality of those subject to such rules, do not infringe Article 7, even if they affect the competitiveness of the traders covered by them.
9. Furthermore, as the Court stated in its judgment of 3 July 1979 (Joined

cases 185 to 204/78 *Van Dam* [1979] ECR 2345, at p. 2361), it cannot be held contrary to the principle of non-discrimination to apply national legislation merely because other Member States allegedly apply less strict rules.
10. The answer to the first question must therefore be that Article 7 of the EEC Treaty must be construed as prohibiting only discrimination on the ground of the nationality of traders. There is, therefore, no infringement of Article 7 even if by means of a statutory provision which makes no distinction directly or indirectly on grounds of nationality, a Member State creates a situation affecting the competitiveness of traders established on its territory compared with traders established in other Member States.

D. LITERATURE

Commission of the European Communities, *Studies Competition and Approximation of Legislation*, Series No 20.

J. Mertens de Wilmars, 'The Case Law of the Court of Justice in relation to the review of legality of economic policy in mixed-economy systems, (1982/1) L.I.E.I. 1.

S. Schepers, 'The legal force of the preamble to the EEC Treaty', (1981) ELRev. 356.

P. VerLoren van Themaat, *Economic Law of the Member States of the European Communities in an economic and monetary union*, Brussels, 1973.

III. The four freedoms

A. FREE MOVEMENT OF GOODS

1. *The Customs Union: all trade in goods*

a. Cases

(1) Art treasures Case I

Commission of the EC v. *Italian Republic*; Case 7/68; Judgment of 10 December 1968; (1968) ECR. p. 428 [1969] CMLR, p. 1.

Facts

Italian Law on the protection of articles of artistic or historic interest contains several provisions relating to the exportation of such articles; in particular, it provides, according to the circumstances, for an absolute prohibition on exportation, the requirements of a licence, a right of pre-emption vested in the State and the imposition on exportation of a progressive tax on the value of the article ranging by successive stages from 8% to 30%.

In January 1960, the Commission asked the Italian Republic to abolish the tax as regards the other Member States by the end of the first stage of the transitional period, that is to say, before 1 January 1962, since it considered that the tax had an effect equivalent to a customs duty on exportation and so was contrary to Article 16 of the EEC Treaty.

The Court held:

1. The scope of the disputed tax

By basing its action on Article 16 of the Treaty, the Commission considers that articles of an artistic, historic, archaeological or ethnographic nature, which are the subject of the Italian Law of 1 June 1939, No 1089, fall under the provisions relating to the customs union. This point of view is disputed by the defendant, which considers that the articles in question cannot be assimilated to 'consumer goods or articles of general use' and are not therefore subject to the provisions of the Treaty which apply to 'ordinary merchandise'; for that reason they are excluded from the application of Article

2. *Elimination of customs duties between the Member States and the setting up of the Common Customs Tariff (EEC Treaty Articles 9–29)*

a. Customs duties

1. CASES

(1) Van Gend – Loos Case

For facts and references see pp. 110, 160.

The Court held:

It follows from the wording and the general scheme of Article 12 of the Treaty that, in order to ascertain whether customs duties or charges having equivalent effect have been increased contrary to the prohibition contained in the said Article, regard must be had to the customs duties and charges actually applied at the date of the entry into force of the Treaty.

Further, with regard to the prohibition in Article 12 of the Treaty, such an illegal increase may arise from a re-arrangement of the tariff resulting in the classification of the product under a more highly taxed heading and from an actual increase in the rate of customs duty.

It is of little importance how the increase in customs duties occurred when, after the Treaty entered into force, the same product in the same Member State was subject to a higher rate of duty.

The application of Article 12, in accordance with the interpretation given above, comes within the jurisdiction of the national court which must enquire whether the dutiable product, in this case ureaformaldehyde originating in the Federal Republic of Germany, is charged under the customs measures brought into force in the Netherlands with an import duty higher than that with which it was charged on 1 January 1958.

. . . . .

b. Charges having an equivalent effect as customs duties

i. CASES

(1) Statistical Levy Case

Commission of the EC v. *Italian Republic*; Case 24/68; Judgment of 1 July 1969; [1969] ECR, p. 199; [1971] CMLR, p. 611.

Facts:

For some time before the entry into force of the EEC Treaty the Italian Republic had levied on goods imported and exported a charge called a 'statistical levy'. The tax is payable at a fixed amount of 10 lire on every 100 kilogrammes or every metric ton to goods or on every animal or vehicle with a minimum of 10 lire payable in each case even for goods in the smallest quantities.

After requesting clarification on this levy from the Italian authorities, the Commission took the view that it constituted a charge having an effect equivalent to customs duties on imports and exports.

The Court held:

The concept of a charge having equivalent effect

3. According to Article 9 of the EEC Treaty, the Community shall be based upon a customs union founded upon the prohibition between Member States of customs duties and of all charges having equivalent effect, and the adoption of a common customs tariff in their relations with third countries.

   Article 12 prohibits the introduction of new customs duties on imports or exports or any charges having equivalent effect. Under Articles 13 and 16 customs duties and charges having equivalent effect on both exports and imports in force between Member States are to be abolished in the manner laid down in those articles.

4. The position of these articles at the beginning of that Part of the Treaty reserved for the foundations of the Community, Article 9 being the first provision appearing at the very beginning of the Title dealing with the free movement of goods and Articles 12, 13 and 16 at the beginning of the section on the elimination of customs duties between Member States, is sufficient to show the fundamental role of the prohibitions laid down therein.

   The important of these prohibitions is such that in order to prevent their circumvention by means of various customs and fiscal measures, the Treaty was intended to prevent any possible failure in their implementation.

5. Article 17 therefore specifies that the prohibitions in Article 9 shall also apply to customs duties of a fiscal nature.

   Article 95, which appears both in that Part of the Treaty which deals with the 'Policy of the Community' and in the Chapter on tax provisions, is intended to fill in any breaches which a fiscal measure might open in the prohibitions laid down, by prohibiting the imposition on imported products of internal taxation in excess of that imposed on domestic products.

6. In prohibiting the imposition of customs duties, the Treaty does not distinguish between goods according to whether or not they enter into competition with the products of the importing country.

   Thus the purpose of the abolition of customs barriers is not merely to eliminate their protective nature, as the Treaty sought on the contrary to give general scope and effect to the rule on the elimination of customs duties and charges having equivalent effect, in order to ensure the free movement of goods.

7. It follows from the systems as a whole and from the general and absolute nature of the prohibition of any customs duty applicable to goods moving between Member States that customs duties are prohibited independently of any consideration of the purpose for which they were introduced and the destination of the revenue obtained there-from.

The justification for this prohibition is based on the fact that any pecuniary charge, however small, imposed on goods by reason of the fact that they cross a frontier constitutes an obstacle to the movement of such goods.

8. The extension of the prohibition of customs duties to charges having equivalent effect is intended to supplement the prohibition against obstacles to trade created by such duties by increasing its efficiency.

The use of these two complementary concepts thus tends, in trade between Member States, to avoid the imposition of any pecuniary charge on goods circulating within the Community by virue of the fact that they cross a national frontier.

9. Thus, in order to ascribe to a charge an effect equivalent to a customs duty, it is important to consider this effect in the light of the objectives of the Treaty, in the Parts, Titles and Chapters in which Articles 9, 12, 13 and 16 are to be found, particularly in relation to the free movement of goods.

Consequently, any pecuniary charge, however small and whatever its designation and mode of application, which is imposed unilaterally on domestic or foreign goods by reason of the fact that they cross a frontier, and which is not a customs duty in the strict sense, constitutes a charge having equivalent effect within the meaning of Articles 9, 12, 13 and 16 of the Treaty, even if it is not imposed for the benefit of the State, is not discriminatory or protective in effect and if the product on which the charge is imposed is not in competition with any domestic product.

10. It follows from all the provisions referred to and from their relationship with the other provisions of the Treaty that the prohibition of new customs duties or charges having equivalent effect, linked to the principle of the free movement of goods, constitutes a fundamental rule which, without prejudice to the other provisions of the Treaty, does not permit of any exceptions.

11. In this respect, it follows from Articles 95 et seq that the concept of a charge having equivalent effect does not include taxation which is imposed in the same way within a State on similar or comparable domestic products, or at least falls, in the absence of such products within the framework of general internal taxation, or which is intended to compensate for such internal taxation within the limits laid down by the Treaty.

Although it is not impossible that in certain circumstances a specific service actually rendered may form the consideration for a possible proportional payment for the service in question, this may only apply in specific cases which cannot lead to the circumvention of the provisions of Articles 9, 12, 13 and 16 of the Treaty.

The disputed charge

12. The defendant emphasizes in the first place that the Commission is wrong

in dividing the statistical levy into two distinct concepts, one relating to imports and the other to exports, when the legal nature of the disputed charge should be determined by taking account of its true nature and not by breaking it down into two distinct charges.

According to the defendant the circumstance that the statistical levy is imposed whenever goods cross the frontier without distinquishing between exports and imports or between domestic and foreign goods ipso facto precludes any possibility of considering it as a charge having an effect equivalent to customs duties since any protection of domestic production or discrimination is eliminated.

13. On the other hand the Commission breaks down the disputed levy into two distinct charges having effects equivalent respectively to a customs duty on imports and to a customs duty on exports and with protective or discriminatory effects although to a very slight degree.
14. It is of no consequence for its designation under the Treaty whether the disputed charge is treated as a general charge or as two distinct charges, one on exports and the other on imports.

    As it is imposed universally on good crossing the frontier, the charge in question hampers the interpenetration at which the Treaty aims and thus has an effect on the free circulation of goods equivalent to a customs duty.

    The very low rate of the charge cannot change its character with regard to the principles of the Treaty which, for the purpose of determining the legality of those charges, do not admit of the substitution of quantitative criteria for those based on the nature of the charge.
15. The Italian Government further maintains that the disputed charge constitutes the consideration for a service rendered and as such cannot be designated as a charge having equivalent effect.

    According to the Italian Government the object of the statistics in question is to determine precisely the actual movements of goods and, consequently, changes the state of the market. It claims that the exactness of the information thus supplied affords importers a better competitive position in the Italian market whilst exporters enjoy a similar advantage abroad and that the special advantages which dealers obtain from the survey justifies their paying for this public service and moreover demonstrates that the disputed charge is in the nature of a 'quid pro quo'.
16. The statistical information in question is beneficial to the economy as a whole and inter alia to the relevant administrative authorities.

    Even if the competitive position of importers and exporters were to be particularly improved as a result, the statistics still constitute an advantage so general, and so difficult to assess, that the disputed charge cannot be regarded as the consideration for a specific benefit actually conferred.
17. It appears from the abovementioned considerations that in so far as the disputed charge is levied on exports it is contrary to Article 16 of the Treaty.

18. With regard to the statistical levy on the import from other Member States of products subject to regulations relating to the common organisation of the markets the abovementioned provisions of such regulations prohibit the levying of any customs duty or charge having equivalent effect on trade between the Member States.

The concept of a 'charge having equivalent effect' accessory to that of 'customs duty' was re-enacted in the abovementioned regulations from Articles 9, 12 and 13 of the Treaty.

Nothing in the said regulations justifies the conclusion that they are intended to confer on this concept a scope different from that which it has within the framework of the Treaty itself, especially as, when those regulations take account of the particular conditions for establishing a common market in agricultural products, they pursue the same objectives as Articles 9 to 13 of the Treaty which they implement.

. . . . .

(2) Capolongo Case

Carmine Capolongo v. *Azienda Agricola Maya*; Case 77/72; Preliminary Ruling of 19 June 1973; [1973] ECR 622; [1974] I CMLR p. 230.

Facts:

Carmine Capolongo bought from Azienda Agricola Maya a large quantity of eggs which were delivered in cardboard containers. The invoice included an item of 2,908 lire described as a tax of 1.75% as 'Contributo Ente Nazionale per la Cellulosa e per la Carta', levied on the containers which had been imported from Germany.

The Ente Nazionale per la Cellulosa e per la Carta is a public corporation comprising producers of paper and cellulose and users of the latter and having the object of promoting the production in Italy of cellulose products and paper which it did by subsidising certain paper using operations and exports. It was financed by a charge levied on cellulose, paper and cardboard, whether produced domestically or imported. Producers and importers were entitled to pass on part of the charge to their customers.

Capolongo objected to paying the charge invoiced to him and after making payment brought an action before the Pretore of Conegliano for its repayment. The Pretore, on receipt of the detailed statement of claim and without having yet heard the defendant, referred 5 questions to the European Court of Justice by order dated 20 November 1972 for a preliminary ruling.

The Court held:

. . . . .

As to the third question

7. It is asked whether the collection of a financial charge on the basis of a percentage calculated by reference to the value of the product imported from other Member States constitutes an infringement of Article 13 (2) of the Treaty or any other rule of the Treaty prohibiting the application of special taxation on imports coming from other Member States.
8. In the absence of accurate information relating to the objectives, nature and methods of collection of the duty in dispute, it must be stated that, in exercise of the powers conferred by Article 177, the Court, having to limit itself to giving an interpretation of the provisions of Community law in question, cannot consider legal acts and provisions of national law, the risk being that the reply will correspond only imperfectly to the circumstances of the case.
9. Article 13 (1) provides that customs duties on imports applying between Member States at the date of the entry into force of the Treaty, shall be progressively abolished during the transitional period in accordance with Articles 14 and 15.

    Articles 14 and 15 contain the provisions necessary to this end, so that by the end of the transitional period all customs duties on imports between Member States will have disappeared.

    Article 13 (2) complements Articles 13 (1) by enacting that charges having an equivalent effect to customs duties on imports, in force between Member States, shall be progressively abolished during the transitional period.
10. Thus the provisions relating to the elimination of customs duties between Member States, which form the first section of the first chapter, entitled 'The Customs Union', are designed to ensure that the objective set out in Article 9 of the Treaty will be realized by the end of the transitional period.

    Although such provisions make certain adjustments and allowances during the transitional period, it follows from their wording that such laws and taxes must in any event be entirely abolished at the latest by the end of the said period.
11. Article 13 (2), therefore, comprises a clear and precise prohibition, as from the end of the transitional period at the latest and for all charges having an effect equivalent to customs duties, on the collecting of the said charges, which prohibition has no reservation allowing States to subject its implementation to a positive measure of domestic law or to an intervention by the institutions of the Community.

This prohibition lends intself, by its very nature, to producing direct effects in the legal relations between Member States and their subjects.
12. It is aimed at any tax demanded at the time of or by reason of importation and which, being imposed specifically on an imported product to the exclusion of the similar domestic product, results in the same restrictive consequences on the free movement of goods as a customs duty by altering the cost price of that product.

Even pecuniary charges intended to finance the activities of an agency governed by public law can constitute taxes having equivalent effect within the meaning of Article 13 (2) of the Treaty.

On the other hand, financial charges within a general system of internal taxation applying systematically to domestic and imported products according to the same criteria are not to be considered as charges having equivalent effect.
13. In the interpretation of the concept 'charge having an effect equivalent to a customs duty on imports', the destination of the financial charges levied must be taken into account.

In effect, when such a financial charge or duty is intended exclusively to support activities which specifically profit taxed domestic products, it can follow that the general duty levied according to the same criteria on the imported product and the domestic product nevertheless constitutes for the former a net supplementary tax burden, whilst for the latter it constitutes in reality a set-off against benefits or aids preciously received.
14. Consequently, a duty within the general system of internal taxation applying systematically to domestic and imported products according to the same criteria, can nevertheless constitute a charge having an effect equivalent to customs duty on imports, when such contribution is intended exclusively to support activities specifically benefit the taxed domestic product.

. . . . .

(3) Bauhuis Case

Bauhuis v. *The Kingdom of the Netherlands*; Case 46/76; Preliminary Ruling of 25 January 1977; [1977] ECR 14.

Facts:

In accordance with provisions of Netherlands Law relating to live-stock (Veewet) the plaintiff in the main action paid fees for veterinary and public health inspections when in November and December 1970 he imported into the Netherlands swine coming from Member States and when from August 1966 to July 1971 he exported swine, swine for breeding, bovine animals, bovine animals for breeding and horses from the Netherlands to other Member States. Since he takes the view that these fees, 588 guilders for the imports and 32,265.90 guilders for the exports, are not payable because they were levied in contra-vention of Community provisions, which prohibit the collection of charges having an effect equivalent to customs on imports and exports, he asks for the total amount of 32,853.90 guilders to be refunded together with interest at the rate allowed by law as from 15 January 1972.

By its judgment of 10 May 1976 the Arondissementsrechtbank, The Hague, before which this action was brought, allowed the claim for a refund of the fees paid when the import inspections were made. As far as the fees levied for the veterinary inspection on the export of the animals in question is concerned, this court, whilst reserving judgment, rejected certain submissions of the Netherlands Government in support of the view that the imposition of these fees complies with Community law but also decided to refer to the Court the following questions:

'Is the phrase /'charges having an effect equivalent to customs duties on exports'/ to be interpreted as including pecuniary charges which are imposed by a Member State in respect of the veterinary and public health inspection of livestock which is intended to be exported to another Member State in so far as such pecuniary charges suffice to cover, and do not exceed, the actual costs of a veterinary and public health inspection which is carried out by authority of the Government:

(a) (as regards bovine animals and swine)
   in compliance with obligations imposed on the exporting Member State by the Council of the European Economic Community in its Directive No 64/432/EEC of 26 June 1964; or
(b) (as regards bovine animals and swine)
   in compliance with the obligations referred to at (a) above, and in addition to ensure that the bovine animals and swine concerned satisfy the particular conditions laid down for the importation thereof by the importing Member State; or
(c) (as regards animals other than bovine animals or swine)
   in order to ensure that the animals concerned satisfy the conditions laid down for the importation thereof by the importing Member State?'

The Court held:

6. It is however advisable to specify first of all the legal framework within which the questions referred have to be answered.
7. Article 9 of the EEC Treaty prohibits between Member States customs duties on imports and exports and all charges having equivalent effect.
8. Under Article 16 Member States shall abolish between themselves customs duties on exports and charges having equivalent effect by the end of the first stage of the transitional period at the latest.
9. The justification for the prohibition of charges having an effect equivalent

to customs duties lies in the fact that any pecuniary charge, however small, impoed on goods by reason of the fact that they cross a frontier constitutes an obstacle to the movement of goods, which is aggravated by the resulting administrative form-alities.
10. Consequently, any pecuniary charge, whatever its designation and mode of application, which is imposed unilaterally on goods by reason of the fact that they cross an frontier and which is not a customs duty in the strict sense, constitutes a charge having equivalent effect within the meaning of Articles 9, 12, 13 and 16 of the Treaty, even if it is not imposed for the benefit of the State.
11. The position would be different only if the charge in question is the consideration for a benefit provided in fact for the exporter representing an amount proportionate to the said benefit or if it related to a general system of internal dues applied systematically in accordance with the same criteria to domestic products and imported products alike.
12. Although Article 36 of the Treaty provides that 'The provisions of Articles 30 to 34 shall not preclude prohibitions or quantitative restrictions on imports ... justified on grounds of ... the protection of health and life of humans, animals ...', this provision constitutes a derogation from the basic rule that all obstacles to the free movement of goods between Member States shall be eliminated and must be interpreted strictly and thus cannot be understood as authorizing measures of a different nature from those referred to in Articles 30 to 34.
13. Consequently, although Article 36 does not prevent veterinary and public health inspections it cannot nevertheless be interpreted as thereby permitting the imposition of charges levied on imported goods subjected to the said inspections and intended to cover the costs thereof.
14. In fact this charge is not intrinsically necessary for the exercise of the power laid down in Article 36 and is thus capable of constituting an additional barrier to intra-Community trade.

. . . . .

c. Internal taxation

i. CASES

(1) Lütticke Case II

Alfons Lütticke v. *Hauptzollamt Saarlouis*; Case 57/65; Preliminary ruling of 16 June 1966; [1966] ECR 209; [1971] CMLR 674.

Facts:

The facts may be summarized as follows:

On 9 October 1963, the undertaking Alfons Lütticke GmbH, of Köln-Deutz, the plaintiff in the main action, requested and customs office, Nennig, to given customs clearance for 15,000 kg of whole milk powder originating in Luxembourg. In granting the request, the customs purposes of 29,815.50 DM, required the plaintiff to pay the sums of 3,279.70 DM as customs duties and 1,323.80 DM as turnover equalization tax ('Umsatzausgleichsteuer').

The plaintiff's representative made an administrative complaint against the second section of that decision, alleging that the turnover equalization tax demanded was unfounded in law. Since 1 February 1956, paragraph 4, No 20 (f), of the Turnover Tax Law ('Umsatzsteuergesetz') has exempted domestic whole milk powder from the internal turnover tax. Pursuant to paragraph 4, No 25, of the Turnover Tax Law, after 30 June 1961 supplies of the basis product, that is to say, milk, were also exempt from the turnover tax, so that the levying of the turnover equalization tax was prohibited under Article 95 of the EEC Treaty.

The Hauptzollamt (Principal Customs Office) by decision of 23 January 1964, rejected the complaint as unfounded and the Lütticke company lodged an appeal against this rejection with the Finanzgericht des Saarlandes.

In its Order of 25 November 1965 the Finanzgericht took the view that the result of the dispute depends, on the one hand, on whether the turnover equalization tax is an internal tax or a charge having equivalent effect to that of customs duties and, on the other hand, on whether the provisions of Article 95 of the Treaty have direct effect so as to create individual rights of which national courts must take account, and it therefore stayed the proceedings and made a reference to the Court of Justice under Article 177 of the Treaty in order to obtain a preliminary ruling on the questions which it formulated as follows:

1. Does the first paragraph of Article 95 of the EEC Treaty have direct effect, creating individual rights of which the national cosurts must take account?

If the answer to this question is in the negative:

2. Does the third paragraph of Article 95 of the EEC Treaty in conjunction with the first paragraph of that Article have direct effect as from 1 January 1962 and create individual rights of whichs the national courts must take account?

If the answer to this second question is also in the negative:

3. Do the first and third paragraphs of Article 95 of the EEC Treaty in conjunction with Articles 12 and 13 thereof have direct effect creating individual rights of which the national courts must take account?

The Court held:

1. The first and second questions

In its first question, the Finanzgericht des Saarlandes requests the Court to rule whether the first paragraph of Article 95 of the Treaty produces direct effects and creates individual rights of which national courts must take account. If a negative answer is given to this question, the Finanzgericht asks whether, as from 1 January 1962, the third paragraph of the same Article, together with the first paragraph, produces the effects and creates the rights mentioned above.

It is necessary to consider the two questions together and first of all to clarify the relationship between the said paragraphs of Article 95.

The first paragraph of Article of Article 95 sets forth, as a general and permanent rule of Community law that Member States shall not impose on the products of other Member States any internal taxation in excess of that imposed on similar domestic products. Such a system, often adopted by the Treaty to ensure the equal treatment of nationals within the Community under national legal systems, constitutes in fiscal matters the indispensable foundation of the Common Market. In order to facilitate the adaptation of national legal systems to this rule, the third paragraph of Article 95 allows Member States a period of grace lasting until the beginning of the second stage of the transitional period, that is to say, until 1 January 1962, to repeal or amend any 'provisions existing when this Treaty enters into force which conflict with the preceding rules'. Article 95 thus contains a general rule provided with a simple suspensory clause with regard to provisions existing when it entered into force. From this it must be concluded that on the expiry of the said period the general rule emerges unconditionally into full force.

The question raised by the Finanzgericht must be considered in the light of the foregoing considerations.

The first paragraph of Article 95 contains a prohibition against discrimination, constituting a clear and unconditional obligation. With the exception of the third paragraph this obligation is not qualified by any condition, or subject, in its implementation or effects, to the taking of any measure either by the institutions of the Community or by the Member States. This prohibition is therefore complete, legally perfect and consequently capable of producing direct effects on the legal relationships between the Member States and persons within their jurisdiction. The fact that this Article describes the Member States as being subject to the obligation of non-discrimination does not imply that individuals cannot benefit from it.

With regard to the third paragraph of Article 95, it indeed imposes an obligation on the Member States to 'repeal' or 'amend' any provisions which conflict with the rules set out in the preceding paragraphs. The said obligation however leaves no discretion to the Member States with regard to the date by which these operations must have been carried out, that is to say, before 1 January 1962. After this date it is sufficient for the national court to find, should the case arise, that the measures implementing the contested national rules of law were adopted after 1 January 1962 in order to be able to apply the first paragraph directly in any event. Thus the provisions of the third paragraph prevent the application of the general rule only with regard to implementing measures adopted before 1 January 1962, and founded upon provisions existing when the Treaty entered into force.

In the oral and written observations which have been submitted in the course of the proceedings, three governments have relied on Article 97 in order to support a different interpretation of Article 95.

In empowering Member States which levy a turnover tax calculated on a cumulative multi-stage tax system to establish average rates for products or groups of products, the said Article thus constitutes a special rule for adapting Article 95 and this rule is, by its nature, incapable of creating direct effects on the relationships between the Member States and persons subject to their jurisdiction. This situation is peculiar to Article 97, and can in no circumstances influence the interpretation of Article 95.

It follows from the foregoing that, notwithstanding the exception in the third paragraph for provisions existing when the Treaty entered into force until 1 January 1962, the prohibition contained in Article 95 produced direct effects and creates individual rights of which national courts must take account.

2. The third question

In its third question, the Finanzgericht requests the Court to rule whether 'the first and third paragraphs of Article 95 of the EEC Treaty in conjunction with Articles 12 and 13 thereof have direct effect creating individual rights of which the national courts must take account'.

Since the question was only raised in the event of the Court's answering the first two questions in the negative, it is unnecessary to give a reply to it. It should however be made clear that Articles 12 and 13 on the one hand and Article 95 on the other cannot be applied jointly to one and the same case. Charges having an effect equivalent to customs duties on the one hand and internal taxation on the other hand are governed by different systems. In this respect it should be noted that a charge intended to offset the effect of internal taxation thereby takes on the internal character of the taxation whose effect it is intended to offset.

. . . . .

(2) Statens Kontrol Case

Statens Kontrol medaedle Metaller v. *Larsen*; Case 142/77; Preliminary ruling of 29 June 1978; [1978] ECR 1554; [1979] 2 CMLR 680.

For the facts see the judgment below.

The Court held:

1. By order of 2 November 1977, which reached the Court on 18 November

1977, Københavns Byret referred to the Court under Article 177 of the EEC Treaty four questions for a preliminary ruling on the interpretation of the concepts of charge having an effect equivalent to a customs duty on exports within the meaning of Article 16 and of internal taxation within the meaning of the first paragraph of Article 85 of the EEC Treaty in relation to the Danish legislation on the control of articles of precious metal.

2. These questions were raised within the context of a dispute between the Statens Kontrol medaedle Metaller (National Authority for the Control of Precious Metals) and two goldsmiths over the payment of the charge introduced to cover the expenses of the supervision of undertakings manufacturing, importing or dealing in articles of precious metal.

3. It results from the file that the dispute brought before the national court is essentially caused by the uncertainties which existed in the Danish legislation as to whether or not precious metal worked in Denmark and exported in the form of articles not bearing a Danish mark must be included in the chargeable consumption on which the taxation of the undertakings is assessed.

4. By judgment of 4 March 1975 Københavns Byret found in favour of the goldsmiths in these cases, acknowledging that there is no need, for the purpose of establishing the basis of the assessment to the tax, to include the consumption of precious metal used in the manufacture of goods exported without the application of their mark.

5. The Statens Kontrol medaedle Metaller appealed against that judgment and the Østre Landsret (Court of Appeal for Eastern Denmark), by judgment of 21 October 1976, dismissed the arguments put forward by the goldsmiths and ruled that the consumption of precious metal exported without application of its mark must be included in the chargeable consumption of the exporting undertaking.

6. As the goldsmiths concerned relied, in the alternative, on the argument that the levying of such a charge was contrary to the EEC Treaty, the Østre Landsret referred the case to Københavns Byret for the examination of that question.

7. As a result of that reference, Københavns Byret referred to the Court four questions for a preliminary ruling worded as follows:
   1. Does a levy which is imposed upon undertakings manufacturing, importing or dealing in articles of precious metal in order to meet the costs of the supervision of such undertakings by the authorities and which is calculated on the basis of the undertakings' consumption of precious metals constitute a charge having an effect equivalent to a customs duty on exports within the meaning of Article 16 of the EEC Treaty when it is imposed upon all undertakings which are subject to such supervision in accordance with provisions whereby one and the same article is only subject to charge on one occasion in Denmark irrespective of whether it is again subject to charge abroad?
   2. Where manufacture is effected for other persons but the manufacturer does not apply his own mark is the answer to Question 1 affected by

the fact that such consumption of precious metal is not included in the calculation of the chargeable value when such goods are manufactured for a Danish owner of a mark since the latter includes such precious metals in the account of his chargeable consumption whilst the consumption must be included when manufacture is for a foreign undertaking which is not subject to the charge in Denmark since such consumption would not otherwise be included in the basis for the Danish levy, still irrespective of whether it is again subject to charge abroad?
3. In his connection is it relevant that the precious metal which is made up in Denmark is supplied to the Danish manufacturer by the foreign customer in question to whom the finished product is re-exported?
4. If such a levy is not regarded as constituting a charge having an effect equivalent to a customs duty on exports is it to be regarded as internal taxation (on the imported quantity of gold) contrary to the first paragraph of Article 95 of the EEC Treaty?

The first, the second and third questions (interpretation of Article 16)

8. It follows from the information supplied by Københavns Byret that the Statens Kontrol medaedle Metaller generally supervises on the national territory the production of articles of precious metal, in other words gold, silver and platinum.
9. The costs of that control are covered inter alia by contributions paid by the undertakings in the form of a charge calculated on the basis of the consumption of precious metal of each undertaking.
10. So far as articles marketed on the national territory are concerned, the metal used by each undertaking and bearing the mark of that undertaking forms the basis of assessment to that charge.
11. Articles not marked by the manufacturer are exempted from the charge where they are transferred to the owner of a mark since in that case the consumption of metal in question is, on account of the undertaking owning the mark.
12. The quantities of metal exported, which are exempted by the law from the duty of marking, must be included in the chargeable consumption of the exporting undertaking, as results from the above-mentioned judgment of the Østre Landsret.
13. This charge is explained by the fact that those quantities of metal, which are subject to the control on the same conditions as metal marketed on the national territory, would otehwise escape all taxation in the absence of the application of a Danish mark.
14. It therefore appears that the system of taxation in question is intended to make subject to tax all precious metal used by Danish undertakings and that for that reason all quantities of metal imported, dealt in on the actual territory of Denmark or exported are included in the chargeable consumption of those undertakings according to the same criteria and without any distinction as to origin or destination.

15. It is therefore a system of internal taxation in the sense in which that expression is used in Article 95 et seq. of the Treaty.
16. Where products intended for export are included in the chargeable consumption of the exporter, the charges levied on that account cannot be described as charges having an effect equivalent to a customs duty on exports, since the characteristics of those duties is that they are imposed specifically on exported products and not on the same products marketed on the national territory, this does not apply in the present case.
17. It follows from the foregoing that the first question must be answered in the negative and that the second and third questions are therefore purposeless.
18. The subject-matter of the dispute must therefore be examined exclusively from the point of view of the system of the Treaty as regards the application, in intra-Community trade, of the provisions on internal taxation to which the fourth question refers.
19. Within this context, it is however appropriate to take into account both the third question on contract work carried out for a foreign customer and an aspect of the first and second questions on the possible effects of double taxation when precious metals are exported to other States.

The fourth question (scope of Article 95)

20. The fourth question calls for examination of the problem whether the rule against discrimination laid down by Article 95 of the Treaty is also applicable when a domestic charge is imposed on a product intended for export and, if the answer is in the affirmative, whether a system of taxation such as applied in Denmark with regard to the control of articles of precious metal is compatible with that rule against discrimination.
21. The wording of Article 95 refers only to the discriminatory application of systems of internal taxation to products imported from other Member States.
22. The application of the same systems of taxation to exports is referred to in Articles 96 to 98 from the point of view of the repayment of excessive taxation which may distort conditions of trade within the common market.
23. It follows from a comparison of those provisions that the aim of the Treaty in this field is to guarantee generally the neutrality of systems of internal taxation with regard to intra-Community trade whenever an economic transaction going beyond the frontiers of a Member States at the same time constitutes the chargeable event giving rise to a fiscal charge within the context of such a system.
24. It therefore seems necessary to interpret Article 95 as meaning that the rule against discrimination which forms the basis of that provision also applies when the export of a product constitutes, within the context of a system of internal taxation, the chargeable event giving rise to a fiscal charge.

25. It would in fact be incompatible with the system of the tax provisions laid down in the Treaty to acknowledge that Member States, in the absence of an express prohibition laid down in the Treaty, are free to apply in a discriminatory manner a system of internal taxation to products intended for export to other Member States.
26. Although it is true that as a general rule the States have no interest in curbing their exports by measures of that kind, it is however impossible to rule out the possibility of such discrimination in cases such as the export of rare products which are particularly valuable or especially sought after.
27. It is therefore appropriate to hold, as the Court of Justice has already indicated in its judgment of 23 January 1975 (*P.J. van der Hulst's Zonen* v. *Produktschap voor Siergewassen*, Case 51/74 [1975] ECR 79, paragraph 34 of the decision), that Article 95, considered in conjunction with the other tax procisions laid down in the Treaty, must be interpreted as also prohibiting any tax discrimination against products intended for export to other Member States.
28. It is appropriate to appraise, in the light of the foregoing, the question whether a system of internal taxation such as the one at issue in the dispute brought before Københavns Byret is compatible with the requirements of the Treaty.
29. In view of the information supplied by the national court, it is impossible to consider as discriminatory a system of levies so arranged that all undertakings using precious metal are obliged to pay their share of tax so that purely national transactions and transactions relating to the import or export of those metals are made subject to tax on the same account.
29. In view of the information supplied by the national court, it is impossible to consider as distriminatory a system of levies so arranged that all undertakings using precious metal are obliged to pay their share of tax so that purely national transactions and transactions relating to the import or export of those metals are made subject to tax on the same account.
30. More particularly, if the application of a mark consitutes the condition for the placing of precious metal into circulation on the national territory with the result that the duty to pay tax is linked to the application of the mark by the undertaking in question there is no discrimination in including in the chargeable consumption of an undertaking the quantities of metal exported by the latter without the application of a mark.
31. The same consideration applies to the case referred to in the third question in which the precious metal made up on the national territory was supplied to the manufacturer by a foreign customer to whom the finished product is re-exported, as long as such a transaction fulfils the conditions to which the national legislation attaches a duty to pay tax in the case of similar operations carried out on the national territory even if, in the absence of the application of a mark on exports, the procedure for taxation is different.
32. It follows from the fist two questions which have been submitted that the national court asks whether an exemption for quantities of precious metal

exported without the application of a mark would be justified if the products in question were intended to undergo a fresh control, with the levying of charges in respect thereof, in the country of destination.
33. It is necessary to observe in this connection that the EEC Treaty contains no provision prohibiting effects of double taxation of this type.
34. Although the abolition of such effects is doubtless desirable in the interest of the freedom of movement of goods, it can however only result from the harmonization of the national systems under Article 99 or possibly Article 100 of the Treaty.
35. At present, Community law does not however contain any rules which prevent a Member State from also including, in the application of a system of taxation intended to finance the control of precious metal, products intended for export.
36. For the same reason, the fact that a system of taxation is arranged so that the same quantity of metal marketed on the national territory can be included only once for the purpose of establishing the basis of assessment to the levy intended to finance the control of precious metal is not such as to make the application of the same tax to exported products appear discriminatory when the procedures for the control and for the taxation of imports in other States are not within the influence of the exporting State.
37. It is therefore necessary to reply as stated above to the questions submitted to this Court by Københavns Byret.

(3) Taxation of alcohol in Ireland Case

Commission v. *Ireland*; Case 55/79; Judgment of 27 February 1980; (1980) ECR 490; [1980] 1 CMLR 734.

For the facts see the judgment below.

The Court held:

. . . . .

2. The facts which gave rise to the action are not contested by Ireland. It is in fact common ground that the legal provisions applicable in Ireland, in particular pursuant to the Imposition of Duties (No 221) (Excise Duties) Order 1975, provide in favour of producers of spirits, beer and made wine for deferment of payment of between four and six weeks according to the product whereas, in the case of the same products from other Member States, the duty is payable either at the date of importation or of delivery from the customs warehouse.

3. The Commission acknowledges that there is no discrimination as regards the rates of duty applicable. On the other hand, it considers that the fact that Irish products are granted deferment of payment beyond the date on which the products are put on the market amounts to conferring on national producers a financial benefit in comparison with importers who are obliged to pay the duty on the actual date on which the products are released to the market. This results, according to the Commission, in a disadvantage to imported products in competition with the corresponding Irish national production.

. . . . .

5. The Government of Ireland claims in its defence that the detailed arrangements for levying the duty have to be adaptable to the different circumstances of home-produced products and imported products. It states that the decisive criterion is the rate of duty applied, whilst the wording of Article 95 merely prohibits the Member States from imposing on the products of other Member States taxation 'in excess' of that imposed on domestic products; to introduce factors which do not appear in its wording is to do violence to that provision.
6. The Government of Ireland relies in addition upon the fact that Irish producers, as consideration for the advantage given them as regards deferment of payment, must accept corresponding disadvantages. Thus, in order to obtain deferred payment, they must pay an additional duty and furnish the authorities with security for payment. It states that it is necessary moreover to take into account the disadvantage suffered by Irish whisky producers in competition with Scotch whisky owing to the divergent exchange rates between the Irish and United Kingdom 'green pounds'.
7. Finally, the Government of Ireland claims once more that the discrimination complained of by the Commission must be abolished with the context of the harmonization of tax legislation and that it does not come within the scope of Article 95.

. . . . .

10. As the Commission has correctly stated, the fact that Irish producers may only benefit from the facilities for deferred payment by paying additional duty and furnishing financial security does not remove that discrimination. Those two obligations are so trifling that their effect is not to compensate for the benefit reserved to Irish producers. Moreover, there is nothing to prevent the Irish authorities from imposing the same additional duty on importers and from requiring the latter to supply similar security.

11. Similarly, the argument based on the difference in the rate of the Irish and United Kingdom 'green pounds' must be rejected. If the Irish authorities consider that the exchange rates in question were not fixed appropriately, they should seek the remedy for that situation by the appropriate means. A monetary situation cannot be corrected by means of discriminatory tax provisions.
12. Finally, it is necessary to reject the argument that discrimination such as that which forms the subject-matter of the application must be eliminated by the procedure for the hormonization of tax legislation under Articles 99 and 100 of the Treaty, rather than by means of Article 95. There is no doubt that obstacles to the free movement of goods may be eliminated by applying the procedure for the harmonization of tax legislation, but the implementation of the provisions of the Treaty relating thereto and in particular of Article 99 cannot be posed as a condition for the application of Article 95, which imposes on Member States with immediate effect the duty to apply their tax legislation without discrimination even before there is any harmonization.
13. It is appropriate however to point out that in particular as regards beer manufactured in Ireland, where the excise duty is imposed on the worts before manufacture, the grant of deferment of payment cannot be considered as discrimination in so far as that deferment corresponds to the period during which the beer must be kept in the brewery in order to mature. The finished product is therefore only in a situation similar to that of the imported product from the date on which it is marketed.

(4) Taxation of alcohol in Denmark Case

Commission of the European Communities v. *Kingdom of Denmark*; Case 171/78; Judgment of 27 February 1980; [1980] ECR 461; [1980] 1 CMLR 688.

Facts:

Danish production of spirits has been during recent years of the order of 7 million litres per annum. It consists essentially of aquavit (or schnapps), the yearly production of which is almost 6 million litres, in other words approximately 85% of the total production of spirits for human consumption in Denmark.

Aquavit (or schnapps) represented 67% in 1972 and 63% in 1977 of the total consumption of spirits in Denmark, which is of the order of 9 million litres per annum.

Imports into Denmark of spirits from the other Member States amounted to 2,300,000 litres in 1975; they were made up essentially, in order, of whisky, vodka, cognac, gin and rum.

The Danish legislation provides for the levying of an excise duty on spirits, the rate of which is different according to whether aquavit (and schnapps), which benefit from a preferential rate, or other spirits are involved. No difference in taxation on the basis of the origin of the products has been established, whether they are of Danish manufacture or imported.

According to Articles 3 and 4 of the law, aquavit (and schnapps) means products which are manufactured from neutral spirits, contain vegetable flavouring matter, have a minimum alcohol content of 40% and an maximum alcohol content of 49.9% of the original volume, contain less than two grammes per 100 millilitres of vegetable extract and do not have the characteristics of gin, vodka, geneva, wacholder and other liqueurs, punch, bitters and beverages treated as such, aniseed spirit, rum, spirits obtained from fruit and others whose typical taste is produced through distillation or maturation.

On 22 December 1975 and Commission asked the Danish authorities for more detailed information on the national system of taxation on spirits which it considered to be incompatible with Article 95 of the EEC Treaty. That information was supplied to it on 17 February 1976. It confirmed that the excise duty on spirits of Dkr. 154.80 per litre of pure ethyl alcohol was reduced to Dkr. 108.60 in the case of aquavit (and schnapps).

In a letter sent to the Danish Government on 26 March 1976, the Commission found in particular that aquavit was a product similar to all other spirits for human consumption, that the manufacture of spirits other than aquavit was virtually non-existent in Denmark, that the increased rate of Dkr. 154.80 per litre of pure ethyl alcohol affected almost exclusively imported spirits and that that discriminatory taxation consituted an infringement of the first paragraph of Article 95 or, at least, of the second paragraph of Article 95 of the EEC Treaty. In those circumstances, it found that the Kingdom of Denmark was failing to fulfil its obligations under the Treaty; consequently, in accordance with the first paragraph of Article 169 of the Treaty, it was requested to submit its observations to the Commission.

The Court held:

The interpretation of Article 95

7. Whilst the criterion indicated in the first paragraph of Article 95 consists in the comparison of tax burdens, whether in terms of the rate, the mode of assessment or other detailed rules for the application thereof, in view of the difficulty of making sufficiently precise comparisons between the products in question, the second paragraph of that article is based upon a more general criterion, in other words the protective nature of the system of internal taxation.
8. The application in this instance of the criterion of similarity, which determines the scope of the prohibition laid down in the first paragraph of Article 95, has given rise to differences of opinion between the parties. According to the Commission all spirits, whatever the raw materials used

for their manufacture, have similar properties and in essence meet the same needs of consumers. Therefore, whatever the specific characteristics of the various products coming within that category and whatever the consumer habits in the various regions of the Community, spirits as finished products represent, from the point of view of consumers, a single general market. It is necessary to observe that this concept is expressed in the proposals submitted by the Commission to the Council for the establishment of a common organization of the market in alcohol, based on the application of a single rate of tax for all the products in question on the basis of their pure alcohol content.

9. This concept is contested by the Government of the three defendant Member States. In their opinion, it is possible to distinguish in the case of spirits various categoriesof product which differ either in terms of the raw materials used or of their typical characteristics or of the consumer habits observed in the various Member States.

10. In this connection, the Commission points out however that the appraisal of the characteristics of the various alcoholic beverages, in the same way as consumer habits, is variable in time and space and that such factors cannot provide valid criteria as regards the Community taken as a whole. It draws attention moreover to the danger of hardening such habits by means of tax classifications made by the Member States.

11. These arguments prompt the following reply from the Court. The application of the provisions of Article 95 to specific national situations forming the subject-matter of the applications submitted by the Commission must be examined in the context of the general state of the market in alcoholic beverages within the Community. In this respect it is necessary to take into account three lines of thought:

   (a) it is impossible, first of all, to disregard the fact that all the products in question, whatever their specific characteristics in other respects, have common generic features. All are the outcome of the distillation procedure; all contain, as a principal characteristic ingredient, alcohol suitable for human consumption at a relatively high degree of concentration. It follows that within the largest group of alcoholic beverages spirits form an identifiable whole united by common characteristics;

   (b) in spite of those common characteristics, it is possible to distinguish within that whole products which have their own more or less pronounced characteristics. Those characteristics spring either from the raw materials used (in this connection it is possible to distinguish in particular spirits distilled from wine, fruit, cereals and sugar-cane), or from manufacturing processes or, again, from the flavourings added. Typical varieties of spirits may in fact be defined by these particular characteristics, so much so that some of them are even protected by registered designations of origin;

   (c) at the same time, it is impossible to disregard the fact that there are, in the case of spirits, in addition to well-defined products which are put to relatively specific uses, other products with less distinct characteristics and wider uses. There are, on the one hand, numerous products derived from what are known as 'neutral' spirits, in other words spirits of all origins including molasses alcohol and potato alcohol; these products owe their individuality only to flavouring additives with a more or less pronounced taste. On the other hand, it is necessary to draw attention to the fact that in the case of spirits there are products which may be consumed in very different forms, either neat or diluted or, again, in the form of mixtures. These products may therefore be in competition with a range of varying size of other alcoholic products of more limited use. A characteristic of the three cases brought before this Court is however the fact that in each there are, in addition to well-defined spirits, one or several products with a broad range of uses.

12. Two conclusions follow from this analysis of the market in spirits. First, there is, in the case of spirits considered as a whole, an indeterminate number of beverages which must be classified as 'similar products' within the meaning of the first paragraph of Article 95, although it may be difficult to decide this in specific cases, in view of the nature of the factors implied by distinguishing criteria such as flavour and consumer habits. Secondly, even in cases in which it is impossible to recognize a sufficient degree of similarity between the products concerned, there are nevertheless, in the case of all spirits, common characteristics which are sufficiently pronounced to accept that in all cases there is at least partial or potential competition. It follows that the application of the second paragraph of Article 95 may come into consideration in cases in which the relationship of similarity between the specific varieties of spirits remains doubtful or contested.

13. It appears from the foregoing that Article 95, taken as a whole, may apply without distinction to all the products concerned. It is sufficient therefore to examine whether the application of a given national tax system is discriminatory or, as the case may be, protective, in other words whether there is a difference in the rate or the detailed rules for levying the tax and whether that difference is likely to favour a given domestic production. It will be necessary to examine within this framework the economic relationships between the products concerned and the characteristics of the tax systems which form the subject-matter of the disputes in the case of each of the applications lodged by the Commission.

14. In the various procedures, the parties have relied, with regard to the distinction between several categories of alcoholic product, upon certain statements made by the Court of Justice in the judgment in the *Hansen & Balle case*, supra, which was delivered at a time when these applications were pending. Reference has been made more particularly to a passage in that judgment which states as follows: 'At the present stage of its development and in the absence of any unification or harmonization of the relevant provisions, Community law does not prohibit Member

States from granting tax advantages, in the form of exemption from or reduction of duties, to certain types of spirits or to certain classes of producers. Indeed, tax advantages of this kind may serve legitimate economic or social purposes, such as the use of certain raw materials by the distilling industry, the continued production of particular spirits of high quality, or the continuance of certain classes of undertakings such as agricultural distilleries'.

15. Since certain of the defendant Governments have relied upon these statements in order to justify their tax system, the Court has asked the Commission questions as to the compatibility with Community law of the differences in the rates of tax applied to various categories of alcoholic beverages and as to its intentions in that respect within the context of the harmonization of tax legislation. The Commission, after re-stating its view that all spirits are similar and its intention to propose the introduction, at least in principle, of a single rate of tax in future Community regulations, draws attention to the fact that the problems linked to the use of certain raw materials, continued high-quality production and the economic structure of manufacturing undertakings to which the Court referred in the abovementioned judgment may be resolved by means of aid to producers or systems of compensation between producers, taking into account the difference in the cost of the raw materials used. It draws attention to the fact that this objective has already been attained within the context of the common organization of the market in wine as regards spirits obtained by distilling wine. According to the Commission, such mechanisms might safeguard the marketing chances of certain products which are handicapped by production costs, without its being necessary to have recourse for this purpose to the procedure of variation in the rates of tax.

16. In view of these observations, the Court points out that although it acknowledged in the judgment in the *Hansen & Balle case*, taking into account the state of development of Community law, that certain tax exemptions or tax concessions are lawful, this is on condition that the Member States using those powers extend the benefit thereof without discrimination to imported products in the same conditions. It is necessary to emphasize that it was acknowledged that those practices were lawful in particular so as to enable productions or undertakings to continue which would no longer be profitable without these special tax benefits because of the rise in poduction costs. On the other hand, the considerations expressed in that judgment cannot be understood as legitimating tax differences which are discriminatory or protective.

. . . . .

The appraisal of the contested tax system

22. The Commission considers that the Danish tax system is discriminatory as regards spirits imported from the other Member States because the bulk of domestic production, consituted by aquavit, benefits from a reduced rate of tax whereas similar or competing alcoholic beverages imported from the other Member States are subject to the highest rate of tax, apart from insignificant quantities which have the specific characteristics of aquavit as defined by the law.
23. In this respect the Commission puts forward the following figures which are not contested by the Danish Government: during 1977, chosen as the reference year, of a total consumption of 9,240,000 litres of pure alcohol, 5,787,000 litres benefited from a reduced rate of tax; of that quantity, 5,728,000 litres were produced in Denmark, whereas 59,000 litres only were imported, in other words approximately 34,000 litres from the Federal Republic of Germany and the rest from third countries. As for other spirits, the consumption of which, expressed in pure alcohol content, was 3,452,000 litres during the reference year, 1,118,000 litres were of domestic production whereas 2,334,000 litres were imported.
24. According to the Commission, those figures show that the reduced rate of tax benefits almost exclusively a type of spirit which represents the bulk of domestic production whereas the heaviest rate of tax applies to all other alcoholic beverages of which the majority are imported products (in other words, approximately two-thirds thereof). As a whole, this tax system therefore clearly discriminates against imported spirits. As such, this system is contrary to the first paragraph of Article 95 of the Treaty, according to which a Member State cannot impose on the products of other Member States internal taxation in excess of that imposed on similar domestic products. If the similarity between aquavit and other spirits referred to by the Danish law is not acknowledged, the Commission considers that the difference created by that law is in any case of such a nature as to afford indirect protection to the domestic production of aquavit within the meaning of the second paragraph of Article 95.
25. The Danish Government contests the opinion put forward by the Commission according to which all spirits for human consumption produced by distillation must be considered as 'similar' products within the meaning of the first paragraph of Article 95. It considers that the Treaty does not prevent the Member States from making classifications between the various alcoholic products so as to apply to those products different rates of tax. The Court of Justice itself, it claims, acknowledged in its judgment in the *Hansen & Balle case*, supra, the power for Member States to create certain differences as regard taxation on spirits. The defendant Government considers that the Danish State is therefore entitled to maintain a difference in the rates of tax on the basis of the special properties which are characteristic of the products listed in both categories laid down in its tax legislation. The Danish Government is of the opinion that consumer habits provide a criterion whereby aquavit may be differentiated from other alcoholic beverages. In support of that statement it produces

market surveys showing that aquavit, by virtue of Danish eating and drinking habits, is consumed principally at meals as an accompaniment to typical dishes so that it cannot be considered as a product equivalent to other spirits.

26. Moreover, the Danish Government draws attention to the fact that the contested tax system makes no distinction between imported products and domestic products. According to their classification in comparison with the categories of tax laid down by the law, the products are taxed at the corresponding rate, whatever their origin; thus imported aquavit benefits from the rate of tax levied on domestic aquavit, whilst other domestic alcoholic beverages are subject to the same rate of tax as imported products.

The shares held by the various products on the market are of no importance for the purposes of appraising whither the law is compatible with Article 95. It thus appears that in the system of the Danish law there is no relationship between the fact that goods cross a frontier and the application of a higher rate of tax.

27. The Danish Government recalls in addition that for a certain period alcoholic beverages were subject to a mixed tax system which involved, in addition to a specific duty, the application of an 'ad valorem' duty. The excise duty levied under the present legislation is in fact nothing more than an adjusted 'ad valorem' duty. This fact explains why aquavit, as an inexpensive product, benefits from a more favourable rate of tax than other spirits whose production costs are higher. Moreover, there is nothing to prevent Denmark from re-introducing the old system; a tax applied according to that method would amount to reducing the tax on aquavit even further whereas spirits with a high production cost, such as whisky and cognac, would be taxed even more heavily.

28. As for the application of the second paragraph of Article 95, the Danish Government states that the real consumer choice is between aquavit and beer, on the one hand, and wine, on the other; the possibilities of substituting aquavit for other spirits and vice versa are on the other hand negligible. For the purposes of the application of the second paragraph of Article 95 the determining criterion is a 'marked cross-elasticity' between products so that a slight increase in the price of one product has the effect of displacing a high proportion of demand to another. The Danish Government recalls in this respect the criteria which the Court applied in order to delimit the markets concerned with a view to the application of the competition rules contained in the Treaty. For its part, the Commission, it claims, has not produced any evidence to establish the existence of a protective effect which is the condition for the application of the second paragraph of Article 95.

29. In the alternative conclusion listed in its defence, the Danish Government requests the Court to limit, if necessary, the declaration that it has failed to fulfil its obligations under the Treaty to those products which, because they have a special affinity with aquavit, must be treated in

the same way as aquavit from the tax point of view, and to dismiss the application with regard to the remainder.
30. In the defence put forward by the Danish Government, it is necessary to reject, as a preliminary, the argument based on the fact that the system in question is nothing more than a transformed system of 'ad valorem' taxation. In fact, every tax system must be appraised in the light of Article 95 on its own merits and not in terms of a tax system which preceded it or which might if necessary be substituted for it. Moreover, it is necessary to emphasize the contradictory nature of the argument put forward in this respect by the Danish Government.

In fact, of the spirits which are subject to the highest rate of tax under Article 3 of the Danish law, there are several products which, being manufactured on the basis of neutral alcohol, may be considered as inexpensive spirits, like aquavit. In a system of 'ad valorem' taxation, they should therefore benefit from the same tax advantages as aquavit. The fact that those products are treated as regards taxation in the same way as products with a higher production cost shows that the tax system at present in force does not have the characteristics of 'ad valorem' taxation.
31. The appraisal of the compatibility of the Danish tax system with Article 95 raises a special problem in that the preferential rate laid down by the Danish legislation benefits a single product defined precisely by the law to the exclusion of all other spirits. It is therefore necessary to appraise the existence of either a relationship of similarity or competition between a single product and an indeterminate number of products some of which are identified by the law whereas others are not specified.
32. In this connection, it is necessary to point out, first, that of the products subject to the highest rate of tax there are several named beverages the characteristics of which are akin to aquavit in that they are normally manufactured from neutral alcohol and owe their characteistic flavour to added flavouring extracts. It is necessary to assume that those products have been listed expressly among the spirits subject to a higher rate of tax precisely because of their similarity. In the case of those beverages there can therefore be no doubt that there has been an infringement of the first paragraph of Article 95.
33. As regards most of the other alcoholic beverages subject under the Danish legislation to the highest rate of tax, it is impossible to establish with certainty how many of them are spirits which may be classified as 'similar' to aquavit within the meaning of the first paragraph of Article 95 and how many of them are products which, although they cannot be classified as similar, are in competition or in substitution relationship with aquavit which is referred to by the second paragraph of the same article.
34. The Court considers that it is not necessary to give a ruling on this matter in order to resolve the present dispute. In fact, even if doubts remain as to the question to what extent the numerous alcoholic products classified by Danish legislation in the most heavily taxed tax category must be

considered as products similar to aquavit within the meaning of the first paragraph of Article 95, it is impossible reasonably to contest that all those beverages are without exception in an least partial competition with the product benefited by the Danish legislation.

35. In fact, as indicated above, the spirituous beverages referred to by the Danish legislation as products obtained by distillation have sufficient characteristics in common with aquavit to constitute at least in certain circumstances an alternative choice for consumers. Because of their varied properties, these beverages are likely to be in competition with aquavit at times. The fact that aquavit is preferred in Denmark by consumers as an accompaniment to certain typical meals does not prevent that beverage from still being used for other purposes or from thus being in at least a partial substitution relationship with an indeterminate number of other types of spirit. It may therefore be said that to the extent to which the spirituous beverages on which the highest tax burden is imposed are not beverages which are similar to aquavit within the first paragraph of Article 95 they are in any case in competition with aquavit as referred to in the second paragraph of Article 95.

36. Viewed by itself, the tax system introduced by the Danish legislation contains incontestable discriminatory or protective characteristics. Although it does not establish any formal distinction according to the origin of the products, it has been adjusted so that the bulk of the domestic production of spirits comes within the most favourable tax category whereas almost all imported products come within the most heavily taxed category. These characteristics of the system are not obliterated by the fact that a very small fraction of imported spirits benefits from the most favourable rate of tax whereas, conversely, a certain proportion of domestic production comes within the same tax category as imported spirits. It therefore appears that the tax system is devised so that it largely benefits a typical domestic product and handicaps imported spirits to the same extent.

37. In conclusion, it is necessary to state that the system of taxation applied to spirits in the Kingdom of Denmark, as follows most recently from the Coordinated Law of 4 April 1978, is incompatible with the requirements of Article 95 of the Treaty, without its being necessary to make a distinction in this respect between the first and the second paragraph of that provision. It follows that the alternative conclusions put forward by the Danish Government in its defence are purposeless.

Similar legal problems have arisen in case 168/78, *Commission* v. *France*; Judgment of 27 February 1980, [1980] ECR 347, and case 169/78, *Commission* v. *Italy*; Judgment of 27 February 1980; [1980] ECR 385.

In the case of France the Court ruled that the French Republic applied discriminatory taxation on geneva and other alcoholic beverages obtained from the distillation of cereals in comparison with spirits obtained from wine and fruit and in the case of Italy the Court ruled that the Italian Republic applied discriminatory taxation of spirits obtained by the distillation of cereals and sugarcane in comparison with spirits obtained from wine and marc.

In case 170/78, *Commission* v. *United Kingdom*; Judgment of 27 February 1980; [1980] ECR 417, the Court came to the conclusion that the U.K. tax system showed a protective trend in favour of beer in comparison to light wine. The Court was however unable to give a definite ruling in view of the uncertainties both as to the characteristics of the competitive relationship between wine and beer and as to the question of the appropriate tax ration between the two products from the point of view of the whole Community. The Court therefore ordered the parties to re-examine the subject-matter of the dispute.

(5) Vinal Case

S.p.A. Vinal v. *S.p.A. Orbat*; Case 46/80; Preliminary ruling of 14 January 1981; [1981] ECR 90; [1981] 3 CMLR 524.

For the facts see the judgment below.

The Court held:

1. By an order of 30 January 1980 which was received at the Court on 4 February 1980 the Pretura Civile (Civil Court), Casteggion, referred to the Court for a preliminary ruling under Article 177 of the EEC Treaty three questions on the interpretation of Article 95 of the EEC Treaty in order to make it possible to assess whether the system of differential taxation applied by virtue of Decree-Law No 1200 of 6 October 1948, as amended by Decree-Law No 836 of 16 September 1955, and Article 3 of Law No 506 of 18 August 1978 to denatured synthetic ethyl alcohol and denatured ethyl alcohol obtained by fermentation is compatible with the requirements of the Treaty.
2. These questions have been submitted in the context of civil proceedings concerning the performance of a contract concluded in January 1980 between the plaintiff in the main action, SpA Vinal, a producer and imported of alcohol, and SpA Orbat, relating to the supply of a consignment of denatured synthetic alcohol from France.
3. The order making the reference for a preliminary ruling shows that SpA Orbat, the defendant in the main action, does not dispute that it is bound to pay the agreed price but challenges the imposition in this case of the special revenue charge of LIT 12,000 per hectolitre of pure alcohol, stating that it is prepared to reimburse the plaintiff only the special charge of LIT 1,000 per hectolitre applicable to denatured alcohol obtained by fermentation. The defendant claims in fact that the levying of the said revenue charge of LIT 12,000 per hectolitre of denatured synthetic alcohol is unlawful by virtue of Article 95 of the EEC Treaty since it constitutes tax discrimination which is prohibited by that provision.
4. In order to decide this dispute the Pretura submitted the following questions to the Court for a preliminary ruling:

(a) Must the first paragraph of Article 95 of the Treaty of Rome be interpreted as meaning that two products derived from different raw materials but capable of being put to the same use and having the same practical application must be considered to be 'similar'?

(b) If the reply to Questions 1 is in the affirmative:

Must the first paragraph of Article 95 of the Treaty of Rome be interpreted as meaning that it must be considered to be prohibited to impose charges which, whilst appearing to place an identical burden on the Community product and the similar domestic product, in fact amount to discrimination in tax matters to the detriment of similar products from other Member States in that the products subject to heavier taxation are exclusively imported and the products subject to lighter taxation are principally domestic?

. . . . .

14. Differential taxation such as that which exists in Italy for denatured synthetic alcohol on the one hand and denatured alcohol obtained by fermentation on the other satisfies these requirements. It appears in fact that that system of taxation pursues an objective of legitimate industrial policy in that it is such as to promote the distillation of agricultural products as against the manufacture of alcohol from petroleum deivates. That choice does not conflict with the rules of Community law or the requirements of a policy decided within the framework of the Community.

15. The detailed provisions of the legislation at issue before the national court cannot be considered as discriminatory since, on the other hand, it is not disputed that imports from other Member States of alcohol obtained by fermentation qualify for the same tax treatment as Italian alcohol produced by fermentation and, on the other hand, although the rate of tax prescribed for synthetic alcohol results in restraining the importation of synthetic alcohol originating in other Member States, it has an equivalent economic effect in the national territory in that it also hampers the establishment of profitable production of the same product by Italian industry.

16. Having regard to the foregoing, the questions submitted by the Pretura, Casteggio, should be answered as follows.

17. With regard to the first and second question, taken together, the reply should be that tax arrangements which impose heavier charges on denatured synthetic alcohol than on denatured alcohol obtained by fermentation on the basis of raw materials and the manufacturing processes employed for the two products are not at variance with the first paragraph of Article 95 of the EEC Treaty if they are applied identically to the two categories of alcohol originating in other Member States. Such tax arrangements are justified even though the products in questions, whilst

derived from different raw materials, are capable of being put to the same uses and have the same practical application.
18. With regard to the third question the reply should be that where, by reason of the taxation of synthetic alcohol, it has been impossible to develop profitable production of that type of alcohol on national territory, the application of such tax arrangements cannot be considered as constituting indirect protection of national production of alcohol obtained by fermentation within the meaning of the second paragraph of Article 95 on the sole ground that their consequence is that the product subject to the heavier taxation is in fact a product which is exclusively imported from other Member States of the Community.

(6) Schul Case I

Gaston Schul Douane Expediteur B.V. v. *Inspecteur der Invoerrechten en Accijnzen:* Case 15/81; Preliminary ruling of 5 May 1982; [1982] ECR 1409.

Facts:

The limited liability company Gaston Schul Douane Expediteur BV, customs forwarding agents, imported a second-hand pleasure and sports boat into the Netherlands on the instructions and on behalf of a private person residing in the Netherlands who had bought it in France from another private person. The Netherlands revenue authority levied on that importation value-added tax at the rate of 18% on the sale price which was the normal rate applied within the country on the sale of goods for valuable consideration. The levying of that tax is the subject of the main action.

The Netherlands authority relied on the Netherlands law of 1968 on turnover tax and in particular Article 1 thereof. According to that provision turnover tax is chargeable on the one hand on goods delivered and services provided within the country by traders in the course of their business and on the other hand on the importation of goods. The provision gives effect to Article 2 of the Second Council Directive No 67/228 of 11 April 1967 on the harmonization of legislation of Member States concerning turnover taxes – structure and procedures for application of the common system of value-added tax (Official Journal, English Special Edition 1967, p. 16), an article whose provisions were substantially incorporated into the above-mentioned Article 2 of the Sixth Council Directive No 77/388 af 17 May 1977.

When the objection to that decision was dismissed on the ground that the tax had been levied in conformity with the Netherlands legislation the company Gaston Schul brought the matter before the Gerechtshof, 's-Hertogenbosch. It claims that the tax is contrary to the provisions of the EEC Treaty, in particular Articles 12 and 13 on the one hand and Article 95 on the other.

In order to be able to assess that submission the Gerechtshof referred to the Court the following questions for a preliminary ruling:

'1. Must the charging by a Member State of turnover tax on the importation of goods from another Member State which are supplied by a private person be regarded as a charge having an effect equivalent to customs duties within the meaning of Article 13 (2) of the Treaty [establishing the European Economic Community] if, on the supply by a private person of goods which are already in that Member State, no charge to turnover tax is made?
2. If Question 1 is answered in the negative, then, within the meaning of Article 95 of the Treaty, must the charging by a Member State of turnover tax on the importation of goods from another Member State which are supplied by a private person be regarded as internal taxation in excess of that imposed on similar domestic products if no turnover tax is charged on the supply of goods which are already in that Member State if they are supplied by a priate person?
3. Should one of the two foregoing questions be answered in the affirmative, must it be assumed that point 2 of Article 2 of the Sixth [Council] Directive on the harmonization of the laws of the Member States relating to turnover taxes is incompatible with the Treaty and therefore invalid in so far as that provision requires Member States to subject the importation of goods from other Member States to value-added tax without making any exception for goods supplied by private persons which, when supplied within the Member State concerned, would not be subject to that tax?
4. Does an affirmative answer to Question 3 mean that a Member State is prohibited from subjecting to value-added tax the importation of goods from another Member State supplied by a private person if the supply of those goods within the Member State by a private person is not subject to that tax?'

The Court held:

2. The limited liabilty company Gaston Schul Douane Expediteur BV, customs forwarding agents, imported a second-hand pleasure and sports boat into the Netherlands on the instructions and on behalf of a private person residing in the Netherlands who had bought it in France from another private person. The Netherlands revenue authority levied on that importation value-added tax at the rate of 18% on the sale price which was the normal rate applied within the country on the sale of goods for valuable consideration. The levying of that tax is the subject of the main action.
3. The Netherlands authority relied on the Netherlands law of 1968 on turnover tax and in particular Article 1 thereof. According to that provision turnover tax is chargeable on the one hand on goods delivered

and services provided within the country by traders in the course of their business and on the other hand on the importation of goods. The provision gives effect to Article 2 of the Second Council Directive No 67/228 of 11 April 1967 on the harmonization of legislation of Member States concerning turnover taxes – structure are procedures for application of the common system of value-added tax (Official Journal, English Special Edition 1967, p. 16), an article whose provisions were substantially incorporated into the above-mentioned Article 2 of the Sixth Council Directive No 77/388 of 17 May 1977.

4. When the objection to that decision was dismissed on the ground that the tax had been levied in conformity with the Netherlands legislation the company Gaston Schul brought the matter before the Gerechtshof, 's-Hertogenbosch. It claims that the tax is contrary to the provisions of the EEC Treaty, in particular Articles 12 and 13 on the one hand and Article 95 on the other.

. . . . .

6. The questions put by the national court are essentially aimed at ascertaining whether it is compatible with the provisions of the Treaty, and in particular with Articles 12 and 13 on the one hand and 95 on the other, for a Member State to levy, pursuant to Community directives, turnover tax in the form of value-added tax on the importation of products from another Member State supplied by a non-taxable person (hereinafter referred to as a 'private person').

. . . . .

8. In order to evaluate the content of those arguments and to supply the factors required for an answer to the questions put to the Court it is necessary to record briefly the characteristics, relevant in this case, of the system of turnover tax in the form of the common system of value-added tax.

9. The common system was established on the basis of Articles 99 and 100 of the Treaty by the First Council Directive No 67/227 of 11 April 1967 on the harmonization of legislation of Member States concerning turnover taxes (Official Journal, English Special Edition 1967, p. 14). It was supplemented by the Second Council Directive No 67/228 of the same date which in turn was replaced by the Sixth Council Directive No 77/388 of 17 May mentioned above.

10. By virtue of Article 2 of the First Directive the principle of the common system of value-added tax consists in the application to goods and services

up to and including the retail stage of a general tax on consumption which is exactly proportional to the price of the goods and services, irrespective of the number of transactions which take place in the production and distribution process before the stage at which the tax is charged. However, value-added tax is chargeable on each transaction only after deduction of the amount of value-added tax borne directly by the cost of the various price components. The procedure for deduction is so arranged by Article 17 (2) of the Sixth Directive that only taxable persons are authorized to deduct from the value-added tax for which they are liable the value-added tax which the goods have already borne.

11. That is the background to Article 2 of the Sixth Directive which provides that the following are to be subject to value-added tax: on the one hand 'the supply of goods or services effected for consideration within the territory of the country by a taxable person acting as such' (point 1) and on the other 'the importation of goods' (point 2). Article 4 of the directive defines 'taxable person' as meaning any person who independently carries out in any place any economic activity such as that of producer, trader, and person supplying services including mining and agricultural activities and activities of the professions. Article 5 defines 'supply of goods' as "the transfer of the right to dispose of tangible property as owner' whereas 'importation of goods' is defined in Articles 7 as 'the entry of goods into the territory of the country'.

12. The Sixth Directive also harmonizes the concepts of chargeable event and chargeability of tax (Aticle 10) and the taxable amount (Article 11). Exemption are provided both for transactions within the country and imports (Articles 13 and 14). Exports and like transactions are exempted from tax (Article 15).

13. It is right to stress that the directives bring about only a partial harmonization of the system of value-added tax. At the present stage of Community law Member States are free inter alia to fix the rate of value-added tax, provided always that the rate applicable on the importation of goods must be that applied to the supply of like goods within the territory of the country (Article 12 of the Sixth Directive).

14. It may be concluded from an analysis of the characteristics of the common system of value-added tax, as set out above, on the one hand that, as regards transactions within a Member State the chargeable event is constituted by the supply of goods for valuable consideration by a taxable person acting as such whereas as regards imports the chargeable event is constituted by the mere entry of the goods into the territory of a Member State whether or not there is a transaction, and irrespective of whether the transaction is carried out for valuable consideration or free of charge, be it by a taxable person or a private person.

15. It follows further that although deliveries for export are themselves exempt from value-added tax, whether carried out by taxable persons or private persons, only taxable persons are authorized to exercise the right to deduct. As a result, only goods delivered for export by taxable persons or on their behalf may be exempted from all value-added tax applied in

the country of exportation, whereas goods delivered for export by private persons remain liable to value-added tax to the extent proportionate to their value at the time of export. Since all imports are subject to value-added tax in the importing country there is in such a case an overlapping of taxes both of the State of exportation and the State of importation.
16. The preliminary questions must be considered on the basis of those aspects of the common system.

The first question: the interpretation of Articles 12 and 13 of the Treaty

17. The first question which the Gerechtshof submits is essentially whether it is compatible with Articles 12 and 13 of the Treaty to levy value-added tax on the importation of products from another Member State supplied by a private person if no such tax is levied on the supply of similar goods by a private person within the territory of the importing Member State.
18. According to established case-law of the Court the prohibition, in relations between Member States, of charges having an effect equivalent to customs duties, covers any tax which is payable on or by reason of importation and which, as it applies specifically to an imported product to the exclusion of a similar domestic product, ultimately produces, by adversely affecting the cost price of the former product, the same effect upon the free movement of goods as a customs duty.
19. The essential characteristic of a charge having an effect equivalent to a customs duty, and the one which, distinguishes it from internal taxation, is therefore that it affects only imported products as such whereas internal taxation affects both imported products and domestic products.
20. The Court has nevertheless recognized that a pecuniary charge payable on a product imported from another Member State and not on an identical or similar domestic product does not constitute a charge having equivalent effect but internal taxation within the meaning of Article 95 of the Treaty if it is part of a general system of internal dues applicable systematically to categories of products according to objective criteria applied without regard to the origin of the products.
21. It is apparent from those considerations that a tax of the kind referred to by the national court does not have the ingredients of a charge having an effect equivalent to customs duties on imports within the meaning of Articles 12 and 13 (2) of the Treaty. Such a tax is part of the system of value-added tax the structure of which, and the essential terms governing its application, have been laid down by the Council in harmonizing directives. Those directives have established a uniform taxation procedure covering systematically and according to objective criteria both transactions carried out within the territory of the Member States and import transactions. It should be pointed out in particular in that respect that the common system makes imports and supplies of like goods within the territory of a Member State subject to the same rate of tax. As a result the tax in question must be considered as an integral part of a general system of internal taxation for the purposes of Article 95 of the Treaty

and its compatibility with Community law must be considered in the context of that article and not of that of Articles 12 et seq. of the Treaty.

22. The first question must therefore be answered to the effect that value-added tax which a Member State levies on the importation of products from another Member State supplied by a private person, where no such tax is levied on the supply of similar products by a private person within the territory of the Member State of importation, does not constitute a charge having an effect equivalent to a customs duty on imports within the meaning of Articles 12 and 13 (2) of the Treaty.

Second question: the interpretation of Article 95 of the Treaty

23. In its second question the Gerechtshof asks in substance whether the levying of value-added tax on the importation of products from another Member State supplied by a private person is compatible with Article 95 of the Treaty where no such tax is payable on the supply of similar products by a private person within the territory of the Member State of importation.

. . . . . .

31. It may be observed that at the present stage of Community law the Member States are free, by virtue of Article 95, to charge the same amount on the importation of products as the value-added tax which they charge on similar domestic products. Nevertheless, this compensation is justified only in so far as the imported products are not already burdened with value-added tax in the Member State of exportation since otherwise the tax on importation would in fact be an additional charge burdening imported products more heavily than similar domestic products.

32. That view derives in the first place from the terms of Article 95 of the Treaty which prohibits not only the direct but also the indirect imposition of internal taxation on products from other Member States in excess of that on similar domestic products. That prohibition would not be complied with if imported products could be subject to the value-added tax applicable to similar domestic products without account being taken of the proportion of value-added tax with which those products are still burdened at the time of their importation.

33. Such an interpretation accords with the need to take account of the objectives of the Treaty which are laid down in Articles 2 and 3 among which appears, in the first place, the establishment of a common market. The concept of a common market as defined by the Court in a consistent line of decisions involves the elimination of all obstacles to intra-Community trade in order to merge the national markets into a single market bringing about conditions as close as possible to those of a

genuine internal market. It is important that not only commerce as such but also private persons who happen to be conducting an economic transaction across national frontiers should be able to enjoy the benefits of that market.
34. Consequently, it is necessary also to take into account the value-added tax levied in the Member State of exportation for the purpose of determining the compatibility with the requirements of Article 95 of a charge to value-added tax on products from another Member State supplied by private persons where the supply of similar products within the territory of the Member State of importation is not so liable. Accordingly, in so far as such an imported product supplied by a private person may not lawfully benefit from a remission of tax on exportation and so remains burdened upon importation with part of the value-added tax paid in the Member State of exportation the amount of value-added tax payable on importation must be reduced by the residual part of the value-added tax of the Member State of exportation which is still contained in the value of the product when it is imported. The amount of this reduction may not, however, be greater than the amount of value-added tax actually paid in the Member State of exportation.
35. The Member States which have taken part in these proceedings have objected to this interpretation on the ground that the value-added tax paid in the Member State of exportation is difficult to check since both the rate of the tax and its basis of assessment may have varied in the course of time.
36. In that regard it should be pointed out that it is for the person who seeks exemption from or a reduction in the value-added tax normally levied on importation to establish that he satisfies the conditions for such exemption or reduction. Accordingly it is open to the Member State of importation to require such an importer to provide the necessary documentary proof that the value-added tax was levied in the Member State of exportation and still burdens the product on importation.
37. Further, the Member States maintained that the establishment of a system ensuring the complete neutrality of internal taxation with regard to intra-community trade could take place only by strict application of the principle of taxation in the Member State of destination and that would mean full remission of tax on all products at the time of exportation. It is for the political institutions of the Community to adopt such a solution since it involves a political choice.
38. Nevertheless although the establishment of a system of complete neutrality in the field of competition involving full remission of tax on exportation is indeed a matter for the Community legislature, so long as such a system is not established Article 95 of the Treaty prevents an importing Member State from applying its system of value-added tax to imported products in a manner contrary to the principles embodied in that article.
39. Finally, it is also necessary to dismiss the objections based on possible

difficulties of a technical and administrative nature which may result from taking into account the value-added tax of the Member State of exportation and those based on the need to prevent fraudulent circumventions and distortions in competition within the Community. The first category of objections must be dismissed since it is for the individual who seeks to claim the benefit of exemption from or reduction in value-added tax on importation to provide proof that the conditions are satisfied. The second category of objections is irrelevant since the levying of the differential amount of value-added tax removes any incentive to deflect trade.

40. The second question must accordingly be answered to the effect that value-added tax which a Member State levies on the importation of products from another Member State supplied by a private person, where no such tax is levied on the supply of similar products by a private person within the territory of the Member State of importation, constitutes internal taxation in excess of that imposed on similar domestic products within the meaning of Article 95 of the Treaty, to the extent to which the residual part of the value-added tax paid in the Member State of exportation which is still contained in the value of the product on importation is not taken into account. The burden of proving facts which justify the taking into account of the tax falls on the importer.

d. Customs legislation

i. CASES

(1) **Turkey tail Case**

Hauptzollamt Hamburg-Oberelbe v. *Firma Paul G. Bollmann*; Case 40/69; Preliminary ruling of 18 February 1970; [1970] ECR 79; [1970] CMLR 141.

Facts:

Defendant Bollmann had imported into Germany goods from the USA described as 'turkey tails'. The German Customs Office originally classified these turkey tails under the tariff heading for 'edible turkey offal' and imposed the appropriate levy for this heading.

A few months later, however, a new decision was taken, classifying turkey tails under the heading 'poultry parts' and requesting Bollmann to pay an additional levy. Bollmann appealed against this decision to the Finanzgericht (Court of Finance) Hamburg which annulled the decision. The appellant chief Customs Office lodged an appeal with the Bundesfinanzhof against the judgment of the Finanzgericht. The Bundesfinanzhof requested the Court of Justice to give a preliminary ruling, not only whether 'turkey tails' should be considered to come under the one or the other heading of the Common

Customs Tariff, but also whether the relevant Community Regulation No 22, establishing the Common Market organization for poultry allowed the national legislation to interpret these definitions autonomously or not.
The latter point raised some questions of principle.

The Court held:

. . . . .

The first question

2. In its first question the Bundesfinanzhof asks the Court whether the correct interpretation of Article 14 of Regulation No 22/62 is that Member States are entitled and obliged to take internal legislative measures to specify which products are subject to the levy by virtue of Article 1 of that regulation and to differentiate between them.
3. According to Article 14 of Regulation No 22/62 'Member States shall take all steps to adapt their laws, regulations, and administrative provisions in such a way that the provisions of the present regulation, unless hereby otherwise provided, may be effectively implemented as from 1 July 1962'.
4. Since Regulation No 22/62, in conformity with the second paragraph of Article 189 of the Treaty, is directly applicable in all Member States, the latter, unless otherwise expressly provided, are precluded from taking steps, for the purpose of applying the regulation, which are intended to alter its scope or supplement its provisions. To the extent to which Member States have transferred legislative powers in tariff matters with the object of ensuring the satisfactory operation of a common market in agriculture they no longer have the powers to adopt legislative provisions in this field.

. . . . .

6. Therefore the answer to the first question must be in the negative.

The second question

7. In the event of the first question's being answered in the negative the Bundesfinanzhof asks the Court whether 'Article 1 of Regulation No 22/62 which mentions some of the goods included in the Common Customs Tariff is to be construed as meaning that national legislatures may interpret the terms by which these goods are described, since the terms by which goods in a customs tariff are described of necessity require interpretation'.

8. As the description of the goods referred to in the regulations establish a common organization of a market is part of Community law its interpretation can only be settled in accordance with Community procedures. Moreover the common organization of the markets in agriculture, such as the one which it is the aim of Regulation No 22/62 to establish progressively, can only achieve their objectives if the provisions adopted for their realization are applied in a uniform manner in all Member States. The descriptions of goods covered by these organizations must therefore have exactly the same range in all Member States.
9. Such a requirement would be placed in jeopardy if, whenever there was a difficulty in the classification of any goods for tariff purposes, each Member State could determine the range covered by the descriptions in question by way of interpretation. Although it is true that in the event of any difficulty in the classification of any goods the national administration may be led to take implementing measures and clarify in the particular case the doubts raised by the description of the goods, it can only do so if it complies with the provisions of Community law and subject to the reservation that the national authorities cannot issue binding rules of interpretation.
10. The second question must therefore be answered in the negative.

(2) Deutsche Bakels Case

Deutsche Bakels GmbH v. *Oberfinanzdirektion München*; Case 14/70; Preliminary ruling of 8 December 1970; [1970] ECR 1008; [1971] CMLR 188.

Facts:

Bakels imported a product called Voltem and claimed that it should be classified in tariff group 38.19 (chemical products). The German customs authorities however, classified it in tariff group 21.07 (products for human consumption) which led to a higher tariff. The EEC tariff classification was not clear so that the Bundesfinanzhof considered to apply the further interpretation given by the German authorities or that given by the Customs Cooperation Council, a world wide organization in which all EEC Members take part. A preliminary ruling was asked on the question whether such interpretation could be used.

The Court held:

The first question

1. By the first question the Court is asked to rule whether, where the Community authorities have not yet issued explanatory notes for head-

ings to the Common Customs Tariff, the explanatory notes issued by national authorities can be recognized as having the force of a binding interpretation of these tariff headings.
3. The Council issued pursuant to Articles 28 and 111 of the EEC Treaty Regulation No 950/68 concerning the Common Customs Tariff, which contains the customs tariff as an annex. The interpretation of the headings of this tariff can only be fixed if the powers vested in the Community are respected. For it follows from the very nature of the Common Customs Tariff that the individual tariff headings must have the same scope in all the Member States. This requirement would be jeopardized if, where there are difficulties in classifying a product for tariff purposes, each Member State were itself able to fix this scope by way of interpretation.
4. Although, where there are difficulties in classifying a product, the national administration may find it advisable to take implementing measures and to elucidate thereby the doubts raised by the description of a product, it may only do so by observing Community law, without the national authorities' being to issue rules of interpretation having binding effect.
5. Accordingly, the first question put by the Bundesfinanzhof must be answered to the effect that even in the absence of an express Community interpretation, the effect of a binding interpretation cannot be attributed to the explanatory notes of the national authorities relating to the headings of the Common Customs Tariff.

The second question

6. In the event of a negative answer to the first question, the Bundesfinanzhof asks the Court to rule whether, where explanatory notes have not yet been issued by the Community for headings to the Common Customs Tariff, the Explanatory Notes to the Brussels Nomen-clature of 1955 on these headings are authoritative.
7. It is accepted that the Common Customs Tariff annexed to Regulation (EEC) No 950/68 is based on the Brussels Nomenclature, which was established by the Convention on Nomenclature for the Classification of Goods in Customs Tariffs of 15 December 1950 to which the Member States were parties.
8. In order to ensure the uniform interpretation and application of the Nomenclature, Articles III and IV of the Convention provide that a Nomenclature Committee under the authority of the Customs Cooperation Council is to issue explanatory notes and classification opinions.
9. These explanatory notes and opinions are a means of interpretation for the original and present meaning and scope of the individual tariff headings. In the absence of relevant provisions issued by the Community, therefore, their authority as regards the interpretation of the Nomenclature cannot be ignored by the institutions called upon to apply the Community provisions incorporating the Brussels Nomenclature.

10. In particular where no Community explanatory notes have yet been issued in respect of the tariff headings to the Common Customs Tariff, the observance of these explanatory notes and opinions is a useful means of ensuring that the common external tariff is uniformly interpreted and applied at all the frontiers of the Common Market. Therefore, the consultation and observance of the explanatory notes and classification opinions promote an approximation of the practices of the authorities entrusted with the execution of the Common Customs Tariff.
11. Accordingly the aims and the structure of the Common Customs Tariff imply that in the absence of the relevant Community provisions the abovementioned explanatory notes and classification opinions should be regarded as an authoritative source for the purposes of the interpretation of the tariff headings contained in Regulation (EEC) No 950/68. The second question put by the Bundesfinanzhof must therefore be answered in the affirmative.

. . . . .

(3) Überseehandel Case

Gesellschaft für Überseehandel GmbH v. *Handelskammer Hamburg*; Case 49/76; Preliminary ruling of 26 January 1977; [1977] ECR 51.

Facts:

1. For several years, the Gesellschaft für Überseehandel GmbH has imported casein, in the form of pieces from the size of a pea to the size of a hazelnut, from the Soviet Union and from Poland. In its establishment in Hamburg it grinds the imported product to different degrees of fineness, sometimes according to the preferences of its customers. The products is then sorted and packed. The casein thus treated is sold to the different consumers. It is used in the human and animal food industry, in the manufacture of glues, colours and other materials capable of being applied in the form of a coating.

From 1967 to June 1972, the Handelskammer (Chamber of Commerce) Hamburg, provided certificates of origin, in accordance with an undertaking to that effect, naming the Federal Republic of Germany as the country of origin of the casein treated by the Company.

Article 5 of Regulation No 802/68 of the Council of 17 June 1968 on the common definition of the context of the origing of goods, OJ (Special Edition, p. 165 provides:

'A product in the production of which two or more countries were concerned shall be regarded as originating in the country in which the last substantial process or operation that is economically justified was performed, having been carried out in an undertaking equipped for the

purpose, and resulting in the manufacture of a new product or representing an important stage of manufacture'.
2. In June 1972, the Handelskammer for the first time withdrew its undertaking, but on 21 July 1972 it again undertook to continue to supply certificates of origin, on the ground that the operations carried out by the company could be considered as the 'last ... process ... economically justified' within the meaning of Article 5 of Regulation No 802/68. It was however stated in the undertaking that it would be reconsidered should new factors, such as a decision of the Community or German authorities acting in pursuance of their powers, later arise so as to justify a different interpretation of the provisions of the aforesaid regulation.

By letter of 15 September 1975, the Handelskammer did in fact withdraw its undertaking. It based its action on a communication from the Federal Minister of Food, Agriculture and Forestry, stating that the grinding, mixing and packing of casein could not be considered as activites conferring a particular origin on the product and thus giving it an origin in the country where they took place.

By decision of 21 January 1976, the Handelskammer rejected a new request made by the Company on 12 January 1976. On 18 March 1976, the Company, having failed in the proceedings which followed, took the dispute to the Verwaltungsgericht (Administrative Court) Hamburg.

By order of 28 May 1976, that court decided to suspend its proceedings and to refer the following question to the Court of Justice under Article 177 of the EEC Treaty:

'Is untreated casein obtained in a third country, which has been rendered fit for use by being ground up in a Member State of the EEC in the way described by the plaintiff in its action, to be regarded as originating in that Member State according to Article 5 of Regulation (EEC) No 803/68 of the Council?'

The Court held:

. . . . .

Article 5 of Regulation No 802/68 provides:

'A product in the production of which two or more countries were concerned shall be regarded as originating in the country in which the last substantial process or operation that is economically justified was performed, having been carried out in an undertaking equipped for the purpose, having been carried out in an undertaking equipped for the purpose, and resulting in the manufacture of a new product or representing an important stage of manufacture.'

It appears from the order for reference that it is not denied that, in accordance with the said provision, the process or operation to which the raw casein is subjected in this case constitutes an activity 'carried out in an undertaking equipped for the purpose', and that it is 'economically justified' because it is necessary for the industrial use of the product.

Thus, the dispute is concerned in essence with the question whether the said activity constitutes a 'substantial' process or operation for the purposes of Article 5 of Regulation No 802/68, resulting in 'the manufacture of a new product' or representing 'an important stage of manufacture'.

It is therefore in respect of this question that an answer should be given to the national court.

4. Although the Court has no jurisdiction under Article 177 of the EEC Treaty to apply the provision of Community law to actual cases, it may nevertheless furnish the national court with the interpretative criteria necessary to enable it to dispose of the dispute.

5. According to the last recital in the preamble to Regulation No 802/68 and to Article 1 of that regulation, a common definition of the concept of the origin of goods constitutes an indispensable means of ensuring the uniform application of the Common Customs Tariff, of quantitative restrictions and of all other measures adopted, in relation to the importation or exportation of goods, by the Community or by the Member States.

For those purposes, Articles 4 and 5 of the regulation base such a definition on objective criteria, making it possible to ensure the uniform application in all the Member States of the concept of the origin of goods and thus to avoid deflections of trade and abuses.

In particular, there can be seen in Article 6 of the regulation the intention to prevent the origin of goods in the production of which two or more countries are concerned from being determined by way of a non-substantial process or operation in such a manner as to defeat the purposes of Article 1 or to circumvent the measures adopted by the Member States in relation to importation or exportation.

In these circumstances, it should not seem sufficient to seek criteria defining the origin of goods in the tariff classification of the processed products, for the Common Customs Tariff has been conceived to fulfil special purposes and not in relation to the determination of the origin of products.

On the contrary, in order to meet the purposes and requirements of Regulation No 802/68, the determination of the origin of goods must be based on a real and objective distinction between raw material and processed product, depending fundamentally on the specific material qualities of each of those products.

6. Therefore, the last process or operation referred to in Article 5 of the regulation is only 'substantial' for the purposes of that provision if the product resulting therefrom has its own properties and a composition of its own, which it did not possess before that process of operation.

In providing that the said process or operation must, in order to confer a particular origin, result in the manufacture of a new product or represent an important stage of manufacture, the above-mentioned Article 5 shows

in fact that activities affecting the presentation of the product for the purposes of its use, but which do not bring about a significant qualitative change in its properties, are not of such a nature as to determine the origin of the said product.
7. The grinding of a raw material such as raw casein to various degrees of fineness cannot be considered as a process or operation for the purposes of Article 5 of Regulation No 802/68, because the only effect of doing so is to change the consistency of the product and its presentation for the purposes of its later use; it does not bring about a significant qualitative change in the raw material.

Furthermore, the quality control by grading to which the ground product is subjected and the manner in which it is packaged relate only to the requirements for marketing the product and do not affect its substantial properties.
8. In its opinion expressed at its meetings of 17 and 18 December 1975 and of 22 to 24 June 1976, the Committee on Origin set up under Article 12 of Regulation No 802/68 has found that the grinding to different degrees of fineness, the sorting and packaging of casein do not constitute activities involving a process or operation conferring on the product resulting from those activities a particular origin for the purposes of the said regulation.

Although opinions expressed by the Committee are not binding, except in so far as the Commission has adopted implementing provisions in application of Article 14 (3) (a) of Regulation No 802/68, nevertheless, until such time as the Commission adopts contrary provisions under subparagraphs (b) and (c) of the said Article 14 (3), they constitute an important criterion for interpreting Article 5 of the said regulation, the scope of which they define in respect of specific cases.
9. It is therefore to be concluded that the cleaning and grinding of a raw material, such as raw casein imported from a third country into a Member State, together with the grading and packaging of the product obtained, do not constitute a substantial process or operation for the purposes of Articles 5 of Regulation No 802/68, and do not confer a Community origin on the said product, according to that regulation.

. . . . .

3. Elimination of quantitative restrictions between Member States and measures having equivalent effect (EEC Treaty Articles 30–35)

a. Cases

(1) Salgoil Case

Salgoil v. *Italian Ministry of Foreign Trade*; Case 13/68; Preliminary ruling of 14 December 1968; [1968] ECR 460; (1969) CMLR 181.

Facts:

An Italian company, Salgoil Ltd., of Milan, appealed to the Rome Court of Appeal to set aside a decision of the Rome Civil Tribunal, which has ruled that it did not have jurisdiction te hear the case brought by the company against the Italian Foreign Trade Ministry, claiming compensation for damage allegedly suffered because of the latter's refusal to permit the importation of a product which it had contracted to buy from a Swiss firm, Rohimag, of Basle.

The appellant company pointed out that at the time the contract was concluded, there were no restrictions on the importation of the product in question. It was only later that the Italian Government made the importation of this product subject to the issue of a license, Salgoil's application for an import license was turned down.

Salgoil Ltd. contended that this action by the Italian Government constituted an infringement of the provisions of the EEC Treaty, in particular Articles 31 and 33, relating to the elimination of quantitative restrictions on trade between Member States.

The appellant company futher submitted that Articles 30 et seq. of the Treaty conferred directly on nationals of Member States personal rights on which they were entitled to rely in any action before a national court.

The Court held:

II – The first question

In its first question the Corte d'Appello, Rome, asks the Court of Justice 'to determine whether the provisions of Article 30 et seq. of the Treaty, especially Article 31, also produce effects on the relationship between a Member State and its nationals'.

In view of the information supplied by the court making the reference, it seems that this question asks only for an interpretation of Articles 30 and 31, the first paragraph and the second sentence of the second paragraph of Article 32, and paragraph (1) and the first subparagraph of paragraph (2) of Article 33.

(a) Article 30 lays down a general prohibition on quantitative restrictions and measures having equivalent effect but states that this is 'without prejudice to the following provisions'.

Amongs these provisions Articles 31, 32 and 33 define the scope of the abovementioned prohibition on a transitional basis. Since the present case relates to a period during which the said provisions were applicable, there is no need to examined the scope of the prohibition laid down by Article 30 after the expiry of the effects of the articles mentioned.

(b) The first paragraph of Article 31 provides: 'Member States shall refrain from introducing between themselves any new quantitative restrictions or measures having equivalent effect'. The second paragraph of the same article defines the degree of liberalisation with reference to which the expression 'new restrictions' must be understood and in so doing it refers to 'decisions of the Council of the Organization for European Economic Cooperation of 14 January 1955'. Furthermore, the said paragraph states that: 'Member States shall supply the Commission, not later than six months after the entry into force of this Treaty, with lists of the products liberalized by them in pursuance of these decisions' and provides that: 'These lists shall be consolidated between Member States'.

Once these lists have been supplied, or at the latest once the time-limit for supplying them has expired, Article 31 contains a clear prohibition, constituting not a duty to act but a duty to refrain from acting. This duty is not accompanied by any reservation whereby its operation depends on a positive measure of national law or on an intervention by the institutions of the Community. The prohibition in Article 31 of its very nature lends itself perfectly to producing direct effect on the legal relationships between Member States and those subject to their jurisdiction. Thus Article 31 creates rights which national courts must protect.

(c) The first paragraph of Article 32 provides: 'In their trade with one another Member States shall refrain from making more restrictive the quotas and measures having equivalent effect existing at the date of the entry into force of this Treaty'.

For reasons analogous to those which have just been set out as regards Article 31, this provision lends itself of its very nature to produce identical effects on the legal relationships between Member States and those subject to their jurisdiction.

(d) The provisions of the last sentence of Article 32 and those of paragraph (1) and the first subparagraph of paragraph (2) of Article 33 are directed at the progressive abolition, during the transitional period, of the quotas and the measures having equivalent effect existing at the date of the entry into force of the Treaty. The last sentence of Article 32 states the principle and Article 33 lays down rules for its application. Therefore the abovementioned provisions should be looked at as a whole. At Article 33 (1) Member States were required, one year after the entry into force of the Treaty, to convert 'any bilateral quotas open to any other Member States into global quotas open without discrimination to all other Member States'. Article 33 (1) also states that the Member States must progressively increase the aggregate of the global quotas at given dates and at a specific rate. Finally the first paragraph of Article 33 (2) specifies, in accordance with analogous criteria, the rate at which the quota for 'a product which has not been liberalized' and for which 'the global quota does not amount to 3% of the national production of the State concerned' is to be raised.

These provisions lay down obligations which are not subject, either as regards their execution or their effects, to the adoption of any measure of the institutions of the Community. However, since they consist of positive obligations, consideration should be given to the question whether the

Member States may in performing them exercise any discretion such as to exclude the abovementioned effects wholly or in part. Some discretion does fall to be exercised by the Member States from the obligation to 'convert any bilateral quotas ... into global quotas' and from the concepts of 'total value' and 'national production'. In fact, since the Treaty gives no indication as to the data on which these figures must be calculated or as to the methods applicable, several solutions may be envisaged. Therefore the last sentence of Article 32 and Article 33 do not apply in a sufficiently precise way for it to be acknowledged that they have the abovementioned direct effect.

(2) Dassonville Case

Procureur du Roi v. *Dassonville*; Case 8/74; Preliminary ruling of 11 July 1974; [1974] ECR 851; [1974] CMLR 436.

Facts:

Belgian law provides that it is prohibited, on pain of penal sanctions, to import, sell or display, have possessions of or transport for the purposes of sale or delivery, spirits bearing a designation of origin duly adopted by the Belgian Government when such spirits are not accompanied by any official documents certifying their right to such a designation.

The designation of origin 'Scotch Whisky' has been duly adopted by the Belgian Government.

In 1970, Gustave Dassonville, a wholesaler in business in France, and his son Benoît Dassonville, who manages a branch of his father's business in Belgium, imported into Belgium 'Scotch whisky' under the brand name 'Johnnie Walker' and 'Vat 69', which Gustave Dassonville had purchased from the French importers and distributors of these two brands of whisky.

On the bottles, the Dassonvilles affixed, with a view to their sale in Belgium, labels bearing in particular the printed words 'British Customs Certificate of Origin', followed by a hand-written note of the number and date of the French excise bond on the permit-register. This excise bond constituted the official document which, according to French rules, had to accompany a product bearing a designation of origin. France does not require a certificate of origin for 'Scotch whisky'.

Although the goods were duly imported into Belgium on the basis of the French documents required and cleared for customs purposes as 'Community goods', the Belgian authorities considered that these documents did not properly satisfy the objective of the Belgian law.

Following this importation, the Public Prosecutor instituted proceedings against the Dassonvilles before a court of summary jurisdiction. It was alleged that they:
– committed forgeries or assisted therein affixing to the bottles the

aforementioned labels, with fraudulent intent to induce belief that they were in possession, quod non, of an official document certifying the origin of the whisy, and made use of forged documents;
- contravened Belgian law by knowingly importing, selling, displaying for sale, holding in their possessing or transporting for the purposes of sale and delivery, whisky bearing a designation duly adopted by the Belgian Government without causing the whisky to be accompanied by an official document certifying its right to such designation.

The Dassonvilles claim that the provisions of Belgian law in the way they are interpreted by the Belgian authorities, are incompatible with the prohibition on quantitative restrictions and measures having equivalenteffect laid down by Article 30 et seq. of the EEC Treaty.

The Court held:

. . . . .

2. By the first question it is asked whether a national provision prohibiting the import of goods bearing a designation of origin where such goods are not accompanied by an official document issued by the government of the exporting country certifying their right to such designation constitutes a measure having an effect equivalent to a quantitative restriction within the meaning of Article 30 of the Treaty.
3. This question was raised within the context of criminal proceedings instituted in Belgium against traders who duly acquired a consignment of Scotch whisky in free circulation in France and imported it into Belgium without being in possession of a certificate of origin from the British customs authorities, thereby infringing Belgian rules.
4. It emerges from the file and from the oral proceedings that a trader, wishing to import into Belgium Scotch whisky which is already in free circulation in France, can obtain such a certificate only with great difficulty, unlike the importer who imports directly from the producer country.
5. All trading rules enacted by Member States which are capable of hindering, directly or indirectly, actually or potentially, intra-Community trade are to be considered as measures having an effect equivalent to quantitative restrictions.
6. In the absence of a Community system guaranteeing for consumers the authenticity of a product's designation of origin, if a Member State takes measures to prevent unfair practices in this connection, it is however subject to the condition that these measures should be reasonable and that the means of proof required should not act as a hindrance to trade between Member States and should, in consequence, be accessible to all Community nationals.

7. Even without having to examine whether or not such measures are covered by Article 36, they must not, in any case, by virtue of the principle expressed in the second sentence of that Article, constitute a means of arbitrary discrimination or a disguised restriction on trade between Member States.
8. That may be the case with formalities, required by a Member State for the purpose of proving the origin of a product, which only direct importers are really in a position to satisfy without facing serious difficulties.
9. Consequently, the requirement by a Member State of a certificate of authenticity which is less easily obtainable by importers of an authentic product which has been put into free circulation in a regular manner in another Member States than by importers of the same product coming directly from the country of origin constitutes a measure having an effect equivalent to a quantitative restriction as prohibited by the Treaty.

(3) Van Tiggele Case

Openbaar Ministerie (Public Prosecutor of the Kingdom of the Netherlands) v. Van Tiggele; Case 82/77; Preliminary ruling of 24 January 1978; [1978] ECR 37; [1978] 2 CMLR 528.

For the facts see the judgment below.

The Court held:

1. By an order of 30 June 1977 which was received at the Court on 5 July 1977 the Gerechtshof Amsterdam, submitted, pursuant to Article 177 of the EEC Treaty, two questions on the interpretation, first, of Articles 30 to 37 of the Treaty concerning the elimination of quantitative restrictions on trade between Member States and, secondly, of Articles 92 to 94 of the Treaty concerning aids granted by States.
2. Those questions were submitted in connection with criminal proceedings instituted against a licensed victualler who was accused of selling alcoholic beverages at prices below the minimum prices fixed by the Produktschap voor Gedestilleerde Dranken pursuant to the Royal Decree of 18 December 1975 (Staatsblad No 746).
3. The regulation of the Produktschap of 17 December 1975 concerning the price of spirits, approved by the Minister for Economic Affairs on 19 December 1975, established within the country a system of minimum retail prices which varied according to each category of spirits.
4. The minimum price for spirits of the kind known as 'new hollands gin' and 'vieux' is calculated on the basis of the manufacturer's catalogue price per unit increased by Hfl 0.60 and by value added tax, the total of which must in no case be lower than a specific amount, namely Hfl 11,25 per litre.

5. The minimum prices of spirits of the type known as 'old hollands gin' is fixed at Hfl 11,25 per litre.
6. The minimum price for all other spirits is the actual purchase price increased by value added tax.
7. Pursuant to Article 7 of the regulation the minimum price, which had at first been fixed at Hfl 11,25, was increased to Hfl 11,70 because of the rise in costs.
8. Article 8 authorizes the President of the Produktschap to grant exemption from the provisions of the regulation in certain cases or categories of cases.
9. It is clear from the statement of reasons on which the Royal Decree of 18 December 1975 is based that the power conferred upon the Produktschap to issue such rules was intended to promote the adaptation of the wine and spirit trade to normal competitive conditions and that such power was to be limited to a period of three years.
10. The first question asks in substance whether Articles 30 to 37 of the Treaty must be interpreted as meaning that the prohibition which they set out covers price-control rules such as those concerned in the present proceedings.
11. Article 30 of the Treaty prohibits in trade between Member States all measures having an effect equivalent to quantitative restrictions.
12. For the purposes of this prohibition it is sufficient that the measures in question are likely to hinder, directly or indirectly, actually or potentially, imports between Member States.
13. Whilst national price-control rules applicable without distinction to domestic products and imported products cannot in general produce such an effect they may do so in certain specific cases.
14. Thus imports may be impeded in particular when a national authority fixes prices or profit margins at such a level that imported products are placed at a disadvantage in relation to identical domestic products either because they cannot profitably be marketed in the conditions laid down or because the competitive advantage conferred by lower cost prices is cancelled out.
15. These are the considerations in the light of which the question submitted must be settled since the present case concerns a product for which there is no common organization of the market.
16. First a national provision which prohibits without distinction the retail sale of domestic products and imported products at prices below the purchase price paid by the retailer cannot produce effects detrimental to the marketing of imported products alone and consequently cannot constitute a measure having an effect equivalent to a quantitative restriction on imports.
17. Furthermore the fixing of the minmum profit margin at a specific amount, and not as a percentage of the cost price, applicable without distinction to domestic products and imported products is likewise incapable of producing an adverse effect on imported products which may be cheaper,

as in the present case where the amount of the profit margin constitutes a relatively insignificant part of the final retail price.
18. On the other hand this is not so in the case of a minimum price fixed at a specific amount which, although applicable without distinction to domestic products and imported products, is capable of having an adverse effect on the marketing of the latter in so far as it prevents their lower cost price from being reflected in the retail selling price.
19. This is the conclusion which must be drawn even though the competent authority is empowered to grant exemptions from the fixed minimum price and though this power is freely applied to imported products, since the requirement that importers and traders must comply with the administrative formalities inherent in such a system may in itself constitute a measure having an effect equivalent to a quantitative restriction.
20. The temporary nature of the application of the fixed minimum prices is not a factor capable of justifying such a measure since it is incompatible on other grounds with Article 30 of the Treaty.
21. The answer to the first question must therefore be that Article 30 of the EEC Treaty must be interpreted to mean that the establishment by a national authority of a minimum retail price fixed at a specific amount and applicable without distinction to domestic products and imported products constitutes, in conditions such as those laid down in the regulation made by the Produktschap voor Gedistilleerde Dranken on 17 December 1975, a measure having an effect equivalent to a quantitative restriction on imports which is prohibited under the said Article 30.

. . . . .

(4) Cassis de Dijon Case

REWE – Zentral AG v. *Bundesmonopolverwaltung für Branntwein*; Case 120/78; Preliminary ruling of 20 February 1970; [1979] ECR 662; [1979] 3 CMLR 494.

Facts:

The principle activity of Rewe-Zentral AG (hereinafter referred to as Rewe), is the importation of goods from other Member States of the Community. On 14 September 1976 it requested authorization from the Bundesmonopolverwaltung für Branntwein (Federal Monopoly for Spirits) to import from France, for the purposes of marketing in the Federal Republic of Germany, certain potable spirits, including the liqueur 'Cassis de Dijon', containing 15 to 20% by volume of alcohol.

By letter of 17 September 1976 the Bundesmonopolverwaltung informed

Rewe that the 'Cassis de Dijon' which it intended to import could not be sold in the Federal Republic of Germany, since Article 100 (3) of the Branntweinmonopolgesetz provides that only potable spirits having a wine-spirit content of at least 32% may be marketed in that country.

Rewe brought an action against that decision before the Verwaltungsgericht Darmstadt; by order of 27 December 1976 that court referred the case to the Hessische Finanzgericht. The Finanzgericht decided, by order of its Seventh Senate of 28 April 1978, pursuant to Article 177 of the EEC Treaty, to stay the proceedings until the Court of Justice has given a preliminary ruling on the following questions:

1. Must the concept of measures having an effect equivalent to quantitative restrictions on imports contained in Article 30 of the EEC Treaty be understood as meaning that the fixing of a minimum wine-spirit content for potable spirits laid down in the German Branntweinmonopolgesetz, the result of which is that traditional products of other Member States whose wine-spirit content is below the fixed limit cannot be put into circulation in the Federal Republic of Germany, also comes within this concept?
2. May the fixing of such a minimum wine-spirit content come within the concept of 'discrimination regarding the conditions under which goods are procured and marketed...between nationals of Member States' contained in Article 37 of the EEC Treaty?

The Court held:

. . . . .

6. The national court is thereby asking for assistance in the matter of interpretation in order to enable it to assess whether the requirement of a minimum alcohol content may be covered either by the prohibition on all measures having an effect equivalent to quantitative restrictions in trade between Member States contained in Article 30 of the Treaty or by the prohibition on all discrimination regarding the conditions under which goods are procured and marketed between nationals of Member States within the meaning of Article 37.
7. It should be noted in this connection that Article 37 relates specifically to State monopolies of a commercial character.

    That provision is therefore irrelevant with regard to national provisions which do not concern the exercise by a public monopoly of its specific function – namely, its exclusive rights – but apply in a general manner to the production and marketing of alcoholic beverages, whether or not the latter are covered by the monopoly in question.

    That being the case, the effect on intra-Community trade of the measure referred to by the national court must be examined solely in relation to the requirements under Article 30, as referred to by the first question.

8. In the absence of common rules relating to the production and marketing of alcohol – a proposal for a regulation submitted to the Council by the Commission on 7 December 1976 (Official Journal C 309, p. 2) not yet having received the Council's approval – it is for the Member States to regulate all matters relating to the production and marketing of alcohol and alcoholic beverages on their own territory.

Obstacles to movement within the Community resulting from disparities between the national law relating to the marketing of the products in question must be accepted in so far as those provisions may be recognized as being necessary in order to satisfy mandatory requirements relating in particular to the effectiveness of fiscal supervision, the protection of public health, the fairness of commercial transactions and the defence of the consumer.

9. The Government of the Federal Republic of Germany, intervening in the proceedings, put forward various arguments which, in its view, justify the application of provisions relating to the minimum alcohol content of alcoholic beverages, adducing considerations relating on the one hand to the protection of public health and on the other to the protection of the consumer against unfair commercial practices.

10. As regards the protection of public health the German Government states that the purpose of the fixing of minimum alcohol contents by national legislation is to avoid the proliferation of alcoholic beverages on the national market, in particular alcoholic beverages with a low alcohol conent, since, in its view, such products may more easily induce a tolerance towards alcohol than more highly alcoholic beverages.

11. Such considerations are not decisive since the consumer can obtain on the market an extremely wide range of weakly or moderately alcoholic products and furthermore a large proportion of alcoholic beverages with a high alcohol content freely sold on the German market is generally consumed in a diluted form.

12. The German also claims that the fixing of a lower limit for the alcohol content of certain liqueurs is designed to protect the consumer against unfair practices on the part of producers and distributors of alcoholic beverages.

This argument is based on the consideration that the lowering of the alcohol content secures a competitive advantage in relation to beverages with a higher alcohol content, since alcohol constitutes by far the most expensive constituent of beverages by reason of the high rate of tax to which it is subject.

Furthermore, according to the German Government, to allow alcoholic products into free circulation wherever, as regards their alcohol content, they comply with the rules laid down in the country of production would have the effect of imposing as a common standard within the Community the lowest alcohol content permitted in any of the Member States, and even of rendering any requirements in this field inoperative since a lower limit of this nature is foreign to the rules of several Member States.

13. As the Commission rightly observed, the fixing of limits in relation to the alcohol content of beverages may lead to the standardization of products placed on the market and of their designations, in the interests of a greater transparency of commercial transactions and offers for sale to the public.

However, this line of argument cannot be taken so far as to regard the mandatory fixing of minimum alcohol contents as being an essential guarantee of the fairness of commercial transactions, since it is a simple matter to ensure that suitable information is conveyed to the purchaser by requiring the display of an indication of origin and of the alcohol content on the packaging of products.

14. It is clear from the foregoing that the requirements relating to the minimum alcohol content of alcoholic beverages do not serve a purpose which is in the general interest and such as to take precedence over the requirements of the free movement of goods, which constitutes one of the fundamental rules of the Community.

In practice, the principle effect of requirements of this nature is to promote alcoholic beverages having a high alcohol content by excluding from the national market products of other Member States which do not answer that description.

It therefore appears that the unilateral requirement imposed by the rules of a Member State of a minimum alcohol content for the purposes of the sale of alcoholic beverages constitutes an obstacle to trade which is incompatible with the provisions of Article 30 of the Treaty.

There is therefore no valid reason why, provided that they have been lawfully produced and marketed in one of the Member States, alcoholic beverages should not be introduced into any other Member State; the sale of such products may not be subject to a legal prohibition on the marketing of beverages with an alcohol content lower than the limit set by the national rules.

15. Consequently, the first question should be answered to the effect that the concept of 'measures having an effect equivalent to quantitative restrictions on imports' contained in Article 30 of the Treaty is to be understood to mean that the fixing of a minimum alcohol content for alcoholic beverages intended for human consumption by the legislation of a Member States also falls within the prohibition laid down in that provision where the importation of alcoholic beverages lawfully produced and marketed in another Member State is concerned.

(4a) Sequel:

Communication from the Commission concerning the consequences of the judgment given by the Court of Justice on 20 February 1979 in Case 120/78 ('*Cassis de Dijon*'); OJ C 256/2 of 3 October 1980.

In the Commission's Communication of 6 November 1978 on 'Safeguarding free trade within the Community', it was emphasized that the free movement of goods is being affected by a growing number of restrictive measures.

The judgment delivered by the Cosurt of Justice on 20 February 1979 in Case 120/78 (the '*Cassis de Dijon*' case), and recently reaffirmed in the judgment of 26 June 1980 in Case 788/79, has given the Commission some interpretative guidance enabling it to monitor more strictly the application of the Treaty rules on the free movement of goods, particularly Articles 30 to 36 of the EEC Treaty.

The Court gives a very general definition of the barriers to free trade which are prohibited by the provisions of Article 30 *et seq.* of the EEC Treaty. These are taken to include 'any national measure capable of hindering, directly or indirectly, actually or potentially, intra-Community trade'.

In its judgment of 20 February 1979 the Court indicates the scope of this definition as it applies to technical and commercial rules.

Any product lawfully produced and marketed in one Member State must, in principle, be admitted to the market of any other Member State.

Technical and commercial rules, even those equally applicable to national and imported products, may create barriers to trade only where those rules are necessary to satisfy mandatory requirements and to serve a purpose which is in the general interest and for which they are an essential guarantee. This purpose must be such as to take precedence over the requirements of the free movement of goods, which constitutes one of the fundamental rules of the Community.

The conclusions in terms of policy which the Commission draws from this new guidance are set out below.

– Whereas Member States may, with respect to domestic products and in the absence of relevant Community provisions, regulate the terms on which such products are marketed, the case is different for products imported from other Member States.

  Any product imported from another Member State must in principle be admitted to the territory of the importing Member State if it has been lawfully produced, that is, conforms to rules and processes of manufacture that are customarily and traditionally accepted in the exporting country, and is marketed in the territory of the latter.

  This principle implies that Member States, when drawing up commercial or technical rules liable to affect the free movement of goods, may not take an exclusively national viewpoint and take account only of requirements confined to domestic products. The proper functioning of the common market demands that each Member State also give consideration to the legitimate requirements of the other Member States.

– Only under very strict conditions does the Court accept exceptions to this principle; barriers to trade resulting from differences between commercial and technical rules are only admissable:
  – If the rules are necessary, that is appropriate and not excessive, in order to satisfy mandatory requirements (public health, protection of con-

sumers or the environment, the fairness of commercial transactions, etc.);
– if the rules serve a purpose in the general interest which is compelling enough to justify an exception to a fundamental rule of the Treaty such as the free movement of goods;
– if the rules are essential for such a purpose to be attained, i.e. are the means which are the most appropriate and at the same time least hinder trade.

The Court's interpretation has induced the Commission to set out a number of guidelines.
– The principles deduced by the Court imply that a Member State may not in principle prohibit the sale in its territory of a product lawfully produced and marketed in another Member State even if the product is produced according to technical or quality requirements which differ from those imposed on its domestic products. Where a product 'suitably and satisfactorily' fulfils the legitimate objective of a Member State's own rules (public safety, protection of the consumer or the environment, etc.), the importing country cannot justify prohibiting its sale in its territory by claiming that the way it fulfils the objective is different from that imposed on domestic products.

In such a case, an absolute prohibition of sale could not be considered 'necessary' to satisfy a 'mandatory requirement' because it would not be an 'essential guarantee' in the sense defined in the Court's judgment.

The Commission will therefore have to tackle a whole body of commercial rules which lay down that products manufactured and marketed in one Member State must fulfil technical or qualitative conditions in order to be admitted to the market of another and specifically in all cases where the trade barriers occasioned by such rules are inadmissible according to the very strict criteria set out by the Court.

The Commission is referring in particular to rules covering the composition, designation, presentation and packaging of products as well as rules requiring compliance with certain technical standards.
– The Commission's work of harmonization will henceforth have to be directed mainly at national laws having an impact on the functioning of the common market where barriers to trade to be removed arise from national provisions which are admissible under the criteria set by the Court.

The Commission will be concentrating on sectors deserving priority because of their economic relevance to the creation of a single internal market.

To forestall later difficulties, the Commission will be informing Member States of potential objections, under the terms of Community law, to provisions they may be considering introducing which come to the attention of the Commission.

It will be producing suggestions soon on the procedures to be followed in such cases.

The Commission is confident that this approach will secure greater freedom of trade for the Community's manufacturers, so strengthening the industrial base of the Community, while meeting the expectations of consumers.

(5) Groenveld Case

Groenveld v. *Produktschap voor Vee en Vlees*; Case 15/79; Judgment of 8 November 1979; [1979] ECR 3409.

Facts:

The undertaking P. B. Groenveld, the plaintiff in the main action, carries on in the Netherlands the business of importing horsemeat and manufacturing smoked horsemeat. On 9 February 1978 it asked the national agency which supervises the production of meat (the Produktschap voor Vee en Vlees [Cattle and Meat Board]) for authority to produce sausages and other preparations from horsemeat, apart from smoked meat. That request was refused pursuant to the Verordening Be- en Verwerking Vlees [Processing and Preparation of Meat Regulation] issued by the board of the Produktschap voor Vee en Vlees on 5 December 1973; Article 3 (1) of that regulation expressly prohibits manufacturers of sausages from having in stock or processing horsemeat and products containing proteins derived from such meat.

Groenveld challenged the refusal of the authorization requested before the College van Beroep voor het Bedrijfsleven [administrative court of last instance in matters of trade and industry]. By an order of 26 January 1979 that court submitted a request to the Court of Justice for a preliminary ruling to establish the following point:

'Must Article 34 of the Treaty establishing the European Economic Community, read possibly in conjunction with any other provision of that Treaty and/or with any principle fundamental to that Treaty, be interpreted to mean that the prohibition on having in stock, preparing and processing horsemeat set out in Article 3 (1) of the Verordening Be- en Verwerking Vlees 1973 of the Produktschap – having regard *inter alia* to the purpose and scope of that prohibition as they have been set out in Point 7 of this order – is incompatible with that article of the Treaty?'

The Court held:

6. Article 34 of the EEC Treaty provides that 'quantitative restrictions on exports, and all measures having equivalent effect, shall be prohibited between Member States'.
7. That provision concerns national measures which have as their specific object or effect the restriction of patterns of exports and thereby the establishment of a difference in treatment between the domestic trade of a

Member State and its export trade in such a way as to provide a particular advantage for national production or for the domestic market of the State in question at the expense of the production or of the trade of other Member States. This is not so in the case of a prohibition like that in question which is applied objectively to the production of goods of a certain kind without drawing a distinction depending on whether such goods are intended for the national market or for export.

8. The foregoing appreciation is not affected by the circumstance that the regulation in question has as its objective, *inter alia*, the safeguarding of the reputation of the national production of meat products in certain export markets within the Community and in non-member countries where there are obstacles of a psychological or legislative nature to the consumption of horsemeat when the same prohibition is applied identically to the product in the domestic market of the State in question. The objective nature of that prohibition is not modified by the fact that the regulation in force in the Netherlands permits the retail sale of horsemeat by butchers. In fact that concession at the level of local trade does not have the effect of bringing about a prohibition at the level of industrial manufacture of the same product regardless of its destination.

(6) Fietje Case

Criminal proceedings against *A. A. Fietje*; Case 27/80; Preliminary ruling of 16 December 1980; [1980] ECR 3839.

For the facts see the judgment below.

The Court held:

1. By a judgment of 19 December 1979, which was received at the Court on 18 January 1980, the Economische Politierechter of the Arrondissementsrechtbank Assen referred to the Court for a preliminary ruling under Article 177 of the EEC Treaty a question on the interpretation of Article 30 of the EEC Treaty which a view to considering the compatibility with Community law of Article 1 of the Netherlands 'Likeurbesluit', in so far as that article makes the use of the word 'likeur' mandatory in the case of the beverages therein defined.
2. The question has been raised in the context of criminal proceedings against a dealer in beverages who is charged with having supplied a beverage, imported from the Federal Republic of Germany and described as 'Berentzen Appel – Aus Apfel mit Weizenkorn 25 vol.%', which did not bear the description 'likeur' even though it fell within the above-mentioned provision.
3. The 'Likeurbesluit' was enacted on the basis of Articles 14 and 15 of the

Netherlands 'Warenwet' of 28 December 1935 (Staatsblad 793). Those articles provide, *inter alia*, that, in order to protect public health or fair trading, general administrative regulations may specify the descriptions which must be used in trade in goods where the goods are of a kind or composition provided for in the regulation.

4. Article 1 (1) of the 'Likeurbesluit' of 11 September 1953 (Staatsblad 466) is at present worded as follows:

'Where it satisfies the provisions of Article 3, any product which has as its characteristic ingredients ethyl alcohol, sugar, aromatic substances and/or fruit juice may and must be described by one of the following words: 'likeur', 'tussenlikeur', 'verloflikeur' (it being permissible, where appropriate, to spell the word 'likeur' as 'liqueur'), or 'likorette', and the last description must be immediately followed by a statement of the percentage by volume of the alcoholic strength at 15°C. These descriptions may be used in conjunction with expressions specifying the taste or the aroma.'

Article 3 of the 'Likeurbesluit' provides that every product described in accordance with Article 1 (1) must have a certain minimum sugar content. It also provides that a product described as 'likeur' must have an alcoholic strength of at least 22% by volume and it lays down different and lower alcoholic strengths for the other products which it mentions. In addition Article 3 contains various other provisions on the composition and quality of the products. According to Article 6, the name specified for the product must appear on any receptacle which is intended or suitable for delivery with the product to the consumer.

5. Article 2 of the 'Likeurbesluit' sets forth a number of exceptions to the obligation to use the descriptions referred to in Article 1. One of these exceptions relates to products 'described with the help of a description generally used under normal commercial practice to describe a liqueur', provided that those liqueurs have an alcoholic strength of not less than 24% by volume and the director of the appropriate government department has given his approval. Other exceptions apply to the beverages which are listed in the article and described by names which for the most part are typically Dutch. Finally, Article 14 (4) of the 'Warenwet' empowers the appropriate ministers to grant exemptions from *inter alia* the rules of the 'Likeurbesluit'.

6. The accused aubmitted that these national rules are incompatible with Article 30 of the EEC Treaty and the Economische Politierechter considered it necessary that, prior to his giving judgment in the criminal proceedings, the Court should give a ruling on the following question:

'Does the concept "measures having an effect equivalent to quantitative restrictions on imports" in Article 30 of the EEC Treaty cover the provisions of Article 1 of the Netherlands Likeurbesluit [Decree on Liqueurs] governing the obligation to use the word "likeur" for beverages defined therein, as a result of which products from other Member States which have the characteristics defined in Article 1 of the Likeurbesluit, but in respect of which there is no obligation to use the description 'likeur' in those Member States, must be labelled differently from importation into the Netherlands?'

7. Before the Court answers the question referred to it, it should be emphasized that, in the absence of common rules relating to the production and marketing of alcohol, it is, in principle, for the Member States to regulate all matters relating to the marketing of alcoholic beverages on their own territory, including the description and labelling of these beverages, subject to any Community measure adopted with a view to approximating national laws in these fields.

8. At the present stage in the development of Community law the factors to which the national court need have regard in its interpretation do not relate therefore to the compatibility with Community law of the obligation to use a particular description in marketing certain alcoholic beverages. As the national court has itself indicated in the wording of the question to the Court of Justice for a preliminary ruling, the issue is whether the extension of such an obligation to beverages imported from the other Member States in such a way as to make it impossible to market the imported product without altering the label under which the beverage is lawfully marketed in the exporting Member State is to be regarded as a measure having an effect equivalent to a quantitative restriction which is prohibited by Article 30 of the Treaty.

9. In order to answer this question it is necessary to consider whether the extension of the national rules is capable of impeding the free movement of goods between Member States and, if so, to what extent such an obstacle is justified on the ground of the public interest underlying the national rules.

10. Although the extension to imported products of an obligation to use a certain name on the label does not wholly preclude the importation into the Member State concerned of products originating in other Member States or in free circulation in those States it may none the less make their marketing more difficult, especially in the case of parallel imports. As the Netherlands Government itself admits in its observations, such an extension of that obligation is thus capable of impeding, at least indirectly, trade between Member States. It is therefore necessary to consider whether it may be justified on the ground of the public interest in consumer protection, which, according to the observations of the Netherlands Government and according to the 'Warenwet', underlies the rules in question.

11. If national rules relating to a given product include the obligation to use a description that is sufficiently precise to inform the purchaser of the nature of the product and to enable it to be distinguished from products with it might be confused, it may well be necessary, in order to give consumers effective protection, to extend this obligation to imported products also, even in such a way as to make necessary the alteration of the original labels of some of these products. At the level of Com-

munity legislation, this possibility is recognized in several directives on the approximation of the laws of the Member States relating to certain foodstuffs as well as by Council Directive 79/112/EEC of 18 December 1978 on the approximation of the laws of the Member States relating to the labelling, presentation and advertising of foodstuffs for sale to the ultimate consumer (OJ 1979, L 33, p. 1).

12. However, there is no longer any need for such protection if the details given on the original label of the imported product have as their content information on the nature of the product and that content includes at least the same information, and is just as capable of being understood by consumers in the importing State, as the description prescribed by the rules of that State. In the context of Article 177 of the EEC Treaty, the making of the findings of fact necessary in order to establish whether there is such equivalence is a matter for the national court.

(7) Oebel Case

For facts and references see at page 252.

The Court held:

11. By the second question the national court asks whether the effects of domestic legislation on working hours in bakeries, such as the German Law in issue, in regard to the export and import of fresh baker's wares are to be regarded as measures having an effect equivalent to quantitative restrictions on imports or exports within the meaning of Articles 30 and 34 of the Treaty.
12. It cannot be disputed that the prohibition in the bread and confectionery industry on working before 4 a.m. in itself constitutes a legitime element of economic and social policy, consistent with the objectives of public interest pursued by the Treaty. Indeed, this prohibition is designed to improve working considitions in a manifestly sensitive industry, in which the production process exhibits particular characteristics resulting from both the nature of the product and the habits of consumers.
13. For these reasons, several Member States of the Community as well as a number of non-member States have introduced similar rules concerning nightwork in this industry. In this regard it is appropriate to mention Convention No 20 of the International Labour Organization of 8 June 1925 concerning nightwork in bakeries which, subject to certain exceptions, prohibits the production of bread, pastries or similar products during the night.
14. The accused maintains that the prohibition on the production of ordinary and fine baker's wares before 4 a.m. constitutes an export barrier prohibited by Article 34 of the Treaty. This is alleged to be the case particularly with regard to products which have to be delivered fresh in time

for breakfast and which must therefore be produced during the night before the day on which they are offered for sale.

15. However, as the Court has already declared in its judgment of 8 November 1979 (Case 15/79 *Groenveld* [1979] ECR 3409), Article 34 concerns national measures which have as their specific object or effect the restriction of patterns of exports and thereby the establishment of a difference in treatment between the domestic trade of a Member State and its export trade, in such a way as to provide a particular advantage for national production or for the domestic market of the State in question.
16. This is clearly not the case with rules such as those in issue, which are part of economic and social policy and apply by virtue of objective criteria to all the undertakings in a particular industry which are established within the national territory, without leading to any difference in treatment whatsoever on the ground of the nationality of traders and without distinguishing between the domestic trade of the State in question and the export trade.

The restrictions on transport and delivery

17. The accused also challenges the prohibition, included in the rules on nightwork at issue before the national court, on the transport and delivery or ordinary and fine baker's wares to consumers or retail shops before 5.45 a.m. He submits that this prohibition constitutes a measure having an effect equivalent to restrictions on both imports and exports, because, on the one hand, it prevents producers established in other Member States from delivering their wares in time to consumers and retail shops in the Federal Republic of Germany, whilst, on the other hand, producers established in the Federal Republic of Germany are prevented from delivery in time to the other Member States.
18. According to the German Government, the sole purpose of the prohibition on transport and delivery before 5.45 a.m. is to ensure compliance with the prohibition on production at night, which might otherwise escape effective control on the part of the authorities. It is alleged to be essential to extend the prohibition to cover products coming from other Member States because otherwise producers established in Germany would be at disadvantage in relation to competition from abroad, which would be contrary to the principle of equality. Therefore, if products from other Member States were to be exempt from such a prohibition, it would be impossible not only to maintain the prohibition for domestic products, but also to maintain the restrictions on production times.
19. In this regard, it must be noted that the restrictive effect of the rules controlling the times for the transport and delivery of ordinary and fine baker's wares, in connection with the control of the hours when those products may be manufactured, must be evaluated in the light of their scope.

20. If such rules are confined to transport for delivery to individual consumers and retail outlets only, without affecting transport and delivery to warehouses or intermediaries, they cannot have the effect of restricting imports or exports between Member States. In this case, indeed, trade within the Community remains possible at alle times, subject to the single exception that delivery to consumers and retailers is restricted to the same extent for all producers, wherever whey are established. Under these circumstances such rules are not contrary to Articles 30 and 34 of the Treaty.
21. The reply to the second question must therefore be that Articles 30 and 34 of the EEC Treaty do not apply to national rules which prohibit the production of ordinary and fine baker's wares and also their transport and delivery to individual consumers and retail outlets during the night up to a certain hour.

. . . . .

The Court ruled:

1. Article 7 of the EEC Treaty must be construed as prohibiting only discrimination on the ground of the nationality of traders. There is, therefore, no infringement of Article 7, even if, by means of a statutory provision which makes no distinction directly or indirectly on grounds of nationality, a Member State creates a situation affecting the competitiveness of traders established on its territory compared with traders established in other Member States.
2. Articles 30 and 34 of the EEC Treaty do not apply to national rules which prohibit the production of ordinary and fine baker's wares and also their transport and delivery to individual consumers and retail outlets during the night up to a certain hour.

(8) Buy Irish Case

Commission v. *Ireland*; Case 249/81; Judgment of 24 November 1982: [1982] ECR 4005.

Facts (as summarized by the Advocate General):

By a letter of 28 May 1979, the Commission opened the procedure laid down in the first paragraph of Article 169 of the EEC Treaty, by inviting the Irish Government to submit its observations on the compatibility with Community law of a series of measures which it had taken in the context of the three-year

programme for the promotion of the sale of Irish products, announced in January 1978. As was stated at pages 3 and 4 of the letter, the measures which the Commission found incompatible with Article 30 were the following:
(a) the introduction of a 'Guaranteed Irish' symbol and the possibility for the consumer to refer any complaints concerning products bearing that symbol to the Irish Goods Council, an association financed and controlled by the Irish Government;
(b) the creation of the 'Shoplink Service', intended to provide the consumer with information on products made in Ireland, by means of five centres located in Dublin, Cork, Limerick, Waterford and Galway;
(c) the promotion of various forms of advertising of Irish products by means of the Irish Goods Council; and
(d) the exhibition facilities available for domestic products only in the Ireland House Trade Centre, Dublin, a body which has equipped space of over 2,000 square metres and is run by the Irish Goods Council.

In conclusion, it seems to me that the established facts of a permanent nature on which attention should be focused in this case are the following: the Irish Government controls and to a considerable extent finances the Irish Goods Council; that Council carries on a wide range of activities for the promotion of the sale of Irish products; the Irish Government has further supported that promotion has further supported that promotion campaign by means of certain promotion campaign by means of certain official statements and through the cooperation of the competent ministers.

The Court held:

27. In the circumstances the two activities in question amount to the establishment of a national practice, introduced by the Irish Government and prosecuted with its assistance, the potential effect of which on imports from other Member States is comparable to that resulting from government measures of a binding nature.
28. Such a practice cannot escape the prohibition laid down by Article 30 of the Treaty solely because it is not based on decisions which are binding upon undertakings. Even measures adopted by the government of a Member State which do not have binding effect may be capable of influencing the conduct of traders and consumers in that State and thus of frustrating the aims of the Community as set out in Article 2 and enlarged upon in Article 3 of the Treaty.
29. That is the case where, as in this instance, such a restrictive practice represents the implementation of a programme defined by the government which affects the national economy as a whole and which is intended to check the flow of trade between Member States by encouraging the purchase of domestic products, by means of an advertising campaign on a national scale and the organization of special procedures applicable solely to domestic products, and where those activities are

attributable as a whole to the government and are pursued in an organized fashion throughout the national territory.

(9) Cinéthèque Case

Cinéthèque SA and Others v. *Fédération Nationale des Cinémas Français*; Cases 60 and 61/84; Preliminary ruling of 11 July 1985; [1985] ECR 2605.

Facts (as summarized by the Advocate General):

Article 89 of French Law No 82-652 of 29 July 1982 on audio-visual communication provides that:
'No cinematographic work being shown in cinemas may simultaneously be exploited in the form of recordings intended for sale or hire for the private use of the public, in particular in the form of video cassettes or video discs, before the expiry of a period to be determined by decree and to run from the date of the issue of the performance certificate. That period shall run from 6 to 18 months. That requirement may be waived subject to conditions to be determined by decree.'

This provision was implemented by Decree 83/4 of 4 January 1983, which fixed the relevant period at one year from the grant of the performance certificate authorizing the showing of the particular film in question. The same Decree provides that this rule may be waived by the Ministry of Culture on the application of the copyright owner after an opinion has been delivered by a committee set up under the auspices of the Centre national de la cinématographie.

There is thus a ban on selling or hiring video-cassettes of any film which is simultaneously being shown, unless a dispensation is granted, for one year from the date of the authorization certificate granted for the film. It is clear that the ban is only on private showing; it does not ban the showing of video-recordings in public, a practice which exists and, the Court is told, is likely to increase. It seems also clear that the ban does not prohibit the production or importation of such video recordings during the year in question. There is a dispute between the parties as to whether the ban can be applied to cassettes intended for export. There is also some doubt, as a matter of interpretation of the French law, as to what constitutes 'simultaneous exploitation' for the purposes of the law and what would be the position if the video cassettes were lawfully shown before a film was shown, if the latter were subsequently authorized to be shown.

According to the Commission, no comparable legislation exists in any other Member State. However, in Germany it is provided by statute that where State subsidies have been granted for a film, no video cassettes or video discs of that film may be distributed within 6 months of its first showing in the cinemas. This was confirmed at the hearing by the representative of the German Government. In Denmark films subsidized by the Danish national film institute are, according to the Commission, subject to a similar prohibition for a one year period. That is stipulated by the national film institute itself.

In addition, in a number of Member States the same result has been achieved by the film industry itself without legislation. Thus, in Italy an agreement between trade associations provides that a film may not be exploited in the form of video-cassettes within 12 months of its first showing in the cinemas. A similar agreement between trade associations has been concluded in Germany and in the Netherlands, where the period is 6 months. In some other Member States a similar ban is laid down on an ad boc basis in contracts for the distribution of films. In such cases the period varies between 3 and 6 months.

The plaintiffs in both these cases claim that these provisions of the French Law are contrary to Articles 30, 34 and 59 of the Treaty.

Case 60/80 Cinéthèque concerns 'Merry Christmas, Mr Lawrence', which is described by the Fédération Nationale des cinémas français as being 'of New Zealand nationality'. The film first appeared in the cinemas in France under the name 'Furyo' on 1 June 1983, although it did not receive its performance certificate until 28 June 1983. Glinwood Films Ltd, the second plaintiffs, are a British company which owned the copyright in the film. It granted to AAA, a French company, the exclusive right to distribute and show the film in French cinemas. By a contract dated 28 July 1983 it granted to Cinéthèque, the first plaintiffs, the exclusive right to produce and sell video-cassettes of the film for a 6 year period starting on 1 October 1983 in France and 1 June 1984 in Belgium and Switzerland. AAA, which had a share in the royalties of the video cassettes, thereupon agreed in writing to this contract concluded between Glinwood and Cinéthèque. Cinéthèque then proceeded to produce the video cassettes, some of which it sold to Discophile Club de France (DCF) and Téléfrance. No request for a waiver of the one-year rule with respect to 'Furyo' was ever made to the Ministry of Culture.

On the basis that the plaintiffs had contravened the French legislation referred to, the Fédération nationale des cinémas français sought and obtained on 19 October 1983 an interim order that the cassettes of the film in the possession of Cinéthèque and of the dealers be seized until the expiry of the one-year period, subject to a waiver being granted by the Ministry of Culture. By the same order Cinéthèque was enjoined from distributing any further copies of the cassettes. That order was confirmed by a second order dated 15 November 1983. Cinéthèque and Glinwood then brought an action against the Fédération nationale to have the order lifted. DCF subsequently intervened of its own volition in support of the plaintiffs and Téléfrance was joined as a co-plaintiff.

The national court submitted i.a. the following question:

In establishing an interval between one mode of distributing cinematographical works and another by a prohibition of the simultaneous exploitation of such works in cinemas and in video-cassette form for a period of one year, save in the case of derogation, are the provisions of Article 89 of the French Law of 29 July 1982, as supplemented by the Decree of 4 January 1983, regulating the distribution of cinematographical works, compatible with the provisions of Article 30 and 34 of the EEC Treaty on the free movement of goods?

The Court held:

20. It must be stated first that, in the light of that information, the national legislation at issue in the main proceedings of these cases forms part of a body of provisions applied in the majority of Member States, whether in the form of contractual, administrative or legislative provisions and of variable scope, but the purpose of which, in all cases, is to delay the distribution of films by means of video-cassettes during the first months following their release in the cinema in order to protect their exploitation in the cinema, which protection is considered necessary in the interests of the profitability of cinematographic production, as against exploitation through video-cassettes. It must also be observed that, in principle, the Treaty leaves it to the Member States to determine the need for such a system, the form of such a system and any temporal restrictions which ought to be laid down.
21. In that connection it must be observed that such a system, if it applies without distinction to both video-cassettes manufactured in the national territory and to imported video-cassettes, does not have the purpose of regulating trade patterns; its effect is not to favour national production as against the production of other Member States, but to encourage cinematographic production as such.
22. Neverthelesss, the application of such a system may create barriers to intra-Community trade in video-cassettes because of the disparities between the systems operated in the different Member States and between the conditions for the release of cinematographic works in the cinemas of those States. In those circumstances a prohibition of exploitation laid down by such a system is not compatible with the principle of the free movement of goods provided for in the Treaty unless any obstacle to intra-Community trade thereby created does not exceed that which is necessary in order to ensure the attainment of the objective in view and unless that objective is justified with regard to Community law.
23. It must be conceded that a national system which, in order to encourage the creation of cinematographic works irrespective of their origin, gives priority, for a limited initial period, to the distribution of such works through the cinema, is so justified.
24. The reply to the questions referred to the Court is therefore that Article 30 of the EEC Treaty must be interpreted as meaning that it does not apply to national legislation which regulates the distribution of cinemato-

graphic works by imposing an interval between one mode of distributing such works and another by prohibiting their simultaneous exploitation in cinemas and in video-cassette form for a limited period, provided that the prohibition applies to domestically produced and imported cassettes alike and any barriers to intra-Community trade to which its implementation may give rise do not exceed what is necessary for ensuring that the exploitation in cinemas of cinematographic works of all origins retains priority over other means of distribution.

4. Public morality, public policy, public security, protection of health, national measures, industrial policy (EEC Article 36)

a. Cases

(1) Art treasures Case I

For references and facts see page 254.

The Court held:

3. The classification of the disputed tax having regard to Article 36 of the Treaty

The defendant relies on Article 36 of the Treaty as authorizing export restrictions which, as in this case, are claimed to be justified on grounds of the protection of national treasures possessing artistic, historic or archaeological value. By reason of its object, scope and effects, the tax in dispute is claimed to fall less within the provisions of the Treaty relating to charges having an effect equivalent to customs duties on exports than within the restrictive measures permitted by Article 36.

In fact, the divergence of view between the Commission and the Italian Government relates, it is argued, not to the objective but to the choice of means. As for the latter, the Italian authorities gave their preference to the levy of a charge which would disturb the functioning of the Common Market less than the application of prohibitions or export restrictions.

Article 36 of the Treaty provides that: 'The provisions of Articles 30 and 34 shall not preclude prohibitions or restrictions on ... exports ... justified on grounds of ... the protection of national treasures possessing artistic, historic or archaeological value'. This provision, both by its position and by an express reference to Articles 30 to 34, forms part of the chapter relating to the elimination of quantitative restrictions between Member States. The subject of that chapter is State intervention in intra-Community trade by measures in the nature of prohibitions, total or partial, on import, export or transit, according to circumstances. It is to such measures that Article 36 refers clearly and solely, as follows from the use of the words 'prohibitions

323

or restrictions'. The prohibitions and restrictions in question are by nature clearly distinguished from customs duties and assimilated charges whereby the economic conditions of importation or exportation are affected without restricting the freedom of decision of those involved in commercial transactions.

The provisions of Title I of Part Two of the Treaty introduced the fundamental principle of the elimination of all obstacles to the free movements of goods between Member States by the abolition of, on the one hand, quantitative restrictions and measures having equivalent effect. Exceptions to this fundamental rule must be strictly construed.

Consequently, in view of the difference between the measures referred to in Article 16 and Article 36, it is not possible to apply the exception laid down in the latter provision to measures which fall outside the scope of the prohibitions referred to in the chapter relating to the elimination of quantitative restrictions between Member States.

Finally, the fact that the provisions of Article 36 which have been mentioned do not relate to customs duties and charges having equivalent effect is explained by the fact that such measures have the sole effect of rendering more onerous the exportation of the products in question, without ensuring the attainment of the object referred to in that article, which is to protect the artistic, historic or archaeological heritage.

In order to avail themselves of Article 36, Member States must observe the limitations imposed by that provision both as regards the objective to be attained and as regards the nature of the means used to attain it.

Consequently, the levy of the disputed tax, which falls outside the limits of Article 36, is incompatible with the provisions of the Treaty.

(2) Centrafarm – Sterling Drug Case

Centrafarm v. *Sterling Drug*; Case 15/74; Preliminary ruling of 31 October 1974; [1974] ECR 1161; [1974] 2 CMLR 480.

Facts:

Sterling Drug, titular holder of national patents in several countries – including the Netherlands and Great Britain – relating to the mode of preparation of a medicament named 'acidum nalidixicum', for the treatment of infections of the urinary passages.

For this product the trade mark 'Negram' is the property, in Great Britain, of the company Sterling-Winthrop Group Ltd. and, in the Netherlands, of a subsidiary of the latter, Winthrop BV.

Centrafarm, of which Mr. de Peijper is a director, imported medicinal preparations manufactured according to the patent method, some of which bore the trade mark Negram, without the agreement of Sterling Drug, from

England and the Federal Republic of Germany, where they had been put onto the market in a regular manner by subsidiaries of Sterling Drug Inc., into the Netherlands where they were offered for sale.

By importing the goods from Great Britain Centrafarm took advantage of a considerable price differential. It appears that in Great Britain the product is sold for half the price at which it sells in the Netherlands.

On 16 June 1971 Sterling Drug submitted to the president of the Arrondissementsrechtbank at Rotterdam, sitting in chambers, an application for the immediate adoption of measures of conservation against the actions of Centrafarm and of its director, and requiring them to refrain from any further infringement of the patent belonging to Sterling Drug, together with several subsidiary requests. The president to the court rejected the application, on the grounds of an interpretation of the law on patents (Octrooiwet) according to which a product is held to have been put into circulation in a regular manner even if it is put into circulation abroad by the titular holder of a Dutch patent. Sterling Drug thereupon brought an appeal before the Gerechtshof (Court of Appeal) at The Hague, which found in favour of Sterling Drug, with the exception of certain of its subsidiary requests.

Centrafarm and de Peijper brought an appeal on a point of law before the Hoge Raad against the judgment of the Gerechtshof.

The Court held:

1. By interim decision of 1 March 1974, registered at the Court on 4 March, the Hoge Raad der Nederlanden (Dutch Supreme Court) referred certain questions by virtue of Article 177 of the EEC Treaty, on patent rights in relation to the provisions of the Treaty and of the Act concerning the Accession of the three new Member States.
2. In the decision making the reference the Hoge Raad set out as follows the elements of fact and of national law in issue in relation to the questions referred:
   – a patentee holds parallel patents in several of the States belonging to the EEC,
   – the products protected by those patents are lawfully marketed in one or more of those Member States by undertakings to which the patentee has granted licences to manufacture and/or sell,
   – those products are subsequently exported by third parties and are marketed and further dealt in in one of those other Member States,
   – the patent legislation in the lastmentioned State gives the patentee the right to take legal action to prevent products thus protected by patents from being there marketed by others, even where there products were previously lawfully marketed in another country by the patentee or by the patentee's licencee.
3. It appears from the proceedings that the main action is concerned with the rights of a proprietor of parallel patents in several Member States

who grants an exclusive licence to sell, but not to manufacture, the patent product in one of those States, while at the same time the patentee does not manufacture the patent product in that same Member State.

As regards question I(a)

4. This question requires the Court to state whether, under the conditions postulated, the rules in the EEC Treaty concerning the free movement of goods prevent the patentee from ensuring that the product protected by the patent is not marketed by others.
5. As a result of the provisions in the Treaty relating to the free movement of goods and in particular of Article 30, quantitative restrictions on imports and all measures having equivalent effect are prohibited between Member States.
6. By Article 36 these provisions shall nevertheless not include prohibitions or restrictions on imports justified on grounds of the protection of industrial or commercial property.
7. Nevertheless, it is clear from this same Article, in particular its second sentence, as well as from the context, that whilst the Treaty does not affect the existence of rights recognized by the legislation of a Member State in matters of industrial and commercial property, yet the exercise of these rights may nevertheless, depending on the circumstances, be affected by the prohibitions in the Treaty.
8. Inasmuch as it provides an exception to one of the fundamental principles of the Common Market, Article 36 in fact only admits of derogations from the free movement of goods where such derogations are justified for the purpose of safeguarding rights which constitute the specific subject matter of this property.
9. In relation to patents, the specific subject matter of the industrial property is the guarantee that the patentee, to reward the creative effort of the inventor, has the exclusive right to use an invention with a view to manufacturing industrial products and putting them into circulation for the first time, either directly or by the grant of licences to third parties, as well as the right to oppose infringements.
10. An obstacle to the free movement of goods may arise out of the existence, within a national legislation concerning industrial and commercial property, of provisions laying down that a patentee's right is not exhausted when the product protected by the patent is marketed in another Member State, with the result that the patentee can prevent importation of the product into his own Member State when it has been marketed in another State.
11. Whereas an obstacle to the free movement of goods of this kind may be justified on the ground of protection of industrial property where such protection is invoked against a product coming from a Member State where it is not patentable and has been manufactured by third parties without the consent of the patentee and in cases where there exist

patents, the original proprietors of which are legally and economically independent, a derogation from the principle of the free movement of goods is not, hwoever, justified where the product has been put onto the market in a legal manner, by the patentee himself or with his consent, in the Member State from which it has been imported, in particular in the case of a proprietor of parallel patents.

12. In fact, if a patentee could prevent the import of protected products marketed by him or with his consent in another Member State, he would be able to partition off national markets and thereby restrict trade between Member States, in a situation where no such restriction was necessary to guarantee the essence of the exclusive rights flowing from the parallel patents.
13. The Plaintiff in the main action claims, in this connection, that by reason of divergences between national legislations and practice, truly identical or parallel patents can hardly be said to exist.
14. It should be noted here that, in spite of the divergences which remain in the absence of any unification of national rules concerning industrial property, the identity of the protected invention is clearly the essential element of the concept of parallel patents which it is for the courts to assess.
15. The question referred should therefore be answered to the effect that the exercise, by a patentee, of the right which he enjoys under the legislation of a Member State to prohibit the sale, in that State, of a product protected by the patent which has been marketed in another Member State by the patentee or with his consent is incompatible with the rules of the EEC Treaty concerning the free movement of goods within the Common Market.

. . . . .

As regards question I(c)

18. This question requires the Court to state whether it makes any difference to the answer given to question I(a) that the patentee and the licencees do or do not belong to the same concern.
19. It follows from the answer given to question I(a) that the factor which above all else characterizes a restriction of trade between Member States is the territorial protection granted to a patentee in one Member State against importation of the product which has been marketed in another Member State by the patentee himself or with his consent.
20. Therefore the result of the grant of a sales licence in a Member State is that the patentee can no longer prevent the sale of the protected products throughout the Common Market.
21. Accordingly, it is of no significance to know whether the patentee and the licencees do or do not belong to the same concern.

As regards question I(d)

22. This question requires the Court to state, in substance, whether the patentee can, notwithstanding the answer given to the first question, prevent importation of the protected product, given the existence of price differences resulting from governmental measures adopted in the exporting country with a view to controlling the price of that product.
23. It is part of the Community authorities' task to eliminate factors likely to distort competition between Member States, in particular by the harmonization of national measures for the control of prices and by the prohibition of aids which are incompatible with the Common Market, in addition to the exercise of their powers in the field of competition.
24. The existence of factors such as these in a Member State, however, cannot justify the maintenance or introduction by another Member State of measures which are incompatible with the rules concerning the free movement of goods, in particular in the field of industrial and commercial property.
25. The questions referred should therefore be answered in the negative.

. . . . .

As regards question I(e)

26. This question requires the Court to state whether the patentee is authorized to exercise the rights conferred on him by the patent, notwithstanding Community rules on the free movement of goods, for the purpose of controlling the distribution of a pharmaceutical product with a view to protecting the public against the risk arising from defects therein.
27. The protection of the public against risks arising from defective pharmaceutical products is a matter of legitimate concern, and Article 36 of the Treaty authorizes the Member States to derogate from the rules concerning the free movement of goods on grounds of the protection of health and life of humans and animals.
28. However, the measures necessary to achieve this must be such as may properly be adopted in the field of health control, and must not constitute a misuse of the rules concerning industrial and commercial property.
29. Moreover, the specific considerations underlying the protection of industrial and commercial properly are distinct from the considerations underlying the protection of the public and any responsibilities which that may imply.
30. The question referred should be answered in the negative.

. . . . .

In its judgment of the same day in case 16/74, *Centrafarm* v. *Winthrop*, [1974] ECR 1183; [1974] 2 CMLR 480; also a request for a preliminary ruling by the Supreme Court of the Netherlands, the court ruled:
1. The exercise, by the owner of a trade mark, of the right which he enjoys under the legislation of a Member State to prohibit the sale, in that state, of a product which has been marketed under the trade mark in another Member State by the trade mark owner or with his consent is incompatible with the rules of the EEC Treaty concerning the free movement of goods within the Common Market.
2. In this connection, it is a matter of no significance that there exist, between the exporting the importing Member States, price differences resulting from governmental measures adopted in the exporting State with a view to controlling the price of the product.
3. The owner of a trade mark relating to a pharmaceutical product cannot avoid the incidence of Community rules concerning the free movement of goods for the purpose of controlling the distribution of the product with a view of protecting the public against defects therein.

. . . . .

(3) De Peijper Case

Officier van Justitie te Rotterdam v. *Adriaan de Peijper*; Case 104/75; Judgment of 20 May 1976; [1976] ECR 633; [1976] 2 CMLR 271

For the facts see the judgment below.

The Court held:

1. By order of 29 September 1975, which reached the Court on 2 October 1975, the Kantonrechter of Rotterdam referred to the Court pursuant to Article 177 of the EEC Treaty two questions concerning the interpretation of Article 30 et seq., and in particular of Article 36, of the said Treaty.
2. These questions were raised during criminal proceedings instituted by the Officier van Justitie for the district of Rotterdam against a Netherlands trader whom he accuses of having infringed the Netherlands public health legislation, on the one hand by supplying pharmacies in that Member State with medicinal preparations which he had imported from the United Kingdom without the consent of the Netherlands authorities and, on the other hand, by failing to have in his possession certain documents connected with these medicinal preparations, namely the 'file' and the 'records' prescribed by the said legislation.
3. Under that legislation 'file' means a document which the importer must

keep for 'every pharmaceutical packaging of a pharmaceutical preparation which he imports' and which must contain detailed particulars concerning the said packaging and especially of the quantitative and qualitative composition as well as the method of preparation; these particulars have to be signed and endorsed 'seem and approved' by 'the person who is responsible for the manufacture abroad'.

4. It is the practice for the importer to produce the 'file' to the competent authorities for 'certification' which at the same time authorizes him to market the packaging in the Netherlands so that only an importer who has the 'file' in his possession can obtain this authorization.

5. Under the Netherlands legislation 'records' mean documents which an importer must have in his possession when he supplies a pharmaceutical preparation which he has imported and which establish that the latter has in fact been manufactured and checked in accordance with the particulars on the abovementioned 'file' and relating to the manufacturing formula as well as the rules for checking the preparation and the substances of which this preparation is composed.

6. It appears that the 'file' relates to the product in general whereas the 'records' refer to each specific batch of the product which the importer wishes to place on the market.

7. The accused in the main proceedings does not deny the matters of which he is accused but argues that he could not comply with the rules in question because he was unable to obtain the documents which are at issue in those proceedings.

8. The explanations for this is that the medicinal preparations in questions were manufactured by a British producer – belonging to a group whose operational centre is in Switzerland –, that the accused in the main proceedings purchased them from a wholesaler established in the United Kingdom and then imported them 'in parallel' into the Netherlands and finally that the said manufacturer or the representative of the group in the Netherlands refused to give the accused the help which was absolutely necessary if the latter was to obtain possession of the abovementioned documents.

9. The main purpose of the questions referred by the national court is to find out whether rules and practice such as the ones in issue are contrary to Community law because they constitute a measure having an effect equivalent to a quantitative restriction which is prohibited by Article 30 of the Treaty and cannot fall within the exception specified in Article 36 of the Treaty in favour of restrictive measures justified on grounds of the protection of health and the life of humans.

The first question

10. The first question envisages a factual situation which the Kantonrechter describes as follows:
    – a pharmaceutical product prepared in accordance with a uniform

method of preparation and qualitative and quantitative composition is lawfully in circulation in several Member States, in the sense that, in pursuance of the national systems of legislation of these States, the requisite authorizations have been granted in relation to that product to the manufacturer 'or the person responsible for putting the product on the market' in the Member State in question;
- the fact that such authorizations have been granted in each of the Member States is made known by general notice given by official publication or in some other way; and
- this product is in every respect similar to a product in respect of which the public health authorities of the Member State into which the first product has been imported already possess the documents relating to the method of preparation and also to the quantitative and qualitative composition, since these documents were produced to them previously by the manufacturer or his duly appointed importer in support of an application for authorization to place them on the market.

11. The Court is asked to rule whether national authorities faced with such a situation adopt a measure equivalent to a quantitative restriction and prohibited by the Treaty when they make the authorization to place a product on the market, for which a parallel importer has applied, conditional upon the production of documents identical with those which the manufacturer or his duly appointed importer has already lodged with them.
12. National measures of the kind in question have an effect equivalent to a quantitative restriction and are prohibited under Article 30 of the Treaty if they are likely to constitute an obstacle, directly or indirectly, actually or potentially, to imports between Member States.
13. Rules of practices which result in imports being channelled in such a way that only certain traders can effect these imports, whereas others are prevented from doing so, constitutes such an obstacle to imports.
14. However, according to Article 36 'the provisions of Articles 30 to 34 shall not preclude prohibitions or restrictions on imports ... justified on grounds of ... the protection of health and the life of humans' which do not 'constitute a means of arbitrary discrimination or a disguised restriction on trade between Member States'.
15. Health and the life of humans rank first among the property or interests protected by Article 36 and it is for the Member States, within the limits imposed by the Treaty, to decide what degree of protection they intend to assure and in particular how strict the checks to be carried out are to be.
16. Nevertheless in emerges from Article 36 that national rules or practices which did restrict imports of pharmaceutical products or are capable of doing so are only compatible with the Treaty to the extent to which they are necessary for the effective protection of health and life of humans.
17. National rules or practices do not fall within the exception specified in Article 36 if the health and life of humans can as effectively protected by measures which do not restrict intra-Community trade so much.

18. In particular Article 36 cannot be relied on to justify rules or practice which, even though they are beneficial, contain restrictions which are explained primarily by a concern to lighten the administration's burden or reduce public expenditure, unless, in the absence of the said rules or practices, this burden or expenditure clearly would exceed the limits of what can reasonably be required.
19. The situation described by the national court must be examined in the light of these considerations.
20. For this purpose a distinction must be drawn between on the one hand the documents relating to a medicinal preparation in general, in this case the 'file' prescribed by the Netherlands legislation, and, on the other hand, those relating to a specific batch of this medicinal preparation imported by a particular trader, in this case the 'records', which have to be kept under the said legislation.
21. With regard to the documents relating to the medicinal preparation in general, if the public health authorities of the importing Member State already have in their possession, as a result of importation on a previous occasion, all the pharmaceutical particulars relating to the medicinal preparation in question and considered to be absolutely necessary for the purpose of checking that the medicinal preparation is effective and not harmful, it is clearly unnecessary, in order to protect the health and life of humans, for the said authorities to require a second trader who has imported a medicinal preparation which is in every respect the same, to produce the above-mentioned particulars to them again.
22. Therefore national rules or practices which lay down such a requirement are not justified on grounds of the protection of health and life of humans within the meaning of Article 36 of the Treaty.
23. With regard to the documents relating to a specific batch of a medicinal preparation imported at a time when the public health authorities of the Member State of importation already, have in their possession a file relating to this medicinal preparation, these authorities have a legitimate interest in being able at any time to carry out a thorough check to make certain that the said batch complies with the particulars on the file.
24. Nevertheless, having regard to the nature of the market for the pharmaceutical product in question, it is necessary to ask whether this objective cannot be equally well achieved if the national administrations, instead of waiting passively for the desired evidence to be produced to them – and in a form calculated to give the manufacturer of the product and his duly appointed representatives an advantage – were to admit, where appropriate, similar evidence and, in particular, to adopt a more active policy which could enable every trader to obtain the necessary evidence.
25. This question is all the more important because parallel importers are very often in a position to offer the goods at a price lower than the one applied by the duly appointed importer for the same product, a fact which, where medicinal preparations are concerned, should, where appropriate, encourage the public health authorities not to place parallel imports at a

disadvantage, since the effective protection of health and like of humans also demands that medicinal preparations should be sold at reasonable prices.
26. National authorities possess legislative and administrative methods capable of compelling the manufacturer or his duly appointed representative to supply particulars making it possible to ascertain that the medicinal preparation which is in fact the subject of parallel importation is identical with the medicinal preparation in respect of which they are already informed.
27. Moreover, simple co-operation between the authorities of the Member States would enable them to obtain on a reciprocal basis the documents necessary for checking certain largely standardized and widely distributed products.
28. Taking into account all these possible ways of obtaining information the national public health authorities must consider whether the effective protection of health and life of humans justifies a presumption of the non-conformity of an imported batch with the description of the medicinal preparation, or whether on the contrary it would not be sufficient to lay down a presumption of conformity with the result that, in appropriate cases, it would be for the administration to rebut this presumption.
29. Finally, even if it were absolutely necessary to require the parallel importer to prove this conformity, there would in any case be no justification under Article 36 for compelling him to do so with the help of documents to which he does not have access, when the administration, or as the case may be, the court, finds that the evidence can be produced by other.
30. The British, Danish and Netherlands Governments are of the opinion that measures such as those which are the subject-matter of the main proceedings are necessary in order to comply with the requirements of Council Directives Nos 65/65/EEC, 75/319/EEC (OJ, English Special Edition 1965, p. 20; OJ L 147 of 9-6-1975, p. 1 and p. 13) concerning the approximation of national provisions relating to proprietary medicinal products.
31. However the sole aim of these directives is to harmonize national provisions in this field; they do not and cannot aim at extending the very considerable powers left to Member States in the field of public health by Article 36.
32. Given a factual situation such as that described in the first question the answer must therefore be that rules or practices which make it possible for a manfuacturer and his duly appointed representatives simply by refusing to produce the 'file' or the 'records' to enjoy a monopoly of the importation and marketing of the product in question must be regarded as being unnecessarily restrictive and cannot therefore come within the exceptions specified in Article 36 of the Treaty, unless it is clearly proved that any other rules or practice would obviously be beyond the means which can reasonably be expected of an administration operation in a normal manner.

The second question

33. By the second question the Court is asked to say whether in principle the answer which must be given to the first question also applies to the case where (a) the process of manufacture and the qualitative and quantitative composition of the medicinal preparation imported by the parallel importer coming from another Member State are different from those of the medicinal preparation bearing the same name and in respect of which the authorities of the Member State into which it has been imported already have these data but (b) 'the differences between the one and the other product are of such minor importance that it is likely that the manufacturer is applying or introducing ... these differences with the conscious and exclusive intention of using these differences ... in order to prevent or impede the possibility of the parallel importation of the proprietary medicinal product'.
34. The competent administration of the importing Member State is clearly entitled to require the manufacturer or his duly appointed importer, when the person concerned applies for an authorization to market the medicinal preparation and lodges the relevant documentation (a) to state whether the manufacturer or, as the case may be, the group of manufacturers to which he belongs, manufacturers under the same name for different Member States several variants of the medicinal preparation and (b) if his answer is in the affirmative, to produce similar documentation for the other variants too, specifying what are differences between all these variants.
35. It is only if the documents produced in this way show that there are differences which have a therapeutic effect that there would be any justification for treating the variants as different medicinal preparations, for the purposes of authorizing them to be placed on the market and as regards producing the relevant documents it being understood that the answer to the first question remains valid as regards each of the authorization procedures which have become necessary.

(4) EMI – CBS Case

EMI Records v. *CBS United Kingdom*; Case 51/75; Preliminary ruling of 15 June 1976; [1976] ECR 909; [1976] 2 CMLR 235.

Facts:

In 1975 three cases, 51, 86 and 96/75 came before the Court by way of references for preliminary rulings under Article 177 of the EEC Treaty by the Chancery Division of the High Court of Justice of England and Wales, by the Sø-og Handelsretten of Copenhagen and by the Landgericht of Cologne.

In each of them the plaintiff in the proceedings before the national Court is

EMI Records Ltd., a wholly owned subsidiary of EMI Limited. EMI Records Limited and EMI Limited are both English companies.

The defendant in each case is a locally incorporated subsidiary of CBS Inc., which is an American company. In the English case the defendant is CBS United Kingdom Limited, in the Danish case it is CBS Records ApS (formerly CBS Grammophon A/S) and in the German case it is CBS Schallplatten GmbH.

The facts may be summarized as follows.

As a result of a number of events and transactions going back to 1894 EMI Records Limited is now in many countries of Europe, Africal, Asia and Australia the registered proprietor of all trae marks for grammophon records consisting of or including the mark 'Columbia'. Those countries include every Member State of the Community except France, where those marks are owned by another subsidiary of EMI Ltd.. CBS Inc. is the proprietor of Columbia trade marks in the USA, in the other countries of North and South America and in a few countries elsewhere.

Both EMI Records Limited and other subsidiaries of EMI Limited on the one hand and CBS Inc. and its subsidiaries on the other hand manufacture and sell records on a large scale. In the countries where it is entitled to the mark Columbia each group sells records extensively under that mark, but does so also under other marks. In the countries where it does not own the mark Columbia each group has, until the event giving rise to the present litigation, sold its records under other marks. In particular the CBS group has sold its records in the Community under the mark CBS.

In some instances, however, the CBS group has imported into the United Kingdom, Denmark and Germany records manufactured in America and bearing, both on the central label of the record itself and on the sleeve, the mark Columbia. In the case of such imported records, that mark has sometimes been obliterated with a sticker (usually or so it seems from the exhibits sent to the Court by the Sø-og Handelsretten, a sticker bearing the mark CBS) but on other occasions the mark Columbia has not been so obliterated, particularly not from the label on the record itself. It is sales of such records, with the mark Columbia visible, that have given rise to the litigation.

The defendants contended that the provisions of the Treaty relating to free movement of goods should be interpreted as precluding EMI Records Limited from invoking its rights to the trade mark Columbia in the Community for the purpose of preventing imports into the Community from outside it of goods bearing that mark.

The defendants' contention was greeted with indignation by EMI Records Ltd. and all seven Member States which intervened in the proceedings and the Commission.

The Court ruled:

1. The principles of Community law and the provisions on the free movement of goods and on competition do not prohibit the proprietor of the same

mark in all the Member States of the Community from exercising his trademark rights, recognized by the national laws of each Member State, in order to prevent the sale in the Community by a third party of products bearing the same mark, which is owned in a third country, provided that the exercise of the said rights does not manifest itself as the result of an agreement or of concerted practices which have as their object or effect the isolation or partitioning of the common market.
2. In so far as that condition is fulfilled the requirement that such third party must, for the purposes of his exports to the Community, obliterate the mark on the products concerned and perhaps apply a different mark forms part of the permissible consequence of the protection which the national law of each Member State afford to the proprietor of the mark against the importation of products from third countries bearing a similar or identical mark.

(5) Terrapin – Terranova Case

Terrapin (overseas) Ltd. v. *Terranova Industrie C.A.*; Case 119/75, Preliminary ruling of 22 June 1976; [1976] ECR 1039; [1976] 2 CMLR 482.

Facts:

See judgment below.

The Court held:

1. By order dated 31 October 1975, received at the Court Registry on the following 5 December, the Bundesgerichtshof referred to the Court for a preliminary ruling under Article 177 of the Treaty the following question on the relation between the provisions of the Treaty on the free movement of goods and the protection given by national laws to the right to a trade-mark and to a commercial name:

    'Is it compatible with the provisions relating to the free movement of goods (Articles 30 and 36 of the EEC Treaty) that an undertaking established in Member State A, by using its commercial name and trade-mark rights existing there, should prevent the import of similar goods of an undertaking established in Member State B if these goods have been lawfully given a distinguishing name which may be confused with the commercial name and trade-mark which are protected in State A for the undertaking established there, if there are no relations between the two undertakings, if their national trade-mark rights arose autonomously and independently of one another (no common origin) and at the present time there exist no economic or legal relations of any kind other than those appertaining to trade-marks between the undertakings?'

2. It appears from the order of reference that the plaintiff in the main action, the respondent to the appeal, is the proprietor in the Federal Republic of Germany of the trade-marks 'Terra', 'Terra Fabrikate' and 'Terranova', registered at the German patents office, the last of these names being simultnaeously used as a commercial name. The plaintiff manufactures and markets finished plaster for facades and other construction materials under these names. The defendant in the main action and appellant in the appeal is an English company specializing in the production of prefabricated houses and components for the construction of such houses which it sells under the name 'Terrapin', which is at the same time the defendant's commercial name. The defendant applied to the German patents office to register the trade-mark 'Terrapin', but Terranova lodged an opposition and by order of the Bundespatentgericht of 3 February 1967 registration was refused on the ground of the risk of confusion with the trade-marks 'Terra' and 'Terranova'. Subsequently Terranova brought an action before the Landgericht München to prohibit the defendant from using the name 'Terrapin' on its products. This action was dismissed by judgment dated 27 November 1972, since the Landgericht considered that the names in question did not cause any real risk of confusion. Terranova brought an appeal before the Bayrisches Oberlandesgericht, Munich, which reversed the judgment of the Landgericht and by judgment dated 27 September 1973 held that there was a risk of confusion and as a result prohibited the defendant from using the name 'Terrapin' and declared that in principle the defendant was bound to make good any damage caused to the plaintiff by the use of the name in question. Terrapin brought an appeal against this judgment before the Bundesgerichtshof.
3. The Bundesgerichtshof considers that the first appellate court rightly found similarity between the products of the two parties and risk of confusion between the names in question with the result that according to German law the judgment of the appellate court and the injunction which it issued against Terrapin must be confirmed.
4. Although this finding has been questioned during the oral procedure the Court does not have to rule on this point since no question has been put to it with regard to the matter. It is right however to stress that the answer given below does not prejudge the qustion whether an allegation by one undertaking as to the similarity of products originating in different Member States and the risk of confusion of trade-marks or commercial names legally protected in these States may perhaps involve the application of Community law with regard in particular to the second sentence of Article 36 of the Treaty. It is for the court of first instance, after considering the similarity of the products and the risk of confusion, to enquire further in the context of this last provision whether the exercise in a particular case of industrial and commercial property rights may or may not constitute a means of arbitrary discrimination or a disguised restriction on trade between Member States. It is for the national court in this respect to ascertain in particular whether the rights in question are in fact exercised

by the proprietor with the same strictness whatever the national origin of any possible infringer.
5. As a result of the provisions in the Treaty relating to the free movement of goods and in particular of Article 30, quantitative restrictions on imports and all measures having equivalent effect are prohibited between Member States. By Article 36 these provisions nevertheless do not preclude prohibitions or restrictions on imports justified on grounds of the protection of industrial or commercial property. However, it is clear from that same article, in particular the second sentence, as well as from the context, that whilst the Treaty does not affect the existence of rights recognized by the legislation of a Member State in matters of industrial and commercial property, yet the exercise of those rights may nevertheless, depending on the circumstances, be restricted by the prohibitions in the Treaty. Inasmuch as it provides an exception to one of the fundamental principles of the common market, Article 36 in fact admits exceptions to the free movement of goods only to the extent to which such exceptions are justified for the purpose of safeguarding rights which constitute the specific subject-matter of that property.
6. It follows from the above that the proprietor of an industrial or commercial property right protected by the law of a Member State cannot rely on that law to prevent the importation of a product which has lawfully been marketed in another Member State by the proprietor himself or with his consent. It is the same when the right relied on is the result of the subdivision, either by voluntary act or as a result of public constraint, of a trade-mark right which originally belonged to one and the same proprietor. In these cases the basic function of the trade-mark to guarantee to consumers that the product has the same origin is already undermined by the subdivision of the original right. Even where the rights in question belong to different proprietors the protection given to industrial and commercial property by national law may not be relied on when the exercise of those rights is the purpose, the means or the result of an agreement prohibited by the Treaty. In all these cases the effect of invoking the territorial nature of national laws protecting industrial and commercial property is to legitimize the insulation of national markets without this partitioning within the common market being justified by the protection of a legitimate interest on the part of the proprietor of the trade-mark or business name.
7. On the other hand in the present state of Community law an industrial or commercial property right legally acquired in a Member State may legally be used to prevent under the first sentence of Article 36 of the Treaty the import of products marketed under a name giving rise to confusion where the rights in question have been acquired by different and independent proprietors under different national laws. If in such a case the principle of the free movement of goods were to prevail over the protection given by the respective national laws, the specific objective of industrial and commercial property rights would be undermined. In the particular situation the requirements of the free movement of goods and the safeguarding of

industrial and commercial property rights must be so reconciled that protection is ensured for the legitimate use of the rights conferred by national laws, coming within the prohibitions on imports 'justified' within the meaning of Article 36 of the Treaty, but denied on the other hand in respect of any improper exercise of the same rights of such a nature as to maintain or effect artificial partitions within the common market.

8. It is appropriate therefore to reply to the question referred to the Court that it is compatible with the provisions of the EEC Treaty relating to the free movement of goods for an undertaking established in a Member State, by virtue of a right to a trade-mark and a right to a commercial name which are protected by the legislation of that State, to prevent the importation of products of an undertaking established in another Member State and bearing by virtue of the legislation of that State a name giving rise to confusion with the trade-mark and commercial name of the first undertaking, provided that there are no agreements restricting competition and no legal or economic ties between the undertakings and that their respective rights have arisen independently of one another.

(6) Ratti Case

For facts and references see at page 181.

The Court held:

36. When, pursuant to Article 100 of the Treaty, Community directives provide for the harmonization of measures necessary to ensure the protection of the health of humans and animals and establish Community procedures to supervise compliance therewith, recourse to Article 36 ceases to be justified and the appropriate controls must henceforth be carried out and the protective measures taken in accordance with the scheme laid down by the harmonizing directive.

(7) Obscence articles Case

Regina v. *Henn and Darby*; Case 34/79; Preliminary ruling of 14 December 1979; [1979] ECR 3810; [1980] 1 CMLR 246.

For the facts see the judgment below.

The Court held:

1. By order of 22 February 1979, received at the Court of Justice on 1 March 1979, the House of Lords, pursuant to Article 177 of the EEC Treaty,

referred to the Court a number of questions concerning the interpretation of Articles 30, 36 and 234 of the Treaty. These questions have arisen in the context of criminal proceedings against the appellants who, on 14 July 1977, were convicted at Ipswich Crown Court of a number of offences. Only one of the charges brought against the appellants is relevant to the present reference – that of being 'knowingly concerned in the fraudulent evasion of the prohibition of the importation of indecent or obscene articles, contrary to section 42 of the Customs Consolidation Act, 1876, and section 304 of the Customs and Exercise Act, 1952'.

2. The articles involved in the charge against the appellants formed part of a consignment of several boxes of obscene films and magazines which had been brought into the United Kingdom on 14 October 1975 by a lorry which arrived at Felixtowe by ferry from Rotterdam. The charge related to six films and seven magazines, all of Danish origin.

3. The appellants appealed against their conviction to the Court of Appeal of England and Wales. That court dismissed their appeals by judgment of 13 July 1978. On 9 November 1978 the House of Lords granted both appellants leave to appeal. On 29 January 1979, after hearing the appellants, the House of Lords decided that it was necessary to refer to the Court of Justice, in accordance with Article 177 of the Treaty, the questions set forth in the order seeking a preliminary ruling.

4. The appellants contended that the United Kingdom had no consistent policy of public morality in regard to indecent or obscene articles. In that respect they pointed to differences in the law applied in the different constituent parts of the United Kingdom. They contended furthermore that a complete prohibition of the importation of indecent or obscene articles resulted in the application to importation or stricter rules than those which applied internally and constituted arbitrary discrimination within the meaning of Article 36 of the Treaty.

5. According to the Agreed Statement of Law accompanying the order seeking the preliminary ruling, it is true that, in this field, the laws of the different parts of the United Kingdom, that is to say, England and Wales, Scotland, Northern Ireland and the Isle of Man, differ from each other and that each is derived from a number of different sources, some of which are to be found in the common law and others in statute.

6. According to the same statement, the various laws of the United Kingdom recognize and apply two different and distinct criteria. The first, referred to in the statement as 'Standard A', relates to the words 'indecent or obscene' which appear in the customs legislation and in certain other legislation and are also used to indicate the ambit of the English common law offence of 'outraging public decency'. These words convey, according to the statement, a single idea, that of offending against recognized standards of propriety' 'indecent' being at the lower end of the scale, and 'obscene' at the upper end.

7. The second criterion, referred to in the statement as 'Standard B', relates to the word 'obscene' as used in the Obscene Publications Acts, 1959 and

1964, (which apply to England and Wales only) and in describing the ambit of certain common law offences in England and Wales, Scotland and Northern Ireland. According to the statement, this word applies to a more restricted class of material, namely that which tends to 'deprave and corrupt' those exposed to the material.
8. The Obscene Publications Acts, 1959 and 1964, create certain offences in regard to the publication of obscene articles but exclude from their field of application 'obscene articles', as defined therin, if their publication is justified on the ground that it is in the interests of science, literature, art or learning or other objects of general concern.
9. The mere possession, for non-commercial purposes, of articles which offend against either Standard A or Standard B is not a criminal offence in any part of the United Kingdom.
10. The relevant provisions concerning the importation of pornographic articles are section 42 of the Customs Consolidation Act, 1876, and section 304 of the Customs and Excise Act 1952. They apply throughout the United Kingdom. Put shortly, they provided that indecent or obscene articles are liable for forfeiture and destruction upon arrival in the United Kingdom and that whoever attempts fraudulently to bring such articles into the United Kingdom shall be guilty of an offence. The seventh schedule to the Customs and Excise Act 1952, provides a procedure for testing before a court the liability of goods to forfeiture.

First question

11. The first question asks whether a law of a Member State which prohibits the import into that State of pornographic articles is a measure having equivalent effect to a quantitative restriction on imports within the meaning of Article 30 of the Treaty.
12. That article provides that 'quantitative restrictions on imports and all measures having equivalent effect' shall be prohibited between Member States. It is clear that his provision includes a prohibition on imports inasmuch as this is the most extreme form of restriction. The expression used in Article 30 must therefore be understood as being the equivalent of the expression 'prohibitions or restrictions on imports' occurring in Article 36.
13. The answer to the first question is therefore that a law such as that referred to in this case constitutes a quantitative restriction on imports within the meaning of Article 30 of the Treaty.

Second and third questions

14. The second and third questions are framed in the following terms:
'2. If the answer to Question 1 is in the affirmative, does the first sentence of Article 36 upon its true construction mean that a Member State may lawfully impose prohibitions on the importation of goods

from another Member State which are of an indecent or obscene character as understood by the laws of the Member State?
 3. In particular:
 (i) is the Member State entitled to maintain such prohibitions in order to prevent, to guard against or to reduce the likelihood of breaches of the domestic law of all constituent parts of the customs territory of the State?
 (ii) is the Member State entitled to maintained such prohibitions having regard to the national standards and characteristics of that State as demonstrated by the domestic laws of the constituent parts of the customs territory of that State including the law imposing the prohibition, notwithstanding variations between the laws of the constituent parts?'

It is convenient to consider these questions together.

15. Under the terms of Article 36 of the Treaty the provisions relating to the free movement of goods within the Community are not to preclude prohibitions on imports which are justified inter alia 'on grounds of public morality'. In principle, it is for each Member State to determine in accordance with its own scale of values and in the form selected by it the requirements of public morality in its territory. In any event, it cannot be disputed that the statutory provisions applied by the United Kingdom in regard to the importation of articles having an indecent or obscene character come within the powers reserved to the Member States by the first sentence of Article 36.

16. Each Member State is entitled to impose prohibitions on imports justified on grounds of public morality for the whole of its territory, as defined in Article 227 of the Treaty, whatever the structure of its constitution may be and however the powers of legislating in regard to the subject in question may be distributed. The fact that certain differences exist between the laws enforced in the different constituent parts of a Member State does not thereby prevent that State from applying a unitary concept in regard to prohibitions on imports imposed, on grounds of public morality, on trade with other Member States.

17. The answer to the second and third questions must therefore be that the first sentence of Article 36 upon its true construction means that a Member State may, in principle, lawfully impose prohibitions on the importation from any other Member State of articles which are of an indecent or obscene character as understood by its domestic laws and that such prohibitions may lawfully be applied to the whole of its national territory even if, in regard to the field in question, variations exist between the laws in force in the different constituent parts of the Member State concerned.

Fourth, fifth and sixth questions

18. The fourth, fifth and sixth questions are framed in the following terms:

'4. If a problem on the importation of goods is justifiable on grounds of public morality or public policy, and imposed with that purpose, can that prohibition nevertheless amount to a means of arbitrary discrimination or a disguised restriction on trade contrary to Article 36?
5. If the answer to Question 4 is in the affirmative, does the fact that the prohibition imposed on the importation of such goods is different in scope from that imposed by the criminal law upon the possession and publication of such goods within the Member State or any part of it necessarily constitute a means of arbitrary discrimination or a disguised restriction on trade between Member States so as to conflict with the requirements of the second sentence of Article 36?
6. If it be the fact that the prohibition imposed upon importation is, and a prohibition such as is imposed upon possession and publication is not, capable as a matter of administration of being applied by customs officials responsible for examining goods at the point of importation, would that fact have any bearing upon the answer to Question 5?'

19. In these questions the House of Lords takes account of the appellants' submissions based upon certain differences between, on the one hand, the prohibition on importing the goods in question, which is absolute, and, on the other, the laws in force in the various constituent parts of the United Kingdom, which appear to be less strict in the sense that the mere possession of obscene articles for non-commercial purposes does not constitute a criminal offence anywhere in the United Kingdom and that, even if it is generally forbidden, trade in such articles is subject to certain exceptions, notably those in favour of articles having scientific, literary, artistic or educational interest. Having regard to those differences the question has been raised whether the prohibition on imports might not come within the second sentence of Article 36.

20. According to the second sentence of Article 36 the restrictions on imports referred to in the first sentence may not 'constitute a means of arbitrary discrimination or a disguised restriction on trade between Member States'.

21. In order to answer the questions which have been referred to the Court it is appropriate to have regard to the function of this provision, which is designed to prevent restrictions on trade based on the grounds mentioned in the first sentence of Article 36 from being diverted from their proper purpose and used in such a way as either to create discrimination in respect of goods originating in other Member States or indirectly to protect certain national products. That is not the purpose of a prohibition, such as that in force in the United Kingdom, on the importation of articles which are of an indecent or obscene character. Whatever may be the differences between the laws on this subject in force in the different constituent parts of the United Kingdom, and notwithstanding the fact that they contain certain exceptions of limited scope, these laws, taken as a whole, have as their purpose the prohibition, or at least, the restraining, of the manufacture and marketing of publications or articles of an in-

decent or obscene character. In these circumstances it is permissible to conclude, on a comprehensive view, that there is no lawful trade in such goods in the United Kingdom. A prohibition on imports which may in certain respects be more strict than some of the laws applied within the United Kingdom cannot be regarded as amounting to a measure designed to give indirect protection to some national product or aimed at creating arbitrary discrimination between goods of this type depending on whether they are produced within the national territory or another Member State.

22. The answer to the fourth question must therefore be that if a prohibition on the importation of goods is justifiable on ground of public morality and if it is imposed with that purpose the enforcement of that prohibition cannot, in the absence within the Member State concerned of a lawful trade in the same goods, constitute a means of arbitrary discrimination or a disguised restriction on trade contrary to Article 36.

23. In these circumstances it is not necessary to answer the fifth and sixth questions.

Seventh question

24. The seventh question asks whether, independently of the questions posed above, a Member State may lawfully impose prohibitions on the importation of such goods from another Member State by reference to obligations arising from the Geneva Convention, 1923, for the suppression of traffic in obscene publications and the Universal Postal Convention (renewed at Lausanne in 1974), which came into force on 1 January 1976), bearing in mind the provisions of Article 234 of the Treaty.

25. Article 234 provides that the rights and obligations arising from agreements concluded before the entry into force of the Treaty between one or more Member States on the one hand, and one or more third countries on the other, are not to be affected by the provisions of the Treaty. However, to the extent to which such agreements are not compatible with the Treaty, the Member State concerned is to take all appropriate steps to eliminate the incompatibilities established.

26. It appears from a comparison of the foregoing considerations with the provisions of the Conventions to which the House of Lords refers that the observance by the United Kingdom of those international Conventions is not likely to result in a conflict with the provisions relating to the free movement of goods if account is taken of the exception made by Article 36 in regard to any prohibitions on imports based on grounds of public morality.

27. The answer to the seventh question should therefore be that, in so far as a Member State avails itself of the reservation relating to the protection of public morality provided for in Article 36 of the Treaty, the provisions of Article 234 do not preclude that State from fulfilling the obligations arising from the Geneva Convention, 1923, for the suppression of traffic

in obscene publications and from the Universal Postal Convention (renewed at Lausanne in 1974, which came into force on 1 January 1976).

(8) Eyssen Case

Officier van Justitie v. *Kaasfabriek Eyssen*; Case 53/80; Preliminary ruling of 5 February 1981; [1981] ECR 409.

Facts:

See the judgment below.

The Court held:

1. By judgment of 13 Decembe 1979, which was received at the Court on 7 February 1980, the Gerechtshof Amsterdam referred to the Court of Justice for a preliminary ruling under Article 177 of the EEC Treaty a question on the interpretation of the provisions of the Treaty on the free movement of goods within the Community, in particular Articles 30, 34 and 36.
2. That question is raised in the course of criminal proceedings instituted by the Netherlands authorities against a Netherlands manufacturer which produces processed cheese both for sale on the domestic market and for export to other Member States and which is charged with having held in stock for the purposes of sale in the District of Alkmaar certain quantities of processed cheese intended for sale and for human consumption containing an additive, namely nisin, which is not one authorized by the Netherlands law applicable in this case.
3. It appears from the papers in the case and from information given during the oral procedure that nisin is an antibiotic formed by certain types of lactic bacteria and occurs naturally in varying quantities in most varieties of cheese. It has the property of preserving the product for a longer period by retarding the process of deterioration due to the presence of butyric bacteria.
4. The provisions of national law with whose breach the manufacturer is charged are in particular those adopted pursuant to the Law on Goods ('Warenwet') of 28 December 1935, which empowers the Government to adopt legislative measures for the purpose of prohibiting the marketing or importation of certain goods under conditions other than those prescribed.
5. Adopted in pursuance of that Law, the Ceneral Order ('Algemeen Besluit') of 11 July 1949 provides, in Article 10 bis (1) thereof, that antibiotics may be added to drinks and foodstuffs only where the competent minister has authorized their use. As far as processed cheese is

concerned, the addition of nisin is not provided for in either the 'Kaasbesluit' [Cheese Order] of 7 November 1959 or the 'Smeltkaasbesluit' [Processed Cheese Order] of 5 November 1959. Under Article 8 (h) of the 'Smeltkaasbesluit', the presence in processed cheese of substances other than those expressly mentioned in Article 1 thereof and those authorized by the 'Kassbesluit' is prohibited.
6. However, by virtue of a government decision ('Vrijstellingsbeschikking') of 19 August 1965, last amended by decision of 14 May 1969, products intended for export are exempt form the prohibition resulting from those rules, including those laid down by the 'Smeltkaasbesluit' of 5 November 1959.
7. When prosecuted under the Law on Economic Offences ('Wet op de Economische Delicten') of 22 June 1950 for a contravention of Article 8 (h) of the 'Smeltkaasbesluit', the accused pleaded in particular that the quantities of nisin used in the present case did not present any danger to public health and that the addition of that substance to cheese was authorized in other Member States. From that the accused thus deduced that the prohibition of the addition of nisin to processed cheese intended for the domestic market, which resulted from the provisions cited above, constituted a breach of the rules of the Treaty regarding the free movement of goods in the Community inasmuch as it amounted to a measure having an effect equivalent to a quantitative restriction within the meaning of Articles 30 to 36 of the Treaty.
8. In order to determine whether that submission was well-founded and thereby to decide the case, the Gerechtshof Amsterdam referred the following question to the Court of Justice:
'Must the requirements contained in the EEC Treaty regarding the free movement of goods within the EEC, notwithstanding the provision in Article 36 of the Treaty regarding a prohibition which is justified on the grounds of the protection of health and the life of humans, be construed to the effect that a provision as contained in Article 8 (h) of the 'Smeltkaasbesluit' containing a prohibition on the presence of additives, including nisin, in processed cheese other than those which the order permits or for which an exemption is granted, is incompatible with those requirements in its entirety or at least as regards the prohibition of adding nisin to processed cheese in respect of both home-produced cheese spread and cheese spread imported into the Netherlands; does it make any difference to the answer that as regards the addition of nisin to pocessed cheese such exemption is granted only for processes cheese which is clearly intended for export?'

. . . . .

13. There can be no dispute that the issue of the addition of preservatives to foodstuffs is embraced by the more general issue of health protection which calls for the adoption of national measures designed to regulate the use of such additives in the interest of the protection of human health. In

the particular case of the addition of nisin to products intended for human consumption, such as processed cheese, it is indeed accepted that the increasingly widespread use of that substance, not only in milk but also in numerous preserved products, has revealed the need, both at national level in certain countries and at international level, to study the problem of the risk which the consumption of products containing the substance presents, or may present, to human health and has led certain international organizations, such as the Food and Agriculture Organization of the United Nations and the World Health Organization, to undertake research into the critical threshold for the intake of that additive. Although those studies have not as yet enabled absolutely certain conclusions to be drawn regarding the maximum quantity of nisin which a person may consume daily without serious risk to his health, this is essentially due to the fact that the assessment of the risk connected with the consumption of the additive depends upon several factors of a variable nature, including, in particular, the dietary habits of each country, and to the fact that the determination of the maximum quantity of nisin to be prescribed for each product must taken account not only of the quantities of nisin added to a particular product, such as processed cheese, but also those quantities added to each of the other preserved products which are intended to satisfy those habits and in which the nisin content may vary in the case of similar products depending on their place of origin, the method of manufacture of the particular need in the market in question for a longer or shorter period of preservation.

14. The difficulties and uncertainties inherent in such an assessment may explain the lack of uniformity in the national laws of the Member States regarding the use of this preservative and at the same time justify the limited scope which the prohibition of the use of the additive in a given product, such as processed cheese, has in certain Member States, including the Netherlands, which prohibit its use in products intended for sale on the domestic market while permitting it in products intended for export to other Member States where the requirements for the protection of human health are assessed differently according to dietary habits of their own population.

15. Whilst it is true that the obstacles to which the disparity of the national laws on the subject give rise in intra-Community trade in the products concerned may be eliminated only by a uniform set of rules adopted at Community level, such rules do not exist at the present stage of Community law. Council Directive 64/54/EEC of 5 November 1963 on the approximation of the laws of the Member States concerning the preservatives authorized for foodstuffs intended for human consumption (Official Journal, English Special Edition 1963–1964, p. 99) in fact merely provides in Article 6 thereof that the directive 'shall not affect the provisions of national laws concerning: ...(b) nisin' and thus by implication allows the Member States to retain in relation to the matter in issue a discretionary power within the limits laid down by the general provisions of Article 36 of the Treaty.

16. From those considerations it follows that whilst it has the effect of hindering trade between Member States in the product concerned, national legislation, such as that referred to by the national court, prohibiting the use of nisin as a preservative in processed cheese intended for the domestic market is included amongst the measures which Article 36 of the Treaty permits Member States to adopt on grounds of the protection of health of humans and for that reason it escapes the prohibitions resulting from Articles 30 and 34 of the Treaty. In view of the uncertainties prevailing in the various Member States regarding the maximum level of nisin which must be prescribed in respect of each preserved product intended to satisfy the various dietary habits it does not appear that the prohibition laid down by such legislation in the case of processed cheese sold on the domestic market and excluding that intended for export to other Member States, constitutes a 'means of arbitrary discrimination or a disguised restriction on trade between Member States' within the meaning of Article 36 cited above.

(9) Commission – Italy Case

Commission v. *Italy*; Case 95/81; Judgment of a June 1982; [1982] ECR 2187.

The Court held:

27. It must be recalled that in accordance with the settled case-law of the Court, Article 36 must be strictly interpreted and the exceptions which it lists may not be extended to cases other than those which have been exhaustively laid down and, furthermore, that Article 36 refers to matters of a non-economic nature.

(10) Campus Oil Case

Campus Oil Limited v. *Minister for Industry and Energy*; Case 72/83; Preliminary ruling of 10 October 1984; [1984] ECR 2727.

Facts:

See the judgment below.

The Court held:

1. By order of 9 December 1982, which was received at the Court on 28 April 1983, the High Court of Ireland referred to the Court for a

preliminary ruling under Article 177 of the EEC Treaty two questions on the interpretation of Articles 30, 31 and 36 of the Treaty in order to enable it to decide whether Irish rules requiring importers of petroleum products to purchase a certain proportion of their requirements at prices fixed by the competent minister from a State-owned company which operates a refinery in Ireland are compatible with the Treaty.
2. Those questions arose in proceedings instituted by six Irish undertakings trading in petroleum products either exclusively or predominantly in Ireland, which supply approximately 14% of the motor spirit market in Ireland and a somewhat higher percentage of other petroleum products, against Ireland and the Irish National Petroleum Corporation (hereinafter referred to as 'the INPC'). In the main action, the six plaintiff undertakings are seeking a declaration in the High Court that the Fuels (Control of Supplies) Order 1982 (hereinafter referred to as 'the 1982 Order') is incompatible with the EEC Treaty.
3. The 1982 Order was made by the Irish Minister for Industry and Energy under powers conferred on him by the Fuels (Control of Supplies) Act 1971, as amended in 1982, for the maintenance and provision of supplies of fuels. The 1982 Order requires any person who imports any of the various petroleum products to which it applies to purchase a certain proportion of their requirements of petroleum products from the INPC at a price to be determined by the Minister taking into account the costs incurred by the INPC.
4. The INPC, whose share capital is owned by the Irish State and whose function is to improve the security of supply of oil within Ireland, purchased, in 1982, the share capital of the Irish Refining Company Limited, owner of the only refinery in Ireland, which is situated at Whitegate, Country Cork. The share capital of the Irish Refining Company Limited, which is capable of supplying from the Whitegate Refinery some 35% of the requirements of the Irish market in refined petroleum products, had until then been owned by four major oil companies which supply the greater part of the Irish market in refined petroleum products. The decision to acquire the Whitegate Refinery by means of the purchase of the capital of the Irish Refining Company Limited was taken after the four major international oil companies announced their intention to close the refinery.
5. The reason given by the Irish Government for acquiring the Irish Refining Company Limited was the need to guarantee, by keeping refining capacity in operation in Ireland, the provision of supplies of petroleum products in Ireland, in view of the fact that if the refinery had closed, all suppliers of refined petroleum products on the Irish market would have been obliged to obtain their supplies from abroad. Approximately 80% of those supplies come from a single source, namely the United Kingdom.
6. The obligation to purchase from the INPC, provided for by the 1982 Order, is intended to ensure that the Whitegate Refinery can dispose of its products. For each person to whom the 1982 Order applies the proportion of requirements covered by the purchasing obligation is

equal, for each type of petroleum product, to the proportion which the Whitegate Refinery's output for a certain period represents of the total requirements for that type of petroleum product during the same period of all the persons to whom the 1982 Order applies. However, each importer is only required to purchase up to a maximum of 35% of its total requirements of petroleum products and 40% of its requirements of each type of petroleum product.
7. The plaintiff undertakings contend, in support of their application in the main action, that the 1982 Order is contrary to Community law and in particular to the prohibition, as between Member States, of quantitative restrictions on imports and all measures having equivalent effect, laid down in Article 30 of the Treaty. The Irish Government and the INPC dispute that the 1982 Order is a measure which comes within the scope of that prohibition and contend that in any event it is justified, under Article 36 of the EEC Treaty, on grounds of public policy and public security inasmuch as it is intended to guarantee the operation of Ireland's only refinery, which is necessary to maintain the country's supplies of petroleum products.
8. In the main action, the detailed circumstances and reasons which led the Irish Minister for Industry and Energy to make the 1982 Order are disputed between the parties. The High Court took the view that before proceeding to inquire into the disputed facts, it was necessry to ask the Court of Justice to rule on the scope of the rules in the EEC Treaty on the free movement of goods as applied to a scheme such as the one at issue in the case. It therefore referred the following questions to the Court:
'1. Are Articles 30 and 31 of the EEC Treaty to be interpreted as applying to a system such as that established by the Fuels (Control of Supplies) Order 1982 in so far as that system requires importers of oil products into a Member State of the European Economic Community (in this case Ireland) to purchase from a State-owned oil refinery up to 35% of their requirements of petroleum oils?
2. If the answer to the foregoing question is in the affirmative, are the concepts of 'public policy' or 'public security' in Article 36 of the Treaty aforesaid to be interpreted in relation to a system such as that established by the 1982 Order so that:
(a) such system as above recited is exempt by Article 36 of the Treaty from the provisions of Articles 30 to 34 thereof, or
(b) such scheme is capable of being so exempt in any circumstances and, if so, in what circumstances?'

. . . . .

16. The obligation placed on all importers to purchase a certain proportion of their supplies of a given product from a national supplier limits to that

extent the possibility of importing the same product. It thus has a protective effect by favouring national production and, by the same token, works to the detriment of producers in other Member States, regardless of whether or not the raw materials used in the national production in question must themselves be imported.

17. As regard the Irish Government's argument regarding the importance of oil for the life of the country, it is sufficient to note that the Treaty applies the principle of free movement to all goods, subject only to the exceptions expressly provided for in the Treaty itself. Goods cannot therefore be considered exempt from the application of that fundamental principle merely because they are of particular importance for the life or the economy of a Member State.

. . . . .

27. Resource to Article 36 is no longer justified if Community rules provide for the necessary measures to ensure protection of the interests set out in that article. National measures such as those provided for in the 1982 Order cannot therefore be justified unless supplies of petroleum products to the Member State concerned are not sufficiently guaranteed by the measures taken for that purpose by the Community institutions.

. . . . .

31. Consequently, the existing Community rules give a Member State whose supplies of petroleum products depend totally or almost totally on deliveries from other countries certain guarantees that deliveries from other Member States will be maintained in the event of a serious shortfall in proportions which match those of supplies to the market of the supplying State. However, this does not mean that the Member State concerned has an unconditional assurance that supplies will in any event be maintained at least at a level sufficient to meet its minimum needs. In those circumstances, the possibility for a Member State to rely on Article 36 to justify appropriate complementary measures at national level cannot be excluded, even where there exist Community rules on the matter.

The scope of the public policy and public security exceptions

32. As the Court has stated on several occasions (see judgment of 12 July 1979, Case 153/78 *Commission* v. *Germany* [1979] ECR 2555, and the other judgments referred to therein), the purpose of Article 36 of the

Treaty is not to reserve certain matters to the exclusive jurisdiction of the Member States; it merely allows national legislation to derogate from the principle of the free movement of goods to the extent to which this is and remains justified in order to achieve the objectives set out in the article.

33. It is in the light of those statements that it must be decided whether the concept of public security, on which the Irish Government places particular reliance and which is the only one relevant in this case, since the concept of public policy is not pertinent, cover reasons such as those referred to in the question raised by the national court.

34. It should be stated in this connection that petroleum products, because of their exceptional importance as an energy source in the modern economy, are of fundamental importance for a country's existence since not only its economy but above all its institutions, its essential public services and even the survival of its inhabitants depend upon them. An interruption of supplies of petroleum products, with the resultant dangers for the country's existence, could therefore seriously affect the public security that Article 36 allows States to protect.

35. It is true that, as the Court has held on a number of occasions, most recently in its judgment of 9 June 1982 (Case 95/81 *Commission* v *Italy* [1982] ECR 2187), Article 36 refers to matters of a non-economic nature. A Member State cannot be allowed to avoid the effects of measures provided for in the Treaty by pleading the economic difficulties caused by the elimination of barriers to intra-Community trade. However, in the light of the seriousness of the consequences that an interruption in supplies of petroleum products may have for a country's existence, the aim of ensuring a minimum supply of petroleum products at all times is to be regarded as transcending purely economic considerations and thus as capable of constituting an objective covered by the concept of public security.

36. It should be added that to come within the ambit of Article 36, the rules in question must be justified by objective circumstances corresponding to the needs of public security. Once that justification has been established, the fact that the rules are of such a nature as to make it possible to achieve, in addition to the objectives covered by the concept of public security, other objectives of an economic nature which the Member State may also seek to achieve, does not exclude the application of Article 36.

5. Literature

L.W. Gormley, *Prohibiting Restrictions on Trade within the EEC*, Amsterdam, 1985.

D. Guy & G. Leigh, *The EEC and Intellectual Property*, London, 1981.

P. Oliver, *Free Movement of Goods in the EEC*, London, 1988.

J. Usher, 'European Communities – the Customs Union', (1980) ELRev. 142.

B. WORKERS

(EEC Treaty Articles 48–51)

1. Free movement of workers

a. General

Article 48 (1) EEC imposes upon the Member States the obligation to secure freedom of movement of workers – i.e. the abolition of discrimination between workers on grounds of nationality – before the end of the transitional period at the latest. In the words of the Court of Justice the main purpose of this provision '... is to assist in the abolition of obstacles to the establishment of a common market in which the nationals of the Member States may move freely within the territory of those States in order to pursue their economic activities.' (Cases 35 and 36/82, *Marson and Jhanjan* v. *Netherlands*, [1982] ECR 3723, at p. 3736).

Article 49 EEC empowers the Council to issue directives or make regulations to bring about, by progressive stages, freedom of movement for workers.

In fact, freedom of movement for workers was secured, for the most part, more than a year before the end of the transitional period. There were three recognisable stages in its development.

The first stage was initiated by Council Regulation 15 of 1961 and by the Council Directive of 16 August 1961, (OJ 1961, 1513/61). The second stage began three years later with the introduction of Council Regulation 38/64 (OJ 1964, 965/64) and of Council Directive 64/240 (OJ 1964, 981/64).

The third stage has seen the enactment of the final Council Regulation 1612/68 (OJ 1968, L 257/2; Sp. Ed 1968 (II), p. 485).

The fourth and current stage concerns the extension and elaboration by the Court of the notion of free movement of workers.

The EEC system to ensure abolition of discrimination between workers was, for all intends and purposes, completed in 1970 with the coming into force of Council Regulation 1251/70 (OJ 1970, L 142/24; Sp. Ed. 1970 (II), p. 402) dealing with the right to remain in a Member State after having been employed in that State.

Regulation 1612/68 has been amended by Council Regulation 312/76 of 9 February 1976 amending the provisions relating to trade union rights of members contained in this regulation. The scope of these provisions has been extended in such a way that eligibility for the administration or management posts of a trade union is now included next to the right to vote in trade union elections.

On 25 July 1977 the Council accepted a directive on the education of the children of migrant workers, Directive 77/486.

On 26 June 1984 the Council adopted a Regulation introducing special measures of Community interest in the field of employment (Reg. 1888/84, OJ 1984, L177/1).

Stage 1

Regulation 15 of 1961 came into force on 1 September 1961, and in keeping with Article 49 (EEC) it initiated the progressive abolition of restrictions on the freedom of movement of workers. During this stage the national labour market enjoyed a three week priority after which vacancies could be filled by workers from other Member States.

Stage 2

This stage began on 1 May 1964 when Regulation 38/64 came into force. There was a great demand for labour at the time, especially in Germany and the Netherlands, so it was not surprising that this Regulation contained fewer restrictions on the migration of labour than Regulation 15.

Stage 3

Regulation 1612/68 was passed more than a year before the end of the transitional period to co-incide with the early completion of the customs union. The Regulation and the accompanying Directive 68/360 brought about the removal of most of the remaining restrictions on the free movement of workers.

Article 1 of the Regulation gives all nationals of Member States the rights to take up employment within the territory of another Member State with the same priority as nationals of that State. The priority of the national labour market has ceased to exist and thus employers of one Member State and nationals of another Member State may directly exchange offers of, and applications for, employment without any discrimination resulting therefrom (Article 1). More worthy of our attention, however, is the fact that Member State nationals are entitled to travel to other Member States to seek employment and that they may remain in the relevant Member State for that purpose for a period of not more than three months. It should be observed that this 'right' is more than what is required by Article 48 (EEC) and, understandably enough, it is not provided for in either Regulation 1612 or Directive 68/360. It is the result of an agreement reached between the Member States meeting within the Council and it is recorded in the minutes of the Council meeting of 16 October 1968, the date on which Regulation 1612 and Directive 68/360 were adopted.

Administrative and legislative practices in Member States which lay down recruiting and eligibility procedures for nationals of other Member States which differ from those applicable to its own nationals are declared inapplicable by Article 3. Quantitative restrictions on the employment of foreign nationals do not apply to nationals of Member States. Nationals of a Member State who seek employment in another Member State are entitled to receive the same assistance from national employment services as nationals of that state. Medical, vocational or other criteria which discriminate on grounds of nationality shall not apply, but a national of one Member State who has received an offer in his own name from an employer in another Member State may be required to undergo a vocational test if the employer specifically requests it when making the offer.

Migrant workers who are nationals of a Member State are entitled to the same rights as national workers as regards conditions of work and employment (including conditions of remuneration and dismissal, and social and tax advantages). Access to vocational retraining schemes is available to Member State nationals on a basis of equality with nationals. Equality of treatment extends to membership of trade unions including the right to take part in union to membership of trade unions including the right to take part in union elections, excluding, however, membership of bodies governed by public law. Member State nationals are entitled to equality of treatment in housing matters and the migrant worker may put his name on the housing list of the area in which he is employed.

Regulation 1612 authorizes the migrant worker to bring with him to his place of employment his spouse, his children below the age of 21, and his dependent relations. The worker is required to have available for his family housing such as is considered normal for national workers, but this requirement must not give rise to discrimination between migrant workers and national workers.

Part II of the Regulation deals with the matching and balancing of vacancies and applications for employment. Article 13 requires the authorities of the Member States to co-operate with each other in the clearing of employment vacancies and in carrying out studies of employment trends. Article 13 (2) requires the designation of specialist services to be trusted with the organisational aspects of the above-mentioned matters. The Member States authorities are also required to co-operate with the Commission and the European Co-ordination Office in the gathering and analysis of information likely to be of guidance to workers of other Member States, regarding living and working conditions and the state of the labour markets in the various Member States.

The European Co-ordination Office, under control of the Commission, is responsible for all the technical duties assigned to the Commission by the Regulation. The other tasks of the Co-ordination office are, essentially, the co-ordination of the Community measures for matching and balancing vacancies and applications for employment, and the dissemination of information on employment vacancies and the availability of labour in the Member States.

Directive 68/360

The rules regulating the issue and validity of work permits and residence permits were contained in Regulation 38, but under the new system these rules are contained in the directive accompanying Regulation 1612. Article 2 of the Directive instructs the Member States to provide their nationals, including those seeking te leave the state for the purpose of employment, with valid passports or identity cards. Nationals of Member States are entitled to enter the territory of another Member State merely on production of a valid passport or identification card and are not required to produce visas or equivalent documents.

The most important feature of Directive 68/360 is that there is no longer the requirement of a work permit for migrant workers. The migrant worker is however required to be in possession of a 'residence permit for a national of a Member State of the EEC'. The grant of a residence permit is conditional on the production by the worker of the following documents:
1. the document with which he entered the state (e.g. passport)
2. a declaration of engagement from the employer or a certificate of employment.

The members of a workers family are entitled to a residence permit in another Member State when they produce:
1. the document with which they entered the state
2. a document proving their relationship to, or dependence upon the worker.

The right to remain

The enactment of Regulation 1271/70 was a decisive step in the establishment of the freedom of movement of workers. The right to remain in the territory of another Member State after being employed there, provided for initially in Article 48 (3) (d) EEC, is described in the preamble to Regulation 1271 as being a corallary to the right to take up employment elsewhere within the Community.

The Regulation is applicable to all nationals of Member States (and their families) who have worked as employed persons in the territory of another Member State (Article 1).

Stage 4

The Court has given a broad meaning to the term 'worker' for the purpose of Article 48 and therefore at present one speaks of the free movement of *persons* (See *e.g.* Case 139/85, *Kempf* v. *Staatssecretaris van Justitie*, [1986] ECR 1741; [1987] CMLR 764)

Notice that there is no reference to the developing case-law regarding the free movement of nationals of non-Member States.

b. Direct applicability of Article 48 and Regulation 1612/68

i. CASES

(1) French Maritime Labour Code Case

For facts and references see pages 242, 666.

The Court held:

35. A correct assessment of the legal position should have led the French authorities to find that since the provisions of Article 48 and of Regulation No 1612/68 are directly applicable in the legal system of every Member State and Community law has priority over national law, these provisions give rise, on the part of those concerned, to rights which the national authorities must respect and safeguard and as a result of which all contrary provisions of internal law are rendered inapplicable to them.

. . . . .

43. The free movement of persons, and in particular workers, constitutes, as appears both from Article 3 (c) of the Treaty and from the place of Articles 48 to 51 in Part Two of the Treaty, one of the foundations of the Community.
44. According to Article 48 (2) in entails the abolition of any discrimination based on nationality, whatever be its nature or extent, between workers of the Member States as regards employment, remuneration and other conditions of work and employment.
45. The absolute nature of this prohibition, moreover, has the effect of not only allowing in each State equal access to employment to the nationals of other Member States, but also, in accordance with the aim of Article 177 of the Treaty, of guaranteeing to the State's own nationals that they shall not suffer the unfavourable consequences which could result from the offer or acceptance by nationals of other Member States of conditions of employment or remunerations less advantageous than those obtaining under national law, since such acceptance is prohibited.
46. It thus follows from the general character of the prohibition on discrimination in Article 48 and the objective pursued by the abolition of discrimination that discrimination is prohibited even if it constitutes only an obstacle of secondary importance as regards the equality of access to employment and other conditions of work and employment.

. . . . .

(2) Van Duyn Case

See page 366.

c. Article 48 (2): abolition of discrimination

i. CASES

(1) Ugliola Case

Württembergische Milchverwertung – Südmilch v. *Ugliola*; Case 15/69; Preliminary ruling of 15 October 1969; [1969] ECR 368; [1970] CMLR 194.

Facts:

Mr. Ugliola, an Italian national, has been working since May 1961 as an employee with W.M.S. AG. He interrupted his work from 6 May 1965 to 14 August 1966 to perform his compulsory military service in Italy and then immediately resumed his job with his former employer.
'The question then arose as to the application in his favour of the German law which guarantees employment during a period of compulsory military service. Under this statute, which has been in force since 31 March 1957, the contract of employment is suspended during the period when the worker is doing his normal military service or a period of recall in the armed forces. Article 6 (1) provides that a worker who subsequently resumes his work with his employer must not suffer any disadvantage in his occupational prospects by reason of any absence connected with the performance of his military service or a period of recall.
If this rule was extended to his period of military service in Italy Ugliola would be entitled, from Christmas 1966, to a larger bonus under the legal provisions applicable to the enterprise to which he belongs. He considers that by virtue of the Council's regultions he is entitled to benefit from the German statutes.

The Court held:

. . . . .

3. The regulations of which interpretation is requested are based upon Article 48 of the Treaty which, in order to ensure the free movement of workers which is essential to the Common Market, prescribes the abolition of any discrimination based on nationality between workers of the Member States as regards employment, remuneration and other conditions of work and employment. This provision is subject to no reservations other than the restrictions set out in paragraph (3) concerning public policy, public security and public health. The Community rules relating to matters of

social security are based on the principle that the law of each Member State must ensure that nationals of other Member States employed within its territory receive all the benefits which it grants to its own nationals.
4. The fulfilment by migrant workers of an obligation for military service owed to their own State is liable to affect their conditions of work and employment in another Member State. Articles 6 (2) and 7 (2) of EEC Regulation No 38/64, Article 5 (3) of Directive No 64/240 of the Council and Article 6 (2) of Directive No 68/360 of the Council provide for the protection of migrant workers against certain consequences affecting their conditions of work and employment which might arise from their being called up for military service. The nature of these consequences remains substantially the same, whether the worker is called up by the State in which he is employed or by another Member State of which he is a national.
5. A national law which is intended to protect a worker who resumes his employment with his former employer from any disadvantages occasioned by his absence on military service, by providing in particular that the period spent in the armed forces must be taken into account in calculating the period of his service with that employer falls within the context of conditions of work and employment. Such a law cannot therefore, on the basis of its indirect connection with national defence, be excluded from the ambit of Article 9 (1) of EEC Regulation No 38/64 and Article 7 of EEC Regulation No 1612/68 on equality of treatment and protection for migrant workers 'in respect of any conditions of employment and work'.
6. Apart from the cases expressly referred to in paragraph (3), Article 48 of the Treaty does not allow Member States to make any exceptions to the equality of treatment and protection required by the Treaty for all workers within the Community by indirectly introducing discrimination in favour of their own nationals alone based upon obligations for military service. Consequently, as a rule of national law protecting workers from the unfavourable consequences, as regards conditions of work and employment in an undertaking, arising out of absence through obligations for military service must also be applied to the nationals of other Member States employed in the territory of the State in question who are subject to military service in their country of origin.
7. Therefore, the abovementioned provisions entitle a migrant worker who is a national of a Member State and who has had to interrupt his employment with an undertaking in another Member State in order to fulfil his obligations for military service in the country of which he is a national, to have the period of his military service taken into account in the calculation of his seniority in that undertaking, to the extent to which the periods of military service in the country of employment are also taken into account for the benefit of national workers.

. . . . .

(2) Sotgiu Case

Sotgiu v. *Deutsche Bundespost*; Case 152/73; Preliminary ruling of 12 February 1974; [1974] ECR 162.

Facts:

Giovanni Sotgiu, of Italian nationality, was engaged as a skilled worker by the Deutsche Budespost. Mr. Sotgiu is paid in accordance with the collective wages agreement for Federal Post Office workers. His family was still living in Italy. From the beginning of his employment he received a separation allowance of 7.50 DM per day, on the same basis as workers of German nationality employed away from home. The separation allowance for workers employed away from their place of residence in the Federal Republic was increased to 10 DM per day with effect from 1 April 1965, but for workers whose residence at the time of their initial employment was situated abroad the amount of the allowance remained at 7.50 DM per day. Mr. Sotgiu, who continued to receive the allowance at the lower rate, brought an action before the Arbeitsgericht (Labour Court), Stuttgart. In support of his action he claimed in particular that he was the victim of discrimination which was forbidden by Regulation 1612/68. The Arbeitsgericht dismissed the action by a judgment of 21 August 1970. Sotgiu's appeal, brought before the Landesarbeitsgericht (the Land Labour Court) for Baden-Württemberg, was rejected by a judgment of 21 April 1972. On 18 May 1972 he lodged a further appeal before the Bundesarbeitsgericht (Federal Labour Court), Stuttgart. This court asked for a preliminary ruling.

The Court held:

. . . . .

4. Taking account of the fundamental nature, in the scheme of the Treaty, of the principles of freedom of movement and equality of treatment of workers within the Community, the exceptions made by Article 48 (4) cannot have a scope going beyond the aim in view of which this derogation was included.

The interests which this derogation allows the Member States to protect are satisfied by the opportunity of restricting admission of foreign nationals to certain activities in the public service.

On the other hand this provision cannot justify discriminatory measures with regard to remuneration or other conditions of employment against workers once they have been admitted to the public service.

The very fact that they have been admitted shows indeed that those interests which justify the exceptions to the principle of non-discrimination permitted by Article 48 (4) are not at issue.

5. It is necessary to establish further whether the extent of the exception provided for by Article 48 (4) can be determined in terms of the designation of the legal relationship between the employee and the employing administration.

In the absence of any distinction in the provision referred to, it is of no interest whether a worker is engaged as a workman (ouvrier), a clerk (employé) or an official (fonctionnaire) or even whether the terms on which he is employed come under public or private law.

These legal designations can be varied at the whim of national legislatures and cannot therefore provide a criterion for interpretation appropriate to the requirements of Community law.

6. The answer to the question put to the Court should therefore be that Article 48 (4) of the Treaty is to be interpreted as meaning that the exception made by this provision concerns only access to posts forming part of the public services and that the nature of the legal relationship between the employee and the employing administration is of no consequence in this respect.

. . . . .

(3) Casagrande Case

Donato Casagrande v. *City of Munich*; Case 9/74; Preliminary ruling of 3 July 1974; [1974] ECR 778; [1974] 2 CMLR 423.

Facts:

The plaintiff, born on 29 December 1953, possesses Italian nationality, as does his mother, and has lived since his birth in Munich. His father, who died on 24 January 1971, was employed as a worker in the Federal Republic of Germany.

The plaintiff in the main proceedings attended the transitional form 10 of the Fridtjof-Nansen-Realschule, Munich, during the school year 1971/1972 up to 30 April 1972.

Under Article 2 of the Bavarian law on educational grants a child who attends the fifth to tenth form of a secondary school and who does not have sufficient means is entitled to receive an 'educational grant' amounting to 70 DM per month.

The plaintiff in the main action claimed this sum from the City of Munich for the appropriate period he attended school.

The defendant in the main action refused the plaintiff the educational grant

by reference to the law in question under which educational grants are payable solely to the following classes of persons:
1. German nationals within the meaning of the Basic Law;
2. Stateless persons;
3. Aliens who permanently reside in Bavarian territory and who are recognised as enjoying the right of asylum.

The Court held:

. . . . .

5. Under Article 12 of Reg. 1612/68 'the children of a national of a Member State who is or has been employed in the territory of another Member State shall be admitted to that State's general educational, apprenticeship and vocational training courses under the same conditions as the nationals of that State, if such children are residing in its territory', and Member States are required to encourage 'all efforts to enable such children to attend these courses under the best possible conditions'.
6. According to the fifth recital of the Regulation, the latter was issued, inter alia, for the reason that 'the right of freedom of movement, in order that it may be exercised, by objective standards, in freedom and dignity, requires ... that obstacles to the mobility of workers shall be eliminated, in particular as regards the worker's right to be joined by his family and the conditions for the integration of that family into the host country'.
7. Such integration presupposes that, in the case of the child of a foreign worker who wishes to have secondary education, this child can take advantage of benefits provided by the laws of the host country relating to educational grants, under the same conditions as nationals who are in a similar position.
8. It follows from the provision in the second paragraph of Article 12, according to which Member States are to encourage all efforts to enable such children to attend the courses under the best possible conditions, that the Article is intended to encourage special efforts, to ensure that the children may take advantage on an equal footing of the education and training facilities available.
9. It must be concluded that in providing that the children in question shall be admitted to educational courses 'under the same conditions as the nationals' of the host state, Article 12 refers not only to rules relating to admission, but also to general measures intended to facilitate educational attendance.
10. The Staatsanwaltschaft of the Verwaltungsgericht, the third party in the main action, stated that educational policy and educational grants were within the competence of Member States.
11. In the Federal Republic of Germany such policy is largely within the

competence of the Länder, and therefore it must be asked whether Article 12 applies not only to the conditions laid down by laws emanating from the central power but also to those arising from measures taken by the authorities of a country which forms part of a Federal State, or of other territorial entities.
12. Although educational and training policy is not as such included in the spheres which the Treaty has entrusted to the Community institutions, it does not follow that the exercise of powers transferred to the Community is in some way limited if it is of such a nature as to affect the measures taken in the execution of a policy such as that of education and training.

. . . . .

Sequel:

A similar problem was discussed in case 68/74, *Alaimo* v. *Préfet du Rhône*, judgment of 29 January 1975, [1975] ECR 113.

The Court ruled in that case that Article 12 of Regulation No 1612/68 must be interpreted as ensuring for the children referred to an equal position with regard to all the rights araising from admission to educational courses.

(4) Choquet in re driving licence Case

Public Prosecutor v. *Michel Choquet in re driving licence*; Case 16/78; Preliminary ruling of 28 November 1978; [1978] ECR 2293; [1979] 1 CMLR 535.

Facts:

Michel Choquet, a French national who resides at Reutlingen in the Federal Republic of Germany and works as an electrician, was involved in a road traffic accident at Reutlingen-Gröningen, on 15 October 1977.

After the public prosecutor for the Landgericht (Regional Court) Tübingen had issued a summons on 15 November 1977, Mr. Choquet was ordered by the Amtsgericht (Local Court) Reutlingen to pay a fine of DM 1600 for dangerous driving and driving without a driving licence.

In order to drive a motor vehicle in the Federal Republic of Germany an official driving licence is necessary, otherwise the driver is liable to punishment pursuant to Articles 2 and 21 of the Strassenverkehrsgesetz (law on road traffic) of 19 December 1952. Under Articles 6 and 7 of the Paris Convention on Motor Traffic of 24 April 1926, in conjunction with the Regulation on International Motor Traffic of 12 November 1934 as amended by the Regulation of 18 April 1940, a foreigner is entitled to drive a motor vehicle within the Federal territory, in accordance with the provisions of his country of origin, with his national driving licence or an international driving licence, for one year after crossing the frontier or from the date of issue of his driving licence. After that period has elapsed a foreigner in the Federal German Republic must hold a German driving licence.

Mr. Choquet, who has been resident in the Federal Republic of Germany since 1 January 1976, holds a French driving licence issued by the Préfecture de l'Aisne on 22 November 1968, but not a German driving licence.

An appeal was lodged on 14 December 1977 with the Amtsgericht Reutlingen, which by an order of 13 February 1978 decided, pursuant to Article 177 of the EEC Treaty, to stay proceedings until the Court of Justice has given a preliminary ruling on the following question:

> Is it compatible with Community law for a Member State of the European Community to require the nationals of other Member States to possess a driving licence issued by the first Member State for driving motor vehicles and, as the case may be, to penalize them for driving without such a driving licence even though such citizens of the Community have a right of residence under Article 48 et seq. of the EEC Treaty and are in possession of an equivalent driving licence from their own country?

The Court ruled:

1. It is not in principle incompatible with Community law for one Member State to require a national of another Member State, who is permanently established in its territory, to obtain a domestic driving licence for the purpose of driving motor vehicles, even if he is in possession of a driving licence issued by the authorities in his State of origin.
2. However, such a requirement may be regarded as indirectly prejudicing the exercise of the right of freedom of movement, the right of freedom of establishment or the freedom to provide services guaranteed by Articles 48, 52 and 59 of the Treaty respectively, and consequently as being incompatible with the Treaty, if it appears that the conditions imposed by national rules on the holder of a driving licence issued by another Member State are not in due proportion to the requirements of road safety.

(5) Saunders Case

Regina v. *Vera Ann Saunders*; Case 175/78; Preliminary ruling of 28 March 1979; (1979) ECR 1134; [1979] 2 CMLR 216.

Facts:

On 21 December 1977 the Crown Court at Bristol, hearing criminal proceedings brought against Vera Ann Saunders, a British subject, on a charge of theft to which she had pleaded guilty, merely bound her over, in accordance with its powers in this connection under section 6 (4) of the Courts Act 1971, to come up for judgment if called upon to do so, it being a condition of her recognizance – this was, moreover, in accordance with the desire which she had herself expressed – that she should proceed to Northern Ireland and not return to England or Wales within three years.

Miss Saunders broke that undertaking; the Crown Court at Bristol before which her case was brought once more wished to know before giving judgment whether its Order of 21 December 1977 was invalid in that it was in derogation of the rights conferred by Article 48 of the Treaty on freedom of movement for workers.

The Crown Court in fact considers first that the defendant must be considered as a worker within the meaning of the Treaty and secondly that its Order of 21 December 1977 did not fall within any of the limitations set out in Article 48 (3) of the Treaty.

By order of 31 July 1978, received at the Court on 16 August 1978, the Crown Court at Bristol requested the Court of Justice to give a preliminary ruling on the following question:

'Whether the Order of this court made in the case of Vera Ann Saunders on 21 December 1977 may constitute a derogation from the right given to a worker under Article 48 of the Treaty establishing the European Economic Community, having regard in particular to the right specified in Article 48 (b) of the said Treaty, and the fact that she appears to be an English national'.

The Court held:

. . . . .

8. Under Article 7, any discrimination on grounds of nationality is prohibited within the scope of application of the Treaty and without prejudice to any special provisions contained therein.
9. In application of that general principle, Article 48 aims to abolish in the legislation of the Member States provisions as regards employment, remuneration and other conditions of work and employment – including the rights and freedoms which that freedom of movement involves pursuant to Article 48 (3) – according to which a worker who is a national of another Member State is subject to more severe treatment or is placed in an unfavourable situation in law or in fact as compared with the situation of a national in the same circumstances.
10. Although the rights conferred upon workers by Article 48 may lead the Member States to amend their legislation, where necessary, even with respect to their own nationals, this provision does not however aim to

restrict the power of the Member States to lay down restrictions, within their own territory, on the freedom of movement of all persons subject to their jurisdiction in implementation of domestic criminal law.
11. The provisions of the Treaty on freedom of movement for workers cannot therefore be applied to situations which are wholly internal to a Member State, in other words, where there is no factor connecting them to any of the situations envisaged by Community law.
12. The application by an authority or court of a Member State to a worker who is a national of that same state of measures which deprive or restrict the freedom of movement of that worker within the territory of that State as a penal measure provided for by national law by reason of acts committed within the territory of that State is a wholly domestic situation which falls outside the scope of the rules contained in the Treaty on freedom of movement for workers.

d. Article 48 (3): limitations on grounds of public policy, public security or public health

i. CASES

(1) Van Duyn Case

Van Duyn v. *Home Office*; Case 41/74; Preliminary ruling of 4 December 1974; [1974] ECR 1346; [1975] CMLR 4.

Facts:

The Church of Scientology is a body established in the United States of America, which functions in the UK through a college at East Grinstead, Sussex. The British Government regards the activities of the Church of Scientology as contrary to public policy. Foreign nationals come to Britain to study Scientology and to work for it.

The Court held:

1. By order of the Vice Chancellor of 1 March 1974, lodged at the Court on 13 June, the Chancery Division of the High Court of Justice of England, referred to the Court, under Article 177 of the EEC Treaty, three questions relating to the interpretation of certain provisions of Community law concerning freedom of movement for workers.
2. These questions arise out of an action brought against the Home Office by a woman of Dutch nationality who was refused leave to enter the

United Kingdom to take up employment as a secretary with the 'Church of Scientology'.
3. Leave to enter was refused in accordance with the policy of the Government of the United Kingdom in relation to the said organization, the activities of which it considers to be socially harmful.

First question

4. By the first question, the Court is asked to say whether Article 48 of the EEC Treaty is directly applicable so as to confer on individuals rights enforceable by them in the courts of a Member State.
5. It is provided, in Article 48 (1) and (2), that freedom of movement for workers shall be secured by the end of the transitional period and that such freedom shall entail 'the abolishment of any discrimination based on nationality between workers of Member States as regards employment, remuneration and other conditions of work and employment'.
6. These provisions impose on Member States a precise obligation which does not require the adoption of any further measures on the part either of the Community institutions or of the Member States and which leaves them, in relation to its implementation, no discretionary power.
7. Paragraph 3, which defines the rights implied by the principle of freedom of movement for workers, subjects them to limitation justified on grounds of public policy, public security or public health. The application of these limitations is, however, subject to judicial control, so that a Member State's right to invoke the limitations does not prevent the provisions of Article 48, which enshrine the principle of freedom of movement for workers, from conferring on individuals rights which are enforceable by them and which the national courts must protect.
8. The reply to the first question must therefore be in the affirmative.

Second question

9. The second question asks the Court to say whether Council Directive No 64/221 of 25 February 1964 on the co-ordination of special measures concerning the movement and residence of foreign nationals which are justified on grounds of public policy, public security or public health is directly applicable so as to confer on individuals rights enforceable by them in the courts of a Member State.
10. It emerges from the order making the reference that the only provision of the Directive which is relevant is that contained in Article 3 (1) which provides that 'measures taken on grounds of public policy or public security shall be based exclusively on the personal conduct of the individual concerned'.

. . . . . .

13. By providing that measures taken on grounds of public policy shall be based exclusively on the personal conduct of the individual concerned, Article 3 (1) of Directive No 64/221 is intended to limit the discretionary power which national laws generally confer on the authorities responsible for the entry and expulsion of foreign nationals. First, the provision lays down an obligation which is not subject to any exception or condition and which, by its very nature, does not require the intervention of any act on the part either of the institutions of the Community or of Member States. Secondly, because Member States are thereby obliged, in implementing a clause which derogates from one of the fundamental principles of the Treaty in favour of individuals, not to take account of factors extraneous to personal conduct, legal certainty for the persons concerned requires that they should be able to rely on this obligation even though it has been laid down in a legislative act which has no automatic direct effect in its entirety.
14. If the meaning and exact scope of the provision raise questions of interpretation, these questions can be resolved by the courts, taking into account also the procedure under Article 177 of the Treaty.
15. Accordingly, in reply to the second question, Article 3 (1) of Council Directive No 64/221 of 25 February 1964 confers on individuals rights which are enforceable by them in the courts of a Member State and which the national courts must protect.

Third question

16. By the third question the Court is asked to rule whether Article 48 of the Treaty and Article 3 of Directive No 64/221 must be interpreted as meaning that
    'a Member State, in the performance of its duty to base a measure taken on grounds of public policy exclusively on the personal conduct of the individual concerned is entitled to take into account as matters of personal conduct:
    (a) the fact that the individual is or has been associated with some body or organization the activities of which the Member State considers contrary to the public good by which are not unlawful in that State;
    (b) the fact that the individual intends to take employment in the Member State with such a body or organization it being the case that no restrictions are placed on nationals of the Member State who wish to take similar employment with such a body or organization'.
17. It is necessary, first, to consider whether association with a body or an organization can in itself constitute personal conduct within the meaning of Article 3 of Directive No 64/221. Although a person's past association cannot in general, justify a decision refusing him the right to move freely within the Community, it is nevertheless the case that present associa-

tion, which reflects participation in the activities of the body or organization as well as identification with its aims and its designs, may be considered a voluntary act of the person concerned and, consequently, as part of his personal conduct within the meaning of the provision cited.

18. This third question further raises the problem of what importance must be attributed to the fact that the activities of the organization in question, which are considered by the Member State as contrary to the public good are not however prohibited by national law. It should be emphasized that the concept of public policy in the context of the Community and where, in particular, it is used as a justification for derogating from the fundamental principle of freedom of movement for workers, must be interpreted strictly, so that its scope cannot be determined unilaterally by each Member State without being subject to control by the institutions of the Community. Nevertheless, the particular circumstances justifying recourse to the concept of public policy may vary from one country to another and from one period to another, and it is therefore necessary in this matter to allow the competent national authorities an area of discretion within the limits imposed by the Treaty.

19. It follows from the above that where the competent authorities of a Member State have clearly defined their standpoint as regards the activities of a particular organization and where, considering it to be socially harmful, they have taken administrative measures to counteract these activities, the Member State cannot be required, before it can rely on the concept of public policy, to make such activities unlawful, if recourse to such a measure is not thought appropriate in the circumstances.

20. The question raises finally the problem of whether a Member State is entitled, on grounds of public policy, to prevent a national of another Member State from taking gainful employment within its territory with a body or organization, it being the case that no similar restriction is placed upon its own nationals.

21. In this connection, the Treaty, while enshrining the principle of freedom of movement for workers without any discrimination on grounds of nationality, admits, in Article 48 (3), limitations justified on grounds of public policy, public security or public health to the rights deriving from this principle. Under the terms of the provision cited above, the right to accept offers of employment actually made, the right to move freely within the territory of Member States for this purpose, and the right to stay in a Member State for the purpose of employment are, among others all subject to such limitations. Consequently, the effect of such limitations, when they apply, is that leave to enter the territory of a Member State and the right to reside there may be refused to a national of another Member State.

22. Furthermore, it is a principle of international law, which the EEC Treaty cannot be assumed to disregard in the relations between Member States, that a State is precluded from refusing its own nationals the right of entry or residence.

23. It follows that a Member State, for reasons of public policy, can, where it deems, necessary, refuse a national of another Member State the benefit of the principle of freedom of movement for workers in a case where such a national proposes to take up a particular offer of employment even though the Member State does not place a similar restriction upon its own nationals.
24. Accordingly, the reply to the third question must be that Article 48 of the EEC Treaty and Article 3 (1) of Directive 64/221 are to be interpreted as meaning that a Member State, in imposing restrictions justified on grounds of public policy, is entitled to take into account, as a matter of personal conduct of the individual concerned the fact that the individual is associated with some body or organization the activities of which the Member State considers socially harmful but which are not unlawful in that State, despite the fact that no restriction is placed upon nationals of the said Member State who wish to take similar employment with these same bodies or organizations.

(2) Bonsignore Case

Carmelo Bonsignore v. *Stadt Köln*; Case 67/74; Preliminary ruling of 26 February 1975; [1975] ECR 304; [1975] 1 CMLR 472.

For facts see the judgment below.

The Court held:

1. By order of 30 July 1974, received at the Court Registry on 14 September 1974, the Verwaltungsgericht Köln referred to the Court, under Article 177 of the EEC Treaty, two questions concerning the interpretation of Article 3 (1) and (2) of Council Directive No 64/221/EEC of 25 February 1964 on the coordination of special measures concerning the movement and residence of foreign nationals which are justified on grounds of public policy, public security or public health (OJ 850).
2. These questions arose within the context of an appeal brought by an Italian national residing in the Federal Republic of Germany against a decision to deport him taken by the Ausländerbehörde (Aliens Authority) following his conviction for an offence against the Firearms Law and for causing death by negligence.

    The order containing the reference shows that the plaintiff in the main action, who was unlawfully in possession of a firearm, accidentally caused the death of his brother by his careless handling of the firearm concerned.

    For this reason the relevant criminal court sentenced him to a fine for an offence against the firearms legislation.

    The Court also found him guilty of causing death by negligence but

imposed no punishment on this count, considering that no purpose would be served thereby in view of the circumstances, notably the mental suffering caused to the individual concerned as a result of the consequences of his carelessness.
3. Following the criminal conviction the 'Ausländerbehörde' (Aliens Authority) ordered the individual concerned to be deported in accordance with the Ausländergesetz (Aliens Law) of 28 April 1965 (Bundesgesetzblatt, Teil I, p. 353), in conjunction with the Gesetz über Einreise und Aufenthalt von Staatsangehörigen der Mitgliedstaaten der Europäischen Wirtschaftsgemeinschaft (Law on the entry and residence of nationals of Member States of the European Economic Community) of 22 July 1969 (Bundesgesetzblatt, Teil I, p. 927), which was adopted in order to implement Directive No 64/221 in the Federal Republic of Germany.
4. The Verwaltungsgericht, which heard the appeal against this decision, considered that by reason of the particular circumstances of the case the deportation could not be justified on grounds of a 'special preventive nature' based either on the facts which had given rise to the criminal conviction or on the present and foreseeable conduct of the plaintiff in the main action.

The Verwaltungsgericht considered that the only possible justification for the measure adopted would be the reason of a 'general preventive nature', which were emphasized both by the Ausländerbehörde and by the representative of the public interest and were based on the deterrent effect which the deportation of an alien found in illegal possession of a firearm would have in immigrant circles having regard to the resurgence of violence in the large urban centres.

. . . . . .

5. According to Article 3 (1) and (2) of Directive No 64/221, 'Measures taken on grounds of public policy or of public security shall be based exclusively on the personal conduct of the individual concerned' and 'Previous criminal convictions shall not in themselves constitute grounds for the taking of such measures'.

These provisions must be interpreted in the light of the objectives of the directive which seeks in particular to coordinate the measures justified on grounds of public policy and for the maintenance of public security envisaged by Articles 48 and 56 of the Treaty, in order to reconcile the application of these measures with the basic principle of the free movement of persons within the Community and the elimination of all discrimination, in the application of the Treaty, between the nationals of the State in question and those of the other Member States.
6. With this in view, Article 3 of the directive provides that measures adopted on grounds of public policy and for the maintenance of public security

against the nationals of Member States of the Community cannot be justified on grounds extraneous to the individual case, as is shown in particular by the requirement set out in paragraph (1) that 'only' the 'personal conduct' of those affected by the measures is to be regarded as determinative.

As departures from the rules concerning the free movement of persons constitute exceptions which must be strictly construed, the concept of 'personal conduct' expresses the requirement that a deportation order may only be made for breaches of the peace and public security which might be committed by the individual affected.

7. The reply to the questions referred should therefore be that Article 3 (1) and (2) of Directive No 64/221 prevents the deportation of a national of a Member State if such deportation is ordered for the purpose of deterring other aliens, that is, if it is based, in the words of the national court, on reasons of a 'general preventive nature'.

. . . . .

(3) Rutili Case

Rutili v. *Minister for the Interior*; Case 36/75; Preliminary ruling of 28 October 1975; [1975] ECR 1219; [1976] 1 CMLR 140.

Facts:

Mr. Roland Rutili, of Italian nationality, was born on 27 April 1940 in Loudun (Vienne), and has been resident in France since his birth, he is married to a French woman and was, until 1968, the holder of a privileged resident's permit and domiciled at Audun-le-Tiche (in the department of Meurthe-et-Moselle), where he worked and engaged in trade union activities.

On 12 August 1968, the Ministry for the Interior made a deportation order against him.

On 10 September 1968 an order was issued requiring him to reside in the department of Puy-de-Dôme.

By orders of 19 November 1968 the Minister for the Interior revoked the deportation and residence orders affecting Mr. Rutili and, on the same date, informed the Prefect of the Moselle of his decision to prohibit Mr. Rutili from residing in the departments of Moselle, Meurthe-et-Moselle, Meuse and Vosges.

On 17 January 1970 Mr. Rutili applied for the grant of a residence permit for a national of a Member State of the EEC.

On 9 July 1970 he appealed to the Tribunal administratif, Paris, against the implied decision refusing him this document.

On 23 October 1970, the Prefect of Police acting on instructions given by the Minister for the Interior on 17 July, granted Mr. Rutili a residence permit for a national of a Member State of the EEC, which was valid until 22 October 1975 but subject to a prohibition on residence in the departments of Moselle, Meurthe-et-Moselle, Meuse and Vosges.

On 16 December 1970, Mr. Rutili brought proceedings before the Tribunal administratif, Paris, for annulment of the decision limiting the territorial validity of his residence permit.

During the proceedings before the Tribunal administratif, it became apparent that Mr. Rutili's presence in the departments of Lorraine was considered by the Minister for the Interior to be 'likely to disturb public policy' and that there were complaints against him in respect of certain activities, the truth of which is, however, contested, which are alleged to consist, in essence, in political actions during the parliamentary elections in March 1967 and the events of May and June 1968 and in his participation in a demonstration during the celebration on 14 July 1968 at Audun-le-Tiche.

By judgement of 16 December 1974, the Tribunal administratif, Paris, decided to stay the proceedings under Article 177 of the EEC Treaty until the Court of Justice had given a preliminary ruling on the following questions:

1. Does the expression 'subject to limitations justified on grounds of public policy' employed in Article 48 of the Treaty establishing the EEC concern merely the legislative decisions which each Member State of the EEC has decided to take in order to limit within its territory the freedom of movement and residence for nationals of other Member States or does it also concern individual decisions taken in application of such legislative decisions?
2. What is the precise meaning to be attributed to the word 'justified'?

The Court ruled:

1. The expression 'subject to limitations justified on grounds of public policy', in Article 48 concerns not only the legislative provisions adopted by each Member State to limit within its territory freedom of movement and residence for nationals of other Member States but concerns also individual decisions taken in application of such legislative provisions.
2. An appraisal as to whether measures designed to safeguard public policy are justified must have regard to all rules of Community law the object of which is, on the one hand, to limit the discretionary power of Member States in this respect and, on the other, to ensure that the rights of persons subject thereunder to restrictive measures are protected.

These limitations and safeguards arise, in particular, from the duty imposed on Member States to base the measures adopted exclusively on the personal conduct of the individuals concerned; to refrain from adopting any measures in this respect which service ends unrelated to the requirements of public policy or which adversely affect the exercise of trade union rights and, finally, unless this is contrary to the interests of the security of the State involved, immediately to inform any person against whom a restrictive measure has been adopted of the grounds on which the decision taken is based to enable him to make effective use of legal remedies.

In particular, measures restricting the rights of residence which are limited to part only of the national territory may not be imposed by a Member State on nationals of other Member States who are subject to the provisions of the Treaty except in the cases and circumstances in which such measures may be applied to nationals of the State concerned.

(4) The German Aliens Act Case

Public Prosecutor v. *Sagulo, Brenca and Bakhouche*; Case 8/77; Preliminary ruling of 14 July 1977; [1977] ECR 1503; [1977] 2 CMLR 585.

Facts:

Mrs. Concetta Sagulo-Avolio is a bookbinder of Italian nationality. On 21 November 1975 she was convicted by the Amtsgericht Reutlingen as a result of proceedings brought against her on 12 November 1975 by the Staatsanwaltschaft (Public Prosecutor's Office) for infringing the second subparagraph of Article 47 (1) of the Ausländergesetz (Aliens Act) of 28 April 1965 (Bundesgesetzblatt 1965 I, p. 353); she was fined DM 100 for having resided in the Federal Republic of Germany between 24 February and 4 September 1975 without a passport or residence permit.

On 28 November 1975 Mrs. Sagulo lodged an appeal before the Amtsgericht Reutlingen against this conviction.

Mr. Gennaro Brenca, a worker, is Italian. On 25 November 1976 the Amtsgericht Reutlingen fined him DM 100 for having resided in the Federal Republic of Germany between 30 February (sic) and 16 June 1976 without a passport or residence permit. Mr. Brenca appealed to the Amtsgericht Reutlingen against this conviction.

Mr. Addelmadjid Bakhouche, who is without occupation, is French. As a member of the French armed forces he was stationed from 22 June 1962 to 14 November 1973 in the Federal Republic of Germany; thereafter he had a valid residence permit from 12 December 1973 to 11 December 1974.

In spite of repeated requests by the competent authorities Mr. Bakhouche did not endeavour to have his residence permit extended; he was remanded in custody charged with an infringement of the Ausländergesetz and on 12 March 1976 the Amstgericht Reutlingen convicted him of this offence and fined him DM 1,200 taking into account the time spent in custody awaiting trial.

On 24 September 1976 the Staatsanwaltschaft brought further proceedings against Mr. Bakhouche before the Amtsgericht Reutlingen for continuing to reside in the Federal Republic of Germany without a residence permit.

By order dated 13 January 1977 the Amtsgericht Reutlingen stayed the proceedings in the three criminal actions pending before it and referred the following questions to the Court for a preliminary ruling under Article 177 of the EEC Treaty:
1. Can the special residence document which has declaratory effect and is referred to in Article 4 of Council Directive 68/360 issued as proof of a right of residence for aliens entitled thereto by virtue of Article 48 et seq. of the EEC Treaty be treated as being on all fours for the purposes of administrative and criminal law with the residence permit issued under the German Ausländergesetz (Aliens Law) with the result that such aliens who do not hold the document authorizing residence under the first or second subparagraph of Article 47 (1) of the Ausländergesetz or who hold such a document which has ceased to be valid can be sentenced under Article 5 of the Ausländergesetz for residence or entry without a valid residence permit, or does such a sentence contravene the EEC Treaty?
2. Is the EEC Treaty contravened if an alien directly entitled under Article 48 of the EEC Treaty and the above mentioned Council Directive is issued only with a residence permit under Article 5 of the Ausländergesetz with the possible adverse effects of Article 47 of that Law?

The Court held:

. . . . .

4. The rights of nationals of a Member State to enter the territory of another Member State and to reside there for the purposes mentioned in the Treaty follows, as the court making the reference rightly states, directly from the Treaty or, as the case may be, from the provision adopted for its implementation. Nevertheless Community law has not deprived Member States of the power to adopt measures to enable the national authorities to have precise information of movements of population in its territory. To enable the Member States to obtain such data and at the same time to put those concerned in a position to prove their legal position with regard to the application of the provisions of the Treaty two formalities are provided for in Articles 2 and 4 of the Directive No 68/360: the persons in question must have a valid identity card or passport and be able to prove their right of residence by a document entitled 'Residence Permit for a National of a Member State of the EEC' which must include the statement set out in the Annex to the directive. Under the third para-

graph of Article 189 of the Treaty it is for the Member States to choose the form and methods to implement the provisions of the directive in their territory either by the adoption of a special law or regulations or by the application of appropriate provisions of their general regulations on aliens. The Member States are also competent to lay down penalties provided for in their general regulations in order to secure observance in their territory of the formalities provided for in Directive No 68/360.
5. If a Member State executes the directive on the basis of its general regulations on the legal status of aliens, it must naturally not adopt administrative or judicial measures which would have the effect of limiting the full exercise of the rights which the Community law guarantees to the nationals of other Member States. In particular it would be incompatible with Community law for a general residence permit to be required or issued having a different scope from the proof of the right of residence by the issue of the special 'Residence Permit' provided for in Article 4 (2) of Directive No 68/360.
6. The imposition of penalties or other coercive measures is therefore ruled out in so far as a person protected by the provisions of Community law does not comply with national provisions which prescribe for such a person possession of a general residence permit instead of the document provided for in Directive No 68/360, since the national authorities should not impose penalties for disregard of a provision which is incompatible with Community law. On the other hand Community law does not preclude the appropriate punishment for infringement by the person concerned of national provisions adopted in conformity with Directive No 68/360.
7. The same applies to the question whether the repeated disregard of provisions which a Member State has adopted in execution of Directive No 68/360 can where appropriate justify increasing the penalties imposed. Community law does not prevent such an increase in penalties which is consistent with general principles of penal law. However this does not affect the obligation of the court to ascertain whether the conditions for such an increase in penalties are fulfilled where there has been a prior conviction on the basis of legal provisions the application of which was not justified under Community law. Even if the force of 'res judicata' does not allow such a prior conviction to be completely nullified its effect cannot be extended in such a way that it is regarded as an aggravating circumstance in connection with a subsequent conviction which is justified under Community law.
8. The questions put to the Court must therefore be answered as follows: The issue of the special residence document provided for in Article 4 of Council Directive No 68/360 has only a declaratory effect and for aliens to whom Article 48 of the Treaty or parallel provisions give rights, it cannot be assimilated to a residence permit such as is prescribed for aliens in general and in connection with the issue of which the national authorities have a discretion. A Member State may not require from a person

enjoying the protection of Community law that he should possess a general residence permit instead of the document provided for in Article 4 (2) of Directive No 68/360 in conjunction with the Annex thereto nor may it impose penalties for the failure to possess such a permit. The force of 'res judicata' arising from a prior conviction arrived at on the basis of national provisions not in accordance with the requirements of Community law cannot justify an increase in the penalties to be imposed for an infringement of the provisions which a Member State has adopted to secure the application of Directive No 68/360 in its territory.

. . . . . .

10. This question concerns in particular the cases where a person who is entitled under Community law to reside in the territory of the country in question neglects to obtain a valid identity card. Since this requirement is expressly contained in Direction No 68/360 the power of Member States to punish infringements of this duty cannot in principle be contested. The court making the reference nevertheless asks in this connection whether it is compatible with Community law and in particular with the prohibition on discrimination in Article 7 of the Treaty to make a person who is subject to Community law liable to the relatively heavy penalties which the general law on aliens provides for such an infringement whereas a national on infringing similar legal provisions is liable only to the considerably lighter penalties which apply to minor offences.
11. The first paragraph of Article 7 of the EEC Treaty states: 'Within the scope of application of this Treaty, and without prejudice to any special provisions contained therein, any discrimination on grounds of nationality shall be prohibited'. With regard to the question put by the court making the reference it should be pointed out that the general principle of Article 7 can only apply subject to the special provisions of the Treaty. These special provisions include the regulations and directives, including among these Directive No 68/360, provided for in Article 49 to bring about, by progressive stages, freedom of movement. In so far as this directive imposes special obligations (such as the possession of a passport or an identity card) on the nationals of a Member State who enter the territory of another Member State or reside there, the persons affected thereby cannot be simply put on the same footing as nationals of the country of residence.
12. There is therefore no objection to such persons being subject to different penal provisions from those applying to nationals who infringe an obligation, possibly having its origin in a law or regulation, to obtain certain identity documents. This conclusion follows all the more forcibly in that several Member States do not impose any such obligation by law on their own nationals so that in these countries there would be no standard of

comparison. In the absence of a criterion which in the present case might be based on the principle of national treatment contained in Article 7 of the Treaty it is nevertheless to be observed that although Member States are entitled to imposed reasonable penalties for infringement by persons subject to Community law of the obligation to obtain a valid identity card or passport, such penalties should by no means be so severe as to cause an obstacle to the freedom of entry and residence provided for in the Treaty. To this extent it cannot be ruled out that the penalties prescribed in general provisions of laws relating to aliens, having regard to the objective of such provisions, are not compatible with the requirements of Community law which is based on the freedom of movement of persons and, apart from certain exceptions, on the general application of the principle of equal treatment with nationals. If a Member State has not adapted its legal provisions to the requirements of Community law in this sphere it is the task for the national court to use its judicial discretion to impose a publishment appropriate to the character and objective of the provisions of Community law the observance of which the penalty is intended to safeguard.

13. The answer to the question raised must therefore be that it is for the competent authorities of each Member State to impose penalties where appropriate on a person subject to the provisions of Community law who has failed to provide himself with one of the documents of identity referred to in Article 3 (1) of Directive No 68/360 but that the penalties imposed must not be disproportionate to the nature of the offence committed.

. . . . .

(5) Bouchereau Case

Regina v. *Pierre Bouchereau*; Case 30/77; Preliminary ruling of 27 October 1977; [1977] ECR 2008; [1977] 2 CMLR 800.

Facts:

See the judgment below.

The Court held:

1. By order of 20 November 1976, received at the Court on 2 March 1977, the Marlborough Street Magistrate's Court, London, referred to the Court of Justice three questions concerning the interpretation of Article

48 of the Treaty and of certain provisions of Council Directive No 64/221/EEC of 25 February 1964 on the co-ordination of special measures concerning the movement and residence of foreign nationals which are justified on grounds of public policy, public security or public health (OJ, English Special Edition 1963–1964, p. 117).
2. The questions arose within the context of proceedings against a French national who had been employed in the United Kingdom since May 1975 and who was found guilty in June 1976 of unlawful possession of drugs, which is an offence punishable under the Misuse of Drugs Act 1971.
3. On 7 January 1976 the defendant had pleaded guilty to an identical offence before another court and had been conditionally discharged for twelve months.
4. The Marlborough Street Magistrates' Court was minded to make a recommendation for deportation to the Secretary of State pursuant to its powers under section 6 (1) of the Immigration Act 1971 and the appropriate notice was served on the defendant, who maintained, however, that Article 48 of the EEC Treaty and the provisions of Directive No 64/221/EEC prevented such a recommendation from being made in that instance.
5. As the national court considered that the action raised questions concerning the interpretation of Community law it referred the matter to the Court of Justice under Article 177 of the Treaty.

The first question

6. The first question asks 'whether a recommendation for deportation made by a national court of a Member State to the executive authority of that State (such recommendation being persuasive but not binding on the executive authority) constitutes a 'measure' within the meaning of Article 3 (1) and (2) of Directive No 64/221/EEC.'

. . . . . .

15. By coordinating national rules on the control of aliens, to the extent to which they concern the nationals of other Member States. Directive No 64/221/EEC seeks to protect such nationals from any exercise of the powers resulting from the exception relating to limitations justified on grounds of public policy, public security or public health, which might go beyond the requirements justifying an exception to the basic principle of free movement of persons.
16. It is essential that at the different stages of the process which may result in the adoption of a decision to make a deportation order that protection may be provided by the courts where they are involved in the adoption of such a decision.

17. It follows that the concept of 'measure' includes the action of a court which is required by the law to recommend in certain cases the deportation of a national of another Member State.
18. When making such a recommendation, therefore, such a court must ensure that the directive is correctly applied and must take account of the limits which it imposes on the action of the authorities in the Member States.
19. That finding is, moreover, in line with the point of view of the Government of the United Kingdom which 'is not suggesting that it would be open to a court of a Member State to ignore the provisions of Article 3 (1) and (2) on any matter coming before the court to which the articles are relevant' but on the contrary accepts 'that the provisions of those articles are directly applicable and confer rights on nationals of Member States to which the national courts must have regard'.

. . . . .

21. For the purposes of the directive, a 'measure' is any action which affects the right of persons coming within the field of application of Article 48 to enter and reside freely in the Member States under the same conditions as the nationals of the host State.
22. Within the context of the procedure laid down by section 3 (6) of the Immigration Act 1971, the recommendation referred to in the question raised by the national court constitutes a necessary step in the process of arriving at any decision to make a deportation order and is a necesary prerequisite for such a decision.
23. Moreover, within the context of that procedure, its effect is to make it possible to deprive the person concerned of his liberty and it is, in any event, one factor justifying a subsequent decision by the executive authority to make a deportation order.
24. Such a recommendation therefore affects the right of free movement and constitutes a measure within the meaning of Article 3 of the directive.

The second question

25. The second question asks 'whether the wording of Article 3 (2) of Directive No 64/221/EEC, namely that previous criminal convictions shall not 'in themselves' constitute grounds for the taking of measures based on public policy or public security means that previous criminal convictions are solely relevant in so far as they manifest a present or future propensity to act in a manner contrary to public policy or public security; alternatively, the meaning to be attached to the expression 'in themselves' in Article 3 (2) of Directive No 64/221/EEC'.
26. According to the terms of the order referring the case to the Court, that question seeks to discover whether, as the defendant maintained before

the national court, 'previous criminal convictions are solely relevant in so far as they manifest a present or future intention to act in a manner contrary to public policy or public security' or, on the other hand, whether, as Counsel for the prosecution sought to argue, although 'the court cannot make a recommendation for deportation on grounds of public policy based on the fact alone of a previous conviction' it 'is entitled to take into account the past conduct of the defendant which resulted in the previous conviction'.

27. The terms of Article 3 (2) of the directive, which states that 'previous criminal convictions shall not in themselves constitute grounds for the taking of such measures' must be understood as requiring the national authorities to carry out a specific appraisal from the point of view of the interests inherent in protecting the requirements of public policy, which does not necessarily coincide with the appraisals which formed the basis of the criminal conviction.

28. The existence of a previous criminal conviction can, therefore, only be taken into account in so far as the circumstances which gave rise to that conviction are evidence of personal conduct constituting a present threat to the requirements of public policy.

29. Although, in general, a finding that such a threat exists implies the existence in the individual concerned of a propensity to act in the same way in the future, it is possible that past conduct alone may constitute such a threat to the requirements of public policy.

30. It is for the authorities and, where appropriate, for the national courts, to consider that question in each individual case in the light of the particular legal position of persons subject to Community law and of the fundamental nature of the principle of the free movement of persons.

The third question

31. The third question asks whether the words 'public policy' in Article 48 (3) are to be interpreted as including reasons of state even where no breach of the public peace or order is threatened or in a narrower sense in which is incorporated the concept of some threatened breach of the public peace, order or security, or in some other wider sense.

32. Apart from the various questions of terminology, this question seeks to obtain a definition of the interpretation to be given to the concept of 'public policy' referred to in Article 48.

33. In its judgment of 4 December 1974 (Case 41/74, *Van Duyn* v. *Home Office*, [1974] ECR 1337, at p. 1350) the Court emphasized that the concept of public policy in the context of the Community and where, in particular, it is used as a justification for derogating from the fundamental principle of freedom of movement for workers, must be interpreted strictly, so that its scope cannot be determined unilaterally by each Member State without being subject to control by the institutions of the Community.

34. Nevertheless, it is stated in the same judgment that the particular cir-

cumstances justifying recourse to the concept of public policy may vary from one country to another and from one period to another and it is therefore necessary in this matter to allow the competent national authorities an area of discretion within the limits imposed by the Treaty and the provisions adopted for its implementation.

35. In so far as it may justify certain restrictions on the free movement of persons subject to Community law, recourse by a national authority to the concept of public policy presupposes, in any event, the existence, in addition to the perturbation of the social order which any infringement of the law involves, of a genuine and sufficiently serious threat to the requirements of public policy affecting one of the fundamental interests of society.

. . . . .

(6) Pecastaing Case

Josette Pecastaing v. *Belgium*; Case 98/79; Preliminary ruling of 5 March 1980; [1980] ECR 707; [1980] 3 CMLR 685.

Facts:

By an order of 18 June 1979 the President of the Tribunal de Première Instance, Liège, in the course of summary proceedings, submitted a series of questions on the interpretation of Articles 8 and 9 of Council Directive No 64/221 of 25 February 1964 on the co-ordination of special measures concerning the movement and residence of foreign nationals which are justified on grounds of public policy, public security or public health in order to determine whether an application submitted by a French national claiming, in civil proceedings, the suspension of an expulsion order issued against her by the Belgian police is admissible.

The Court ruled:

1. Article 8 of Council Directive No 64/221 of 25 February 1964 on the co-ordination of special measures concerning the movement and residence of foreign nationals which are justified on grounds of public policy, public security or public health covers all the remedies available in a Member State in respect of acts of the administration, within the framework of the judicial system and the division of jurisdiction between judicial bodies in the State in question.

   That provision imposes on the Member States the obligation to provide for the persons covered by the directive protection by the courts which is not less than that which they make available to their own nationals as regards appeals against acts of the administration, including, if appropriate, suspension of the acts appealed against.

On the other hand there may not be inferred from Article 8 of Directive No 64/221 an obligation for the Member States to permit an alien to remain in their territory for the duration of the proceedings, so long as he is able nevertheless to obtain a fair hearing and to present his defence in full.

2. The procedure concerning the consideration of the decision and concerning the opinion referred to in Article 9 of Directive No 64/221, which is intended to mitigate the effect of deficiencies in the remedies referred to in Article 8, is not intended to confer upon the courts additional powers concerning suspension of the measures referred to by the directive or to empower them to review the urgency of an expulsion order.

The performance of these duties by the national courts is governed by Article 8 of the directive.

The scope of that provision nevertheless may not be restricted by measures taken by a Member State under Article 9 of the directive.

e. Article 48 (4): employment in public service

i. CASES

(1) Sotgiu Case

See page 360.

(2) Belgian employment in public service Case

Commission v. *Kingdom of Belgium*; Case 149/79; Judgment of 17 December 1980; [1980] ECR 3898; [1981] 2 CMLR 413.

Facts:

It was brought to the notice of the Commission that the possession of Belgian nationality had been required as a condition of entry for posts with Belgian local authorities or public undertakings (such as the City of Brussels, the Commune of Auderghem, the Société Nationale des Chemins de Fer Belges (Belgain National Railways Company) and the Société Nationale des Chemins de Fer Vicinaux (National Local Railways Company) irrespective of the nature of the duties to be performed.

The Commission considered that a practice of that kind was incompatible with the provisions of Community law guaranteeing the free movement of workers within the Community.

In the Commission's opinion the only exception allowed to that principle is that provided by Article 48 (4) of the EEC Treaty in the case of 'employment in the public service', an exception which must, however, be construed as covering only posts implying actual participation in the exercise of official authority by those occupying them. In the Commission's view the posts in question (being in the case of the vacancies advertised by the railways for unskilled workers, loaders, platelayers and so on and, in the case of the vacancies advertised by the City of Brussels and the Commune of Auderghem, for hospital nurses, children' nurses, night-watchmen, architects, skilled workmen such as plumbers, carpenters and electricians, semi-skilled workmen and so on) are no different from similar post in private undertakings carrying on an industrial or commercial occupation.

The Court held:

. . . . .

9. Article 48 (4) of the Treaty provides that 'the provisions of this article shall not apply to employment in the public service'.
10. That provision removes from the ambit of Article 48 (1) to (3) a series of posts which involve direct or indirect participation in the exercise of powers conferred by public law and duties designed to safeguard the general interests of the State or of other public authorities. Such posts in fact presume on the part of those occupying them the existence of a special relationship of allegiance to the State and reciprocity of rights and duties which from the foundation of the bond of nationality.
11. The scope of the derogation made by Article 48 (4) to the principles of freedom of movement and equality of treatment laid down in the first three paragraphs of the article should therefore be determined on the basis of the aim pursued by that article. However, determining the sphere of application of Article 48 (4) raises special difficulties since in the various Member States authorities acting under powers conferred by public law have assumed responsibilities of an economic and social nature or are involved in activities which are not identifiable with the functions which are typical of the public service yet which by their nature still come under the sphere of application of the Treaty. In these circumstances the effect of extending the exception contained in Article 48 (4) to posts which, whilst coming under the State or other organizations governed by public law, still do not involve any association with tasks belonging to the public service properly so called, would be to remove a considerable number of posts from the ambit of the principles set out in the Treaty

and to create inequalities between Member States according to the different ways in which the State and certain sectors of economic life are organized.
12. Consequently it is appropriate to examine whether the posts covered by the action may be associated with the concept of public service within the meaning of Article 48 (4), which requires uniform interpretation and application throughout the Community. It must be acknowledged that the application of the distinguishing criteria indicated above gives rise to problems of appraisal and demarcation in specific cases. It follows from the foregoing that such a classification depends on whether or not the posts in question are typical of the specific activities of the public service in so far as the exercise of powers conferred by public law and responsibility for safeguarding the general interests of the State are vested in it.
13. Where, in the case of posts which, although offered by public authorities, are not within the sphere to which Article 48 (4) applies, a worker from another Member State is, like a national worker, required to satisfy all other conditions of recruitment, in particular concerning the competence and vocational training required, the provisions of the first three paragraphs of Article 48 and Regulation No 1612/68 do no allow him to be debarred from those posts simply on the grounds of his nationality.
14. In support of the argument put forward by the Belgian Government and supported by the interveners to the effect that the exception clause in Article 48 (4) of the Treaty has general scope covering all the posts in the administration of a Member State, that government has invoked the special provisions of Article 8 of Regulation No 1612/68 by which a worker from another Member State 'may be excluded from taking part in the management of bodies governed by public law and from holding an office governed by public law'.
15. Far from supporting the case of the Belgian Government that provision confirms on the contrary the interpretation of Article 48 (4) given above. Indeed, as the Belgian Government itself admits, Article 8 of Regulation No 1612/68 is not intended to debar workers from other Member States from certain posts, but simply permits them to be debarred in some circumstances from certain activities which involve their participation in the exercise of power conferred by public law, such as – to use the examples given by the Belgian Government itself – those involving 'the presence of trade-union representatives on the boards of administration of many bodies governed by public law with powers in the economic sphere'.
16. The Belgian Government further mentions that the constitutional laws of certain Member States refer expressly to the problem of employment in the public service, the principle being the exclusion of non-nationals, save for any possible derogations. Such is also, it claims, the effect of Article 6 of the Belgian Constitution by which 'Belgians ... only shall be admitted to civil and military posts save in special cases for which exception may be made'. The Belgian Government has itself stated that it

does not deny that 'Community rules override national rules' but it believes that the similarity between the constitutional laws of those Member States should be used as an aid to interpretation to cast light on the meaning of Article 48 (4) and to reject the interpretation given to that provision by the Commission, which would have the effect of creating conflict with the constitutional provisions referred to.

17. The French Government has propounded an argument of similar tenor, drawing attention to the principles applied in French law on the public service, which is founded on a comprehensive idea based on the requirement of French nationality as a condition of entry to any post in the public service appertaining to the State, municipalities or other public establishments, without any possibility of making a distinction on the basis of the nature and the characteristics of the post in question.

18. It is correct that Article 48 (4) is indeed intended to operate, in the scheme of the provisions on freedom of movement for workers, to take account of the existence of provisions of the kind mentioned. But at the same time, as is admitted in the observations of the French Government, the demarcation of the concept of 'public service' within the meaning of Article 48 (4) cannot be left to the total discretion of the Member States.

19. Irrespective of the fact that the wording of the Belgian Constitution does not rule out the possibility of exceptions being made to the general requirement of the possession of Belgian nationality, it should be recalled, as the Court has constantly emphasized by its case-law, that recourse to provisions of the domestic legal systems to restrict the scope of the provisions of Community law would have the effect of impairing the unity and efficacy of that law and consequently cannot be accepted. That rule, which is fundamental to the existence of the Community, must also apply in determining the scope and bounds of Article 48 (4) of the Treaty. Whilst it is true that that provision takes account of the legitimate interest which the Member States have in reserving to their own nationals a range of posts connected with the exercise of powers conferred by public law and with the protection of general interests, at the same time it is necessary to ensure that the effectiveness and scope of the provisions of the Treaty on freedom of movement of workers and equality of treatment of nationals of all Member States shall not be restricted by interpretations of the concept of public service which are based on domestic law alone and which would obstruct the application of Community rules.

20. Finally, the Belgian and French Governments argue that the exclusion of foreign workers from posts which do not at the outset involve any participation in the exercise of powers conferred by public law becomes necessary, for instance, if recruitment takes place on the basis of service regulations and the holders of the posts are eligible for a career which in the higher grades involves duties and responsibilities involving the exercise of powers conferred by public law. The German and British Governments add that such an exclusion is also necessitated by the fact that flexibility in assignment to posts is a characteristic of the public

service and the duties and responsibilities of an employee may consequently change, not only on promotion, but also after a transfer within the same branch, or to a different branch at the same level.
21. Those objections do not however take account of the fact that, in referring to posts involving the exercise of powers conferred by public law and the conferment of responsibilities for the safeguarding of the general interests of the State, Article 48 (4) allows Member States to reserve to their nationals by appropriate rules entry to posts involving the exercise of such powers and such responsibilities within the same grade, the same branch or the same class.
22. The argument of the German Government on that last point, to the effect that any exclusion of nationals of other Member States from promotion or transfer to certain posts in the public service would have the effect of creating discrimination within such service, does not take into consideration the fact that the interpretation which that government puts on Article 48 (4), and which has the effect of debarring those nationals from the totality of posts in the public service, involves a restriction on the rights of such nationals which goes further than is necessary to ensure observance of the objectives of the provision as construed in the light of the foregoing considerations.
23. The Court takes the view that, in general, so far as the posts in dispute are concerned, information available in this case, which has been provided by the parties during the written and oral procedures, does not enable a sufficiently accurate appraisal to be made of the actual nature of the duties involved so as to make it possible to identify, in the light of the foregoing considerations, those of the posts which do not come within the concept of public service within the meaning of Article 48 (4) of the Treaty.
24. In these circumstances the Court does not consider itself to be in a position at this stage to give a decision on the allegation that the Belgian Government has failed to fulfil its obligations. Consequently it invites the Commission and the Kingdom of Belgium to re-examine the issue between them in the light of the foregoing considerations and to report to the Court, either jointly or separately, within a specified period, either any solution to the dispute which they succeed in reaching together or their respective viewpoints, having regard to the matters of law arising from this judgment. An opportunity will be provided for the interveners to submit their observations to the Court on any such report or reports at the appropriate time.

2. *Social security*

a. General

Article 51 EEC obliges the Council of the EEC to adopt such measures in the field of social security as are necessary to provide for the free movement of workers. This obligation was fulfilled by the enactment in 1958 of Council Regulations 3 and 4 (OJ 1958, 561/58, and OJ 1958, 597/58), both of them being modifications of the European Convention on the Social Security of Migrant Workers, signed on 9 December 1957 within the framework of the ECSC. Regulation 3 contained substantive rules for the co-ordination of the social security systems and Regulation 4 (an implementing Regulation) provided administrative measures for the implementation of Regulation 3.

After 13 years of problems the Court of Justice was called upon to give preliminary rulings on many of the provisions of Regulation 3 and 4 and both Regulations were amended on very many occasions – Regulations 3 and 4 were replaced by Regulation 1408/71 (OJ 1971, L 149/1) and Regulation 574/72 (an implementing Regulation, OJ 1972 L 74/1). Both of these Regulations came into force in 1 October 1972.

The basic principle of the EEC social security Regulations is that, for the realisation of the purposes of Article 51 EEC Treaty, they only provide for a co-ordination of the national social security legislations, without either creating one European social security system (with European funds, European institutions etc.) or achieving a harmonization of the different national social security legislations. Although one does not aim at harmonization, the Regulations have a considerable influence in the national social security systems, banning discrimination between own nationals and nationals of other Member States and requiring them to relinquish certain territorial restrictions.

Regulation 1408/71 deals successively with three questions, namely:
1) the scope of application of the Regulations
2) the problem of the applicable legislation
3) specific provisions for the different branches of social security.

1) The scope of application

This matter is looked at from two aspects: namely, what kind of person is covered by the Regulations 1408/71 and 574/72 (personal scope) and what kind of law (material scope).

Concerning the personal scope, the Regulations make reference to 'workers'. The Court of Justice has decided that the concept of worker arises not from national law but from Community law. Without defining the term, the Court has interpreted this concept widely by saying that it refers to all those who, as such and under whatever description, are covered by the different national systems of social security (*Hoekstra-Unger case*). What does this expression mean exactly?

Some clearness was provided by a later case, the *Janssen case*. Here the Court decided that *independent* workers belong under the scope of application of the Regulations if they are affiliated to a social security system for all workers (wage-earners).

It follows that within the scope of application falls everyone, who *by way of his social insurance*, has to be regarded as a wage-earner, independently from the fact how he has to be qualified from the point of view of labour law. In other words, the regulations are covering all the persons who are given social protection identical or comparable to that of workers in the sense of labour law. So the Court seems to be giving more a definition of a 'social insured person' than a definition of worker. The (new) definition of worker in Article 1 sub a of Regulation 1408/71 corresponds with this jurisprudential development. The problem of distinction between those independent workers who belong under the scope of Regulation 1408/71 and those who do not, does no longer exist since – as from July 1982 – the scope of Regulations 1408/71 and 574/72 will be extended to independent workers (see for the Commission proposal: OJ 18-1-1978. (14)).

As regards the adjective 'migrant' (worker) the Court decided that it is not only the migrant worker stricto sensu (i.e. the worker who changes his residence) who comes within the personal scope, but also any worker who goes to another Member States for whatever reason – be it a family visit, holiday etc., (see *Unger Case* and *Hessische Knappschaft Case*).

In line with this jurisprudential development Regulation 1408/71 does not refer only to migrant workers but also to workers moving within the Community.

Concerning the material scope of application, the Regulations refer to all social security law within the EEC, regardless of the method of financing (by tax or by premiums) and regardless of whether it is a general system for all workers, or a specific system for a special group of workers (e.g. the system for miners in France). The European classification of the different branches of social security is mentioned in Article 4 of Regulation 1408/71.

Some exceptions are made for particular social security systems – such as those for civil servants, independent workers and also supplementary systems, which are mostly based on collective agreement (e.g. supplementary pensions). These types of systems do not belong under the material scope of the Regulations.

A special problem is the distinction between social security and social and medical aid, the latter not being regarded as social security and therefore not belonging under the material scope of the Regulations. The view of the Court of Justice is that social aid benefits are characterised both by the fact that the real criterion for application is the need for the benefit and that such benefit makes no demand for labour or insurance qualifications. Social security on the other hand makes no individual decisions – leaves no judgment margin to the executive body – and gives the person concerned a legally defined position.

However, difficulties in classification have arisen in connection with those legal systems which have legislation carrying the features of both social security and social aid. The Court has decided that those types of 'mixed' legislation belong under the material scope of the Regulations.

2) The applicable legislation

In order to prevent conflicts of laws or legal gaps within the co-ordination of the national social security systems, it is first of all necessary to determine that, given a social security situation with Community aspects, there is always a national legislation applicable and preferably that one only. The main principle of the Regulations on this point is that the legislation of the Member State where the worker is employed, is the law to be applied.

Although this principle does not seem to be very complicated, it has given rise to some difficulties. There are in fact two possible interpretations: the first being that there is an obligation on the Member State to apply its law without prohibiting the other Member States to apply their law, (the obligatory effect).

The alternative interpretation is that this principle indicates exclusively the law of the 'workland' as the applicable law, prohibiting the other Member States to apply their law (the exclusive effect). The theory of the obligatory effect is inspired by the idea that the worker should always be covered by a social security system, that of the exclusive effect by the idea of preventing double premium-levy.

In connection with the premium-levy the Court ruled that the determination of the applicable legislation (as regulated in Article 12 of Regulation No 3 and Article 13 of Regulation No 1408/71) has an exclusive effect, as follows from the *Perenboom-case* (Case 102/76, [1977] ECR 815):

'Both Article 12 of Regulation No 3 and Article 13 of Regulation No 1408/71 prevent the State of residence from requiring payment, under its social legislation, of contributions on the remuneration received by a worker in respect of work performed in another Member State and therefore subject to the social legislation of that State'.

This case certainly means a turn back in respect of earlier cases (*Nonnemacher*, Case 92/63, [1964] ECR p. 287 and *Van der Vecht*, Case 19/67, [1967] ECR p. 352), where double premium-levy was admitted, if it brought about a 'supplementary protection'.

The double premium-levy and the notion of 'supplementary protection' however gave rise to a lot of difficulties.

It is however quite probably that, when it concerns *benefits* of social security, the determination of the applicable legislation has on the contrary an *obligatory* effect. For a good understanding it is necessary here to realize that contribution and benefit are not always coupled in social security systems, in the sense that the payment of contributions is a necessary condition for the award of the benefit. Consequently, a prohibition of double premium-levy does not exclude the possibility of a cumulative benefit.

The principle of obligatory effect in respect of benefits, can be derived from the *Massonet-case*, which concerned Article 12 of Regulation No 3:
'That provisions, which is designed to settle conflicts of laws both positive and negative, which may arise in the field of the application of the regulation, does not authorize a national insurance either expressly or by implication to reduce the benefits which are due to a worker or those entitled under him under national legislation alone'.

It can be argued that, where the determination of an applicable legislation has also as object to settle positive conflicts of law (i.e. the situation that more than one Member State is able to apply its law), this determination has an exclusive effect, also in respect of benefits.

However, taking account of both the *Massonet-case* and the *Perenboom-case*, it is probable that the settling of positive conflicts of law only concerns the premium-levy and that the settling of negative conflicts of law (i.e. the situation that no Member State is able to apply its law) concerns both benefits and premium-levy.

However, to the main principle that the applicable law is the law of the workland, there exists a number of exceptions. Some exceptions are enumerated in Article 13, sub 2 (b), (c) and (d) of Regulation No 1408/71, (seamen, civil servants, workers called up for military service), others in Article 14 of Regulation No 1408/71 (detached workers, workers in international transport, commercial travellers working in two or more Member States). Special provisions have been made for all these categories because the 'workland principle' does not provide a satisfactory solution.

A very important exception is that of the detached worker, that is a worker who, because of his employer, is temporarily employed within the territory of another Member State. This worker is still subject, under certain conditions, to the law of the original Member State. The reason for this exception is to favour reciprocal economic penetration without administrative complications, which would be the case if the detached worker should be subject for a short period to the legislation of another country.

The question has arisen whether a worker, sent into another Member State by a secretarial bureau, should be considered as a detached worker in the sense of Article 14 sub 1 (a) of Regulation No 1408/71. The Court has answered this question positively, like in the case where the worker has merely been engaged to work in the territory of another Member State. (Manpower-case, 35/70, (1970) ECR, pp. 1255).

3) Specific provisions for the different branches of social security

Title III of Regulation No 1408/71 makes specific provisions in relation to each of the following branches of social security:
– sickness and maternity
– invalidity
– old age pensions and decease pensions
– labour-accidents and professional diseases
– death grants
– unemployment
– family allowances and children's supplements (including orphans' allowances.

These provisions start with the principle that there is a 'competent State', which is the State whose law is applicable in a certain situation as mentioned above. The competent State, however, may not always be the only Member State involved if a social security situation with Community aspects arises.

According to the specific provisions other Member States may be involved as well *e.g.*:
a. In the case of sickness and maternity the benefits are almost always en-

joyed in the State of residence even when this is another one than the competent State (nevertheless the competent State must refund the amount of those benefits). The worker may also be permitted to enter a Member State other than his State of residence to undergo medical treatment which he cannot be given in his State of residence. It is also possible for urgent medical treatment to be given during a stay in a Member State other than the State of residence.
(Articles 19, 20 and 22 of Regulation 1408/71).
b. In the case of invalidity, decease and old-age pensions it may happen that the whole pension is not provided by the competent State but that several Member States contribute a portion thereof relative to the period of insurance in that particular Member State.
(Pro-rata tempore benefits, mentioned below).
c. In the case of unemployment it is permitted for the worker – with some restrictions – to go into another Member State for a maximum of three months to look for employment.
(Article 69 of Regulation 1408/71).
d. In the case of family allowances the worker is entitled to the allowances available under the law of the competent State, even where members of the family live within the territory of another Member State. However, if the competent State is France and the members of the family live within the territory of another Member State, the family allowances are given according to the law of that Member State. (France refunds the amount of the allowances).
(Articles 73 and 75 of Regulation No 1408/71).
But apart from these complications regarding the Member States involved, the specific provisions have certain features in common i.e., taking into account the period of insurance fulfilled in other Member States both to acquire the right to benefits (completing the qualifying period) and to calculate the amount of the benefits. The latter feature is only of importance in those branches of social security where the amount of the benefit is calculated according to periods of insurance – such as in the case of invalidity-, decease- and old-age pensions. In this field the regulations deal with 'pro-rata temporis' benefits. These benefits, also called 'Pro-rata benefits' are calculated as follows:

First of all, every Member State involved, (i.e., every Member State where the worker fulfilled periods of insurance or residence) calculates the amount of benefit to which the worker should have been entitled, if he had fulfilled all these periods only in that Member State. This amount is called the 'theoretical amount' (Article 46 par. 2 sub a of Regulation 1408/71).

After that, every Member State involved calculates the real amount of benefit which he must give, by taking into account such a part of his theoretical amount, as corresponds with the relation of the periods fulfilled under his legislation to the total of the periods, fulfilled within the Community. This amount is called the 'pro rata benefit'. (Article 64 par. 2 sub b of Regulation No 1408/71).

However, if the amount of benefit, obtained solely under the law of the Member State concerned (so completely independent from Community law) is higher than the amount of the pro-rata benefit, the first mentioned amount should be given by that Member State (Article 46 par. 1 of Regulation No 1408/71). This is the consequence of the principle enhanced by the Court of Justice, that social security rights, obtained solely under national law, should not be affected by Community law. This principle, which has already been mentioned above in relation to the determination of the applicable leglisation, has found a clear expression in the *Petroni-Case*, and has developed as one of the basic features of the coordination of the social security schemes within the Community.

b. Cases

(1) Hoekstra-Unger Case

Mrs. Hoekstra-Unger v. *Bestuur der Bedrijfsvereniging voor Detailhandel en Ambachten*; Case 75/63; Preliminary ruling of 19 March 1964; [1964] ECR 183; [1964] CMLR 330.

Facts:

By the terms of her contract of employment in Amsterdam, the appellant, in conformity with the relevant law (the 'Ziektewet') was compulsory insured against illness. The Ziektewet appears among the legislative provisions on social security in the Netherlands, which are listed in Appendix B of EEC Regulation No 3 and to which Regulation No 3 applies. When this compulsory insurance expired, the appellant was accepted by the respondent, as from 15 January 1962, as a beneficiary of the voluntary insurance provided for by that law. This arrangement was made under Article 64 (1) of the Ziektewet.

While visiting her parents in Münster on 25 February 1962 the appellant fell ill and required inmmediate medical treatment and was unable to carry on any professional activity. On 28 March 1962 she returned to the Netherlands, where, in accordance with the Ziektewet, she claimed insurance payments in respect of her inability to work.

By a decision of 18 April 1962, the respondent refused payment of the costs of the illness incurred while the appellant had been in Germany, from 25 February to 18 March 1962, on the grounds that, by Article 11 (2) (a) of the Regulation on the payment of the costs of illness voluntary insured persons have the right of payment of the costs of illness during residence abroad only if for the purpose of convalescence, they have been allowed so to reside abroad, in accordance with the circumstances provided in the regulatory provisions; and in the present case, no such authorization had been given.

The Raad van Beroep (social court of first instance) at Amsterdam found in favour of the respondent. The appellant appealed against this decision to the Centrale Raad van Beroep and, basing her argument on Article 19 (1) of Regulation No 3, submitted that the abovementioned provision did not apply to her case.

The Centrale Raad thereupon, requested the Court, under Article 177 of the EEC Treaty, to give a preliminary ruling interpreting the effect of Regulation No 3.

The Court held:

. . . . .

Articles 48 to 51 of the Treaty, by the very fact of establishing freedom of movement for 'workers', have given Community scope to this term.

If the definition of this term were a matter within the competence of national law, it would therefore be possible for each Member State to modify the meaning of the concept of 'migrant worker' and to eliminate at will the protection afforded by the Treaty to certain categories of persons.

Moreover, nothing in Articles 48 to 51 of the Treaty leads to the conclusion that these provisions have left the definition of the term 'worker' to national legislation. On the contrary, the fact that Article 48 (2) mentions certain elements of the concept of 'workers', such as employment and remuneration, shows that the Treaty attributes a Community meaning to that concept. Articles 48 to 51 would therefore be deprived of all effect and the abovementioned objectives of the Treaty would be frustrated if the meaning of such a term could be unilaterally fixed and modified by national law.

The concept of 'workers' in the said Articles does not therefore relate to national law, but to Community law.

The expression 'wage-earner or assimilated worker', used by Regulation No 3 has a meaning only within the framework and the limits of the concept of 'workers' provided for in the Treaty to the application of which this Regulation is limited. The said expression, which is intended to clarify the concept of 'workers' for the purposes of Regulation No 3, has therefore like that concept, a Community meaning. Even if, for the sake of argument, the expression 'wage-earner or assimilated worker' appeared in the legislation of each of the Member States, it could not possibly have a comparable meaning and rôle, so that it is impossible to establish the meaning by reference to similar expressions which may appear in national legislation. The concept of 'wage-earner' or 'assimilated worker' has thus a Community meaning, referring to all those who, as such and under whatever description, are covered by the different national systems of social security.

When national law offers to individuals who have been deprived of their employment the opportunity to adhere voluntarily to the social security system for wage-earners and such adherence has been proffered and accepted, this measure can be considered in certain circumstances as intending to protect the persons concerned in their capacity as 'workers' within the meaning of the Treaty and to confer on this protection the safeguards of Regulation No 3. This applies if the above-mentioned benefit is granted to the persons concerned on the grounds that they previously possessed the status of 'worker' and that they are capable of re-acquiring that status. Therefore, such persons may be considered as 'wage-earners or assimilated workers' within the meaning of Regulation No 3, there being no provision of this Regulation conflicting with this interpretation.

. . . . .

(2) Hessische Knappschaft Case

Hessische Knappschaft v. *Maison Singer et fils*; Case 44/65; Preliminary ruling of 9 December 1965; [1965] ECR 969; [1966] CMLR 94–95.

Facts:

On 24 September, Herr Gassner, a German national spending his holidays in France, was killed following a collision between his motorcycle and a cattle truck belonging to Maison Singer et Fils and being driven by a servant of that firm.

In its capacity as a social security organ, the Hessische Knappschaft paid to the successors of the victim benefits for which it had claimed repayment, in particular from Maison Singer, by virtue of a subrogation to the rights of the said successors, which took place by application of the German laws and Article 52 of Regulation No 3.

In a judgment of 4 October 1963, the Tribunal de Grande Instance of Strasbourg (Chambre Civile) dismissed the action brought against Maison Singer et Fils among other things on the ground that Regulation No 3 related to migrant workers, whereas the victim, according to the statements of the Hessische Knappschaft itself, was on holiday in France when he suffered the accident.

On appeal the Courd'Appel de Colmar asked for a preliminary ruling.

The Court held:

. . . . .

Under Article 51 of the Treaty, the Council 'shall ... adopt such measures in the field of social security as are necessary to provide freedom of movement for workers'. Article 51 is included in the Chapter entitled 'Workers' and situated in Title III ('Free movement of persons, services and capital') in Part Two of the Treaty ('Foundations of the Community'). The establishment of as complete a freedom of movement of workers as possible, which thus forms part of the 'foundations' of the Community, therefore constitutes the ultimate objective of Article 51 and thereby conditions the exercise of the power which it confers upon the Council.

It would not be in conformity with that spirit to limit the concept of 'worker' solely to migrant workers stricto sensu or solely to workers required to move for the purpose of their employment. Nothing in Article 51 imposes such distinctions, which would in any case tend to make the application of the rules in question impracticable.

On the other hand, the system adopted by Regulation No 3, which consists in abolishing as far as possible the territorial limitations on the application of the different social security schemes, certainly corresponds to the objectives of Article 51 of the Treaty.

(3) Costa Case

Mrs. Luciana Costs v. *Belgian State*; Case 39/74; Preliminary ruling of 13 November 1974; [1974] ECR 1260.

Facts:

Mrs. Luciana Mazzier, neé Costa, an Italian national married to a Belgian and residing in Belgium since July 1956, made an application to the Belgian authorities on 29 September 1971 for the payment of an allowance for the handicapped provided for under the Belgian Law of 27 June 1969. The Belgian State refused to grant Mrs. Mazzier the benefit of this law, on the grounds that the person interested cannot by reason of her nationality benefit from the provisions for equal treatment with the State's own nationals, otherwise than under the provisions of the European Interim Agreement of 11 December 1953 on Social Security Schemes in respect of old-age, invalidity and survivors, and that she does not satisfy the conditions of Article 2 of the said agreement. On 13 May 1972 Mrs. Mazzier appealed against this decision to the Tribunal de Travail of Liège, which Tribunal decided by judgment of 29 March 1974 to stay the proceedings and to refer among others the following preliminary question to the Court:

'Is the legislation on allowances for the handicapped (Law of 27 June 1969) social assistance legislation falling, ratione materiae, within the ambit of Article 2 (3) of Regulation No 3?'

The Court held:

. . . . .

6. Although it may seem desirable, from the point of view of the application of the Regulation, to distinguish between legislation concerning social security and assistance respectively, the possibility cannot be excluded that by reason of the persons covered thereby, its objectives and its manner of application, a legislation may at the same time fall within both categories, and thus not be amenable to any overall classification.
7. Whilst in some of its features, legislation concerning the grant of benefits to handicapped persons is akin to social assistance, especially when the need is the essential criterion in its implementation and there are no conditions as to periods of employment, of membership or of contributions, yet it is nevertheless close to social security to the extent that, departing from the consideration of each case on its merits – a characteristic feature of assistance – it confers upon beneficiaries a legally defined position.
8. In view of the widely-drawn definition of people entitled to benefit, such a legislation fulfils in fact a double function, which is on the one hand to guarantee a minimum income to handicapped persons who are entitled outside the social security system and, on the other hand, to provide supplementary means to persons entitled to social security benefits who are permanently incapacitated from work.
9. Under the provisions of Article 2 (1) (b) thereof, Regulation No 3 applies to 'invalidity benefits, including benefits granted for the purpose of maintaining or improving earning capacity'.
10. Under Article 1 (s) of the same Regulation, the term benefits shall be interpreted in the widest possible sense as mening all benefits 'including all fractions thereof chargeable to public funds, increments, revaluation allowances or supplementary allowances'.
11. Accordingly, a national legislation giving a legally protected right to a benefit for the handicapped falls, as regards the persons covered by Regulation No 3, within the area of social security within the meaning of Article 51 of the Treaty and of the Community Regulations thereunder.

(4) Janssen Case

Janssen v. *Landsbond der Christelijke Mutualiteiten*; Case 23/71; Judgment of 27 October 1971; [1971] ECR 863; [1972] CMLR 13.

Facts:

Mr. Janssen, a Belgian national now resident in Belgium, worked in France as a wage-earning agricultural worker from 16 October 1967 to 31 December 1968. During that period he was properly affiliated in that country to the Mutualité Sociale de la Somme. From 1 January 1970, Mr. Janssen stopped working in France and became a 'helper' on the agricultural holding of his father. He became affiliated, as from that date, as an independent worker, to the Alliance Nationale des Mutualités Chrétiennes. During that same month of January his wife went into hospital, for the birth of a baby, at the Bilzen Clinic. Mr. Janssen claimed from the above-mentioned insurance fund the repayment of the appropriate costs, but the fund rejected his claim on the ground that the insured had not completed the waiting period laid down in section 25 of the Arrêté Royal of 30 July 1964 on sickness insurance of independent workers (viz. six months). Mr. Janssen disputed the validity of the rejection citing EEC Regulations 3 and 4.

The Arbeidsrechtbank (Labour Court) of Tongeren, to which the dispute was taken, decided by judgment of 30 April 1971, to stay proceedings and request the Court of Justice under Article 177:

> to give a preliminary ruling on the interpretation of the words 'and assimilated', used in the EEC Regulations 3 and 4, and more particularly on the question whether helpers, in the sense of the Belgian social security legislation, considered as independent workers, are subject to the application of these regulations as being assimilated to workers contractually engaged to an employer.

The Court held:

. . . . .

3. The scope of Regulation No 3 is set out, as regards the persons to whom it applies, by Article 4, which provides that 'the provisions of this Regulation shall apply to wage-earners or assimilated workers who are or have been subject to the legislation of one or more of the Member States . . .'.
4. Reference is made to that provision in Article 1 of Regulation No 4, which was adopted to implement Regulation No 3.
5. This provisions is based on a wide conception of the persons to whom it applies inasmuch as it subjects to the provisions of the regulation not only wage-earners within the strict sense of the word but in addition all those assimilated to such workers.
6. In this respect, Article 4 follows a general tendency of the social law of Member States to extend the benefits to social security in favour of new categories of persons by reason of identical risks.
7. However, the exact measure of this assimilation can only be determined in terms of the national legislations to which Regulation No 3 refers.
8. Such an assimilation takes place on every occasion on which, as the result of the effect of national legislation, the provisions of a general scheme of social security are extended to a category of persons other than the wage-earners referred to by the said regulation, whatever may be the forms or methods employed by the national legislature.

9. The extension of these provisions must entitle those benefiting from it to a degree of protection against one or more risks comparable to that granted in respect of the risk concerned under the general scheme.

. . . . .

(5) Massonet Case

Caisse de pension des employés privés, Luxembourg v. *Helga Massonet*; Case 50/75; Preliminary ruling of 25 November 1975; [1975] ECR 1482.

Facts:

Mr. Bernard Weber of Luxembourg nationality, who was born on 25 July 1930, died on 14 September 1967 leaving a widow, Mrs. Helga Massonet and two children born in 1963 and 1965. He had worked from 1954 to 1962 in the Grand Duchy of Luxembourg where he paid contributions for 67 months; from October 1965 to 1 September 1967 he was affiliated to the Bundesversicherungsanstalt für Angestellte, Berlin, in respect of employment in Germany for 13 months.

The Bundesversicherungsanstalt granted the widow a pension with effect from 1 September 1967. It based the calculation of that pension on the Law known as the Angestelltenversicherungsgesetz and on Regulations Nos 3 and 4 (EEC) concerning social security for migrant workers. In the first place it decided that in accordance with paragraph 45 (2) of that Law, the widow had a right to an increased pension, known as 'erhöhte Hinterbliebenenrente' since the widow was responsible for at least one child who had a right to an orphan's pension. For that reason it took into account not only the insurance months actually completed by Mr. Weber, but also the number of months remaining between the date of his death and the date on which he would have attained 55 years of age, a period called the 'Zurechnungszeit', which is in the present case 215 months.

The Bundesversicherungsanstalt first determined the amount of the benefit to which Mrs. Weber would have been entitled if all the previous periods had been completed under its own legislation and then fixed the amount which it was its duty to pay in proportion to the duration of the periods actually completed under German legislation in relation to the total duration of the periods completed under the legislation of the two Member States concerned.

The Caisse de pension des employés privés Luxembourg, for its part granted Mrs. Weber a pension as from the same date. Whilst calculating advances of this pension it had taken into account the special increases provided for in case of premature death, in accordance with Article 4 of the Law of 25 October 1968 which was concerned with the reform of invalidity and death insurance within the contributory pension schemes. Later the Caisse de pension changed its mind and refused to include the special increase in question in the calculation of the Luxembourg pension. The latter are due to a widow who is bringing up a child and whose husband dies before attaining 55 years of age. They are granted for all complete calendar months remaining from the beginning of the entitlement to a pension until the completion of the fifty-fifth year of age. They are fixed at 1.6% of the normal monthly minimum social wage during the periods preceding the completion of the fifty-fifth year of age and at 1.4% of the minimum monthly social wage increasee by 20% for the subsequent period, subject to certain special provisions.

Mrs. Weber than made an appeal against the decision of the Caisse de Pension to the Conseil arbitral des assurances sociales which by a judgment of 20 December 1972 decided that she was entitled to the special increases. By order of 4 July 1974, the Conseil supérieur des assurances sociales upheld the judgment of the Conseil arbitral des assurances sociales.

The Caisse de pension appealed against that order to the Cour supérieure de Justice, which decided, in a judgment of 15 May to stay the proceedings and in accordance with Article 177 of the EEC Treaty to ask the Court of Justice to give a preliminary ruling among others on the following question:

1. (a) Can Regulation No 3 of the EEC concerning social security for migrant workers and more particularly Article 12, according to which wage-earners employed in the territory of a Member State are subject to the legislation of that State, affect (and if so in what conditions and to what extent) a provision of the domestic legislation of a Member State of the EEC providing that in case of successive, alternate or cumulative affiliation to contributory pension schemes, special increase in pension on the grounds of the premature death of an affiliated person must be paid by the pension institution to which the insured person was last affilated, and can it, where appropriate, have the effect of releasing the institution thus designated from the internal point of view by domestic legislation wholly or partially from its obligation to bear the cost of the special increases applicable?

   (b) What, more particularly, is the reply to be given when in a first State the right to the increase is acquired solely under domestic legislation and without its being necessary to have recourse to the process known as aggregation, whilst in a second State in which there has been later affiliation, the right is available only through recourse to aggregation, it being furthermore established that the amount of the increase to be paid by the social institution of the first State is not dependent upon the duration of affiliation but is constituted by a fixed sum of money payable for each month still remaining until the time when the deceased person would have attained fifty-five years of age?

The Court held:

. . . . .

13. The first question asks whether Regulation No 3 and more especially Article 12 according to which wage-earners employed in the territory of one Member State shall be subject to the legislation of that State may affect a provision of the internal legislation of a Member State providing that in case of successive alternative or cumulative affiliations to contributory pensions schemes, special increases in pension because of the premature death of a person affiliated must be paid by the pensions institution to which the insured person was last affiliated, and, according to the circumstances, have the effect of freeing the institution thus designated at national level by national legislation, from its obligation to bear the relevant special increases.
14. More specifically it is asked what is the reply to be given when in a first State the right to the increase is acquired by virtue of national legislation alone, and without there being any need to have recourse to the so-called aggregation procedure, whilst in a second State in which there has been a subsequent affiliation, the right is acquired only through recourse to aggregation.
15. The purpose of Article 12 of Regulation No 3, according to which the worker is subject to the legislation of the State where he is employed, is to avoid any plurality or purposeless overlapping of contributions and liabilities which would result from the simultaneous or alternate application of several legislative systems and, moreover, preventing those concerned, in the absence of legislation applying to them, from remaining without protection in the matter of social security.
16. That provision, which is designed to settle conflicts of laws both positive and negative, which may arise in the field of the application of the regulation, does not authorize a national insurance institution either expressly or by implication to reduce the benefits which are due to a worker or those entitled under him under national legislation alone.

(6) Petroni Case

Mrs. Silvana Amarelli (née Petroni) v. l'Office National des pensions pour Travailleurs salariés; Case 24/75; Preliminary ruling of 21 October 1975; [1975] ECR 1159.

Facts:

Mr. Raffaele Petroni, an Italian national, worked for 17 years as a miner in Belgium and for seven years as an employed person in Italy. As from 1

January 1973 he was awarded in Belgium an old age pension which, calculated solely under Belgian legislation, would have amounted to Bfrs 34,358 per annum, whilst in his country of origin, to which he had returned, he received an old age pension granted under the general pension scheme which, after aggregation and apportionment, amounts to Lit 251,420 per annum.

When it came to calculating the Belgian pension, the competent institution, initially, in accordance with the first subparagraph of Article 46 (1) of Regulation No 1408/71, calculated the pension on the basis of Belgian law alone, which gave the figure quoted above. Then, in accordance with the second subparagraph of Article 46 (1), it calculated the same pension by aggregating the Belgian and Italian periods and apportioning them. That calculation produced a total amount (described by Article 46 (2) as the 'theoretical amount') of Bfrs 45,812 and an apportioned amount of Bfrs 32,450. In accordance with the last sentence of the second subparagraph of Article 46 (1) it was the higher amount (in the present case Bfrs 34,358) which was taken into consideration. However, to this amount the competent institution applied Article 46 (3), according to which the total sum of the Belgian pension and the Italian pension must be limited to the higher theoretical amount of the two pensions. These theoretical amounts, consisting of the aggregated total before apportionment were for the Italian pension Lit 465,920 and for the Belgian pension, Bfrs 45,812 that is, Lit 594,181. The total sum of the pensions cannot exceed the latter figure and as that total gave a result of Lit 445,623 (= Bfrs 34,358) + Lit 254,420 = Lit 697,043, the competent Belgian institute, relying upon the second subparagraph of Article 46 (3), reduced the Belgian pension correspondingly and put it at Bfrs 26,427.

Mr. Petroni's widow to whom that decision was notified on 13 February 1974, appealed against it on 20 February 1974. After the death of Mrs Petroni, her daughters continued the proceedings before the Belgian court with a view to establishing that since Mr. Petroni's right to the Belgian pension existed independently of the insurance periods completed by him in Italy, the reduction was unjustified and that Article 46 (3), at least if it is interpreted and applied as was done by the Belgian institution, is contrary to Article 51 of the Treaty.

The Tribunal du travail of Brussels, taking the view that the outcome of the proceedings depended upon a decision concerning the validity, and, if necessary the interpretation of a provision of Community law, decided by a judgment of 24 February 1975 to stay the proceedings and to make a reference to the Court of Justice of the European Communities in accordance with Article 177 of the EEC Treaty in respect of among others the following questions:
1. Is Article 46 (3) of Regulation No 1408/71 EEC of the Council in conformity with Article 51 of the Treaty of Rome of 25 March 1947 and must it therefore be applied by the relevant institutions of the Member States?
2. If the above question is answered in the affirmative is that provision applicable:
    (a) to a pension granted to a migrant worker on the basis of insurance periods which are not duplicated by any of the periods forming the

basis for calculating the pensions granted in other countries of the Community?

. . . . .

The Court held:

. . . . .

10. These questions ask whether Article 46 (3) of Regulation No 1408/71 of the Council is in conformity with Article 51 of the Treaty and, if so, whether it must be applied to the pension granted to a migrant worker on the basis of insurance periods not duplicated by any of the periods used as the basis for calculating the pension granted in other countries of the Community.
11. The regulations in the field of social security for migrant workers have as their basis, their framework and their bounds Articles 48 to 51 of the Treaty.
12. Article 51 requires the Council to adopt in the field of social security measures as are 'necessary' to provide freedom of movement for workers, providing for the aggregation, in particular for the purpose of acquiring and attaining and retaining the right to benefit and of calculating the amount of benefits, of all periods taken into account under the laws of the several countries.
13. The aim of Articles 48 to 51 would not be attained if, as a consequence of the exercise of their right to freedom of movement, workers were to lose advantages in the field of social security guaranteed to them in any event by the laws of a single Member State.
14. Article 51 of the Treaty deals essentially with the case in which the laws of one Member State do not by themselves allow the person concerned the right to benefits by reason of the insufficient number of periods completed under its laws, or only allow him benefits which are less than the maximum.
15. To remedy this situation it provides, in respect of a worker who has been successively or alternately subject to the laws of two or more Member States, for aggregation of the insurance periods completed under the laws of each of such States.
16. The aggregation and apportionment cannot therefore be carried out if their effect is to diminish the benefits which the person concerned may claim by virtue of the laws of a single Member State on the basis solely of the insurance periods completed under those laws, always provided that this method cannot lead to a duplication of benefits for one and the same period.
17. Aggregation is not applied even in cases where insurance periods completed in the State concerned coincide with insurance periods completed in another Member State.
18. That interpretation is expressly confirmed by Article 45 of Regulation

No 1408/71 according to which an institution of a Member State whose legislation makes the acquisition, retention or recovery of the right to benefits conditional upon the completion of periods of insurance or of residence shall take into account periods of insurance or of residence completed in other Member States only 'to the extent necessary'.
19. Thus, adopting Regulation No 1408/71, the Council intended to align the implemented rules which it lays down with the requirements of Article 51 of the Treaty.
20. Article 46 (3) appears to be a rule limiting overlapping and the Council, in the exercise of the powers which it holds under Article 51 concerning the coordination of the social security schemes of the Member States, has the power, in conformity with the provisions of the Treaty, to lay down detailed rules for the exercise of rights to social benefits which the persons concerned derive from the Treaty.
21. However, a limitation on the overlapping of benefits which would lead to a diminution of the rights which the persons concerned already enjoy in a Member State by virtue of the application of the national legislation alone is incompatible with Article 51.
22. It is therefore proper to conclude that Article 46 (3) is incompatible with Article 51 of the Treaty to the extent to which it imposes a limitation on the overlapping of two benefits acquired in different Member States by a reduction in the amount of the benefit acquired under national legislation alone.

(7) Pinna Case

Pietro Pinna v. *Caisse d'allocations familiates de la Savoie*; Case 41/84; Preliminary ruling of 15 January 1986: [1986] ECR 1.

Facts:

The French Cour de Cassation asks the Court to interpret Article 73 (2) of Regulation (EEC) No 1408/71 on the application of social security schemes to employed persons and their families moving within the Community, providing that: 'A worker subject to French legislation shall be entitled, in respect of members of his family residing in the territory of a Member State other than France, to the family allowances provided for by the legislation of the Member State in whose territory those members of the family reside. In particular the court making the reference wishes to know whether the provision is still valid.

The Court held:

19. As regards a migrant worker employed in one Member State but whose family resides in another Member States, Regulation No 1408/71 introduced a distinction between workers employed in France and workers

employed in other Member States. Article 73 (1) provides that a worker subject to the legislation of a Member State other than France is to be entitled to the family benefits provided for by the legislation of the first Member State for members of his family residing in the territory of another Member State as though they were residing in the territory of the first State. Article 73 (2) provides that (see *facts* above).

20. As regards the difference in treatment between workers to whom Article 73 (1) applies and workers subject to the arrangements laid down in Article 73 (2), it must be observed that Article 51 of the Treaty provides for the coordination, not the harmonization, of the legislation of the Member States. As a result, Article 51 leaves in being differences between the Member States' social security systems and consequently, in the rights of persons working in the Member States. It follows that substantive and procedural differences between the social security systems of individual Member States, and hence in the rights of persons working in the Member States, are unaffected by Article 51 of the Treaty.

21. Nevertheless, the achievement of the objective of securing free movement for workers within the Community, as provided for by Articles 48 to 51 of the Treaty is facilitated if conditions of employment, including social security rules, are as similar as possible in the various Member States. That objective will, however, be imperilled and made more difficult to realize if unnecessary differences in the social security rules are introduced by Community law. It follows that the Community rules on social security introduced pursuant to Article 51 of the Treaty must refrain from adding to the disparities which already stem from the absence of harmonization of national legislation.

22. Article 73 of Regulation No 1408/71 creates two different systems for migrant workers depending on whether they are subject to French legislation or to the legislation of another Member State. Accordingly, it adds to the disparities caused by national legislation, and, as a result, impedes the achievement of the aims set out in Articles 48 to 51 of the Treaty.

23. More specifically with regard to the assessment of the validity of Article 73 (2) itself, it must be stated that the principle of equal treatment prohibits not only overt discrimination based on nationality but all covert forms of discrimination which, by applying other distinguishing criteria, in fact achieve the same result.

24. That is precisely the case when the criterion set out in Article 73 (2) is used in order to determine the legislation applicable to the family benefits of a migrant worker. Although as a general rule the French legislation employs the same criterion to determine the entitlement to family benefits of a French worker employed in French territory, that criterion is by no means equally important for that category of workers, since the problem of members of the family residing outside France arises essentially for migrant workers. Consequently, the criterion is not of such a nature as to secure the equal treatment laid down by Article 48 of the Treaty and therefore may not be employed within the context of the coordination of national legislation which is laid down in Article 51 of

the Treaty with a view to promoting the free movement of workers within the Community in accordance with Artice 48.
25. It follows that Article 73 (2) of Regulation No 1408/71 is invalid in so far as it precludes the award to employed persons subject to French legislation of French family benefits for members of their family residing in the territory of another Member State.

3. Literature

M. Forde, 'Social assistance and the EEC's Regulations', LIEI 1978/1, 9.
M. Forde, 'The self-employed and the EEC social security rules', *The Industrial Law Journal* 1979, p. 1.
A. M. Govers, 'The material and personal applicational scope of EEC Regulation 1408/71', LIEI 1979/2, 65.
H. Knorpel, 'Social security cases in the Court of Justice of the European Communities 1978–1980', (1981) CMLRev. 579.
M. Morgan, 'EEC Social security of the migrant worker', 1980 NLJ, 731.
A. Page, 'The scope of community and national rules against the overlapping of social security benefits', (1980) CMLRev. 211.
P. Watson, 'Free movement of workers and social security', (1980) ELRev., 485.
D. Wyatt, 'The social security rights of migrant workers and their families', 1977 CML Rev. 411.

See Materials on the Law of the European Communities, Chapter Three. No. 26 Regulation No 1408/71. No. 27 Regulation No 574/72.

C. RIGHT OF ESTABLISHMENT AND THE FREEDOM TO PROVIDE SERVICES

(EEC Treaty Articles 52–66)

1. Right of establishment

a. Cases

(1) Costa – ENEL Case

For facts and references see at pages 114, 121, 161, 573.

The Court held:

. . . . .

On the interpretation of Article 53

By Article 53 the Member States undertake not to introduce any new restrictions on the right of establishment in their territories of nationals of other Member States, save as otherwise provided in the Treaty. The obligation thus entered into by the States simply amounts legally to a duty to not to act, which is neither subject to any conditions, nor, as regards its execution or effect, to the adoption of any measure either by the States or by the Commission. It is therefore legally complete in itself and is consequently capable of producing direct effects on the relations between Member States and individuals. Such as express prohibition which came into force with the Treaty throughout the Community, and thus became an integral part of the legal system of the Member States, forms part of the law of those States and directly concerns their nationals, in whose favour it has created individual rights which national courts must protect.

The interpretation of Article 53 which is sought requires that it be considered in the context of the Chapter relating to the right of establishment in which it accurs. After enacting in Article 52 that 'restrictions on the freedom of establishment of nationals of a Member State in the territory of another Member State shall be abolished by progressive stages', this chapter goes on in Article 53 to provide that 'Member States shall not introduce any new restrictions on the right of establishment in their territories of nationals of other Member States'. The question is, therefore, on what conditions the nationals of other Member States have a right of establishment. This is dealt with by the second paragraph of Article 52, where it is stated that freedom of establishment shall include the right to take up and pursue activities as self-employed person and to set up and manage undertakings 'under the conditions laid down for its own nationals by the law of the country where such establishment is effected.

Article 53 is therefore satisfied so long as no new measure subjects the establishment of nationals of other Member States to more severe rules than those prescribed for nationals of the country of establishment, whatever the legal system governing the undertaking.

. . . . .

(2) Reyners Case

Reyners v. *the Belgian State*; Case 2/74; Preliminary ruling of 21 June 1974; [1974] ECR 648; [1974] 2 CMLR 305.

Facts:

The plaintiff, born in Brussels of Dutch parents, has retained his Dutch nationality, although resident in Belgium, where he has been educated and been made Docteur en Droit Belge. It has not been possible for the plaintiff to be admitted to the practice of the profession of avocat in Belgium. The Belgian Code Judiciaire provides i.a. that no one may hold the title of avocat nor practice that profession unless he is a Belgian and holds the diploma of docteur en droit. Dispensations from the condition of nationality may be granted in cases determined by the King, on the advice of the General Council of the Ordre of avocats. Reynders has made several unsuccessful applications for dispensation from the condition of nationality. He finally applied to the Conseil d'Etat of Belgium, and the Conseil d'Etat stayed the proceedings and asked for a preliminary ruling.

Reynders invoked Articles 52, 54, 55 and 57 of the EEC Treaty.

The Court held:

. . . . .

24. The rule on equal treatment with nationals in one of the fundamental legal provisions of the Community.
25. As a reference to a set of legislative provisions effectively applied by the country of establishment to its own nationals, this rule is, by its essence, capable of being directly invoked by nationals of all Member States.
26. In laying down that freedom of establishment shall be attained at the end of the transitional period, Article 52 thus imposes an obligation to attain a precise result, the fulfilment of which had to be made easier by, but not made dependent on, the implementation of a programme of progressive measures.
27. The fact that this progression has not been adhered to leaves the obligation itself intact beyond the end of the period provided for its fulfilment.
28. This interpretation is in accordance with Article 8 (7) of the Treaty, according to which the expiry of the transitional period shall constitute the latest date by which all the rules laid down must enter into force and all the measures required for establishing the common market must be implemented.
29. It is not possible to invoke against such an effect the fact that the Council has failed to issue the directives provided for by Articles 54 and 57 or the fact that certain of the directives adtually issued have not fully attained the objective of non-discrimination required by Article 52.
30. After the expiry of the transitional period the directives provided for by the Chapter on the right of establishment have become superfluous with regard to implementing the rule on nationality, since this is henceforth sanctioned by the Treaty itself with direct effect.
31. These directives have however not lost all interest since they preserve an important scope in the field of measures intended to make easier the effective exercise of the right of freedom of establishment.

32. It is right therefore to reply to the question raised that, since the end of the transitional period, Article 52 of the Treaty is a directly applicable provision despite the absence in a particular sphere, of the directives prescribed by Articles 54 (2) and 57 (1) of the Treaty.
33. The Conseil d'Etat has also requested a definition of what is meant in the first paragraph of Article 55 by 'activities which in that State are connected, even occasionally, with the exercise of official authority'.
34. More precisely, the question is whether, within a profession such as that of avocat, only those activities inherent in this profession which are connected with the exercise of official authority are excepted from the application of the Chapter on the right of establishment, or whether the whole of this profession is excepted by reason of the fact that it comprises activities connected with the exercise of this authority.
35. The Luxembourg Government and the Ordre national des avocats de Belgique consider that the whole profession of avocat is exonerated from the rules in the Treaty on the right of establishment by the fact that it is connected organically with the functioning of the public service of the administration of justice.
36. This situation (is argued) results both from the legal organization of the Bar, involving a set of strict conditions for admission and discipline, and from the functions performed by the avocat in the context of judicial procedure where his participation is largely obligatory.
37. These activities, which make the advocate an indispensable auxiliary of the administration of justice, form a coherent whole, the parts of which cannot be separated.
38. The Plaintiff in the main action for his part, contends that at most only certain activities of the profession of avocat are connected with the exercise of official authority and that they alone therefore come within the exception created by Article 55 to the principle of free establishment.
39. The German, Belgian, British, Irish and Dutch Governments, as well as the Commission, regard the exception contained in Article 55 as limited to those activities alone within the various professions concerned which are actually connected with the exercise of official authority, subject to their being separable from the normal practice of the profession.
40. Differences exist, however, between the Governments referred to as regards the nature of the activities which are thus excepted from the principle of the freedom of establishment, taking into account the different organization of the professions corresponding to that of avocat from one Member State to another.
41. The German Government in particular considers that by reason of the compulsory connection of the Rechtsanwalt' with certain judicial processes, especially as regards criminal or public law, there are such close connections between the profession of Rechtsanwalt and the exercise of judicial authority that large sectors of this profession, at least, should be excepted from freedom of establishment.
42. Under the terms of the first paragraph of Article 55 the provisions of the

Chapter on the right of establishment shall not apply 'so far as any given Member State is concerned, to activities which in that State are connected, even occasionally, with the exercise of official authority'.
43. Having regard to the fundamental character of freedom of establishment and the rules on equal treatment with nationals in the system of the Treaty, the exceptions allowed by the first paragraph of Article 55 cannot be given a scope which would exceed the objective for which this exemption clause was inserted.
44. The first paragraph of Article 55 must enable Member States to exclude non-nationals from taking up functions involving the exercise of official authority which are connected with one of the activities of self-employed persons provided for in Article 52.
45. This need is fully satisfied when the exclusion of nationals is limited to those activities which, taken on their own, constitute a direct and specific connection with the exercise of official authority.
46. An extension of the exception allowed by Article 55 to a whole profession would be possible only in cases where such activities were linked with that profession in such a way that freedom of establishment would result in imposing on the Member State concerned the obligation to allow the exercise, even occasionally, by non-nationals of functions appertaining to official authority.
47. This extension is on the other hand not possible when, within the framework of an independent profession, the activities connected with the exercise of official authority are separable from the professional activity in question taken as a whole.
48. In the absence of any directive issued under Article 57 for the purpose of harmonizing the national provisions relating, in particular, to professions such as that of avocat, the practice of such profession remains governed by the law of the various Member States.
49. The possible application of the restrictions on freedom of establishment provided for by the first paragraph of Article 55 must therefore be considered separately in connection with each Member State having regard to the national provisions applicable to the organization and the practice of this profession.
50. This consideration must however take into account the Community character of the limits imposed by Article 55 on the exceptions permitted to the principle of freedom of establishment in order to avoid the effectiveness of the Treaty being defeated by unilateral provisions of Member States.
51. Professional activities involving contacts, even regular and organic, with the courts, including even compulsory cooperation in their functioning, do not constitute, as such, connection with the exercise of official authority.
52. The most typical activities of the profession of avocat, in particular, such as consultation and legal assistance and also representation and the defence of parties in court, even when the intervention or assistance of the

avocat is compulsory or is a legal monopoly, cannot be considered as connected with the exercise of official authority.
53. The exercise of these activities leaves the discretion of judicial authority and the free exercise of judicial power intact.
54. It is therefore right to reply to the question raised that the exception to freedom of establishment provided for by the first paragraph of Article 55 must be restricted to those of the activities referred to in Article 52 which in themselves involve a direct and specific connection with the exercise of official authority.
55. In any case it is not possible to give this description, in the context of a profession such as that of avocat, to activities such as consultation and legal assistance or the representation and defence of parties in court, even if the performance of these activities is compulsory or there is a legal monopoly in respect of it.

(3) Royer Case

Public prosecutor v. *Jean Noël Royer*; Case 48/75; Preliminary ruling of 8 April 1976; [1976] ECR 510; [1976] 2 CMLR 619.

Facts:

In pursuance of instructions from the Procureur Général of Liège concerning the suppression of gangsterism and the adoption of measures against international criminals, Mr. Jean Noël Royer, a tradesman of French nationality was, on 18 January 1972, 'detected' in Grâce-Hollogne since the month of November 1971 without having completed the administrative formalities of entry on the population register and that, in France, he had been prosecuted for various armed robberies committed between 1959 and 1966 and sentenced to two years' imprisonment for procuring.

On 24 January 1972, acting on the instructions from the general administration of the Sûreté, Aliens Department, the Belgian Police Judiciare served on Royer in order to leave the country on the ground that he was unlawfully resident there, the forbidding him to return.

In compliance with the order to leave the country, Royer went to Aachen where he remained until 10 February 1972.

The Belgian Police Judiciaire once again detected the presence of Royer in Grâce-Hollogne on 11 March 1972. The local Gendarmerie arrested him on 27 April 1972.

Royer was put under arrest for having disobeyed the order to leave the country and the prohibition on returning, and was handed over to the office of the Procureur Général and committed to prison on 18 April 1972.

In 1973 Royer was again summoned and charged before the Tribunal de première instance of Liège for having, between 10 February and 27 April 1972, re-entered and resided in Belgium without having been authorized by the Minister of Justice in the manner determined by the Royal Decree of 21 December 1965 relating to conditions of entry, of residence and establishment for aliens in Belgium.

Deciding that the case raised questions of the interpretation of various provisions of Community law on the freedom of movement for workers, on the right of establishment and on the freedom to provide services, the 11th Chamber of the Tribunal de première instance of Liège (tribunal correctionnel) in a judgment, the grounds of which were given at length, of 6 May 1975, decided, pursuant to Article 177 of the EEC Treaty, to stay the proceedings until the Court of Justice had given a preliminary ruling.

The Court held:

. . . . .

11. The facts submitted by the national court and the choice of the provisions of Community law of which it seeks interpretation allows of different hypotheses according to whether the accused falls within the provisions of Community law by virtue of an occupations which he carried out himself or by virtue of a post which he had himself found for or again as the husband of a person subject to the provisions of Community law because of her occupation so that the accused's position may be regulated by either:
    a) the chapter of the Treaty concerning workers and, more especially Article 48 which was implemented by Regulation (EEC) No 1612/68 of the Council of 15 October 1968 on freedom of movement for workers within the Community (OJ English Special Edition 1968 (II) p. 475) and Council Directive No 68/360/EEC or
    b) the chapters concerning the right of establishment and freedom to provide services, in particular Articles 52, 53, 56, 62 and 66 implemented by Council Directive No 73/148 of 21 May 1973 concerning the removal of restrictions on the movement and residence of nationals of the Member States within the Community for establishment and provision of services (OJ, L.172, p. 14).
12. Nevertheless comparison of these different provisions shows that they are based on the same principles both in so far as they concern the entry into and residence in the territory of Member States of persons covered by Community law and the prohibition of all discrimination between them on grounds of nationality.
13. In particular Article 10 of Regulation (EEC) No 1612/68, Article 1 of Directive No 68/360 and Article 1 of Directive No 63/148 extend in identical terms the application of Community law relating to entry into

the residence in the territory of the Member States to the spouse of any person covered by these provisions.
14. Further, Article 1 of Directive No 64/221 states that the directive shall apply to any national of a Member State who resides in or travels to another Member State of the Community either in order to pursue an activity as an employed or self-employed person or as a recipient of services, and his or her spouse and members of their family.
15. It is apparent from the foregoing that substantially identical provisions of Community law apply in a case such as the one at issue if there exists either with regard to the party concerned or his spouse a connection with Community law under any of the above-mentioned provisions.
16. The questions referred by the Tribunal de première instance will be answered in the light of these considerations and without prejudice to the national court's right to determine the situation before it with respect to provisions of Community law.

The first, second, third and fourth questions (source of rights) conferred by the Treaty in respect of entry into the residence in the territory of the Member States)

17. The first, second, third and fourth questions seek to determine, with particular regard to Article 48 of the Treaty and Directives Nos 64/221 and 68/360 the source of the right of any nationals of a Member State of enter into and reside in the territory of another Member State and the effect on the exercise of this right of powers exercised by the Member States with regard to the supervision of aliens.
18. More particularly, it is asked in this connection.
    (a) whether this right is conferred directly by the Treaty or other provisions of Community law or whether it only arises by means of a residence permit issued by the competent authority of a Member State recognizing the particular position of a national of another Member State with respect to Community law;
    (b) whether it is to be inferred from Article 4 (1) and (2) of Directive No 68/360 that Member States are obliged to issue a residence permit once the person concerned is able to produce proof that he or she is covered by the provisions of Community law;
    (c) whether the failure by a national of a Member State to comply with the legal formalities for the control of aliens constitutes in itself conduct endangering public policy or public security and whether such conduct may therefore justify a decision ordering expulsion or the provisional deprivation of an individual's liberty.
26. Article 4 of Directive No 68/360 provides that 'Member States shall grant the right of residence in their territory' to the persons referred to and further states that as 'proof' of this right an individual residence permit shall be issued.
27. Further the preamble to Directive No 73/148 states that freedom of establishment can be fully attained only 'if a right of permanent resid-

ence is granted to the persons who are to enjoy freedom of establishment' and that freedom to provide services entails that persons providing and receiving services should have 'the right of residence for the time during which the services are being provided'.

28. These provisions show that the legislative authorities of the Community were aware that, while not creating new rights in favour of persons protected by Community law, the regulation and directives concerned determined the scope and detailed rules for the exercise of rights conferred directly by the Treaty.

29. It is therefore evident that the exception concerning the safeguard of public policy and public health contained in Articles 48 (3) and 56 (1) of the Treaty must be regarded not as a condition precedent to the acquisition of the right of entry and residence but as providing the possibility, in individual cases where there is sufficient justification of imposing restrictions on the exercise of a right derived directly from the Treaty.

30. In view of these considerations the specific questions referred by the national court may be answered as follows.

31. It follows from the foregoing that the right of nationals of a Member State to enter the territory of another Member State and reside there for the purposes intended by the Treaty – in particular to look for or pursue an occupation or activities as employed or self-employed persons, or to rejoin their spouse or family – is a right conferred directly by the Treaty, or, as the case may be, by the provisions adopted for its implementation.

32. It must therefore be concluded that this right is acquired independent of the issue of a residence permit by the competent authority of a Member State.

33. The grant of this permit is therefore to be regarded not as a measure giving rise to rights but as a measure by a Member State serving to prove the individual position of a national of another Member State with regard to provisions of Community law.

. . . . .

(4) Thieffry Case

Jean Thieffry v. *Conseil de l'Ordre des Avocats à la Cour de Paris*; Case 71/76; Preliminary ruling of 28 April 1977; [1977] ECR 776; [1977] 2 CMLR 373.

Facts:

See judgment below.

The Court held:

. . . . .

7. Under Article 3 of the Treaty, the activities of the Community include, inter alia, the abolition of obstacles to freedom of movement for persons and services.
8. With a view to attaining this objective, the first paragraph of Article 52 provides that restrictions on the freedom of establishment of nationals of a Member State shall be abolished by progressive stages in the course of the transitional period.
9. Under the second paragraph of the same article, freedom of establishment includes the right to take up activities as self-employed persons, under the conditions laid down for its own nationals by the law of the country where such establishment is effected.
10. Article 53 emphasizes the irreversible nature of the liberalization achieved in this regard at any give time, by providing that Member States shall not introduce any new restrictions on the right of establishment in their territories of nationals of other Member States.
11. With a view to making it easier for persons to take up and pursue activities as self-employed persons, Article 57 assigns to the Council the duty of issuing directives concerning, first, the mutual recognition of diplomas, and secondly, the coordination of the provisions laid down by law or administrative action in Member States concerning the taking up and pursuit of activities as self-employed persons.
12. That article is therefore directed toward reconciling freedom of establishment with the application of national professional rules justified by the general good, in particular rules relating to organization, qualifications, professional ethics, supervisions and liability, provided that such application is effected without discrimination.
13. In the General Programme for the abolition of restrictions on freedom of establishment, adopted on 18 December 1961 pursuant to Article 54 of the Treaty, the Council proposed to eliminate not only overt discrimination, but also any form of disguised discrimination, by designation of Title III (B) as restrictions which are to be eliminated, 'Any requirements imposed, pursuant to any provision laid down by law, regulation or administrative action or in consequence of any administrative practice, in respect of the taking up or pursuit of an activity as self-employed person where, although applicable irrespective of nationality, their effect is exclusively or principally to hinder the taking up or pursuit of such activity by foreign nationals' (OJ English Special Edition, Second Series, IX, p. 8).
14. In the context of the abolition of restrictions on freedom of establishment that programme provides useful guidance for the implementation of the relevant provisions of the Treaty.

15. It follows from the provisions cited taken as a whole that freedom of establishment, subject to observance of professional rules justified by the general good, is one of the objectives of the Treaty.
16. In so far as Community law makes no special provision, these objectives may be attained by measures enacted by the Member States, which under Article 5 of the Treaty are bound to take 'all appropriate measures, whether general or particular, to ensure fulfilment of the obligations arising out if this Treaty or resulting from action taken by the institutions of the Community', and to abstain 'from any measure which could jeopardize the attainment of the objectives of this Treaty'.
17. Consequently, if the freedom of establishment provided for by Article 52 can be ensured in a Member State either under the provisions of the laws and regulations in force, or by virtue of the practices of the public service or of professional bodies, a person subject to Community law cannot be denied the practical benefit of that freedom solely by virtue of the fact that, for a particular profession, the directives provided for by Article 57 of the Treaty have not yet been adopted.
18. Since the practical enjoyment of freedom of establishment can thus in certain circumstances depend upon national practice or legislation, it is incumbent upon the competent public authorities – including recognized professional bodies – to ensure that such practice or legislation is applied in accordance with the objectives defined by the provisions of the Treaty relating to freedom of establishment.
19. In particular, there is an unjustified restriction on that freedom where, in a Member State, admission to a particular profession is refused to a person covered by the Treaty who holds a diploma which has been recognized as an equivalent qualification by the competent authority of the country of establishment and who furthermore has fulfilled the specific conditions regarding professional training in force in that country, solely by reason of the fact that the person concerned does not possess the national diploma corresponding to the diploma which he holds and which has been recognized as an equivalent qualification.
20. The national court specifically referred to the effect of a recognition of equivalence 'by the university authority of the country of establishment', and in the course of the proceedings the question has been raised whether a distinction should be drawn, as regards the equivalence of diplomas, between university recognition, granted with a view to permitting the pursuit of certain studies, and a recognition having 'civil effect', granted with a view to permitting the pursuit of a professional activity.
21. It emerges from the information supplied in this connection by the Commission and the governments which took part in the proceedings that the distinction between the academic effect of and the civil effect of the recognition of foreign diplomas is acknowledged, in various forms, in the legislation and practice of several Member State.
22. Since this distinction falls within the ambit of the national law of the different States, it is for the national authorities to assess the consequences

thereof, taking account, however, of the objectives of Community law.
23. In this connection it is important that, in each Member State, the recognition of evidence of a professional qualification for the purposes of establishment may be accepted to the full extent compatible with the observance of the professional requirements mentioned above.
24. Consequently, it is for the competent national authorities, taking account of the requirements of Community law set out above, to make such assessments of the facts as will enable them to judge whether a recognistion granted by a university authority can, in addition to its academic effect, constitute valid evidence of a professional qualification.
25. The fact that a national legislation provides for recognition of equivalence only for university purposes does not of itself justify the refusal to recognize such equivalence as evidence of a professional qualification.
26. This is particularly so when a diploma recognized for university purposes is supplemented by a professional qualifying certificate obtained according to the legislation of the country of establishment.
27. In these circumstances, the answer to the question referred to the Court should be that when a national of one Member State desirous of exercising a professional activity such as the profession of advocate in another Member State has obtained a diploma in his country of origin which has been recognized as an equivalent qualification by the competent authority under the legislation of the country of establishment and which has thus enabled him to sit and pass the special qualifying examination for the profession in question, the act of demanding the national diploma prescribed by the legislation of the country of establishment constitutes, even in the absence of the directives provided for in Article 57, a restriction incompatible with the freedom of establishment guaranteed by Article 52 of the Treaty.

. . . . .

(5) Patrick Case

Richard Hugh Patrick v. *Ministre des Affaires Culturelles*; Case 11/77; Preliminary ruling of 28 June 1977; [1977] ECR 1205; [1977] 2 CMLR 523.

Facts:

Article 2 (2) of the French law of 31 December 1940 governing the title and profession of architect provides as follows:
'Nationals of foreign countries shall be authorized to practice the profession of architect in France subject to the conditions of reciprocity laid down

by diplomatic conventions and to production of a certificate equivalent to the certificate required for French architects.

... Foreigners not covered by the provisions of a convention may, exceptionally, receive the said authorization'.

The law adds that foreign architects who have been thus authorized shall not be members of the Order of Architects but shall nevertheless be subject to its discipline.

A decree of the Minister for Cultural Affairs dated 22 June 1964 recognized the certificates issued in the United Kingdom by the Architectural Association as an equivalent qualification within the meaning of the aforesaid Law although there is no reciprocal convention between the United Kingdom and France relating to the practice of the profession of architect.

Richard Patrick, a British subject, who has held the certificate of the Architectural Association since 29 May 1961, wished to transfer his office to France and applied for authorization to practice his profession there as an architect. His application was, however, rejected by decision of the Minister for Cultural Affairs dated 9 August 1973 on the ground that such authorization 'pursuant to the actual provisions of the Law of 31 December 1940 continues to be exceptional if there is no convention of reciprocity between France and the applicant's country of origin'.

On 8 October 1963 Patrick brought an application, based on Article 7 of the EEC Treaty, for annulment of this decision before the Tribunal Administratif Paris.

The Tribunal Administratif, Paris, held that the settlement of the dispute raised questions of interpretation of Community law, and, by order of Community law on 9 August 1973, the day on which the contested decision was taken, a British subject was entitled to invoke in his favour the benefit of the right of establishment to practice the profession of architect in a Member State of the Community'.

The Court held:

. . . . .

8. Under the provisions of Article 52 of the Treaty, freedom of establishment shall include the right to take up activities as self-empolyed persons and to pursue them 'under the conditions laid down for its own nationals by the law of the country where such establishment is effected'.
9. As the Court of Justice held in its judgment of 21 June 1974 (*Reyners* v. *Belgium*, Case 2/74 (1974) ECR 631), the rule on equal treatment with nationals is one of the fundamental legal provisions of the Community and, as a reference to a set of legislative provisions effectively applied by the country of establishment to its own nationals, this rule is, by its essence, capable of being directly invoked by nationals of all the other Member States.

10. In laying down that, in the case of the old Member States and their nationals, freedom of establishment shall be attained at the end of the transitional period, Article 52 thus imposes an obligation to attain a precise result, the fulfilment of which had to be made easier by, but not made dependent on, the implementation of a programme of progressive measures.
11. The fact that this progression has not been adhered to leaves the obligation itself intact beyond the end of the period provided for its fulfilment.
12. It is not possible to invoke against the direct effect of the rule on equal treatment with nationals contained in Article 52 the fact that the Council has failed to issue the directives provided for by Articles 54 and 57 or the fact that certain of the directives actually issued have not fully attained the objectives of non-discrimination required by Article 52.
13. After the expiry of the transitional period the directives provided for by the chapter on the right of establishment have become superfluous with regard to implementing the rule on nationality, since this is henceforth sanctioned by the Treaty itself with direct effect.
14. In the absence of transitional provisions concerning the right of establishment in the Treaty of Assession of 22 January 1972, the principle contained in Article 52 has, in the case of the new Member States and their nationals, been fully effective since the entry into force of the said Treaty, that is, since 1 January 1973.
15. Thus a Member State cannot, after 1 January 1973, make the exercise of the right to free establishment by a national of a new Member State subject to an exceptional authorization in so far as he fulfils the conditions laid down by the legislation of the country of establishment for its own nationals.
16. In this connection the legal requirement, in the various Member States, relating to the possession of qualifications for admission to certain professions constitutes a restriction on the effective exercise of the freedom of establishment the abolition of which is, under Article 47 (1), to be made easier by directives of the Council for the mutual recognition of diplomas, certificates and other evidence of formal qualifications.
17. Nevertheless, the fact that those directives have not yet been issued does not entitle a Member State to deny the practical benefit of that freedom to a person subject to Community law when the freedom of establishment provided for by Article 52 can be ensured in that Member State by virtue in particular of the provisions of the laws and regulations already in force.
18. The answer to the question referred to the Court must therefore be that, with effect from 1 January 1973, a national of a new Member State who holds a qualification recognized by the competent authorities of the Member State of establishment as equivalent to the certificate issued and required in that State enjoys the right to be admitted to the profession of architect and to practice it under the same conditions as nationals of the Member State of establishment without being required to satisfy any additional conditions.

(6) Auer Case

Ministre Public v. *Vincent Auer*; Case 136/78; Preliminary ruling of 7 February 1979; [1979] ECR 447; [1979] 2 CMLR 373.

Facts:

Mr. Auer, who was born in Austria, studied veterinary medicine first in Vienna (Austria), then in Lyon and finally at the University of Parma, where he was awarded the degree of doctor of veterinary medicine on 1 December 1956 and was granted a provisional practicing certificate by the competent authority on 11 March 1957.

Mr. Auer took up residence in Mulhouse in 1958 where he practiced veterinary medicine, first under the direction of a French veterinary surgeon and then on his own account, when he became a naturalized Frenchman he requested the application to himself of Decree 62–1481 of 27 November 1962 'relating to the medical and surgical treatment of animals by veterinary surgeons who have acquired or re-acquired French nationality'.

Section 1 of that decree provides that 'An authorization to undertake the medical and surgical treatment of animals may be granted by order of the Minister for Agriculture to veterinary surgeons who have acquired or re-acquired French nationality who do not hold the State doctorate referred to in section 340 of the Rural Code. A committee convened by the Minister for Agriculture shall examine the qualifications and deliver its opinion as to the professional competence and integrity of candidates'.

When the application was made to the Committee established by the 1962 decree it delivered on adverse opinion, mainly on the ground that the degree which the person concerned was awarded by the University of Parma was not equivalent to the French university degree of doctor of veterinary medicine.

Although each of Mr. Auer's applications was turned down he set himself up in practice as a veterinary surgeon and on 17 October 1974 was found guilty by the Tribunal de Grande Instance, Mulhouse, of unlawfully practicing as a veterinary surgeon and holding himself out as a veterinary surgeon. The same court against found him guilty of the same offences on 17 December 1977.

When the accused appealed to the Cour d'Appel, Colmar, that court, as it was of the opinion that the proceedings raised questions relating to the interpretation of Community law, referred to the Court of Justice the following question for a preliminary ruling:

'Does the fact that a person who has acquired the right to practice the profession of veterinary surgeon in a Member State of the European Community and who, after acquiring that right, has adopted the nationality of another Member State is forbidden to practice the said profession in the second Member State constitute a restriction on the freedom of establishment provided for by Article 52 of the Treaty of Rome and, in relation to the taking up of activities as self-employed persons, by Article 57 of that Treaty?'

The Court held:

. . . . .

10. The situation referred to by the national court is that of a natural person who is a national of the Member State in which he actually resides, and who is invoking the provisions of the Treaty relating to freedom of establishment with a view to being authorized to practice the profession of veterinary surgeon there, whereas, he does not possess the degrees required of nationals for that purpose but possesses degrees and qualifications acquired in another Member State which allow him to practice that profession in that other Member State.
11. It should also be stated that the question refers to the situation as it existed at a time when Article 57 (1) of the Treaty relating to mutual recognition of diplomas, certificates and other qualifications had not yet been applied as regards the practice of the profession of veterinary surgeon.
12. This matter has subsequently been dealt with by Council Directive No 78/1026 of 18 December 1978 concerning the mutual recognition of diplomas, certificates and other evidence of formal qualifications in veterinary medicine, including measures to facilitate the effective exercise of the right of establishment ana freedom to provide services (Official Journal No L 362, p. 1), supplemented by Council Directive No 78/1027 of the same date concerning the coordination of provisions laid down by law, regulation or administrative action in respect of the activities of veterinary surgeons (Official Journal No L 362, p. 7).
13. According to Article 18 of the first and Article 3 of the second of these directives Member States have a period of two years in which to bring into force the measures necessary to comply with them, dating from the notification of the directives.
14. Consideration must therefore be given to the question whether, and if so to what extent, nationals of the Member State in which they were established were entitled, at the time in question, to rely on the provisions of Articles 53 to 57 of the Treaty in situations such as those described above.
15. These provisions must be interpreted in the light of their place in the general structure of the Treaty and of its objectives.
16. Under Article 3 of the Treaty the activities of the Community with a view to the establishment of the Common Market include, inter alia, the abolition of obstacles to freedom of movement for persons and services.
17. In the words of Article 7 of the Treaty, within the scope of its application, any discrimination on grounds of nationality is prohibited.
18. Thus freedom of movement for persons is intended to contribute to the establishment of a common market, in which nationals of the Member States have opportunity to carry on their economic activities by estab-

lishing themselves or by providing services in any place within the territory of the Community.
19. As regards freedom of establishment, the realization of this objective is in the first place brought about in Article 52 of the Treaty which provides, first, that 'restrictions on the freedom of establishment of nationals of a Member State in the territory of another Member State shall be abolished by progressive stages in the course of the transitional period' and, secondly, that such freedom of establishment shall include the right to take up and pursue activities as self-employed persons, 'under the conditions laid down for its own nationals by the law of the country where such establishment is effected'.
20. In so far as it is intended to ensure, within the transitional period, with direct effect, the benefit of national treatment, Article 52 concerns only – and can concern only – in each member State the nationals of other Member States, those of the host Member State coming already, by definition, under the rules in question.
21. However, it may be seen from the provisions of Articles 54 and 57 of the Treaty that freedom of establishment is not completely ensured by the mere application of the rule of national treatment, as such application retains all obstacles other than those resulting from the non-possession of the nationality of the host State and, in particular, those resulting from the disparity of the conditions laid down by the different national laws for the acquisition of an appropriate professional qualification.
22. With a view to ensuring complete freedom of establishment, Article 54 of the Treaty provides that the Council shall draw up a general programme for the abolition of existing restrictions on such freedom and Article 57 provides that the Council shall issue directives for the mutual recognition of diplomas, certificates and other evidence of qualifications.
23. It follows from the general structure both of the General Programmes of 18 December 1961, drawn up in implementation of Articles 54 and 63 of the Treaty (Official Journal, English Special Edition, Second Series, IX, pp. 3 and 7) and of the directives issued in implementation of those programmes, that the field of application, ratione personae, of the measures for securing freedom of establishment and freedom to provide services is to be determined on each occasion without distinction based on the nationality of those concerned.
24. This idea, in particular to the extent to which it relates to the effects of mutual recognition of diplomas, certificates and other qualifications, is in conformity with the general rule set out in Article 7 of the Treaty according to which, within the scope of application of the Treaty, any discrimination on grounds of nationality is prohibited.
25. Moreover, in so far as the practice of the profession of veterinary surgeon is concerned, this idea was fully confirmed by a declaration concerning the definition of the persons covered by the directives, which was recorded in the minutes of the meeting of the Council during which the directives relating to the mutual recognition of diplomas and the

co-ordination of provisions laid down by law, regulation or administrative action in respect of the activities of veterinary surgeons were adopted.

26. That declaration states that: 'The Council reaffirms that it is to be understood that freedom of establishment, particularly for the holders of certificates obtained in other Member States, must be accorded on the same terms to nationals of other Member States and to nationals of the Member States concerned, as is the case with other directives.

27. It appears, both from the wording of the question referred to the Court and from the recitals to the decision of the national court, that that court would also like to know whether the fact that the person concerned has acquired French nationality by naturalization at a date subsequent to that on which he had obtained the Italian degrees and qualifications on which he relies, was of such a nature as to influence the reply to the question which it has put.

28. There is no provision of the Treaty which, within the field of application of the Treaty, makes it possible to treat nationals of a Member State differently according to the time at which or the manner in which they acquired the nationality of that State, as long as, at the time at which they rely on the benefit of the provisions of Community law, they possess the nationality of one of the Member States and that, in addition, the other conditions for the application of the rule on which they rely are fulfilled.

29. Hence, in assessing the rights of a national of a Member State, in periods both prior and subsequent to that referred to in the directives cited above, the date on which he acquired the status of a Member State is irrelevant as long as he possesses it at the time at which he relies upon the provisions of Community law, the enjoyment of which is linked to the status of a national of a Member State.

30. It follows from the considerations set out above the Article 52 of the Treaty must be interpreted as meaning that for the period prior to the date on which the Member States are required to have taken the measures necessary to comply with Council Directives Nos 78/1026 and 78/1027 of 18 December 1978, the nationals of a Member State cannot rely on that provision with a view to practicing the profession of veterinary surgeon in that Member State on any conditions other than those laid down by national legislation.

31. This answer in no way prejudges the effects of the above-mentioned directives from the time at which the Member States are required to have complied with them.

(7) Knoors Case

Knoors v. *Staatssecretaris voor Economische Zaken*; Case 115/78; Preliminary ruling of 7 February 1979; [1979] ECR 407; [1979] 2 CMLR 357.

Facts:

In the Netherlands the activities of self-employed persons in manufacturing and processing industries, in particular those of central heating contractor, plumber and water fitter, are governed by the Vestigingswet Bedrijven (Establishment of Undertakins Act) 1954.

Section 4 (1) of that Act provides that the practice, without an authorization from the relevant Chamber of Commerce and Industry, of certain trades in the sphere of self-employment in the processing industries may be forbidden by general provisions of public administration in the form of decrees relating to establishment.

As regards operations as a contractor in central heating, plumbing and water fitting, prohibitions on the practice of those trades without an authorization from the relevant Chamber of Commerce and Industry are laid down by section 7 of the Vestigingsbesluit verwarmings- en aanverwante bedrijven (Establishment of Heating and Associated Business Decree) 1960 and by sections 19 and 27 of the Vestigingsbesluit bouwnijverheidsbedrijven (Establishment in Building Trade Decree) 1958.

These decrees impose various conditions on the grant of an authorization from the Chamber of Commerce and Industry, in particular that of skill in the trade concerned.

Section 15 (1) of the Establishment Act 1954 provides that the Minister for Economic Affairs may grant exemption from a prohibition on the practice of a trade referred to in a decree relating to establishment 'if the provisions of a directive of the Council of the European Communities with regard to the establishment of natural persons and companies in the territory of one of the Member States of the European Economic Community or with regard to the provision of services by natural persons and companies in that territory require such exemption'.

In pursuance of that provision, J. Knoors, a Dutch national, residing at Dilsen/Stokkem (Belgium), where since 13 March 1970 he has been carrying on trade as a central heating contractor and sanitary contractor and plumber as the head of an independent undertaking. applied to the Kamer van Koophandel en Fabrieken voor de Mijnstreek (Chamber of Commerce and Industry for the Mining Region), whose office is at Heerlen, for an exemption from the prohibition on practicing in the Netherlands, as head and administrator of a business, the trades of central heating contractor, plumber and water fitter.

The Secretary of State for Economic affairs on 31 January 1977 sent Mr. Knoors a decision rejecting his application on the ground that, as a Dutch national, he could not be considered in the Netherlands as being a 'beneficiary' within the meaning of Article 4 (1) (a) of Council Directive 64/429 of 7 July 1964 concerning the attainment of freedom of establishment and freedom to provide services in respect of activities of self-employed persons in manufacturing and processing industries falling within ISIC Major Groups 23–40 (Industry and small craft industries) (1963–64, OJ Special Edition 155).

On 14 April 1977, Mr. Knoors had appealed from the decision of the Secretary of State for Economic Affairs of 31 January 1977 to the College van Beroep voor het Bedrijfsleven (administrative court of last instance in matters of trade and industry).

That court, by decision of 9 May 1978, stayed the proceedings and in pursuance of Article 177 of the EEC Treaty put the following question to the Court of Justice for a preliminary ruling:

'Must Directive 64/427/EEC of the Council of the European Economic Community of 7 July 1964 be interpreted as meaning that the expression 'beneficiaries' as referred to and as defined in Article 1 (1) of the directive also includes persons who possess and have always possessed solely the nationality of the host Member State?'

The Court held:

8. The definition of the persons to whom Directive No 64/427 applies depends, first, on the actual aim of that directive and, secondly, on the provisions which form its basis and its framework, namely the General Programmes for the abolition of restrictions on freedom to provide services and freedom of establishment of 18 December 1961 (OJ. English Special Edition, Second Series, IX, pp. 3 and 7 respectively) as well as on the relevent provisions of the Treaty.
9. Directive No 64/427 is intended to facilitate the realization of freedom of establishment and of freedom to provide services in a large group of trade activities relating to industry and small craft industries, pending the harmonization of the conditions for access to the trades in question in the various Member States, which is an indispensable precondition for complete freedom in this sphere.
10. More particulary that directive takes account of the difficulties resulting from the fact that, in certain Member States, certain of the activities in question may be freely taken up and pursued, whilst other Member States apply more or less strict conditions involving the possession of specialized training for admission to certain trades.
11. With a view to resolving the problems created by this disparity, Article 3 of the directive provides that, where, in a Member State, the taking up or pursuit of any activity referred to in the directive is dependent on the possession of certain qualifications, 'that Member State shall accept as sufficient evidence of such knowledge and ability the fact the activity in question has been pursued in another Member State'.
12. That article further states what is to be understood by 'pursuing' an activity, in particular by fixing minimum periods during which it must have been practiced.
13. As a counterpart, Article 5 of the same directive dealing with Member States in which the taking up of one of the activities in question is not subject to the possession of any given trade qualifications, governs the situation of persons coming from a Member State where such qualifications are required.

14. The persons to whom the directive applies are essentially defined by Article 1 (1) under which 'Member States, acting in accordance with the provisions hereinafter laid down, shall adopt the following transitional measures in respect of establishment or provision of services in their territories by natural persons or companies or firms covered by Title I of the general programmes (hereinafer called 'beneficiaries') wishing to engage in activities as self-employed persons in manufacturing and processing industries'.
15. The General Programme for the abolition of restrictions on freedom to provide services, in the first indent of Title I, defines as beneficiaries the 'nationals of Member States who are established within the Community', without making any distinction as to the nationality or residence of the persons concerned.
16. The same idea is expressed by Title I of the General Programme for the abolition of restrictions on freedom of establishment, which designates as beneficiaries, in the first and third indents, the 'nationals of Member States' without any distinctions as regards nationality or residence.
17. It may therefore be stated that Directive No 64/427 is based on a broad definition of the 'beneficiaries' of its provisions, in the sense that the nationals of all Member States must be able to avail themselves of the liberalizing measures which it lays down, provided that they come objectively within one of the situations provided for by the directive, and no differentiation of treatment on the basis of their residence or nationality is permitted.
18. Thus the provisions of the directive may be relied upon by the nationals of all the Member States who are in the situations which the directive defines for its application, even in respect of the State whose nationality they possess.
19. This interpretation is justified by the requirements flowing from freedom of movement for persons, freedom of establishment and freedom to provide services, which are guaranteed by Article 3 (c), 48, 52 and 59 of the Treaty.
20. In fact, these liberties, which are fundamental in the Community system, could not be fully realized if the Member States were in a position to refuse to grant the benefit of the provisions of Community law to those of their nationals who have taken advantage of the facilities existing in the matter of freedom of movement and establishment and who have acquired, by virtue of such facilities, the trade qualifications referred to by the directive in a Member State other than that whose nationality they possess.
21. In contesting this solution the Netherlands Government states, first, that the first paragraph of Article 52 provides for the abolition of 'restrictions on the freedom of establishment of nationals of a Member State' and, secondly, that according to the second paragraph of the same article, freedom of establishment is to include the right to take up activities as self-employed persons under the conditions laid down by the law of the country where such establishment is effected 'for its own nationals'.

22. It is claimed that those provisions of the Treaty show that the nationals of the host State are not regarded by the Treaty as being beneficiaries of the liberalization measures for which provision is made and that they therefore remain entirely subject to the provisions of their national legislation.
23. Moreover, the Netherlands Government draws attention to the risk that the nationals of a Member State might evade the application of their national provisions in the matter of training for a trade if they were authorized to avail themselves, as against their own national authorities, of the facilities created by the directive.
24. Although it is true that the provisions of the Treaty relating to establishment and the provision of services cannot be applied to situations which are purely internal to a Member State, the position nevertheless remains that the reference in Article 52 to 'nationals of a Member State' who wish to establish themselves 'in the territory of another Member State' cannot be interpreted in such a way as to exclude the benefit of Community law a given Member State's own nationals when the latter, owing to the fact that they have lawfully resided on the territory of another Member State and have there acquired a trade qualification which is recognized by the provisions of Community law, are, with regard to their State of origin, in a situation which may be assimilated to that of any other persons enjoying the rights and liberties guaranteed by the Treaty.
25. However, it is not possible to disregard the legitimate interest which a Member State may have in preventing certain of its nationals, by means of facilities created under the Treaty, from attempting wrongly to evade the application of their national legislation as regards training for a trade.
26. In this case, however, it should be borne in mind that, having regard to the nature of the trades in question, the precise conditions set out in Article 3 of Directive No 64/427, as regards the length of periods during which the activity in question must have been pursued, have the effect of excluding, in the fields in question, the risk of abuse referred to by the Netherlands Government.
27. Moreover, it should be emphasized that it is always possible for the Council, by virtue of the powers conferred upon it by Article 57 of the Treaty, to remove the causes of any abuses of the law by arranging for the harmonization of the conditions of training for a trade in the various Member States.
28. The answer to be given to the question referred to the Court should therefore be that Council Directive No 64/427 of 7 July 1964 laying down detailed provisions concerning transitional measures in respect of activities of self-employed persons in manufacturing and processing industries falling with ISIC Major Groups 23–40 (Industry and small craft industries) must be understood to mean that persons who possess the nationality of the host Member State are also 'beneficiaries' within the meaning of Article 1 (1) of the directive.

(8) Broekmeulen Case

Broekmeulen v. *The Huisarts Registratie Commissie (General Practitioners Registration Committee)*; Case 246/80; Preliminary ruling of 6 October 1981 1981 [ECR] 2311.

Facts:

A doctor of Netherlands nationality, Dr. Broekmeulen, who, having obtained a diploma of doctor of medicine, surgery and obstetrics at the Catholic University of Louvain, Belgium, was authorized by the Netherlands Secretary of State for Health and the Environment to practice medicine in the Netherlands; however the Huisarts Registratie Commissie (General Practitioners Registration Committee, hereinafter referred to as 'the Registration Committee') refused to register him as a Huisarts (General Practitioner).

The Court ruled:

Council Directive No 75/362 is to be interpreted as meaning that a national of a Member State who has obtained a diploma listed under Article 3 of the directive in another Member State and who, by that token, may practise general medicine in that other Member State is entitled to establish himself as a general practitioner in the Member State of which he is a national, even if that Member State makes entry to that profession by holders of diplomas of medicine obtained within tis own borders subject to additional training requirements.

(9) Klopp Case

Ordre des Avocats au Barreau de Paris v. *Klopp*: Case 107/83; Preliminary ruling of 12 July 1984; [1984] ECR 2971.

Facts:

See the judgment below.

The Court held:

1. By a judgment of 3 May 1983 which was received at the Court on 6 June 1983, the French Cour de Cassation [Court of Cassation] referred to the Court for a preliminary ruling under Article 177 of the EEC Treaty a question as to the interpretation of Article 52 *et seq.* of EEC Treaty in relation to access to the legal profession.

2. The question was raised in proceedings between the Ordre des Avocats au Barreau de Paris [the Paris Bar Association] and Mr. Klopp, a German national and a member of the Düsseldorf Bar. Mr. Klopp had applied to take the oath as an *avocat* and to be registered for the period of practical training at the Paris Bar whilst remaining a member of the Düsseldorf Bar and retaining his residence and chambers there.
3. By an order of 17 March 1981 the Council of the Paris Bar Association [hereinafter referred to as 'the Paris Bar Council'] rejected his application on the ground that although Mr. Klopp satisfied all the other requirements for admission as an *avocat*, especially as regards his personal and formal qualifications, he did not satisfy the provisions of Article 83 of Decree No 72/468 (Journal Officiel de la République Française of 11 June 1972) and Article 1 of the Internal Rules of the Paris Bar which provide that an *avocat* may establish chambers in one place only, which must be within the territorial jurisdiction of the *tribunal de grande instance* [regional court] with which he is registered.
4. Article 83 of the aforesaid decree provides that: 'An *avocat* shall establish his chambers within the territorial jurisdiction of the *tribunal de grande instance* with which he is registered'. Article 1 of the Internal Rules of the Paris Bar provides: 'An *avocat* of the Paris Bar must genuinely practise his profession,' that 'in order to practise the profession, he must be a registered legal practitioner or trainee and must have his chambers in Paris or in the *départements* of Hauts-de-Seine, Seine-Saint-Denis or Val-de-Marne' and that 'apart from his principal chambers be may establish a second set of chambers within the same geographical area.'
5. When the Cour d'Appel [Court of Appeal], Paris, set aside the decision of the Paris Bar Council by judgment of 24 March 1982 the Council appealed to the Court of Cassation, which, taking the view that the case raised a question concerning the interpretation of Community law, stayed the proceedings and requested the Court of Justice under Article 177 of the EEC Treaty to give a preliminary ruling:

> 'by way of interpretation of Article 52 *et seq*. of the Treaty of Rome, on whether, in the absence of any directive of the Council of the European Communities coordinating provisions governing access to and exercise of the legal profession, the requirement that a lawyer who is a national of a Member State and who wishes to practise simultaneously in another Member State must maintain chambers in one place only, a requirement imposed by the legislation of the country where he wishes to establish himself and intended to ensure the proper administration of justice and compliance with professional ethics in that country, constitutes a restriction which is incompatible with the freedom of establishment guaranteed by Article 52 of the Treaty of Rome.'

. . . . . .

17. It should be emphasized that under the second paragraph of Article 52 freedom of establishment includes access to and the pursuit of the activities of self-employed persons 'under the conditions laid down for its own nationals by the law of the country where such establishment is effected.' It follows from that provision and its context that in the absence of specific Community rules in the matter each Member State is free to regulate the exercise of the legal profession in its territory.
18. Nevertheless that rule does not mean that the legislation of a Member State may require a lawyer to have only one establishment throughout the Community territory. Such a restrictive interpretation would mean that a lawyer once established in a particular Member State would be able to enjoy the freedom of the Treaty to establish himself in another Member State only at the price of abandoning the establishment he already had.
19. That freedom of establishment is not confined to the right to creat a single establishment within the Community is confirmed by the very words of Article 52 of the Treaty, according to which the progressive abolition of the restrictions on freedom of establishment applies to restrictions on the setting up of agencies, branches or subsidiaries by nationals of any Member States established in the territory of another Member State. That rule must be regarded as a specific statement of a general principle, applicable equally to the liberal professions, according to which the right of establishment includes freedom to set up and maintain, subject to observance of the professional rules of conduct, more than one place of work within the Community.
20. In view the special nature of the legal profession, however, the second Member State must have the right, in the interests of the due administration of justice, to require that lawyers enrolled at a Bar in its territory should practise in such a way as to maintain sufficient contact with their clients and the judicial authorities and abide by the rules of the profession. Nevertheless such requirements must not prevent the nationals of other Member States from exercising properly the right of establishment guaranteed them by the Treaty.
21. In that respect it must be pointed out that modern methods of transport and telecommunications facilitate proper contact with clients and the judicial authorities. Similarly, the existence of a second set of chambers in another Member State does not prevent the application of the rules of ethics in the host Member State.
22. The question must therefore be answered to the effect that even in the absence of any directive coordinating national provisions government access to and the exercise of the legal profession, Article 52 *et seq.* of the EEC Treaty prevent the competent authorities of a Member State from denying, on the basis of the national legislation and the rules of professional conduct which are in force in that State, to a national of another Member State the right to enter and to exercise the legal profession solely on the ground that he maintains chambers simultaneously in another Member State.

(10) Daily Mail Case

The Queen v. H. M. Treasury and Commissioners of Inland Revenue ex parte Daily Mail; Case 81/87: Preliminary ruling of 27 September 1988 (not yet published).

Facts:

See the judgment below.
   The National court submitted i.a. the following questions:
1. Do Articles 52 and 58 of the EEC Treaty preclude a Member State from prohibiting a body corporate with its central management and control in that Member State from transferring without prior consent or approval that central management and control to another Member State in one or both of the following circumstances, namely where:
   (i) payment of tax upon profits or gains which have already arisen may be avoided;
   (ii) were the company to transfer its central management and control, tax that might have become chargeable had the company retained its central management and control in that Member State would be avoided?
2. Does Council Directive 73/148/EEC give a right to a corporate body with its central management and control in a Member State to transfer without prior consent or approval its central management and control to another Member State in the conditions set out in Question 1? If so, are the relevant provisions directly applicable in this case?

The Court held:

First question

11. The first question seeks in essence to determine whether Articles 52 and 58 of the Treaty give a company incorporated under the legislation of a Member State and having its registered office there the right to transfer its central management and control to another Member State. If that is so, the national court goes on to ask whether the Member State of origin can make that right subject to the consent of national authorities, the grant of which is linked to the company's tax position.

. . . . .

15. Faced with those diverging opinions, the Court must first point out, as it has done on numerous occasions, that freedom of establishment constitutes one of the fundamental principles of the Community and that

the provisions of the Treaty guaranteeing that freedom have been directly applicable since the end of the transitional period. Those provisions secure the right of establishment in another Member State not merely for Community nationals but also for the companies referred to in Article 58.

16. Even though those provisions are directed mainly to ensuring the foreign nationals and companies are treated in the host Member State in the same way as nationals of that State, they also prohibit the Member State of origin from hindering the establishment in another Member State of one of its nationals or of a company incorporated under its legislation which comes within the definition contained in Article 58. As a Commission rightly observed, the rights guaranteed by Articles 52 *et seq.* would be rendered meaningless if the Member State of origin could prohibit undertakings from Leaving in order to establish themselves in another Member State. In regard to natural persons, the right to leave their territory for that purpose is expressly provided for in Directive 73/148, which is the subject of the second question referred to the Court.

17. In the case of a company, the right of establishment is generally exercised by the setting-up of agencies, branches or subsidiaries, as is expressly provided for in the second sentence of the first paragraph of Article 52. Indeed, that is the form of establishment in which the applicant engaged in this case by opening an investment management office in the Netherlands. A company may also exercise its right of establishment by taking part in the incorporation of a company in another Member State, and in that regard Article 221 of the Treaty ensures that it will receive the same treatment as nationals of that Member State as regards participation in the capital of the new company.

18. The provision of United Kingdom law at issue in the main proceedings imposes no restriction on transactions such as those described above. Nor does it stand in the way of a partial or total transfer of the activities of a company incorporated in the United Kingdom to a company newly incorporated in another Member State, if necessary after winding-up and, consequently, the settlement of the tax position of the United Kingdom company. It requires Treasury consent only where such a company seeks to transfer its central management and control out of the United Kingdom while maintaining its legal personality and its status as a United Kingdom company.

19. In that regard it should be borne in mind that, unlike natural persons, companies are creatures of the law and, in the present state of Community law, creatures of national law. They exist only by virtue of the varying national legislation which determines their incorporation and functioning.

20. As the Commission has emphasized, the legislation of the Member States varies widely in regard to both the factor providing a connexion to the national territory required for the incorporation of a company and the question whether a company incorporated under the legislation of a Member State may subsequently modify that connecting factor. Certain

States require that not merely the registered office but also the real head office, that is to say the central administration of the company, should be situated on their territory, and the removal of the central administration from that territory thus presupposes the winding-up of the company with all the consequences that winding-up entails in company law and tax law. The legislation of other States permits companies to transfer their central administration to a foreign country but certain of them, such as the United Kingdom, make that right subject to certain restrictions, and the legal consequences of a transfer, particularly in regard to taxation, vary from one Member State to another.

21. The Treaty has taken account of that variety in national legislation. In defining, in Article 58, the companies which enjoy the right of establishment, the Treaty places on the same footing, as connecting factors, the registered office, central administration and principal place of business of a company. Moreover, Article 220 of the Treaty provides for the conclusion, so far as is necessary, of agreements between the Member States with a view to securing *inter alia* the retention of legal personality in the event of transfer of the registered office of companies from one country to another. No convention in this area has yet come into force.

22. It should be added that none of directives on the co-ordination of company law adopted under Article 54 (3) (g) of the Treaty deal with the differences at issue here.

23. It must therefore be held that the Treaty regards the differences in national legislation concerning the required connecting factor and the question whether – and if so how – the registered office or real head office of a company incorporated under national law may be transferred from one Member State to another as problems which are not resolved by the rules concerning the right of establishment but must be dealt with by future legislation or conventions.

24. Under those circumstances, Articles 52 and 58 of the Treaty cannot be interpreted as conferring on companies incorporated under the law of a Member State a right to transfer their central management and control and their central administration to another Member State while retaining their status as companies incorporated under the legislation of the first Member State.

25. The answer to the first part of the first question must therefore be that in the present state of Community law Articles 52 and 58 of the Treaty, properly construed, confer no right on a company incorporated under the legislation of a Member State and having its registered office there to transfer its central management and control to another Member State.

26. Having regard to that answer, there is no need to reply to the second part of the first question.

Second question

27. In its second question, the national court asks whether the provisions of

Council Directive 73/148 of 21 May 1973 on the abolition of restrictions on movement and residence within the Community for nationals of Member States with regard to establishment and the provision of services give a company a right to transfer its central management and control to another Member State.
28. It need merely be pointed out that regard that the title and provisions of that directive refer solely to the movement and residence of national persons and that the provisions of the directive cannot, by their nature, be applied by analogy to legal persons.
29. The answer to the second question must therefore be that Directive 73/148, properly construed, confers no right on a company to transfer its central management and control to another Member State.

2. Freedom to provide services

a. Cases

(1) Van Binsbergen Case

J. H. M. van Binsbergen v. *Bestuur van de Bedrijfsvereniging voor de Metaalnijverheid* (Board of Trade Association of the Engineering Industry); Case 33/74; Preliminary ruling of 3 December 1974; [1974] ECR, p. 1310; [1975]1 CMLR 298.

Facts:

The Raad van Beroep (court of first instance in social security matters) of Roermond dismissed an action brought by Van Binsbergen against the Board concerning the application of the Law on Unemployment (Werkloosheidswet).

By power of attorney dated 5 July 1972, Van Binsbergen authorised M. G. J. M. Kortmann, a Dutch national established in the Netherlands, to bring, on his behalf, an appeal against the decision before the Centrale Raad van Beroep (court of last instance in social security matters) and to represent him in the proceedings before that court.

On 30 November 1973, the Assistant Registrar of the Centrale Raad van Beroep informed Kortmann that he was no longer entitled to act as Van Binsbergen's representative ad litem or adviser. Dutch law provides that only persons established in the Netherlands can act as legal representatives or advisers; during the course of the proceedings Kortmann had transferred his habitual residence to Belgium.

Kortmann invoked Article 59 of the EEC Treaty providing for the progressive abolition, during the transitional period, of restrictions on freedom to provide services within the Community.

The Centrale Raad van Beroep decided to ask for a preliminary ruling.

The Court held:

. . . . .

The actual scope of Articles 59 and 60

6. The Court is requested to interpret Articles 59 and 60 in relation to a provision of national law whereby only persons established in the territory of the State concerned are entitled to act as legal representatives before certain courts or tribunals.
7. Article 59, the first paragraph of which is the only provision in question in this connection, provides that: 'Within the framework of the provisions set out below, restrictions on freedom to provide services within the Community shall be progressively abolished during the transitional period in respect of nationals of Member States who are established in a State of the Community other than that of the person for whom the services are intended'.
8. Having defined the concept 'services' within the meaning of the Treaty in its first and second paragraphs, Article 60 lays down in the third paragraph that, without prejudice to the provisions of the chapter relating to the right of establishment, the person providing a service may, in order to provide that service, temporarily pursue in activity in the State where the service is provided, under the same conditions as are imposed by that State on its own nationals.
9. The question put by the national court therefore seeks to determine whether the requirement that legal representatives be permanently established within the territory of the State where the service is to be provided can be reconciled with the prohibition, under Articles 59 and 60, on all restrictions on freedom to provide services within the Community.
10. The restrictions to be abolished pursuant to Articles 59 and 60 include all requirements imposed on the person providing the service by reason in particular of his nationality or of the fact that he does not habitually reside in the State where the service is provided, which do not apply to persons established within the national territory or which may prevent or otherwise obstruct the activities of the person providing the service.
11. In particular, a requirement that the person providing the service must be habitually resident within the territory of the State where the service is to be provided may, according to the circumstances, have the result

of depriving Article 59 of all useful effect, in view of the fact that the precise object of that Article is to abolish restrictions on freedom to provide services imposed on persons who are not established in the State where the service is to be provided.

12. However, taking into account the particular nature of the services to be provided, specific requirements imposed on the person providing the service cannot be considered incompatible with the Treaty where they have as their purpose the application of professional rules justified by the general good – in particular rules relating to organization, qualifications, professional ethics, supervision and liability – which are binding upon any person established in the State in which the service is provided, where the person providing the service would escape from the ambit of those rules being established in another Member State.

13. Likewise, a Member State cannot be denied the right to take measures to prevent the exercise by a person providing services whose activity is entirely or principally directed towards its territory of the freedom guaranteed by Article 59 for the purpose of avoiding the professional rules of conduct which would be applicable to him if he were established within that State; such a situation may be subject to judicial control under the provisions of the chapter relating to the right of establishment and not of that on the provision of services.

14. In accordance with these principles, the requirement that persons whose functions are to assist the administration of justice must be permanently established for professional purposes within the jurisdiction of certain courts or tribunals cannot be considered incompatible with the provisions of Articles 59 and 60, where such requirement is objectively justified by the need to ensure observance of professional rules of conduct connected, in particular, with the administration of justice and with respect for professional ethics.

15. That cannot, however, be the case when the provision of certain services in a Member State is not subject to any sort of qualification or professional regulation and when the requirement of habitual residence is fixed by reference to the territory of the State in question.

16. In relation to a professional activity the exercise of which is similarly unrestricted within the territory of a particular Member State, the requirement of residence within that State constitutes a restriction which is incompatible with Articles 59 and 60 of the Treaty if the administration of justice can satisfactorily be ensured by measures which are less restrictive, such as the choosing of an address for service.

17. It must therefore be stated in reply to the question put to the Court that the first paragraph of Article 59 and the third paragraph of Article 60 of the EEC Treaty must be interpreted as meaning that the national law of a Member State cannot, by imposing a requirement as to habitual residence within that State, deny persons established in another Member State the right to provide services, where the provision of services is not subject to any special condition under the national law applicable.

The question of the direct applicability of Articles 59 and 60

18. The Court is also asked whether the first paragraph of Article 59 and the third paragraph of Article 60 of the EEC Treaty are directly applicable and create individual rights which national courts must protect.
19. This question must be resolved with reference to the whole of the chapter relating to services, taking account, moreover, of the provisions relating to the right of establishment to which reference is made in Article 66.
20. With a view to the progressive abolition during the transitional period of the restrictions referred to in Article 59, Article 63 has provided for the drawing up of a 'general programme' – laid down by Council Decision of 18 December 1961 (OJ 1962, p. 32) – to be implemented by a series of directives.
21. Within the scheme of the chapter relating to the provision of services, these directives are intended to accomplish different functions, the first being to abolish, during the transitional period, restrictions on freedom to provide services, the second being to introduce into the law of Member States as set of provisions intended to facilitate the effective exercise of this freedom, in particular by the mutual recognition of professional qualifications and the coordination of laws with regard to the pursuit of activities as self-employed persons.
22. These directives also have the task of resolving the specific problems resulting from the fact that where the person providing the service is not established, on a habitual basis, in the State where the service is performed he may not be fully subject to the professional rules of conduct in force in that State.
23. As regards the phased implementation of the chapter relating to services, Article 59, interpreted in the light of the general provisions of Article 8 (7) of the Treaty, expresses the intention to abolish restrictions on freedom to provide services by the end of the transitional period, the latest date for the entry into force of all the rules laid down by the Treaty.
24. The provisions of Article 59, the application of which was to be prepared by directives issued during the transitional period, therefore became unconditional on the expiry of that period.
25. The provisions of that article abolish all discrimination against the person providing the service by reason of his nationality or the fact that he is established in a Member State other than that in which the service is to be provided.
26. Therefore, as regards at least the specific requirement of nationality or of residence, Articles 59 and 60 impose a well-defined obligation, the fulfilment of which by the Member States cannot be delayed or jeopardized by the absence of provisions which were to be adopted in pursuance of powers conferred under Articles 63 and 66.
27. Accordingly, the reply should be that the first paragraph of Article 59 and the third paragraph of Article 60 have direct effect and may therefore be relied on before national courts, at least in so far as they seek to

abolish any discrimination against a person providing a service by reason of his nationality or of the fact that he resides in a Member State other than that in which the service is to be provided.

(2) Walrave-Koch Case

Bruno Walrave and Norbert Koch v. *Association Union Cycliste Internationale, Koninklijke Nederlandse Wielren Unie and Federacion Espagnola Ciclismo*; Case 36/74; Preliminary ruling of 12 December 1974; [1974] ECR 1420; [1976]1 CMLR 320.

Facts:

It is the practice of the plaintiffs in the main action, both of whom are Dutch, to offer their services for remuneration to act as pacemakers on motorcycles in medium distance cycle races with so-called stayers, who cycle in the lee of the motorcylce. They provide these services under agreements with the stayers or the cycling association or with organizations outside the sport (sponsors). These competitions include the world championships, the rules of which, made by the first defendant, include a provisions that 'as from 1973 the pacemaker must be of the same nationality as the stayer'. The plaintiffs in the main action consider that this provision is incompatible with the Treaty of Rome in so far as it prevents a pacemaker of one Member State from offering his services to a stayer of another Member State.

The Court held:

. . . . .

3. These questions were raised in an action directed against the Union Cycliste Internationale and the Dutch and Spanish cycling federations by two Dutch nationals who normally take part as pacemakers in races of the said type and who regard the aforementioned provision of the rules of UCI as discriminatory.
4. Having regard to the objectives of the Community, the practice of sport is subject to Community law only in so far as it constitutes an economic activity within the meaning of Article 2 of the Treaty.
5. When such activity has the character of gainful employment or remunerated service it comes more particularly within the scope, according to the case, of Articles 48 to 51 or 59 to 66 of the Treaty.

6. These provisions, which give effect to the general rule of Article 7 of the Treaty, prohibit any discrimination based on nationality in the performance of the activity to which they refer.
7. In this respect the exact nature of the legal relationship under which such services are performed is of no importance since the rule of non-discrimination covers in identical terms all work or services.
8. This prohibition however does not affect the composition of sport teams, in particular national teams, the formation of which is a question of purely sporting interests and as such has nothing to do with economic activity.
9. This restriction on the scope of the provisions in question must however remain limited to its proper objective.
10. Having regard to the above, it is for the national court to determine the nature of the activity submitted to its judgment and to decide in particular whether in the sport in question the pacemaker and stayer do or do not constitute a team.

. . . . .

12. The questions raised relate to the interpretation of Articles 48 and 59 and to a lesser extent to Article 7 of the Treaty.
13. Basically they relate to the applicability of the said provisions to legal relationships which do not come under public law, the determination of their territoria scope in the light of rules of sport emanating from a world-wide federation and the direct applicability of certain of those provisions.
14. The main question in respect of all the Articles referred to is whether the rules of an international sporting federation can be regarded as incompatible with the Treaty.
15. It has been alleged that the prohibitions in these Articles refer only to restrictions which have their origin in acts of an authority and not to those resulting from legal acts of persons or associations who do not come under public law.
16. Articles 7, 48, 59 have in common the prohibition, in their respective spheres of application, of any discrimination on grounds of nationality.
17. Prohibition of such discrimination does not apply to the action of public authorities but extends likewise to rules of any other nature aimed at regulating in a collective manner gainful employment and the provisions of services.
18. The abolition as between Member States of obstacles to freedom of movement for persons and to freedom to provide services, which are fundamental objectives of the Community contained in Article 3 (c) of the Treaty, would be compromised if the abolition of barriers of national origin could be neutralized by obstacles resulting from the exercise of

their legal autonomy by associations or organizations which do not come under public law.
19. Since, moreover, working conditions in the various Member States are governed sometimes by means of provisions laid down by law or regulation and sometimes by agreements and other acts concluded or adopted by private persons, to limit the prohibitions in question to acts of a public authority would risk creating inequality in their application.
20. Although the third paragraph of Article 60, and Articles 62 and 64, specifically relate, as regards the provision of services, to the abolition of measures by the State, this fact does not defeat the general nature of the terms of Article 59, which makes no distinction between the source of the restrictions to be abolished.
21. It is established, moreover, that Article 48, relating to the abolition of any discrimination based on nationality as regards gainful employment, extends likewise to agreements and rules which do not emanate from public authorities.
22. Article 7 (4) of Regulation No 1612/68 in consequence provides that the prohibition on discrimination shall apply to agreements and any other collective regulations concerning employment.
23. The activities referred to in Article 59 are not to be distinguished by their nature from those in Article 48, but only by the fact that they are performed outside the ties of a contract of employment.
24. The single distinction cannot justify a more restrictive interpretation of the scope of the freedom to be ensured.
25. It follows that the provisions of Articles 7, 48 and 59 of the Treaty may be taken into account by the national court in judging the validity or the effects of a provision inserted in the rules of a sporting organization.
26. The national court then raises the question of the extent to which the rule on non-discrimination may be applied to legal relationships established in the context of the activities of a sporting federation of world-wide proportions.
27. The Court is also invited to say whether the legal position may depend on whether the sporting competition is held within or outside the Community.
28. By reason of the fact that it is imperative, the rule on non-discrimination applies in judging all legal relationships in so far as these relationships, by reason either of the place where they are entered into or of the place where they take effect, can be located within the territory of the Community.
29. It is for the national judge to decide whether they can be so located, having regard to the facts of each particular case, and, as regards the legal effect of these relationships, to draw the consequences of any infringement of the rule on non-discrimination.

. . . . .

31. As has been shown above, the objective of Article 59 is to prohibit in the sphere of the provision of services, inter alia, any discrimination on the grounds of the nationality of the person providing the services.
32. In the sector relating to services, Article 59 constitutes the implementation of the non-discrimination rule formulated by Article 7 for the general application of the Treaty and by Article 48 for gainful employment.
33. Thus, as has already been ruled (Judgment of 3 December 1974 in case 33/74, *Van Binsbergen*) Article 59 comprises, as at the end of the transitional period, an unconditional prohibition preventing in the legal order of each Member State, as regards the provision of services – and in so far as it is a question of nationals of Member States – the imposition of obstacles or limitations based on the nationality of the person providing the services.
34. It is therefore right to reply to the question raised that as from the end of the transitional period the first paragraph of Article 59, in any event in so far as it refers to the abolition of any discrimination based on nationality, create individual rights which national courts must protect.

(3) Van Wesemael Case

Ministère Public a.o. v. *Van Wesemael and Poupaert*; Cases 110 and 111/78; Preliminary ruling of 18 January 1979; [1979] ECR 48; [1979]3 CMLR 87.

Facts:

See the judgment below.

The Court held:

1. By two judgments both delivered on 21 March 1978 and received at the Court of Justice on 8 May 1978, the Tribunal de Première Instance de Tournai referred under Article 177 of the EEC Treaty several questions on the interpretation of Council Directive 67/43/EEC of 12 January 1967 (Official Journal, English Special Edition 1967, p. 3) and of certain provisions of the EEC Treaty relating to freedom to provide services.
2. These questions were raised in the context of two cases of criminal proceedings each against a person established in Belgium and a French employment agent for entertainers established in France, who are charged with having infringed the provisions of Articles 6 and 20 of the Belgian Arrêté Royal of 28 November 1975 relating to the operation of fee-charging employment agencies for entertainers.
3. It provides that, 'the operation of a fee-charging employment agency for

entertainers shall be subject to the grant of a licence by the Minister responsible for employment', and that, 'foreign employment agencies for entertainers may not, in the absence of a reciprocal convention between Belgium and their country, place anyone in employment in Belgium except through a fee-charging employment agency holding a licence'.
4. In each of the two cases the first accused in charged with having, for the purpose of engaging entertainers, resorted to a fee-charging employment agency situated in France the operator of which does not hold a licence in Belgium, and the second accused is charged with having placed persons in employment in that State without acting through an agency holding a licence in Belgium.
5. The accused pleaded that the aforementioned provisions of national law were incompatible with the Treaty in that they restricted the freedom to provide services referred to in Articles 52, 55, 59 and 60.

. . . . .

24. The first paragraph of Article 59 of the Treaty provides that '... restrictions on freedom to provide services within the Community shall be progressively abolished during the transitional period in respect of nationals of Member States ...' of the Community.
25. In laying down that freedom of provide services shall be attained by the end of the transitional period, that provision, interpreted in the light Article 8 (7) of the Treaty, imposes an obligation to attain a precise result, the fulfilment of which had to be made easier by, but no dependent on, the implementation of a programme of progressive measures.
26. If follows that the essential requirements of Article 59 of the Treaty, which was to be implemented progressively during the transitional period by means of the directives referred to in Article 63, became directly and unconditionally applicable on the expiry of that period.
27. Those essential requirements, which lay down the freedom to provide services, abolish all discrimination against the person providing the service by reason of his nationality or the fact that he is established in a Member State other than that in which the service is to be provided.
28. Taking into account the particular nature of certain services to be provided, such as the placing of entertainers in employment, specific requirements imposed on persons providing services cannot be considered incompatible with the Treaty where they have as their purpose the application of professional rules, justified by the general good or by the need to ensure the protection of the entertainer, which are binding upon any person established in the said State, in so far as the person providing the service is not subject to similar requirements in the Member State in which he is established.
29. However, when the pursuit of the employment agency activity at issue

is made subject to the State in which the service is provided to the issue of a licence and to supervision by the competent authorities, that State may not, without failing to fulfil the essential requirements of Article 59 of the Treaty, impose on the persons providing the service who are established in another Member State any obligation either to satisfy such requirements or to act through the holder of a licence, except where such requirement is objectively justified by the need to ensure observance of the professional rules of conduct and to ensure the said protection.
30. Such a requirement is not objectively justified when the service is provided by an employment agency which comes under the public administration of a Member State or when the person providing the service is established in another Member State and in that State holds a licence issued under conditions comparable to those required by the State in which the service is provided and his activities are subject in the first State to proper supervision covering all employment agency activity whatever may be the Member State in which the service is provided.

. . . . .

(4) Debauve Case

Procureur du Roi v. *Debauve*; Case 52/79; Preliminary ruling of 18 March 1980; [1980] ECR 853; [1981]2 CMLR 362.

Facts:

See the judgment below.

The Court held:

1. By a judgment of 23 February 1979, which was received at the Court on 3 April 1979, the Tribunal Correctionnel, Liège, referred two questions under Article 177 of the EEC Treaty for a preliminary ruling on the interpretation of Articles 59 and 60 of the Treaty with regard to certain problems concerning the transmission of commercial advertisements by cable television.
2. Those questions have arisen out of criminal proceedings brought before the Tribunal de Police, Liège, against three persons for infringement of a prohibition on the transmission of television broadcasts in the nature of commercial advertising and implicating two Belgian companies, vicariously liable in civil law for the three accused, who are officers of those companies. Those proceedings were begun on the particular

initiative of three associations representing consumers or cultural interests and by a certain number of natural persons who intervened as civil parties before the Tribunal de Police. When that court acquitted the accused and the companies liable in civil law, the three associations and certain other civil parties as well as the Ministère Public appealed to the Tribunal Correctionnel.
3. It is apparent from the file that the two companies in question provide, with the authority of the Belgian administration, a cable television diffusion service covering part of Belgium. Television sets belonging to subscribers to the service are linked by cable to a central aerial having special technical features which enable Belgian broadcasts to be picked up as well as certain foreign broadcasts which the subscribers cannot always receive with a private aerial, and which furthermore improve the quality of the pictures and sound received by the subscribers.
4. The prosecutions relate to the diffusion in Belgium by means of the system of cable television installed there of broadcasts effected by broadcasting stations established outside Belgium to the extent to which they contain commercial advertising material. Belgian legislation prohibits national radio and television broadcasting organizations, which have a legal monopoly on broadcasting, from making broadcasts in the nature of commercial advertising. In regard to cable television, Article 21 of the Royal Decree of 24 December 1966 (Moniteur Belge of 24 January 1967) also prohibits the transmission of broadcasts in the nature of commercial advertising.
5. The judgment making the reference states that in practice cable television distributors have disregarded that prohibition and have transmitted foreign programmes without excising advertisements; this practice has been tolerated by the Belgian Government, which has not imposed any penalty or withdrawn any authorizations; it also states that a large number of Belgian television viewers can pick up foreign programmes without the help of the relay systems set up by the cable television diffusion companies.
6. It is in the light of those factual circumstances that the Tribunal Correctionel has formulated its questions relating to Articles 59 and 60 of the Treaty. It believes that the application of the prohibition in question might have an effect upon the freedom to provide services at the Community level. In fact, according to the Tribunal, foreign broadcasting organizations derive an appreciable part of their revenue from advertising placed with them by advertisers so that the excision of advertisements in Belgium might cause those advertsiers to restrict or discontinue their commercial advertising; furthermore, advertisers, whether traders or manufacturers, established in neighbouring countries would obtain a more restricted coverage of the Belgian market to which they hitherto directed their advertising and on which they offered their services.

. . . . .

8. Before examining those questions the Court recalls that it has already ruled in its judgment of 30 April 1974 (Case 155/73, *Sacchi*, (1974) ECR 490) that the broadcasting of television signals, including those in the nature of advertisements, comes, as such, within the rules of the Treaty relating to services. There is no reason to treat the transmission of such signals by cable television any differently.
9. However, it should be observed that the provisions of the Treaty on freedom to provide services cannot apply to activities whose relevant elements are confined within a single Member State. Whether that is the case depends on findings of fact which are for the national court to establish. Since the Tribunal Correctionnel has concluded that in the given circumstances of this case the services out of which the prosecutions brought before it arose are such as to come under provisions of the Treaty relating to services, the questions referred to the Court should be examined from the same point of view.

. . . . .

11. According to the first paragraph of Article 59 of the Treaty restrictions on freedom to provide services within the Community shall be progressively abolished during the transitional period in respect of nationals of Member States of the Community. The strict requirement of that provision involve the abolition of all discrimination against a provider of services on the grounds of his nationality or of the fact that he is established in a Member State other than that where the service is to be provided.
12. In view of the particular nature of certain services such as the broadcasting and transmission of television signals, specific requirements imposed upon providers of services which are founded upon the application of rules regulating certain types of activity and which are justified by the general interest and apply to all persons and undertakings established within the territory of the said Member State cannot be said to be incompatible with the Treaty to the extent to which a provider of services established in another Member State is not subject to similar regulations there.
13. From information given to the Court during these proceedings it appears that the television broadcasting of advertisements is subject to widely divergent systems of law in the various Member States, passing from alomst total prohibition, as in Belgium, by way of rules comprising more or less strict restrictions, or systems affording broad commercial freedom. In the absence or any approximation of national laws and taking into account the considerations of general interest underlying the restrictive rules in this area, the application of the laws in question cannot be regarded as a restriction upon freedom to provide services so long as those laws treat all such services identically whatever their origin

or the nationality or place of establishment of the persons providing them.
14. A prohibition of the type contained in the belgian legislation referred to by the national court should be judged in the light of those considerations. It must be stressed that the prohibition on the transmission of advertisements by cable television contained in the Royal Decree referred to above cannot be examined in isolation. A review of all the Belgian legislation on broadcasting shows that prohibition is the corollary of the ban on the broadcasting of commercial advertisements imposed on the Belgian broadcasting organizations. This is also the way in which the judgment making the references sets out the relevant legislation, indicating that the Royal Decree prohibits the transmission of advertisements in order to maintain conformity with the scheme imposed on the national broadcasting organizations.
15. In the absence of any harmonization of the relevant rules, a prohibition of this type falls within the residual power of each Member State to regulate, restrict or even totally prohibit television advertising on its territory on grounds of general interest. The position is not altered by the fact that such restrictions or prohibitions extend to television advertising originating in other Member States in so far as they are actually applied on the same terms to national television organizations.
16. The answer must therefore be that Articles 59 and 60 of the Treaty do not preclude national rules prohibiting the transmission of advertisements by cable television – as they prohibit the broadcasting of advertisements by television – if those rules are applied without distinction as regards the origin, whether national or foreign, of those advertisements, the nationality of the person providing the service, or the place where he is established.

. . . . .

(5) Webb Case

Public Prosecutor v. *Alfred Webb*; Case 279/80; Preliminary ruling of 17 December 1971; [1981] ECR 3305.

Facts:

Alfred Webb, who is the manager of a company incorporated under English law and established in the United Kingdom, holds a licence under United Kingdom law for the provision of manpower. The company provides technical staff for the Netherlands in particular. The staff are recruited by the company and made available, temporarily and for consideration, to undertakings located in the Netherlands, no contract of employment being entered into as between such staff and the undertakings.

In February 1978 the company had on three occasions, not being in possession of a licence issued by the Netherlands Minister for Social Affairs, supplied workers for undertakings in the Netherlands, for considerations and otherwise than in pursuance of a contract of employment concluded with the latter, for the performance of work usually carried on in those undertakings.

The Court held:

. . . . .

7. The substance of the first question raised by the national court is whether the concept of 'services': contained in Article 60 of the Treaty extends to the supply of manpower within the meaning of the Netherlands legislation cited above.
8. According to the wording of the first paragraph of Article 60 of the Treaty the expression 'services' means services which are normally provided for remuneration, in so far as they are not governed by the provisions relating to freedom of movement for goods, capital and person. In the second paragraph of the article examples of activities covered by the expression 'services' are listed.
9. Where an undertaking hires out, for remuneration, staff who remain in the employ of that undertaking, no contract of employment being entered into with the user, its activities constitute an occupation which satisfies the conditions laid down in the first paragraph of Article 60. Accordingly they must be considered a 'service' within the meaning of that provision.
10. The French Government has sought to emphasize in this connection the special nature of the activity in question, which although covered by the expression 'services' in Article 60 of the Treaty ought to receive special consideration inasmuch as it may be covered as well both by provisions concerning social policy and by those concerning the free movement of persons. Whilst employees of agencies for the supply of manpower may in certain circumstances be covered by the provisions of Articles 48 to 51 of the Treaty and the Community regulations adopted in implementation thereof, that does not prevent undertakings of that nature which employ such workers from being undertakings engaged in the provision of services, which therefore come within the scope of the provisions of Article 59 et seq. of the Treaty. As the Court already declared, in particular in its judgment of 3 December 1974 (*Van Binsbergen*, Case 33/74 [1974] ECR 1299), the special nature of certain services does not remove them from the ambit of the rules on the freedom to supply services.

11. The reply to the first question must therefore be that the expression 'services' in Article 60 of the Treaty includes the provision of manpower within the meaning of the Wet op het ter Beschikking stellen van Arbeidskrachten.

(6) Coditel Case I

Coditel v. *Ciné Vog Films*; Case 62/79; Preliminary ruling of 18 March 1980; [1980] ECR 881.

Facts:

Ciné Vog Films, a cinematographic film distribution company, acquired under a contract made with the producer, the company La Boétie, the exclusive right to show the film 'Le Boucher' publicly in Belgium in all its versions in the form of cinerma performances and television broadcasts. At a later date La Boétie assigned the right to broadcast the film on television in the FRG to the German television broadcasting station. The Belgian cable television companies, Coditel, picked up directly on their aerial at their reception sites in Belgium the film 'La Boucher' when broadcasted in the FRG and distributed the film by cable to their subscribers. A Brussels Court decided subsequently that Coditel was guilty of infringing the copyright held by Ciné Vog. The cable television companies appealed against that judgment. They relied, interalia, upon the incompatibility of the exclusive right granted by La Boétie to Ciné Vog and the exercise of that right with the provisions of the EEC Treaty on competition (Article 85), on the one hand, and on the freedom to provide services (Article 59), on the other. Having decided that the submission based upon Article 59 raised the problem of the interpretation of that provision, the national court submitted the following questions:
'1. Are the restrictions prohibited by Article 59 of the Treaty establishing the European Economic Community only those which prejudice the provision of services between nationals established in different Member States, or do they also comprise restrictions on the provision of services between nationals established in the same Member State which however concern services the substance of which originates in another Member State?
2. If the first limb of the preceding question is answered in the affirmative, is it in accordance with the provisions of the Treaty on freedom to provide services for the assignee of the performing right in a cinematographic film in one Member State to rely upon his right in order to prevent the defendant from showing that film in that State by means of cable television where the film thus shown is picked up by the defendant in the said Member State after having been broadcast by a third party in another Member State with the consent of the original owner of the right?'

The Court held:

15. Whilst Article 59 of the Treaty prohibits restrictions upon freedom to provide services, it does not thereby encompass limits upon the exercise of certain economic activities which have their origin in the application of national legislation for the protection of intellectual property, save where such application constitutes a means of arbitrary discrimination or a disguished restriction on trade between Member States. Such would be the case if that application enabled parties to an assignment of copyright to create artificial barriers to trade between Member States.
16. The effect of this is that, whilst copyright entails the right to demand fees for any showing or performance, the rules of the Treaty cannot in principle constitute an obstacle to the geographical limits which the parties to a contract of assignment have agreed upon in order to protect the author and his assigns in this regard. The mere fact that those geographical limits may coincide with national frontiers does not point to a different solution in a situation where television is organized in the Member States largely on the basis of legal broadcasting monopolies, which indicates that a limitation other than the geographical field of application of an assignment is often impracticable.
17. The exclusive assignee of the performing right in a film for the whole of a Member State may therefore rely upon his right against cable television diffusion companies which have transmitted that film on their diffusion network having received it from a television broadcasting station established in another Member State, without thereby infringing Community law.
18. Consequently the answer to the second question referred to the Court by the Cour d'Appel, Brussels, should be that the provisions of the Treaty relating to the freedom to provide services do not preclude an assignee of the performing right in a cinematographic film in a Member State from relying upon his right to prohibit the exhibition of that film in that State, without his authority, by means of cable diffusion if the film so exhibited is picked up and transmitted after being broadcast in another Member State by a third party with the consent of the original owner of the right.

(7) Coditel Case II

Codital v. *Ciné Vog Films*; Case 262/81; Preliminary ruling of 6 October 1982; [1982] ECR 3381.

Facts:

See *Coditel I* above. The national court submitted the following question:
'Where a company which is the proprietor of the rights of exploitation of a

cinematographic film grants a contract to a company in another Member State an exclusive right to show that film in that State, for a specified period, is that contract liable, by reason of the rights and obligations contained in it and of the economic and legal circumstances surrounding it, to constitute an agreement, decision or concerted practice which is prohibited between undertakings pursuant to the first and second paragraphs of Article 85 of the Treaty or are those provisions inapplical 'e either because the right to show the film is part of the specific subject-matter of copyright and accordingly Article 36 of the Treaty would be an obstacle to the application of Article 85, or because of the right relied upon by the assignee of the right to show the film derives from a legal status which confers on the assignee protection *erga omnes* and which does not fall within the class of agreements and concerted practices referred to by the said Article 85?'

The Court held:

13. The distinction, implicit in Article 36, between the existence of a right conferred by the legislation of a Member State in regard to the protection of artistic and intellectual property, which cannot be affected by the provisions of the Treaty, and the exercise of such right, which might constitute a disguised restriction on trade between Member States, also applies where that right is exercised in the context of the movement of services.

(8) Luisi and Carbone Case

Luisi and Carbone v. *Ministero del Tesoro*; Cases 286/82 and 26/83; Preliminary Ruling of 31 January 1984; [1984] ECR 377.

Facts:

Graziani Luisi and Giuseppe Carbone, the plaintiffs in the main proceedings, Italian nationals residing in Italy, had both used abroad means of payment to an exchange value of Italian Lires that exceeded the limits to the export of foreign currency as authorized by the Italian legislation. The Ministero del Tesoro imposed on Luisi and Carbone for infringements of that legislation fines equal to the difference between the amount of currency exported and the maximum permitted limit (Lit 500,000 per annum).

Before the national court the plaintiffs contested the validity of the provisions of Italian legislation on which the fines were based, on the ground that those provisions were incompatible with Community law. In Case 286/82 the plaintiff in the main proceedings, Mrs Luisi, stated that she had exported the currency in question for the purpose of various visits to France and the Federal Republic of Germany as a tourist and in order to receive medical treatment in the latter country. In Case 26/83 the plaintiff in the main proceedings, Mr Carbone, stated that the foreign currency purchased by him had been used for a stay of three months in the Federal Republic of Germany as a tourist. Both plaintiffs submitted that the restrictions on the export of means of payment in foreign currency for the purpose of tourism or medical treatment were contrary to the provisions of the EEC Treaty relating to current payments and the movement of capital.

In its first order, dated 12 July 1982 (Case 286/82), the Tribunale di Genova stated that the transactions for which Italian law imposed a ceiling on transfers of foreign currency, namely tourism and travel for the purposes of business, education and medical treatment, fell within the invisible transactions listed in Annex III to the Treaty. Payments made in connection with such transactions therefore fell within the first subparagraph of Article 106 (3) of the Treaty, which required Member States to refrain from introducing any new restrictions between themselves, notwithstanding which the contested Italian legislation was adopted in 1974. It appeared appropriate, however, to determine the exact scope of that provision in relation to those governing movements of capital, in particular as regards the extent to which the latter provisions apply to physical transfers of bank notes.

Seeking information on that point, the Tribunale submitted the following questions to the Court for a preliminary ruling:

'In the case of exportation by residents travelling abroad for the purpose of tourism, business, education or medical treatment of foreign State and bank notes and credit instruments in foreign currency, do persons subject to Community law have the benefit of rights which Member States are obliged to respect by virtue of the 'standstill' provisions contained in the first subparagraph of Article 106 (3) of the EEC Treaty, regard being had to the fact that the transaction in question is one of the invisible transactions listed in Annex III to the said Treaty?

Or, by virtue of the reference made in the second subparagraph of Article 106 (3) of the Treaty, do the abovementioned circumstances, which, from an objective point of view, constitute a transfer of currency in cash, fall within the definition of the movements of capital which, pursuant to the provisions of Articles 67 and 68 of the Treaty and the related directives adopted by the Council on 11 May 1960 and 18 December 1962, are not subject to compulsory liberalization, with the result that control measures and penalties imposed by a Member State, in this case administrative penalties, are lawful?'

and

'In the case of exportation, by resident travellers going abroad for the purpose of tourism, of foreign bank notes, or credit instruments in foreign currency, do Community nationals benefit from rights which the Member States are bound to respect by virtue of the directly applicable provision contained in Article 106 (1) of the EEC Treaty, on the assumption that tourism is to be regarded as falling within the scope of the movement of services and that transfers of currency to cover tourist expenses are to be treated as current payments which must therefore be deemed to be liberalized in the same way as the services with which they are connected; or, if the transaction in question falls within the category of invisible transactions listed in Annex III to the EEC Treaty and, by virtue of the reference made by the second subparagraph of Article 106 (3), the transaction constitutes a transfer of cash, does it fall within the category of movements of capital which under the provisions of Articles 67 and 68 of the Treaty and of the relevant directives adopted by the Council on 11 May 1960 and 18 December 1962, need not necessarily be liberalized, with the result that in that sphere Member States may impose controls and penalties of an administrative nature?'

The Court held:

(a) 'Services' and 'invisible transactions'

9. According to Article 60 of the Treaty, services are deemed to be 'services' within the meaning of the Treaty where they are normally provided for remuneration, in so far as they are not governed by the provisions relating to freedom of movement for goods, capital and persons. Within the context of Title III of Part Two of the Treaty ('Free movement of persons, services and capital'), the free movement of persons includes the movement of workers within the Community and freedom of establishment within the territory of the Member States.
10. By virtue of Article 59 of the Treaty, restrictions on freedom to provide such services are to be abolished in respect of nationals of Member States who are established in a Member State other than that of the person for whom the service is intended. In order to enable services to be provided, the person providing the service may go to the Member State where the person for whom it is provided is established or else the latter may go to the State in which the person providing the service is established. Whilst the former case is expressly mentioned in the third paragraph of Article 60, which permits the person providing the service to pursue his activity temporarily in the Member State where the service is provided, the latter case is the necessary corollary thereof, which fulfils the objective of liberalizing all gainful activity not covered by the free movement of goods, persons and capital.
11. For the implementation of those provisions, Title II of the General Programme for the Abolition of Restrictions on Freedom to Provide Services (Official Journal, English Special Edition, Second Series IX, p. 3), which was drawn up by the Council pursuant to Article 63 of the Treaty on 18 December 1961, envisages *inter alia* the repeal of provisions laid down by law, regulation or administrative action which in any Member State govern, for economic purposes, the entry, exit and residence

of nationals of Member States, where such provisions are not justified on grounds of public policy, public security or public health and are liable to hinder the provision of services by such persons.

12. According to Article 1 thereof, Council Directive 64/221/EEC of 25 February 1964 on the coordination of special measures concerning the movement and residence of foreign nationals which are justified on grounds of publicy policy, public security or public health (Official Journal, English Special Edition 1963–1964, p. 117) applies *inter alia* to any national of a Member State who travels to another Member State 'as a recipient of services'. Council Directive 73/148/EEC of 21 May 1973 on the abolition of restrictions on movement and residence within the Community for nationals of Member States with regard to establishment and the provision of services (Official Journal 1973, L 172, p. 14) grants both the provider and the recipient of a service a right of residence coterminous with the period during which the service is provided.

13. By basing the General Programme for the Abolition of Restrictions on the Freedom to provide Services partly on Article 106 of the Treaty, its authors showed that they were aware of the effect of the liberalization of services on the liberalization of payments. In fact, the first paragraph of that article provides that any payments connected with the movement of goods or services are to be liberalized to the extent to which the movement of goods and services has been liberalized between Member States.

14. Among the restrictions on the freedom to provide services which must be abolished, the General Programme mentions, in section C of Title III, impediments to payments for services, particularly where, according to section D of Title III and in conformity with Article 106 (2), the provision of such services is limited only by restrictions in respect of the payments therefor. By virtue of section B of Title V of the General Programme, those restrictions were of be abolished before the end of the first stage of the transitional period, subject to a proviso permitting limits on 'foreign currency allowances for tourists' to be retained during that period. Those provisions were implemented by Council Directive 63/340/EEC of 31 May 1963 on the abolition of all prohibitions on or obstacles to payments for services where the only restrictions on exchange of services are those governing such payments (Official Journal, English Special Edition 1963–1964, p. 31). Article 3 of that directive also refers to foreign exchange allowances for tourists.

15. However, both the General Programme and the aforesaid directive reserve the right for Member States to verify the nature and genuineness of transfers of funds and of payments and to take all necessary measures in order to prevent contravention of their laws and regulations, 'in particular as regards the issue of foreign currency to tourists'.

16. It follows that the freedom to provide services includes the freedom, for the recipients of services, to go to another Member State in order to receive a service there, without being obstructed by restrictions, even in relation to payments and that tourists, persons receiving medical

treatment and persons travelling for the purpose of education or business are to be regarded as recipients of services.
17. Article 106 (3) provides for the progressive abolition of restrictions on transfers connected with the 'invisible transactions' listed in Annex III to the Treaty. As the national court correctly stated, that list includes, *inter alia*, business travel, tourism, private travel for the purpose of education and private travel on health grounds.
18. However, since that paragraph is merely subordinate to paragraphs (1) and (2) of Article 106, as is apparent from the second subparagraph thereof, it cannot be applied to the four types of transaction in question.

(9) Gravier Case

See at page 601.

(10) German insurance Case

Commission v. *Federal Republic of Germany*; Case 205/84; Judgment of 4 December 1986; [1986] ECR 3775.

Facts:

By an application lodged at the Court Registry on 14 August 1984 the Commission of the European Communities brought an action before the Court under Article 169 of the EEC Treaty for a declaration that,
(a) by applying the Versicherungsaufsichtsgesetz (Insurance Supervision Law) as amended by the Vierzehntes Änderungsgesetz (Fourteenth Law amending the Versicherungsaufsichtsgesetz) of 29 March 1983 which provides that where insurance undertakings in the Community wish to provide services in the Federal Republic of Germany in relation to direct insurance business, other than transport insurance, through salesmen, representatives, agents or other intermediaries, such persons must be established and authorized in the Federal Republic of Germany and which provides that insurance brokers established in the Federal Republic of Germany may not arrange contracts of insurance for persons resident in the Federal Republic of Germany with insurers established in another Member State, the Federal Republic has failed to fulfil its obligations under Articles 59 and 60 of the EEC Treaty;
(b) by bringing into force and applying the Vierzehntes Änderungsgesetz zum Versicherungsaufsichtsgesetz, which was intended to transpose into national Law Council Directive 78/473/EEC of 30 May 1978 on the coordination of Laws, regulations and administrative provisions relating to Community co-insurance, the Federal Republic of Germany has failed to fulfil its obligations under Articles 59 and 60 of the EEC Treaty and

under the aforementioned directive in so far as that law provides in relation to the Community co-insurance operations that the leading insurer (in the case of risks situated in the Federal Republic of Germany) must be established in that State and authorized there to cover the risk insured also as sole insurer;

(c) by the fixing through the Bundesaufsichtsamt für das Versicherungswesen (Federal Insurance Supervision Office), in the context of the transposition into national law of the aforementioned directive, excessively high thresholds in respect of the risks arising the connexion with fire insurance, civil liability aircraft insurance and general civil liability insurance, which may be the subject of Community co-insurance, so that as a result co-insurance as a service is excluded in the Federal Republic of Germany for risks below those thresholds, the Federal Republic of Germany has failed to fulfil its obligations under Articles 1 (2) and 8 of the said directive and under Articles 59 and 60 of the EEC Treaty.

The Court held:

2. The provision of services in the context of insurance

18. According to the first paragraph of Article 59 of the EEC Treaty, the abolition of restrictions on the freedom to provide services within the Community concerns all services provided by nationals of Member States who are established in a State of the Community other than that of the person for whom the services are intended. The first paragraph of Article 60 provides that services are to be considered to be 'services' within the meaning of the Treaty where they are normally provided for remuneration, in so far as they are not governed by the provisions relating to freedom of movement for goods, capital and persons.

19. Those articles require the abolition of all restrictions on the free movement of the provision of services, as thus defined, subject nevertheless to the provisions of Article 61 and those of Articles 55 and 56 to which Article 66 refers. Although those provisions are not at issue in these proceedings, the Italian Government has made the observation that, according to Article 61 (2), the liberalization of insurance services connected with movements of capital must be effected in step with the progressive liberalization of the movement of capital. In that respect it should however be pointed out that the First Council Directive for the implementation of Article 67 of the Treaty of 11 May 1960 (Official Journal, English Special Edition 1959–1962, p. 49) already provided that Member States were to grant all foreign exchange authorizations required for capital movements in respect of transfers in performance of insurance contracts as and when freedom of movement in respect of services was extended to those contracts in implementation of Articles 59 and 60 et seq. of the Treaty.

20. Although the rules on movements of capital are therefore not of such

a nature as to restrict the freedom to conclude insurance contracts in the context of the provision of services under Articles 59 and 60, it is, however, necessary to determine the scope of those articles in relation to the provisions of the Treaty on the right of establishment.
21. In that respect, it must be acknowledged that an insurance undertaking of another Member State which maintains a permanent presence in the Member State in question comes within the scope of the provisions of the Treaty on the right of establishment, even if that presence does not take the form of a branch or agency, but consists merely of an office managed by the undertaking's own staff or by a person who is independent but authorized to act on a permanent basis for the undertaking, as would be the case with an agency. In the light of the aforementioned definition contained in the first paragraph of Article 60, such an insurance undertaking cannot therefore avail itself of Articles 59 and 60 with regard to its activities in the Member State in question.
22. Similarly, as the Court held in its judgment of 3 December 1974 (Case 33/74, *van Binsbergen* v. *Bedrijfsvereniging Metaalnijverheid* [1974] ECR 1299) a Member State cannot be denied the right to take measures to prevent the exercise by a person providing services whose activity is entirely or principally directed towards its territory of the freedom guaranteed by Article 59 for the purpose of avoiding the professional rules of conduct which would be applicable to him if he were established within that State. Such a situation may be subject to judicial control under the provisions of the chapter relating to the right of establishment and not of that on the provision of services.
23. Finally, it should be mentioned that since the scope of Articles 59 and 60 is defined by reference to the places of establishment or of residence of the provider of the services and of the person for whom they are intended, special problems may arise where the risk covered by the insurance contract is situated on the territory of a Member State other than that of the policy-holder, as the person for whom the services are intended. The Court does not propose in these proceedings to consider such problems, which were not the subject of argument before it. The following examination therefore concerns only insurance against risks situated in the Member State of the policy-holder (hereinafter referred to as 'the State in which the service is provided').
24. It follows from the foregoing that in order to give judgment in these proceedings it is necessary to consider only the provision of services relating to contracts of insurance against risks situated in a Member State concluded by a policy-holder established or residing in that State with an insurer who is established in another Member State and who does not maintain any permanent presence in the first State or direct his business activities entirely or principally towards the territory of that State.

3. The conformity of the contested requirements with Articles 59 and 60 of the Treaty

25. According to the well-established case-law of the Court, Articles 59 and 60 of the EEC Treaty became directly applicable on the expiry of the transitional period, and their applicability was not conditional on the harmonization or the co-ordination of the laws of the Member States. Those articles require the removal not only of all discrimination against a provider of a service on the grounds of his nationality but also all restrictions on his freedom to provide services imposed by reason of the fact that he is established in a Member State other than that in which the service is to be provided.

26. Since the German Government and certain other of the Governments intervening in its support have referred to the third paragraph of Article 60 as a basis for their contention that the State of the person insured can also apply its supervisory legislation to insurers established in another Member State, it should be added, as the Court made clear in particular in its judgment of 17 December 1981 (Case 279/80, *Webb*, [1981] ECR 3305), that the principal aim of that paragraph is to enable the provider of the service to pursue his activities in the Member State where the service is given without suffering discrimination in favour of the nationals of the State. However, it does not follow from that paragraph that all national legislation applicable to nationals of that State and usually applied to the permanent activities of undertakings established therein may be similarly applied in its entirety to the temporary activities of undertakings which are established in other Member States.

27. The Court has nevertheless accepted, in particular in its judgments of 18 January 1979 (Joined Cases 110 and 111/78, *Ministère Public and Another* v. *van Wesemael and Others*, [1979] ECR 35) and 17 December 1981 (Case 279/80, *Webb*, cited above), that regard being had to the particular nature of certain services, specific requirements imposed on the provider of the services cannot be considered to be incompatible with the Treaty where they have as their purpose the application of rules governing such activities. However, the freedom to provide services, as one of the fundamental principles of the Treaty, may be restricted only by provisions which are justified by the general good and which are applied to all persons or undertakings operating within the territory of the State in which the service is provided in so far as that interest is not safeguarded by the provisions to which the provider of a service is subject in the Member State of his establishment. In addition, such requirements must be objectively justified by the need to ensure that professional rules of conduct are complied with and that the interests which such rules are designed to safeguard are protected.

28. It must be stated that the requirements in question in these proceedings, namely that an insurer who is established in another Member State, authorized by the supervisory authority of that State and subject to the supervision of that authority, must have a permanent establishment within the territory of the State in which the service is provided and that he must obtain a separate authorization from the supervisory authority of

that State, constitute restrictions on the freedom to provide services inasmuch as they increase the cost of such services in the State in which they are provided, in particular where the insurer conducts business in that State only occasionally.

29. It follows that those requirements may be regarded as compatible with Articles 59 and 60 of the EEC Treaty only if it is established that in the field of activity concerned there are imperative reasons relating to the public interest which justify restrictions on the freedom to provide services, that the public interest is not already protected by the rules of the State of establishment and that the same result cannot be obtained by less restrictive rules.

(a) The existence of an interest justifying certain restrictions on the freedom to provide insurance services.

30. As the German Government and the parties intervening in its support have maintained, without being contradicted by the Commission or the United Kingdom and Netherlands Governments, the insurance sector is a particularly sensitive area from the point of view of the protection of the consumer both as a policy-holder and as an insured person. This is so in particular because of the specific nature of the service provided by the insurer, which is linked to future events, the occurrence of which, or at least the timing of which, is uncertain at the time when the contract is concluded. An insured person who does not obtain payment under a policy following an event giving rise to a claim may find himself in a very precarious position. Similarly, it is as a rule very difficult for a person seeking insurance to judge whether the likely future development of the insurer's financial position and the terms of the contract, usually imposed by the insurer, offer him sufficient guarantees that he will receive payment under the policy if a claimable event occurs.

31. It must also be borne in mind, as the German Government has pointed out, that in certain fields insurance has become a mass phenomenon. Contracts are concluded by such enormous numbers of policy-holders that the protection of the interests of insured persons and injured third parties affects virtually the whole population.

32. Those special characteristics, which are peculiar to the insurance sector, have led all the Member States to introduce legislation making insurance undertakings subject to mandatory rules both as regards their financial position and the conditions of insurance which they apply, and to permanent supervision to ensure that those rules are complied with.

33. It therefore appears that in the field in question there are imperative reasons relating to the public interests which may justify restrictions on the freedom to provide services, provided, however, that the rules of the State of establishment are not adequate in order to achieve the necessary level of protection and that the requirements of the State in which the service is provided do not exceed what is necessary in that respect.

(b) The question of whether the public interest is already protected by the rules of the State of establishment.

34. The Commission and the United Kingdom and Netherlands Governments maintain that, in any event since the adoption of the First Co-ordination Directives, namely Directives 73/239 and 79/267, the supervision by the authorities of the State of establishment to a large extent meets the considerations of protection mentioned above.
35. In that respect it should be observed *in limine* that according to their preambles and the wording of their provisions, those two directives are intended to facilitate the setting-up of branches or agencies in a Member State other than that in which the head office is situated. They lay down rules governing the relationship between, on the one hand, the legislation and the supervisory authority of the State in which the head office is situated, and, on the other hand, the legislation and the supervisory authority of States in which the undertaking has set up branches or agencies; but they do not concern the activities pursued by the undertaking in the context of the provision of services within the meaning of the Treaty. Consequently the provisions of those directives cannot be applied to the relationship between the State of establishment, where the head office, branch or agency is situated, and the State in which the service is provided. That relationship is considered only in the proposal for a second directive.
36. It is however necessary to consider whether the two 'First Directives' have nevertheless provided for conditions for conducting insurance business which are sufficiently equivalent throughout the Community and means of supervision which are sufficiently effective for the restrictions imposed by the States in which the services are provided on the undertakings providing them to be entirely, or at least partially, abolished.
37. As regards the financial position of insurance undertakings, the two directives contain very detailed provisions on the free assets of the undertaking, in other words its own capital resources. Those provisions are intended to ensure that the undertaking is solvent and the directives require the supervisory authority of the Member State in which the head office is situated to verify the state of solvency of the undertaking 'with respect to its entire business'. That expression must be construed as also covering business conducted in the context of the provision of services. It follows that the State in which the service is provided is not entitled to carry out such verifications itself, but must accept a certificate of solvency drawn up by the supervisory authority of the Member State in whose territory the head office of the undertaking providing the service is situated. According to the German Government, which has not been contradicted by the Commission, that is the case in the Federal Republic of Germany.
38. On the other hand, the two directives did not harmonize the national rules concerning technical reserves, in other words financial resources

which are set aside to guarantee liabilities under contracts entered into and which do not form part of the undertaking's own capital resources. The directives expressly left the necessary harmonization in that respect to later directives. Thus under Directives 73/239 and 79/267 it is for each country in which business is carried on to lay down rules according to its own law for the calculation of such reserves and for determining the nature of and valuing the assets which represent such reserves. The assets covering business conducted in the Member State in which the service is provided must be localized in that State and their existence monitored by the supervisory authority of that State, although the directives provide that the State in which the head office is situated must verify that the balance sheet of the undertaking shows equivalent and matching assets to the underwriting liabilities assumed in all the countries in which it undertakes business. The abolition of that requirement of localization is proposed only in the draft for a second directive which concerns in particular the harmonization of national provisions relating to technical reserves.

39. In the course of the proceedings before the Court, the German Government and the Governments intervening in its support have shown that considerable differences exist in the national rules currently in force concerning technical reserves and the assets which represent such reserves. In the absence of harmonization in that respect and of any rule requiring the supervisory authority of the Member State of establishment to supervise compliance with the rules in force in the State in which the service is provided, it must be recognized that the latter State is justified in requiring and supervising compliance with its own rules on technical reserves with regard to services provided within its territory, provided that such rules do not exceed what is necessary for the purpose of ensuring that policy-holders and insured persons are protected.

40. Finally, the two 'First Co-ordination Directives' make no provision for harmonization of the conditions of insurance and leave to each Member State in which business is conducted the task of ensuring that its own mandatory rules are complied with in respect of business carried on within its territory. The proposal for a second directive defines the scope of such mandatory rules and excludes their application to certain types of commercial insurance which are defined in detail. In view of the considerable differences existing between national rules in that respect it must be stated that, in this connexion too and subject to the same reservation, the Member State in which the service is provided is justified in requiring and verifying compliance with its own rules in respect of services provided within its territory.

41. It must therefore be recognized that, in the present state of Community law, the considerations described above relating to the protection of policy-holders and insured persons justify the application by the Member State in which the service is provided of its own legislation concerning technical reserves and the conditions of insurance, provided that the

requirements of that legislation do not exceed what is necessary to ensure the protection of policy-holders and insured persons. It therefore remains to consider whether it is necessary for such supervision to be effected under an authorization procedure and on the basis of a requirement that the insurance undertaking should have a permanent establishment in the State in which the service is provided.

(c) The necessity of an authorization procedure

42. The Commission does not dispute that the State in which the service is provided is entitled to exercise a certain control over insurance undertakings which provide services within its territory. At the hearing it even accepted that it was permissible to provide for certain measures of supervision of the undertaking concerned to be applied prior to its conducting any business in the context of the provision of services. It nevertheless maintained that such supervision should take a form less restrictive than that of authorization. It did not however explain how such a system might work.
43. The German Government and the Governments intervening in its support maintain that the necessary supervision can be carried out only by means of an authorization procedure which makes it possible to investigate the undertaking before it commences its activities, to monitor those activities continuously and to withdraw the authorization in the event of the serious and repeated infringements.
44. In that respect it should be noted that in all the Member States the supervision of insurance undertakings is organized in the form of an authorization procedure and that the necessity of such a procedure is recognized in the two 'First Co-ordination Directives' as regards the activities to which they refer. In each of those directives Article 6 thereof provides that each Member State must make the taking-up of the business of insurance in its territory subject to an official authorization. An undertaking which sets up branches and agencies in Member States other than that in which its head office is situated must therefore obtain an authorization from the supervisory authority of each of those States.
45. It must also be observed that the proposal for a second directive provides for the retention of that system. The undertaking must obtain an official authorization from each Member State in which it wishes to conduct business in the context of the provision of services. Although, according to that proposal, the authorization must be obtained from the supervisory authority of the State of establishment, that authority must first consult the authority of the State in which the service is to be provided and send it all the relevant papers. The proposal also envisages permanent co-operation between the two supervisory authorities, thus making it possible, in particular, for the authority of the State of establishment to take all appropriate measures, which may extend to withdrawal of the authorization, to put an end to the infringements which

have been notified to it by the supervisory authority of the State in which the service is provided.

46. In those circumstances the German Government's argument to the effect that only the requirement of an authorization can provide an effective means of ensuring the supervision which, having regard to the foregoing considerations, is justified on grounds relating to the protection of the consumer both as a policy-holder and as an insured person, must be accepted. Since a system such as that proposed in the draft for a second directive, which entrusts the operation of the authorization procedure to the Member State in which the undertaking is established, working in close co-operation with the State in which the service is provided, can be set up only by legislation, it must also be acknowledged that, in the present state of Community law, it is for the State in which the service is provided to grant and withdraw that authorization.

47. It should however be emphasized that the authorization must be granted on request to any undertaking established in another Member State which meets the conditions laid down by the legislation of the State in which the service is provided, that those conditions may not duplicate equivalent statutory conditions which have already been satisfied in the State in which the undertaking is established and that the supervisory authority of the State in which the service is provided must take into account supervision and verifications which have already been carried out in the Member State of establishment. According to the German Government, which has not been contradicted on that point by the Commission, the German authorization procedure conforms fully to those requirements.

48. It is still necessary to consider whether the requirement of authorization which, under the Insurance Supervision Law, applies to any insurance business other than transport insurance, is justified in all its applications. In that respect it has been pointed out, in particular by the United Kingdom Government, that the free movement of services is of importance principally for commercial insurance and that with regard to that particular type of insurance the grounds relating to the protection of policy-holders relied on by the German Government and the Governments intervening in its support do not apply.

49. It follows from the foregoing that the requirement of authorization may be maintained only in so far as it is justified on the grounds relating to the protection of policy-holders and insured persons relied upon by the German Government. It must also be recognized that those grounds are not equally important in every sector of insurance and that there may be cases where, because of the nature of the risk insured and of the party seeking insurance, there is no need to protect the latter by the application of the mandatory rules of his national law.

50. However, although it is true that the proposal for a second directive takes account of those considerations by excluding *inter alia* commercial insurance, which is defined in detail, from the scope of the mandatory

rules of the State in which the service is provided, it must also be observed that, in the light of the legal and factual arguments which have been presented before it, the Court is not in a position to make such a general distinction and to lay down the limits of that distinction with sufficient precision to determine the individual cases in which the needs of protection, which are characteristic of insurance business in general, do not justify the requirement of an authorization.

51. It follows from the foregoing that the Commission's first head of claim must be rejected in so far as it is directed against the requirement of authorization.

(d) The necessity of establishment

52. If the requirement of an authorization constitutes a restriction on the freedom to provide services, the requirement of a permanent establishment is the very negation of that freedom. It has the result of depriving Article 59 of the Treaty of all effectiveness, a provision whose very purpose is to abolish restrictions on the freedom to provide services of persons who are not established in the State in which the service is to be provided (see in particular the judgment of 3 December 1974, cited above, and the judgments of 26 November 1985 in Case 39/75, *Coenen* v. *Sociaal-Economische Raad*, [1975] ECR 1547, and 10 February 1982 in Case 76/81, *Transporoute* v. *Minister of Public Works*, [1982] ECR 417). If such a requirement is to be accepted, it must be shown that it constitutes a condition which is indispensable for attaining the objective pursued.

53. In that respect, the German Government points out in particular that the requirement of an establishment in the State in which the service is provided makes it possible for the supervisory authority of that State to carry out verifications *in situ* and to monitor continuously the activities carried or by the authorized insurer and that, without that requirement, the authority would be unable to perform its task.

54. The Court has already stressed in its decisions, most recently in its judgment of 3 February 1983 (Case 29/82, *Van Luipen*, [1983] ECR 151), that considerations of an administrative nature cannot justify derogation by a Member State from the rules of Community law. That principle applies with even greater force where the derogation in question amounts to preventing the exercise of one of the fundamental freedoms guaranteed by the Treaty. In this instance it is therefore not sufficient that the presence on the undertaking's premises of all the documents needed for supervision by the aurthorities of the State in which the service is provided may make it easier for those authorities to perform their task. It must also be shown that those authorities cannot, even under an authorization procedure, carry out their supervisory tasks effectively unless the undertaking has in the aforesaid State a permanent establishment at which all the necessary documents are kept.

55. That has not been shown to be the case. As has been stated above, Community law on insurance does not, as it stands at present, prohibit the State in which the service is provided from requiring that the assets representing the technical reserves covering business conducted on its territory be localized in that State. In that case the presence of such assets may be verified *in situ*, even if the undertaking does not have any permanent establishment in the State. As regards the other conditions for the conduct of business which are subject to supervision, it appears to the Court that such supervision may be effected on the basis of copies of balance sheets, accounts and commercial documents, including the conditions of insurance and schemes of operation, sent from the State of establishment and duly certified by the authorities of that Member State. It is possible under an authorization procedure to subject the undertaking to such conditions of supervision by means of a provision in the certificate of authorization and to ensure compliance with those conditions, if necessary by withdrawing that certificate.

56. It has therefore not been established that the considerations acknowledged above concerning the protection of policy-holders and insured persons make the establishment of the insurer in the territory of the State in which the service is provided an indispensable requirement.

57. As regards the Commission's first head of claim, it must therefore be concluded that the Federal Republic of Germany has failed to fulfil its obligations under Articles 59 and 60 of the Treaty by providing in the Versicherungsaufsichtsgesetz that where insurance undertakings in the Community wish to provide services in relation to direct insurance business, other than transport insurance, through salesmen, representatives, agents or other intermediaries, they must have an establishment in its territory; however, that failure does not extend to compulsory insurance and insurance for which the insurer either maintains a permanent presence equivalent to an agency or a branch or directs his business entirely or principally towards the territory of the Federal Republic of Germany.

B. The Commission's second head of claim

58. In its second head of claim the Commission seeks a declaration that the Federal Republic has failed to fulfil its obligations not only under Articles 59 and 60 of the Treaty but also under Directive 78/473 on Community co-insurance. However, that head of claim, like the first, is based on the proposition that the requirements of authorization and establishment are contrary to Articles 59 and 60 of the Treaty with regard to all insurance business. In the Commission's view there are therefore no grounds for distinguishing in that respect between the position of the insurer in general and that of the leading insurer in particular. Thus, according to the Commission, the Federal Republic of Germany infringed those articles when, in transposing Directive 78/473 into national

law, it exempted only the other co-insurers, and not the leading insurer, from those requirements.
59. The Commission admits that the directive is ambiguous on that point but it claims that it must be interpreted in a manner consistent with the Treaty. That was acknowledged by the Member States in their joint statement in the minutes of the Council meeting of 23 May 1978. Consequently, the directive can in the Commission's view in no way be regarded as requiring the leading insurer to be authorized and to be established in the Member State in which the risk is situated.
60. For its part, the German Government refers to the distinction made in Directive 78/473 between the leading insurer and the other co-insurers. The provisions of that directive regarding the leading insurer, and in particular Article 2 (1) (c) thereof inasmuch as it refers to Directive 73/239, show that the country of the risk may require that the leading insurer be established and authorized in its territory so that he is in a position to cover the whole risk as sole insurer. In the German Government's view, therefore, the German legislation does not infringe Directive 78/473 or Articles 59 and 60 of the EEC Treaty.
61. It is true that the aforesaid provision of the directive provides that 'the leading insurer is authorized in accordance with the conditions laid down in the First Co-ordination Directive, i.e. he is treated as if he were the insurer covering the whole risk'. The directive does not however indicate in which Member State the leading insurer must be authorized and it follows from what the Court has said under A above that, according to Community law, an insurer who is already authorized and established in a Member State need not necessarily be established in another Member State in order to be able to cover the whole of a risk situated in the territory of that State.
62. As the Court held in its judgment of 13 December 1983 (Case 218/82 *Commission* v. *Council*, [1983] ECR 4063), when the wording of secondary Community law is open to more than one interpretation, preference should be given to the interpretation which renders the provision consistent with the Treaty rather than the interpretation which leads to its being incompatible with the Treaty. Consequently, the directive should not be construed in isolation and it is necessary to consider whether or not the requirements in question are contrary to the abovementioned provisions of the Treaty and to interpret the directive in the light of the conclusions reached in that respect.
63. As regards the insurance sector in general, the Court has already held in this case that the requirement of establishment is incompatible with Articles 59 and 60 of the Treaty. Consequently, such a requirement in relation to the leading insurer can find no basis in Directive 78/473. It is therefore sufficient to consider whether the requirement that the leading insurer must be authorized in the country of the risk is in conformity with Community law.
64. In that respect consideration of the first head of claim has shown that the

requirement that an insurance undertaking providing services must be authorized in the State in which the service is provided can be regarded as compatible with the Treaty only in so far as it is justified on grounds relating to the protection of the consumer both as a policy-holder and as an insured person. According to Article 1 (2) thereof, Directive 78/473 concerns only insurance against risks which by reason of their nature or size call for the participation of several insurers for their coverage. Moreover, according to Article 1 (1) the directive applies only to Community co-insurance operations relating to certain of the risks listed in the annex to Directive 73/239. For example, it does not concern either life assurance or accident and sickness insurance or road traffic civil liability insurance. The directive is concerned with insurance which is taken out only by large undertakings or groups of undertakings which are in a position to assess and negotiate insurance policies proposed to them. Consequently the arguments based on consumer protection do not have the same force as in connexion with other forms of insurance.

65. Consideration of the first head of claim has shown, in addition, that the requirement of authorization in the State in which the service is provided is not justified where the undertaking providing the services already satisfies equivalent conditions in the Member State in which it is established and where there exists a system of co-operation between the supervisory authorities of the Member States concerned ensuring effective supervision of compliance with such conditions also as regards the provision of services. According to the preamble to Directive 78/473, the directive is intended to establish the minimum co-ordination necessary to facilitate the effective pursuit of Community co-insurance business and to organize special co-operation between the supervisory authorities of the Member States and between those authorities and the Commission which, for the provision of services in the insurance business in general, is provided for only in the proposal for a second directive.

66. Moreover, a difference of treatment in that respect between the leading insurer and other co-insurers does not appear objectively justified. Although it is for the leading insurer to negotiate the contract and to ensure its performance, there is nothing to prevent him from covering a much smaller part of the risk than that covered by the other co-insurers.

67. In those circumstances and in the case of the insurance to which Directive 78/473 on co-insurance applies, not only the requirement that the leading insurer be established but also the requirement that he be authorized, which are laid down in the Insurance Supervision Law, are contrary to Articles 59 and 60 of the Treaty and therefore also to the directive.

68. It must therefore be held that the Federal Republic of Germany has failed to fulfil its obligations under Articles 59 and 60 of the EEC Treaty and under Council Directive 78/473 in so far as the provisions of its legislation require, with regard to Community co-insurance, that where the risks are situated in the Federal Republic of Germany the leading insurer must be established and authorized there.

3. Literature

D. Lasok, *The Professions and Services in the EEC,* Deventer, 1986.
B. Sundberg-Weitman, *Discrimination on grounds of nationality,* Amsterdam, 1977.

D. CAPITAL

(EEC Treaty Articles 67–73)

1. Cases

(1) Thompson Case

Regina v. Thompson, Johnson and Woodiwiss; Case 7/78; Judgment of 23 November 1978; [1978] ECR 2247.

Facts:

The appellants were charged before the Crown Court at Canterbury with being knowingly concerned in a fraudulent evasion of the prohibition on importation imposed by the import of Goods (Control) Order 1954, contrary to section 304 (b) of the Customs and Excise Act 1952, in relation to certain goods, namely 1,500 Krugerrand gold coins. The appellant Johnson was also charged with seven other offences of a similar nature (in relation to 1,900 Kruggerrand gold coins), and the appellants Johnson and Woodiwiss were charged with conspiracty to evade the prohibition imposed by the Export of Goods (Control) Order 1970, on the exportation of 40.39 tonnes of coins of silver alloy minted in the United Kingdom.

At an early stage in the trial the appellant Woodiwiss pleaded guilty. Subsequently all three submitted that there was no case for them to answer, on the basis that the relevant prohibitions on importation and exportation were invalid as being in conflict with the Treaty of Rome. The trial Judge rejected the submission and refused to refer the question which arose to the Court for a preliminary interpretation under Article 177 of the Treaty. The appellants then pleaded guilty to the remaining charges.

They subsequently appealed to the Court of Appeal (Criminal Division) which by order of 15 December 1977, registered in the Court Registry on 16 January 1978, referred questions to the Court under Article 177 of the Treaty.

The Court held:

. . . . .

19. An examinations of the questions asked shows that, even if these questions have been formulated so as to lay emphasis on the description of the coins in question as 'capital', their actual purpose is to find out whether these coins are goods falling within the provisions of Articles 30 to 37 of the Treaty or constitute a means of payment falling within the scope of other provisions.
20. Understood in this way, these questions must be considered in the context of the general system of the Treaty.
21. An analysis of this system shows that the rules relating to the free movement of goods and, in particular, Articles 30 et seq. concerning the elimination of quantitative restrictions and measures having equivalent effect, must be considered not only with reference to the specific rules relating to transfers of capital but with reference to all the provisions of the Treaty relating to monetary transfers, which can be effected for a great variety of purposes, of which capital transfers only comprise one specific category.
22. Although Articles 67 to 73 of the Treaty, which are concerned with the liberalization of movements of capital, assume special importance as far as one of the aims set out in Article 3 of the Treaty is concerned, namely the abolition of obstacles to freedom of movement for capital, the provisions of Articles 104 to 109, which are concerned with the overall balance of payments and which for this reason relate to all monetary movements, must be considered as essential for the purpose of attaining the free movement of goods, services or capital which is of fundamental importance for the attainment of the Common Market.
23. In particular, Article 106 provides that 'Each Member State undertakes to authorize, in the currency of the Member State in which the creditor or the beneficiary resides, any payments connected with the movement of goods, services or capital, and any transfers of capital and earnings, to the extent that the movement of goods, services, capital and persons between Member States has been liberalized pursuant to this Treaty'.
24. The aim of this provision is to ensure that the necessary monetary transfers may be made both for the liberalization of movements of capital and for the free movement of goods, services and persons.
25. It must be inferred from this that under the system of the Treaty means of payment are not to be regarded as goods falling within the purview of Articles 30 to 37 of the Treaty.
26. Silver alloy coins which are legal tender in Member State are, by their very nature, to be regarded as means of payment and it follows that their transfer dies not fall within the provisions of Articles 30 to 37 of the Treaty.
27. Although doubts may be entertained on the question whether Krugerrands are to be regarded as means of legal payment it can nevertheless be noted that on the money markets of those Member States which permit dealings in these counts they are treated as being equivalent to currency.

28. Their transfer must consequently be designated as a monetary transfer which does not fall within the provisions of the said Articles 30 to 37.
29. Having regard to the above-mentioned considerations it is unnecessary to deal with the question under what circumstances the transfer of these two categories of coins might possibly designated either as a movement of capital or as a current payment.
30. Question 1 (c) refers to silver alloy coins of a Member State, which have been legal tender in that State and which, although no longer legal tender, are protected as coinage from destruction.
31. Such coins cannot be regarded as means of payment within the meaning stated above, with the result that they can be designated as goods falling within the system of Articles 30 to 37 of the Treaty.
32. It is for the Member States to mint their own coinage and to protect it from destruction.
33. The Court's file shows that in the United Kingdon the melting down or destruction of national coins is prohibited, even if they are no longer legal tender.
34. A ban on exporting such coins with a view to preventing their being melted down or destroyed in another Member State is justified on grounds of public policy within the meaning of Article 36 of the Treaty, because it stems from the need to protect the right to mint coinage which is traditionally regarded as involving the fundamental interests of the State.

(2) Casati Case

Public Prosecutor v. *Guerrino Casati*; Case 203/80; Preliminary ruling of 11 November 1981 [1981] ECR 2595.

Facts: see the judgment below.

The Court held:

1. By order of 6 October 1980, received at the Court Registry on 16 October 1980, the Tribunale (District Court), Bolzano, referred to the Court for a preliminary ruling, pursuant to Article 177 of the EEC Treaty, several questions on the interpretation of Articles 67, 69, 71, 73 and 106 of the EEC Treaty and on the existence of various principles of Community law, to enable it to adjudicate on the compatibility of certain provisions of Italian exchange control legislation with those articles principles.
2. The questions have been raised in connection with criminal proceedings brought against an Italian national, residing in the Federal Republic of Germany, who is charged with attempting to export from Italy, without the authorization prescribed by Italian exchange control legislation, *inter*

alia, the sum of DM 24,000, which was found in his possession on 16 July 1979 at the frontier between Italy and Austria. The accused in the main proceedings stated that he had previously imported that sum of money into Italy, without declaring it, with a view to purchasing equipment which he needed for his business in Germany and was obliged to re-export the currency because the factory at which he intended to buy the equipment was closed for the holidays.

3. Article 14 of the Italian Decreto Ministeriale (Ministerial Decree) of 7 August 1978 (Gazetta Ufficiale No 220 of 8 August 1978) provides that foreign bank notes may be freely imported. Article 13 of the same decreto ministeriale provides that the exportation of foreign bank notes by a non-resident is permitted up to the amount previously imported or the amount lawfully acquired in Italy, which must be proved in accordance with the procedures laid down by the Minister for Foreign Trade. Those procedures were laid down in particular by Circular No A/100 of 3 May 1974 of the Ufficio Italiano dei Cambi (Italian Foreign Exchange Department), Article 11 of which provides that non-residents may export the amount of money they declared on Form V2 on entry into Italy.

4. According to Article 1 of Law No 159 of 30 April 1976, the unauthorized exportation of currency of a value exceeding Lit 500,000 is punishable by a term of imprisonment of one to six years and by a fine of between two and four times the value of the currency exported. Before 1976, those infringements were no more than administrative infringements, not offences, and attracted only administrative penalties, consisting of fines of up to five times the value of the effects exported.

. . . . .

8. The first question concerns the effects of Article 67 and, more particularly, Article 67 (1), after the expiry of the transitional period. That article heads the chapter on capital which belongs to Title II, 'Free movement of persons, services and capital', incorporated in Part Two of the EEC Treaty, entitled 'Foundations of the Community'. The general scheme of those provisions is in keeping with the list, set out in Article 3 of the EEC Treaty, of the methods provided for the attainment of the Community's objectives. Those methods include, according to Article 3 (c) 'the abolition, as between Member States, of obstacles to freedom of movement for persons, services and capital'. Thus the free movement of capital constitutes, alongside that of persons and services, one of the fundamental freedoms of the Community. Furthermore, freedom to move certain types of capital is, in practice, a pre-condition for the effective exercise of other freedoms guaranteed by the Treaty, in particular the right of establishment.

9. However, capital movements are also closely connected with the econ-

omic and monetary policy of the Member States. At present, it cannot be denied that complete freedom of movement of capital may undermine the economic policy of one of the Member States or create an imbalance in its balance of payments, thereby impairing the proper functioning of the Common Market.
10. For those reasons, Article 67 (1) differs from the provisions on the free movement of goods, persons and services in the sense that there is an obligation to liberalize capital movements only 'to the extent necessary to ensure the proper functioning of the Common Market'. The scope of that restriction, which remained in force after the expiry of the transitional period, varies in time and depends on an assessment of the requirements of the Common Market and on an appraisal of both the advantages and risks which liberalization might entail for the latter, having regard to the stage it has reached and, in particular, to the level of integration attained in matters in respect of which capital movements are particularly significant.
11. Such an assessment is, first and foremost, a matter for the Council, in accordance with the procedure provided for by Article 69. The Council has adopted two directives under that article, the first on 11 May 1960 (Official Journal, English Special Edition 1959–1962, p. 49) and the second, which adds to and amends the first, on 18 December 1962 (Official Journal, English Special Edition 1963–1964, p. 5). All the movements of capital are divided into four lists (A, B, C & D) annexed to the directives. In the case of the movements covered by Lists A and B, unconditional liberalization is prescribed by the directives. However, in the case of the movements covered by List C, the directives authorize the Member States to maintain or to re-impose the exchange restrictions in existence on the date of the entry into force of the first directive if the freedom of movement of capital is capable of forming an obstacle to the achievement of the economic policy objectives of the State concerned. Finally, in the case of the movements referred to in list D, the directives do not require the Member States to adopt any liberalizing measures. List D covers, inter alia, the physical importation and exportation of financial assets, including bank notes.
12. The conclusion must be drawn that the obligation contained in Article 67 (1) to abolish restrictions on movements of capital cannot be defined, in relation to a specific category of such movements, in isolation from the Council's assessment under Article 69 of the need to liberalize that category in order to ensure the proper functioning of the Common Market. The Council has so far taken the view that it is unnecessary to liberalize the exportation of bank notes, the operation with which the accused in the main proceedings is charged, and there is no reason to suppose that, by adopting that position, it has overstepped the limits of its discretionary power.
13. The answer to the first question should therefore be that Article 67 (1) must be interpreted as meaning that restrictions on the exportation of

bank notes may not be regarded as abolished as from the expiry of the transitional period, irrespective of the provisions of Article 69.
14. The second question put by the national court concerns the safeguard clause contained in Article 73. The purpose of that article is to enable a Member State to introduce, subject to certain conditions and in accordance with certain procedures, restrictions which that State would otherwise be obliged to refrain from imposing under the general rules governing movements of capital. It is inapplicable in the case of restrictions the introduction of which is already permitted under those rules.
15. In view of the answer to the first question, it is sufficient to state in reply to the second question that failure to have recourse to the procedures provided for by Article 73 in regard to restrictions imposed on capital movements which the Member State concerned is not obliged to liberalize under the rules of Community law does not constitute an infringement of the EEC Treaty.
16. In its third question, the national court asks essentially whether a principle of Community law or any provision of the Treaty guarantees the right of non-residents to re-export currency previously imported and not used.
17. To begin with it is necessary to observe that, as the replies given to the first two questions show, the extent to which capital movements are liberalized and exchange restrictions gradually abolished does not depend on a general principle but is governed by the provisions of Articles 67 and 69 of the EEC Treaty and by those of the aforesaid directives of 11 May 1960 and 18 December 1962 adopted to give effect to those articles. However, it is necessary to consider whether, in matters where, according to those provisions, there is so far no obligation to liberalize movements of capital – for example, transfers of currency – individuals may derive rights which the Member States are bound to respect, either from the standstill provisions contained in Article 71 of the EEC Treaty or from Article 106 of the EEC Treaty, both of which are referred to by the national court, though in another context, in its sixth and eighth questions.
18. According to the first paragraph of Article 71, the Member States must endeavour to avoid introducing within the Community any new exchange restrictions on the movement of capital and must endeavour not to make existing rules more restrictive.
19. By using the term 'shall endeavour', the wording of that provision departs noticeably from the more imperative forms of wording employed in other similar provisions concerning restrictions on the free movement of goods, persons and services. It is apparent from that wording that, in any event, the first paragraph of Article 71 does not impose on the Member States an unconditional obligation capable of being relied upon by individuals.
20. Capital movements account for only a part of the transactions involving transfers of currency. With good reason, therefore, the national court

draws attention to Article 106 which is designed to ensure that the necessary transfers of currency may be made both for the liberalization of capital movements and for the free movement of goods, services and persons and which, moreover, does not contain the same restrictions as those expressly provided for by the provisions already considered.

21. More specifically, in its sixth question, the national court refers to the standstill obligation contained in the first sub-paragraph of Article 106 (3). According to that provision, the Member States undertake not to introduce between themselves any new restrictions on transfers connected with the so-called 'invisible' transactions listed in Annex III to the Treaty.

22. In that regard, it is necessary to recall that the defendant in the main proceedings has stated that he intended to re-export a sum of money previously imported with a view to making purchases of a commercial nature, not an amount corresponding to a transaction actually listed in Annex III.

23. The answer to the questions relating to Article 106 (3) should therefore be that the latter provision is inapplicable to the reexportation of a sum of money previously imported with a view to making purchases of a commercial nature if such purchases have not in fact been effected.

24. The order referring the matter to the Court contains no express reference to the first two paragraphs of Article 106. In view of the alleged purpose of the importation of the sum of money in question, those two paragraphs are significant in relation to the third question. According to those provisions, the Member States undertake to authorize on the expiry of the transitional period, any payments connected with, inter alia, the movement of goods. The first two paragraphs of Article 106 are thus designed to ensure the free movement of goods in practice by authorizing all the transfers of currency necessary to achieve that aim. However, those provisions do not require the Member States to authorize the importation and exportation of bank notes for the performance of commercial transactions, if such transfers are not necessary for the free movement of goods. In connection with commercial transactions, that method of transfer which, moreover, is not in conformity with standard practice, cannot be regarded as necessary to ensure such free movement.

25. In the light of the foregoing considerations, the answer to the third question should be that the right of non-residents to re-export bank notes which were previously imported with a view to performing commercial transactions but have not been used is not guaranteed by any principle of Community law or by any provisions of Community law relating to capital movements or by the rules of Article 106 concerning payments connected with the movement of goods.

Possible limits set by Community law to national rules of criminal law and procedure

26. In its fourth, fifth and sixth questions, the national court asks in substance whether penalties of the kind provided for by Italian exchange control legislation are incompatible with the principles of proportionality and non-discrimination which form part of Community law. The eighth question raises the problem of the freedom to provide evidence in criminal proceedings.

27. In principle, criminal legislation and the rules of criminal procedure are matters for which the Member States are still responsible. However, it is clear from a consistent line of cases decided by the Court, that Community law also sets certain limits in that area as regards the control measures which it permits the Member States to maintain in connection with the free movement of goods and persons. The administrative measures or penalties must not go beyond what is strictly necessary, the control procedures must not be conceived in such a way as to restrict the freedom required by the Treaty and they must not be accompanied by a penalty which is so disproportionate to the gravity of the infringement that it becomes an obstacle to the exercise of that freedom.

28. Certain situations which are comparable to those considered in that case-law may arise, in connection with capital movements and transfers of currency, in relation to control measures maintained by the Member States for example under Article 5 of the First Directive for the implementation of Article 67 of the Treaty, but only in connection with transactions liberalized under Community law. The limits set by that case-law are designed to prevent the freedoms guaranteed by Community law from being eroded by the control measures which Community law permits the Member States to maintain. That is not the case in these proceedings. It is apparent from the replies to the other questions referred to the Court for a preliminary ruling that the transaction in question has not been liberalized either by the provisions of the Treaty or by the directives adopted for their implementation. In such circumstances, the aforesaid case-law is inapplicable.

29. The reply to those questions should therefore be that with regard to capital movements and transfers of currency with the Member States are not obliged to liberalize under the rules of Community law, those rules do not restrict the Member States' power to adopt control measures and to enforce compliance therewith by means of criminal penalties.

(3) Luisi and Carbone Case

For facts and references see at pages 450, 582.

The Court held:

(b) "Current payments' and 'movements of capital'

19. The national court has pointed out that the physical transfer of bank notes is included in List D in the annexes to the two directives which the Council adopted pursuant to Article 69 of the Treaty in relation to the movement of capital (Official Journal, English Special Edition 1959–1962, p. 49, and 1963–1964, p. 5). List D enumerates the movements of capital for which the directives do not require the Member States to adopt any liberalizing measure. The question therefore arises whether the reference in that list to the physical transfer of bank notes implies that such a transfer itself constitutes a movement of capital.
20. The Treaty does not specify what is to be understood by the movement of capital. However, in the annexes to the two above-mentioned directives a list is given of the various movements of capital, together with a nomenclature. Although the physical transfer of financial assets, in particular bank notes, is included in that list, that does not mean that any such transfer must in all circumstances be regarded as a movement of capital.
21. The general scheme of the Treaty shows, and a comparison between Articles 67 and 106 confirms, that current payments are transfers of foreign exchange which constitute the consideration within the context of an underlying transaction, whilst movements of capital are financial operations essentially concerned with the investment of the funds in question rather than remuneration for a service. For that reason movements of capital may themselves give rise to current payments, as is implied by Articles 67 (2) and 106 (1).
22. The physical transfer of bank notes may not therefore be classified as a movement of capital where the transfer in question corresponds to an obligation to pay arising from a transaction involving the movement of goods or services.
23. Consequently, payments in connection with tourism or travel for the purposes of business, education or medical treatment cannot be classified as movements of capital, even where they are effected by means of the physical transfer of bank notes.

(c) The extent to which the payments referred to in Article 106 of the Treaty have been liberalized

24. As regards the movement of services, Article 106 (1) provides that payments relating thereto must be liberalized to the extent to which the movement of services itself has been liberalized between Member States in accordance with the Treaty. By virtue of Article 59 of the Treaty, restrictions on the freedom to provide services within the Community were to be abolished during the transitional period. As from the end of that period, any restrictions on payments relating to the provision of services must therefore be abolished.
25. Consequently, payments relating to tourism and travel for the purposes

of business, education or medical treatment have been liberalized since the end of the transitional period.

26. This interpretation finds confirmation in Article 54 of the Act of Accession of 1979, by virtue of which the Hellenic Republic is authorized to maintain restrictions on transfers relating to tourism, but only within certain limits and only until 31 December 1985. That article implies that without that derogation the transfers in question would have had to be liberalized immediately.

(d) Control measures in respect of transfers of foreign currency

27. The last aspect of the problem raised in these cases concerns the question whether, and if so to what extent, Member States have retained the power to subject liberalized transfers and payments to control measures applicable to the transfer of foreign currency.
28. In that respect, it should be noted in the first place that the liberalization of payments provided for in Article 106 compels Member States to authorize the payments referred to in that provision in the currency of the Member State in which the creditor or beneficiary resides. Payments made in the currency of a third country are not therefore covered by that provision.
29. It should also be noted that Article 2 of Directive 63/340, cited above, states that the liberalization measures provided for in the directive do not limit the right of Member States to 'verify the nature and genuineness of payments'. This proviso appears to be inspired by the fact that, at that time, payments relating to the movements of goods and services and movements of capital were not yet fully liberalized.
30. However, even though the transitional period has ended that liberalization has not yet been fully accomplished. The Council directives provided for in Article 69 of the Treaty with a view to attaining the free movement of capital have not yet in fact abolished all the restrictions in that area, whilst Article 67, which provides for that freedom, must, as the Court held in its judgment of 11 November 1981 (Case 203/80 *Casati* [1981] ECR 2595), be interpreted as meaning that even after the expiry of the transitional period restrictions on the export of foreign currency may not be regarded as having been abolished, irrespective of the terms of the directives adopted pursuant to Article 69.
31. In those circumstances, Member States have retained the power to impose controls on transfers of foreign currency in order to verify that transfers do not in fact constitute movements of capital, which have not been liberalized. That power is particularly important since it is bound up with the responsibility which Member States have in relation to monetary matters under Articles 104 and 107 of the Treaty, a responsibility which implies that appropriate measures may be adopted in order to prevent the flight of capital or other speculation of that kind against their currencies.

32. Articles 108 and 109 of the Treaty provide for the measures to be taken and the procedures to be followed where a Member State is in difficulties or is seriously threatened with difficulties as regards its balance of payments. However, those provisions, which are to remain operative even after the free movement of capital has been fully achieved relate only to periods of crisis.
33. In the absence of any crisis and until the free movement of capital has been full achieved, it must therefore be acknowledged that Member States are empowered to verify that transfers of foreign currency purportedly intended for liberalized payments are not diverted from that purpose and used for unauthorized movements of capital. In that connection, Member States are entitled to verify the nature and genuineness of the transactions or transfers in question.
34. Controls introduced for that purpose must, however, be kept within the limits imposed by Community law, in particular those deriving from the freedom to provide services and to make payments relating thereto. Consequently, they may not have the effect of limiting payments and transfers in connection with the provision of services to a specific amount for each transaction or for a given period, since in that case they would interfere with the freedoms recognized by the Treaty. For the same reason, such controls may not be applied in such a manner as to render those freedoms illusory or to subject the exercise thereof to the discretion of the administrative authorities.
35. These findings do not preclude a Member State from fixing flat-rate limits below which no verification is carried out and from requiring proof, in the case of expenditure exceeding those limits, that the amounts transferred have actually been used in connection with the provision of services, provided however that the flat-rate limits so determined are not such as to affect the normal pattern of the provision of services.
36. It is for the national court to determine in each individual case whether the controls on transfers of foreign currency which are at issue in proceedings before it are in conformity with the limits thus defined.
37. On the basis of all the foregoing considerations, it may be stated in reply to the questions submitted for a preliminary ruling that Article 106 of the Treaty must be interpreted as meaning that:
Transfers in connection with tourism or travel for the purposes of business, education or medical treatment constitute payments and not movements of capital, even where they are affected by means of the physical transfer of bank notes;
Any restrictions on such payments are abolished as from the end of the transitional period;
Member States retain the power to verify that transfers of foreign currency purportedly intended for liberalized payments are not in reality used for unauthorized movements of capital;
Controls introduced for that purpose may not have the effect of limiting payments and transfers in connection with the provision of services to a

specific amount for each transaction or for a given period, or of rendering illusory the freedoms recognized by the Treaty or of subjecting the exercise thereof to the discretion of the administrative authorities;
Such controls may involve the fixing of flat-rate limits below which no verification is carried out, whereas in the case of expenditure exceeding those limits proof is required that the amounts transferred have actually been used in connection with the provision of services, provided however that the flat-rate limits so determined are not such as to affect the normal pattern of the provision of services.

(4) Brugnoni Case

Luisi Brugnoni and Roberto Ruffinengo v. *Cassa di risparmio di Genova e Imperia*; Case 157/85; Preliminary ruling of 24 June 1986; [1986] ECR 2013.

Facts: see the judgment below.

The Court held:

1. By an order of 16 May 1985, which was received at the Court on 23 May 1985, the Pretura di Genova referred to the Court for a preliminary ruling under Article 177 of the EEC Treaty three questions on the interpretation of Articles 67, 68, 73 and 108 of the EEC Treaty and of the First and Second Council Directives, of 11 May 1960 and 18 December 1962, for the implementation of Article 67 of the Treaty in order to enable it to give judgment on the compatibility with Community law of certain Italian legislative provisions on exchange regulation.
2. Those questions were raised in proceedings relating to the purchase of foreign securities by Luigi Brugnoni, an Italian resident. In November 1984, Mr. Brugnoni instructed the Cassa di risparmio di Genova e Imperia through his agent, Roberto Ruffinengo, to purchase DM 5,000 worth of bonds issued by the European Coal and Steel Community, which were quoted on the foreign stock exchange. In pursuance of those instructions the Cassa di risparmio deposited the bonds with the Deutsche Bank in Frankfurt for the account of Messrs Brugnoni and Ruffinengo and debited them with safe custody charges. It also debited them with an amount in lire equivalent to 50%, subsequently reduced to 30%, of the value of the securities, for the purposes of the deposit provided for by Italian exchange rules. Mr. Brugnoni and Mr. Ruffinengo brought an action against the Cassa di risparmio before the Pretura di Genova for an order requiring it to deliver up the securities and repay the sums withheld for the deposit and safe custody charges.
3. The plaintiffs did not deny that the bank had acted in compliance with the

Italian legislation. That legislation does in fact lay down special rules regarding the purchase and holding of foreign securities. Article 5 of Law No 786 of 25 July 1956 (Gazzetta Ufficiale della Repubblica Italiana No 192 of 2 August 1956) provides that Italian residents may not, except with ministeral authorization, hold shares in companies having their registered office outside Italian territory or hold shares or bonds issued or payable abroad. A Ministerial Decree of 12 March 1981 implementing that Law (Gazzetta Ufficiale, Supplement No 82 of 24 March 1981) authorizes, subject to certain conditions, the purchase by Italian residents of shares and bonds issued or payable abroad. Those conditions include the compulsory payment of a deposit and the lodging of the securities with an approved bank.

4. Article 15 of the aforesaid Decree provides that residents purchasing such securities must pay into a blocked, interest-free account with the bank through which the transaction is carried out a sum equal to 50% of the value of the investment. In 1984 that amount was reduced to 30% for purchase of bonds issued by the Community institutions and quoted on the foreign stock exchange. Article 20 of the Decree provides that bonds and shares issued or payable abroad must be entrusted to the custody of an approved bank. However, that condition is deemed to be fulfilled where the approved bank lodges the securities with a foreign bank in its own name and for the account of the owners of the securities.

5. The plaintiffs in the main proceedings submitted that national legislation was contrary to Community law and in particular to Articles 67 and 68 of the Treaty which deal with the free movement of capital. They acknowledge that the liberalization of capital movements was to be carried out according to the timetable laid down by the Council in directives adopted under Article 69 of the Treaty but pointed out that the two directives already adopted in 1960 and 1962 for the implementation of Article 67 contained an annex classifying all capital movements into four categories in List A, B, C and D, List B setting out transactions which were to be unconditionally liberalized. Those transactions included the acquisition by residents of foreign securities dealt in on a stock exchange.

6. The defendant, the Cassi di risparmio, contended before the Pretura di Genova that Commission Decision No 85/16/EEC of 19 December 1984 (Official Journal 1985, L 8, p. 34) had specifically authorized the Italian Republic to continue to apply certain protective measures. Those protective measures included the lodging of a 30% interest-free deposit on transactions in foreign securities issued by the Community institutions. They also required the securities in question to be held for at least one year; hence the necessity for them to be kept in safe custody for verification purposes.

7. The Pretura di Genova considered that it was necessary, for the purposes of reaching a correct decision in the case pending before it,to refer the three following questions to the Court for a preliminary ruling:

'(1) In the case of the acquisition by residents of foreign securities which are dealt in on a stock exchange and denominated in foreign currency or of foreign bonds denominated in foreign currency, do subjects of Community law enjoy rights which the Member States are bound to respect by virtue of directly applicable rules of Community law where such operations must be treated as one of the liberalized movements of capital because they appear in List B in the annexes to the Council Directives of 11 May 1960 and 18 December 1962 for the implementation of Article 67 of the EEC Treaty? If so, can restrictive measures imposed by national law which affect the performance of the contract and the right to dispose of the asset acquired, with particular reference to the requirement for securities to be deposited with banks authorized to act as depositories and administrators pursuant to Article 5 of Decree Law No 476 of 6 June 1956, which was converted into Law No 786 of 25 July 1956, and to Article 20 of the Ministerial Decree of 12 March 1981, be regarded as compatible with Community law?

Or, as the operation at issue is one of the capital movements mentioned in Commission Decision No 85/16/EEC and in view of the reference in that decision to Article 108 (3) of the Treaty, does the operation fall into the category of capital movements which the Member States may still subject to restrictions in accordance with Articles 67 and 68 of the Treaty, with the result that the restrictive measure introduced by the Member State is lawful in that context even though it imposes penal sanctions?

(2) Does the fact that the Italian Government did not observe the consultative procedure provided for in Article 73 of the Treaty when adopting or continuing measures restricting capital movements which the Member State concerned must liberalize constitute an infringement of the EEC Treaty in view of Commission Decisions Nos 74/287/EEC, 75//355/EEC and 85/16/EEC?

(3) Must the authorization contained in Commission Decision No 85/16/EEC of 19 December 1984 authorizing the Italian Republic to continue to apply certain protective measures be interpreted, in view of the express reference to Decisions Nos 74/287/EEC and 75/355/EEC, as a further extension of the preceding authorizations, that is to say the authorizations in force since 1974, or, in view of the wording of Article 1 thereof and having regard to the taking effect of the decision as provided for in the second paragraph of Article 191 of the Treaty, must it be interpreted as a new authorization which is not therefore applicable to operations carried out before 19 December 1984?'

. . . . .

C – Applicability of Article 73 of the Treaty

26. Article 73 provides for consultations and, if necessary, protective measures in the event that movements of capital lead to disturbances in the functioning of the capital market in any Member State. However, Commission Decisions Nos 74/287, 75/355 and 85/16, the decisions at issue in this case, were adopted pursuant to Article 108. That article provides for consultation, mutual assistance between the Member States and, if necessary, protective measures where a Member State is in difficulties or is seriously threatened with difficulties as regards its balance of payments either as a result of an overall disequilibrium in its balance of payments or as a result of the type of currency at its disposal.
27. A comparison of those two provisions shows that the substantive requirements of Article 73 differ from those of Article 108 and that the decisions which may be adopted or authorized are not the same in each case. It must therefore be concluded that the same applies as regards the procedures to be followed. Those procedures cannot therefore be regarded as cumulative.
28. Consequently, the answer to this question must be that the procedures provided for in Article 73 of the Treaty are not applicable to decisions and measures taken by a Member State and by the Commission pursuant to Article 108 of the Treaty.

2. Literature

P. Oliver/J. P. Baché, 'Free movement of capital between the Member States: Recent developments', (1989) CML Rev. 61

Chapter Five

Policy of the community

I. Introduction

Part three of the EEC Treaty is entitled 'Policy of the Community'. In this part one finds elements both of 'negative integration' (Common Market) and of 'positive integration' (approximation of policies). Indeed, the Common Market finds its necessary complement in the first Title of this Third Part which under the heading 'Common Rules' is concerned with the rules on competition (both the famous Articles 85 and 86 applicable to enterprises, and the rules on State aids), with the impact which tax provisions have on the 'Common market-freedoms', and with the 'Approximation of laws' between Member States without which a common market could be realised only in terms of the starkest 'free for all'.

The remaining Titles, on the other hand, are concerned with 'positive integration', viz. the elaboration of common policies between the Member States by which the economy is deliberately steered in certain directions which, by common consent, are deemed desirable. Here a distiction may be made between the 'classic' policies, which had their place in the Treaty right from the beginning, and those policies which gained recognition more recently and reference to which was thus inserted into the Treaty only recently, at the entry into force of the Single European Act.

Into the former category enter Titles II ('Economic Policy', comprising both 'internal policies' such as conjunctural policy and balance of payments, and 'commercial policy' on which the Community's position in world trade relations is based), III ('Social Policy', comprising i.a. the famous Article 119 dealing with discrimination against women) and IV ('The European Investment Bank'). The recent additions include Titles V ('Economic and Social Cohesion'), VI ('Research and Technological Development') and VII ('Environment'). Whereas the latter two need no further comment here, it may be noted that the notion of 'economic and social cohesion' is meant to translate into action the feeling that it is in the interest of all Member States that gaps in economic development between various parts of the Community be reduced.

II. Competition policy

A. Rules applying to undertakings

1. Principles common to Articles 85 and 86

a. Scope of application of Articles 85 and 86

i. Ratione territorii

aa. Cases

(1) Woodpulp Case

A. Ahlström Osakeyhtiö and Others v. *Commission*; Joined Cases 89, 104, 114, 116, 117, 125–129/85; Judgment of 27 September 1988 (not yet published).

Facts:

See judgment below.

The Court held:

1. By applications lodged at the Court Registry between 4 and 30 April 1985, wood pulp producers and two associations of wood pulp producers, all having their registered offices outside the Community, brought an action under the second paragraph of Article 173 of the EEC Treaty for the annulment of Decision IV/29.725 of 19 December 1984 (Official Journal 1985 No. L 85, p. 1), in which the Commission had established that they had committed infringements of Article 85 of the Treaty and imposed fines on them.
2. The infringements consisted of: concertation between those producers on prices announced each quarter to customers in the Community and on actual transaction prices charged to such customers (Article 1 (1) and (2) of the decision); price recommendations addressed to its members by the Pulp, Paper and Paperboard Export Association of the United States (formerly named Kraft Export Association and hereinafter referred to as 'KEA'), an association of a number of United States producers (Article 1 (3)); and, as regards Fincell, the common sales organization of some ten Finnish producers, the exchange of individualized data concerning prices with certain other wood pulp producers within the framework of the Research and Information Centre for the European Pulp and Paper Industry which is run by the trust company Fides of Switzerland (Article 1 (4)).

3. In paragraph 79 of the contested decision the Commission set out the grounds which in its view justify the Community's jurisdiction to apply Article 85 of the Treaty to the concentration in question. It stated first that all the addresses of the decision were either exporting directly to purchasers within the Community or were doing business within the Community through branches, subsidiaries, agencies or other establishments in the Community. It further pointed out that the concertation applied to the vast majority of the sales of those undertakings to and in the Community. Finally it stated that two-thirds of total shipments and 60% of consumption of the product in question in the Community had been affected by such concertation. The Commission concluded that 'the effect of the agreements and practices on prices announced and/or charged to customers and on resale of pulp within the EEC was therefore not only substantial but intended, and was the primary and direct result of the agreements and practices'.

. . . . .

5. A number of applicants have raised submissions regarding the Community's jurisdiction to apply its competition rules to them. On 8 July 1987 the Court decided in the first instance to hear the parties' submissions on this point. By order of 16 December 1987 the Court joined the cases for the purposes of the oral procedure and the judgment.

. . . . .

Incorrect assessment of the territorial scope of Article 85 of the Treaty and incompatibility of the decision with public international law

(a) The individual undertakings

11. In so far as the submission concerning the infringement of Article 85 of the Treaty itself is concerned, it should be recalled that provision prohibits all agreements between undertakings and concerted practices which may affect trade between Member States and which have as their object or effect the restriction of competition within the Common Market are prohibited.
12. It should be noted that the main sources of supply of wood pulp are outside the Community, in Canada, the United States, Sweden and Finland and that the market therefore has global dimensions. Where wood pulp producers established in those countries sell directly to purchasers

established in the Community and engage in price competition in order to win orders from those customers, that constitutes competition within the Common Market.
13. It follows that where those producers concert on the prices to be charged to their customers in the Community and put that concertation into effect by selling at prices which are actually co-ordinated, they are taking part in concertation which has the object and effect of restricting competition within the Common Market within the meaning of Article 85 of the Treaty.
14. Accordingly, it must be concluded that by applying the competition rules in the Treaty in the circumstances of this case to undertakings whose registered offices are situated outside the Community, the Commission has not made an incorrect assessment of the territorial scope of Article 85.
15. The applicants have submitted that the decision is incompatible with public international law on the grounds that the application of the competition rules in this case was founded exclusively on the economic repercussions within the Common Market of conduct restricting competition which was adopted outside the Community.
16. It should be observed that an infringement of Article 85, such as the conclusion of an agreement which has had the effect of restricting competition within the Common Market, consists of conduct made up of two elements, the formation of the agreement, decision or concerted practice and the implementation thereof. If the applicability of prohibitions laid down under competition law were made to depend on the place where the agreement, decision or concerted practice was formed, the result would obviously be to give undertakings an easy means of evading those prohibitions. The decisive factor is therefore the place where it is implemented.
17. The producers in this case implemented their pricing agreement within the Common Market. It is immaterial in that respect whether or not they had recourse to subsidiaries, agents, sub-agents, or branches within the Community in order to make their contacts with purchasers within the Community.
18. Accordingly the Community's jurisdiction to apply its competition rules to such conduct is covered by the territoriality principle as universally recognized in public international law.
19. As regards the argument based on the infringment of the principle of non-interference, it should be pointed out that the applicants who are members of KEA have referred to a rule according to which where two States have jurisdiction to lay down and enforce rules and the effect of those rules is that a person finds himself subject to contradictory orders as to the conduct he must adopt, each State is obliged to exercise its jurisdiction with moderation. The applicants have concluded that by disregarding that rule in applying its competition rules the Community has infringed the principle of non-interference.

20. There is no need to enquire into the existence in international law of such a rule since it suffices to observe that the conditions for its application are in any event not satisfied. There is not, in this case, any contradiction between the conduct required by the United States and that required by the Community since the Webb-Pomerene Act merely exempts the conclusion of export cartels from the application of United States antitrust laws but does not require such cartels to be concluded.
21. It should further be pointed out that the United States authorities raised no objections regarding any conflict of jurisdiction when consulted by the Commission pursuant to the OECD Council Recommendation of 25 October 1979 concerning Co-operation between Member Countries on Restrictive Business Practices affecting International Trade (Acts of the Organization, Vol. 19, p. 377).
22. As regards the argument relating to disregard of international comity, it suffices to observe that it amounts to calling in question the Community's jurisdiction to apply its competition rules to conduct such as that found to exist in this case and that, as such, that argument has already been rejected.
23. Accordingly it must be concluded that the Commission's decision is not contrary to Article 85 of the Treaty or to the rules of public international law relied on by the applicants.

ii. Ratione materiae

aa. Cases

(1) Züchner Case

G. Züchner v. *Bayerische Vereins bank AG*; Case 172/80; 14 July 1981: [1981] ECR 2021.

Facts:

See the judgment below.

The Court held:

2. From the file forwarded by the national court it appears that the holder of a bank account with the Bayerische Vereinsbank in Rosenheim, Federal Republic of Germany, drew a cheque on the bank on 17 July 1979 in the amount of DM 10 000 in favour of a payee resident in Italy. The bank debited his account of respect of the transfer with a 'service charge' (Bearbeitungsgebühr) of DM 15, representing 0.15% of the sum transferred.

3. The holder of the account considered that the imposition of such a charge ran counter to the provisions of the EEC Treaty and sued the bank before the Amtsgericht Rosenheim for repayment of the charge.
4. He maintained, *inter alia*, that the imposition of the charge was incompatible with Articles 85 and 86 of the Treaty because it was part of a concerted practice followed by all or most banks both in the Federal Republic of Germany and in other Community States, which was contrary to the rules on competition and capable of affecting trade between the Member States.
5. In order to clarify that last point, in particular, the national court decided to refer the following question to the Court of Justice for a preliminary ruling pursuant to Article 177 of the Treaty:
'In transfers of capital and other payments between banks within the common market, is the debiting of a general service charge at a rate of 0.15% of the sum transferred a concerted practice which may affect trade, and therefore contrary to Articles 85 and 86 of the EEC Treaty?'.
6. The defendant in the main action raised the initial objection in the course of the oral procedure that the question of interpretation raised by the national court was without purpose because the Treaty provisions on competition did not apply, at least to a great extent, to banking undertakings. It maintained that by reason of the special nature of the services provided by such undertakings and the vital role which they play in transfers of capital they must be considered as undertakings 'entrusted with the operation of services of general economic interest' within the meaning of Article 90 (2) and thus are not subject, pursuant to that provision, to the rules on competition in Articles 85 and 86 of the Treaty. It also relied in support of its argument on the provisions in Article 104 et seq. of the Treaty concerning 'Economic policy'.
7. Although the transfer of customers' funds from one Member State to another normally performed by banks is an operation which falls within the special task of banks, particularly in connexion with international movements of capital, that is not sufficient to make them undertakings within the meaning of Article 90 (2) of the Treaty unless it can be established that in performing such transfers the banks are operating a service of general economic interest with which they have been entrusted by a measure adopted by the public authorities.
8. As to Article 104 et seq. of the Treaty, those provisions in no way have the effect of exempting banks from the competition rules of the Treaty. They appear in Chapter 2 of Title II of the Treaty, which concerns 'Balance of payments', and are restricted to stipulating that there must be coordination between the Member States on economic policy, and to that end they provide for collaboration between the appropriate national administrative departments and the central banks of the Member States in order to attain the objectives of the Treaty.
9. In the light of all those considerations the objection raised by the defendant in the main proceedings must therefore be dismissed.

10. The question of interpretation was raised by the national court with reference to the debiting of a uniform service charge of 0.15% on the relevant transactions. The question arose with regard to both Article 85 and Article 86 of the Treaty. In view of the fact that the order submitting the reference considers only the existence of a concerted practice as a possible infringement of Community rules on competition and having regard to the fact that Article 86 deals with the abuse of a dominant position and does not cover the existence of concerted practices, to which solely the provisions of Article 85 apply, examination of the question which has been referred to the Court must be restricted to the latter article.
11. According to Article 85 (1) of the Treaty: 'The following shall be prohibited as incompatible with the common market: all agreements between undertakings decisions by associations of undertakings and concerted practices which may affect trade between Member States and which have as their object or effect the prevention, restriction of distortion of competition within the common market'.
12. As the Court has stated, in particular in its judgment of 14 July 1972 (Case 48/69 *Imperial Chemical Industries Ltd* v. *Commission* [1972] ECR 619) a concerted practice within the meaning of Article 85 (1) of the Treaty is a form of coordination between undertakings which, without having reached the stage where an agreement properly so called has been concluded, knowingly substitutes practical cooperation between them for the risks of competition.
13. The Court also stated, in its judgment of 16 December 1975 (Joined Cases 40 to 48, 50, 54 to 56, 111, 113 and 114/73, *Suiker Unie* v. *Commission* [1975] ECR 1663, at p. 1942) that the criteria of coordination and cooperation necessary for the existence of a concerted practice in no way require the working out of an actual 'plan' but must be understood in the light of the concept inherent in the provisions of the Treaty relating to competition, according to which each trader must determine independently the policy which he intends to adopt on the common market and the conditions which he intends to offer to his customers.
14. Although it is correct to say that this requirement of independence does not deprive traders of the right to adapt themselves intelligently to the existing or anticipated conduct of their competitors, it does however strictly preclude any direct or indirect contract between such traders, the object or effect of which is to create conditions of competition which do not correspond to the normal conditions of the market in question, regard being had to the nature of the products or services offered, the size and number of the undertakings and the volume of the said market.
15. The applicant in the main proceedings is of the opinion that in this case there is a concerted practice consisting in the debiting by all or most banks within the common market, or at least in the Federal Republic of Germany, of a uniform service charge for transfers of sums of a similar amount to other Member States.

16. The defendant in the main proceedings has not denied that, for transfers of funds of this nature a charge at the same rate is imposed by other banks, both in the Federal Republic of Germany and in other Member States. It has however pointed out that this similarity of conduct is not the result of an agreement or concerted practice between those banks, the object or effect of which is to produce results prohibited by Article 85 of the Treaty. It has explained that the justification for imposing the charge lies in the costs involved in such transfers owing in particular to the complex nature of the exchange transactions involved, and it has observed, in addition, that the charge uniformly levied in respect of every transfer above a certain amount represents only a partial contribution towards the total cost of the transfers usually effected.

17. The fact that the charge in question is justified by the costs involved in all transfers abroad normally effected by banks on behalf of their customers, and that it therefore represents partial reimbursement of such costs, debited uniformly to all those who make use of such service, does not exclude the possibility that parallel conduct in that sphere may, regardless of the motive, result in coordination between banks which amounts to a concerted practice within the meaning of Article 85 of the Treaty.

18. Such a practice is capable, precisely because of the fact that it covers international transactions, of affecting 'trade between Member States' within the meaning of the above-mentioned article, the concept of 'trade' used in that article having a wide scope which includes monetary transactions.

19. Moreover, it would fall within the prohibition in Article 85 (1) of the Treaty if it were established that its object or effect was to affect significantly conditions of competition in the market in monetary transfers by banks from one Member State to another.

20. That would be the case, in particular, if a concerted practice enabled the banks participating in it to congeal conditions in their present state thus depriving their customers of any genuine opportunity to take advantage of services on more favourable terms which would be offered to them under normal conditions of competition.

21. That is question of fact which only the court adjudicating on the substance of the case has jurisdiction to decide. In doing so, it must consider whether between the banks conducting themselves in like manner there are contacts or, at least, exchanges of information on the subject of, *inter alia* the rate of the charges actually imposed for comparable transfers which have been carried out or are planned for the future and whether, regard being had to the conditions of the market in question, the rate of charge uniformly imposed is no different from that which would have resulted from the free play of competition. Consideration must also be given to the number and importance in the market in monetary transactions between Member States of the banks participating in such a practice, and the volume of transfers on which the charge in question is imposed as compared with the total volume of transfers made by the banks from one member country to another.

22. On all those grounds, the reply to the question which has been referred

to the Court must be that parallel conduct in the debiting of a uniform bank charge on transfers by banks from one Member State to another of sums from their customers' funds amounts to a concerted practice prohibited by Article 85 (1) of the Treaty of it is established by the national court that such parallel conduct exhibits the features of coordination and cooperation characteristic of such a practice and if that practice is capable of significantly affecting conditions of competition in the market for the services connected with such transfers.

(2) Asjes (Nouvelles Frontières) Case

Ministère Public v. *Lucas Asjes and Others*; Joined Cases 209–213/84; Preliminary ruling of 30 April 1986; [1986] ECR 1425.

See at page 672.

iii. Ratione temporis

aa. Cases

(1) Sirena Case

Sirena v. *Eda*; Case 40/70; Preliminary ruling of 10 February 1971; [1971] ECR 69.

Facts:

By order dated 12 June 1970, which reached the Court of Justice on 31 July 1970, the Tribunale Civile e Penale, Milan, referred to the Court under Article 177 of the EEC Treaty two questions concerning the interpretation of Articles 85 and 86 of the said Treaty. The Court is asked to decide whether Articles 85 and 86 of the Treaty are 'applicable to the effects of a contract of assignment of a trade-mark, made before the Treaty entered into force', and whether those articles must be interpreted 'as preventing the proprietor of a trade-mark lawfully registered in one Member State from exercising the absolute right derived from the trade-mark to prohibit third parties from importing, from other countries of the Community, products bearing the same trade-mark, lawfully attached to them in their place of origin'.

The Court held:

12. If the restrictive practices arose before the Treaty entered into force, it is

both necessary and sufficient that they continue to produce their effects after that date.

b. The concept of trade between Member States

i. Cases

(1) Grundig Case

Etablissements Consten SA and Grundig-Verkaufs GmbH v. *EEC Commission;* Cases 56 and 58/64; Judgment of 13 July 1966; [1966] ECR 341; [1966] CMLR 418; Competition Law CM/M/III/5.

Facts:

On 23 September 1964, the Commission took a decision prohibiting the exclusive dealing agreement concluded between the German manufacturer of radio, TV and recording equipment Grundig-Verkaufs GmbH and the French firm Etablissements Consten SA. The agreement provided for exclusive distribution with absolute protection of Consten's sales territory (France). The territorial protection arrangement was designed to make Consten sole supplier of Grundig products in France. For this purpose, Grundig had imposed an export ban on all its dealers in other countries, so that French purchasers could buy Grundig products only from Consten. In addition, Grundig and Consten had signed a supplementary agreement on the use of a special trademark (Gint) in France the purpose of which was also to hinder the importation by firms other than Consten into France.

Consten had sought to protect its exclusive dealing system by taking action on the basis of the French law on unfair competition (which contained a provision for the protection on exclusive dealing systems) and on the basis of infringement of the Gint trademark against several parallel importers. One of the undertakings concerned was the Paris firm UNEF. Consten won its action at first instance.

UNEF appealed against this decision and, in the meantime, submitted a complaint against Frundig and Consten to the European Commission. When the Commission commenced an action under Regulation No 17 the Court of Appeal in Paris suspended proceedings pending the decision of the Commission, Grundig and Consten appealed to the Court of Justice in Luxembourg against the unfavourable decision of the Commission.

The Court held:

. . . . .

The complaints relating to the concept of 'agreements ... which may affect trade between Member States'.

The applicants and the German Government maintain that the Commission has relied on a mistaken interpretation of the concept of an agreement which may affect trade between Member States and has not shown that such trade would have been greater without the agreement in dispute.

The defendant replies that this requirement in Article 85 (1) is fulfilled once trade between Member States develops, as a result of the agreement, differently from the way in which it would have done without the restriction resulting from the agreement, and once the influence of the agreement on market conditions reaches a certain degree. Such is the case here, according to the defendant, particularly in view of the impediments resulting within the Common Market from the disputed agreement as regards the exporting and importing of Grundig products to and from France.

The concept of an agreement 'which may affect trade between Member States' is intended to define, in the law governing cartels, the boundary between the areas respectively covered by Community law and national law. It is only to the extent to which the agreement may affect trade between Member States that the deterioration in competition caused by the agreement falls under the prohibition of Community law contained in Article 85; otherwise it escapes the prohibition.

In this connection, what is particularly important is whether the agreement is capable of constituting a threat, either direct or indirect, actual or potential, to freedom of trade between Member States in a manner which might harm the attainment of the objectives of a single market between States. Thus the fact that an agreement encourages an increase, even a large one, in the volume of trade between States is not sufficient to exclude the possibility that the agreement may 'affect' such trade in the abovementioned manner. In the present case, the contract between Grundig and Consten, on the one hand by preventing undertakings other than Consten from importing Grundig products into France, and on the other hand by prohibiting Consten from re-exporting those products to other countries of the Common Market, indisputably affects trade between Member States. These limitations on the freedom of trade, as well as those which might ensue for third parties from the registration in France by Consten of the GINT trade mark, which Grundig places on all its products, are enough to satisfy the requirement in question.

Consequently, the complaints raised in this respect must be dismissed.

Sequel

The Court annulled the decision of the Commission in so far as in Article 1 of its decision it declared that the whole of the contract between Consten and Grundig constituted an infringement of the provisions of Article 85. The Court held that most of the provision of the contract die not infringe Article 85 (1), but dismissed the remaining applications of Grundig and Consten.

(2) LTM – MBU Case

La Technique Minière v. *Maschinenbau Ulm*; Preliminary ruling of 30 July 1966; Case 56/65; [1966] ECR 235; [1966] CMLR 357; Competition Law CM/M/III/4.

Facts:

The French company La Technique Minière (LTM), which was engaged in the sale of material for public works contracts, purchased from the German company Maschinenbau Ulm (MBU) 37 levellers which were to be delivered over a period of two years. The contract provided the MBU granted the LTM 'the exclusive sales right' of the levellers 'for France'.

The parties agreed that 'the supply of machines liable to compete with the goods mentioned in the exclusivity clause could only be carried out with the agreement of Maschinenbau Ulm', and Technique Minière undertook 'to ensure the good working of a repairs service and to set up a good stock of spare parts'.

After delivery by MBU to LTM of six levellers, LTM asked the Court for the nomination of an expert to examin 'whether the machines were unsuitable for the use for which they were intended and unsalable to French customers'. The expert found they complied 'with the terms of the order' and were 'perfectly salable on the French market', and the Tribunal de Commerce de la Seine, at the suit of MBU, gave judgment on 8 January 1964 rejecting two objections of inadmissibility brought by LTM, one of which was based on the EEC Treaty, and declaring annulled the contract in question in so far as it was not executed, the latter company to bear the liability.

LTM appealed against that judgment, asking the Cour d'Appel de Paris to declare the contract 'absolutely void' as contrary to Article 85 of the EEC Treaty or, in the alternative, to stay proceedings until the European Court had given an interpretation of the said Article and implementing regulations under Article 177.

MBU then pleaded that notification to the EEC Commission was not compulsory for contract which were not subject to Article 85 (1) and that only a sole distribution contract, which partitioned the market completely, could fall under the application of that provision, whereas in this case competition was capable of taking place in France through parallel imports and the rights of LTM to export the levellers in question.

The Paris Court of Appeal decided to stay proceedings and to ask for a preliminary ruling by the Court of Justice. It submitted the following questions:

'1. What interpretation should be given to Article 85 (1) of the Treaty of Rome and to the Community regulations adopted in implementation thereof with regard to agreements which have not been notified and which whilst granting an 'exclusive right of sale',
– do not prohibit the concessionaire from re-exporting to any other markets of the EEC the goods which he has acquired from the grantor;

- do not include an undertaking by the grantor to prohibit his concessionaries in other countries of the Common Market from selling his products in the territory which is the primary responsibility of the concessionaire with whom the agreement is made;
- do not fetter the right of dealers and consumers in the country of the concessionaires to obtain supplies through parallel imports from concessionaires or suppliers in other countries of the Common Market;
- require the concessionaire to obtain the consent of the grantor before selling machines likely to compete with the goods with which the concession is concerned?
2. Does the expression 'automatically void' in Article 85 (2) of the Treaty of Rome mean that the whole of an agreement containing a clause prohibited by Article 85 (1) is void, or is it possible for the nullity to be limited to the prohibited clause alone?'

The Court held:

. . . . .

The effects on trade between Member States.

The agreement must also be one which 'may affect trade between Member States'.

This provision, clarified by the introductory words of Article 85 which refer to agreements in so far as they are 'incompatible with the Common Market', is directed to determining the field of application of the prohibition by laying down the condition that it may be assumed that there is a possibility that the relization of a single market between Member States might be impeded. It is in fact to the extent that the agreement may affect trade between Member States that the interference with competition caused by that agreement is caught by the prohibitions in Community law found in Article 85, whilst in the converse case it escapes those prohibitions. For this requirement to be fulfilled it must be possible to foresee with a sufficient degree of probability on the basis of a set of objective factors of law or of fact that the agreement in question may have an influence, direct or indirect, actual or potential, on the pattern of trade between Member States. Therefore, in order to determine whether an agreement which contains a clause 'granting an exclusive right of sale' comes within the field of application of Article 85, it is necessary to consider in particular whether it is capable of bringing about a partitioning of the market in certain products between Member States and thus rendering more difficult the interpenetration of trade which the Treaty is intended to create.

. . . . .

(3) VCH Case

Vereniging van Cementhandelaren v. *EC Commission*; Judgment of 17 October 1972; Case 8/72; [1972] ECR 977; [1973] CMLR 7; Competition Law CM/M/III/36.

Facts:

On 4 April 1928 the Vereeniging van Cementhandelaren (the Association of cement dealers) was founded in Amsterdam. Its objects were in particular to conclude agreements and to defend the interests of its members on the Dutch cement market both generally and as againt the manufacturers.

On 30 October the Association (VCH) notified to the EC Commission under Article 5 (1) of Regulation No 17 a series of agreements and decisions concerning the sale of cement in Holland. On 17 December 1965 several amendments and additions to the foregoing were also notified to the Commission.

Following various communications sent by the VCH to the Commission, including those of 29 September 1967, 9 September 1968 and 4 February 1969, the latter began examining conformity with Article 85 EEC of certain texts. This culminated in a communication of plaints by the Commission to the VCH on 26 January 1970, to which the VHC replied by letter of 29 May 1970. The Commission asked some further questions on 22 October 1970 which were answered by a letter from the VHC of 16 December 1970. An oral hearing was held at the Commission on 17 March 1971. Then after obtaining the opinion of the Consultative Committee on Cartels and Monopolies, the Commission issued a decision on 16 December 1971, holding that certain texts violated Article 85 (1) and could not be granted exemption under Article 85 (3) and ordering the violation to be terminated.

The VCH appealed against the Commission Decision.

The Court held:

(b) Influence on trade between Member States

26. According to the applicant association, the Community nonetheless has no jurisdiction to appraise the cartel to which the contested decision relates because it is a purely national cartel, limited to the territory of the Netherlands, which does not apply in any way to imports or exports and which consequently has no influence over the patterns of trade between Member States.
27. In this respect, it emphasizes more especially the fact that the total production of cement in the Netherlands far from satisfies the needs of the Netherlands economy and leaves a substantial need for imports, that furthermore there is, apart from its members, a large number of cement

sellers not affiliated to it and that therefore there is no danger of intra-Community trade being affected.
28. According to Article 85 (1) all agreements which have as their object of effect the prevention, restriction or distortion of competition are incompatible with the Treaty once they may affect trade between Member States.
29. An agreement extending over the whole of the territory of a Member State by its very nature has the effect of reinforcing the compartmentalization of markets on a national basis, thereby holding up the economic interpretation which the Treaty is designed to bring about and protecting domestic production.
30. In particular, the provisions of the agreement which are mutually binding on the members of the applicant association and the prohibition by the association on all sales to resellers who are not authorized by it make it more difficult for producers or sellers from other Member States to be active in or penetrate the Netherlands market.
31. It appears therefore that the objection based on the fact that trade between Member States is not capable of being affected by the decision of the applicant association must be rejected.
32. It follows from the foregoing that the complaints based on an alleged infringement of the rules of the Treaty must be dismissed.

. . . . .

(4) Windsurfing Case

Windsurfing International Inc. v. *Commission*; Case 193/83; Judgment of 25 February 1986; [1986] ECR 611.

Facts:

See the judgment below.

The Court held:

2. Windsurfing International is a company founded by Mr Hoyle Schweitzer, a key figure in the development of sailboards, an apparatus composed of a 'board' (a hull made of synthetic materials equipped with a centreboard) and a 'rig' (an assemblage consisting essentially of a mast, a joint for the mast, a sail and spars) which makes it possible to combine the art of surfing with the sport of sailing. The company's turnover derives partly from the proceeds of the sale of sailboards which it manufactures and

partly from the income arising out of licences which it has granted to other undertakings. In the 1970's Windsurfing International extended its operations to Europe, where it initially submitted patent claims in certain member countries of the European Community, namely the United Kingdom and the Federal Republic of Germany.
3. The scope of the patent for invention granted to Windsurfing International in the Federal Republic of Germany in 1978, following a patent claims procedure begun in 1969, has always been a matter of dispute. It is again in dispute in these proceedings because Windsurfing International argues that the clauses at issue in its licensing agreements are linked to the exercise of its patent rights and must therefore enjoy the protection which the EEC Treaty affords to industrial property rights, while this is denied by the Commission.
4. On 1 January 1973, when its patent application was still being examined by the German Patent Office [Bundespatentamt], Windsurfing International granted to Ten Cate, a Netherlands undertaking, an exclusive temporary licence for the production and sale in Europe of sailboards incorporating its know-how. Ten Cate was also granted the right to use the word marks 'Windsurfer' and 'Windsurfing' and a design mark ('logo') showing a stylized representation of a sail.
5. In 1976 and 1977 respectively, Ten Cate granted to the German undertakings Ostermann and Shark sub-licences for the exploitation of the German patent already applied for and also, in Ostermann's case, of any patent subsequently applied for in Europe. Windsurfing International does not accept that Ten Cate was entitled to enter into those two agreements. In 1978 they were taken over by Windsurfing International, which then concluded licensing agreements with other German undertakings, namely Akutec on 1 July 1978, SAN and Klepper on 1 January 1979 and Marker on 21 August 1980.

. . . . .

8. . . . the Commission considered it necessary to initiate a proceeding for the infringement of the competition rules against Windsurfing International . . . That proceeding resulted in the decision of 11 July 1983 whereby the Commission found that certain clauses in the licensing agreements originally concluded between Windsurfing International and Ostermann, Shark, Akutec, SAN, Klepper and Marker constituted an infringement of Article 85 (1) of the EEC Treaty and imposed upon Windsurfing International a fine of 50 000 ECU.

. . . . .

10. Windsurfing International has brought an action against that decision in which it challenges both the Commission's findings of fact and its legal assessment of the clauses which it found incompatible with Article 85 (1) of the Treaty.

. . . . .

B — *Obstacle to intra-Community trade*

95. Windsurfing International further argues that even though certain clauses in the licensing agreements may have been of such a nature as to restrict competition, they could not have had any appreciable effect on trade between Member States.
96. That argument must be rejected. Article 85 (1) of the Treaty does not require that each individual clause in an agreement should be capable of affecting intra-Community trade. Community law on competition applies to agreements between undertakings which may affect trade between Member States; only if the agreement as a whole is capable of affecting trade is it necessary to examine which are the clauses of the agreement which have as their object or effect a restriction or distortion of competition.
97. In a case such as the present one, in which there is no doubt as to the significance of the agreements at issue for trade between Member States, it is therefore unnecessary to examine whether each clause restricting competition, taken in isolation, may affect intra-Community trade.

c. The notion of undertaking

i. Decisions

(1) Reuter – BASF Decision

Decision of the Commission of 26 July 1976; O.J. No L 254, of 17 September 1976; (1976)2 CMLR D 44; Competition Law CM/M/I/106.

Facts:

Acting on a complaint from Mr. Gottfried Reuter, a research chemist and entrepreneur, the Commission decided that the contractual restraint on competition imposed on him when he sold the Elastomer Group to BASF infringed Article 85 (1) of the EEC Treaty.

The Decision was based on the following facts. Between 1969 and 1971 Mr Reuter, of Lemförde, near Hannover, sold his entire shareholding in the Swiss limited company Elastomer AG, which he owned, to BASF AG, Ludwigshafen. Elastomer was the holding company of a group of firms with plants in several countries both within and outside the Community. The group manufactures polyurethanes, which are synthetic substances increasingly used in a large number of industries for the production of various finished goods. The commercial value of the group consisted primarily of the knowhow and goodwill developed by Mr. Reuter. In the contract of sale dated 25 June 1971 Mr. Reuter undertook that for a period of eight years he would refrain from engaging in any direct or indirect activities in the field covered by the contract, whether in Germany or elsewhere. All activities relating to polyurethanes, research and development, manufacture, industrial application and marketing were included in this restraint. Every form of activity was prohibited, including the holding of shares in other undertakings and the making of association and consultancy agreements.

The Commission found that the restriction on research and development was intended to eliminate Mr. Reuter as a potential competitor from the polyurethane market, and was thereby a clear infringement of Community competition law.

The restriction on commerical activities – manufacture, application of knowhow and sales – which, taken separately might have been acceptable subject to certain conditions, such as being for a reasonable duration, was considered by the Commission to have become unlawful by the time of the Commission Decision, five years after the business had been transferred.

The Commission ruled

. . . . .

The agreement of 18 June 1971 containing the non-competition clause is an agreement between undertakings. Dr. Reuter is also to be regarded as an undertaking for the purpose of Article 85, since he engages in economic activity through those firms of the Elastomer group which remain under his control, by exploiting the results of his own research and as commercial advisor to third parties.

(2) Christiani and Nielsen Decision

Decision of the Communision of 18 June 1969 on an application for a negative clearance under Article 2 of Regulation No 17; J O No 165, 5 July 1969, p. 12; [1969] CMLR D 36; Competition Law CM/M/I/20.

Facts:

The firms concerned are the Danish company Christiani and Nielsen, Copenhagen, and its Netherlands subsidiary Christiani & Nielsen, The Hague, which have concluded an agreement under which the parent company makes available to its subsidiary its experience, know-how, and in certain cases the services of its technical staff.

The provision of the agreement most directly concerning the rules of competition is that preventing Christiani & Nielsen, The Hague, from exercising its activity outside Netherlands territory without the agreement of the parent company. The Commission nevertheless felt that the agreement in question did not restrict competition, since Christiani & Nielsen of The Hague, although a company with a legal personality of its own, was an integral part of the parent company economically and financially. The two companies were not therefore competing with each other. In these circumstances, the restriction preventing the subsidiary from operating outside the country where its registered office was situated ultimately did no more than apportion work within the economic entity constituted by the Christiani & Nielsen international group.

Christiani & Nielsen (The Hague) is a limited liability company governed by Dutch law. It follows a given economic object and to that end disposes of an organisation comprising staff and material and immaterial elements. Further, it bears the risk and the responsibility of the work which it carries out. The relations between the subsidiary and the parent company are governed by the agreement at present under examination, which sets out obligations bindings each of the two companies and which cannot be terminated without the assent of both parites.

For Article 85 (1) of the Treaty to apply, there should, between the undertakings in question, be competition which is capable of being restricted. This requirement is not necessarily fulfilled, in relations between two undertakings which carry on their activities in the same sector, by the mere fact of the existence of a separate legal personality for each of the undertakings. In that respect, it is imperative to know whether, on the factual level, autonomous activity of the subsidiary with regard to the parent company is possible on the economic plane.

The company Christiani & Nielsen (Copenhagen) created the company Christiani & Nielsen (The Hague) in order to carry out in optimum conditions on Dutch territory the work in which it has specialised. It was considerations of management which led this undertaking, the activity of which is international, to create subsidiaries in different countries rather than establishing there branches or agencies. That is a piece of marketing strategy which cannot have the effect of causing us to consider, in the present case, a wholly owned subsidiary as an economic entity which can enter into competition with its parent company.

In addition, Christiani & Nielsen (Copenhagen) has the right to nominate directors of Christiani & Nielsen (The Hague) and to give directives to its subsidiary, which is obliged to carry them out. Christiani & Nielsen (The Hague) is therefore an integral part of the economic whole making up the Christiani & Nielsen group.

The unity of the economic organisation of the parent company and the subsidiary is emphasised by the exchange of information, inventions, patents, know-how and by the permanent collaboration between the two undertakings.

In view of the foregoing, the division of markets laid down in the agreements is, in the end, only the distribution of tasks within a single economic entity. It could not be expected in this case that one part of this entity, albeit enjoying separate legal personality, should enter into competition with the parent company. Christiani & Nielsen (Copenhagen), even without any contract, would always have the power to determine the behaviour of Christiani & Nielsen (The Hague), of which it holds the whole of the share capital.

It follows from these factors that the agreement in question cannot have the object or effect of preventing, restricting or distorting competition within the Common Market.

In these circumstances, the information available to the Commission does not permit it to conclude that the agreement in the case is covered by Article 85 (1) and therefore the negative clearance may be granted.

The Commission decided:

1. There is no ground for the Commission, according to the information made available to it, to intervene under the provisions of Article 85 (1) of the Treaty instituting the European Economic Community with regard to the agreement concluded on 25 August 1931 and renewed on 20 March 1959 between Christiani & Nielsen (Copenhagen) and Christiani & Nielsen (The Hague).
2. The present decision is addressed to the company Christiani & Neilsen of Copenhagen, Denmark, and to the company Christiani & Nielsen of the Hague, Holland.

2. Article 85

a. Agreements

i. Cases

(1) LTM – MBU Case

Facts and references see pp. 494, 517.

The Court held:

The necessity for an agreement 'between undertakings'

In order to fall within this prohibition, an agreement must have been made between undertakings. Article 85 (1) makes no distinction as to whether the parties are at the same level in the economy (so-called horizontal agreements), or at different levels (so-called vertical agreements). Therefore an agreement containing a clause 'granting an exclusive right of a sale' may fulfil this condition.

b. Decisions by associations of undertakings

i. Cases

(1) Fedetab Case

Heintz von Ladewyck Sàrl and others v. *Commission*; joined cases 209 to 215 and 218/78; [1981] ECR 3250; [1981] 3 CMLR 134.

Facts:

The applicants sought annulment of a Commission Decision which had found that the applicants all members of the non-profit-making Féderation Belgo-Luxembourgeoise des Industries du Tabac, Brussels had committed various infringements of Article 85. The measures condemned by the Decision related to the manufacture and distribution of manufactured tobacco products in Belgium.

The Court held:

. . . . .

85. Jubilé and Vander Elst maintain that the Commission infringed Articles 85 and 190 of the Treaty by wrongly regarding the recommendation as having constituted an agreement between undertakings or a decision of an association of undertakings or as having imposed obligations on the applicants. To constitute such an agreement the recommendation would have had to involve features making it a binding contract under national law. In the present case it is not such a contract since the binding element is lacking.
86. That argument cannot be accepted. In the present case the applicant members of FEDETAB informed the Commission that they wished to be party to the notification of the recommendation and during the proceedings before the Court they admitted that they had complied with it since 1 December 1975. It follows that the recommendation is a faithful

87. expression of the applicants' intention to conduct themselves on the Belgian cigarette market in conformity with the terms of the recommendation. The necessary conditions for the application of Article 85 (1) are therefore satisfied.
87. Certain applicants including the intervener AGROTAB complain further that the Commission wrongly treated the recommendation as a decision of an association of undertakings within the meaning of Article 85 (1). The recommendation is said to have been made by FEDETAB, a non-profit-making association which as such does not trade.
88. That argument cannot be accepted either. It is apparent from Article 8 of the statutes of FEDETAB that the decisions taken by it are binding on its members. Further, Article 85 (1) also applies to associations in so far as their own activities or those of the undertakings belonging to them are calculated to produce the results which it aims to suppress. Since several manufacturers have expressly stated that they are complying with the provision of the recommendation, it cannot escape Article 85 of the Treaty simply because it has been made by a non-profit-making association.
89. Nor is it possible to accept the argument to the effect that the recommendation has no binding effect and that the decision is wrong in referring in paragraph 61 to a genuine mandatory rule of conduct for all firms in the industry. Apart from the fact that pursuant to Article 8 of the statutes of FEDETAB the provisions of the recommendation are binding on its members, it is necessary also to point out that compliance with the recommendation by seven undertakings, the applicants in the present cases, who control a substantial part of the total cigarette sales in Belgium, has a profound influence on competition in the market in question.

. . . . .

c. Concerted practices

i. Cases

(1) Züchner Case

Facts and references see p. 487.

The Court held:

11. According to Article 85 (1) of the Treaty: 'The following shall be prohibited as incompatible with the common market: all agreements between undertakings decisions by associations of undertakings and concerted

practices which may affect trade between Member States and which have as their object or effect the prevention, restriction of distortion of competition within the common market'.

12. As the Court has stated, in particular in its judgment of 14 July 1972 (Case 48/69 *Imperial Chemical Industries Ltd* v. *Commission* [1972] ECR 619) a concerted practice within the meaning of Article 85 (1) of the Treaty is a form of coordination between undertakings which, without having reached the stage where an agreement properly so called has been concluded, knowingly substitutes practical cooperation between them for the risks of competition.

13. The Court also stated, in its judgment of 16 December 1975 (Joined Cases 40 to 48, 50, 54 to 56, 111, 113 and 114/73, *Suiker Unie* v. *Commission* [1975] ECR 1663, at p. 1942) that the criteria of coordination and co-operation necessary for the existence of a concerted practice in no way require the working out of an actual 'plan' but must be understood in the light of the concept inherent in the provisions of the Treaty relating to competition, according to which each trader must determine independently the policy which he intends to adopt on the common market and the conditions which he intends to offer to his customers.

14. Although it is correct to say that this requirement of independence does not deprive traders of the right to adapt themselves intelligently to the existing or anticipated conduct of their competitors, it does however strictly preclude any direct or indirect contract between such traders, the object or effect of which is to create conditions of competition which do not correspond to the normal conditions of the market in question, regard being had to the nature of the products or services offered, the size and number of the undertakings and the volume of the said market.

d. Object or effect

i. Cases

(1) Grundig Case

Facts and references see pages 492, 518.

The Court held:

Besides, for the purpose of applying Article 85 (1), there is no need to take account of the concrete effects of an agreement once it appears that it has as its object the prevention, restriction or distortion of competition.

Therefore the absence in the contested decision of any analysis of the effects of the agreement on competition between similar products of different makes does not, of itself, constitute a defect in the decision.

e. Competition

i. Cases

(1) Metro Case I

Metro SB- Grossmärkte GmbH & Co KG v. *Commission*; Case 26/76; Judgment of 25 October 1977; [1977] ECR 1903; [1978] 2 CMLR 1.

Facts:

Metro applied to the Court of Justice for annulment of the Commission Decision exempting the selective distribution system established by SABA for distributing its electronic equipment for the leisure market. SABA refuses to supply Metro for it does not fulfil the conditions for appointment as a SABA wholesaler. The Commission approved Metro's exclusion by its Decision.

The Court held:

. . . . .

19. The applicant maintains that Article 2 of the contested decision is vitiated by misuse of powers inasmuch as the Commission has failed to recognize 'what is protected under Article 85 (namely) freedom of competition for the benefit of the consumer, not the coincident interests of a manufacturer and a given group of traders who wish to secure selling prices which are considered to be satisfactory by the latter'.

    Furthermore, if it were to be considered that an exemption from the prohibition might be granted in respect of the distribution system in dispute pursuant to Article 85 (3), the applicant maintains that the Commission has misapplied that provision by granting an exemption in respect of restrictions on competition which are not indispensable to the attainment of the objectives of improving production or distribution or promoting technical or economic progress and which lead to the elimination of competition from self-service wholesale traders.

A – Misuse of powers

20. The requirement contained in Article 3 and 85 of the EEC Treaty that competition shall not be distorted implies the existence on the market of workable competition, that is to say the degree of competition necessary

to ensure the observance of the basic requirements and the attainment of the objectives of the Treaty, in particular and creation of a single market achieving conditions similar to those of a domestic market.

In accordance with this requirement the nature and intensiveness of competition may vary to an extent dictated by the products or services in question and the economic structure of the relevant market sectors.

In the sector covering the production of high quality and technically advanced consumer durables, where a relatively small number of large- and medium-scale producers offer a varied range of items which, or so consumers may consider, are readily interchangeable, the structure of the market does not preclude the existence of a variety of channels of distribution adapted to the peculiar characteristics of the various producers and to the requirements of the various categories of consumers.

On this view the Commission was justified in recognizing that selective distribution systems constituted, together with others, as aspect of competition which accords with Article 85 (1), provided that resellers are chosen on the basis of objective criteria of a qualitative nature relating to the technical qualifications of the reseller and his staff and the suitability of his trading premises and that such conditions are laid down uniformly for all potential resellers and are not applied in a discriminatory fashion.

21. It is true that in such systems of distribution price competition is not generally emphasized either as an exclusive or indeed as a principal factor.

This is particularly so when, as in the present case, access to the distribution network is subject to conditions exceeding the requirements of an appropriate distribution of the products.

However, although price competition is so important that it can never be eliminated it does not constitute the only effective form of competition or that to which absolute priority must in all circumstances be accorded.

The powers conferred upon the Commission under Article 85 (3) show that the requirements for the maintenance of workable competition may be reconciled with the safeguarding of objectives of a different nature and that to this end certain restrictions on competition are permissible, provided that they are essential to the attainment of those objectives and that they do not result in the elimination of competition for a substantial part of the Common Market.

For specialist wholesalers and retailers the desire to maintain a certain price level, which corresponds to the desire to preserve, in the interests of consumers, the possibility of the continued existence of this channel of distribution in conjunction with new methods of distribution based on a different type of competition policy, forms one of the objectives which may be pursued without necessarily falling under the prohibition contained in Article 85 (1), and, if it does fall thereunder, either wholly or in part, coming within the framework of Article 85 (3).

This argument is strengthened if, in addition, such conditions promote improved competition inasmuch as it relates to factors other than prices.

22. Although the figures submitted by both sides concerning the existence of price competition amongst SABA distributors ultimately indicate that the price structure is somewhat rigid, they do not, especially in view of the existence at the same time of competition between products of the same brand (intra-brand competition) and the existence of effective competition between different brands, permit the conclusion that competition has been restricted or eliminated on the market in electronic equipment for leisure purposes.

Nevertheless, the Commission must ensure that this structural rigidity is not reinforced, as might happen if there were an increase in the number of selective distribution networks for marketing the same product.

Since the Commission granted the desired exemption only for a period expiring on 21 July 1980 it retains the possibility of reconsidering within a reasonable time the consequences of this aspect of its decision.

In those circumstances the submission based on the existence of a misuse of powers must be rejected.

(2) Remia Case

Remia BV and others v. *Commission*; Case 42/84; Judgment of 11 July 1985; [1985] ECR 2545.

Facts:

See the judgment below.

The Court held:

2. The public limited company NV Verenigde Bedrijven Nutricia (hereinafter referred to as 'Nutricia'), whose registered office is in the Netherlands, is a manufacturer of health and baby foods. In 1974 it acquired two undertakings which become its subsidiaries, Remia BV (hereinafter referred to as 'Remia'), which belonged to Mr de Rooij and was principally a manufacturer of Remia sauces, margarine and materials for the baking industry, and Luycks Producten BV (hereinafter referred to as 'Luycks'), a manufacturer of sauces under the Luycks brand name and of condiments. From 1974 to 1976 both subsidiaries retained their own sales divisions and continued their existing production.

3. In early 1977 Nutricia decided to review the arrangements under which its subsidiaries' products were marketed in order to improve their profitability, particularly in view of the financial difficulties experienced by Luycks. From 1977 to 1978 Luycks and Remia kept their legal status and production unchanged but the management of the sales divisions of both subsidiaries was modified as part of a rationalization scheme.

4. In 1979 Nutricia undertook a restructuring of its production facilities, concentrating sauce production at Remia while leaving the production of pickles and condiments with Luycks. The re-organization was undertaken partly in the hope of making it easier to find buyers for Remia and Luycks.
5. By an agreement of 31 August 1979 Nutricia transferred Remia, thus restructured, back to Mr de Rooij, its former proprietor, and the undertaking was later renamed New Remia. That agreement is referred to as 'the sauce agreement'. By a second agreement dated 6 June 1980 Nutricia transferred its Luycks subsidiary, as restructured, to the undertaking Zuid-Hollandse Conservenfabriek (hereinafter referred to as 'Zuid'), and Luycks was re-named Luycks-Zuid and then Sluyck. Zuid is a subsidiary of the American company Campbell. The agreement of 6 June 1980 is referred to as 'the pickles agreement'.
6. Both transfer agreements contained non-competition clauses intended to protect the purchasers from competition from the vendor on the same market immediately after the transfers.
7. By clause 5 of the sauce agreement Nutricia undertook for a period of 10 years not to engage directly or indirectly in the production or sale of sauces on the Netherlands market and to guarantee Lucyks's compliance with that undertaking. As a transitional arrangement, Luycks was given the right to manufacture and sell sauces for export and even, to a very limited extent, on the Netherlands market, but only until 1 July 1980.
8. Clause V (1) (f) in the pickles agreement concluded between Nutricia and Zuid extended to Luycks-Zuid the restriction contained in clause 5 of the sauce agreement. Furthermore, under clause IX, Nutricia undertook for a period of five years not to engage 'directly or indirectly ... in any production or sale of pickles or condiments in European countries.'
9. The Campbell company let it be known to the applicants that it regarded the non-competition clause imposed on Luycks as contrary to Article 85 of the EEC Treaty, and this prompted them to notify the two transfer agreements to the Commission in June and July 1981 and to request, not negative clearance, but an exemption under Article 85 (3) of the EEC Treaty.
10. By a decision dated 12 December 1983, the Commission, taking the view that the duration and scope of the non-competition clauses mentioned above were excessive and that the clauses constituted a restriction on competition, affected trade between Member States and were not eligible for exemption under Article 85 (3), refused the applicants' request for an exemption.
11. Those are the circumstances in which the applicants brought this action, by which they ask the Court to declare the contested decision void, declare 'that the non-competition clause referred to in Article 1 of the decision does not infringe Article 85 (1) of the EEC Treaty and in any case not as from 1 October 1983 and that in any event the Commission wrongly failed to apply Article 85 (3)' ...

The application of Article 85 (1) of the EEC Treaty

17. It should be stated at the outset that the Commission has rightly submitted — and the applicants have not contradicted it on that point — that the fact that non-competition clauses are included in an agreement for the sale of an undertaking is not of itself sufficient to remove such clauses from the scope of Article 85 (1) of the Treaty.
18. In order to determine whether or not such clauses come within the prohibition in Article 85 (1), it is necessary to examine what would be the state of competition if those clauses did not exist.
19. If that were the case, and should the vendor and the purchaser remain competitors after the transfer, it is clear that the agreement for the transfer of the undertaking could not be given effect. The vendor, with his particularly detailed knowledge of the transferred undertaking, would still be in a position to win back his former customers immediately after the transfer and thereby drive the undertaking out of business. Against that background non-competition clauses incorporated in an agreement for the transfer of an undertaking in principle have the merit of ensuring that the transfer has the effect intended. By virtue of that very fact they contribute to the promotion of competition because they lead to an increase in the number of undertakings in the market in question.
20. Nevertheless, in order to have that beneficial effect on competition, such clauses must be necessary to the transfer of the undertaking concerned and their duration and scope must be strictly limited to that purpose. The Commission was therefore right in holding that where those conditions are satisfied such clauses are free of the prohibition laid down in Article 85 (1).

. . . . .

45. As regards the submission alleging that the contested decision contains a mistaken appraisal of the facts of the case in so far as it refuses a request for an exemption under Article 85 (3), it should be observed that, as the Court held in its judgment of 17 January 1984 in Joined Cases 43 and 63/82 (cited above), where an exemption is being applied for under Article 85 (3) it is in the first place for the undertakings concerned to present to the Commission the evidence intended to establish the economic justification for an exemption.

(3) Philip Morris-Rothmans Case

British American Tobacco Company Ltd. and R.J. Reynolds Industries Inc. v.

Commission; Cases 142/84 and 156/84; Judgment of 17 November 1987 (not yet published).

Facts:

See the judgment below.

The Court held:

1. By applications lodged at the Court Registry on 4 and 20 June 1984 respectively, British-American Tobacco Company Ltd., whose head office is in London, and R.J. Reynolds Industries Inc., Winston Salem, North Carolina (USA), brought two actions pursuant to Article 173(2) EEC for the annulment of the decision contained in the Commission's letters no. SG(84)D/3946 of 22 March 1984 concerning Cases IV/30.342 and IV/30.926, rejecting the applications made by the applicants pursuant to Article 3(2) of Regulation 17 and declaring that certain agreements concluded between Philip Morris Inc. (hereinafter referred to as Philip Morris), New York, and Rembrandt Group Ltd. (hereinafter referred to as Rembrandt), Stellenbosch, Republic of South Africa, do not infringe Articles 85 and 86 EEC. The applicants also ask the Court to order the Commission to alter its position with regard to those applications in order to comply with the judgment of the Court.
2. By orders of 28 November 1984 the Court granted Philip Morris and Rembrandt leave to intervene in support of the Commission's conclusions. By an order of 26 September 1984 the Court joined the cases for the purposes of the oral procedure and of the judgment.
3. The applications submitted by the applicants pursuant to Article 3(2) of Regulation 17 were directed against agreements between Philip Morris and Rembrandt under which Philip Morris bought from Rembrandt, for $350 million, 50 per cent. of the shares in Rothmans Tobacco (Holdings) Ltd. (hereinafter referred to as Rothmans Holdings), a holding company wholly owned by Rembrandt which held a sufficiently large shareholding in Rothmans International plc (hereinafter referred to as Rothmans International) to control the latter company, and important manufacturer of cigarettes on the Community market, especially in the Benelux countries. Under those agreements Philip Morris acquired an indirect share of 21.9 per cent. in the profits of its competitor Rothmans International.
4. Those agreements (hereinafter referred to as the 1981 agreements) also contained conditions intended to maintain a balance between the parties with regard to their direct or indirect shareholdings in Rothmans International and gave each of the parties a 'right of first refusal' in the event of the disposal by the other party of its shareholding in Rothmans Holdings.

5. With regard to management, the 1981 agreements gave the two parties the right to appoint an equal number of members to the board of directors of Rothmans Holdings. They provided that Rembrandt was to retain the management functions which it had exercised until then in relation to the commercial activities of Rothmans International, and that information of a competitive nature was not to be made available to Philip Morris, but they also contained provisions for co-operation between Philip Morris and Rothmans International in sectors such as joint distribution and manufacture, technical know-how and research, and so forth.
6. Following complaints lodged by the applicants, among others, the Commission issued a statement of objections to Philip Morris and Rembrandt to the effect that the 1981 agreement infringed both Articles 85 and 86 of the Treaty. After negotiations with the Commission, Philip Morris and Rembrandt finally replaced those agreements with new agreements intended to remove the cause for the Commission's objections. It is those agreements (hereinafter referred to as the 1984 agreements) which are the subject-matter of the contested Commission decisions; the Commission did not consider it necessary to adopt a decision concerning the original 1981 agreements, since they had been rescinded and replaced by the 1984 agreements.
7. Under the 1984 agreements, Philip Morris abandoned its shareholding in Rothmans Holdings in exchange for a direct shareholding in Rothmans International. That holding is 30.8 per cent. but represents only 24.9 per cent. of the votes, whereas Rembrandt's holding, also 30.8 per cent., represents 43.6 per cent. of the votes.
8. Like the 1981 agreements, the new agreements give each party a right of first refusal if the other disposes of its shareholding. Furthermore, in the case of a disposal to third parties a party must dispose of the whole of its shareholding, and may transfer it only to a single independent purchaser or to ten or more independent purchasers. If Rembrandt disposes of its shareholding to a single purchaser, that purchaser must make an identical offer for Philip Morris's shareholding. Finally, where one or other of the parties disposes of its shareholding, the agreements provide for the possibility of an equal division of voting rights in Rothmans International.
9. The 1984 agreements were accompanied by a number of undertakings given by the parties to the Commission. Those undertakings given by the parties to the Commission. Those undertakings are intended in particular to ensure that Philip Morris is not represented in the management of Rothmans International and that information concerning the Rothmans International group which might influence the behaviour of the Philip Morris group in the competitive relationship between the two groups within the Community is not made available to Philip Morris. Furthermore, Philip Morris undertook to inform the Commission of any amendment to the agreements and of any increase in its shareholding in Rothmans International or any circumstances in which it would obtain 25 per cent. or more of the voting rights in Rothmans International. In the two

latter cases the Commission may require a 'hold separate' arrangement with regard to the respective interests of Rothmans International and Philip Morris so as to ensure maintenance of the *status quo* for a period of three months, during which the Commission may determine what further measures, if any, are appropriate.

...

The application of Article 85

32. The applicants argue in substance that where a company acquires a substantial shareholding, albeit a minority one, in a competing company it must be presumed that there will be a restrictive effect on competition. The acquisition of such a shareholding inevitably has an influence on the commercial behaviour of the companies concerned, particularly in a stagnant and highly oligopolistic market such as that for cigarettes, where any attempt to increase the market share of one company will be at the expense of its competitiors. The establishment of links between two of the largest firms on the market for cigarettes will destroy the competitive balance.
33. According to the applicants, the transactions in question not only has the effect of restricting competition but was intended to do so. That is clear from the relationship between the agreements in issue and the original 1981 agreements which provided for commercial co-operation between the parties. It was by means of the rights which it obtained under the original agreements that Philip Morris was able to acquire a direct shareholding in Rothmans International, and there is no indication that the idea of commercial co-operation was abandoned, especially since the price paid by Philip Morris remained the same. The intention of Philip Morris and Rothmans International to co-operate on the Community market is confirmed, moreover, by the fact that they have agreements to co-operate in Indonesia, Malaysia and the Philippines.
34. The applicants also submit that the anti-competitive effect and intention of the agreements at issue are reinforced by the clauses providing for a right of first refusal in the event that one of the parties should wish to dispose of its shareholding in Rothmans International. Those clauses are intended to preserve for Philip Morris the possibility of acquiring control of Rothmans International, and show that its acquisition of an equity interest is not a simple passive investment. The fact that the exercise of the rights granted by those clauses would be contrary to Article 85 is sufficient in itself to justify a finding that the object of the agreements is to restrict competition.
35. Finally, the undertakings required by the Commission are, according to the applicants, in no way sufficient to rid the agreements of their anti-competitive nature. First of all, the undertakings regarding the existing management of Rothmans International do not prevent Philip Morris from exerting informal influence in its capacity as a substantial share-

holder in Rothmans International. Furthermore, the undertakings regarding the separation of the interests of Philip Morris and Rothmans International should Philip Morris exercise its right of first refusal concern the period following an infringement of Article 85 and would not even apply if Philip Morris gained effective control of Rothmans International on the sale of Rembrandt's shareholding to at least ten purchasers independent of each other and of Philip Morris.

36. It should be recalled that the agreements prohibited by Article 85 are those which have as their object or effect the prevention, restriction or distortion of competition within the Common Market.

37. Although the acquisition by one company of an equity interest in a competitor does not in itself constitute conduct restricting competition, such an acquisition may neveretheless serve as an instrument for influencing the commercial conduct of the companies in question so as to restrict or distort competition on the market on which they carry on business.

38. That will be true in particular where, by the acquisition of a shareholding or through subsidiary clauses in the agreement, the investing company obtains legal or *de facto* control of the commercial conduct of the other company or where the agreement provides for commercial co-operation between the companies or creates a structure likely to be used for such co-operation.

39. That may also be the case where the agreement gives the investing company the possibility of reinforcing its position at a later stage and taking effective control of the other company. Account must be taken not only of the immediate effects of the agreement but also of its potential effects and of the possibility that the agreement may be part of a long-term plan.

40. Finally, every agreement must be assessed in its economic context and in particular in the light of the situation on the relevant market. Moreover, where the companies concerned are multinational corporations which carry on business on a world-wide scale, their relationships outside the Community cannot be ignored. It is necessary in particular to consider the possibility that the agreement in question may be part of a policy of global co-operation between the companies which are party to it.

f. De minimis

i. Cases

(1) Völk — Vervaecke Case

Franz Völk v. *Etablissements J. Vervaecke*; Preliminary ruling of 9 July 1969; Case 5/69; [1969] ECR 295; [1969] CMLR 273; Competition Law CM/M/III/11.

Facts:

Völk, trading under the name of Josef Erd & Co., manufacturers of washing machines under the trademark 'Konstant'. Vervaecke is an undertaking distributing household electrical appliances.

On 15 September 1963 the two undertakings concluded an agreement in which Völk granted Vervaecke the exclusive right to sell its products in Belgium and Luxembourg. Vervaecke undertook to place a monthly order for about 80 appliances with Völk. Völk undertook to protect Vervaecke's sales territory against parallel imports. The agreement was supplemented several times during 1964.

After some time the parties disagreed about the execution of the contract and Völk started proceedings before a German court against Vervaecke. The German court of first instance, the Landesgericht, Kempten, found for Völk. Vervaecke appealed against this judgment to the Oberlandesgericht Munich. Vervaecke submitted in both instances that the agreement was in violation of Article 85 since it contained clauses granting absolute territorial protection, Völk on the other hand considered that those provisions were valid because the proportion of the market which he had acquired in Belgium and in Luxembourg and that which he had in fact endeavoured to acquire was extremely small.

On 5 December 1968 the Oberlandesgericht, Munich, decided to ask the Court, under Article 177 of the EEC Treaty, to give a ruling on the following question:

'In determining whether the disputed conctract of 15 December 1963, as amended on 1 January 1964 and 11 March 1964, falls within the prohibition set out in Article 85 (1) of the EEC Treaty, must regard be had to the proportion of the market which the plaintiff in fact acquired or ultimately endeavoured to acquire in the Member States of the European Economic Community, in particular in Belgium and in Luxembourg, the sales sector for which the defendant enjoys 'absolute protection?'

The Court held:

. . . . .

5/7 If an agreement is to be capable of affecting trade between Member States it must be possible to foresee with a sufficient degree of probability on the basis of a set of objective factors of law or of fact that the agreement in question may have an influence, direct or indirect, actual or potential, on the pattern of trade between Member States in such a way that it might hinder the attainment of the objectives of a single market between States. Moreover the prohibition in Article 85 (1) is applicable only if the agreement in question also has as its object or effect the prevention, restriction or distortion of competition within the Common Market. Those conditions must be understood by reference to the actual circumstances of the agreement. Consequently an agreement falls outside the prohibition in Article 85 when it has only an insignificant effect on the markets, taking into account the weak position which the persons concerned have on the market of the product in question. Thus an exclusive dealing agreement, even with absolute territorial protection, may, having regard to the weak position of the persons concerned on the market in the products in question in the area covered by the absolute protection, escape the prohibition laid down in Article 85 (1).

Sequel:

The Oberlandesgericht, Munich, in a judgment of 19 November 1969, ruled in favour of Völk. The Court considered the agreement to be valid.

For the Commission's point of view on the de minimis rule consult the Commission notice of 19 December 1977 concerning agreements, decisions and concerted practices of minor importance which do not fall under Article 85 (1) of the EEC Treaty.

See however the Commission's refusal to apply this notice in re *Advocaat Zwarte Kip*.

In re *SABA*, for references see above page 398, where Article 85 (1) applied, the share of the market of the undertakings concerned ranged in the Federal Republic of Germany for the various types of equipment from 1.8% to 11.9% and the share of the market in other Member States was less than 1%.

In Case 22/71, *Béguelin Import Co.* v. *Import Export SA* the Court of Justice clarified its holding in the *Völk-Vervaecke* case in its judgment of 25 November 1971; [1971] ECR 960:

'In order to come within the prohibition imposed by Article 85 the agreement must affect trade between Member States and the free play of competition to an appreciable extent'.

g. Nullity

i. Cases

(1) Haecht Case II

Brasserie de Haecht v. *Wilkin-Janssen*; Case 48/73; [1973] ECR 77; [1973] CMLR 287; Competition Law CM/M/III/37.

Facts:

The Commercial Court of Liège, in the proceedings brought before it by the brewery company de Haecht against the café proprietors Wilkin and Janseen, has asked a second time for a preliminary ruling under Article 177 of the EEC Treaty. The Court would now like to have answers to the following questions:
1. 'Must a procedure under Articles 2, 3 and 6 of Regulation No 17 be considered to be initiated by the Commission from the moment when it acknowledged receipt of a request for a negative clearance or of notification for the purposes of obtaining exemption under Article 85 (3) of the EEC Treaty?'
2. 'Can notification of a standard contract referring to legal arrangements made in 1968 be considered as notification of a similar contract entering into during 1963?'
3. 'Is the nullity of contracts exempted from notification to be deemed to take effect from the date when one of the contracting parties duly brings an action for it or merely from the date of the judgment or the decision of the Commission which establishes it?'

The Court held:

On the third question

24. This question is concerned with whether nullity be virtue of Article 85 (2) of agreements exempted from notification is deemed to take effect from the date when one of the contracting parties duly claimed it or merely from the date of the judgment or the decision of the Commission establishing it.
25. It follows from the general considerations above that Article 85 (2) renders agreements and decisions prohibited pursuant to that Article automatically void.
26. Such nullity is therefore capable of having a bearing on all the effects, either past or future, of the agreement or decision.
27. Consequently, the nullity provided for in Article 85 (2) is of retroactive effect.

(2) LTM — MBU Case

For facts and references see pp. 494, 502.

The Court held:

The second question relating to the interpretation of Article 85 (2)

Article 85 (2) provides that 'Any agreements or decisions prohibited pursuant to this Article shall be automatically void'. This provision, which is intended to ensure compliance with the Treaty, can only be interpreted with reference to its purpose in Community law, and it must be limited to this context. The automatic nullity in question only applies to those parts of the agreement affected by the prohibition, or to the agreement as a whole if it appears that those parts are not severable from the agreement itself. Consequently any other contractual provisions which are not affected by the prohibition, and which therefore do not involve the application of the Treaty, fall outside Community law.

h. Article 85 (3)

i. Cases

(1) Grundig Case

For facts and references see pp. 492, 505.

The Court held:

The complaints concerning the application of Article 85 (3)
The conditions of application.

The applicants, supported on several points by the German Government, allege inter alia that all the conditions for application of the exemption, the existence of which is denied in the contested decision, are met in the present case. The defendant starts from the premise that it is for the undertakings concerned to prove that the conditions required for exemption are satisfied.

The undertakings are entitled to an appropriate examination by the Commission of their requests for Article 85 (3) to be applied. For this purpose the Commission may not confine itself to requiring from undertakings proof of the fulfilment of the requirements for the grant of the exemption but must, as a matter of good administration, play its part, using the means available to it, in ascertaining the relevant facts and circumstances.

Furthermore, the exercise of the Commission's powers necessarily implies complex evaluations on economic matters. A judicial review of these evaluations must take account of their nature by confining itself to an examination of the relevance of the facts and of the legal consequences which the Commission deduces therefrom. This review must in the first place be carried out in respect of the reasons given for the decisions which must set out the facts and considerations on which the said evaluations are based.

The contested decision states that the principal reason for the refusal of exemption lies in the fact that the requirement contained in Article 85 (3) (a) is not satisfied.

The German Government complains that the said decision does not answer the question whether certain factors, especially the advance orders and the guarantee and after-sales services, the favourable effects of which were recognized by the Commission, could be maintained intact in the absence of absolute territorial protection.

The contested decision admits only by way of assumption that the sole distributorship contract in question contributes to an improvement in production and distribution. Then the contested decision examines the question 'whether an improvement in the distribution of goods by virtue of the sole distribution agreement could no longer be achieved if parallel imports were admitted'. After examining the arguments concerning advance orders, the observation of the market and the guarantee and after-sales services, the decision concluded that 'no other reason which militates in favour of the necessity for absolute territorial protection has been put forward or hinted at'.

The question whether there is an improvement in the production or distribution of the goods in question, which is required for the grant of exemption, is to be answered in accordance with the spirit of Article 85. First, this improvement cannot be identified with all the advantages which the parties to the agreement obtain from it in their production or distribution activities. These advantages are generally indisputable and show the agreement as in all respects indispensable to an improvement as understood in this sense. This subjective method, which makes the content of the concept of 'improvement' depend upon the special features of the contractual relationships in question, is not consistent with the aims of Article 85. Furthermore, the very fact that the Treaty provides that the restriction of competition must be 'indispensable' to the improvement in question clearly indicates the importance which the latter must have. This improvement must in praticular show appreciable objective advantages of such a character as to compensate for the disadvantages which they cause in the field of competition.

The argument of the German Government, based on the premise that all those features of the agreement which favour the improvement as conceived by the parties to the agreement must be maintained intact, presupposes that the question whether all those features are not only favourable but also indispensable to the improvement of the production or distribution of the goods in question has already been settled affirmatively. Because of this the argument not only tends to weaken the requirement of indispensability but also amongst other consequences to confuse solicitude for the specific interests of the parties with the obejctive improvements contemplated by the Treaty.

In its evaluation of the relative importance of the various factors submitted for its consideration, the Commission on the other hand had to judge their effectiveness by reference to an objectively ascertainable improvement in the production and distribution of the goods, and to decide whether the resulting benefit would suffice to support the conclusion that the consequent restrictions upon competition were indispensable. The argument based on the necessity to maintain intact all arrangements of the parties in so far as they are capable of contributing to the improvement sought cannot be reconciled with the view propounded in the last sentence. Therefore, the complaint of the Federal Government, based on faulty premises, is not such as can invalidate the Commission's assessment.

. . . . .

(2) VBVB – VBBB Case

Vereeniging ter Bevordering van het Vlaamse Boekwezen, VBVB, and Vereeniging tot Bevordering van de Belangen des Boekhandels, VBBB, v. *Commission*; Joined Cases 43 and 63/82; Judgment of 14 January 1984 [1984] ECR 19.

Facts:

The Vereeniging ter Bevordering van de Belangen des Boekhandels (hereinafter referred to as 'the Dutch Association') is an association of publishers, book wholesalers, booksellers, importers of books and book-club operators who are established in the Netherlands. Its object is to protect the common interests of booksellers and publishers and to promote cooperation in the book trade in the widest sense, in particular by laying down and administering binding rules governing the book trade in the Netherlands with the object of determining standards and practices for bookselling in the Netherlands and encouraging their observance and application.

The Vereniging ter Bevordering van het Vlaamse Boekwezen (hereinafter referred to as 'the Flemish Association'), an association having its place of business in Antwerp, is a federation, possessing legal personality, of publishers, booksellers, sole distributors of domestic and foreign publishing houses and members of allied trades and is established in the Dutch-speaking part of Belgium. Its object is to protect the interests of the book trade in the widest sense; with that aim in view it has drawn up and administers binding rules concerning trade in Dutch-language books in Belgium.

The essential feature of the national rules is a resale price maintenance system, collectively applied, which is binding on the members of the associations. The associations are empowered to conclude with national or foreign organizations binding agreements relating to the book trade.

On 21 January 1949 the Dutch and Flemish Associations made an agreement (amended on 2 June 1958) relating to trade in Dutch-language books between Belgium and the Netherlands.

The agreement concluded between the two associations was notified to the Commission, in pursuance of Article 5 of Regulation No 17 of the Council of 6 February 1962, the first regulation implementing Articles 85 and 86 of the Treaty (Official Journal, English Special Edition 1959–1962, p. 87) by the Dutch Association on 30 October 1962 and by the Flemish Association on 3 November 1962, together with the relevant national rules. At that time they made an application for negative clearance for both the transnational agreement and the domestic systems.

Article 1 of the decision states that the agreement between the two associations, making provision for collective exclusive dealing and collective resale price maintenance in trade in Dutch-language books between Belgium and the Netherlands, infringes Article 85 (1) of the EEC Treaty. Article 2 states that the application for exemption under Article 85 (3) of the Treaty is dismissed. Article 3 requires the two associations of undertakings to bring the infringement established to an end forthwith. Article 4 requires the two associations of undertakings to inform their members and affiliates and other parties recognized by or registered with them of the Commission decision and of the fact that the restrictions on competition laid down in the agreement have been brought to an end and stating the practical effects which will result as regards trade in Dutch-language books between Belgium and the Netherlands; they were required to send the Commission a draft notice for that purpose within four months of the receipt of the Commission decision.

The Court held:

The Commission's refusal to follow up the applicants' alternative proposals

51. As indicated above, the applicants submitted to the Commission certain alternative proposals set out in paragraphs 24 to 31 of the preamble to the decision. They complain that those proposals, which might have mitigated the effect of the resale price maintenance system, were not accepted by the Commission which, for its part, did not put forward any specific proposals which might have made an exemption possible.
52. In this connection it must be stated first of all that the purpose of the preliminary administrative procedure is to prepare the way for the Commission's decision on the infringement of the rules of competition, but that the procedure also presents an opportunity for the undertakings concerned to adapt the practices at issue to the rules of the Treaty. In the event of an exemption's being applied for under Article 85 (3) it is in the first place for the undertakings concerned to present to the Commission the evidence intended to establish the economic justification for an exemption and, if the Commission has objections to raise, to submit alternatives to it. Although it is true that the Commission, for its part, may give the undertakings indications as regards any possible solutions, it is not legally required to do so, still less is it bound to accept proposals which it deems incompatible with the conditions laid down in Article 85 (3).
53. This submission must therefore be dismissed.

3. *Article 86*

a. Relevant market

i. Cases

(1) United Brands Case

Judgment of 14 February 1978; Case 27/76; [1978] ECR 207; [1978] I CMLR 429; Competition Law CM/M/III/71.

The Court held:

Chapter I – The existence of a dominant position

Section I – The relevant market

10. In order to determine whether UBC has a dominant position on the banana market it is necessary to define this market both from the standpoint of the product and from the geographic point of view.
11. The opportunities for competition under Article 86 of the Treaty must be considered having regard to the particular features of the products in question and with reference to a clearly defined geographic area in which it is marketed and where the conditions of competition are sufficiently homogenous for the effect of the economic power of the undertaking concerned to be able to be evaluated.

Paragraph 1. The Product Market

12. As far as the product market is concerned it is first of all necessary to ascertain whether, as the applicant maintains, bananas are an integral part of the fresh fruit market, because they are reasonable interchangeable by consumers with other kinds of fresh fruit such as apples, oranges, grapes, peaches, strawberries, etc. or whether the relevant market consists solely of the banana market which includes both bananas and unlabelled bananas and is a market sufficiently homogeneous and distinct from the market of other frensh fruit.
13. The applicant submits in support of its argument that bananas compete with other fresh fruit in the same shops, on the same shelves, at prices which can be compared, satisfying the same needs: consumption as a dessert or between meals.
14. The statistics produced show that consumer expenditure on the purchase of bananas is at its lowest between June and December when there is a plentyful supply of domestic fruit on the market.
15. Studies carried out by the Food and Agriculture Organization (FAO)

(especially in 1975) confirm that the price of apples for example has a statistically appreciable impact on the consumption of bananas in the Federal Republic of Germany.

16. Again according to these studies some easing of prices is noticeable at the end of the year during the 'orange season'.
17. The seasonal peak period when there is a plentiful supply of other fresh fruit exert an influence not only on the prices but also on the volume of sales of bananas and consequently on the volume of imports thereof.
18. The applicant concludes from these findings that bananas and other fresh fruit form only one market and that UBC's operations should have been examined in this context for the purpose of any application of Article 86 of the Treaty.
19. The Commission maintains that there is a demand for bananas which is distinct from the demand for other fresh fruit especially as the banana is a very important part of the diet of certain sections of the community.
20. The specific qualities of the banana influence customer preference and induce him not to readily accept other fruits as a substitute.
21. The Commission draws the conclusion from the studies quoted by the applicant that the influence of the prices and availabilities of other types of fruit on the prices and availabilities of bananas on the relevant market is very ineffective and that these effects are too brief and too spasmodic for such other fruit to be regarded as forming part of the same market as bananas or as a substitute therefor.
22. For the banana to be regarded as forming a market which is sufficiently differentiated from other fruit markets it must be possible for it to be singled out by such special features distinguishing it from other fruits that it is only to a limited extent interchangeable with them and is only exposed to their competition in a way that is hardly perceptible.
23. The ripening of bananas takes place the whole year round without any season having to be taken into account.
24. Throughout the year production exceeds demand and can satisfy it at any time.
25. Owing to this particular feature the banana is a privileged fruit and its production and marketing can be adapted to the seasonal fluctuation of other fresh fruit which are known and can be computed.
26. There is no unavoidable seasonal substitution since the consumer can obtain this fruit all the year around.
27. Since the banana is a fruit which is always available in sufficient quantities the question whether it can be replaced by other fruits must be determined over the whole of the year for the purpose of ascertaining the degree of competition between it and other fresh fruit.
28. The studies of the banana market on the Court's file show that on the latter market there is no significant long term cross-elasticity any more than – as has been mentioned – there is any seasonal substitutability in general between the banana and all the seasonal fruits, as this only exists between the banana and two fruits (peaches and table grapes) in one of the countries (West Germany) of the relevant geographic market.

29. As far as concerns the two fruits available and in the case of the second there is only a relative degree of substitutability.
30. This small degree of substitutability is accounted for by the specific features of the banana and all the factors which influence consumer choice.
31. The banana has certain characteristics, appearance, taste, softness, seedlessness, easy handling, a constant level of production which enable it to satisfy the constant needs of an important section of the population consisting of the very young, the old and the sick.
32. As far as prices are concerned two FAO studies show that the banana is only affected by the prices – falling prices – of other fruits (and only of peaches and table grapes) during the summer months and mainly in July and then by an amount not exceeding 20%.
33. Although it cannot be denied that during these months and some weeks at the end of the year this product is exposed to competition from others fruits, the flexible way in which the volume of imports and their marketing on the relevant geographic market is adjusted means that the conditions of competition are extremely limited and that its price adapts without any serious difficulties to this situation where supplies of fruit are plentiful.
34. It follows from all these considerations that a very large number of consumers having a constant need for bananas are not noticeably or even appreciably enticed away from the consumption of this product by the arrival of other fresh fruit on the market and that even the personal peak periods only affect it for a limited period of time and to a very limited extent from the point of view of substitutability.
35. Consequently the banana market is a market which is sufficiently distinct from the other fresh fruit markets.

Paragraph 2. The geographic market

36. The Commission has taken the Federal Republic of Germany, Denmark, Ireland, the Netherlands and the BLEU as the geographic market and it is in respect of this market that it is necessary to consider whether UBC has the power to hinder effective competition.
37. It takes the view that that the economic conditions in this part of the Community allow importer/distributors of bananas to market their products there in the ordinary course without there being any significant economic barriers for UBC to overcome compared with other importer/distributors.
38. The other Member States of the Community (France, Italy, the United Kingdom) must however be excluded from this geographic definition of the market notwithstanding the significant presence of UBC in these States, because of the special circumstances relating to import arrangements and trading conditions and the fact that bananas of various types and origin are sold there.
39. The applicant point out that the geographic market where an undertaking's economic and commercial power is taken into consideration

should only comprise areas where the conditions of competition are homogeneous.
40. Although the Commission had good reason to exclude France, Italy and the United Kingdom from the said market it failed to take account of the differences in the conditions of competition in the other Member States which should have led it to come to the same conclusions with regard to the latter as it came to in the case of the three countries referred to above.
41. In fact three substantially different systems of customs duty apply in the Member States concerned: a zero tariff in Germany covering a banana quota which meets most of this country's requirements, a transitional tariff in Ireland and Denmark and the Common Customs Tariff of 20% for imports into Benelux.
42. The Commission has not either taken account of the consumer habits of the Member States concerned the annual consumption of fresh fruits per capita in Germany is equal to 2.5 times that of Ireland and twice that of Denmark), differing commercial patterns, concentrations and monetary points of view.
43. The applicant draws the conclusion from all these findings that the geographic market taken by the Commission includes areas in which the conditions of competition are so different that they cannot be considered as constituting a single market.
44. The conditions for the application of Article 86 to an undertaking in a dominant position presuppose the clear determination of the substantial part of the Common Market in which it may be able to engage in abuses which hinder effective competition and this is an area where the objective conditions of competition applying to the product in question must be the same for all traders.
45. The Community has not established a common organization of the agricultural market in bananas.
46. Consequently import arrangements vary considerably from one Member State to another and reflect a specific commercial policy peculiar to the States concerned.
47. This explains why for example the French market owing its national organization is restricted upstream by a particular import arrangement and obstructed downstream by a retail price monitored by the Administration.
48. This market, in addition to adopting certain measures relating to a 'target price' ('prix objectif') fixed each year and to packaging and grading standards and the minimum qualities required, reserves about two thirds of the market for the production of the overseas departments and one third to that of certain countries enjoying preferential relations with France (Ivory Coast, Madagascar, Cameron) the bananas whereof are imported dutyfree, and it includes a system the running of which is entrusted to the 'Comité interprofessionel bananier' ('C.I.B.').
49. The United Kingdom market enjoys 'Commonwealth preferences', a system of which the main feature is the maintenance of a level of production favouring the developing countries of the Commonwealth and of a price

paid to the associations of producers directly linked to the selling price of the green banana charged in the United Kingdom.

50. On the Italian market, since the abolition in 1965 of the State Monopoly responsible for marketing bananas, a national system of quota restrictions has been introduced, the Ministry for Shipping and the Exchange Control Office supervising the imports and the charterparties relating to the foreign ships which carry the bananas.
51. The effect of the national organization of these three markets is that the applicant's bananas do not compete on equal terms with the other bananas sold in these States which benefit from a preferential system and the Commission was right to exclude these three national markets from the geographic market under consideration.
52. On the other hand the six other States are markets which are completely free, although the applicable tariff provisions and transport costs are of necessity different but not discriminatory, and in which the conditions of competition are the same for all.
53. From the standpoint of being able to engage in free competition these six States form an area which is sufficiently homogeneous to be considered in its entirety.
54. UBC has arranged for its subsidiary in Rotterdam – UBC BV – to market its products. UBC BV is for this purpose a single centre for the whole of this part of the Community.
55. Transport costs do not in fact stand in the way of the distribution policy chosen by UBC which consists in selling f.o.b. Rotterdam and Bremerhaven, the two ports where the bananas are unloaded.
56. These are factors which go to make relevant market a single market.
57. It follows from all these considerations that the geographic market as determined by the Commission which constitutes a substantial part of the common market must be regarded as the relevant market for the purpose of determining whether the applicant may be in a dominant position.

. . . . .

b. Dominant position

i. Cases

(1) Hoffmann – La Roche (vitamins) Case

Hoffmann – La Roche v. *Commission*; Case 85/76; judgment of 13 February 1979; [1979] ECR 461.

Facts:

See the judgment below.

The Court held:

1. The principal claim in the application lodged on 27 August 1976 by the Swiss company Hoffmann-La Roche & Company AG (hereinafter referred to as 'Roche'), whose principal place of business is at Basle, is the annulment of Commission Decision of 9 June 1976 (IV/29.020 – Vitamins) relating to a proceeding under Article 86 of the EEC Treaty, which was served upon the applicant on 14 June 1976 and published in the Official Journal of the European Communities L 223 of 16 August 1976, and the alternative claim is the annulment of Article 3 of that decision which imposes upon the applicant a fine of 300 000 units of account, being 1 098 000 Deutschmarks.

   In that decision the Commission finds that Roche has a dominant position within the Common Market, within the meaning of Article 86 of the Treaty, on the markets in vitamins A, B_2, B_3 (pantothenic acid), B_6, C, E and H (biotin) and that it has abused that position and thereby infringed the said article, by concluding, from 1964 onwards and in particular during the years 1970 to 1974 inclusive, with 22 purchasers of these vitamins agreements which contain an obligation upon purchasers, or by the grant of fidelity rebates offer them an incentive, to buy all or most of their requirements of vitamins exclusively or in preference from Roche (Article 1 of the decision). That decision enjoins Roche to terminate the infringement forthwith (Article 2) and orders it to pay the above-mentioned fine (Article 3).

. . . . .

38. Article 86 is an application of the general objective of the activities of the Community laid down by Article 3 (f) of the Treaty namely, the institution of a system ensuring that competition in the Common Market is not distorted.

    Article 86 prohibits any abuse by an undertaking of a dominant position in a substantial part of Common Market in so far as it may affect trade between Member States.

    The dominant position thus referred to relates to position of economic strength enjoyed by an undertaking which enables it to prevent effective competition being maintained on the relevant market by affording it the power to behave to an appreciable extent independently of its competitors, its customers and ultimately of the consumers.

39. Such a position does not preclude some competition, which it does where there is a monopoly or a quasi-monopoly, but enables the undertaking which profits by it, if not to determine, at least to have an appreciable influence on the conditions under which that competition will develop, and in any case to act largely in disregard of it so long as such conduct does not operate to its detriment.

A dominant position must also be distinguished from parallel courses of conduct which are preculiar to oligopolies in that in an oligopoly the courses of conduct interact, while in the case of an undertaking occupying a dominant position the conduct of the undertaking which derives profits from that position is to a great extent determined unilaterally.

The existence of a dominant position may derive from several factors which, taken separately, are not necessarily determinative but among these factors a highly important one is the existence of very large market shares.

40. A substantial market share as evidence of the existence of a dominant position is not a constant factor and its importance varies from market to market according to the structure of these markets, especially as far as production, supply and demand are concerned.

Even though each group of vitamins constitutes a separate market, these different markets, as has emerged from the examination of their structure, nevertheless have a sufficient number of features in common to make it possible for the same criteria to be applied to them as far as concerns the importance of the market shares for the purpose of determining whether there is a dominant position or not.

41. Furthermore although the importance of the market shares may vary from on market to another the view may legitimately be taken that very large shares are in themselves, and save in exceptional circumstances, evidence of the existence of a dominant position.

An undertaking which has a very large market share and holds it for some time, by means of the volume of production and the scale of the supply which it stands for – without those having much smaller market shares being able to meet rapidly the demand from those who would like to break away from the undertaking which has the largest market share – is by virtue of that share in a position of strength which makes it an unavoidable trading partner and which, already because of this secures for it, at the very least during relatively long periods, that freedom of action which is the special feature of a dominant position.

42. The contested decision has mentioned besides the market shares a number of other factors which together with Roche's market shares would secure for it in certain circumstances, a dominant position.

These factors which the decision classifies as additional criteria are as follows:
 (a) Roche's market shares are not only large but there is also a big disparity between its shares and those of its next largest competitors (Recitals 5 and 21 to the decision);
 (b) Roche produces a far wider range of vitamins than its competitors (Recital 21 to the decision);
 (c) Roche is the world's largest vitamin manufacturer whose turnover exceeds that of all the other producers and is at the head of a multinational group which in terms of sales is the world's leading pharmaceuticals producer (Recitals 5, 6, and 21 to the decision);

(d) Although Roche's patents for the manufacture of vitamins have expired Roche, since it has played a leading role in this field, still enjoys technological advantages over its competitors of which the highly developed customer information and assistance service which it has is evidence (Recitals 7 and 8 to the decision);
(e) Roche has a very extensive and highly specialized sales network (Recital 21 to the dicision);
(f) There is no potential competition (Recital 21 to the decision).

Furthermore during the proceedings before the Court the Commission adduced as a factor establishing Roche's dominant position the latter's ability, notwithstanding lively competition, to maintain its market shares substantially intact.

43. Before considering whether the factors taken into account by the Commission can in fact be confirmed in Roche's case it is necessary to ascertain, since the applicant challenges their relevance, whether these factors, in the light of the special features of the relevant markets and of the market shares, are of such a kind as to disclose the existence of a dominant position.

44. In this connexion it is necessary to reject the criterion based on retention of market shares, since this may just as well result from effective competitive behaviour as from a position which ensures that Roche can behave independently of competitors, and the Commission, while admitting that there is competition, has not mentioned the factors which may account for the stability of market shares where it has been found to exist.

However if there is a dominant position then retention of the market shares may be a factor disclosing that this position is being maintained, and, on the other hand, the methods adopted to maintain a dominant position may be an abuse within the meaning of Article 86 of the Treaty.

45. The fact that Roche produces a far wider range of vitamins than its competitors must similarly be rejected as being immaterial.

The Commission regards this as a factor establishing a dominant position and asserts that 'since the requirements of many users extend to several groups of vitamins, Roche is able to employ a sales and pricing strategy which is far less dependent than that of the other manufacturers on the conditions of competition in each market'.

46. However the Commission has itself found that each group of vitamins constitutes a specific market and is not, or at least not to any significant extent, interchangeable with any other group or with any other products (Rectial 20 to the decision) so that the vitamins belonging to the various groups are as between themselves products just as different as the vitamins compared with other products of the pharmaceutical and food sector.

Moreover it is not disputed that Roche's competitors, in particular those in the chemical industry, market besides the vitamins which they manufacture themselves, other products which purchasers of vitamins also want, so that the fact that Roche is in a position to offer several

groups of vitamins does not in itself give it any advantage over its competitors, who can offer, in addition a less or much less wide range of vitamins, other products which are also required by the purchasers of these vitamins.
47. Similar considerations lead also to the rejection as a relevant factor of the circumstance that Roche is the world's largest vitamin manufacturer, that its turnover exceeds that of all the other manufacturers and that it is at the head of the largest pharmaceuticals group in the world.

In the view of the Commission these three considerations together are a factor showing that there is a dominant position, because 'it follows that the applicant occupies a preponderant position not only within the Common Market but also on the world market; it therefore enjoys very considerable freedom of action, since its position enables it to adapt itself easily to the developments of the different regional markets. An undertaking operating throughout the markets of the world and having a market share which leaves all its competitors far behind it does not have to concern itself unduly about any competitors within the Common Market'.

Such reasoning based on the benefits reaped from economics of scale and on the possibility of adopting a strategy which varies according to the different regional markets is not conclusive, seeing that it is accepted that each group of vitamins constitutes a group of separate products which require their own particular plant and form a separate market, in that the volume of the overall production of products which are different as between themselves does not give Roche a competitive advantage over its competitors, especially over those in the chemical industry, who manufacture on a world scale other products as well as vitamins and have in principle the same opportunities to set off one market against the other as are offered by a large overall production of products which differ from each other as much as the various groups of vitamins do.
48. On the other hand the relationship between the market shares of the undertaking concerned and of its competitors, especially those of the next largest, the technological lead of an undertaking over its competitors, the existence of a highly developed sales network and the absence of potential competition are relevant factors, the first because it enables the competitive strength of the undertaking in question to be assessed, the second and third because they represent in themselves technical and commercial advantages and the fourth because it is the consequence of the existence of obstacles preventing new competitors from having access to the market.

As far as the existence or non-existence of potential competition is concerned it must however be observed that, although it is true – and this applies to all the groups of vitamins in question – that because of the amount of capital investment required the capacity of the factories is determined according to the anticipated growth over a long period so that access to the market by new producers is not easy, account must also be taken of the fact that the existence of considerable unused manufacturing capacity creates potential competition between established manufacturers.

Nevertheless Roche is in this respect in a privileged position because, as it admits itself, its own manufacturing capacity was, during the period covered by the contested decision, in itself sufficient to meet world demand without this surplus manufacturing capacity placing it in a difficult economic or financial situation.

49. It is in the light of the preceding considerations that Roche's shares of each of the relevant markets, complemented by those factors which in conjunction with the market shares make it possible to show that there may be a dominant position, must be evaluated.

Finally it will also be necessary to consider whether Roche's submission relating to the implication of its conduct on the market, mainly as far as concerns prices, are of such a kind as to alter the findings to which the examination of the market shares and the other factors taken into account might lead.

c. Abuse

i. Cases

(1) Hoffmann – La Roche (vitamins) Case

Facts and references see at p. 526.

The Court held:

Section 3: The determination, in the light of Article 86 of the Treaty, of the legal nature of the undertakings to obtain supplies exclusively from Roche and of the system of rebates

89. An undertaking which is in a dominant position on a market and ties purchasers – even if it does so at their request – by an obligation or promise on their part to obtain all or most of their requirements exclusively from the said undertaking abuses its dominant position within the meaning of Article 86 of the Treaty, whether the obligation in question is stipulated without further qualification or whether it is undertaken in consideration of the grant of a rebate.

   The same applies if the said undertaking, without tying the purchasers by a formal obligation, applies, either under the terms of agreements concluded with these purchasers or unilaterally, a system of fidelity rebates, that is to say discounts conditional on the customer's obtaining all or most of its requirements – whether the quantity of its purchases be large or small – from the undertaking in a dominant position.

90. Obligations of this kind to obtain supplies exclusively from a particular undertaking, whether or not they are in consideration of rebates or of the

granting of fidelity rebates intended to give the purchaser an incentive to obtain his supplies exclusively from the undertaking in a dominant position, are incompatible with the objective of undistorted competition within the Common Market, because – unless there are exceptional circumstances which may make an agreement between undertakings in the context of Article 85 and in particular of paragraph (3) of that article, permissible – they are not based on an economic transaction which justifies this burden or benefit but are designed to deprive the purchaser of or restrict his possible choices of sources of supply and to deny other producers access to the market.

The fidelity rebate, unlike quantity rebates exclusively linked with the volume of purchases from the producer concerned, is designed through the grant of a financial advantage to prevent customers from obtaining their supplies from competing producers.

Furthermore the effect of fidelity rebates is to apply dissimilar conditions to equivalent transactions with other trading parties in that two purchasers pay a different price for the same quantity of the same product depending on whether they obtain their supplies exclusively from the undertaking in a dominant position or have several sources of supply.

Finally these practices by an undertaking in a dominant position and especially on an expanding market tend to consolidate this position by means of a form of competition which is not based on the transactions effected and is therefore distorted.

91. For the purpose of rejecting the finding that there has been an abuse of a dominant position the interpretation suggested by the applicant that an abuse implies that the use of the economic power bestowed by a dominant position is the means whereby the abuse has been brought about cannot be accepted.

The concept of abuse is an objective concept relating to the behaviour of an undertaking in a dominant position which is such as to influence the structure of a market where, as a result of the very presence of the undertaking in question, the degree of competition is weakened and which, through recourse to methods different from those which condition normal competition in products or services on the basis of the transactions of commercial operators, has the effect of hindering the maintenance of the degree of competition still existing in the market or the growth of that competition.

d. Concentration

i. Cases

(1) Continental Can Case

Europemballage Corporation and Continental Can Company Inc. v. Commission; Case 6/72; Judgment of 21 February 1973; [1973] ECR 215.

Facts:

Continental Can Company Inc. (Continental) of New York (USA), a company manufacturing metal packages, packaging materials of paper and plastic and machines for manufacturing and using these packages, by successive purchases during the year 1969, brought its share in Schmalbach-Lubeca-Werke AG (SLW) of Brunswick (Germany) to 85.8% of the nominal capital.

During the same year, Continental contemplated the formation, with The Metal Box Company Ltd (MB) of London, of a European holding company for packaging, in which the licensees of Continental in the Netherlands and in France, Thomassen & Drijver-Verblifa N.V. (TDV) of Deventer and J.J. Carnaud and Forges de Basse-Indre (Carnaud) of Paris, would be invited to participate. However, Carnaud indicated, at the end of August 1969, that it could not participate in the contemplated holding company.

On 16 February 1970, an agreement was signed between Continental and TDV whereby it was agreed:
(a) that Continental would set up in Delaware (USA) a company (subsequently called Europemballage Corporation) to which it would transfer its interests in SLW;
(b) that Continental would induce Europemballage to offer to the shareholders of TDV other than MB and Carnaud, a sum of 140 florins cash for each TDV share of 20 florins nominal value. Each TDV shareholder offering his shares would also receive a certificate granting him a preferential right to purchase ordinary shares in Europemballage when these should be offered to the public. Continental would provide Europemballage with the necessary funds for such a purchase by acquiring additional shares in Europemballage.

In implementation of this agreement:
– on 20 February 1970, a company called Europemballage Corporation (Europemballage) was set up in Wilmington, under the legislation of the state of Delaware. This company opened an office in New York and another in Brussels;
– on 16 March 1970, TDV published the take-over bid made by Europemballage.

In March and April, the Commission drew the attention of the undertakings concerned to the possible incompatibility of the transaction contemplated with the provisions of Article 86 of the Treaty, and to the legal and financial consequences which might thereby arise for these companies. MB then indicated that it was postponing its contemplated transaction with Europemballage.

On 8 April 1970, Europemballage carried out the purchase of the shares and debentures of TDV offered up to that date, thus bringing the initial share of Continental in TDV to 91.07%.

On 9 April 1970, the Commission decided to open of its own motion a procedure (in application of Article 3 (1) of Regulation No 17/62) against Continental and its subsidiary Europemballage concerning the acquisition by the latter of the majority of the shares in TDV. On completion of that procedure the Commission made, on 9 December 1971, a decision under Article 86 of the Treaty which, having set out the reasons on which it was based concerning the characteristics of the undertakings in question, their mutual links on a personal, financial, contractual and technical level and, particularly as regards SLW and TDV, the characteristics of their production, their sales on their respective markets, the exports of one company into the territory of the other, their competitive situation, etc., provides as follows:

'Article 1

It is found that Continental Can Company Inc. of New York, which holds through the medium of its subsidiary, Schmalbach-Lubeca-Werke AG of Brunswick, a dominant position over a substantial part of the Common Market on the market for light packaging for preserved meat, fish and crustacea and on the market in metal caps for glass jars, has abused this dominant position by the purchase made in April 1970 by its subsidiary Europemballage Corporation of approximately 80% of the shares and convertible debentures of the Dutch undertaking Thomassen & Drijver-Verblifa N.V. of Deventer. This purchase has had the effect of practically eliminating competition in the above-mentioned packaging products over a substantial part of the Common Market.

Article 2

Continental Can Company Inc. is required to put an end to the infringement of Article 86 of the Treaty establishing the EEC found in Article 1. For this purpose it must submit proposals to the Commission before 1 July 1972.

Article 3

This decision is addressed to Continental Can Company Inc. in New York.'

The Court held:

C – On Article 86 of the Treaty and abuse of a dominant position

18. In Article 1 and 2 of the Commission's decision of 9 December 1971 Continental Can is blamed for having infringed Article 86 of the EEC Treaty by abusing the dominant position which it allegedly held through Schmalbach-Lubeca-Werke AG of Brunswick (hereinafter called SLW) in a substantial part of the Common Market in the market for light metal containers for meat, meat products, fish and crustacea as well as in the market for metal closures for glass jars. According to Article 1 the abuse consists in Continental having acquired in April 1970, through its subsidiary Europemballage, about 80% of the shares and debentures of

TDV. By this acquisition competition in the containers mentioned was practically eliminated in a substantial part of the Common Market.
19. The applicants maintain that the Commission by its decision, based on an erroneous interpretation of Article 86 of the EEC Treaty, is trying to introduce a control of mergers of undertakings, thus exceeding its powers. Such an attempt runs contrary to the intention of the authors of the Treaty, which is clearly seen not only from a literal interpretation of Article 86, but also from a comparison of the EEC Treaty and the national legal provisions of the Member States. The examples given in Article 86 of abuse of a dominant position confirm this conclusion, for they show that the Treaty refers only to practices which have effects on the market and are to the detriment of consumers or trade partners. Further, Article 86 reveals that the use of economic power linked with a dominant position can be regarded as an abuse of this position only if it constitutes the means through which the abuse is effected. But structural measures of undertakings – such as strengthening a dominant position by way of merger – do not amount to abuse of this position within the meaning of Article 86 of the Treaty. The decision contested is, therefore, said to be void as lacking the required legal basis.
20. Article 86 (1) of the Treaty says 'Any abuse by one or more undertakings of a dominant position within the common market or in a substantial part of it shall be prohibited as incompatible with the common market in so far as it may affect trade between Member States'. The question is whether the word 'abuse' in Article 86 refers only to practices of undertakings which may directly affect the market and are detrimental to production or sales, to purchasers or consumers, or whether this word refers also to changes in the structure of an undertaking, which lead to competition being seriously disturbed in a substantial part of the Common Market.
21. The distinction between measures which concern the structure of the undertaking and practices which affect the market cannot be decisive, for any structural measure may influence market conditions, if it increases the size and the economic power of the undertaking.
22. In order to answer this question, one has to go back to the spirit, general scheme and wording of Article 86, as well as to the system and objectives of the Treaty. These problems thus cannot be solved by comparing this Article with certain provisions of the ECSC Treaty.
23. Article 86 is part of the chapter devoted to the common rules on the Community's policy in the field of competition. This policy is based on Article 3 (f) of the Treaty according to which the Community's activity shall include the institution of a system ensuring that competition in the Common Market is not distorted. The applicants' argument that this provision merely contains a general programme devoid of legal effect, ignores the fact that Article 3 considers the pursuit of the objectives which it lays down to be indispensable for the achievement of the Community's tasks. As regards in particular the aim mentioned in (f), the

Treaty in several provisions contains more detailed regulations for the interpretation of which this aim is decisive.

24. But if Article 3 (f) provides for the institution of a system ensuring that competition in the Common Market is not distorted, then it requires *a fortiori* that competition must not be eliminated. This requirement is so essential that without it numerous provisions of the Treaty would be pointless. Moreover, it corresponds to the precept of Article 2 of the Treaty according to which one of the tasks of the Community is 'to promote throughout the Community a harmonious development of economic activities'. Thus the restraints on competition which the Treaty allows under certain conditions because of the need to harmonize the various objectives of the Treaty, are limited by the requirements of Articles 2 and 3. Going beyond this limit involves the risk that the weakening of competition would conflict with the aims of the Common Market.

25. With a view to safeguarding the principles and attaining the objectives set out in Article 2 and 3 of the Treaty, Article 85 to 90 have laid down general rules applicable to undertakings. Article 85 concerns agreements between undertakings, decisions of associations of undertakings and concerted practices, while Article 86 concerns unilateral activity of one or more undertakings. Articles 85 and 86 seek to achieve the same aim on different levels, *viz.* the maintenance of effective competition within the Common Market. The restraint of competition which is prohibited if it is the result of behaviour falling under Article 85, cannot become permissible by the fact that such behaviour succeeds under the influence of a dominant undertaking and results in the merger of the undertakings concerned. In the absence of explicit provisions one cannot assume that the Treaty, which prohibits in Article 85 certain decisions of ordinary associations of undertakings restricting competition without eliminating it, permits in Article 86 that undertakings, after merging into an organic unity, should reach such a dominant position that any serious chance of competition is practically rendered impossible. Such a diverse legal treatment would make a breach in the entire competition law which could jeopardize the proper functioning of the Common Market. If, in order to avoid the prohibitions in Article 85, it sufficed to establish such close connections between the undertakings that they escaped the prohibition of Article 85 without coming within the scope of that of Article 86, then, in contradiction to the basic principles of the Common Market, the partitioning of a substantial part of this market would be allowed. The endeavour of the authors of the Treaty to maintain in the market real or potential competition even in cases in which restraints on competition are permitted, was explicitly laid down in Article 85 (3) (b) of the Treaty. Article 86 does not contain the same explicit provisions, but this can be explained by the fact that the system fixed there for dominant positions, unlike Article 85 (3), does not recognize any exemption from the prohibition. With such a system the obligation to observe the basic objec-

tives of the Treaty, in particular that of Article 3 (f), results from the obligatory force of these objectives. In any case Articles 85 and 86 cannot be interpreted in such a way that they contradict each other, because they serve to achieve the same aim.

26. It is in the light of these considerations that the condition imposed by Article 86 is to be interpreted whereby in order to come within the prohibition a dominant position must have been abused. The provision states a certain number of abusive practices with it prohibits. The list merely gives examples, not an exhaustive enumeration of the sort of abuses of a dominant position prohibited by the Treaty. As may further be seen from letters (c) and (d) of Article 86 (2), the provision is not only aimed at practices which may cause damage to consumers directly, but also at those which are detrimental to them through their impact on an effective competition structure, such as is mentioned in Article 3 (f) of the Treaty. Abuse may therefore occur if an undertaking in a dominant position strengthens such position in such a way that the degree of dominance reached substantially fetters competition, i.e. that only undertakings remain in the market whose behaviour depends on the dominant one.

27. Such being the meaning and the scope of Article 86 of the EEC Treaty, the question of the link of causality raised by the applicants which in their opinion has to question exist between the dominant position and its abuse, is of no consequence, for the strengthening of the position of an undertaking may be an abuse and prohibited under Article 86 of the Treaty, regardless of the means and procedure by which it is achieved, if it has the effects mentioned above.

4. Member States and Articles 85 and 86

a. Cases

(1) Leclerc Case

Association des centres distributeurs Édouard Leclerc and others v. *Sàrl 'Au blé vert' and others*; Case 229/83; Judgment of 10 January 1985; [1985] ECR 1.

Facts:

See the judgment below.

The Court held:

1. By a judgment of 28 September 1983, which was received at the Court on 10 October 1983, the Cour d'Appel [Court of Appeal], Poitiers, referred

a question to the Court under Article 177 of the EEC Treaty for a preliminary ruling on the interpretation of various rules of Community law, in particular the provisions relating to free competition in the Common Market and Articles 3 (f) and 5 of the EEC Treaty, so as to enable it to assess the compatibility with Community law of national legislation requiring all retailers to abide by the selling prices for books fixed by the publisher or importer.

2. The question was raised in proceedings between Association des Centres distributeurs Édouard Leclerc (hereinafter referred to as 'Leclerc') and Thouars distribution, part of the Leclerc Group, on the one hand, and various booksellers in Thouars and Union syndicale des libraires de France [French booksellers' association], on the other. The dispute concerns the need to comply with the retail prices for books fixed under Law No 81–766 of 10 August 1981 on book prices (Journal Officiel de la République Française of 11 August 1981).

3. Leclerc has retail outlets throughout France which initially sold groceries but have extended their business to cover other products including books. The outlets have the reputation of charging low prices. It appears that Thouars distribution, like other distributors in the Leclerc group, has sold books at prices undercutting the prices fixed under the aforementioned legislation.

4. Under the Law of 10 August 1981 all publishers or importers of books are required to fix retail prices for the books which they publish or import. Retailers must charge an effective price for sales to the public of between 95% and 100% of that price. The law exempts certain private and public entities, such as libraries and educational establishments, from having to pay that price and it authorizes clearance sales, subject to certain conditions. If the provisions of the law are contravened competitors and various types of association may seek an injunction or claim damages; criminal proceedings may also be brought.

5. As far as imported books are concerned, the last paragraph of Article 1 of the law provides that 'where imported books were published in France the retail price fixed by the importer shall be no less than that fixed by the publisher'. Decree No 81-1068 of 3 December 1981 (Journal Officiel de la République Française of 4 December 1981), issued pursuant to the Law of 10 August 1981, further provides that the principal distributor of imported books who must comply with the requirement laid down in Article 8 of the Law of 21 June 1943 – namely the requirement that a complete copy must be deposited with the Ministry of the Interior – is deemed to be the importer.

. . . . .

The application of Articles 3 (f), 5 and 85 of the EEC Treaty

10. Leclerc maintains that the French Law on book prices does not introduce

State price controls but rules restricting price competition, since the prices are freely fixed by publishers and importers. Hence the law should be considered first from the point of view of the rules on competition laid down in the Treaty. In that regard, Leclerc submits that the law establishes a collective system of price maintenance which undertakings are precluded from establishing by Article 85 (1) of the Treaty and which is contrary to the system of undistorted competition in the Common Market which Article 3 (f) designates as one of the aims of the Community. The second paragraph of Article 5 of the Treaty therefore imposes on Member States an obligation to refrain from adopting such measures, since they are likely to render Article 85 ineffective by enabling private undertakings to circumvent the constraints embodied therein and are thus likely to jeopardize the attainment of one of the aims of the Treaty.

11. The French Government considers that Article 3 (f) and 5 of the Treaty merely lay down general principles and do not in themselves give rise to obligations. Article 85, on the other hand, applies, in its view, only to certain practices on the part of undertakings and cannot be construed, even in conjunction with Articles 3 (f) and 5, as prohibiting Member States from adopting measures which might have an effect on free competition. The limitation of price competition at retailer level – price competition at publisher level being moreover free – should be examined in the light of Article 30 *et seq.*, the only potentially relevant Treaty provisions in this case.

12. The Commission considers that Articles 3 (f) and 5 cannot be interpreted in such a manner as to deprive Member States of all power in the economic sphere by prohibiting them from interfering with free competition. Since Article 85 concerns only practices on the part of undertakings and not State measures, it would only be the exceptional case – where a Member State required or facilitated the conclusion of prohibited agreements, heightened their impact by extending them to third parties or pursued the specific aim of enabling undertakings to circumvent the Community competition rules– that the adoption of such State measures could constitute a failure to fulfil the obligations arising under the second paragraph of Article 5 of the Treaty. The Commission therefore considers that the compatibility with the Treaty of legislation of the type in question is to be considered solely in the light of Article 30 *et seq.*

13. In accordance with the aim laid down in Article 3 (f) of the Treaty, the following are incompatible with the Common Market and prohibited by virtue of Article 85 (1) of the Treaty: all agreements between undertakings, decisions by associations of undertakings and concerted practices which may affect trade between Member States and which have as their object or effect the prevention, restriction or distortion of competition within the Common Market, and in particular those which directly or indirectly fix purchase or selling prices or any other trading conditions. Thus, Article 85 (1) covers agreements, decisions and concerted practices in restraint of competition between undertakings, subject to exemptions granted by the Commission under Article 85 (3) of the Treaty.

14. Whilst it is true that the rules on competition are concerned with the conduct of undertakings and not with national legislation, Member States are none the less obliged under the second paragraph of Article 5 of the Treaty not to detract, by means of national legislation, from the full and uniform application of Community law or from the effectiveness of its implementation measures; nor may they introduce or maintain in force measures, even of a legislative nature, which may render ineffective the competition rules applicable to undertakings (cf. judgment of 13 February 1969 in Case 14/68, *Wilhelm* v. *Bundeskartellamt*, [1969] ECR 1, and judgment of 16 November 1977 in Case 13/77, *Inno* v. *ATAB*, [1977] ECR 2115).
15. However, legislation of the type at issue does not require agreements to be concluded between publishers and retailers or other behaviour of the sort contemplated by Article 85 (1) of the Treaty; it imposes on publishers and importers a statutory obligation to fix retail prices unilaterally. Accordingly, the question arises as to whether national legislation which renders corporate behaviour of the type prohibited by Article 85 (1) superfluous, by making the book publisher or importer responsible for freely fixing binding retail prices, detracts from the effectiveness of Article 85 and is therefore contrary to the second paragraph of Article 5 of the Treaty.
16. The French Government, while maintaining that Article 85 of the Treaty is not applicable to legislative measures, seeks to justify the legislation at issue on the ground that its aim is to protect books as cultural media from the adverse impact that untrammelled competition in retail prices would have on the diversity and cultural level of publishing. The French Government further maintains that such legislation is necessary both in order to conserve specialist booksellers in the face of competition from other distribution channels which rely on a policy of reduced margins and a limited range of titles and in order to prevent a small number of large distributors from being able to impose their will on publishers to the detriment of poetic, scientific and creative works. It is therefore indispensable in order to preserve books as an instrument of culture and has counterparts in most of the Member States.
17. The Commission, which also considers that Article 85, even in conjunction with Article 5, does not apply to a case such as this, does not share the French Government's assessment of the state of competition in the book trade. It contests the utility and desirability of special national rules for the book trade. Nevertheless, it recognizes that publishers and booksellers have retail price maintenance agreements or practices in most Member States, even though the various national systems exhibit considerable differences, from one Member State to another, as regards their application and detailed rules.
18. It may be observed that the Commission, which has publicly stated its intention to investigate all those systems and practices, has not yet succeeded in bringing that investigation to a conclusion or in determining

what approach to adopt with regard to the exercise in this sphere of the powers conferred on it by the Treaty and by Regulation No 17 of 30 October 1962. Moreover, it has so far failed to submit any proposal for action to the Council. Nor has it initiated any proceed under Article 85 of the Treaty with a view to prohibiting national systems practices for fixing book prices.

B. Public enterprise (EEC Treaty Article 90)

1. Cases

(1) Port de Mertert Case

Public prosecutor of Luxembourg v. *Muller et al.*; Case 10/71; Preliminary ruling of 14 July 1971; [1971] ECR 723; Competition Law CM/M/III/24.

Facts:

J.P. Hein et Fils, a general partnership engaged in dredging the Moselle River, had to terminate this activity following the canalization of that waterway. In order to reconvert its operations, it asked the Luxembourg Ministry of Transport for permission to increase the size of the transshipment dock it has owned since 1940 so that it could be used for the loading and unloading of ships using the canalised Moselle. On 7 April 1965, it was given 'provisional and revocable' permission, following a favourable opinion given by the International Moselle Commission, but this permission was revoked on 28 July of the same year.

Following discussions between the parties regarding the legality of the revocation, the Hein firm, early in 1967, received permission from the Ministry of Transport to use its dock for loading and unloading certain materials from its own sand and gravel pits or quarries for its own account.

In a decision of 20 February 1970, the District Court (Magistrate's Section) of Luxembourg found Mrs. Madeleine Muller and Messrs. Alphonse Hein, Eugène Hein, and André Hein, partners in the firm of J.P. Hein et Fils, criminally liable for having performed for third parties transhipment involving products that were not covered by the government permission of February 1967, in violation of the Luxembourg Law on the operation of the Moselle River port of Mertert.

The Court held:

. . . . .

9. Article 90 (1) imposes a general prohibition on Member States, in respect of public undertakings to which they grant special or exclusive rights, against enacting or maintaining in force any measure contrary to the rules contained in the Treaty, in particular to those rule provided for in Article 7 and Articles 85 to 94.
10. However, Article 90 (2) provides that undertakings entrusted with the operation of services of general economic interest shall be subject to these rules, and in particular to the rules on competition, in so far as the application of such rules does not obstruct the performance, in law or in fact, of the particular tasks assigned to those undertakings, but subject to the condition that the development of trade must not be affected to such an extent as would be contrary to the interests of the Community.
11. An undertaking which enjoys certain privileges for the accomplishment of the task entrusted to it by law, maintaining for this purpose close links with the public authorities, and which is responsible for ensuring the navigability of the State's most important waterway, may fall within this provision.
12. To answer the questions referred, therefore, it is necessary to consider whether Article 90 (2) is of such a nature as to create individual rights which the national courts must protect.
13. Article 90 (2) does not lay down an unconditional rule.
14. Its application involves an appraisal of the requirements, on the one hand, of the particular task entrusted to the undertaking concerned and, on the other hand, the protection of the interests of the Community.
15. This appraisal depends on the objectives of general economic policy pursued by the States under the supervision of the Commission.
16. Consequently, and without prejudice to the exercise by the Commission of the powers conferred by Article 90 (3), Article 90 (2) cannot at the present stage create individual rights which the national courts must protect.

. . . . .

(2) Sacchi Case

Public prosecutor v. *Giuseppe Sacchi*; Case 155/73; Preliminary ruling of 30 April 1974; [1974] ECR 431; [1974] CMLR 204.

Facts:

Under Italian law television is a monopoly granted by the State to Radio Audizione Italiana (hereinafter called RAI), which involves on the one hand the monopoly of televised commercial advertising and on the other hand the prohibitions on any other person or undertaking from receiving, for the purpose of their retransmission, audio-visual signals transmitted either from the national territory or from foreign stations.

Mr. Sacchi, who has an unauthorized television relay undertaking (TELE-BIELLA), alleged that this system did not conform with the EEC Treaty insofar as cable television was concerned. After he had refused to pay the license fee on receivers for television relay, a refusal which Italian law treats as an offence, he was charged with 'being in possession in premises open to the public outside his place of residence of some television sets used for reception of transmission by cable without having paid the prescribed licence fee'.

The Court held:

. . . . .

14. Article 90 (1) permits Member States inter alia to grant special or exclusive rights to undertakings.

    Nothing in the Treaty prevents Member States, for considerations of public interest, of a non-economic nature, from removing radio and television transmissions, including cable transmissions, from the field of competition by conferring on one or more establishments an exclusive right to conduct them.

    However, for the performance of their tasks these establishments remain subject to the prohibitions against discrimination and, to the extent that this performance comprises activities of an economic nature, fall under the provisions referred to in Article 90 relating to public undertakings and undertakings to which Member States grant special or exclusive rights.

    It is therefore the same as regards an extension of exclusive rights following a new intervention by this State.
15. Moreover, if certain Member States treat undertakings entrusted with the operation of television, even as regards their commercial activities, in particular advertising, as undertakings entrusted with the operation of sevices of general economic interest, the same prohibitions apply, as regards their behaviour within the market, by reason of Article 90 (2), so long as it is not shown that the said prohibitions are incompatible with the performance of their tasks.
16. In the fourth question the national court has cited a certain number of acts capable of amounting to abuse within the meaning of Article 86.
17. Such would certainly be the case with an undertaking possessing a mono-

poly of television advertising, if it imposed unfair charges or conditions on users of its services or if it discriminated between commercial operators or national products on the one hand, and those of other Member States on the other, as regards access to television advertising.
18. The national court has in each case to ascertain the existence of such abuse and the Commission has to remedy it within the limits of its powers.

Even within the framework of Article 90, therefore, the prohibitions of Article 86 have a direct effect and confer on interested parties rights which the national courts must safeguard.

. . . . .

(3) British Telecom Case

Italian Republic v. *Commission*; Case 41/83; Judgment of 20 March 1985; [1985] ECR 873.

Facts (as summarized by the Advocate General):

The Italian Government, acting on the basis of Article 173 of the EEC Treaty, has asked the Court to declare void a decision of 10 December 1982, in which the Commission declared certain provisions, adopted successively by the United Kingdom Post Office and by British Telecommunications (hereinafter jointly referred to as 'BT') and designed to curtail the activities of messageforwarding agencies, to be contrary to Article 86 of the Treaty.

Thus the applicant State is not the one in which the undertaking in question has its seat. On the contrary, the Government of the United Kingdom intervened in the proceedings in support of the Commission. Furthermore, BT, which had not implemented the provisions complained of, did not incur any fine, and indeed refrained from seeking the Court's censure of a decision with which it had 'unilaterally' complied in advance. . . . . .

BT, which in 1981 succeeded the United Kingdom Post Office and which, since the hearing in this case, has been in the limelight on the London Stock Exchange, is an undertaking to which the United Kingdom granted a statutory monopoly on the management of telecommunications systems. In order to perform its tasks it was assigned rule-making powers which it exercises by way of 'schemes'.

It was in the context of those tasks that BT encountered the activities of message-forwarding agencies. Those agencies, combining and advanced technology with 'UK tariffs [which were] ... more attractive' than those prevailing abroad, offered the public a new service, handling the reception and transmission, on behalf of third parties, of a volume of messages the charge for which was unrelated to the chargeable length of use of the public network.

They provide, therefore, an expediting service, offering a twofold advantage to those using it; unusually low prices and speed of transmission.

BT considered itself obliged to counter those activities and, availing itself of its rule-making powers, adopted the contested schemes in pursuance *inter alia* of the obligations laid upon it by the International Telecommunication Convention.

That Convention (hereinafter referred to as the 'ITC'), which was signed in 1947 in Atlantic City and re-negotiated at Malaga-Torremolinos in 1973, set up the International Telecommunications Union (hereinafter referred to as the 'ITU'), of which all the States in the Community are members.

Repeating the main points of Article 20-1 of the 1947 Convention, the Convention of 1973, at Article 44-1, provides as follows:

'The Members are bound to abide by the provisions of this Convention and the Administrative Regulations.'

The Convention further sets up an International Telegraph and Telephone Consultative Committee ('the CCITT'), the duties of which

'... shall be to study technical, operating and tariff questions relating to telegraphy and telephony and to issue recommendations on them'.

As a 'recognized private operating agency', BT belongs to that committee.

In October 1976, the CCITT issued Recommendation F 60, Section 3.5 of which is worded as follows:

'Administrative and recognized private operating agencies should refuse to make the telex service available to a telegraph forwarding agency which is known to be organized for the purpose of sending or receiving telegrams for retransmission by telegraphy with a view to evading the full charges due for the complete route. [Such] administrations shall refuse to provide international telex service to a customer whose activity would be regarded as an infringement of the functions of an administration in providing a public telecommunications service.'

On the strength of that text, BT supplemented the two earlier schemes, which had been introduced in order to prohibit the charge made by the forwarding agencies from being 'such that it enables the originator of the message to send it more cheaply than if he had sent it by means of a telex call made by him directly to the person for whom the message was ultimately intended', with Scheme T1/1978, which was repealed and repeated by a scheme adopted in 1981 under which the international forwarding of messages by the United Kingdom was forbidden *per se*.

Those are the four schemes which the contested decision of the Commission treated as being in contravention of Article 86 of the Treaty establishing the European Economic Community.

The Court held:

I – Submissions to the effect that BT's schemes are not open to appraisal for their compatibility with Article 86 of the Treaty

1. The applicability of the Community rules on competition in the light of the activities covered by the decision at issue

16. The Italian Republic argues that Article 86 of the Treaty applies solely to the activities of business concerns carried out under private law, and not to rule-making activities carried out pursuant to a statute by a public body functioning in conformity with conditions laid down by central government. Inasmuch as the contested decision is directed, not to BT's conduct in its capacity as a body responsible for the operation of certain equipment or as a supplier of telecommunication services to users, but rather to its rule-making activities under the Post Office Art 1969 and the British Telecommunications Art 1981, the applicant takes the view that the Commission has misapplied Article 86. The rule-making activities complained of can, at most, provide the basis for an action against the United Kingdom under Articles 90 or 169 of the Treaty.

17. The Commission, supported in its conclusions and arguments by the United Kingdom, contends that the provision of telecommunications services is a business activity. Although United Kingdom statute law empowered BT to have recourse to schemes, it did so solely for the purpose of establishing the charges and conditions subject to which such services are offered. The schemes at issue therefore perform the same function as contractual terms, and were freely adopted by BT pursuant to the powers vested in it and without any intervention on the part of the United Kingdom authorities. Even if the United Kingdom could be held responsible in these circumstances, that would have the effect, at most, of diminishing the undertaking's responsibility for the purposes of calculating the fine, but would not prevent the Community rules on competition from being applied to it.

18. It should be noted in the first place that the applicant does not dispute that, despite BT's status as a nationalized industry, its management of public telecommunications equipment and its placing of such equipment at the disposal of users on payment of a fee do indeed amount to a business activity which as such is subject to the obligations imposed by Article 86 of the Treaty.

19. In the second place it should be observed that, by virtue of Section 28 of the Post Office Act 1969 and then of Section 21 of the British Telecommunications Act 1981, the power conferred on BT to introduce schemes has been strictly limited to laying down provisions relating to the scale of charges and other terms and conditions under which it provides services for users. In the light of the wording of those provisions it must further be acknowledged that the United Kingdom legislature in no way predetermined the content of the schemes, which is freely determined by BT.

20. In those circumstances, the schemes referred to by the contested decision must be regarded as an integral part of BT's business activity. The submission to the effect that it was not in law open to the Commission to appraise them for their compatibility with Article 86 of the Treaty must therefore be rejected.

2. The question whether the Community rules on competition are applicable in view of the monopoly held by BT

21. The applicant argues that, by virtue of Article 222 of the Treaty, which provides that the Treaty 'shall in no way prejudice the rules in Member States governing the system of property ownership', Member States are free to determine, in their international systems, the activities which are reserved to the public sector and to create national monopolies. Thus BT is entitled to preserve its monopoly by preventing the operation of private agencies wishing to provide services covered by that monopoly. By condemning the schemes adopted by BT in that regard as being incompatible with Article 86, the Commission therefore infringed Article 222 of the Treaty.
22. It is apparent from the documents before the Court that, whilst BT has a statutory monopoly, subject to certain exceptions with regard to the management of telecommunication networks and to making them available to users, it holds no monopoly over the provision of ancillary services such as the retransmission of messages on behalf of third parties. At all events, it must be observed that the schemes adopted by BT are not designed to suppress any private agencies which may be created in contravention of its monopoly but seek solely to alter the conditions in which such agencies operate. Accordingly, Article 222 of the Treaty did not prevent the Commission from appraising the schemes in question for their compatibility with Article 86 thereof.
23. The submission based on infringement of Article 222 of the Treaty must therefore be rejected.

C. STATE AID (EEC ARTICLES 92–94)

1. Cases

(1) French rediscount Case

See at page 574.

(2) French textile industry Case

France v. *Commission of the EC*; Case 47/69; Judgment of 25 June 1970; [1970] ECR 493–497; [1970] CMLR 362.

Facts:

In 1965, the French Government instituted a system of aid for the textile industry, financed by a special tax on sales of textile products, both national and imported. The Commission recognized that the aid provided in the context of this system was compatible with Article 92 of the EEC Treaty, but that its method of financing was not.

It therefore made a Decision on 18 July 1968, requiring the French Government either to abolish the whole system of aid or to modify its method of financing to bring it into conformity with the Treaty.

The French Government thereupon brought this application for an annulment of the decision.

The Court held:

. . . . .

3. Under Article 93 (2) of the Treaty, if the Commission finds 'that aid granted by a State or through State resources is not compatible with the Common Market having regard to Article 92 or that such aid is being misused, it shall decide that the State concerned shall abolish or alter such aid within a period of time to be determined by the Commission'.
4. This provision, by thus taking into account the connection which may exist between the aid granted by a Member State and the method by which it is financed through the resources of that State, does not therefore allow the Commission to isolate the aid as such from the method by which it is financed and to disregard this method if, in conjunction with the aid in its narrow sence, it renders the whole incompatible with the Common Market.
5. Under Article 92 (1): 'Any aid granted by a Member State or through State resources in any form whatsoever which distorts or threatens to distort competition by favouring certain undertakings or the production of certain goods shall, in so far as it affects trade between Member States, be incompatible with the Common Market'.
6. Nevertheless under Article 92 (3) (c): 'The following may be considered to be compatible with the Common Market: ... aid to facilitate the development of certain economic activities or of certain economic areas, where such aid does not adversely affected trading conditions to an extent contrary to the common interest'.
7. In order to determine whether an aid 'affects trade between Member States', distorts or threatens to distort competition by favouring certain undertakings or the production of certain goods' and 'adversely affects trading conditions to an extent contrary to the common interest', it is

necessary to consider all the legal and factual circumstances surrounding that aid, in particular whether there is an imbalance between the charges imposed on the undertakings or producers concerned on the one hand and the benefits derived from the aid in question on the other.

8. Consequently the aid cannot be considered separately from the effects of its method of financing.

9. The Commission therefore had power to decide whether the French Republic should abolish or alter the disputed system of aid as a whole.

The second submission

10. The French Government claims that Articles 12 and 95 are alone applicable in this case and can afford no grounds for objecting to the charge in question, since it was levied both on national and imported products and did not have any effects equivalent to a customs duty.

11. This argument amounts to asserting that when an aid is financed by internal taxation, this method of financing can only be examined in relation to its compatibility with Article 95 and that the requirements of Articles 92 and 93 must be disregarded.

12. However these two types of provision have different aims in view.

13. The fact that a national measure complies with the requirements of Article 95 does not imply that it is valid in relation to other provisions, such as those of Articles 92 and 93.

14. When an aid is financed by taxation of certain undertakings or certain producers, the Commission is required to consider not only whether the method by which it is financed complies with Article 95 of the Treaty but also whether in conjunction with the aid which it services it is compatible with the requirements of Articles 92 and 93.

15. The French Government further maintains that in admitting that the French textile industry needed aid, the Commission could not refuse it without contradicting itself nor require an alteration of the method whereby it was financed since on the one hand this method does not adversely affect trade to an extent contrary to the common interest, and on the other hand the same result could be achieved if the aid in question, instead of being serviced by a charge designed for the purpose, were serviced by budgetary means financed by the value-added tax.

16. It may be that aid properly so-called, although not in conformity with Community law, does not substantially affect trade between States and may thus be acknowledged as permissible but that the disturbance which it creates is increased by a method of financing it which would render the scheme as a whole incompatible with a single market and the common interest.

17. In its appraisal the Commission must therefore take into account all those factors which directly or indirectly characterize the measure in question, that is, not only aid, properly so-called, for selected national activities, but also the indirect aid which may be constituted both by the method of

financing and by the close connection which makes the amount of aid dependent upon the revenue from the charge.
18. If such a system whereby an aid is serviced by a charge designed for that purpose, were to become general, it should have the effect of opening a loophole in Article 92 of the Treaty and of reducing the Commission's opportunities of keeping the position under constant review.
19. In fact it leads to a system of permanent aids, the amount of which is unforeseeable and which would be difficult to review.
20. By automatically increasing the amount of national aid in proportion to the increase in the revenue from the charge and more expecially the revenue from the charge levied on competing foreign products, the method of financing in question has a protective effect which goes beyond aid properly so-called.
21. In particular, the more Community undertakings succeed in increasing sales in a Member State by marketing efforts and by price-cutting, the more they have to contribute under the system of the servicing charge to an aid which is essentially intended for those of their won competitors who have not made such efforts.
22. Thus the Commission was entitled to take the view that the fact that foreign undertakings can have access to research work done in France could not eliminate the adverse effects on the Common Market of an aid incorporating a charge designed to service it.
23. Therefore it has rightly decided that this aid, whatever might be the rate of the said charge, has the effect, because of the method by which it is financed, of adversely affecting trade to an extent contrary to the common interest within the meaning of Article 92 (3) (c).

. . . . .

(3) Italian textile industry Case

Italian Republic v. *Commission*; Case 173/73; Judgment of 2 July 1974; [1974] ECR 715; [1974] 2 CMLR 593.

Facts:

The Italian Republic and the Commission disagreed about the validity of Italian measures in relation to the textile industry.

The Court held:

. . . . .

6. It is accepted that though Article 20 of Italian Law No 1101 created an innovation with regard to the previous legal position of the Italian textile industry and small crafts, there was no prior notification to the Commission of the adoption of this provision as prescribed by Article 93 (3).

   After having sought the comments of the Italian authorities and of experts in the other Member States, the Commission, considering that the provision in issue constituted an aid within the meaning of Articles 92 and 93, adopted the contested Decision.

7. In order to ensure the progressive development and functioning of the common market in accordance with the provisions of Article 92, Article 93 provides for constant review of aids granted or planned by the Member States, an operation which assumes constant cooperation between these States and Commission.

   Article 93 (2) envisages the case where during the course of such a review the Commission finds that aid granted by a Member State is not compatible with the provisions of Article 92, provides for the situation to be resolved by decision of the Commission subject to appeal to the Court of Justice.

   Because the Article is based on the idea of cooperation, the Commission must, in such a case, allow the State concerned a period of time within which to comply with the decision taken.

   However, in the situation envisaged by Article 93 (3) where a proposed aid is considered incompatible with Article 92, the fixing of a time limit is unnecessary, as the aid in question cannot be put into effect.

8. The submissions amount to the assertion that a new aid granted by a Member State in contravention of paragraph (3) must be treated in the same way as aids granted legally and, consequently, should be subject only to the procedure prescribed by Article 93 (2), including the compulsory fixing of a time limit.

   This interpretation of Article 93 is however unacceptable because it would have the effect of depriving the provisions of Article 93 (3) of their binding force and even that of encouraging their non-observance.

9. Moreover, the spirit and general scheme of Article 93 imply that the Commission, when it establishes that an aid has been granted or altered in disregard of Paragraph (3), must be able, in particular when it considers that this aid is not compatible with the common market having regard to Article 92, to decide that the State concerned must abolish or alter it, without being bound to fix a period of time for this purpose and with the possibility of referring the matter to the Court if the State in question does not comply with the required speed.

   In such a case, the means of recourse open to the Commission are not restricted to the more complicated procedure under Article 169.

   Consequently, the submission that the Decision is intended to take direct effect in the internal legal order of the Italian Republic is unfounded, since Article 2 of the Decision stipulates that: 'This Decision is addressed to the Italian Republic'. From this wording it emerges that the

Decision is intended to impose the obligation laid down in Article 1 on the State concerned.

. . . . .

13. The aim of Article 92 is to prevent trade between Member States from being affected by benefits granted by the public authorities which, in various forms, distort or threaten to distort competition by favouring certain undertakings or the production of certain goods.

   Accordingly, Article 92 does not distinguish between the measures of State intervention concerned by reference to their causes or aims but defines them in relation to their effects.

   Consequently, the alleged fiscal nature or social aim of the measure in issue cannot suffice to shield it from the application of Article 92.

. . . . .

16. The argument that the contested reduction is not a 'State aid', because the loss of revenue resulting from it is made good through funds accruing from contributions paid to the unemployment insurance funds, cannot be accepted.

    As the funds in question are financed through compulsory contributions imposed by State legislation and as, as this case shows, they are managed and apportioned in accordance with the provisions of that legislation, they must be regarded as State resources within the meaning of Article 92, even if they are administered by institutions distinct from the public authorities.

17. As to the argument that the social charge devolving upon employers in the textile sector are higher in Italy than in the other Member States, it should be observed that, in the application of Article 92 (1), the point of departure must necessarily be the competitive position existing within the common market before the adoption of the measure in issue.

    This position is the result of numerous factors having varying effects on production costs in the different Member States.

    Moreover, Articles 92 to 102 of the Treaty provide for detailed rules for the abolition of generic distortions resulting from difference between the tax and social security systems of the different Member States whilst taking account of structural difficulties in certain sectors of industry.

    On the other hand, the unilateral modification of a particular factor of the cost of production in a given sector of the economy of a Member State may have the effect of disturbing the existing equilibrium.

    Consequently, there is no point in comparing the relative proportions of total production costs which a particular category of costs represents, since the decisive factor is the reduction itself and not the category of costs to which it relates.

. . . . .

(4) Steinike Case

Steinike und Weinlig v. *Federal Republic of Germany*; Case 78/76; Preliminary ruling of 22 March 1977; [1977] ECR 595; [1977] 2 CMLR 688.

Facts:

See the judgment below.

The Court held:

1. By order dated 10 June 1976, received at the Court Registry on 2 August 1976, the Verwaltungsgericht Frankfurt am Main raised various questions under Article 177 of the EEC Treaty relating to the interpretation of Articles 9, 12, 13, 92, 93 and 95 of the EEC Treaty. These questions have arisen in an action between a German undertaking, the plaintiff in the main action, and the Federal Republic of Germany, represented by Bundesamt für Ernährung und Forstwirtschaft; they relate to the compatibility with Community law of a charge of DM 20,000 levied on the plaintiff on the processing of citrus concentrates imported from Italy and various third countries. This charge is intended, along with other funds of a different kind, to finance the Absatzförderungsfonds der deutschen Land-, Forst, und Ernährungswirtschaft (hereinafter called 'the Fund') set up by a Federal Law of 26 June 1969. Under Paragraph 2 of this law the purpose of the Fund is, with the help of a body financed and controlled by it and functioning under the name 'Centrale Marketing-Gesellschaft der deutschen Agrarwirtschaft', to 'promote centrally by the use of modern means and methods the sale and use of products of the German agricultural and food industry and of German forestry by opening up and fostering markets at home and abroad'. The aid is given to the German food industry independently of whether its products are made from domestic raw material or from semi-finished products of domestic origin or from other Member States. The Commission, which under Article 93 (3) of the Treaty was informed in advance by the Federal Republic of the intended introduction of this aid, has raised no objection to it with result that the said legal provisions have

been adopted regularly from the point of view of the procedure laid down in Article 93.
2. The plaintiff in the main action takes the view that the charges demanded of it infringe the Treaty and are not payable because on the one hand the purpose is to finance aid incompatible with Article 92 of the Treaty and on the other hand since they were levied on the processing of citrus concentrates from other Member States although there is no similar product in the country of import they are either charges having an equivalent effect to a customs duty prohibited by Articles 9, 12 and 13 of the Treaty or internal taxation discriminating against a product from another Member State contrary to Article 95.
3. The Federal Law of 23 March 1972 provides that the contested contribution shall not be levied in respect of processing in a German undertaking of 'products which do not grow naturally in the climatic conditions of the territory to which this Law (on the Fund) applies'; citrus concentrates are thus exempted from the contribution. The contested contribution applies however to citrus concentrates which were imported and processed before the law of 32 March 1972 entered into force.
4. The questions referred for a preliminary ruling must be answered in this light.

The first question

5. The Verwaltungsgericht asks first whether the procedural rules prescribed in Article 93 of the EEC Treaty preclude a national court from obtaining a preliminary ruling on Article 92 of the EEC Treaty and subsequently from deciding upon the application of this provision. This question is concerned with how far the national courts can invoke Article 92 of the Treaty in the legal systems of the Member States whether it be at the behest of parties or of their own motion.
6. Article 92 (1) provides: 'Save as otherwise provided in this Treaty, any aid granted by a Member State or through State resources in any form whatsoever which distorts or threatens to distort competition by favouring certain undertakings or the production of certain goods shall, in so far as it affects trade between Member States, be incompatible with the common market'. Article 92 (2) lists three kinds of aid which are not affected by the prohibition in Article 92 (1) and Article 92 (3) lists three further kinds of aid which may in certain circumstances be considered to be compatible with the Common Market and empowers the Council to specify other categories which may be exempted from the prohibition in Article 92 (1).
7. Further the third subparagraph of Article 93 (2) of the Treaty provides: 'On application by a Member State, the Council, may, acting unanimously, decide that aid which that State is granting or intends to grant shall be considered to be compatible with the common market, in derogation from the provisions of Article 92 or from the regulations provided for

in Article 94, if such a decision is justified by exceptional circumstances. If, as regards the aid in question, the Commission has already initiated the procedure provided for in the first subparagraph of this paragraph, the fact that the State concerned has made its application to the Council shall have the effect of suspending that procedure until the Council has made its attitude known'. The Council may under Article 94 of the Treaty 'make any appropriate regulations for the application of Articles 92 and 93 and may in particular determine the conditions in which Article 93 (3) shall apply and the categories of aid exempted from this procedure'. Finally regard must be had to the powers given to the Council by Article 12 in respect of agricultural products.
8. These provisions show that the prohibition in Article 92 (1) is neither absolute nor unconditional since Article 92 (3) and Article 93 (2) give the Commission a wide discretion and the Council extensive power to admit aids in derogation from the general prohibition in Article 92 (1).
9. In judging in these cases whether State aid is compatible with the common market complex economic factors subject to rapid change must be taken into account and assessed. Article 93 of the Treaty therefore provides for a special procedure whereby the Commission shall keep aid under constant review. With regard to aid existing before the Treaty entered into force Article 93 (2) provides that the Commission may decide that the State concerned shall abolish or alter the aid within a period of time to be determined by the Commission. With regard to new aid which the Member States intend to introduce a special procedure is provided and if it is not followed the aid is not regarded as being regularly introduced. The conclusion to be drawn from all these considerations is that the intention of the Treaty, in providing through Article 93 for aid to be kept under constant review and supervised by the Commission, is that the finding that an aid may be incompatible with the common market is to be determined, subject to review by the Court, by means of an appropriate procedure which it is the Commission's responsibility to set in motion.
10. The parties concerned cannot therefore simply, on the basis of Article 92 alone, challenge the compatibility of an aid which Community law before national courts or ask them to decide as to any compatibility which may be the main issue in actions before them or may arise as a subsidiary issue. There is this right however where the provisions of Article 92 have been applied by the general provisions provided for in Article 94 or by specific decisions under Article 93 (2).
11. The plaintiff in the main action claims that Article 12 of Regulation No 865/68 of the Council of 28 June 1968 on the common organization of the market in products processed from fruit and vegetables is a specific implementing measure of the aforesaid kind enabling individuals to rely on Article 92 before national courts for the purpose of finding that State aid is incompatible with the common market and in particular with the relevant organization of the market.

12. The said Article 12 provides: 'Save as otherwise provided in this regulation, Articles 92, 93 and 94 of the Treaty shall apply to the production and trade in the products listed in Article 1'.
13. In accordance with Article 42 of the Treaty, Article 12 declares that the provisions of Articles 92 to 94 shall apply to the agricultural products coming within the ambit of Regulation No 865/68 without however altering the nature and scope of these provisions.
14. The limitations mentioned above on reliance on Article 92 do not however mean that cases cannot come before national courts requiring them to interpret (making use if necessary of the procedure under Article 177 of the Treaty) and apply the provisions contained in Article 92, but nevertheless they cannot be called upon to find that such State aid is incompatible save in the case of aid introduced contrary to Article 93 (3). Thus a national court may have cause to interpret and apply the concept of aid contained in Article 92 in order to determine whether State aid introduced without observance of the preliminary examination procedure provided for in Article 93 (3) ought to have been subject to this procedure. In any case under Article 177 of the Treaty the national courts which make a reference for a preliminary ruling must themselves decide whether the questions referred are necessary to enable judgment to be given.
15. The answer to the first question is therefore that the provisions of Article 93 do not preclude a national court from referring a question on the interpretation of Article 92 of the Treaty to the Court of Justice if it considers that a decision thereon is necessary to enable it to give judgment; in the absence of implementing provisions within the meaning of Article 94 however a national court does not have jurisdiction to decide an action for a declaration that existing aid which has not been the subject of a decision by the Commission requiring the Member State concerned to abolish or alter it or that a new aid which had been introduced in accordance with Article 93 (3) is incompatible with the Treaty.

The second question

16. Secondly the national court asks whether the expression 'undertakins or the production of certain goods' in Article 92 of the EEC Treaty is restricted to private business or also includes non-profit-making institutions governed by public law.
17. Article 90 (1) of the Treaty provides: 'In the case of public undertakings and undertakings to which Member States grant special or exclusive rights, Member States shall neither enact nor maintain in force any measure contrary to the rules contained in this Treaty, in particular to those rules provided for in Article 7 and Articles 85 to 94'. Article 90 (2) provides: 'Undertakings entrusted with the operation of services of general economic interest or having the character of a revenue-producing monopoly shall be subject to the rules contained in this Treaty, in par-

ticular to the rules on competition, in so as the application of such rules does not obstruct the performance, in law or in fact, of the particular tasks assigned to them. The development of trade must not be affected to such an extent as would be contrary to the interests of the Community'.
18. From this is follows that save for the reservation in Article 90 (2) of the Treaty, Article 92 covers all private and public undertakings and all their production.

The third and fourth questions

19. Thirdly, the national court asks whether the concept 'any aid granted through State resources' is satisfied even if the State agency itself receives aid from the State or private undertakings. The fourth question asks whether there is aid in the sense of granting a gratuitous advantage if the recipient of aid is not a private undertaking but a State agency, and whether it can be said to be grauitous when the charge on the individual undertaking is insignificant in relation to the total amount of contributions.
20. These two questions must be taken together.
21. The prohibition contained in Article 92 (1) covers all aid granted by a Member State or through State resources without its being necessary to make a distinction whether the aid is granted directly by the State or by public or private bodies established or appoined by it to administer the aid. In applying Article 92 regard must primarily be had to the effects of the aid on the undertakings or producers favoured and not the status of the institutions entrusted with the distribution and administration of the aid.
22. A measure adopted by the public authority and favouring certain undertakings or products does not lose the character of a gratuitous advantage by the fact that it is wholly or partially financed by contributions imposed by the public authority and levied on the undertakings concerned.

The fifth question

23. The fifth question asks whether competition is distorted and trade between Member States affected if the market research and advertising carried on by the State agency in its own country and abroad is also carried on by similar institutions of other Community countries.
24. Any breach by a Member State of an obligation under the Treaty in connection with the prohibition laid down in Article 92 cannot be justified by the fact that other Member States are also failing to fulfil this obligation. The effects of more than one distortion of competition on trade between Member States do not cancel one another out but ac-

cumulate and the damaging consequences to the common market are increased.

. . . . .

(5) Philip Morris Case

Philip Morris Holland BV v. *Commission*; Case 730/79; Judgment of 17 Setpember 1980; [1980] ECR 2687 [1981] CMLR 321.

Facts:

By a letter of 4 October 1978 the Government of the Netherlands gave notice to the Directorate-General for Competition of its intention to grant Philip Morris Holland (hereinafter referred to as 'PMH'), a Netherlands subsidiary of the Philip Morris International group of companies aid to increase the production capacity of its factory at Bergen op Zoom where it manufactures cigarettes.

The aid in question, called 'an addition premium for major schemes' ('grote projecten toeslag'), was introduced by Article 6 of the Netherlands Law of 29 June 1978 on the promotion and guidance of investment (Wet Investeringsrekening, Staatsblad No 368, 1978). This aid is granted in respect of investment schemes for which more than Hfl 300 000 000 have been paid. The amount depends on the number of jobs created and is limited to 4% of the value of the investment concerned.

Since the Commission considered this arrangement to be general system of aid it met with its approval subject to prior notification of all cases of application of such aid, as provided for in Article 93 (3) of the Treaty and taking into account the principles laid down by Article 92 thereof.

After the Commission had obtained certain supplementary information from the Netherlands Government it decided on 14 December 1968 to initiate the procedure provided for in Article 93 (2). At that stage only the Netherlands Government was invited to submit its observations. At a later stage the Commission asked the other Member States and other interested parties, including on 28 February 1979 PMH, for their views.

The latter submitted its written comments on 29 March 1979. Discussions took place on 29 May 1979 during which the applicant was given the opportunity to answer certain more detailed questions put by the Commission and the latter's objections to the granting of the aid.

The circumstances in which Philip Morris International made its investment decisions are as follows: the PMH factory at Eindhoven was to be closed and its production capacity transferred to the PMH factory at Bergen-op-Zoom. The total manufacturing capacity was to be raised from 11 400 million to

16 000 million cigarettes per year leading to a 40% increase in the production capacity of the company and an increase of approximately 13% in the total production of cigarettes in the Netherlands. This extension and modernization would require an investment of 60.7 million EUA, the value of the aid being 2.4 million EUA. The parties are not in agreement as to the number of new jobs which would be created as a result of this operation: according to the Commission there would only be five, according to the applicant there would be 475.

Context of the case: the cigarette market

There is a very large trade in cigarettes in the Member States. In the Community 481 100 million cigarettes were sold in 1977 and 480 300 million in 1978. Aggregate intra-Community exports of cigarettes represent about 11% of total consumption within the Community. In 1968 the Member States exporting the most cigarettes were the Federal Republic of Germany and the Netherlands, accounting for about 44% and 36% respectively of intra-Community exports. The Federal Republic of Germany exports about 16% of its total production whilst the Netherlands 55%. The countries which are the main importers of cigarettes are Italy, France and the Netherlands.

Philip Morris is the second largest group of tobacco manufacturers in the world after British American Tobacco Company (hereinafter referred to as 'BAT'). In the Community, Philip Morris has manufacturing and marketing subsidiaries in Belgium, France, Germany, the Netherlands and the United Kingdom. In the common market its main competitors with the exception of local and State-controlled companies, are BAT, Rothmans and Reynolds. PMH informed the Commission that it was not in a position to supply an estimate of its share of the Community market.

Philip Morris is a relative newcomer to the European market. It started trading in the Netherlands in 1969. PMH estimates that after completing the investment in question it will produce 50% of all the cigarettes manufactured in the Netherlands and it hopes to export over 80% of its total production to the other Member States.

The value of exports of cigarettes in 1977 from the Netherlands totalled 94 million EUA, which is 27% of all Community exports, whilst the value of imports of cigarettes into the Netherlands was 63.7 million EUA, which is 24.4% of all intra-Community imports of cigarettes. Therefore the Netherlands had a trade surplus as far as concerns cigarettes of 30.3 million EUA.

The Commission by a Decision of 27 July 1979, having regard to the fact that the proposed aid was likely to affect trade and distort competition between Member States by favouring the undertaking in question within the meaning of Article 92(1) of the Treaty, decided that the Kingdom of the Netherlands should refrain from implementing its proposal to grant 'the additional premium for major schemes' to investment made at Bergen-op-Zoom by 'the Dutch subsidiary of a multi-national tobacco manufacturer'.

The Court held:

. . . . .

Admissibility of the application

5. The Commission does not dispute the applicant's right as a potential recipient of the aid referred to in the decision to bring an action for a declaration that the decision is void even though it is addressed to a Member State.

. . . . .

9. The applicant maintains that, in order to decide to what extent specific aid is incompatible with the common market, it is appropriate to apply first of all the criteria for deciding whether there are any restrictions on competition under Article 85 and 86 of the Treaty. The Commission must therefore first determine the 'relevant market' and in order to do so must take account of the product, the territory and the period of time in question. It must then consider the pattern of the market in question in order to be able to assess how far the aid in question in a given case affects relations between competitors. But these essential aspects of the matter are not found in the disputed decision. The decision does not define the relevant market either from the standpoint of the product or in point of time. The market pattern and moreover for that matter, the relations between competitors resulting therefrom which might in a given case be distorted by the disputed aid, have not been specified at all.
10. It is common ground that when the applicant has completed its planned investment it will account for nearly 50% of the cigarette production in the Netherlands and that it expects to export over 80% of its production to other Member States. The 'additional premium for major schemes' which the Netherlands Government proposed to grant the applicant amounted to Hfl. 6.2 million (2.3 million EUA) which is 3.8% of the capital invested.
11. When State financial aid strengthens the position of an undertaking compared with other undertakings competing in intra-Community trade the latter must be regarded as affected by that aid. In this case the aid which the Netherlands Government proposed to grant was for an undertaking organized for international trade and this is proved by the high percentage of its production which it intends to export to other Member States. The aid in question was to help to enlarge its production capacity and consequently to increase its capacity to maintain the flow of

trade including that between Member States. On the other hand the aid is said to have reduced the cost of converting the production facilities and has thereby given the applicant a competitive advantage over manufacturers who completed or intend to complete at their own expense a similar increase in the production capacity of their plant.

12. These circumstances, which have been mentioned in the recitals in the preamble to the disputed decision and which the applicant has not challenged, justify the Commission's deciding that the proposed aid would be likely to affect trade between Member States and would threaten to distort competition between undertaking established in different Member States.

13. It follows from the foregoing considerations that the first submission must be rejected in substance and also as far as concerns the inadequacy of the statement of reasons on which the decision was based.

. . . . .

16. According to the applicant it is wrong for the Commission to lay down as a general principle that aid granted by a Member State to undertakings only falls within the derogating provisions of Article 92 (3) if the Commission can establish that the aid will contribute to the attainment of one of the objectives specified in the derogations, which under normal market conditions the recipient firms would not attain by their own actions. Aid is only permissible under Article 92 (3) of the Treaty if the investment plan under consideration is in conformity with the objectives mentioned in subparagraphs (a), (b) and (c).

17. This argument cannot be upheld. On the one hand it disregards the fact that Article 92 (3), unlike Article 92 (2), gives the Commission a descretion by providing that the aid which it specifies 'may' be considered to be compatible with the common market. On the other hand it would result in Member States' being permitted to make payments which would improve the financial situation of the recipient undertaking although they were not necessary for the attainment of the objectives specified in Article 92 (3).

18. It should be noted in this connection that the disputed decision explicitly states that the Netherlands Government has not been able to give nor has the Commission found any grounds establishing that the proposed aid meets the conditions laid down to enforce derogations pursuant to Article 92 (3) of the EEC Treaty.

19. The applicant maintains that the Commission was wrong to hold that the standard of living in the Bergen op Zoom area is not 'abnormally low' and that this area does not suffer serious 'under-employment' within the meaning of Article 92 (3) (a). In fact in the Bergen-op-Zoom region the

under-employment rate is higher and the per capital income lower than the national average in the Netherlands.

20. As far as concerns Article 92 (3) (b) the applicant disputes the Commission's assertion that the system of an 'additional premium' cannot be compared to aid intended to 'remedy a serious disturbance in the economy of a Member State', and that to take any other view would allow the Netherlands in the context of an economic downturn and large-scale unemployment throguhout the whole Community to effect to their advantage investments likely to be made in other Member States in a less favourable situation.

21. In the applicant's view it is impossible to answer the question whether there is a serious disturbance in the economoy of a Member State and, if so, whether a specific national aid remedies that disturbance by considering, as the Commission has done, whether the investment by the undertaking to which the aid from the particular Member State relates may if necessary be effected in other Member States in a less favourable situation than that Member State.

22. Finally the applicant challenges the Commission's statement in the decision that an examination of the cigarette manufacturing industry in the Community and in the Netherlands shows that market conditions alone and without State intervention seem apt to ensure a normal development and that the disputed aid cannot therefore be considered as facilitating the development within the meaning of Article 92 (3) (c).

23. The applicant takes the view that, in principle, the question whether 'without state intervention' market conditions alone are such as to ensure a normal development of production in a Member State and in the Community is irrelevant. The only thing that matters is to ascertain whether the aid facilitates development or not. Furthermore the statement of the reasons on which the decision is based is incomprehensible and contradictory.

24. These arguments put forward by the applicant cannot be upheld. It should be borne in mind that the Commission has a discretion the exercise of which involves economic and social assessments which must be made in a Community context.

25. That is the context in which the Commission has with good reason assessed the standard of living and serious under-employment in the Bergen-op-Zoom area, not with reference to the national average in the Netherlands but in relation to the Community level. As far as concerns the applicant's argument base on Article 92 (3) (b) of the Treaty the Commission could very well take the view, as it did, that the investment to be effected in this case was not 'an important project of common European interest' and that the proposed aid could not be likened to aid intended 'to remedy a serious disturbance in the economy of a Member State', since the proposed aid would have permitted the transfer to the Netherlands, of an investment which could be effected in other Member States in a less favourable situation that that of the Netherlands where the national level of unemployment is one of the lowest in the Community.

26. As far as concerns Article 92 (3) (c) of the Treaty the arguements submitted by the applicant are not relevant. The compatibility with the Treaty of the aid in question must be determined in the context of the Community and not of a single Member State. The Commission's assessment is based for the most part on the finding that the increase in the production of cigarettes envisaged would be exported to the other Member States, in a situation where the growth of consumption has slackened and this did not permit the view that trading conditions would remain unaffected by this aid to an extent contrary to the common interest. This assessment is justified. The finding that market conditions in the cigarette manufacturing industry seem apt, without State intervention, to ensure a normal development, and that the aid cannot therefore be regarded as 'facilitating' de development is also justified when the need for aid is assessed from the standpoint of the Community rather than of a single Member State.

(6) Intermills Case

SA Intermills v. *Commission*; Case 323/82; Judgment of 14 November 1984; [1984] ECR 3809.

Facts (as summarized by the Advocate General);

In Case 323/82, ... , the Court is required essentially to decide how State holdings in undertakings must be appraised on the basis of Article 92 of the EEC Treaty. The action brought by the applicant, and supported by the interveners, seeks a declaration that Commission Decision 82/670/EEC of 22 July 1982 on aid granted by the Belgian Government to a paper-manufacturing undertaking (Official Journal 1982, L 280, p. 30) is void. In fact, the action challenges solely the second paragraph of Article 1 of that decision, which states that the aid in the form of the acquisition by the Belgian Government of a holding in the undertaking in question is incompatible with the common market under Article 92 of the EEC Treaty, and Article 2 of the decision. Article 2 provides as follows:

'The Kingdom of Belgium shall inform the Commission within three months of the date of notification of this decision of the measures it has taken to ensure that the aid referred to in the second paragraph of Article 1 does not continue to distort competition in the future.'

The Court held:

29. Article 92 (1) provides that 'Save as otherwise provided in this Treaty, any aid granted by a Member State or through State resources in any form whatsoever which distorts or threatens to distort competition by

favouring certain undertakings or the production of certain goods shall, in so far as it affects trade between Member States, be incompatible with the common market'.
30. Article 92 (3) (c), to which the contested decision refers, states that aid 'to facilitate the development of certain economic activities' may be considered to be compatible with the common market, provided that such aid does not adversely affect trading conditions to an extent contrary to the common interest.
31. It is clear from the provisions cited that the Treaty applies to aid granted by a State or through State resources 'in any form whatsoever'. It follows that no distinction can be drawn between aid granted in the form of loans and aid granted in the form of a holding acquired in the capital of an undertaking. Aid taking either form falls within the prohibition laid down in Article 92 where the conditions set out in that provision are fulfilled.
32. As the Commission has itself acknowledged, the granting of aid, especially in the form of capital holdings acquired by the State or by public authorities, cannot be regarded as being automatically contrary to the provisions of the Treaty. Thus, irrespective of the form in which aid is granted, be it as a loan or as a capital holding, it is the Commission's task to examine whether it is contrary to Article 92 (1) and, if so, to assess whether there is any possibility of its being exempt under Article 92 (3), giving the grounds on which its decision is based accordingly.

(7) COFAZ Case

Cofaz SA and others v. *Commission*; Case 169/84: Judgment of 28 January 1986; [1986] ECR 409.

Facts:

See the judgment below.

The Court held:

1. By application lodged at the Court Registry on 2 July 1984, Compagnie française de l'azote (Cofaz) SA, Société Cdf Chimie azote et fertilisants SA and Société chimique de la Grande Paroisse SA brought an action under the second paragraph of Article 173 of the EEC Treaty in which they requested the Court to declare void the decision of 17 April 1984 whereby the Commission terminated the procedure initiated under Article 93 (2) of the EEC Treaty against the tariff structure for natural gas prices

in the Netherlands by letter of 4 November 1983 addressed to the Netherlands Government.
2. The Commission challenged the admissibility of the application, without expressly raising an objection of inadmissibility under Article 91 of the Rules of Procedure. The Court, pursuant to Article 92 (2) of those Rules, decided to give a decision on the admissibility of the application first without considering the substance of the case.
3. On 1 June 1983 the Syndicat professionnel de l'industrie des engrais azotés (SPIEA) [Trade Association of Producers of Nitrate Fertilizers, hereinafter referred to as 'the Syndicat'], acting *inter alia* on behalf of the applicants, submitted a complaint to the Commission against the application by the Netherlands of a preferential tariff system to Netherlands producers of nitrate fertilizers for the supply of natural gas intended for the manufacture of ammonia. The Belgian and French Governments, together with a German undertaking, also raised objections to that preferential tariff system which were transmitted to the Commission.
4. On 25 October 1983 the Commission decided to initiate the procedure under Article 93 (2) of the EEC Treaty against the aforesaid tariff system. According to the Commission, the aid scheme in question was a system whereby the Netherlands Government, through Gasunie [the Gas Board], granted special rebates by means of a two-tier tariff structure which had the effect of reducing the cost of natural gas used as a feedstock for Netherlands ammonia producers. By letter of 4 November 1983, the Commission informed the Netherlands Government that it had initiated the above-mentioned procedure. By Notice dated 1 December 1983 given in accordance with Article 93 (2) of the EEC Treaty to the parties concerned regarding a tariff structure for natural gas prices in the Netherlands (Official Journal 1983, C 327, p. 3), the Commission invited those parties to submit their comments.
5. Availing itself of the possibility offered in the aforementioned notice, the Syndicat again made representations to the Commission in a letter dated 6 January 1984 and in its observations confirmed its complaint and provided further particulars thereof.
6. At the same time as the procedure provided for by Article 93 (2), the Commission set in motion the procedure under Article 170 of the EEC Treaty, in response to a complaint from the French Government directed against the same tariff system. In accordance with the procedure under Article 170, the Commission delivered a reasoned opinion on 13 March 1984 in which it found that, by granting through Gasunie a preferential tariff for the supply of natural gas to Netherlands producers of ammonia and of nitrate fertilizers, the Kingdom of the Netherlands had failed to fulfil its obligations under Article 93 of the Treaty. Moreover, the Commission reserved its position with regard to the attitude which it would adopt in connection with the procedure initiated under Article 93 (2).

7. In a memorandum dated 28 March 1984, the Syndicat, still acting on behalf of the applicants, made further representations to the Commission and raised a number of objections to the system of natural gas tariffs which had in the meantime been amended by Gasunie.
8. By telex message of 14 April 1984 the Netherlands Government informed the Commission that Gasunie had again amended its industrial tariff structure with retroactive effect from 1 November 1983, thereby abolishing the two tariff systems to which the Syndicat had objected in its complaint of 1 June 1983 and in its observations of 6 January 1984, on the one hand, and in its memorandum of 28 March 1984 on the other.
9. Taking the view that the new tariff system established by Gasunie was compatible with the common market, the Commission decided at its meeting on 17 April 1984 to terminate the procedure which had been initiated under Article 93 (2) of the EEC Treaty against the tariff system established by Gasunie. It notified the Netherlands Government of its decision by letter of 18 May 1984. The applicants had already been informed of that decision, through the Syndicat, by letter of 24 April 1984 which was couched in terms broadly similar to those used in the letter addressed to the Netherlands Government.
10. The Commission came to the conclusion that the new tariff system was compatible with the common market essentially for the following reasons: Gasunie had abolished the two-tier tariff system and had added to its internal industrial tariff structure (namely tariffs B – E) a new tariff, known as tariff F, for the benefit of the major industrial users in the Netherlands. In order to qualify for that new tariff, users had to consume at least 600 million cubic metres of gas per year and operate 90% of the time or more and they had to accept total or partial interruptions of supplies at Gasunie's discretion or supplies of natural gas having different calorific values. The new tariff, tariff F, formed an integral part of the general tariff structure for users in the Netherlands and did not discriminate between sectors. The value of the rebate granted to the undertakings eligible for the new tariff (by comparison with tariff E) was even lower than the total value of the savings made by Gasunie on account of the volume of consumption by those undertakings and the other aforementioned conditions of the new tariff system. Tariff F was therefore justified in economic terms.
11. After considering the Commission's letter of 24 April 1984, the Syndicat replied on 22 May 1984 setting out its objections to the Commission's decision to terminate the procedure in question. In its letters of 26 and 27 June 1984, the Commission refuted those objections.
12. It is the decision of 17 April 1984 terminating the procedure under Article 93 (2) that the applicants are seeking to have annulled in this application under the second paragraph of Article 173 of the EEC Treaty. In their application they maintain that the Commission's decision is vitiated by manifest errors in the assessment of essential information, particularly with regard to the appraisal of the total value of the savings made by Gasunie as a result of the conditions for the application of the new tariff.

In their view, tariff F is merely an attempt to maintain in a different guise the previous tariff system.

13. The Commission considers that the contested decision is not of individual concern to the applicants, within the meaning of the second paragraph of Article 173. It does not deny that in different circumstances an action may be admissible where it is brought by an undertaking other than that to which a decision terminating an investigation procedure initiated under Article 93 (2) is addressed, but submits that the possibility of bringing proceedings in this case should be interpreted restrictively. In its view, there are no attributes peculiar to the applicants which differentiate them from all other persons. Neither the fact of being ammonia producers nor the fact that they were allegedly treated in a discriminatory manner is sufficient, in the Commission's view, to distinguish them individually. In any event, since Articles 92 and 93 of the Treaty did not confer a right on individuals, a decision based on those articles in no way affects the legal position of individuals. Finally, the Commission maintains that the decision is not of individual concern to the applicants because they are not the only producers of nitrate fertilizers in the Community.

14. The Commission considers that the applicants' involvement in the initiation of the administrative procure does not individually distinguish them either. They merely provided some information and that cannot be compared to the role by complainants in a procedure under Regulation No 17 of the Council of 6 February 1962 (Official Journal, English Special Edition 1959–62, p. 87) or under Council Regulation (EEC) No 3017/79 of 20 December 1979 (Official Journal 1979, L 339, p. 1). Articles 92, 93 and 94 do not confer a specific status on the applicants. However, even on the assumption that the applicants had a right to request the Commission to bring to an end an aid which was allegedly incompatible with the common market, that would not in itself demonstrate that they had an interest in challenging a decision establishing that the aid was not incompatible with the common market. Since the Court has recognized the direct effect of Article 93 (3), inasmuch as it establishes procedural criteria which the national courts can apply and confers rights on individuals which the national courts must protect, it follows, in the Commission's view, that an infringement of Article 93 (3) may be penalized directly by the national courts. The applicants are not, therefore, denied any redress whatsoever.

15. The Commission concludes this line of reasoning with a reference to the case-law of the Court, according to which the Commission enjoys a broad discretion with regard to the application of Article 92. It follows, in its view, first that Article 92 does not have direct effect, and secondly that the Commission alone is responsible for initiating the procedure under Article 93 (2).

16. With regard to the question whether the contested decision is of direct concern to the applicants, the Commission emphasizes that the mere fact that they are competing with undertakings allegedly in receipt of State aid

does not constitute a specific circumstance enabling them to claim that the decision affects their position on the market. In the Commission's view, however, a specific circumstance of that kind is necessary, according to the case-law of the Court, in order for proceedings under Article 173 to be brought. Moreover, the competitive position of the applicants is directly dependent on the gas tariffs charged by their supplier, namely Gaz de France, and not on the gas tariffs which Gasunie charges to Netherlands producers.

17. The applicants maintain on the contrary that from the inception of the procedure until the adoption of the contested decision the issue had remained the same, namely the assessment of a rebate granted to certain users of natural gas in the Netherlands. They consider that the decision is of individual concern to them inasmuch as they are placed at a serious disadvantage by the favourable competitive position enjoyed by their Netherlands competitors. Furthermore, they contend that their involvement in the initiation and course of the procedure distinguishes them individually for the purposes of Article 173. They maintain that the Commission itself recognized their involvement by notifying the contested decision to them. According to the applicants, an undertaking which is adversely affected by an aid has a right similar to that conferred by Article 3 (2) of Regulation No 17 of the Council to request the Commission to give a decision on the legality of the aid.

18. The applicants also consider that the contested decision is of direct concern to them, first because they claim to be detrimentally affected by a distortion of competition, and secondly because that adverse impact is the result of the Commission's decision. In so far as the products manufactured by the Netherlands producers are marketed within the Community, the applicants claim that the decision affects their position on the market.

19. In the applicants' view, it is apparent from the recent case-law of the Court that account should be taken of the principles on which Articles 164 and 173 are based. Accordingly, the absence of regulations which accord the applicants specific rights during the administrative procedure is not a decisive factor. Moreover, the applicants consider that the contested decision is of direct concern to them on the ground that it entered into force immediately, without being implemented by any Community or national measure.

20. It should be stated, by way of a preliminary observation, that in order to examine the admissibility of the application and without considering the substance of the case, it is necessary to take as a basis the applicants' contentions to the effect that tariff F, which was added by Gasunie to its industrial tariff structure and was applied to natural gas supplied to the major users in the Netherlands, constitutes an aid granted by the Netherlands Government in favour of the three Netherlands producers of ammonia and nitrate fertilizers.

21. In the first place it must be borne in mind that, in accordance with the

second paragraph of Article 173, a natural or legal person may, under the conditions set out in the first paragraph of that article, institute proceedings against a decision addressed to another person only if that decision is of direct and individual concern to the former. Accordingly, the applicants' right of action depends on whether the decision addressed to the Netherlands Government whereby the Commission terminated the procedure initiated under Article 93 (2) against the Netherlands is of direct and individual concern to them.

22. It is clear from a consistent line of decisions of the Court that persons other than those to whom a decision is addressed may claim to be concerned within the meaning of the second paragraph of Article 173 only if that decision affects them by reason of certain attributes which are peculiar to them, or by reason of circumstances in which they are differentiated from all other persons, and by virtue of these factors distinguishes them individually just as in the case of the person addressed (judgment of 15 July 1963 in Case 25/62 *Plaumann* v. *Commission* [1963] ECR 95).

23. More particularly, as regards the circumstances referred to in that judgment, the Court has repeatedly held that where a regulation accords applicant undertakings procedural guarantees entitling them to request the Commission to find an infringement of Community rules, those undertakings should be able to institute proceedings in order to protect their legitimate interests (judgments of 25 October 1977 in Case 26/76 *Metro* v. *Commission* [1977] ECR 1875, 5 October 1983 in Case 191/82 *Fediol* v. *Commission* [1983] ECR 2913, and 11 October 1983 in Case 210/81 *Demo-Studio Schmidt* v. *Commission* [1983] ECR 3045).

24. In its judgment of 20 March 1985 in Case 264/82 (*Timex Corporation* v. *Council and Commission* [1985] ECR 849) the Court pointed out that it was necessary to examine in that regard the part played by the undertaking in the administrative proceedings. The Court accepted as evidence that the measure in question was of concern to the undertaking, within the meaning of the second paragraph of Article 173 of the EEC Treaty, the fact that the undertaking was at the origin of the complaint which led to the opening of the investigation procedure, the fact that its views were heard during that procedure and the fact that the conduct of the procedure was largely determined by its observations.

25. The same conclusions apply to undertakings which have played a comparable role in the procedure referred to in Article 93 of the EEC Treaty provided, however, that their position on the market is significantly affected by the aid which is the subject of the contested decision. Article 93 (2) recognizes in general terms that the undertakings concerned are entitled to submit their comments to the Commission but does not provide any further details.

26. With regard to the position of the applicants whilst the Commission's investigation concerning the aid in question was in progress, it should be noted that on 1 June 1983 they lodged a complaint with the Commission

concerning the preferential tariff system in favour of Netherlands producers of nitrate fertilizers. In their complaint, they laid particular emphasis on their competitive position in relation to the three Netherlands producers and on the adverse effects of the aid. Moreover, the applicants complied with the Commission's request to submit their comments under Article 93 (2).

27. With regard to the impact of economic factors as a whole on the market in nitrate fertilizers, the applicants have pointed out that, according to their calculations, the preferential tariff system represents an annual transfer of approximately Hfl. 165 million to the three Netherlands producers of ammonia. According to the applicants in France the cost of natural gas represents approximately 80% of the ex-works cost price of ammonia which, in its turn, is the raw material from which nitrate fertilizers are manufactured. They have also argued that they compete directly with the three Netherlands producers of nitrate fertilizers who, between 1978 and 1982, more than triplied their volume of exports of nitrate fertilizers to France and whose share of the French market rose between 1980 and 1982 from 9% to 21.7%.

28. It is not for the Court, at this stage of the procedure, when it is considering whether the application is admissible, to make a definitive finding on the competitive relationship between the applicants and the Netherlands undertakings. It is sufficient to note that the applicants have adduced pertinent reasons to show that the Commission's decision may adversely affect their legitimate interests by seriously jeopardizing their position on the market in question.

29. In those circumstances, the fact that, according to the Commission, a fourth undertaking which is not in competition with the applicants also qualifies for tariff F is immaterial. Again on the assumption that the aid in question falls within the scope of Article 92, the advantage gained from a tariff system by an outside undertaking not in competition with the applicants does not detract from the validity of the argument that a system of that kind may distort or threaten to distort competition between the other undertakings and does not affect the substantive nature of the damage allegedly sustained by the applicants.

30. As regards the question whether the Commission's decision to terminate the procedure is of direct concern to the applicants, it is sufficient to observe that the decision has left intact all the effects of the tariff system set up, whilst the procedure sought by the applicants would lead to the adoption of a decision to abolish or amend that system. In those circumstances, it must be held that the contested decision is of direct concern to the applicants.

31. It follows that the contested measure is a decision of direct and individual concern to the applicants, within the meaning of the second paragraph of Article 173 of the Treaty.

32. For all those reasons, the application must be declared admissible and the proceedings must take their course.

D. LITERATURE

I. van Bael/J. F. Bellis, *Competition Law of the EEC*, Bicester, 1987.
C. W. Bellamy/G. D. Child, *Common Market Law of Competition*, London, 1987.

III. Approximation of Laws

A. ARTICLE 100

1. Cases

(1) Enka Case

For facts and references see p. 43.

The Court held:

. . . . .

9. The Court has already found in its judgment of 1 February 1977 in Case 51/76 (*Verbond van Nederlandse ondernemingen* v. *Inspecteur der Invoerrechten en Accijnzen* [1977] ECR 113) that where the Community authorities have, by directive, imposed on Member States the obligation to pursue a particular course of conduct, the effectiveness of such an act would be weakened if individuals were prevented from relying on it before their national courts and if the latter were prevented from taking it into consideration as an element of Community law.
10. That is especially so when the individual invokes a provision of a directive before a national court in order that the latter shall rule whether the competent national authorities, in exercising the choice which is left to them as to the form and the methods for implementing the directive, have kept within the limits of their discretion as set out in the directive.
11. It emerges from the third paragraph of Article 189 of the Treaty that the choice left to the Member States as regards the form of the measures and the methods used in their adoption by the national authorities depends upon the result which the Council or the Commission wishes to see achieved.
12. As regards the harmonization of the provisions relating to customs matters laid down in the Member States by law, regulation or administrative action, in order to bring about the uniform application of the Common Customs Tariff it may prove necessary to ensure the

absolute identity of those provisions which govern the treatment of goods imported into the Community, whatever the Member State across whose frontier they are imported.

. . . . .

(2) Denkavit Case II

Denkavit Futtermittel v. *Minister für Ernährung des Landes Nordrhein-Westfalen*; Case 251/78; Preliminary ruling of 8 November 1979; [1979] ECR 3388; [1980] 3 CMLR 513.

Facts:

Denkavit imported into the Federal Republic of Germany from the Netherlands feeding-stuffs containing products of animal origin – in this case substitute milk-based feeding-stuffs (Milchaustauschfutter). Denkavit called in question the compatibility of certain provisions of the regulation of 18 September 1957 of the Land in question on animal health measures applicable on the importation and transit of feeding-stuffs containing products of animal origin from abroad (hereinafter referred to as the 'Viehseuchenverordnung (regulation on infectious diseases of animals) 1957' with Article 30 and 36 and also with Article 9 of the Treaty relating respectively to the prohibition of measures having an effect equivalent to quantitative restrictions and of charges having an effect equivalent to customs duties in intra-Community trade and also with the provisions of Regulation (EEC) No 804/68 of the Council of 27 June 1968 on the common organization of the market in milk and milk products (Official Journal, English Special Edition 1968 (I), p. 176) and of Regulation (EEC) No 2725/75 of the Council of 29 October 1975 on the common organization of the market in cereals (Official Journal L 281, p. 1) which enact or imply the same prohibitions.

The Court held:

. . . . .

13. As far as concerns the field of application of Article 36 the national court asks, in the first place, whether that provision may still be invoked by a Member State even though Community directives or regulations make arrangements for supervision having the same objectives as those provided for by the national provisions adopted in accordance with the said Article 36.
14. The Court of Justice has held in its judgment of 5 October 1977 in Case

5/77, *Carlo Tedeschi* v. *Denkavit Commerciale* s.r.l. (1977) ECR 1556 that Article 36 is not designed to reserve certain matters to the exclusive jurisdiction of Member States but only permits national laws to derogate from the principle of the free movement of goods to the extent to which such derogation is and continues to be justified for the attainment of the objectives referred to in that article. Consequently when, in application of Article 100 of the Treaty, Community directives provide for the harmonization of the measures necessary to guarantee the protection of animal and human health and when they establish procedures to check that they are observed, recourse to Article 36 is no longer justified and the appropriate checks must be carried out and the protective measures adopted within the framework outlined by the harmonizing directive.

. . . . .

(3) Hormones Case

United Kingdom v. *Council*; Case 68/86; Judgment of 23 February 1988 (not yet reported).

See at p. 654.

B. Article 102

1. Cases

(1) Costa-ENEL Case

For facts and references see pages 114, 121, 161, 406

The Court held:

On the interpretation of Article 102

Article 102 provides that, where 'there is reason to fear' that a provision laid down by law may cause 'distortion', the Member State desiring to proceed therewith shall 'consult the Commission'; the Commission has power to recommend to the Member States the adoption of suitable measures to avoid the distortion feared.

This Article, placed in the chapter devoted to the 'Approximation of Laws', is designed to prevent the differences between the legislation of the different nations with regard to the objectives of the Treaty from becoming more pronounced. By virtue of this provision, Member States have limited their freedom of initiative by agreeing to submit to an appropriate procedure of consultation. By binding themselves unambiguously to prior consultation with the Commission in all those cases where their projected legislation might create a risk, however slight, of a possible distortion, the States have undertaken an obligation to the Community which binds them as States, but which does not create individual rights which national courts must protect. For its part, the Commission is bound to ensure respect for the provisions of this Article, but this obligation does not give individuals the right to allege, within the framework of Community law and by means of Article 177 either failure by the State concerned to fulfil any of its obligations or breach of duty on the part of the Commission.

C. LITERATURE

Approximation of Laws under Article 100 of the EEC Treaty, Select Committee on the European Communities, House of Lords, session 1977–78, 22nd report (London, H.M.S.O., 1978).
Close, G., 'Harmonisation of Laws: use or abuse of the powers under the EEC Treaty', 3 E. L. Rev. 1978, 462–481.
Easson, A. J., 'EEC Directives for the Harmonisation of Laws: Some Problems of Validity, Implementation and Legal Effects', 1 Yb. Eur. Law 1984, 1–44.
Slot, P. J., *Technical and administrative obstacles to trade in the EEC*, Leiden, 1975.

See Materials on the law of the European Communities, Chapter Five.
No 14 Extract of the Council Directive 72/166/EEC of 24 April 1972 on the approximation of the laws of the Member States relating to insurance against civil liability in respect of the use of motor vehicles, and to the enforcement of the obligation to insure against such liability.
No 15 Reply to Written Question No 614/79 of 30 November 1979 on Harmonization.

IV. Economic, social and environment policies

A. ECONOMIC POLICY

1. Cases

(1) French rediscount case

Commission of the EC v. *French Republic*; Joined cases 6–11/69; Judgment of 10 December 1969; [1969] ECR 538–546; [1970] CMLR 63.

Facts:

The Banque France has for some years granted a rediscount rate for export credits, including that for steel products, more favourable than the rate for internal credits. From 1964 the Commission requested that this advantage for credits based on the member countries of the European Communties should be removed, since in its opinion the disparity in rates constituted an aid which was incompatible with the Common Market. The French Government, without admitting that the advantage given to its exporters was incompatible with the Treaties, made it know by letter of 13 May 1968 that it was examining the conditions under which the advantage could be removed as from 1 July 1968.

On 12 June 1968, because of the serious social crisis being experienced by France and so as to assist its exporters, the French Government informed the Commission that it expected it to approve the reduction by one point of the liquidation rate for credits based on exports, which was then 3 per cent, while the internal discount rate was 3.5 per cent. On 24 June 1968 the Permanent Representative of France informed the Commission that his Government was forced, as a safeguard measure, to take from 1 July 1968 and up to 31 January 1969 particularly a fresh reduction of the dediscount rate on exports, bringing the latter from 3 to 2 per cent. In a letter dated 27 June 1968 the Permanent Representative of France stated that the measures taken were based, as regards EEC products, on Chapter 2 (balance of payments) of Title II of Part 3 of the EEC Treaty, and more precisely on Articles 108 (1) and 109, and, as regards ECSC products, that the question was still under examination.

The Commission, in its reply of 28 June 1968, recalled that in order to meet the French requests, the appropriate Community procedures should be activated and declared that for its part it was opening the consultations provided for in Articles 37 and 67 of the ECSC Treaty and carrying out the procedure provided for in Article 108 of the EEC Treaty.

On 30 June 1968 the Banque de France reduced the rediscount rate for all export credits from 3 to 2 per cent, until 31 December 1968.

After consultations with both the Consultative Committee and the Council, the Commission took Decision 914/68/ECSC of 6 July 1968 authorizing France to grant certain aids to the steel industry. On 31 July 1968 there came the EEC Decision 68/301/EEC of the Commission which authorized France to take various safeguard measures in accordance with Article 108 (3) of the Treaty and providing, in absolutely identical terms to those cited above, the possibility of a preferential rediscount rate for all credits relating to export operations.

On 5 November 1968 the French Minister of Foreign Affairs informed the President of the Commission of the intention of the French Government to maintain the rediscount rate for export credits at 2 per cent, until 31 December 1968. Since the internal rediscount rate remained fixed at 5 per cent, a gap of 3 per cent was maintained after 31 October 1968 contrary to the provisions of Decisions 68/301/EEC and 914/68/EEC.

The Commission considered that in these circumstances France had violated the obligations by which it was bound under the Treaties and invited the French Government, in accordance with the provisions of Article 88 ECSC and Article 169 EEC, to present its observations on the matter. On 13 December 1968 the Permanent Representative of France stated that because of circumstances and in order to avoid upsets in the plans of French undertakings, it had not been possible to make the increase in the rate, required by the Commission on the date laid down, but that it was the intention of the French Government to raise, as from 31 December 1968, the rediscount rate on exports to 4%.

Since it was not satisfied by these observations, and the gap between the two rates had in the meanwhile risen to four points because of the increase of the general rate from 5 to 6%, the Commission on 18 December 1968 issued a reasoned opinion under Article 169 of the EEC Treaty. The Commission measures to comply with the opinion. As France let the time limit pass without altering the criticised measures, the Commission brought action 6/69 on 31 January 1969.

The Commission also took a decision under Article 88 of the ECSC Treaty. This Decision also granted the French Government a time limit of 21 days to comply with the obligation contained in Decision 914/68/ECSC. The French Government appealed against this Decision (action 11/69).

The Court held:

. . . . .

14. Although under Article 104 of the Treaty Member States are responsible for ensuring the equilibrium of their total balance of payments and for maintaining confidence in their currency, their obligation under Articles 105 and 107 is no less to coordinate their economic policies for this purpose and to treat their policies on exchange as a matter fo common concern.
15. Articles 108 (3) and 109 (3) confer powers of authorization or intervention on the Community institutions which would be otiose if the Member States were free, on the pretext that their action related only to monetary policy, unilaterally to derogate from their obligations under the provisions of the Treaty and without being subject to control by the institutions.
16. The solidarity which is at the basis of these obligations as of the whole of the Community system in accordance with the undertaking provided for in Article 5 of the Treaty, is continued for the benefit of the States in the procedure for mutual assistance provided for in Article 108 where a Member State is seriously threatened with difficulties as regards its balance of payments.
17. The exercise or reserved powers cannot therefore permit the unilateral adoption of measures prohibited by the Treaty.

18. Under Article 92 the Member States have agreed that any aid granted by them in any form whatsoever which distorts or threatens to distort competition is incompatible with the Common Market.
19. It cannot be otherwise under Article 92 (3) (b) except in the case of a serious disturbance in the economy of a Member State and subject to the conditions laid down in Article 93, that it to say, after a decision of the Commission and, where appropriate, of the Council.
20. A preferential rediscount rate for exports, granted by a State in favour only of national products exported and for the purpose of helping them to compete in other Member States with products originating in the latter, constitutes an aid within the meaning of Article 92 the observance of which it is the Commission's task to ensure.
21. Neither the fact that the preferential rate in question is applicable to all national products exported and only to them nor the fact that in establishing it the French Government may have resolved to approximate the rate to those applied in the other member countries can remove from the measure in question the character of an aid which is prohibited except in the cases and procedures provided for by the Treaty.
22. As a result prior authorization by the Commission was necessary to establish or retain a preferential rediscount rate on exports and by making it subject to appropriate conditions the Commission has not impinged on the powers reserved to the Member States.
23. There is even less ground for challenging the necessity for this authorization in so far as by its communication of 12 June 1968 the French Government itself applied to the Commission to 'retain and even increase' the privileged rediscount rate for exports to the other countries of the Community.
24. In view of the definitive nature of the decision in question it is not necessary to consider the other submissions which the French Government has put forward outside the procedures and time-limits laid down in the Treaty and the observance of which is required in the interest both of the States themselves and of the Community.
25. The Government of the French Republic further pleads that the retention beyond 1 November 1968 of the difference between the preferential rediscount rate and the general rate constitutes a new protective measure within the meaning of Article 109 of the Treaty justified by the fresh monetary crisis which occurred during the authumn of 1968.
26. It says that the Commission could not interrupt the effects of this measure by pursuing proceedings for failure by a State to fulfil its obligations which related to a situation overtaken by events and that by delivering the reasoned opinion of 18 December without having regard to the new circumstances, it infringed Article 109 of the Treaty.
27. This submission is admissible since it is based on new factors subsequent to the decision of 23 July 1968.
28. In the event of urgency and when a decision of the Council within the meaning of Article 108 (2) is not forthcoming immediately, Article 109

allows, as a precaution, unilateral action by a Member State and leaves this latter to decide the circumstances which render such action necessary.

29. However, since they relate to measures of derogation which are likely to cause disturbances in the functioning of the Common Market, they are both exceptional and precautionary and therefore only temporary pending an examination of their validity, which must take place as soon as possible, and any action which may be taken under Articles 108 and 109.

30. In the event of unilateral action by a State derogating from the provisions of the Treaty, intervention by the Community institutions as soon as possible meets a fundamental requirement for the functioning of the Common Market.

31. Observance of this requirement requires that a State which takes advantage of the exceptional power contained in Article 109 (1) should immediately – or not later than when such measures enter into force – inform the Commission and the other Member States and make express reference to this provision.

32. These provisions, which are to be derived from the very nature of the unilateral protective measures, have not been observed in the present case.

33. Although the content of the verbal communication of 5 November 1968 is disputed by the parties and has not been clearly established, it is however common ground that the letter from the French Government dated 13 December 1968 justifies the retention of the difference in question only on the ground of the necessity of avoiding disruption of the forward planning of French undertakings and the consideration that the increase in the general rediscount rate from 5% to 6% which occurred after 12 November 1968 raised in a different way the question of fixing the rediscount rate for exports.

34. The submission based on Article 109 is therefore unfounded.

. . . . .

(2) Balkan Import-Export Case

Balkan Import-Export GmbH v. *Hauptzollamt Berlin-Packhof*; Case 5/73; Preliminary ruling of 24 October 1973; [1973] ECR 1107.

Facts:

Regulation No 974/71 of the Council of 12 May 1971 (OJ L 106, of 12 May 1971, p. 1) provides for the application of a system of compensatory amounts in trade with other Member States and third countries.

When the plaintiff in the main action imported 13.590 kg of Bulgarian white cheese of sheep's milk, tariff heading No 04.04-E-1-3-4-50, into the Federal Republic of Germany, the Hauptzollamt of Berlin Packhof by notice of 27 March 1972 under the said Regulation claimed in addition to a levy and the turnover tax on the import a compensatory amount of 6183.45 DM, or 45.50 DM per 100 kg.

The plaintiff in the main action brought an action before the Finanzgericht of Berlin for the annulment of the notice of recovery of the compensatory dury, disputing the validity of Regulation No 974/71.

Accordingly the Finanzgericht of Berlin, by order of 19 January 1973, asked the Court the following questions:

'Is Regulation (EEC) No 974/71 of the Council of 12 May 1971 concerning 'certain measures of conjunctural policy to be taken in the agricultural sector as a result of the temporary widening of the fluctuation margins of the currencies of certain Member States' (OJ, 12 May 1971, L 106, p. 1), or are the Regulations implementing it, viz. Regulations (EEC) No 1013/71, 1014/71 and 548/72 of the Commission, valid, in so far as they provide for the making and computation of compensatory amounts for the import of milk products from Bulgaria?'

The Court held:

(a) The legal basis of Regulation (EEC) No 974/71

11. This question concerns, first, whether the validity of the above Regulation could be affected by the fact that it is based on Article 103 of the Treaty, which does not touch on the common agricultural policy, the latter being governed by the specific provisions of Articles 38 to 47 of the Treaty, and that in any case, the said Article 103 authorizes only the adoption of conjunctural measures, which the disputed measures are not.

12. Article 40 of the Treaty states that Member States shall bring the common agricultural policy into force by the end of the transitional period at the latest and that, in order to attain the objectives set out in Article 39, a common organization of agricultural markets is to be established.

The same Article provides that this common organization may include any measures required and in particular regulation of prices, aids for production and marketing, storage and carry-over arrangements and common machinery for stabilizing imports and exports.

By virtue of the third paragraph of Article 43 (2), the Council shall (on a proposal from the Commission and after consulting the Assembly, acting, after the end of the second stage of the transitional period, by a qualified majority) make regulations, issue directives, or take decisions in this sphere.

It is evident from these provisions that the powers conferred for implementing the common agricultural policy do not relate merely to possible

structural measures but extend equally to any immediate short-term economic intervention required in this area of production, and that the Council is empowered to resort to them in accordance with the decision-making procedures there set out.
13. On the other hand, Article 103 refers to Member States' conjunctural policies, which they must regard as a matter of common concern.

Consequently it does not relate to areas already subject to common rules, as is the organization of agricultural markets.

The real object envisaged by Article 103 is the coordination of Member States' conjunctural policies, and, according to the terms of paragraph 2 of that Article, the adoption of common measures appropriate to the situation.
14. The floating of the exchange rates for the German and Dutch currencies, deemed essential if the wave of speculative capital into the Federal Republic and the Netherlands was to be checked, imperilled the unity of the common market and made measures designed to safeguard the machinery and objectives of the common agricultural policy imperative.

The introduction of compensatory amounts was not intended to provide extra protection, but to maintain uniform prices, the foundation of the present organization of the markets, despite the temporary departure from fixed parities, thus preventing the collapse of the intervention price system and preserving the normal flow of trade in agricultural products both within the Community and with third countries.

These measures, intended to compensate temporarily for the harmful effects of national monetary measures, so that the process of economic integration may meanwhile continue its progress, are of an essentially transitory nature and would normally have had to adopted by virtue of the powers conferred on the Council by Articles 40 and 43 and in accordance with the procedures set out therein, in particular after consulting the Assembly.
15. However, owing to the time needed to give effect to the procedures laid down in Articles 40 and 43, a certain amount of trade might then have passed free of the regulations, and this could jeopardize the relevant common organizations of the market.

There being no adequate provision in the common agricultural policy for adoption of the urgent measures necessary to counteract the monetary situation described above, it is reasonable to suppose that the Council was justified in making interim use of the powers conferred on it by Article 103 of the Treaty.

Consequently – while the suddenness of the events with which the Council was faced, the urgency of the measures to be adopted, the seriousness of the situation and the fact that these measures were adopted in an area intimately connected with the monetary policies of Member States (the effects of which they had partially to offset) all prompted the Council to have recourse to Article 103 – Regulation No 2746/72 shows that this state of affairs was only a temporary one, since the legal basis for the measure was eventually found in other provisions of the Treaty.

(b) The form in which the disputed measure was adopted

16. The next question is whether Regulation No 974/71 is invalid on the ground that Article 103 of the Treaty, notably in paragraph 3, authorizes the adoption of measures only in the form of a directive of decision, not in the form of a regulation.

    It is alleged that such an interpretation is borne out by the wording of Article 103 and is justified in view of the fact that in the realm of conjunctural policy no more than a coordinating rôle has been given to the Institutions.

17. Although by Article 103 (1) Member States are bound to regard their conjunctural policies as a matter of common concern, the wording does not preclude Community Institutions from having power to lay down themselves, without prejudice to other procedures set out in the Treaty, conjunctural measures on matters within the spheres of their competence.

    On the contrary, Article 103 (2), by declaring that the Council may, 'acting unanimously ... decide upon the measures appropriate to the situation', confers on that body – subject to the condition referred to above – the powers mecessary to adopt, in principle, any conjunctural measures which may appear to be needed in order to safeguard the objectives of the Treaty.

    Without some such faculty, the natural concomitant of any kind of economic administration, the Institutions of the Community would find it impossible to accomplish the tasks entrusted to them in this field.

18. The phrase 'measures appropriate to the situation' in Article 103 (2) means that as regards form, too, the Council may choose whichever seems best suited to the case in hand.

    Subject to the requirement of a unanimous decision, Article 103 (2) refers to the general procedures whereby the Council may exercise its powers, described in Articles 145, 155 and 189, including therefore, its right to delegate to the Commission the implementation of Regulations it has laid down.

    Article 103 (3) differs from Article 103 (2) in that, as the use of the phrase 'where required' shows, it envisages the possibility that the Council might not be able to reach the unanimity required to carry into effect the rules for the application of the conjunctural measures decided on. In that circumstance only, these rules would be binding on Member States as far as they concerned the result to be obtained, but would have to leave to the national authorities the choice of form and method.

. . . . .

(3) Luisi and Carbone Case

See at pages 450, 474.

B. SOCIAL POLICY

1. Cases

(1) Defrenne Case II

Defrenne v. *Sabena*; Case 43/75; Judgment of 18 March 1976; [1976] ECR 471.

Facts:

Miss Gabrielle Defrenne was engaged as an air hostess by Sabena on 10 December 1951. On 1 October 1963 her employment was confirmed by a new contract of employment which gave her the duties of 'Cabin Steward and Air Hostess – Principal Cabin Attendant'.

Miss Defrenne gave up her duties on 15 February 1968 in pursuance of the sixth paragraph of Article 5 of the contract of employment entered into by air crew employed by Sabena, which stated that contracts held by women members of the crew shall terminate on the day on which the employee in question reaches the age of 40 years.

When Miss Defrenne left she received an allowance on termination of service.

On 9 February 1970 Miss Defrenne brought an action before the Conseil d'Etat of Belgium for the annulment of the Royal Decree of 3 November 1969 which laid down special rules governing the acquisition of the right to a pension by air crew in civil aviation.

This action gave rise, following a request for a preliminary ruling, to a judgment of the Court of Justice of 25 May 1971 (Case 80/70, [1971] ECR 445), in which the Court ruled: 'A retirement pension established within the framework of a social security scheme laid down by legislation does not constitute consideration which the worker receives indirectly in respect of his employment from his employer within the meaning of the second paragraph of Article 119 of the EEC Treaty'.

Miss Defrenne had previously brought an action before the Tribunal du Travail of Brussels on 13 March 1968 for compensation for the loss she had suffered in terms of salary, allowance on termination of service and pension as a result of the fact that air hostesses and male members of the air crew performing identical duties did not receive equal pay.

The Court held:

The first question (direct effect of Article 119)

4. The first question asks whether Article 119 of the Treaty introduces 'directly into the national law of each Member State of the European Community the principle that men and women should receive equal pay for equal work and does it therefore, independently of any national provision, entitle workers to institute proceedings before national courts in order to ensure its observance?
5. If the answer to this question is in the affirmative, the question further enquires as from what date this effect must be recognized.
6. The reply to the final part if the first question will therefore be given with the reply to the second question.
7. The question of the direct effect of Article 119 must be considered in the light of the nature of the principle of equal pay, the aim of this provision and its place in the scheme of the Treaty.
8. Article 119 pursues a double aim.
First, in the light of the different stages of the development of social legislation in the various Member States, the aim of Article 119 is to avoid a situation in which undertakings established in States which have actually implemented the principle of equal pay suffer a competitive disadvantage in intra-Community competition as compared with undertakings established in States which have not yet eliminated discrimination against somen workers as regards pay.
10. Secondly, this provision forms part of the social objectives of the Committee, which is not merely an economic union, but is at the same time intended, by common action, to ensure social progress and seek the constant improvement of the living and working conditions of their peoples, as is emphasized by the Preamble to the Treaty.
11. This aim as accentuated by the insertion of Article 119 into the body of a chapter devoted to social policy whose preliminary provision, Article 117, marks 'the need to promote improved working conditions and an improved standard of living for workers, so as to make possible their harmonization while the improvement is being maintained'.
12. This double aim, which is at once economic and social, shows that the principle of equal pay forms part of the foundations of the Community.
13. Furthermore, this explains why the Treaty has provided for the complete implementation of this principle by the end of the first stage of the transitional period.
14. Therefore, in interpreting this provision, it is impossible to base any argument on the dilatoriness and resistance which have delayed the actual implementation of this basic principle in certain Member States.
15. In particular, since Article 119 appears in the context of the harmonization of working conditions while the improvement is being maintained,

the objection that the terms of this article may be observed in other ways than by raising the lowest salaries may be set aside.

16. Under the terms of the first paragraph of Article 119, the Member States are bound to ensure and maintain 'the application of the principle that men and women should receive equal pay for equal work'.

17. The second and third paragraphs of the same article add a certain number of details concerning the concepts of pay and work referred to in the first paragraph.

18. For the purpose of the implementation of these provisions a distinction must be drawn within the whole area of application of Article 119 between, first, direct and overt discrimination which may be identified solely with the aid of the criteria based on equal work and equal pay referred to by the article in question and, secondly, indirect and disguised discrimination which can only be identified by reference to more explicit implementing provisions of a Community or national character.

19. It is impossible not to recognize that the complete implementation of the aim pursued by Article 119, by means of the elimination of all discrimination, direct or indirect, between men and women workers, not only as regards individual undertakings but also entire branches of industry and even of the economic system as a whole, may in certain cases involve the elaboration of criteria whose implementation necessitates the taking of appropriate measures at Community and national level.

20. This view is all the more essential in the light of the fact that the Community measures on this question, to which reference will be made in answer to the second question, implement Article 119 from the point of view of extending the narrow criterion or 'equal work', in accordance in particular with the provisions of Convention No 100 on equal pay concluded by the International Labour Organization in 1951, Article 2 of which establishes the principle of equal pay for work 'of equal value'.

21. Among the forms of direct discrimination which may be identified solely by reference to the criteria laid down by Article 119 must be included in particular those which have their origin in legislative provisions or in collective labour agreements and which may be detected on the basis of a purely legal analysis of the situation.

22. This applies even more in cases where men and women receive unequal pay for equal work carried out in the same establishment or service, whether public or private.

23. As is shown by the very findings of the judgment making the reference, in such a situation the court is in a position to establish all the facts which enable it to decide whether a woman worker is receiving lower pay than a male worker performing the same tasks.

24. In such situation, at least, Article 119 is directly applicable and may thus give rise to individual rights which the courts must protect.

25. Furthermore, as regards equal work, as a general rule, the national legislative provisions adopted for the implementation of the principle

of equal pay as a rule merely reproduce the substance of the terms of Article 119 as regards the direct forms of discrimination.

26. Belgian legislation provides a particularly opposite illustration of this point, since Article 14 of Royal Decree No 40 of 24 October 1967 on the employment of women merely sets out the right of any female worker to institute proceedings before the relevant court for the application of the principle of equal pay set out in Article 119 and simply refers to that article.

27. The items of Article 119 cannot be relied on th invalidate this conclusion.

28. First of all, it is impossible to put forward an argument against its direct effect based on the use in this article of the word 'principle', since, in the language of the Treaty, this term is specifically used in order to indicate the fundamental nature of certain provisions, as is shown, for example, by the heading of the first part of the Treaty which is devoted to 'Principles' and by Article 113, according to which the commercial policy of the Community is to be based on 'uniform principles'.

29. If this concept were to be attenuated to the point of reducing it to the level of a vague declaration, the very foundations of the Community and the coherence of its external relations would be indirectly affected.

30. It is also impossible to put forward arguments based on the fact that Article 119 only refers expressly to 'Member States'.

31. Indeed, as the Court has already found in other contexts, the fact that certain provisions of the Treaty are formally addressed to the Member States does not prevent rights from being conferred at the same time on any individual who has an interest in the performance of the duties thus laid down.

32. The very wording of Article 119 shows that it imposes on States a duty to bring about a specific result to be mandatorily achieved within a fixed period.

33. The effectiveness of this provision cannot be affected by the fact that the duty imposed by the treaty has not been discharged by certain Member States and that the joint institutions have not reacted sufficiently energetically against this failure to act.

34. To accept the contrary view would be to risk raising the violation of the right to the status of a principle of interpretation, a position the adoption of which would not be consistent with the task assigned to the Court by Article 164 of the Treaty.

35. Finally, in its reference to 'Member States', Article 119 is alluding to those States in the exercise of all those of their functions which may usefully contribute to the implementation of the principle of equal pay.

36. Thus, contrary to the statements made in the course of the proceedings this provision is far from merely referring the matter to the powers of the national legislative authorities.

37. Therefore, the reference to 'Member States' in Article 119 cannot be interpreted as excluding the intervention of the courts in direct application of the Treaty.

38. Furthermore it is not possible to sustain any objection that the application by national courts of the principle of equal pay would amount to modifying independent agreements concluded privately or in the sphere of industrial relations such as individual contracts and collective labour agreements.
39. In fact, since Article 119 is mandatory in nature, the prohibition on discrimination between men and women applies not only to the action of public authorities, but also extends to all agreements which are intended to regulate paid labour collectively, as well as to contracts between individuals.
40. The reply to the first question must therefore be that the principle of equal pay contained in Article 119 may be relied upon before the national courts and that these courts have a duty to ensure the protection of the rights which this provision vests in individuals, in particular as regards those types of discrimination arising directly from legislative provisions or collective labour agreements, as well as in cases in which men and women receive unequal pay for equal work which is carried out in the same establishment or service, whether private or public.

The second question (implementation of Article 119 and powers of the Community and of the Member States)

41. The second question asks whether Article 119 has become 'applicable in the internal law of the Member States by virtue of measures adopted by the authorities of the European Economic Community', or whether the national legislature must 'be regarded as alone competent in this matter'.
42. In accordance with what has been set out above, it is appropriate to join to this question the problem of the date from which Article 119 must be regarded as having direct effect.
43. In the light of all these problems it is first necessary to establish the chronological order of the measures taken on a Community level to ensure the implementation of the provision whose interpretation is requested.
44. Article 119 itself provides that the application of the principle of equal pay was to be uniformly ensured by the end of the first stage of the transitional period at the latest.
45. The information supplied by the Commission reveals the existence of important differences and discrepancies between the various States in the implementation of this principle.
46. Although, in certain Member States, the principle had already largely been put into practice before the entry into force of the Treaty, either by means of express constitutional and legislative provisions or by social practices established by collective labour agreements, in other States its full implementation has suffered prolonged delays.
47. In the light of this situation, on 30 December 1961, the eve of the expiry of the time-limit fixed by Article 119, the Member States adopted a Resolution concerning the harmonization of rates of pay of men and women which was intended to provide further details concerning certain

aspects of the material content of the principle of equal pay, while delaying its implementation according to a plan spread over a period of time.
48. Under the terms of that Resolution all discrimination, both direct and indirect, was to have been completely eliminated by 31 December 1964.
49. The information provided by the Commission shows that several of the original Member States have failed to observe the terms of that Resolution and that, for this reason, within the context of the tasks entrusted to it by Article 155 of the Treaty, the Commission was led to bring together the representatives of the governments and the two sides of industry in order to study the situation and to agree together upon the measures necessary to ensure progress towards the full attainment of the objective laid down in Article 119.
50. This led to be drawing up of successive reports on the situation in the original Member States, the most recent of which, dated 18 July 1973, recapitulates all the facts.
51. In the conclusion to that report the Commission announced its intention to initiate proceedings under Article 169 of the Treaty, for failure to take the requisite action, against those of the Member States who had not by that date discharged the obligations imposed by Article 119, although this warning was not followed by any further action.
52. After similar exchanges with the competent authorities in the new Member States the Commission stated in its report dated 17 July 1974 that, as regards those States, Article 119 had been fully applicable since 1 January 1973 and that from that date the position of those States was the same as that of the original Member States.
53. For its part, in order to hasten the full implementation of Article 119, the Council on 10 February 1975 adopted Directive No 75/117 on the approximation of the laws of the Member States relating to the application of the principle of equal pay for men and women (OJ L 45, 19).
54. This Directive provides further details regarding certain aspects of the material scope of Article 119 and also adopts various provisions whose essential purpose is to improve the legal protection of workers who may be wronged by failure to apply the principle of equal pay laid down by Article 119.
55. Article 8 of this Directive allows the Member States a period of one year to put into force the appropriate laws, regulations and administrative provisions.
56. It follows from the express terms of Article 119 that the application of the principle that men and women should receive equal pay was to be fully secured and irreversible at the end of the first stage of the transitional period, that is, by 1 January 1962.
57. Without prejudice to its possible effects as regards encouraging and accelerating the full implementation of Article 119, the Resolution of the Member States of 30 December 1961 was ineffective to make any valid modification of the time-limit fixed by the Treaty.
58. In fact, apart from any specific provisions, the Treaty can only be modi-

fied by means of the amendment procedure carried out in accordance with Article 236.
59. Moreover, it follows from the foregoing that, in the absence of transitional provisions, the principle contained in Article 119 has been fully effective in the new Member States since the entry into force of the Accession Treaty, that is, since 1 January 1973.
60. It was not possible for this legal situation to be modified by Directive No 75/117, which was adopted on the basis of Article 100 dealing with the approximation of laws and was intended to encourage the proper implementation of Article 119 by means of measures to be taken on the national level, in order, in particular, to eliminate indirect forms of discrimination, but was unable to reduce the effectiveness of that article or modify its temporal effect.
61. Although Article 119 is expressly addressed to the Member States in that it imposes on them a duty to ensure, within a given period, and subsequently to maintain the application of the principle of equal pay, that duty assumed by the States does not exclude competence in this matter on the part of the Community.
62. On the contrary, the existence of competence on the part of the Community is shown by the fact that Article 119 sets out one of the 'social policy' objectives of the Treaty which form the subject of Title III, which itself appears in Part Three of the Treaty dealing with the 'Policy of the Community'.
63. In the absence of any express reference in Article 119 to the possible action to be taken by the Community for the purposes of implementing the social policy, it is appropriate to refer to the general scheme of the Treaty and to the courses of action for which it provided, such as those laid down in Articles 100, 155 and, where appropriate, 235.
64. As has been shown in the reply to the first question, no implementing provision, whether adopted by the insitutions of the Community or by the national authorities, could adversely affect the direct effect of Article 119.
65. The reply to the second question should therefore be that the application of Article 119 was to have been fully secured by the original Member States as from 1 January 1962, the beginning of the second stage of the transitional period, and by the new Member States as from 1 January 1973, the date of entry into force of the Accession Treaty.
66. The first of these time-limits was not modified by the Resolution of the Member States of 30 December 1961.
67. As indicated in reply to the first question, Council Directive No 75/117 does not prejudice the direct effect of Article 119 and the period fixed by that Directive for compliance therewith does not affect the time-limits laid down by Article 119 of the EEC Treaty and the Accession Treaty.
68. Even if the areas in which Article 119 has no direct effect, that provision cannot be interpreted as reserving to the national legislature exclusive power to implement the principle of equal pay since, to the extent to

which such implementation is necessary, it may be relieved by a combination of Community and national measures.

The temporal effect of this judgment

69. The Government of Ireland and the United Kingdom have drawn the Court's attention to the possible economic consequences of attributing direct effect to the provisions of Article 119, on the ground that such a decision might, in many branches of economic life, result in the introduction of claims dating back to the time at which such effect came into existence.
70. In view of the large number of people concerned with claims, which undertakings could not have foreseen might seriously affect the financial situation of such undertakings and even drive some of them to bankrupcy.
71. Although the practical consequences of any judicial decision must be carefully taken into account, it would be impossible to go so far as to diminish the objectivity of the law and compromise its future application on the ground of the possible repercussions which might result, as regards the past, from such a judicial decision.
72. However, in the light of the conduct of several of the Member States and the views adopted by the Commission and repeatedly brought to the notice of the circles concerned, it is appropriate to take exceptionally into account the fact that, over a prolonged period, the parties concerned have been led to continue with practices which were contrary to Article 119, although not yet prohibited under their national law.
73. The fact that, in spite of the warnings given, the Commission did not initiate proceedings under Article 160 against the Member States concerned on grounds of failure to fulfil an obligation was likely to consolidate the incorrect impression as to the effects of Article 119.
74. In these circumstances, it is appropriate to determine that, as the general level at which pay would have been fixed cannot be known, important considerations of legal certainty affecting all the interests involved, both public and private, make it impossible in principle to reopen the question as regards the past.
75. Therefore, the direct effect of Article 119 cannot be relied on in order to support claims concerning pay periods prior to the date of this judgment, except as regards those workers who have already brought legal proceedings or made an equivalent claim.

(2) Defrenne Case III

Defrenne v. *Sabena*; Case 149/77; Judgment of 15 June 1978; (1978) ECR 1376.

See *Defrenne Case II* at page 582.

Facts:

On 16 September 1976 Miss Defrenne lodged an appeal before the Cour de Cassation, Belgium, against the judgment of the Cour du Travail, Brussels, of 23 April 1975 in so far as that judgment upheld the judgment of the Tribunal du Travail, Brussels, of 17 December 1970 on the second and third heads of claim (which sought an order to Sabena to pay a supplementary allowance on termination of service and compensation for the damage suffered as regards her pension).

By judgment of 28 November 1977 the Cour de Cassation, Belgium, Third Chamber, decided, in pursuance of Article 177 of the EEC Treaty, to stay the proceedings until the Court of Justice had given a preliminary ruling on the following question:

'Must Article 119 of the Treaty of Rome which lays down the principle that "men and women should receive equal pay for equal work" be interpreted by reason of the dual economic and social aim of the Treaty as prescribing not only equal pay but also equal working conditions for men and women, and, in particular, does the insertion into the contract of employment of an air hostess of a clause bringing the said contract to an end when she reaches the age of 40 years, it being established that no such limit is attached to the contract of male cabin attendants who are assumed to do the same work, constitute discrimination prohibited by the said Article 119 of the Treaty of Rome or by a principle of Community law if that clause may have pecuniary consequences, in particular, as regards the allowance on termination of service and pension?'

The Court held:

. . . . .

15. The field of application of Article 119 must be determined within the context of the system of the social provisions of the Treaty, which are set out in the chapter formed by Article 117 et seq.
16. The general features of the conditions of employment and working conditions are considered in Articles 117 and 118 from the point of view of the harmonization of the social systems of the Member States and of the approximation of their laws in that field.
17. There is no doubt that the elimination of discrimination based on the sex of workers forms part of the programme for social and legislative policy which was clarified in certain respects by the Council Regulation of 21 January 1974 (Official Journal C 13, p. 1).
18. The same thought also underlies Council Directive No 76/207/EEC of 9 February 1976 on the implementation of the principle of equal treatment for men and women as regards access to employment, vocational training and promotion and working conditions (Official Journal L 39, p. 40).

19. In contrast to the provisions of Articles 117 and 118, which are essentially in the nature of a programme, Article 119, which is limited to the question of pay discrimination between men and women workers, constitutes a special rule, whose application is linked to precise factors.
20. In these circumstances it is impossible to extend the scope of that article to elements of the employment relationship other than those expressly referred to.
21. In particular, the fact that the fixing of certain conditions of employment – such as a special age-limit – may have pecuniary consequences is not sufficient to bring such conditions within the field of application of Article 119, which is based on the close connection which exists between the nature of the services provided and the amount of remuneration.
22. That is a fortiori true since the touchstone which forms the basis of Article 119 – that is, the comparable nature of the services provided by workers of either sex – is a factor as regards which all workers are ex hypothesi on an equal footing, whereas in many respects an assessment of the other conditions of employment and working conditions involves factors connected with the sex of the workers, taking into account considerations affecting the special position of women in the work process.
23. It is, therefore, impossible to widen the terms of Article 119 to the point, first, of jeopardizing the direct applicability which that provision must be acknowledged to have in its own sphere and, secondly, of intervening in an area reserved by Articles 117 and 118 to the discretion of the authorities referred to therein.
24. The reply to the first part of the question must therefore be that Article 119 of the Treaty cannot be interpreted as prescribing, in addition to equal pay, equality in respect of the other working conditions applicable to men and women.

The second part of the question – the existence of a general principle prohibiting discrimination based on sex in conditions of employment and working conditions.

25. The second part of the question asks whether, apart from the specific provisions of Article 119, Community law contains any general principle prohibiting discrimination based on sex as regards the conditions of employment and working conditions of men and women.
26. The Court has repeatedly stated that respect for fundamental personal human rights is one of the general principles of Community law, the observance of which it has a duty to ensure.
27. There can be no doubt that the elimination of discrimination based on sex forms part of those fundamental rights.
28. Moreover, the same concepts are recognized by the European Social Charter of 18 November 1961 and by Convention No 111 of the International Labour Organization of 25 June 1958 concerning discrimination in respect of employment and occupation.

29. Attention must be drawn in this regard to the fact that in its judgment of 7 June 1972 in Case 20/71 *Sabbatini (née Bertoni)* v. *European Parliament* ((1972) ECR 345) and 20 February 1975 in Case 21/74 *Airola* v. *Commission of the European Communities* ((1975) ECR 221), the Court recognized the need to ensure equality in the matter of working conditions for men and women employed by the Community itself, within the context of the Staff Regulations of Officials.
30. On the other hand, as regards the relationships of employer and employee which are subject to national law, the Community had not, at the time of the events now before the Belgian courts, assumed any responsibility for supervising and guaranteeing the observance of the principle of equality between men and women in working conditions other than remuneration.
31. As has been stated above, at the period under consideration Community law contained only the provisions in the nature of a programme laid down by Articles 117 and 118 of the Treaty, which relate to the general development of social welfare, in particular as regards conditions of employment and working conditions.
32. It follows that the situation before the Belgian courts is governed by the provisions and principles of internal and international law in force in Belgium.
33. The reply to the second part of the question must therefore be that at the time of the events which form the basis of the main action there was, as regards the relationships between employer and employee under national law, no rule of Community law prohibiting discrimination between men and women in the matter of working conditions other that the requirements as to pay referred to in Article 119 of the Treaty.

(3) Macarthys – Smith Case

Macarthys Ltd. v. *Wendy Smith*; Case 129/79; Judgment of 20 March 1980; [1980] ECR 1286; [1980]2 CMLR 205.

For facts see the judgment below

The Court held:

1. By order of 25 July 1979, received at the Court on 10 August 1979, the Court of Appeal in London referred to the Court for a preliminary ruling under Article 177 of the EEC Treaty four questions concerning the interpretation of Article 119 of the EEC Treaty and Article 1 of Council Directive No 75/117 of 10 February 1975 on the approximation of the laws of the Member States relating to the application of the principle of equal pay for men and women.

2. It appears from the file that the respondent in the main action, Mrs. Wendy Smith, was employed as from 1 March 1976 by Macarthys Limited, wholesale dealers in pharmaceutical products, as a ware-house manageress at a weekly salary of £50. She complains of discrimination in pay because her predecessor, a man, whose post she took up after an interval of four months, received a salary of £60 per week.

. . . . .

The interpretation of Article 119 of the EEC Treaty.

9. According to the first paragraph of Article 119 the Member States are obliged to ensure and maintain 'the application of the principle that men and women should receive equal pay for equal work'.
10. As the Court indicated in the Defrenne judgment of 8 April 1976, that provision applies directly, and without the need for more detailed implementing measures on the part of the Community or the Member States, to all forms of direct and overt discrimination which may be identified solely with the aid of the criteria of equal work and equal pay referred to by the article in question. Among the forms of discrimination which may be thus judicially identified, the Court mentioned in particular cases where men and women receive unequal pay for equal work carried out in the same establishment or service.
11. In such a situation the decisive test lies in establishing whether there is a difference in treatment between a man and a woman performing 'equal work' within the meaning of Article 119. The scope of that concept, which is entirely qualitative in character in that it is exclusively concerned with the nature of the services in question, may not be restricted by the introduction of a requirement of contemporaneity.
12. It must be acknowledged, however, that, as the Employment Appeal Tribunal properly recognized, it cannot be ruled out that a difference in pay between two workers occupying the same post but at different periods in time may be explained by the operation of factors which are unconnected with any discrimination on grounds of sex. That is a question of fact which it is for the court or tribunal to decide.
13. Thus the answer to the first question should be that the principle that men and women should receive equal pay for equal work, enshrined in Article 119 of the EEC Treaty, is not confined to situations in which men and women are contemporaneously doing equal work for the same employer.
14. The second question put by the Court of Appeal and expresses in terms of alternatives concernes the framework within which the existence of possible discrimination in pay may be established. This question is intended to enable the court to rule upon a submission made by the respondent in the main action and developed by her before the Court of

Justice to the effect that a woman may claim not only the salary received by a man who previously did the same work for her employer but also, more generally, the salary to which whe would be entitled were she a man, even in the absence of any man who was concurrently performing, or had previously performed, similar work. The respondent in the main action defined this term of comparison by reference to the concept of what she described as 'a hypothetical male worker'.

15. It is clear that the latter proposition, which is the subject of Question 2 (a), is to be classed as indirect and disguised discrimination, the identification of which, as the Court explained in the Defrenne judgment, cited above, implied comparative studies of entire branches of industry and therefore requires, as a prerequisite, the elaboration by the Community and national legislative bodies of criteria of assessment. From that it follows that, in case of actual discrimination falling within the scope of the direct application of Article 119, comparisons are confined to parallels which may be drawn on the basis of concrete appraisals of the work actually performed by employees of different sex within the same establishment or service.

16. The answer to the second question should therefore be that the principle of equal pay enshrined in Article 119 applies to the case where it is established that, having regard to the nature of her services, a woman has received less pay than a man who was employed prior to the woman's period of employment and who did equal work for the employer.

17. From the foregoing it appears that the dispute brought before the national court may be decided within the framework of an interpretation of Article 119 of the Treaty alone. In those circumstances it is unnecessary to answer the questions submitted in so far as they relate to the effect and to the interpretation of Directive No 75/117.

(4) Jenkins Case

Jenkins v. *Kingsgate*; Case 96/80; Preliminary ruling of 31 March 1981; [1981] ECR 922.

For facts see the judgment below.

The Court held:

. . . . .

2. The questions were raised in the course of a dispute between a female employee working part-time and her employer, a manufacturer of wom-

en's clothing, against whom she claimed that she was receiving an hourly rate of pay lower than that paid to one of her male colleagues employed full-time on the same work.

3. Mrs. Jenkins took the view that such a difference in pay contravened the equality clause incorporated into her contract of employment by virtue of the Equal Pay Act 1970, Section 1 (2) (a) of which provides for equal pay for men and women en every case where 'a woman is employed on like work with a man in the same employment'.

4. The Industrial Tribunal, hearing the case at first instance, held in its decision of 5 February 1979 that in the case of part-time work the fact that the weekly working hours amounted, as in that case, to 75% of the full working hours was sufficient to constitute a 'material difference' between part-time work and full-time work within the meaning of Section 1 (3) of the abovementioned Act, according to which:

'An equality clause shall not operate in relation to a variation between the woman's contract and the man's contract if the employer proves that the variation is genuinely due to a material difference (other than the difference of sex) between her case and his.'

5. The plaintiff in the main action appealed against that decision to the Employment Appeal Tribunal, which decided that the dispute raised problems concerning the interpretation of Community law and referred a number of questions to the Court for a preliminary ruling.

6. According to the information in the order making the reference, prior to 1975 the employer did not pay the same wages to male and female employees but the hourly rates of pay were the same whether the work was part-time or full-time. From November 1975 the pay for full-time work (that is to say, the pay for those working 40 hours per week) became the same for male and female employees but the hourly rate for part-time work was fixed at a rate which was 10% lower than the hourly rate of pay for full-time work.

9. It appears from the first three questions and the reasons stated in the order making the reference that the national court is principally concerned to know whether a difference in the level of pay for work carried out part-time and the same work carried out full-time may amount to discrimination of a kind prohibited by Article 119 of the Treaty when the category of part-time workers is exclusively or predominantly comprised of women.

10. The answer to the questions thus understood is that the purpose of Article 119 is to ensure the application of the principle of equal pay for men and women for the same work. The differences in pay prohibited by that provision are therefore exclusively those based on the difference of the sex of the workers. Consequently the fact that part-time work is paid at an hourly rate lower than pay for full-time work does not amount per se to discrimination prohibited by Article 119 provided that the hourly rates are applied to workers belonging to either category without discrimination based on sex.

11. If there is no such distinction, therefore, the fact that work paid at time rates is remunerated at an hourly rate which varies according to the number of hours worked per week does not offend against the principle of equal pay laid down in Article 119 of the Treaty in so far as the difference in pay between part-time work and full-time work as attributable to factors which are objectively justified and are in no way related to any discrimination based on sex.
12. Such may be the case, in particular, when by giving hourly rates of pay which are lower for part-time work than those for full-time work the employer is endeavouring, on economic grounds which may be objectively justified, to encourage full-time work irrespective of the sex of the worker.
13. By contrast, if it is established that a considerably smaller percentage of women than of men perform the minimum number of weekly working hours required in order to be able to claim the full-time hourly rate of pay, the inequality in pay will be contrary to Article 119 of the Treaty where, regard being had to the difficulties encountered by women in arranging to work that minimum number of hours pay week, the pay policy of the undertaking in question cannot be explained by factors other than discrimination based on sex.
14. Where the hourly rate of pay differs according to whether the work is part-time or full-time it is for the national courts to decide in each individual case whether, regard being had to the facts of the case, its history and the employer's intention, a pay policy such as that which is at issue in the main proceedings alghough represented as a difference based on weekly working hours is or is not in reality discrimination based on the sex of the worker.
15. The reply to the first questions must therefore be that a difference in pay between full-time workers and part-time workers does not amount to discrimination prohibited by Article 119 of the Treaty unless it is in reality merely an indirect way of reducing the level of pay of part-time workers on the ground that group of workers is composed exclusively or predominantly of women.

Fourth question

16. In the fourth and last question, the national court asks whether the provisions of Article 119 of the Treaty are directly applicable in the circumstances of this case.
17. As the Court has stated in previous decisions (judgment of 8 April 1976 in Case 43/75, *Defrenne* (1976) ECR 455; judgment of 27 March 1980 in Case 129/79, *Wendy Smith* (1980) ECR 1275 and judgment of 11 March 1981 in Case 69/80, *Worringham*), Article 119 of the Treaty applies directly to all forms of discrimination which may be identified solely with the aid of criteria of equal work and equal pay referred to by the article in question, without national or Community measures being required to

define them with greater precision in order to permit of their application. Among the forms of discrimination which may be thus judicially identified, the Court mentioned in particular cases where men and women receive unequal pay for equal work carried out in the same establishment or service, public or private.
18. When the national court is able, using the critieria of equal work and equal pay, without the operation of Community or national measures, to establish that the payment of lower hourly rates of remuneration for part-time work than for full-time work represents discrimination based on difference of sex the provisions of Article 119 of the Treaty apply directly to such a situation.

Article 1 of Council Directive 75/117/EEC of 10 February 1975

19. The national courts also raises with regard to Article 1 of Council Directive 75/117/EEC of 10 February 1975 the same questions of interpretation as those examined above in relation to Article 119 of the Treaty.
20. As may be seen from the first recital in the preamble the primary objective of the above-mentioned directive is to implement the principle that men and women should receive equal pay which is 'contained in Article 119 of the Treaty'. For that purpose the fourth recital states that 'it is desirable to reinforce the basic laws by standards aimed at facilitating the practical application of the principle of equality'.
21. The provisions of Article 1 of that directive are confined, in the first paragraph, to restating the principle of equal pay set out in Article 119 of the Treaty and specify in the second paragraph, the conditions for applying that principle where a job classification system is used for determining pay.
22. It follows, therefore, that Article 1 of Council Directive 75/117/EEC which is principally designed to facilitate the practical application of the principle of equal pay outlined in Article 119 of the Treaty in no way alters the content or scope of that principle as defined in the Treaty.

(5) Garland Case

Garland v. *British Rail Engineering*; Case 12/81; Preliminary ruling of 9 February 1982; [1982] ECR 359.

Facts:

The appellant in the main action, Mrs. Garland, is a married woman employed by British Rail Engineering Limited, the whole of the shareholding in which is held by the British Ralways Board, a public authority charged by statute with the duty of providing railway services in Great Britain.

During the period of their employment all employees of British Rail Engineering enjoy certain valuable travel facilities which are also extended to their spouses and dependent children.

On retirement former employees, men and women, continue to enjoy travel facilities but they are reduced in comparison with those which they enjoyed during the period of their employment. However, although male employees continue to be granted facilities for themselves and for their wives and dependent children as well, female employees no longer have such facilities granted in respect of their families.

The Court held:

. . . . .

4. To assist in answering the first question it is first of all necessary to investigate the legal nature of the special travel facilities at issue in this case which the employer grants although not contractually bound to do so.
5. It is emportant to note in this regard that in paragraph 6 of its judgment of 25 May 1971 in Case 80/70 *Defrenne* (1971) ECR 445, at p. 451, the Court stated that the concept of pay continued in the second paragraph of Article 119 comprises any other consideration, whether in cash or in kind, whether immediate or future, provided that the worker receives it, albeit indirectly, in respect of his employment from his employer.
6. According to the order making the reference for a preliminary ruling, when male employees of the respondent undertaking retire from their employment on reaching retirement age they continue to be granted special travel facilities for themselves, their wives and their dependent children.
7. A feature of those facilities is that they are granted in kind by the employer to the retired male employees or his dependents directly or indirectly in respect of his employment.
8. Moreover, it appears from a letter sent by British Rail Engineering to the trade unions on 4 December 1975 that the special travel facilities granted after retirement must be considered to be an extension of the facilities granted during the period of employment.
9. It follows from those considerations that rail travel facilities such as those referred to by the House of Lords fulfil the criteria emabling them to be trated as pay within the meaning of Article 119 of the EEC Treaty.
10. The argument that the facilities are not related to a contractual obligation is immaterial. The legal nature of the facilities is not important for the purposes of the application of Article 119 provided that they are granted in respect of the employment.

11. It follows that where an employer (although not bound to do so by contract) provides special travel facilities for former male employees to enjoy after their retirement this constitutes discrimination within the meaning of Article 119 against former female employees who do not receive the same facilities.

(6) Burton Case

Arthur Burton v. *British Railways Board*; Case 19/81; Preliminary ruling of 16 February 1982; [1982] ECR 555.

For facts see the judgment below.

The Court held:

1. By an order of 16 January 1981, which was received at the Court on 4 February 1981 the Employment Appeal Tribunal referred to the Court for a preliminary ruling under Article 177 of the EEC Treaty three questions concerning the interpretation, with regard to payment of voluntary redundancy benefit, of Article 119 of the Treaty, Article 1 of Council Directive No 75/117/EEC of 10 February 1975 on the approximation of the laws of the Member States relating to the application of the principle of equal pay for men and women (Official Journal No L 45, p. 19) and Articles 1 (1), 2 (1) of Council Directive No 76/207/EEC of 9 February 1976 on the implementation of the principle of equal treatment for men and women as regards access to employment, vocational training and promotion, and working conditions (Official Journal No L 39, P. 40).
2. According to the case-file Mr. Burton, the plaintiff in the main action, is an employee of the British Railway Board (hereinafter referred to as 'The Board'), a body established by the Transport Act 1962 and responsible for operating the railway system in Great Britain.
3. As a result of an internal re-organization the Board made an offer of voluntary redundancy to some of its employees. A memorandum was drawn up embodying the terms of a collective agreement between management and the recognized trade unions on the terms on which certain aspects of the re-organization were to be carried out. Paragraph 6 of the memorandum provides as follows:
'Staff aged 60/55 (Male/Female) may leave the service under the Redundancy and Resettlement arrangements when the Function in which (they are) employed has been dealt with under Organization Planning'.
4. In August 1979 Mr. Burton applied for voluntary redundancy but his application was rejected on the ground that he was under the minimum age of 60 specified for male employees by the above-mentioned memo-

randum. Mr. Burton therefore claimed that he was treated less favourable than female employees inasmuch as the benefit would have been granted to a woman of his age (58).
5. After the rejection of his application Mr. Burton complained to an Industrial Tribunal under the provisions of the Equal Pay Act 1970, as last amended by the Sex Discrimination Act 1975. The Industrial Tribunal rejected Mr. Burton's claim and he appealed to the Employment Appeal Tribunal. In the course of the appeal it was conceded on his behalf that by virtue of section 6 (4) of the Sex Discrimination Act 1975 it is not contrary to the Act for an employer to treat a male employee less favourable than he treats famale employees as regards access to voluntary redundancy benefit. However, Mr. Burton contended that section 6 (4) must be construed as subject to the enforceable Community rights conferred by Article 119 of the Treaty, Article 1 of Directive No 85/117 on equal pay and Articles 1, 2 and 5 of Directive No 76/207 on equal treatment.
7. The principal issue raised by those questions is whether the requirement that a male worker should have reached the age of 60 in order to be eligible for payment of a voluntary redundancy benefit whereas women workers become eligible at the age of 55 amounts to discrimination prohibited by Article 119 of the Treaty or by Article 1 of Directive No 75/117 or, at least, by Directive No 76/207 and, if so, whether the relevant provision of Community law may be relied upon in the national courts.
8. Consequently the question of interpretation which has been referred to the Court concerns not the benefit itself, but whether the conditions of access to the voluntary redundancy scheme are discriminatory. That is a matter covered by the provision of Directive No 76/207 to which reference was made by the national court, and not by those of Article 119 of the Treaty or Directive No 75/117.
9. According to Article 5 (1) of Directive No 76/207 application of the principle of equal treatment with regard to working conditions, including the conditions governing dismissal, means that men and women are to be guaranteed the same conditions without discrimination on grounds of sex. In the context of the directive the word 'dismissal' must be widely construed so as to include termination of the employment relationship between a worker and his employer, even as part of a voluntary redundancy scheme.
10. In deciding whether the difference in treatment of which the plaintiff in the main action complains is discriminatory within the meaning of that directive account must be taken of the relationship between measures such as that at issue and national provisions on normal retirement age.
11. Under United Kingdom legislation the minimum qualifying age for a State retirement pension is 60 for women and 65 for men.
12. From the information supplied by the United Kingdom Government in the course of the proceedings it appears that a worker who is permitted by the Board to take voluntary early retirement must do so within the

five years preceding the normal minimum age of retirement, and that he may receive the following benefits: (1) the lump sum calculated in accordance with the provisions of the Redundancy Payments Act 1965, (2) a lump sum calculated on the basis of the total length of his employment with the Board, and (3) 25% of the sum of the first two amounts. In addition he is entitled up to the minimum retiring age to an early retirement pension equal to the pension to which he would have been entitled had he attained the minimum statutory retirement age and to an advance, repayable at the minimum retiring age, equal to the sum to which he becomes entitled at that age.
13. Council Directive No 79/7/EEC of 19 December 1978 on the progressive implementation of the principle of equal treatment for men and women in matters of social security (Official Journal 1979 No L 6, p. 24), which was adopted with particular reference to Article 235 of the Treaty, provides in Article 7 that the directive shall be without prejudice to the right of Member States to exclude from its scope the determination of pensionable age for the purpose of granting old-age and retirement pensions and the possible consequences thereof for other benefits.
14. It follows that the determination of a minimum pensionable age for social security purposes which is not the same for men as for women does not amount to discrimination prohibited by Community law.
15. The option given to workers by the provisions at issue in the present instance is tied to the retirement scheme governed by United Kingdom social security provisions. It enables a worker who leaves his employment at any time during the five years before he reaches normal pensionable age to receive certain allowances for a limited period. The allowances are calculated in the same manner regardless of the sex of the worker. The only difference between the benefits for men and those for women stems from the fact that the minimum pensionable age under the national legislation is not the same for men as for women.
16. In the circumstances the different age conditions for men and women with regard to access to voluntary redundancy cannot be regarded as discrimination within the meaning of Directive No 76/207.

(7) Marshall Case

See at page 189.

(8) Gravier Case

Françoise Gravier v. *City of Liège*; Case 293/83; Preliminary ruling of 13 February 1985, [1985] ECR 593.

Facts:

See the judgment below.

The Court held:

3. It appears from the documents in the proceedings that in Belgium, pursuant to Article 12 of the Law of 29 May 1959 amending certain provisions of the laws on education (Moniteur Belge of 19 June 1959), primary and secondary education is free of charge in the State system and in subsidized establishments, and institutions of post secondary or higher education may charge only low registration fees intended to finance their social services. Each year since the academic year 1976–77, however, the laws setting out the national education budget have, in derogation from Article 12, authorized the Minister to establish 'an enrolment fee for foreign pupils and students whose parents are not resident in Belgium and who attend a State educational institution or an institution supported by the State at pre-school, primary, special, secondary, higher (short or long type) and technical (second and third degree) level'.
4. On the basis of such a provision – in this case Article 15 of the 1983 budget law – the Minister for Education issued circular No 83.24 G of 30 June 1983 (Moniteur Belge of 3 February 1984), which laid down 'for the year 1983–84, as for previous years, an enrolment fee ... or pupils and students who are not of Belgian nationality and who attend an institution of full-time artistic education organized or subsidized by the State'. The circular exempts from the obligation to pay the fee *inter alia* students having one parent to Belgian nationality, students of Luxembourg nationality, and students whose father or mother resides in Belgium and carries on a principal occupation or receives social security income or a pension and pays income tax there.
5. The plaintiff in the main proceedings, Françoise Gravier, who is of French nationality and whose parents reside in France, went to Belgium in 1982 in order to study strip cartoon art at the Académie Royale des Beaux-Arts in Liège, in a four-year course of higher art education. For the 1982–83 academic year she sought exemption from payment of the enrolment fee of BFR 24 622 demanded of foreign students in higher art education. By a letter of 7 October 1983 the Académie Royale informed her that her request had been rejected on the ground that 'all foreign students must be aware that such education is not free of charge and must anticipate payment of an enrolment fee'.
6. After her request was rejected, Miss Gravier was asked to pay the fee for the academic years 1982–83 and 1983–84. Since the sums demanded were not paid in time, her enrolment for the 1983–84 year was refused. As a result her Belgian residence permit was not extended. It was in

those circumstances that she brought proceedings before the President of the Tribunal de Première Instance, Liège, claiming exemption from payment of the fee and the issuance of all certificates necessary for the extension of her stay in Belgium.
7. During the proceedings before the President of the Tribunal, the plaintiff challenged the validity of the circulars which imposed the enrolment fee in question. She argued that she could not be obliged to pay a fee which was not required of Belgian nationals since on the one hand such an obligation constituted discrimination on grounds of nationality prohibited by Article 7 of the Treaty and on the other hand a national of another Member State going to Belgium to study must be free to do so as a person to whom services are provided according to Article 59 of the Treaty.
8. The defendant in the main proceedings, the City of Liège, ensured that a provisional registration certificate was issued to the plaintiff, who was thus able to comply with Belgian residence formalities. It took the view, however, that it was for the Belgian State and the Communauté Française, third parties, to reply to the claim made with regard to the circulars concerning payment of the fee.

. . . . .

(The national court submitted *i.a.* the following question:

Is it in accordance with Community law to consider that nationals of Member States of the European Community who enter the territory of another Member State for the sole purpose of duly following courses there in an institution offering instruction relating in particular to vocational training fall, with regard to that institution, within the scope of Article 7 of the Treaty of Rome of 25 March 1957?)

. . . . .

19. The first remark which must be made in that regard is that although educational organization and policy are not as such included in the spheres which the Treaty has entrusted to the Community institutions, access to and participation in courses of instruction and apprenticeship, in particular vocational training, are not unconnected with Community law.
20. Article 7 of Regulation no 1612/68 of the Council of 15 October 1968 on freedom of movement for workers within the Community (Official Journal, English Special Edition 1968 (II), p. 475) provides that a worker

who is a national of a Member State and who is employed in another Member State is to have access to training in vocational schools and retraining centres in that country by virtue of the same right and under the same conditions as national workers. Article 12 of the regulation provides that the children of such workers are to be admitted to that State's general educational apprenticeship and vocational training course under the same conditions as the nationals of that State.

21. With regard more particularly to vocational training, Article 128 of the Treaty provides that the Council is to lay down general principles for implementing a common vocational training policy capable of contributing to the harmonious development both of the national economies and of the common market. The first principle established in Council Decision No 63/266/EEC of 2 April 1963 laying down those general principles (Official Journal, English Special Edition 1963–1964, p. 25) states that 'the general principles must enable every person to receive adequate training, with due regard for freedom of choice of occupation, place of training and place of work'.

22. The particular attention which the Community institutions have given to problems of access to vocational training and its improvement throughout the Community may be seen, moreover, in the 'general guidelines' which the Council laid down in 1971 for drawing up a Community programme on vocational training (Official Journal, English Special Edition, Second Series IX, p. 50), in the resolution of the Council and of the Ministers for Education meeting within the Council of 13 December 1976 concerning measures to be taken to improve the preparation of young people for work and to facilitate their transition from education to working life (Official Journal C 308, p. 1) and the Council resolution of 11 July 1983 concerning vocational training policies in the European Community in the 1980s (Official Journal C 193, p. 2).

23. The common vocational training policy referred to in Article 128 of the Treaty is thus gradually being established. It constitutes, moreover, an indispensible element of the activities of the Community, whose objectives include *inter alia* the free movement of persons, the mobility of labour and the improvement of the living standards of workers.

24. Access to vocational training is in particular likely to promote free movement of persons throughout the Community, by enabling them to obtain a qualification in the Member State where they intend to work and by enabling them to complete their training and develop their particular talents in the Member State whose vocational training programmes include the special subject desired.

25. It follows from all the foregoing that the conditions of access to vocational training fall within the scope of the Treaty.

26. The answer to the first question must therefore be that the imposition on students who are nationals of other Member States, of a charge, a registration fee or the so-called 'minerval' as a condition of access to vocational training, where the same fee is not imposed on students who

are nationals of the host Member State, constitutes discrimination on grounds of nationality contrary to Article 7 of the Treaty.

C. ENVIRONMENT

1. Cases

(1) Italian sulphur Case

Commission v. *Italian Republic*; Case 92/79, Judgment of 18 March 1980 [1980] ECR 1115; SEW (1980) 461.

Facts:

In this case the Court recognised that there is a legal basis for environmental policy of the Community. At that time the Articles 130 R-130T had not yet been introduced by the Single European Act in the EEC Treaty.

The Court held:

8. As regards the observations of the Italian Government concerning the powers of the Community in the matter, it should be observed that the directive has been adopted not only within the Programme of Action of the Communities on the Environment; it also comes under the General Programme for the elimination of technical barriers to trade which result from disparities between the provisions laid down by law, regulation or administrative action in Member States, adopted by the Council on 28 May 1969. In this sense it is validly founded upon Article 100. Furthermore it is by no means ruled out that provisions on the environment may be based upon Article 100 of the Treaty. Provisions which are made necessary by considerations relating to the environment and health may be a burden upon the undertakings to which they apply and if there is no harmonization of national provisions on the matter, competition may be appreciably distorted.

Sequel:

Subsequently environmental policy has been considered as an essential objective of the Community. The Court argues that there are imperative reasons relating to environmental protection which justify restrictions on the free movement of goods, if the conditions of proportionality and non-discrimination are fulfilled.

(2) Waste oil Case

Procureur de La République and Association de défense des brûleurs d'huiles usagées; Case 240/83; Preliminary ruling of 7 February 1985; [1985] ECR 531.

Facts:

See the judgment below.

The Court held:

1. By judgment of 23 March 1983, which was received at the Court on 24 October 1983, the Tribunal de Grande Instance [Regional Court], Créteil, referred to the Court for a preliminary ruling under Article 177 of the EEC Treaty two questions on the interpretation and validity of Council Directive No 75/439/EEC of 16 June 1975 on the disposal of waste oils (Official Journal 1975 L 194, p. 23), in order to ascertain whether French Decree No 79-981 of 21 November 1979 laying down rules for the recovery of waste oil (Journal Officiel de la République Francaise of 23 November 1979, p. 2900) and its implementing orders were compatible with Community legislation inasmuch as they contained provisions prohibiting the use of such oils as fuel.
2. On the basis of those French provisions the Procureur de la République [Public Prosecutor] applied to the Tribunal de grande instance, Créteil, for the dissolution of the Association de défense des brûleurs d'huiles usagées [Association for the defence of the interests of burners of waste oils, hereinafter referred to as 'the Association'], on the ground that its aim and objects were unlawful. The Association's object is to defend the interests of manufacturers, dealers and users of stoves and heating appliances which burn both fuel oil and waste oil, such burning being prohibited by the French legislation.
3. Articles 2 to 4 of Directive No 75/439/EEC require Member States to take the necessary measures to ensure the safe collection and disposal of waste oils, preferably by recycling. Article 5 of the Directive provides as follows: 'Where the aims defined in Articles 2, 3 and 4 cannot otherwise be achieved, Member States shall take the necessary measures to ensure that one or more undertakings carry out the collection and/or disposal of the products offered to them by the holders, where appropriate in the zone assigned to them by the competent authorities.' Article 6 (1) thereof further provides that 'any undertaking which disposes of waste oils must obtain a permit'. In addition, Articles 13 and 14 provide that an indemnity, financed in accordance with the 'polluter pays' principle and not exceeding the actual yearly costs, may be granted to under-

takings collecting and/or disposing of waste oils, as compensation for the obligations imposed on them under Article 5.
4. In pursuance of the directive, on 21 November 1979 the French Government adopted Decree No 79-981 laying down rules for the recovery of waste oils, together with the two above-mentioned implementing orders of the same date. Under those provisions French territory was divided into zones and a system was established for the approval both of waste-oil collectors and of the undertakings responsible for disposing of waste oils. Under Article 3 of Decree No 79-981, holders of waste oils must either deliver them to collectors approved pursuant to Article 4 thereof, or make them directly available to a disposal undertaking which has obtained the approval required by Article 8, or else perform the disposal themselves if they have been granted such an approval. Article 6 of the decree requires collectors to surrender the oils collected to approved disposal undertakings. Article 7 lays down that 'the only permitted methods for disposing of waste oils ... are recycling or regeneration under economically acceptable conditions, or else industrial use as fuel'. With respect to such industrial use, the second paragraph of Article 2 of the implementing order on the conditions for the disposal of waste oils provides that disposal by burning must take place 'in a plant which has been approved for the purposes of environmental protection'.
5. Since the legislation in question was adopted pursuant to Directive No 75/439, the Association raised before the national court the question whether that directive could constitute a legal basis for the prohibition of the burning of waste oils. Furthermore, doubts were expressed as to the validity of the directive in the light of certain fundamental principles of Community law.
6. In those circumstances, the Tribunal de Grande Instance, Créteil, stayed the proceedings and submitted to the Court a request for a preliminary ruling on the interpretation and validity of Directive No 75/439/EEC, in the following terms: 'Is the directive in conformity with the principles of freedom of trade, free movement of goods and freedom of competition, established by the Treaty of Rome, in view of the fact that Articles 5 and 6 of the directive empower the administrative authorities of the States to draw up zones which are assigned to one or more undertakings approved by those authorities and charged by them with the collection and the disposal of waste, and the fact that Articles 13 and 14 authorize the granting of subsidies?

In addition, does the directive provide legal grounds justifying the prohibition of the burning of waste oils?

. . . . .

12. In the first place it should be observed that the principle of freedom of

trade is not to be viewed in absolute terms but is subject to certain limits justified by the objectives of general interest pursued by the Community provided that the rights in question are not substantively impaired.

13. There is no reason to conclude that the directive has exceeded those limits. The directive must be seen in the perspective of environmental protection, which is one of the Community's essential objectives. It is evident, particularly from the third and seventh recitals in the preamble to the directive, that any legislation dealing with the disposal of waste oils must be designed to protect the environment from the harmful effects caused by the discharge, deposit or treatment of such products. It is also evident from the provisions of the directive as a whole that care has been taken to ensure that the principles of proportionality and non-discrimination will be observed if certain restrictions should prove necessary. In particular, Article 5 of the directive permits the creation of a system of zoning 'where the aims defined in Articles 2, 3 and 4 cannot otherwise be achieved'.

14. In the second place, as far as the free movement of goods is concerned, it should be stressed that the directive must be construed in the light of the seventh recital in the preamble thereto, which states that the treatment of waste oils must not create barriers to intra-Community trade. As the Court has already ruled in its judgment of 10 March 1983 (Case 172/82, *Fabricants Raffineurs d'Huile de Graissage* v. *Inter-Huiles*, [1983] ECR 555) dealing with the same zoning scheme, an exclusive right of that kind does not automatically authorize the Governments of the Member States to establish barriers to exports. Indeed, such a partitioning of the markets is not provided for in the Council Directive and would be contrary to the objectives laid down therein.

15. It follows from the foregoing that the measures prescribed by the directive do not create barriers to intra-Community trade, and that in so far as such measures, in particular the requirement that permits must be obtained in advance, have a restrictive effect on the freedom of trade and of competition, they must nevertheless neither be discriminatory nor go beyond the inevitable restrictions which are justified by the pursuit of the objective of environmental protection, which is in the general interest. That being so, Articles 5 and 6 cannot be regarded as incompatible with the fundamental principles of Community law mentioned above.

(3) Danish bottle Case

Commission v. *Denmark*; Case 302/86; judgment of 20 September 1988 (not yet published).

*Facts and judgment:**

* Unofficial text: English translation not yet available.

The Commission of the European Communities brought an action for a declaration that by introducing and applying a system under which all containers of beer and soft drinks must be returnable the Kingdom of Denmark had failed to fulfil its obligations under Article 30 of the EEC Treaty.

An essential feature of the system is that manufacturers must market beer and soft drinks only in containers which are returnable. The container must be approved by the National Agency for the Protection of the Environment.

The system was subsequently amended to allow, providing a deposit and collection system was established, the use of non-approved containers to a limit of 3 000 hectolitres per producer per annum and as part of transactions carried out by foreign producers to test the market.

In the present case the Danish Government submitted that the said system is justified by the imperative need to protect the environment.

In that respect the Court observed that it had already held that environmental protection is 'one of the Community's essential objectives' which as such may justify certain limitations to the principle of free movement of goods. That view had moreover been confirmed by the Single European Act.

However it had also to be remembered that if a Member State had a choice between various measures suitable to achieve the same aim it must choose the means which involved the least obstacles to free trade.

In that respect it was to be observed that although the returnable system for approved containers guarantees a maximum rate of re-use and thus a very appreciable environmental protection since empty containers may be returned to any retailer of beverages, while non-approved containers may be returned only to the retailer who had sold the drinks in view of the impossibility of setting up such a complete organization for them too.

Nevertheless the system of returnable non-approved containers was calculated to protect the environment and as far as imports were concerned concerns only limited quantities of beverages in relation to the quantity of beverages consumed in the country because of the restrictive effect on imports of the requirement that containers should be returnable.

In those circumstances a limitation of the quantity of products which may be marketed by importers was disproportionate to the objective pursued.

The Court held:
'1. By restricting, by Order No. 95 of 16 March 1984, to 3 000 hl per producer per annum the quantity of beer and soft drinks which may be marketed in non-approved containers, the Kingdom of Denmark has failed, in relation to imports of those products from other Member States, to fulfil its obligations under Article 30 of the EEC Treaty;
2. The remainder of the application is dismissed;
3. The parties and the intervener are ordered to pay their own costs.'

D. LITERATURE

D. Van der Meersch, 'The Single European Act and the Environmental

Policy of the European Economic Community', (1987) *European Law Review* 407.
A. Nollkaemper, 'The European Community and International Environmental co-operation', (1987/2) L.I.E.I. 55.
R.J.H. Smits, 'Some aspects of the monetary law of the European Community', (1982/2) L.I.E.I. 39.

V. Sectorial policy

A. AGRICULTURE

(EEC Treaty Articles 38–47)

1. Objectives

a. Cases

(1) Balkan Import-Export Case

Balkan Import-Export GmbH v. Hauptzollamt Berlin-Packhof; Case 5/73.

For references and facts see pages 578, 659.

The Court held:

. . . . .

(d) Contravention of Articles 39 (1) (c), 40 (3) (second paragraph) of the Treaty

. . . . .

24. Article 39 of the Treaty sets out various objectives of the common agricultural policy.
    In pursuing these objectives, the Community Institutions must secure the permanent harmonization made necessary by any conflicts between these

aims taken individually and, where necessary, allow any one of them temporary priority in order to satisfy the demands of the economic factors or conditions in view of which their decisions are made.

If, owing to developments in the monetary situation, preference happens to be given to the interests of the agricultural community, the Council does not in so doing contravene Article 39.

Moreover, it has not been established that the measures questioned gave rise to prices which would appear obviously unreasonable on selling to consumers.

25. According to the second paragraph of Article 40 (3) of the Treaty, the common organization of the market shall be limited to pursuit of the objectives set out in Article 39 and shall exclude any discrimination between producers or consumers within the Community.

It appears from the reference to this provision made by the national court that the latter contemplated the possibility that discrimination had occurred between producers and consumers to the detriment of the consumers.

Article 40 refers only to discrimination between producers or between consumers, while the balance to be held between the conflicting interests of these two groups is dealt with in Article 39.

The Council did not, therefore, contravene Article 40 by adopting the measures in dispute.

(2) Eridania Case II

Eridania zuccherifici nazionali SpA and Others v. *Cassa conguaglio zucchero and the Italian Ministry of Finance and Treasury*; Case 250/84; Preliminary ruling of 22 January 1986; [1986] ECR 134.

For the facts see the judgment below.

The Court held:

2. ... In 1982 the plaintiffs in the main proceedings received demand for the payment of sugar production levies pursuant to Articles 24 and 28 of Regulation No 1785/81. In their action they request the tribunale di Roma to declare that those levies are not payable owing to the unlawfulness of those two article and to order the defendants to repay with interest the levies already paid.
3. Considering that its decision depended on the answer to the question whether or not Articles 24 and 28 of Regulation No 1785/81 are valid, the tribunale di Roma stayed the proceedings and referred the following questions to the Court:
    (a) Inasmuch as it requires Italian producers to pay a levy for the sale of

sugar at a guaranteed price calculated on the basis of the production quotas fixed in Article 24, is Article 28 of Council Regulation (EEC) No 1785/81 unlawful as being contrary to the prohibition of discrimination laid down in Articles 7 and 40 (3) of the EEC Treaty and contrary to the principle of proportionality having regard to the aim laid down in Article 39 (1) (b) of that Treaty?

. . . . .

8. As from 1 July 1981 the aforesaid regulations were replaced by Council Regulation No 1785/81 of 30 June 1981. That regulation, at issue in the present case distinguishes between three types of quota: the A quota, which represent consumption within the Community, may be freely marketed on the common market and the disposal of A quota sugar is guaranteed by the intervention price, the B quota is the quantity of sugar produced in excess of the basic quota ('A quota') without exceeding the 'maximum quota', which is equal to the A quota multiplied by a coefficient; it may also be freely marketed on the common market but without an intervention price guarantee, or exported to non-member countries with export aid; that aid, equal to the difference between the intervention price and the price of sugar on the world market, is paid in the form of export refunds, finally, the C quota, which is the quantity produced in excess of the 'maximum quota' (A and B quotas), may be marketed only in non-member countries and no export aid may be granted.

Regulation No 1785/81 also reformed the system for financing the costs of exporting sugar. First, it introduced the principle of 100% producer responsibility – they must bear all of the costs of disposing on export markets of sugar on which refunds have been granted. Secondly, not only sugar produced under the B quota but also sugar produced under the A quota was made subject to the production levy.

The first question

The alleged discrimination

11. In its first question the national court is in effect asking whether the levy imposed on Italian producers under Articles 14 and 28 of Regulation No 1785/81 is contrary to the prohibition of discrimination laid down in Articles 7 and 40 (3) of the EEC Treaty.
12. The plaintiffs in the main proceedings and the Italian Government suggest that this question should be answered in the affirmative. They contend that the discrimination arises from the fact that the total of the charges connected with the financing of the quota system is calculated on

the basis of consumption within the Community, whereas the charges to be borne by the individual undertakings are calculated on the basis of their actual production during the reference period. The application of different criteria as regards the total of the charges and their division between individual undertakings means that the A quota allocated to Italy, which is subject to a levy of only 2%, is fixed at a level which is much lower than internal consumption in Italy.

. . . . .

19. The Court would first observe that, as the Council and Commission has explained, the quota system for the production of sugar is an essential part of the common organization of the markets in that commodity. At a time when surpluses exist on both the common market and the world market, the quota system curbs production and aligns it as closely as possible with internal consumption while promoting regional specialization. To that end, it provides for the disposal at guaranteed prices of qualifying quantities by means of a system for financing the costs of disposal, which are borne jointly by all the producers. That financial system is designed in such a way that the A quota, which represents internal consumption, attracts only a minimal levy whereas the B quota, which is mainly for export, is subject to a much higher levy in order to finance the necessary refunds whilst discouraging production.
20. In those circumstances, the Council was justified in dividing the quotas between the individual undertakings on the basis of their actual production. Indeed, such a distribution of the burden is consistent with the principle of regional specialization, which is one of the foundations of the common market and which requires production to occur at the place that is economically the most suitable. It is also consistent with the principle of solidarity between producers, since production is a legitimate criterion for assessing the economic strength of producers and the benefits which they derive from the system.
21. The fact that the distribution of the burden between undertakings on the basis of their production gives rise to an A quota for Italy which is lower than its internal consumption and also a particularly high ratio between the levies paid and its B quota cannot lead to a different assessment. On the contrary, those consequences are due to the requirement that, in a common market characterized by regional specialization, production in the individual Member States must be able to develop independently of the level of consumption in those States. Those consequences cannot therefore constitute discrimination.
22. The complaint of discrimination is even more unsustainable if the provisions at issue are considered in their legislative context. It was precisely in order to lessen the disparities arising from Italy's specific structural

difficulties that the Council linked the quota system to various specific measures taking the form of aid to Italian producers, such as a higher basic quantity at the outset, a higher intervention price and allowing national aid to be granted to them.

23. The plaintiffs in the main proceedings and the Italian Government also claim that the rules in question are discriminatory inasmuch as the average quota allocated to Italian establishments is lower than the average quota allocated to the establishments in the Community (29 233 tonnes as against 51 873 tonnes). Consequently, the fixed costs to be borne by Italian producers are higher than those borne by producers in other Member States and this situation has led to the insolvency of a number of Italian undertakings.

24. In reply the Council and the Commission point out that the production quotas are not allocated to establishments but to undertakings and that on average Italian undertakings have the highest A quotas in the Community. However, they do not dispute that the costs of sugar production in Italy are higher than the Community average.

25. It must be borne in mind in this regard that the aim of the quota system is not to support the least profitable undertakings but to provide a degree of control over production whilst re-orientating it towards the needs of the market. There is therefore justification for not taking account of differences in production costs when quotas are allocated between the individuals producers; that is particularly true when, as in the present case, the quota system is linked to a set of measures designed to offset at least some of the structural difficulties of the poorer regions.

2. Field of application

a. Cases

(1) König Case

Hauptzollamt Bielefeld v. *König*; Case 185/73; Preliminary ruling of 29 May 1974; [1974] ECR 616.

Facts:

Article 38 (3) of the Treaty provides:

The product subject to the provisions of Articles 39 to 46 are listed in Annex II to this Treaty. Within two years of the entry into force of this Treaty, however, the Council shall, acting by a qualified majority on a proposal from the Commission, decide what products are to be added to this list.

EEC Regulation No 7a/59 adding certain products to the list in Annex II, adopted pursuant to Article 38 (3), was published in the Official Journal on 30 January 1961 (OJ 1961, p. 71).

Article 1 of the Regulation purports to 'add to the list in Annex II to the Treaty' the following products, under Nos. 22.08 and 22.09 in the Brussels Nomenclature:

Ethyl alcohol or neutral spirits, whether or not denatured, of any strength, obtained from agricultural products listed in Annex II to the Treaty, excluding liqueurs and other spirituous beverages and compound alcoholic preparations (known as 'concentrated extracts') for the manufacture of beverages.

The Court held:

As to the second question

9. The second question asks whether the Council was permitted to add ethyl alcohol to the said list without regard to its alcoholic strength.
10. The national court, forming the view that only those products could be added to the list which complied with the definition of agricultural products given in the first paragraph of Article 38, expresses doubt as to whether ethyl alcohol can come within this definition, by reason of the fact that alcohols of a strength of less than 80° would, in practice, be subjected after their distillation to an additional process, that is, dilution with water.
11. The intervening governments deny that the Council had, in any circumstances, acting within the scope of Article 38 (3), the option of adding alcohol to the list in question . . .

    They suggest that the concept of first-stage processing should be interpreted as being restricted to a single operation on the raw material.
12. According to the definition in Article 38 (1), agricultural products are 'the products of the soil, of stockfarming and of fisheries and products of first-stage processing directly related to these products'.

    Paragraph (3) of that Article provides that the products subject to the provisions of Article 39 to 46 are listed in Annex II to the Treaty.

    In this list appear, not only the principal agricultural products, but also a certain number of foodstuffs, the remoteness of which in industrial terms from the basic agricultural products goes beyond the point of first-stage processing as understood in a restricted sense.

    The element common to these products resides in the close economic interdependence between them and the basic products, so that it would not be justifiable to apply the agricultural system to the basic products, while applying to the processed products the general rules of the Treaty.
13. The definition of agricultural products, placed at the head of the Title devoted to agriculture, would be devoid of practical meaning if it were not to be interpreted, as regards the power of the Council to fill the gaps

with which Article 38 (3) is concerned, in the light of the aims of the common agricultural policy and with reference to the products with which the authors of the Treaty considered that policy to be concerned.

The concept of 'products of first-stage processing directly related' to basic products must, accordingly, be interpreted as implying a clear economic interdependence between basic products and products resulting from a productive process, irrespective of the number of operations involved therein.

Processed products which have undergone a productive process, the cost of which is such that the price of the basic agricultural raw materials becomes a completely marginal cost, are therefore excluded.

14. There is no reason to consider that ethyl alcohol falls within this category
 . . .

(2) Santa Anna Case

Société Santa Anna Azienda Agricole v. *INPS and SCAU*; Case 85/77; Preliminary ruling of 28 February 1978; [1978] ECR 538; [1978] 3 CMLR 67.

For the facts see the judgment below.

The Court held:

. . . . .

2. It appears from the order for reference that the plaintiff company in the main action which carries on in Italy the business of raising poultry and laying hens brought an action in the national court against the Instituto della Previdenza Sociale (hereinafter referred to as 'the Instituto') for a declaration of its right to be classified for the purpose of social security contributions in respect of the labour it employs as an agricultural and not industrial undertaking and therefore to make payment only to the Servizio dei Contributi Agricoli Unificati of the above-mentioned contributions at the rates applicable to agricultural undertakings which it seems are less than those applicable to industrial undertakings and demanded of the plaintiff company by the Instituto.

3. First it is necessary to consider Question 1 (b) put by the national court which asks whether the Community has adopted a Community concept of an agricultural holding for the purpose of identifying holdings of this nature and whether the Member States are accordingly obliged to employ the concepts provided in the Treaty and the said regulations in order to identify the agricultural holdings to which the principles laid

down at Community level and those evolued by the various national legal systems with regard to social security.
4. An answer in the negative to the first part of this question would render the other questions superfluous.

. . . . .

8. ... since the Treaty contains no precise definition of agriculture and still less of agricultural holding, it is for the Community institutions to work out, where appropriate, for the purposes of the rules deriving from the Treaty such a definition of agricultural holding.
9. Although the words 'agricultural holding' are used in various places in the Community rules, including the regulations referred to in the order for reference, adopted by the Council or in certain cases by the Commission, in the sphere of agriculture, the definition of these words, is far from being uniform throughout these rules, which are in any case heterogenous, but on the contrary varies according to the specific pursued by the Community rules in question.

. . . . .

14. It follows from the above that it is impossible to find in the provisions of the Treaty or in the rules of secondary Community law any general uniform Community definition of 'agricultural holding' universally applicable in all the provisions laid down by law and regulation relating to agricultural production.
15. Since in the absence of such a definition the above-mentioned question must be answered in the negative, it becomes unnecessary to answer the other questions put by the national court.

(3) CILFIT Case II

CILFIT v. *Ministerio della Sanita*; Case 77/83; Preliminary ruling of 29 February 1984; [1984] ECR 1257.

For the facts see the judgment below.

The Court held:

2. That question was raised in an action brought by the company CILFIT and 54 other companies, importers of wool, established in Italy, for the recovery of sums which they had paid in respect of health-inspection levies. The plaintiffs in the main action maintain that the Italian legislation on health-inspection levies could not apply to imports of wool from non-member countries since such goods were made subject to a common organization of the market by Regulation No 827/68, Article 2 of which provides that in trade with non-member countries the levying of any charge having effect equivalent to a customs duty is prohibited.
3. Regulation No 827/68 applies, according to Article 1 thereof, to the products listed in the annex thereto. They include 'ex 05.15 B animal products not elsewhere specified or included'. The national court wishes to know whether wool comes under that category of product.
4. The recitals in the preamble to Regulation No 827/68 state that a common organization of the market, involving an special system of rules, has been established for many of the products listed in Annex II to the Treaty and that appropriate provisions must also be adopted, within the framework of the common organization of the markets, so as to permit the establishment of a single market for all the other products listed in that annex.
5. If follows that the object of the regulation is to establish a common organization of the markets for products in Annex II to the Treaty not yet governed by other common organizations. Annex II contains, according to Article 38 (3) of the Treaty, the list of products subject to the provisions of Articles 39 and 46 of the Treaty relating to the Common Agricultural Policy.
6. Although therefore Article 1 of the regulation provides that the common organization established by the regulation is to cover the products listed in the annex thereto and although that annex contains, *inter alia*, the following description: 'ex 05.15 B animal products not elsewhere specified or included; deal animals of Chapter I, unfit for human consumption', those words cannot have a meaning different from that which they have in Annex II to the Treaty which also contains them.
7. Since there are no Community provisions explaining the concepts contained in Annex II to the Treaty and that annex adopts word for word certain headings of the Common Customs Traiff, it is appropriate to refer to the established interpretations and methods of interpretation relating to the Common Customs Tariff in order to interpret the annex. Annex II itself refers moreover to the headings and subheadings of the tariff to identify the products listed.

. . . . .

3. The Common Agricultural Policy and the general rules on the free movement of goods

a. Cases

(1) Charmasson Case

Charmasson v. *Minister of Economic Affairs and Finance*; Case 48/74; Preliminary ruling of 10 December 1974; [1974] ECR 193; [1975]2 CMLR 1393.

Facts:

The French banana market is by virtue of State measures reserved to the national production and to that of third countries which 'maintain special relationships' with France. The quantities resulting from such production are normally sufficient to satisfy the needs of French consumers. Any deficit is made up by opening a quota.

On 26 April 1969 Mr. Charmasson complained to the Commission with a view to having it intervene with the French Government to establish that there had been a violation of provisions of the Treaty of Rome and of the Yaoundé Convention of 20 July 1963 (OJ 1964 No 93, p. 1431) insofar as the importation into France, from Somalia and Surinam is concerned.

The Court held:

On the first question

6. The first question asks whether the existence in a Member State of a national market organization within the meaning of Article 43, 45 and 46 if the Treaty is such as to preclude the application of Article 33 of the Treaty in the case of the products concerned, that is to say whether the national market organizations for the agricultural sector may obstruct the rules as to the progressive elimination of quotas.
7. (a) Article 38 (2) of Title II of the Treaty provides that 'save as otherwise provided in Articles 39 to 46, the rules laid down for the establishment of the Common Market shall apply to agricultural products'.
8. It appears from this provision, particularly if considered in conjunction with Article 42, that agricultural products are, in the absence of any contrary provision, subject to the rules relating to the establishment of the Common Market, which include Article 33.
9. Under the provisions of Article 40 (1) Member States shall, by the end of the transitional period at the lates, bring the common agricultural policy into force.

. . . . .

14. It follows from Article 40 (1) of the Treaty that the common organization of agricultural markets shall develop gradually during the transitional period and be accompanied, pursuant to Article 38 (4), by the evelopment of the common agricultural market in conformity with the fundamental objectives of the Treaty; in particular that mentioned in Article 3 (d).
15. Accordingly, while the Treaty provides that the national organization may be kept in existence pending the establishment of a common organization, this was nevertheless only envisaged until the end of the transitional period, the date by which the common agricultural policy must be finally established.
16. Besides, these same provisions seem to show that during this period the national organization must adapt itself to the fullest possible extent to the requirements of the common market with a view to facilitating the establishment of the common agricultural policy.
17. Accordingly, the derogations which a national organization may effect from the general rules of the Treaty are only permissible provisionally, to the extent necessary to ensure its functioning, without however impeding the adaptations which are involved in the establishment of the common agricultural policy.
18. The fact that this policy has not been finally established within the period fixed by Article 40 (1) of the Treaty demonstrated rather than justifies the anomalies that could result from keeping in existence a national organization conceived by the Treaty as a measure having a transitional character.
19. In these circumstances, the adaptation of a national organization to the rules provided for the establishment of the common market is all the more necessary since the absence of a common agricultural policy is contrary to the requirement of Article 3 (d) of the Treaty.
20. Consequently, whilst a national organization of the market existing at the date of coming into force of the Treaty could, during the transitional period, preclude the application of Article 33 thereof, to the extent that such application would have impaired its functioning. This cannot, however, be the case after the expiration of that period, when the provisions of Article 33 must be fully effective.

(2) Commissionaires Réunies – Ramel Case

Société les Commissionaires Réunies v. *Receveur des Douanes* and *Les Fils de Henri Ramel* v. *Receveur des Douanes*; Cases 80 and 81/77; Preliminary ruling of 20 April 1978; [1978] ECR 940.

For the facts see the judgment below.

The Court held:

. . . . .

3. (Questions) have been raised in proceedings brought against the French customs authorites by wine traders who imported into France between the beginning of September 1975 and March 1976 consignments of wine from Italy which proceedings contest whether a duty of FF 1.13 per degree on each hectolitre introduced with effect from 12 September 1975 by Decree No 75/846 of 11 September 1975 of the President of the Republic (Journal Officiel de la République Française of a12 September 1974) and imposed at the time of the said imports was in accord with the Treaty.

. . . . .

First question

14. The first question asks in substance whether Article 31 (2) of Regulation No 816/70 is valid in so far as it authorizes producer Member States to prescribe and to levy, after the end of the transitional period and in the circumstances that it specifies, having an effect equivalent to customs duties in intra-Community trade on a product falling within Annex II of the Treaty, in the present case table wine.
15. The answer to this question requires the interpretation of Article 38 (2) of the EEC Treaty which reads: 'Save as otherwise provided in Articles 39 to 46, the rules laid down for the establishment of the Common Market shall apply to agricultural products'.

. . . . .

19. The objectives of free movement and of the Common Agricultural Policy should not be set one against the other nor in order of preference but on the contrary combined and the principle of free movement should prevail save when the special requirements of the agricultural sector call for adaptations.

. . . . .

23. As is stressed by Article 38 (1) of the Treaty, placed at the head of the title devoted to the Common Agricultural Policy, the Common Market shall extend to agricultural and trade in agricultural products.
24. The abolition between Member States of customs duties and charges having equivalent effect constitutes a fundamental principle of the Common Market applicable to all products and goods with the result that, as has been found by the Court in its judgment of 13 November 1964 (Joined Cases 90 & 91/63 Commission v. Grand Duchy of Luxembourg and Kingdom of Belgium (1964) ECR 625, at p. 633) 'any possible exception, which in any event must be strictly construed, must be clearly laid down'.

. . . . .

26. Therefore in order that the exception provided for in Article 38 (2) should apply to the introduction of charges having an effect equivalent to customs duties in intra-Community trade at the end of the transitional period, it is necessary to find in Articles 39 to 46 a provisions which either expressly or by necessary implication provides for or authorizes the introduction of such charges.
27. Articles 39 to 46 contain no provision of this nature.

. . . . .

35. It is clear from ... these provisions and their relationship inter se that the extensive power, in particular of a sectorial and regional nature, granted to the Community institutions in the conduct of the Common Agricultural Policy must, in any event as from the end of the transitional period, be exercised from the perspective of the unity of the market to the exclusion of any measure compromising the abolition between Member States of customs duties and quantitative restrictions or charges or measures having equivalent effect.

4. The rules of competition

a. Cases

(1) Frubo Case

Nederlandse Vereniging voor de Fruit en Groentenimporthandel, Nederlandse Bond van Grossiers in Zuidvruchten en ander geïmporteerd Fruit (Frubo) v.

EEC Commission; Case 71/74; Judgment of 15 May 1975; [1975] ECR 579; [1975]2 CMLR 123; Competition Law CM/M/III/46.

Facts:

Restrictive provisions of an agreement which set up a system of auction sales in Rotterdam for certain types of fruit (mainly citrus fruit) imported into the Netherlands are the subjects of this Commission decision. The agreement was concluded between an association of the main Dutch fruit importers (Nederlandse Vereniging voor de Fruit en Groentenimporthandel) and an association of virtually all the Dutch fruit wholesalers (Nederlandse Bond van Grossiers in Zuidvruchten en ander geïmporteerd fruit). In order to be allowed to take part in auctions, through which most (roughly 80%) of the citrus fruit sold in the Netherlands is handled dealers had to comply with the conditions imposed by the agreement. The main restriction, apart from a set of technical provisions as to the organization of auction sales, consisted of the obligation for importers and wholesalers to market citrus fruit grown in non-Member Countries and intended for sale in the Netherlands only through the Rotterdam auction sales.

The Court held:

. . . . .

First submission as to substance

22. The applicants contend that, because the disputed Decision withheld application of Article 2 of Regulation No 26 to the disputed agreement on the ground that the agreement was not essential for the attainment of the objectives laid down under Article 39, the Decision infringed not only Article 2 but also Articles 39, 40 and 85 of the Treaty.
23. The stabilization of markets referred to in Article 39 covers not only adjustment of supply to demand in order to develop Community production but also the compatibility of trade in products imported from third countries with paragraphs (c), (d) and (e) of the said Article.
24. The agreement did, in fact, have the beneficial effect of concentrating the supply of and demand for fruit imported from third countries in the Rotterdam import auctions and thus of ensuring the stability of the market, the availability of supplies and their reaching consumers at reasonable prices.
25. The exception provided for under Article 2 (1) of Regulation No 26,

however, applies only to agreements 'necessary for attainment of the objectives set out in Article 39 of the Treaty'.
26. The applicants have not shown in what respect their agreement, which is concerned with products coming from third countries, can be necessary to 'increase agricultural productivity' or to 'ensure a fair standard of living for the agricultural community', as the first two objectives of the common agricultural policy are expressed.
27. In consequence, the Commission could reasonably regard Article 2 of Regulation No 26 as inapplicable.

. . . . .

5. The Common Agricultural Policy

a. The market organization

i. Cases

(1) Deutsche Getreide Case

Deutsche Getreide und Futtermittel HandelsgesllschaftGmbH v Hauptzollamt Hamburg-Altona; Case 31/70; Preliminary ruling of 15 December 1970; [1970] ECR 1063; [1971] CMLR 205.

Facts:

In January 1963 the plaintiff company, an important business with an office in Hamburg, applied for customs clearance of maize imported from the USA. The company stated that the maize had been damaged by moisture in transit and its value reduced by 25 per cent. In spite of this the competent customs office imposed a levy in accordance with Regulation No 19 of the Council, then in force, concerning the gradual establishment of a common organization of the market in cereals, at the rate stated in the import licence, i.e. the full amount.

The plaintiff company considered that this was unjustified and contended that the levy should be reduced in accordance with the reduction value.

The Court held:

. . . . .

5. Regulation No 19 and the other provisions made to establish a common organization of agricultural markets have introduced a system of regulated prices in this sector in order to attain the objectives laid down in Articles 39 and 40 of the Treaty.

Within the framework of this system Regulation No 19 has imposed levies on imports from third countries corresponding to the difference between the prices prevailing on the world market and the prices prevailing in the importing Member State.

These levies are derived from the Treaty and not from national law, are simultaneously applicable in all the Member States and not within only one of them and they act as regulators of the market not within the national framework but within that of a common organization; they are determined by reference to a price level fixed according to the objectives of the Common Market and to fluctuating rates which are capable of variation with changes in the economic situation.

In particular, under the provisions of Article 10 (2) of Regulation No 19 the amount of the levy on each product is the difference between the c.i.f. price determined on the basis of the most favourable prices at which the goods can be bought on the world market and the threshold price in the importing Member State.

The latter price is fixed annually by the Member States for a standard quality for the category of cereals in question, whilst the cif price is fixed on the basis of international prices adjusted by reference to differences in quality which may exist by comparison with the standard quality for which the threshold price is fixed.

6. The result of the system which has thus been established is that the levies, which have been calculated on the basis of weight values and having regard to standard qualities, are standard charges which do not take account of individual characteristics of the products imported.

Products of a quality lower than the standard quality are therefore subject to this levy in the same way as products of a higher quality.

(2) Handelsgesellschaft case

For references and facts see pages 82, 174.

The Court held:

. . . . .

5. By the first question the Verwaltungsgericht asks whether the undertaking to export based on the third subparagraph of Article 12 (1) of

Regulation No 120/67, the lodging of a deposit which accompanies that undertaking and forfeiture of the deposit should exportation not occur during the period of validity of the export licence comply with the law.

6. According to the terms of the thirteenth recital of the preamble to Regulation No 120/67, 'the competent authorities must be in a position constantly to follow trade movements in order to assess market trends and to apply the measures ... as necessary' and 'to that end, provision should be made for the issue of import and export licences accompanied by the lodging of a deposit guaranteeing that the transactions for which such licences are requested are effected'. It follows from these considerations and from the general scheme of the regulation that the system of deposits is intended to guarantee that the imports and exports for which the licences are requested are actually effected in order to ensure both for the Community and for the Member States precise knowledge of the intended transactions.

7. This knowledge, together with other available information on the state of the market, is essential to enable the competent authorities to make judicious use of the instruments of intervention, both ordinary and exceptional, which are at their disposal for guaranteeing the functioning of the system of prices instituted by the regulation, such as purchasing, storing and distributing, fixing denaturing premiums and export refunds, applying protective measures and choosing measures intended to avoid deflections of trade. This is all the more imperative in that the implementation of the common agricultural policy involves heavy financial responsibilities for the Community and the Member States.

8. It is necessary, therefore, for the competent authorities to have available not only statistical information on the state of the market but also precise forecasts on future imports and exports. Since the Member States are obliged by Article 12 of Regulation No 120/67 to issue import and export licences to any applicant, a forecast would lose all significance if the licences did not involve the recipients in an undertaking to act on them. And the undertaking would be ineffectual if observance of it were not ensured by appropriate means.

9. The choice for that purpose by the Community legislature of the deposit cannot be criticized in view of the fact that machinery is adapted to the voluntary nature of requests for licences and that it has the dual advantage over other possible systems of simplicity and efficacy.

10. A system of mere declaration of exports effected and of unused licences, as proposed by the plaintiff in the main action, would by reason of its retrospective nature and lack of any guarantee of application, be incapable of providing the competent authorities with sure data on trends in the movement of goods.

11. Likewise, a system of fines imposed a posteriori would involve considerable administrative and legal complications at the stage of decision and of execution, aggravated by the fact that the traders concerned may be beyond the reach of the intervention agencies by reason of their resid-

ence in another Member State, since Article 12 of the Regulation imposes on Member States the obligation to issue the licences to any applicant 'irrespective of the place of his establishment in the Community'.
12. It therefore appears that the requirement of import and export licences involving for the licences an undertaking to effect the proposed transactions under the guarantee of a deposit constitutes a method which is both necessary and appropriate to enable the competent authorities to determine in the most effective manner their interventions on the market in cereals.
13. The principle of the system of deposits cannot therefore be disputed.

(3) South African maize Case

Coopérative Agricole d'Approvisionnement des Avirons (Réunion) v. *Receveur des Douanes [Collector of Customs], Saint Denis, and Director Régional des Douanes [Regional Director of Customs], Réunion*; Case 58/86; Preliminary ruling of 26 March 1987; (not yet published).

For the facts see the judgment below.

The Court held:

3. In order to decide that dispute the Tribunal d'Instance, Saint-Denis, stayed the proceedings and submitted the following questions to the Court:
   '1. In so far as the import levy instituted by Regulation No. 2727/75 of the Council may be regarded as a variable duty equal to the difference between the prices ruling outside and within the Community and in so far as its purpose is to stabilize the market by compensating for the difference between a lower world price and a higher Community price, is the application of such a levy to a given product not contrary to the spirit of the Community rules and incompatible with the nature of the levy when the real purchase price does not correspond to the fictitious reference price and exceeds not only the latter but also the Community price?'

. . . . .

question 1

5. In its first question, the Tribunal d'Instance asks in substance whether the import levy instituted by Regulation No. 2727/75 of the Council on the common organization of the market in cereals is applicable where

the real purchase price does not correspond to the fictitious reference price and exceeds not only the latter but also the Community price.

6. The plaintiff in the main proceedings submits that the economic and geographical situation of the island of Réunion makes it necessary to import maize from South Africa at a c.i.f. price substantially exceeding the Community threshold prices. In those circumstances, it contends, the application of the levy is contrary to the spirit of the Community legislation.

7. The Commission, on the other hand, argues that in view of the objectives pursued by that legislation the system of levies cannot take account of the prices actually agreed for each individual importation.

8. As the Court held in its judgment of 13 December 1967 in Case 17/67, *Neumann* v *Hauptzollamt Hof/Saale*, [1967] ECR 441, 'since the levy is based on the Treaty and not on national law, is applicable simultaneously in all Member States and not only in one, acts as a regulatory device for markets not in a national context but in a common organization, is defined with reference to a price level fixed in the light of the objectives of the Common Market ... , it therefore appears as a charge regulating external trade connected with a common price policy ...'.

9. The aim of the levies is to ensure, by eliminating the difference between prices inside and outside the Community, that Community preference is observed and that the objectives of the Common Agricultural Policy are attained. The system of levies disregards the prices agreed in individual transactions and it is consequently for traders to plan their imports in the light of the legislation in force.

10. The answer to the first question must therefore be that the import levy laid down by Regulation No. 2727/75 on the common organization of the market in cereals is applicable even where the real purchase price does not correspond to the fictitious reference price and exceeds not only the latter but also the Community price.

. . . . .

question 3 (b)

19. In the second part of its third question, the Tribunal d'Instance asks in substance whether the circumstances surrounding the importation of maize into Réunion constitute 'special circumstances' within the meaning of the first paragraph of Article 13 of Council Regulation No. 1340/79 so as to justify the repayment of levies charged on those imports.

21. The Commission contends that article is not applicable in this case. In its view the expression 'special circumstances' refers to the claimant's individual situation in relation to the customs administration and not to objective situations which might be relied on by an indefinite number of economic operators. Article 13 of Regulation No. 1430/79 must not become a means whereby a Council regulation can be amended by Com-

mission decisions. If that were to happen the Commission would enjoy a broad discretion which would seriously prejudice the division of powers between the institutions.
22. As the Court has held, Article 13 of Regulation No. 1430/79 is 'a general equitable provision designed to cover situations other than those which had most often arisen in practice and for which special provision could be made when the regulation was adopted' (judgment of 15 December 1983 in Case 283/82, *Papierfabrik Schoellershammer* v *Commission*, [1983] ECR 4219; judgment of 15 May 1986 in Case 160/84, *Oryzomyli Kavallas* v *Commission*, [1986] ECR 1633.

The article is intended to apply where the circumstances characterizing the relationship between a trader and the administration are such that it would be inequitable to require the trader to bear a loss which he normally would not have incurred. As the Commission rightly observes, the geographical and economic situation of Réunion is of an objective nature and affects an indefinite number of traders, and hence the circumstances in which maize is imported into that territory cannot be regarded as 'special circumstances' within the meaning of Article 13 cited above.

b. The procedures, Management Committee

i. Cases

(1) Köster Case

See at page 18.

(2) Rey Soda Case

Rey Soda v. *Cassa Conguaglio Zucchero*; Case 23/75; Preliminairy ruling of 30 October 1975; [1975] ECR 1279.

For the facts see the judgment below.

The Court held:

2. It appears from the order for reference that the answer to the questions is intended to enable the national court to judge whether the levying by the Cassa Conguaglio Zucchero of a tax on sugar stocks held by the Italian industrial users on the change-over to the 1974/75 sugar year conforms with Community law.
3. Since the tax on sugar stocks was introduced by an Italian decree-law referring to the aforesaid regulations of the Commission, the national court asks the Court in its first question whether Article 6 of Regulation

(EEC) No 834/74 must be interpreted as meaning that it contains no authority for Italy to impose pecuniary charges on users of sugar, and for the benefit of beet growers.

4. In the second question the national court asks the Court to say whether this provision was adopted illegally inasmuch as a charge of the kind authorized must be expressly approved by the Council of Ministers.

5. Since these two questions are closely related it is appropriate to join them for the purposes of the answer.

. . . . .

15. (I)t is proper to examine in the first place whether Article 37 (2) of Regulation No 1009/67 could supply a valid legal basis for the provisions in question adopted by the Commission.

16. Article 37 (1) provides:
'The Council ... shall, in respect of sugar in stock on 1 July 1968 adopt provisions concerning the measures needed to offset the difference between national sugar prices and prices valid from 1 July 1968' (date on which the common system of prices established by this regulation becomes applicable).

17. Article 37 (2) provides:
'The requisite provisions to prevent the sugar market from being disturbed as a result of an alteration in price level at the changeover from one marketing year to the next may be adopted in accordance with the pricedure laid down in Article 40' (that is to say, according to the so-called Management Committee procedure).

18. The similarity in powers reserved to the Council on the changeover to the first sugar year and conferred on the Commission for the purpose of subsequent marketing years is explained by the Council in the 15th recital to this regulation.

19. It is there explained:
'Whereas the transition to the system established by this Regulation must be effected as smoothly as possible; whereas to this end certain transitional measures may prove necessary; whereas the same need may arise at each change-over from one marketing year to the next; whereas provision must therefore be made for the possibility of adopting appropriate measures'.

20. Accordingly under Article 37 (2) the Commission is given the power to adopt, just as the Council did in Regulation No 769/68 laying down the measures necessary to offset the difference between Community prices from July 1968 (OJ 1968, L 143, p. 14), a measure of equalization in order to prevent the market from being disturbed as a result of an alteration in price level on the change-over from one sugar year to the next.

21. In the present case the Council decided that the application of the new conversion rate of the Italian lira in relation to the unit of account should be related in the sugar market to the beginning of the 1974/1975 sugar year, thus leaving to the Commission the obligation to take account of it in adopting provisions which might be necessary to avoid a disturbance in the Italian market.
22. The attainment of the objective of Article 37 (2) which consists in enabling the Commission to prevent the disturbances which a substantial alteration in the prices of sugar might have on the markets, in the present case the Italian market, would be frustrated if the Commission did not also have to take account of the alteration of the prices expressed in the national currency.
23. A substantial increase in Community prices expressed in national currency could encourage excessive stocking.
24. A provision requiring holders of quantities exceeding certain limits to pay a tax on these stocks was in itself a measure likely to discourage excessive stocking and to encourage a regular supply to consumers provided that the measure was announced in good time and expressed in forcible and precise terms.
25. Nevertheless Article 37 (2) of the basic regulation enabling the Commission to take, in accordance with the consultation procedure of the Management Committee, measures directly applicable in a Member State, cannot be interpreted as enabling the Commission to impose upon a Member State the obligation to draw up, under the guise of implementation measures, essential basic rules which would not to subject to any control by the Council.
26. Thus under the system established by Article 37 (2) of the basic regulation it is for the Commission, when it decides after consultation with the Management Committee to require certain holders of sugar of a Member State to pay a tax on the stocks, itself to determine in a precise manner the essential basic rules.
27. Since the effects of an announcement of a tax to discourage excessive stocking of a product depends to a large extent on the rate of the tax, the announcement must show, in addition to the parties liable, the bases of the calculation of the tax.
28. Accordingly in fulfilling the obligation which is placed on it under Article 37 (2), the Commission should have fixed the basis of the calculation of the tax and the categories of persons liable and submitted this decision to the Management Committee for its opinion.
29. Accordingly the Commission was validly enabled by Article 37 (2) to adopt, after receiving a favourable opinion from the Management Committee, a provision providing for the imposition of a pecuniary charge on holders of stocks of sugar in a Member State as a result of an alteration in the common prices and in these prices expressed in national currencies, at the change-over to a new sugar year in so far as this provision itself fixed the essential basic rules.

30. Next it is necessary to examine whether the Commission has validly used this power in the present case.
31. Article 6 of Regulation No 834/74 provides that:
    '1. Italy shall take national measures to prevent disturbances on the market resulting from the increase on 1 July 1974 in the price of sugar expressed in Italian lire. These provisions shall consist in particular of a payment to beet growers of the increased value of stocks.
    2. The measures referred to in (this) Article which have been adopted or are to be adopted shall be communicated in writing to the Commission before 5 June 1974.'
32. Although the first paragraph of this article requires Italy to make a payment to beet growers, it does not define what is meant by the concepts 'increased value' and 'stocks'.
33. It is therefore necessary to examine whether the context and the Community precedents are such as to give a precise content to this provision.
34. In Regulation (EEC) No 750/68 of the Council of 18 June 1968 laying down general rules for offsetting storage costs for sugar it is explained that although sugar is normally held in store by sugar manufacturers, in some Member States it is also held in store by persons engaged in other businesses.
35. In the recitals to Regulation (EEC) No 748/68 of the Council of 18 June 1968 laying down general rules for postponing part of the sugar production to the following marketing year (OJ No 137, p. 1) it is explained that the manufacturer who carries forward sugar 'can obtain a price equal to the intervention price valid for that marketing year' and 'under Article 37 (2) of Regulation No 1009/67 EEC in the event of an alteration of price levels ... measures may be adopted to offset the price difference in respect of sugar in store on 1 July'.
36. It follows that the concept of stocks in regard to sugar covers mainly stocks held by manufacturers.
37. The stocks held by industrial users, just as those of other consumers, do not as a general rule, come under common organization of the markets since, once sugar has arrived at this stage, the production and marketing cycle is finished.
38. Although as a general rule an industrial user of sugar does not stock within the meaning of the agricultural regulations, but holds only those quantities which by reason of the nature and time-schedules of his activity are necessary for a normal production, he may nevertheless be encouraged in certain circumstances to engage in speculative stocking and thus disturb the market.
39. Thus although Regulation No 769/68 of the Council exempted the quantities of sugar which these industries require for a normal working period of 4 weeks from the tax established by this regulation, it nevertheless subjected these industries to a tax on the remainder of their stocks.
40. In order to avoid disturbances on the market in France, Regulation No 1244/71 of the Commission provided for the levying of a tax on stocks

notified on 1 July 1971, but exempted stocks regarded as working stock of users up to a maximum amount of 20 000 metric tons.

41. Although the last recital to Regulation No 834/74, in explaining that the measures which Italy is required to take must 'result in the removal of any incentive to excessive stocking' may give the impression that working or normal stocks of industrial users are exempt, it is nevertheless necessary that this should be stated clearly as was done in previous Community regulations.

42. The Commission has claimed that Article 6 of Regulation No 834/74, in not making any distinction, was intended to apply to all sugar stocks without distinction, including the working stock of industrial users.

43. It says that this argument is confirmed by Regulation No 1495/74 of the Commission which imposes an obligation to declare on 'All holders in Italy at 00.00 hours on 1 July 1974, *on whatever basis*, ...'.

44. An obligation to declare of this kind is compatible with exemption of working stocks as it was in the previous Community regulations.

45. Article 6 of Regulation No 834/74, either taken alone or in conjunction with Regulation No 1495/74 or in the light of previous Community regulations, cannot be interpreted as defining the classes of traders subject to the tax.

46. It must be concluded from this that the Commission, having defined the aim of the measures which the Italian authorities were required to take, should have determined in respect of each class of business, having regard to the size of the undertakings, what was to be understood by 'excessive stocking'.

47. Moreover, since the concept of 'increased value' is a new term in agricultural regulations, as the Commission explained in the course of the proceedings, the method of calculating this increased value requires precise rules.

48. In addition, by not specifying the bases of the calculation of the tax in the provision in question and leaving Italy to choose them, the Commission discharged itself of its own responsibility to adopt the basic rules and to submit them by way of the Management Committee procedure to the approval if need be of the Council.

49. Therefore the answer to the first two questions from the national court must be that Article 6 of Regulation No 834/74 is invalid.

c. Monetary complications

i. Cases

(1) Malt Case

Malt GmbH v. *Hauptzollamt (Principal Customs Office Düsseldorf)*; Case 236/84; Preliminary ruling of 24 June 1986; [1986] ECR 1939.

For the facts see the judgment below.

The Court held:

1. By an order of 13 September 1984, which was received at the Court on 19 September 1984, the Finanzgericht Düsseldorf referred to the Court for a preliminary ruling under Article 177 of the EEC Treaty a question on the validity of a monetary compensatory amount fixed by Commission Regulation No 481/82 of 26 February 1982 for high quality fresh, chilled or frozen beef and veal, ... imported under a Community tariff quota opened by Council Regulation No 3715/81 of 21 December 1981.

. . . . .

4. The defendant decided to charge monetary compensatory amounts pursuant to Commission Regulation No 481/82 of 26 February 1982 amending monetary compensatory amounts, and Malt challenged that decision first by lodging an objection with the defendant and then, after its objection was rejected, by bringing an action before the Finanzgericht Düsseldorf, on the ground that goods imported under the tariff quota in question could not give rise to the charging of monetary compensatory amounts.

. . . . .

7. Malt takes the view that Regulation No 481/82 is unlawful in so far as it provides for the application of monetary compensatory amounts to beef and veal imported within the Community tariff quota for high-quality beef and veal. It considers that the charging of monetary compensatory amounts is at variance with Article 1 (3) of Regulation No 974/71 of the Council of 12 May 1971 on certain measures of conjunctural policy to be taken in agriculture following the temporary widening of the margins of fluctuation for the currencies of certain Member States. ... In the first place, it is not justified by the existence or threat of disturbances in intra-Community trade. ...

. . . . .

14. In order to resolve that difference of views, it must be pointed out first of all that as regards trade between Member States the purpose of monetary

compensatory amounts is to correct the effects of variations in unstable rates of exchange which, within a system of organization of the markets in agricultural products, based on common prices, are likely to cause disturbances in trade in such products (see judgment of 15 October 1985 in Case 125/84 *Continental Irish Meat* v. *Minister for Agriculture* [1985] ECR 3441). The need to safeguard intra-Community trade requires that monetary compensatory amounts should be applied not only in intra-Community trade but also in trade with non-member countries (judgment of 15 October 1980 in Case 4/79 *Providence Agricole de la Champagne* v. *ONIC* [1980] ECR 2823). As far as imports of agricultural products from non-member countries are concerned, it is true that monetary compensatory amounts are not to constitute a protective component at the external frontiers of the Community and hence differ entirely from the system of levies or customs duties. Nevertheless it is equally true that monetary compensatory amounts applied to products imported from non-member countries have the same regulatory function as those applied to Community products, namely to neutralize the harmful effect which short-term fluctuations in the rates of exchange of the currencies of the various Member States in relation to the representative rate of such currencies have on the system of single prices. In that regard it should be stated that the fixing of monetary compensatory amounts is unlawful if, in their absence, there would be no reason to fear disturbances in intra-Community trade arising from imports from non-member countries or if the imposition of compensatory amounts includes a protective component.

15. As regards the possibility of disturbances in intra-Community trade in agricultural products, this requires the evaluation of a complex economic situation which the Commission has a broad discretion in carrying out, as the Court has consistently held (see judgment of 22 January 1976 in Case 55/75 *Balkan-Import-Export* v. *Hauptzollamt Berlin-Packhof* [1976] ECR 19, and judgment of 12 December 1985 in Case 208/84 *Vonk's Kaas* v. *Minister van Landbouw* [1985] ECR 4025). The Commission is not obliged to decide case by case or separately for each product and exporting country whether there is a risk of disturbance but may decide that question by an evaluation of a general nature. The Court's exercise of its power of review is then limited to examining whether that evaluation contains a manifest error or constitutes a misuse of powers or whether the Commission clearly exceeded the bounds of its discretion.

16. On that point it must be remembered that according to the judgments of the Court (judgment of 9 March 1978 in Case 79/77 *Kühlhaus-Zentrum* v. *Hauptzollamt Hamburg-Harburg* [1978] ECR 611; judgment in *Providence Agricole de la Champague* v. *ONIC* cited above), the Commission must always ensure that the application of monetary compensatory amounts is limited to what is strictly necessary in order to neutralize the effects of currency fluctuations between the Member States, in particular in the case of products imported from non-member countries under a quota and free of the levy. However, that limitation cannot be inter-

preted as meaning that the Commission may ignore the risk of deflections of trade in agricultural products within the Community when products from non-member countries are involved. Such an interpretation would run counter to Article 1 (3) of Regulation No 974/71.
17. In this instance the Community tariff quota in question was not allocated between the Member States. There were therefore grounds for fearing that imports from non-member countries would be made exclusively in the Member States with the strongest currencies, in particular Germany. Importers carrying out the operation would then have been able to sell the products at a profit in a Member State with a weak currency by virtue of the fact that, in the event of delivery in that State, they would have received the negative monetary compensatory amounts applicable for Member States with weak currencies without in any way infringing the Community rules.
18. The Commission has further indicated that according to its calculations Community producers produce annually some 50 000 tonnes of high-quality beef and veal comparable to that imported under the tariff quota. In addition it has supplied statistics showing that there were imports of high-quality beef and veal covered by the tariff quota in question into most of the Member States, thus showing that there was a demand for that product almost everywhere in the Community.
19. Those considerations, together with the calculations and statistics just mentioned, justify the conclusion that the placing on the Community market free of monetary compensatory amounts of 21 000 tonnes of meat imported under the tariff quota might have had repercussions on that market. It was not unreasonable to suppose that traders might divert the flow of imports of the meat in question into the Community by importing it through a Member State with a strong currency, in particular Germany, which would have provoked disturbances in intra-Community trade and jeopardized the system of intervention laid down for beef and veal by Council Regulation No 805/68 of 27 June 1968 on the common organization of the market in beef and veal (Official Journal, English Special Edition 1968 (I), p. 187).
20. In alleging that the monetary compensatory amounts had an additional protective effect, Malt has challenged only the application of monetary compensatory amounts to the imports at issue in this case. In view of the fact that the compensatory amounts at issue have the same regulatory function in intra-Community trade as in trade with non-member countries, the allegation that the monetary compensatory amounts have an additional protective effect cannot be accepted.
21. With regard to the contention that monetary compensatory amounts may not be applied to the quota in question because imports under the tariff quota opened by Council Regulation No 136/82 are exempt from monetary compensatory amounts by virtue of Note 2 to Part 3 of Annex I to Commission Regulation No 481/82, on account of the special nature of that trade, it must be pointed out first of all that the Court has con-

sistently held that there exists no general principle obliging the Community, in its external relations, to accord to non-member countries equal treatment in all respects, nor any right by virtue of which traders rely on the prohibition of discrimination where the difference of treatment between traders is an automatic consequence of the different treatment accorded to non-member countries (judgment in *Balkan-Import-Export* v. *Hauptzollamt Berlin-Packhof* cited above; judgment of 28 October 1982 in Case 52/81 *Faust* v. *Commission* [1982] ECR 3745). The mere fact that the application of monetary compensatory amounts is not expressly excluded in the case of imports under Council Regulation No 217/81 although it is excluded in the case of imports of frozen beef and veal under Regulation No 136/82 and of buffalo meat under Regulation No 481/82 does not in itself constitute discrimination.

6. The C.A.P. and national law

a. Execution by national authorities – execution and subdelegation

i. Cases

(1) Beauport Case

Société des Usines de Beauport v. *Council of Ministers*; Joined Cases 103–109/78; Judgment of 18 Januari 1979; [1979] ECR 122.

For the facts see the judgment below.

The Court held:

1. The applications ... are for the annulment of Council Regulation (EEC) No 298/78 of 13 February 1978 amending Regulation (EEC) No 3331/74 on the allocation and alteration of the basic quotas for sugar.

. . . . .

3. Article 24 of Regulation (EEC) No 3330/74 of the Council of 19 December 1974 on the common organization of the market in sugar provides for the allocation by Member States of basic quotas to undertakings; Article 24 (3) stipulates that 'the Council ... shall adopt the general rules for the application of this article and any derogations therefrom'.

. . . . .

5. Article 2 of (R)egulation (No 3331/74) provides for derogations from Article 24 of Regulation (EEC) No 3330/74.

. . . . .

7. The contested regulation amended Article 2 of Regulation No 3331/74 by adding to the two existing paragraphs a paragraph 3 which provides as follows:
'3. By way of derogation from the first, second and third subparagraphs of Article 24 (2) of Regulation No 3330/74 and paragraph 1 of this article, the French Republic may . . . reduce the basic quota for each undertaking established in these departments by a quantity not exceeding, for the entire period 1 July 1977 to 30 June 1980, 10% of the basic quota applicable to each undertaking during the 1976/77 sugar marketing year. . . .

. . . . .

9. The applicants consider that their 'established rights' have been adversely affected by Regulation (EEC) No 298/78 and request its annulment under Article 173 of the Treaty.

. . . . .

Admissibility

11. (The Council) maintains that the applications for annulment do not comply with the conditions laid down in the second paragraph of Article 173 of the Treaty in that the contested measure does not constitute a decision adopted in the form of a regulation and is not of either direct or individual concern to the applicants.

. . . . .

21. Although it is true that they could have been concerned by the use which the Member State might make of the derogating rule adopted, paragraph 3 added to that article nevertheless provides expressly that 'the French Republic may . . .' reduce the basic quota for each undertaking', thus leaving to that Member State the decision whether or not to reduce the

basic quotas and, if the answer is in the affirmative, to decide whether the basic quotas of all or of certain undertakings are to be reduced.

. . . . .

b. The necessity of uniform application: force majeure

i. Cases

(1) Kampffmeyer Case III

Kampffmeyer v. *Einfuhr – und Vorratstelle für Getreide*; Case 158/73; Preliminary ruling of 30 January 1974; [1974] ECR 101.

For facts see the judgment below.

The Court held:

1. ... The main action is an appeal against a declaration of forfeiture of deposit in an amount corresponding to the quantity of bran not imported by the plaintiffs, made on the ground that the loss of an import licence following dispatch by non-registered letter does not constitute a case of force majeure, the risk of which loss falling upon the holder of the licence.
2. Regulation No 120/67 of the Council, dated 13 June 1967 (OJ No 117 of 19 June 1967, p. 2269), which is the basic regulation on the common organization of the market in cereals, states in the 13th recital of its preamble that 'the competent authorities must be in a position constantly to follow trade movements in order to assess market trends and to apply the measures laid down in this Regulation as necessary'.

    Article 12 of the same Regulation provides that 'imports into Community or exports therefrom ... shall be subject to the submission of an import or export licence ... the issue of such licences shall be conditional on the lodging of a deposit guaranteeing that importation or exportation is effected during the period of validity of the licence; the deposit shall be forfeited in whole or in part if the transaction is not effected, or is only partially effected, within that period'.

With regard to the first question

3. The first question posed is whether Article 2 (1), first sentence, in conjunction with Article 15 (4) of Regulation No 1373/70/EEC of the Commission must be interpreted as meaning that when an import licence is lost, not only does the right to import lapse but also the obligation to do so, with the result that the security must be released, or as meaning

that when the import licence is lost the right lapses but the obligation remains, with the result that the security is forfeit.

. . . . .

5. It is apparent from these provisions that the system of lodging deposits is intended to ensure completion of the imports and exports for which licences or certificates are requested, so that both the Community and the Member States may be certain of knowing exactly what transactions are intended.

In view of the obligation imposed on Member States by Article 12 of the basic Regulation No 120/67 to issue import and export licences to any applicant, any forecast would be meaningless if the licences did not impose non recipients an obligation to act in accordance therewith.

The system established pursuant to the principles contained in the basic Regulation No 120/67 by the implementing Regulation No 1373/70 releases traders from their undertaking only in cases where the import or export transaction cannot be carried out during the period of validity of the licence as a result of a case of force majeure.

6. The answer to the first question therefore should be that Articles 2 (1) and 15 (4) of Regulation (EEC) No 1373/70 of the Commission must not be interpreted as meaning that loss of an import licence automatically entails the lapse of the obligation to import created by its issue.

With regard to the first part of the second question

7. The first part of the second question asks whether the loss of the licence constitutes a case of force majeure within the meaning of Article 18 of Regulation No 1373/70 of the Commission.
8. Since the concept of force majeure differs in content in different areas of the law and in its various spheres of application, the precise meaning of this concept has to be decided by reference to the legal context in which it is intended to operate.

Any interpretation of the concept of force majeure employed in the Regulation must therefore take account of the special nature of the relationships at public law existing between the importers and the national administration, as well as of the objectives of that Regulation.

It is apparent from these objectives, as well as from the actual provisions of the regulations in question, that the concept of force majeure is not limited to cases of absolute impossibility.

9. The public interest, which requires as accurate a forecast as possible of import trends in each Member State and justifies the deposit of security against the grant of authorization to import, must be reconciled to the necessity of not hampering trade between States by too rigid obligations, a necessity which also derives from the public interest.

The threat of forfeiture of security is intended to encourage the fulfilment of the obligation to import by importers enjoying the authorization and thus to ensure the accurate forecasting of import trends required by the general interest mentioned above.

It follows that, in principle, an importer who has exercised all reasonable care is released from the obligation to import when external circumstances render it impossible for him to complete the importation within the period of validity.

10. The answer to the first part of the second question should therefore be that the loss of such an import licence constitutes a case of force majeure within the meaning of Article 18 of Regulation No 1373/70 when such loss occurs despite the fact that the titular holder of the licence has taken all the precautions which could reasonably be expected of a prudent and diligent trader.

c. The competence of the national legislation

i. Limits of national competence

aa. Cases

(1) Amsterdam Bulb Case

Amsterdam Bulb v. *Produktschap voor Siergewassen*; Case 50/76; Preliminary ruling of 2 February 1977; [1977] ECR 137; [1977] 2 CMLR 218.

For the facts see the judgment below.

The Court held:

1. By order of 15 June 1976, received at the Court on 17 June, the College van Beroep voor het Bedrijfsleven requested the Court to give a preliminary ruling on the interpretation of Regulations (EEC) Nos 234/68 of the Council of 27 February 1968 (OJ English Special Edition 1968 (I) p. 26), 1767/68 of the Commission of 6 November 1968 (OJ English Special Edition 1968 (III), p. 530) and 369/75 of the Commission of 10 February 1975 (OJ L 41, 1975, p. 1) to the extent to which they concern the system of minimum prices for exports of flower bulbs.
2. The Court is asked to rule whether the provisions of those regulations 'or any other provisions or principles of European law' forbid the adoption by a competent national organization of rules fixing export prices for flower bulbs which, whilst in part in conformity with the Community regulations, contain provisions which do not appear to those regulations and have no legal foundation therein.
3. In addition to the provisions which are identical to those contained in the

Community regulations the national rules contain provisions which:
- impose a minimum export price for flower bulbs of a smaller size than those for which Regulation No 369/75 fixes minimum export prices;
- impose a minimum export price in respect of flower bulbs other than those for which Regulation No 369/75 fixes minimum export prices;
- Grant exemptions, in certain cases, to the provisions of the national rules;
- provide penal sanctions in respect of infringements of the rules.

. . . . .

The Court ruled:

1. The Member States may neither adopt nor allow national organizations having legislative power to adopt any measure which would conceal the Community nature and effects of any legal provision from the persons to whom it applies.
2. The lowest minimum export price fixed for the product in question by Regulation No 369/75 is also applicable to products which are larger than the minimum size but smaller than the sizes expressly listed in the annex to that regulation.
3. A national provision which fixes minimum prices for exports to third countries of certain varieties of bulbs other than those for which the Commission has fixed minimum prices in Regulation No 369/75, which does not create exemptions from the Community system, does not limit its scope and seeks to achieve the same aim, that is, the stabilization of prices in trade with third countries, cannot be regarded as incompatible with Community law.
4. In the absence of any provisions in the Community rules providing for specific sanctions to be imposed on individuals for a failure to observe those rules, the Member States are competent to adopt such sanctions as appear to them to be appropriate.
5. The Member States may not, either directly or through the intermediary of organizations set up or recognized by them authorize any exemption from the minimum prices fixed by the Community.

(2) Pigs Marketing Board – Redmond Case

(Northern Ireland) Pigs Marketing Board v. *Redmond*; Case 83/78; Preliminary ruling of 29 November 1978; [1978] ECR 2347; [1979]1 CMLR 177.

Facts:

In Northern Ireland marketing of pigs is governed by the Pigs Marketing Scheme (Northern Ireland) 1933, which is administered by the pigs Marketing Board (Northern Ireland). In particular the system requires producers not to sell pigs weighing over 77 kg live weight (or over 56.5 kg dead weight), known as 'bacon pigs', except to or through the agency of the Pigs Marketing Board. Movement of Pigs Regulations (Northern Ireland) 1972, which prohibit any transport of bacon pigs otherwise than to one of the Board's purchasing centres, a destination for which the producer must be in possession of a document authorizing transport. Any offence against the regulations is punishable by a term of imprisonment not exceeding three months and/or a fine of £200; the pigs may be forfeit.

The Court held:

. . . . .

55. It follows that, having regard to the structure of Regulation No 2759/75, which is now in force, the provisions of the Treaty relating to the abolition to tariff and commercial barriers to intra-Community trade and in particular Articles 30 and 34 on the abolition of quantitative restrictions and of all measures having equivalent effect on imports and exports are to be regarded as an integral part of the common organization of the market.
56. As the Court has stated in its judgment of 18 May 1977 in Case 111/75 *Officier van Justitie* v. *Van den Hazel* [1977] ECR at p. 909) once the Community has, pursuant to Article 40 of the Treaty, legislated for the establishment of the common organization of the market in a given sector, Member States are under an obligation to refrain from taking any measure which might undermine or create exceptions to it.
57. With a view to applying that statement in the case of the Pigs Marketing Scheme it should be borne in mind that the common organization of the market in pigment, like the other common organizations, is based on the concept of an open market to which every producer has free access and the functioning of which is regulated solely by the instruments provided for by that organization.
58. Hence any provisions or national practices which might alter the pattern of imports or exports or influence the formation of market prices by preventing producers from buying and selling freely within the State in which they are established, or in any other Member State, in conditions laid down by Community rules and from taking advantage directly of intervention measures or any other measures for regulating the market laid down by the common organization are incompatible with the principles of such organization of the market.
59. Any action of this type, which is brought to bear upon the market by a body set up by a Member State and which does not come within the arrangements made by Community rules cannot be justified by the pursuit of special objectives of economic policy, national or regional, the

common organization of the market, as emerges from the third recital in the preamble to Regulation No 2759/75, is intended precisely to attain such objectives on the Community scale in conditions acceptable for the whole of the Community and taking account of the needs of all its regions.

60. Any intervention by a Member State or by its regional or subordinate authorities in the market machinery apart from such intervention as may be specifically laid down by the Community regulation runds the risk of obstructing the functioning of the common organization of the market and of creating unjustified advantages for certain groups of producers or consumers to the prejudice of the economy of other Member States or of other economic groups within the Community.

. . . . .

The Court ruled:

1. A marketing system on a national or regional scale set up by the legislation of a Member State and administered by a body which, by means of compulsory powers vested in it, is empowered to control the sector of the market in question or a part of it by measures such as subjecting the marketing of the goods to a requirement that the producer shall be registered with the body in question, the prohibition of any sale otherwise than to that body or through its agency on the conditions determined by it, and the prohibition of all transport of the goods in question otherwise than subject to the authorization of the body in question are to be considered as incompatible with the requirements of Articles 30 and 34 of the EEC Treaty and of Regulation No 2759/75 on the common organization of the market in pigmeat.
2. The provisions of Articles 30 and 34 of the EEC Treaty and of Regulation No 2759/75 are directly applicable and confer on individuals rights which the courts of Member States must protect.
3. The effects described above applied, according to the terms of the Act of Accession and in particular of Articles 2, 42 and 60 (1) thereof, to the whole of the territory of the United Kingdom as from 1 February 1973.

ii. Restrictions of production

aa. Cases

(1) Van den Hazel Case

Officier van Justitie v. *Van den Hazel*; Case 111/76; Preliminary ruling of 18 May 1977; [1977] ECR 901; [1980]3 CMLR 12.

For the facts see the judgment below.

The Court held:

. . . . .

2. The national rules referred to in the question restrict for the second half of 1974 the slaughter of poultry by fixing quotas calculated in terms of a reference period.
3. In connection with criminal proceedings instituted against the operator of a poultry slaughter-house for having slaughtered more poultry than the quota permitted him by the Produktschap, the institution governed by public law controlling the organization of the market in this sector, the question arose whether the rules which, it was charged, the accused had infringed were compatible with Regulation No 123/67 of the Council or with Articles 30 to 37 of the Treaty.

. . . . .

6. The organization of the market in poultrymeat established by Regulation No 123/67 of the Council prohibits, with regard to the internal market, State aids, any customs duty or charge having equivalent effect and any quantitative restriction or measure having equivalent effect and covers rules for marketing but it does not establish an intervention system in any form whatsoever.

. . . . .

Community law cited by the national court.

13. Once the Community has, pursuant to Article 40 of the Treaty, legislated for the establishment of the common organization of the market in a given sector, Member States are under an obligation to refrain from taking any measure which might undermine or create exceptions to it.
14. In its communication of 23 January 1967 to the Council the Commission justified the absence of all measures of intervention from its proposal for a regulation on the organization of the market in poultrymeat by the consideration that, because of the nature of the production in this sector and of the structure and marketing of such production, together with the

large part played by variable elements in the production costs, 'intervention on the market in eggs and poultrymeat is not desirable'.
15. In the same document the Commission also observed that the rapid adaptation of the volume of production to demand which, it maintained, is characteristic of the market in poultrymeat means that 'before the intervention machinery intended to withdraw from the market a certain quantity of goods can bring about positive results, forces pertaining to the production process intself are already in operation to adjust prices to a normal level'.
16. It may be inferred from those considerations that the absence of measures concerning the withdrawal, where necessary, of products to from the market does not stem from an omission or from an intention to leave measures of this nature to the appraisal of the Member States but is rather the consequence of a considered choice of economic policy of relying essentially on market forces to attain the desired balance.

. . . . .

18. It thus follows from the general tenor of the regulation that, as regards the internal trade of the Community, the organization of the market in the product in question is based upon freedom of commercial transactions under conditions of genuine competition.
19. Even if the national restrictions on slaughter must be regarded as referring to the production and not to the marketing of the products they are also prohibited by Article 2 of Regulation No 123/67 as amounting to withdrawal of the products from the market and as constituting quantitative restrictions capable of affecting, potentially at any rate, the system of trade as it has been set up by the organization of the market established by Regulation No 123/67.

iii. Regulation of prices

aa. Cases

(1) Galli Case

Publico Ministerio v. *Filippo Galli*; Case 31/74; Preliminary ruling of 23 January 1975; [1975] ECR 59; [1975] 1 CMLR 211.

For facts see the judgment below.

The Court held:

. . . . .

2. These questions have arisen in the context of criminal proceedings against a dealer charged with having contravened, through the sale of cereals and flours derived from oil seeds, the provisions of Italian Decree Law No 425 of 24 July 1973 (Gazetta Ufficiale No 189 of 24.7.1973) controlling the prices of goods produced or distributed by large scale undertakings.
3. This Decree Law required commercial undertakings producing or distributing goods sold according to weight, measure or number and having a turnover in the first six months of 1973 in excess of five thousand million lire to submit a price return which could be changed only sixty days after notification to the competent authorities and provided that the latter raised no objection during this same period of time.

. . . . .

8. Regulation No 120/67 on cereals, adopted within the framework of organization of the market within the meaning of Article 40 of the EEC Treaty.
   This common organization of the market is intended, as is emphasized repeatedly in the preamble to Regulation No 120/67, to create for the Community a 'single market' in cereals subject to common administration.
9. In order to bring about this singel market, the regulation established a system comprising a set of material rules and of powers including a framework of organization calculated to meet all foreseeable situations.
10. In fact, a central place in this system is held by the 'price ... system', provided for by Article 1 of the regulation and applicable, by way of Article 2 (3), at the production and wholesale stage.

. . . . .

15. Such a system excludes any national system of regulation impeding directly or indirectly, actually or potentially, trade within the Community.
    Consequently, as concerns more particularly the price system, any national provisions, the effect of which is to distort the formation of

prices as brought about within the framework of the Community provisions applicable, are incompatible with the regulation.

16. Apart from the substantive provisions relating to the functioning of the common organization of the market in the sector under consideration, Regulation No 120/67 comprises a framework of organization designed in such a way as to enable the Community and Member States to meet all manners of disturbances.

17. In this connection, it must first be stressed that it is one of the objectives of Article 39 (1) of the Treaty that supplies reach consumers at reasonable prices.

18. Articles 19 and 20 of the regulation have therefore made express provisions for such cases by empowering the Council to take all necessary measures where the Community market is disturbed or threatened with disturbances by price rises on the world market which jeopardize the normal functioning of the price machinery established by the regulation.

. . . . .

23. A Member State cannot base the justification for its unilateral intervention in the movement of prices in the sector in question on the provisions of Article 103 of the Treaty relating to conjunctural policy.

24. Article 103, which refers to Member States' conjunctural policies, does not relate to those areas already subject to common rules such as the organization of agricultural markets.

25. It is necessary to examine next whether the preceding consideration are also applicable to the market in oils and fats dealt with in Regulation No. 136/66.

. . . . .

27. Although the incompatibility of national measures intended to influence the formation of prices may be particularly apparent in the case of market organizations comprising a Community price formation system, it is none the less true that the very existence of a common organization of the market in the sense of Article 40 (2) (c) has the effect of precluding Member States from adopting in the sector in question unilateral measures capable of impeding intra-Community trade.

. . . . .

29. It must be concluded that in sectors covered by a common organization of the market – even more so when this organization is based on a common price system – Member States can no longer interfere through national provisions taken unilaterally in the machinery of price formation as established under the Common organization.
30. It is apparent, therefore, that a national system which by freezing prices and subjecting their alteration to administrative authorization, has the effect of modifying the formation or prices as provided for in the context of the common organization of the market, is incompatible both with the regulations in question and with the general provision of the second paragraph of Article 5 of the Treaty according to which Member States must abstain from 'any measure which could jeopardize' the attainment of the objectives of the Treaty.
34. ... It must however be stated that the price system established by Regulations Nos 120/67 and 136/66 is applicable solely at the production and wholesale stage, with the result that these provisions leave Member States free – without prejudice to other provisions of the Treaty – to take the appropriate measures relating to price formation at the retail and consumption stages, on condition that they do not jeopardize the aims or functioning of the common organization of the market in question.

(2) Russo Case

Russo v. *AIMA*; Case 60/75; Preliminary ruling of 22 January 1976; [1976] ECR 45.

For facts see the judgment below.

The Court held:

1. By an order of 2 May 1975 which was registered at the Court on 7 July 1975 the Pretore di Bovino submitted to the Court of Justice, pursuant to Article 177 of the EEC Treaty, various questions on the interpretation of Regulation No 120/67 of the Council of 13 June 1967 on the common organization of the market in cereals (OJ Special English Edition 1967, p. 33).

   The questions were referred in the context of an action initiated by an Italian producer of durum wheat against the State agency for intervention on the agricultural market (AIMA).

   The producer claims that he has been injured by the actions of the AIMA in that it purchased large quantities of durum wheat on the world market and resold them to Italian producers of macaroni, spaghetti and similar products ('pasta products') at prices considerably below the

purchase prices and indeed below the intervention price fixed pursuant to the provisions concerning the common organization of the market in cereals.
2. The purpose of this action, which was undertaken in the context of the anti-inflation policy of the Italian Government, was to provide supplies for the pasta industry at prices which would ensure that production was profitable despite the maximum prices imposed on the finished products at the wholesale and retail stages.

    The action was taken at a period when prices on the world market were appreciably higher than prices fixed under Community rules, whereby all exports of durum wheat, Community production of which is insufficient to meet requirements, were prohibited to third countries.

    It is clear from the file that, on the one hand, the resale price charged by AIMA to the pasta industry was approximately Lit. 13,000 per quintal, that is to say, it was below the target price of about Lit. 16,400 and indeed below the intervention price of about Lit. 15,000 and that, on the other hand, the plaintiff in the main action obtained a price of Lit. 17,000 per quintal for a quantity of durum wheat sold in January 1975.
3. In the first two questions the national court asks essentially whether the purchase of durum wheat by a Member State on the world market and its resale at prices below the purchase price, and even below the intervention price is compatible with the common organization of the market in cereals.

    The third, fourth and fifth question concern the individual position of traders in the event of unlawful interference by the State in the machinery of price formation prescribed by the common organization of the market and the consequences to be drawn if such interference were to result in an infringement of the rights accorded to these traders by Community rules.
4. These questions have been referred to the Court as a result of non-compulsory intervention by the State on the market in cereals, the aims of which was not to influence directly the formation of prices, on that market but to check the rise in prices of certain foodstuffs made from durum wheat at consumer level.
5. Such intervention by a Member State is compatible with the common organization of the market in cereals only in so far as it does not jeopardize the objectives or operation of that organization.

    Since one of the principal objectives of the organization is to guarantee to producers a price based on the target price this objective is jeopardized where the actions of the State agency are of such a nature as to influence conditions on the market and to induce a tendency to force prices below that level.

    It must therefore be concluded that the action of a Member State by purchasing durum wheat on the world market and subsequently reselling it on the Community market at a price lower than the target price is incompatible with the common organization of the market in cereals
6. This situation does not however imply that a specific producer can claim

that he has suffered damage where he has sold his products above the target price, thereby obtaining the advantages which the regulation is intended to produce.

In fact under Community rules an individual producer may claim that he should not be prevented from obtaining a price approximating to the target price and in any event not lower than the intervention price.

Regulation No 120/67 is in fact intended to shield the development of Community agricultural production from fluctuations in world prices and thereby to ensure a fair standard of living for the agricultural community and to stabilize markets by means of Community levies and refunds, protecting the operation of the common agricultural market against the risks of the world market.

7. That regulation is therefore not intended to guarantee to persons concerned the right to profit from random market trends when the level of world prices exceeds that considered desirable for the attainment of the objectives of the common organization.

Consequently, an individual farmer may not claim that he has suffered damage under Community law if the price which he has actually obtained on the market exceeds the target price.

8. It is for the national court to decide on the basis of the facts of each case whether an individual producer has suffered such damage.

9. If such damage has been caused through an infringement of Community law the State is liable to the injured party of the consequences in the context of the provisions of national law on the liability of the State.

. . . . .

(3) Irish excise duty Case

Irish creamery milk suppliers Association v. *Ireland*; Case 36 and 71/80; Preliminary ruling of 10 March 1981; [1981] ECR.746.

For the facts see the judgment below.

The Court held:

1. By an order of 25 October 1979 which was received at the Court on 28 January 1980 the High Court of Ireland referred to the Court for a preliminary ruling under Article 177 of the EEC Treaty two questions, one of which concerns the interpretation of the said Article 177 whilst the other seeks elucidation on the features of interpretation of Community law which it requires in order to decide whether a temporary excise duty of 2% imposed by the Government of Ireland in 1979 on the value of certain

agricultural products was in conformity with that law. By an order of 29 November 1979 which was received at the Court on 6 March 1980 the same national court raised almost identical questions in another case before it.

. . . . .

11. The purpose of this question from the High Court is to elicit the features of interpretation of Community law necessary in order to decide whether the duty is compatible with Community law, and in particular with the provisions of the Treaty prohibiting charges having an effect equivalent to customs duties, with those relating to the common agricultural policy and with the regulations of the common organization of the markets in the sectors covering the products subject to the duty. Since all the products chargeable are subject to Community rules on the common organization of markets it is appropriate to consider the duty first in relation to those rules.

. . . . .

13. Whilst the parties to the main action express differing views on the precise reasons which led the Government of Ireland to introduce the duty, they agree that it forms part of an incomes policy which is designed to divide up the tax burden between the various sectors of the working population. As the Government of Ireland and the Commission correctly argue, nothing in the common organization of markets is opposed, in principle, to such a national policy. According to Article 39 (2) (c) of the Treaty, in working out the common agricultural policy account shall be taken of 'the fact that in the Member States agriculture constitutes a sector closely linked with the economy as a whole'. The common agricultural policy is not intended, therefore, to shield those engaged in agriculture from the effects of a national incomes policy. Moreover, the fixing of common prices within the framework of the common organization of markets does not serve to guarantee to agricultural producers a net price independently of any taxation imposed by the national authorities, and the very wording of Article 39 (1) (b) shows that the increase in individual earnings of persons engaged in agriculture is envisaged as being primarily the result of the structural measures described in subparagraph (a).

. . . . .

15. Nevertheless, the methods used to implement a national incomes policy which includes, among other persons, agricultural producers would be incompatible with the Treaty and with the rules on the common organization of markets if these methods interfered with the functioning of the machinery employed by those organizations in order to achieve their ends. The real problem posed by the duty in question in relation to those rules is therefore whether, apart from the taxation of the incomes of agricultural producers envisaged by the Government of Ireland and precisely because of the basis of its assessment and the way in which it is collected, it has produced other effects capable of obstructing the functioning of the machinery established by the organizations in question.
16. On that point the plaintiffs in the main action in Case 36/80 contend that according to the consistent case-law of the Court even the potential effects of a national measure may render it incompatible with the Treaty. As far as the duty in question is concerned they place special emphasis on its potential effects on the formation of market prices and on market supply. They also support the arguments put forward by the cattle exporter who is the plaintiff in Case 71/80, that such effects have in fact appeared on the market in cattle. Owing to what the plaintiff describes as the special situation of the market in cattle in Ireland, exporters have not been able to pass the duty on to producers. Moreover, a very considerable number of cattle were sold and slaughtered just prior to the introduction of the duty, whereas market supplies decreased subsequently, and the result was an increase in imports from Northern Ireland of cattle which were exempt from the duty if sold to a processing undertaking within 14 days of their importation. The abolition of the duty produced the opposite effects. According to the plaintiffs in the two main actions the duty thus affected the machinery for the formation of market prices, market supply and intra-Community trade, at least in the cattle sector.

. . . . .

19. It is for the national court to decide whether the charge which it is called upon to consider has in fact had effects which obstruct the working of the machinery established by the common organizations of the market. With a view to the decision which has to be made in that respect by the national court it is, however, possible to identify certain features of Community law.
20. The essential aim of the machinery of the common organizations in question is to achieve price levels at the production and wholesale stages which take into account both the interests of Community production as a whole in the relevant sector and those of consumers, and which guarantee market supplies without encouraging over-production. Those aims might

be jeopardized by national measures adopted unilaterally, which have an appreciable influence, even if unintentionally, on price levels on the national market at the same stages, or on supplies on that market. In the case of a duty such as the one in this case, the risk of such influence depends not only on its rate and the period for which it is in force, but equally on the situation on the market in question and, as regards supplies, above all on how general its effect is, that is to say, the number of agricultural products to which it applies. A short-term duty on a large number of products may be neutral in the sense that it does not alter the structure of agricultural production. On the other hand, if the duty encourages producers to replace some of the production of the goods subject to the duty by production of other goods not subject thereto, the duty is liable to create distortion on a number of markets.

iv. Harmonization of national legislation

aa. Cases

(1) Hormones Case

United Kingdom v. *Council*; Case 68/86; Judgment of 23 February 1988 (not yet published).

Facts:

On 31 December 1985 the Council adopted Dir. No. 85/649/EEC prohibiting the use in lifestock farming of certain substances having a hormonal action. This directive was based on the EEC Treaty 'and in particular Article 43 thereof'.

The U.K. brought an action for annulment against the directive, basing itself, *inter alia*, on the lack of a sufficient legal basis.

The Court held:

. . . . .

Legal basis

4. The applicant, supported in all essential respects by the Danish

Government, claims that the contested directive, which was adopted by a qualified majority on the basis of Article 43 of the Treaty, should have been based not only on that article, but also on Article 100, which requires unanimity on the part of the Council. It considers that it was necessary to base the directive at issue on those two articles since, in addition to having agricultural policy objectives, it was designed, *inter alia*, for the purpose of approximating the provisions laid down by law, regulation or administrative action in the Member States to safeguard the interests and health of consumers. In the applicant's view, that aim is not covered by Article 43 of the Treaty but comes under Article 100. Previous practice on the part of the Council bears out the need for that dual legal basis.
5. The Council, the defendant, and the Commission, intervening, do not deny that one aspect of the directive at issue deals with the harmonization of national laws with a view to the protection of consumers and public health, but consider that that does not cause it to fall outside the sphere of the Common Agricultural Policy and that it is therefore covered by Article 43 of the Treaty.
6. It should be pointed out first of all that in this case the argument with regard to the correct legal basis is not a purely formal one, inasmuch as Articles 43 and 100 of the Treaty entail different rules regarding the manner in which the Council may arrive at its decision. The choice of the legal basis could thus affect the determination of the content of the contested directive.
7. Consequently, in order to determine whether the submission based on the alleged insufficiency of the legal basis of the directive at issue is well-founded it is necessary to consider whether the Council had the power to adopt it on the basis of Article 43 alone.
8. By virtue of Article 38 of the Treaty, the provisions of Articles 30 to 46 apply to the products listed in Annex II to the Treaty.
9. Article 43, moreover, must be interpreted in the light of Article 39, which sets out the objectives of the Common Agricultural Policy, and Article 40, which governs its implementation, providing, *inter alia*, that in order to attain the objectives set out in Article 39 a common organization of agricultural markets is to be established and that that organization may include all measures required to attain those objectives (judgment of 21 February 1979 in Case 138/78, *Stölting* v. *Hauptzollamt Hamburg-Jonas*, [1979] ECR 713).
10. The agricultural policy objectives set out in Article 39 of the Treaty include in particular the increasing of productivity by promoting technical progress and by ensuring the rational development of agricultural production and the optimum utilization of the factors of production. Moreover, Article 39 (2) (b) and (c) provides that in working out the Common Agricultural Policy account must be taken of the need to effect the appropriate adjustments by degrees and the fact that in the Member States agriculture constitutes a sector closely linked with the economy as

a whole. It follows that agricultural policy objectives must be conceived in such a manner as to enable the Community institutions to carry out their duties in the light of developments in agriculture and in the economy as a whole.
11. Measures adopted on the basis of Article 43 of the Treaty with a view to achieving those objectives under a common organization of the market as provided for in Article 40 (2) may include rules governing conditions and methods of production, quality and marketing of agricultural products. The common organizations of the markets contain many rules in that regard.
12. Efforts to achieve objectives of the Common Agricultural Policy, in particular under common organizations of the markets, cannot disregard requirements relating to the public interest such as the protection of consumers or the protection of the health and life of humans and animals, requirements which the Community institutions must take into account in exercising their powers.
13. Finally, it must be observed that according to Article 42 of the Treaty the rules on competition are to apply to production of and trade in agricultural products only to the extent determined by the Council within the framework of provisions adopted pursuant to Article 43. Consequently, in adopting such provisions the Council must also take into consideration the requirements of competition policy.
14. It follows from the provisions discussed above, taken as a whole, that Article 43 of the Treaty is the appropriate legal basis for any legislation concerning the production and marketing of agricultural products listed in Annex II to the Treaty which contributes to the achievement of one or more of the objectives of the Common Agricultural Policy set out in Article 39 of the Treaty. There is no need to have recourse to Article 100 of the Treaty where such legislation involves the harmonization of provisions of national law in that field.
15. As the Court has pointed out, in particular in its judgments of 29 November 1978 (Case 83/78, *Pigs Marketing Board* v. *Redmond*, [1978] ECR 2347) and 26 June 1979 (Case 177/78, *Pigs and Bacon Commission* v. *McCarren*, [1979] ECR 2161), Article 38 (2) of the Treaty gives precedence to specific provisions in the agricultural field over general provisions relating to the establishment of the common market.
16. Consequently, even where the legislation in question is directed both to objectives of agricultural policy and to other objectives which, in the absence of specific provisions, are pursued on the basis of Article 100 of the Treaty, that article, a general one under which directives may be adopted for the approximation of the laws of the Member States, cannot be relied on as a ground for restricting the field of application of Article 43 of the Treaty.
17. It is on the basis of the foregoing considerations that it must be determined whether or not the contested directive falls within the scope of Article 43 of the Treaty as described above.
18. In that regard, it must first be observed that there are common

organizations of the markets in the sectors of beef and veal (Regulation No. 805/68 of the Council of 27 June 1968, Official Journal, English Special Edition 1968 (I), p. 187), pigmeat (Regulation No. 2759/75 of the Council of 29 October 1975, Official Journal 1975 No. L 282, p. 1) and sheepmeat and goatmeat (Council Regulation No. 1837/80 of 27 June 1980, Official Journal 1980 No. L 183, p. 1), and that Article 2 of each of those regulations provides for the adoption of Community measures designed to promote better organization of production, processing and marketing, and to improve quality.
23. That finding cannot be affected by the fact, on which the applicant places some reliance, that the Council departed from its practice of basing measures in the field in question on Articles 43 and 100 of the Treaty.
24. On that point, it should be borne in mind that, as the Court held in its judgment of 26 March 1987 (in Case 45/86, *Commission* v. *Council*, [1987] ECR not yet reported), in the context of the organization of the powers of the Community the choice of the legal basis for a measure must be based on objective factors which are amenable to judicial review. A mere practice on the part of the Council cannot derogate from the rules laid down in the Treaty. Such a practice cannot therefore create a precedent binding on Community institutions with regard to the correct legal basis.
25. The applicant's first submission must therefore be rejected.

. . . . .

Sequel:

The outcome of the case was that the directive which had been adopted by means of the written procedure, was declared to be void, because of infringement of the Council's Rules of Procedure.

According to Article 6, para. 1, of the Council's Rules of Procedure the written procedure may only be applied when all the members of the Council accept it. As in the present case two Member States had expressly opposed it, the rule of Article 6, para. 1, had not been compiled with.

7. *Market Organization and individuals*

a. Protection of price level

i. Cases

(1) Russo Case

See page 649.

b. Non discrimination

i. Cases

(1) The Lion Case

Lion Loiret and Heantjens v. *Fonds d'Intervention*; Joined Cases 292 and 293/81; Preliminary ruling of 28 October 1982; [1982] ECR 3887.

Facts:

Regulation No 3330/74 of the Council of 19 December 1974 on the common organization of the market in sugar established a common system for trade with non-member countries, including measures intended to cover the difference between the prices applied outside and inside the Community, where world prices are lower than Community prices.

As regards exports of sugar outside the Community, the first subparagraph of Article 12 (1) of Regulation No 3330/74 provides that all exports are to be made conditional upon the submission of an export licence issued by Member States to any applicant, irrespective of the place of his establishment in the Community.

According to the fourth subparagraph of Article 12 (1) of the regulation the issue of a lience is conditional on the lodging of a deposit guaranteeing that the exportation will be effected during the period of validity of the licence and that the deposit is to be forfeited in full or in part if the transaction is not effected or is only partially effected within that period.

According to Article 19 (1) and (2) of the regulation, in the case of exports the difference between the quotations or prices on the world market and the prices in the Community may be covered by an export refund which is to be the same for the entire Community but may be varied according to destination.

The refund may be fixed in advance. In such cases, the advance-fixing is to be noted on the licence, which serves as a supporting document for the advance-fixing (second subparagraph of Article 12 (1)).

. . . . .

The second question

22. The second question submitted by the Tribunal Administratif seeks to determine whether Regulation No 3016/78 is vitiated by discriminatory measures which render it invalid. It is apparent from the explanations given by the plaintiffs that the second question stems from a twofold

objection raised before the Tribunal Administratif: on the one hand, the plaintiffs complain that the Commission has created special rules applicable to the sugar market without adopting parallel provisions for other market sectors; on the other hand, they claim that the Commission has made no provision for any adjustment of the refunds in favour of traders who opted for advance fixing, and therefore for certainty in their dealings, whilst for other traders the conversion rate which is valid on the day of the exportation is automatically applied.

23. Both those objections are based on the second paragraph of Article 40 (3) of the Treaty, by virtue of which common organizations of the markets must 'exclude any discrimination between producers or consumers within the Community'.

24. It is appropriate to point out in that regard that, in the first place, the fact that Regulation No 3016/78 is specific to the sugar market and that apparently there are no similar provisions for other market sectors cannot be described as discrimination. It is sufficient to note that each of the common organizations of the market embodies features specific to it and the organization of the market in sugar is moreover characterized by the particularly complex nature of its provisions. As a result, a comparison of the technical rules and procedures adopted in order to regulate the various sectors of the market cannot constitute a valid basis for the purpose of proving the complaint of discrimination between dissimilar products, which are subject to different rules and which, moreover, in no way compete with each other.

25. As regards the difference between the treatment of traders who have availed themselves of advance fixing and the treatment of other traders, the complaint of discrimination is once again misconceived since the purpose of advance fixing is precisely to crystallize, at the request of traders, the amount of the refund and of the monetary compensatory amounts at a date prior to the day of the exportation. The resultant difference of treatment is merely the consequence of a choice between two systems offered to traders under the regulation and they may choose one or the other freely according to their own requirements.

26. It is apparent therefore that the complaint of discrimination raised by the plaintiffs is without foundation and that the validity of Regulation No 3016/78 cannot be called in question in that regard.

(2) Balkan Import-Export Case

See pages 578, 610.

(3) Eridania Case II

See page 611.

c. The right freely to pursue a trade or profession and the right to property

i. Cases

(1) Hauer Case

Liselotte Hauer v. *Land Rheinland-Pfalz*; Case 44/79; Preliminary ruling of 13 December 1979; [1979] ECR 3740; [1980] 3 CMLR 42.

For the facts see the judgment below.

Regulation No 1162/76 of 17 May 1976. imposes a prohibition for a period of three years on all new planting of vines.

The Court held:

. . . . .

4. For her part, the plaintiff in the main action considers that the authorization applied for should be granted to her on the ground that the provision of Regulation No 1162/76 are contrary to her right to property and to her right freely to pursue a trade or profession, rights which are guaranteed by Articles 12 and 14 of the Grundgesetz of the Federal Republic of Germany.

. . . . .

The protection of fundamental rights in the Community legal order

13. In its order making the reference, the Verwaltungsgericht states that if Regulation No 1162/76 must be interpreted as meaning that it lays down a prohibition of general application so as to include even land appropriate for wine growing, that provision might have to be considered inapplicable in the Federal Republic of Germany owing to doubts existing with regard to its compatibility with the fundamental rights guaranteed by Articles 14 and 12 of the Grundgesetz concerning, respectively, the right to property and the right freely to pursue trade and professional activities.
14. As the Court declared in its judgment of 17 December 1970, *Internationale Handeslgesellschaft* [1970] ECR 1125, the question of a possible infringement of fundamental rights by a measure of the Community law itself. The introduction of special criteria for assessment stemming from the legislation or constitutional law of a particular Member State would,

by damaging the substantive unity and efficacy of Community law, lead inevitably to the destruction of the unity of the Common Market and the jeopardizing of the cohesion of the Community.
15. The Court also emphasized in the judgment cited, and later in the judgment of 14 May 1974, *Nold* [1974] ECR 491, that fundamental rights form an integral part of the general principles of the law, the observance of which it ensures; that in safeguarding those rights, the Court is bound to draw inspiration from constitutional traditions common to the Member States, so that measures which are incompatible with the fundamental rights recognized by the constitutions of those States are unacceptable in the Community; and that, similarly, international treaties for the protection of human rights on which the Member States have collaborated or of which they are signatories, can supply guidelines which should be followed within the framework of Community law. That conception was later recognized by the joint declaration of the European Parliament, the Council and the Commission of 5 April 1977, which, after recalling the case-law of the Court, refers on the one hand to the rights guaranteed by the constitutions of the Member States and on the other hand to the European Convention for the Protection of Human Rights and Fundamental Freedoms of 4 November 1950 (Official Journal 1977 No C 103, p. 1).
16. In these circumstances, the doubts evinced by the Verwaltungsgericht as to the compatibility of the provisions of Regulation No 1162/76 with the rules concerning the protection of fundamental rights must be understood as questioning the validity of the regulations in the light of Community law. In this regard, it is necessary to distinguish between, on the one hand, a possible infringement of the right to property and, on the other hand, a possible limitation upon the freedom to pursue a trade or profession.

The question of the right to property

17. The right to property is guaranteed in the Community legal order in accordance with the ideas common to the consitutions of the Member States, which are also reflected in the first Prorocol to the European Convention for the Protection of Human Rights.
18. Article 1 of that Protocol provides as follows:
    'Every natural or legal person is entitled to the peaceful enjoyment of his possession. No one shall be deprived of his possessions except in the public interest and subject to the conditions provided for by law and by the general principles of international law.
    The proceedings provisions shall not, however, in any way impair the right of a State to enforce such laws as it seems necessary to control the use of property in accordance with the general interest or to secure the payment of taxes or other contributions or penalties.'
19. Having declared that persons are entitled to the peaceful enjoyment of

their property, that provision envisages two ways in which the rights of a property owner may be impaired, according as the impairment is intended to deprive the owner of his right or to restrict that the prohibition on new planting cannot be considered to be an act depriving the owner of his property, since he remains free to dispose of it or to put to other use which are not prohibited. On the other hand, there is no doubt that that prohibition restricts the use of the property. In this regard, the second paragraph of Article 1 of the Protocol provides an important indication in so far as it recognizes the right of a State 'to enforce such laws as it deems necessary to control the use of property in accordance with the general interest'. Thus the Protocol accepts in principle the legality of restrictions upon the use of property, whilst at the same time limiting those restrictions to the extent to which they are deemed 'necessary' by a State for the protection of the 'general interest'. However, that provision does not enable a sufficient precise answer to be given to the question submitted by the Verwaltungsgericht.

20. Therefore, in order to be able to answer that question, it is necessary to consider also the indications provided by the constitutional rules and practices of the ten Member States. One of the first points to emerge in this regard is that those rules and practices permit the legislature to control the use of private property in accordance with the general interest. Thus some constitutions refer to the obligations arising out of the ownership of property (German Grundgesetz, Article 14 (2) first sentence), to its social function (Italian constitution, Article 42 (2), to the subordination of its use to the requirements of the common good (German Grundgesetz, Article 14 (2), second sentence, and the Irish constitution, Article 43.3.2°), or of social justice (Irish constitution, Article 43.2.1°). In all the Member States, numerous legislative measures have given concrete expression to that social function of the right to property. Thus in all the Member States there is legislation on agriculture and forestry, the water supply, the protection of the environment and town and country planning, which imposes restrictions, sometimes appreciable, on the use of real property.

21. More particularly, all the wine-producing countries of the Community have restrictive legislation, albeit of differeing severity, concerning the planting of vines, the selection of varieties and the methods of cultivation. In none of the countries concerned are those provisions considered to be incompatible in principle with the regard due to the right to property.

22. Thus it may be stated, taking into account the constitutional precepts common to the Member States and consistent legislative practices, in widely varying spheres, that the fact that Regulation No 1162/76 imposed restrictions on the new planting of vines cannot be challenged in principle. It is a type of restriction which is known and accepted as lawful, in identical or similar forms, in the constitutional structure of all the Member States.

23. However, that finding does not deal completely with the problem raised by the Verwaltungsgericht. Even if it is not possible to dispute in principle the Community's ability to restrict the exercise of the right to property in the context of a common organization of the market and for the purposes of a structural policy, it is still necessary to examine whether the restrictions introduced by the provisions in dispute in fact correspond to objectives of general interest pursued by the Community or whether, with regard to the aim pursued, they constitute a disproportionate and intolerable interference with the rights of the owner, impinging upon the very substance of the right to property. Such in fact is the plea submitted by the plaintiff in the main action, who considers that only the pursuit of a qualitative policy would permit the legislature to restrict the use of wine-growing property, with the result that she possesses an unassailable right from the moment that it is recognized that her land is suitable for wine growing. It is therefore necessary to identify the aim pursued by the disputed regulation and to determine whether there exists a reasonable relationship between the measures provided for by the regulation and the aim pursued by the Community in this case.

. . . . .

25. Taken as a whole, those measures show that the policy initiated and partially implemented by the Community consists of a common organization of the market in conjunction with a structural improvement in the wineproducing sector. Within the framework of the guidelines laid down by Article 39 of the Treaty that action seeks to achieve a double objective, namely, on the one hand, to establish a lasting balance on the wine market at a price level which is profitable for producers and fair to consumers and, secondly, to obtain an improvement in the quality of wines marketed. In order to attain that double objective of quantitative balance and qualitative improvements, the Community rules relating to the market in wine provide for an extensive range of measures which apply both at the production stage and at the marketing stage for wine.
26. In this regard, it is necessary to refer in particular to the provisions of Article 17 of Regulation No 816/70, reenacted in an extended form by Article 31 of Regulation No 337/79, which provide for the establishment by the Member States of forecasts of planting and production, coordinated within the framework of a compulsory Community plan. For the purpose of implementing that plan measures may be adopted concerning the planting, re-planting, grubbing-up or cessation of cultivation of vineyards.
27. It is in this context that Regulation No 1162/76 was adopted. It is apparent from the preamble to that regulation and from the economic

circumstances in which it was adopted, a feature of which was the information as from the 1974 harvest of permanent production surplusses, that the regulation fulfils a double function: on the one hand, it must enable an immediate brake to be put on the continued increase in the surpluses; on the other hand, it must win for the Community institutions the time necessary for the implementation of a structural policy designed to encourage high-quality production, whilst respecting the individual characteristics and needs of the different wineproducing regions of the Community, through the selection of land for grape growing and the selection of grape varieties, and through the regulation of production methods.

28. It was in order to fulfil that two fold purpose that the Council introduced by Regulation No 1162/76 a general prohibition on new plantings, without making any distinction, apart from certain narrowly defined exceptions, according to the quality of the land. It should be noted that, as regards its sweeping scope, the measure introduced by the Council is of a temporary nature. It is designed to deal immediately with a conjunctural situation characterized by surpluses, whilst at the same time preparing permanent structural measures.

29. Seen in this light, the measure criticized does not entail any undue limitation upon the exercise of the right to property. Indeed, the cultivation of new vineyards in a situation of continuous over-production would not have any effect, from the economic point of view, apart from increasing the volume of the surpluses; further, such an extension at that stage would entail the risk of making more difficult the implementation of a structural policy at the Community level in the event of such a policy resting on the application of criteria more stringent than the current provisions of national legislation concerning the selection of land accepted for wine growing.

30. Therefore it is necessary to conclude that the restriction imposed upon the use of property by the prohibition on the new planting of vines for a limited period by Regulation No 1162/76 is justified by the objectives of general interest pursued by the Community and does not infringe the substance of the right to property in the form in which it is recognized and protected in the Community legal order.

The question of the freedom to pursue trade or professional activities.

31. The applicant in the main action also submits that the prohibition on new plantings imposed by Regulation No 1162/76 infringes her fundamental rights in so far as its effect is to restrict her freedom to pursue her occupation as a wine-grower.

32. As the Court has already stated in its judgment of 14 May 1974, *Nold*, referred to above, although it is true that guarantees are given by the constitutional law of several Member States in respect of the freedom to

pursue trade or professional activities, the right thereby guaranteed, far from constituting an unfettered prerogative, must likewise be viewed in the light of the social function of the activities protected thereunder. In this case, it must be observed that the disputed Community measure does not in any way affect access to the occupation of wine-grower, or the freedom to pursue that occupation on land at present devoted to winegrowing. To the extent to which the prohibition on new plantings affects the free pursuit of the occupation of winegrowing, that limitation is no more than the consequence of the restriction upon the exercise of the right to property, so that the two restrictions merge. Thus the restriction upon the free pursuit of the occupation of wine-growing, assuming that it exists, is justified by the same reasons which justify the restriction placed upon the use of property.

33. Thus it is apparent from the foregoing that consideration of Regulation No 1162/76, in the light of the doubts expressed by the Verwaltungsgericht, has disclosed no factor of such a kind as to affect the validity of that regulation on account of its being contrary to the requirements flowing from the protection of fundamental rights in the Community.

d. Legitimate Expectations

i. Cases

(1) CNTA Case

See above page 102.

See Materials on the law of the European Communities Chapter Five part III A.

8. Literature

Avery, 'The Common Agricultural Policy: a turning point?' CML Rev. (1984) 481–505.

Barents, 'Hormones and the Growth of Community Agricultural law: Some Reflections on the Hormones Judgement (Case 68/86), LIEI 1988/1, p. 1–19.

Barents, 'The System of deposits in Community Agricultural law: Efficiency v. Proportionality', 10 ElRev. (1985), 239–249.

Snyder, *Law of the Common Agricultural Policy*, London, 1985.

Usher, *Legal Aspects of Agriculture in the European Community*, Oxford, 1988.

1. Cases

(1) ERTA Case

See at pages 6, 51, 169, 245, 676.

(2) French maritime labour code Case

See at pages 242, 356.

(3) Opinion of the Court (1/76)

See at pages 23, 676.

(4) Belgian Railway subsidies Case

Commission v. *Belgium*; Case 156/77; Judgment of 12 October 1978; [1978] ECR 1881.

For the facts see the judgment below.

The Court held:

1. By application lodged on 21 December 1977, the Commission requests the Court for a declaration that 'by not complying with the Commission Decision of 4 May 1976 on aid from the Belgian Government to the Société Nationale des Chemins de Fer Belges (SNCB) for through international railway tariff for coal and steel within the period laid down by the Commission, the Kingdom of Belgium has failed to fulfil an obligation under the Treaty'.
2. In Article 1 of its decision of 4 May 1976 (Official Journal 1976, No L 229, p. 24), the Commission declared that the financial aid granted by the Kingdom of Belgium to the SNCB under Article 3 (2) of Regulation (EEC) No 1170/70 of the Council of 4 June 1970 on the granting of aids for transport by rail, road and waterway, as amended by Regulation (EEC) No 1473/75 of 20 May 1975 (Official Journal 1975, No L 152, p. 1) is not compatible with the Common Market to the extent that it should be granted under Article 4 of the said regulation.
3. It also decided that the Kingdom of Belgium should take the necessary action, as soon as possible and at the most within three months, either to

terminate the aid in question or to modify its legal base in order that that aid might be granted under the provisions of Article 4 of Regulation No 1107/70.
4. As the Kingdom of Belgium did not comply with the decision, the Commission lodged this application before the Court of Justice pursuant to the second subparagraph of Article 93 (2) of the Treaty.

Admissibility

5. The Kingdom of Belgium objects that the application is inadmissible on the ground that it has no legal basis in the second subparagraph of Article 83 (2) of the Treaty.
6. In support of that objection it maintains that the compensation referred to both in Article 3 (2) and in Article 4 of Regulation No 1170/70, constituting aid within the meaning of Article 77 of the Treaty, is, by virtue of that provision, removed from the scope of Article 92 of the Treaty, the first paragraph of which specifies expressly that it applies 'save as otherwise provided in this Treaty'.
7. It claims that as the Commission's intervention in the present case cannot, therefore, be justified within the context of Article 92 of the Treaty, Article 93 cannot provide a valid legal basis for the present application.
8. Although in its defence the Belgian Government put forward this objection as 'a mere observation' made not 'as a defence but solely in order better to determine the problems relating to the substance of the case', it is however necessary to examine the validity of that objection.
9. By this objection, the Kingdom of Belgium claims in substance that the Commission Decision of 4 May 1976 is defective for lack of competence, a defect which, as it is one of those referred to in Article 173 of the Treaty, cannot, for the reasons given below, be examined within the context of this procedure.
10. Moreover, the effect of the application of Article 77 of the Treaty, which acknowledges that aid to transport is compatible with the Treaty only in well-defined cases which do not jeopardize the general interests of the Community, cannot be to exempt aid to transport from the general system of the Treaty concerning aid granted by the States and from the controls and procedures laid down therein.
11. To this effect, Article 3 (1) of Regulation No 1170/70, which was not amended by the above-mentioned Regulation No 1473/75, enumerates the cases and conditions in which an aid granted under Article 77 of the Treaty may be justified pursuant to that provision and Article 2 thereof specifies that "Articles 92 to 94 of the Treaty shall apply to aids granted for transport by rail, road and inland waterway'.
12. Since the Commission's action in this case was motivated by the finding that the aid in question comes within the prohibition laid down in Article 92 of the Treaty the application lodged as a result of that action therefore

has its legal basis in the second subparagraph of Article 93 (2) of the Treaty. The objection of inadmissibility raised by the Kingdom of Belgium is therefore unfounded.

The substance of the case

14. The Kingdom of Belgium claims essentially that the initiation of a procedure on the basis of Article 93 of the Treaty against the aid in question is all the more unjustified in the present case, since the Commission has not established that this aid fulfils the conditions of incompatibility laid down in Article 92 (1).
15. Therefore the Kingdom of Belgium contests the validity of the present application by calling in question the legality of the decision of 4 May 1976 by which the Commission declared that the aid in question was incompatible with the common market.
16. The Commission maintains that since the Belgian Government did not lodge against that decision an application for annulment within the period of two months laid down by the third paragraph of Article 173 of the Treaty it is therefore now barred from contesting the legality of that decision within the context of these proceedings.
17. Article 92 (2) of the Treaty, which gives the Commission the necessary power to ensure application of an compliance with the principle laid down in Article 92, provides for a special procedure enabling that institution to give a ruling, apart from the exceptional and specific case referred to in the third subparagraph of Article 93 (2), as to the compatibility with the Treaty of both aid granted by the State or through State responses and, pursuant to Article 93 (3), of plans to grant or alter aid and to decide if necessary that is should be abolished or altered.
18. For this purpose, the first paragraph of Article 93 (2) provides that if, after giving notice to the parties concerned to submit their comments, the Commission finds that aid is not compatible with the common market having regard to Article 92, or that such aid is being misused, 'it shall decide that the State concerned shall abolish or alter such aid within a period of time to be determined by the Commission'.
19. Such a decision is under the fourth paragraph of Article 189 of the Treaty, 'binding in its entirety upon those to whom it is addressed.'

    In so far as the Member State to whom it is addressed considers that it is inable to comply with that decision because it is legally unfounded it may contest the legality thereof by having recourse to the legal remedies available to it under Article 173 of the Treaty on the conditions laid down by that provision.
21. In view of the fact that the periods within which applications must be lodged are intended to safeguard legal certainty by preventing Community measures which involve legal effects from being called in question indefinitely, it is impossible for a Member State which has allowed the

strict time-limit laid down in the third paragraph of Article 173 to expire without contesting by the means under that Article 184 of the Treaty when an application is lodged by the Commission on the basis of the second subparagraph of Article 93 (2) of the Treaty.
22. First, the objection provided for in Article 184 of the Treaty is limited under that provision to proceedings 'in which a regulation of the Council or of the Commission is in issue' and can in no way be invoked by a Member State to whom an individual decision has been addressed.
23. Secondly, it follows from the wording of the second subparagraph of Article 93 (2) of the Treaty, in particular from the words 'in derogation from the provisions of Articles 169 and 170', that the purpose of the application referred to therein may only be a declaration that the Member State concerned has failed to comply with a Commission decision compelling it to abolish or alter an aid within a specific period, whereas in the case of Articles 169 and 170 the application is directed against any failure of a Member State to fulfil one of its obligations under the Treaty.
24. In these circumstances, to permit a Member State to whom a decision adopted under the first subparagraph of Article 93 (2) has been addressed to call in issue the validity of that decision when an application referred to in the second subparagraph of Article 93 (2) has been lodged, in spite of the expiry of the period laid down in the third paragraph of Article 173 of the Treaty, would be impossible to reconcile with the principles governing the legal remedies established by the Treaty and would jeopardize the stability of that system and the principle of legal certainty upon which it is based.
25. Although it is true that the validity of a Community measure may be called in question by means of the procedure for obtaining a preliminary ruling referred to in Article 177 of the Treaty, in spite of the expiry of the period laid down in the third paragraph of Article 173 such a procedure, which is laid down in respect of all measures adopted by the institutions and corresponds solely to the requirements of the national courts, is nevertheless subject to objectives and rules different from those which govern the applications referred to in Article 173 of the Treaty, and cannot justify a derogation from the principle of the time-barring of applications as a result of the expiry of the period within which proceedings must be brought, without thereby depriving Article 173 of its legal significance.
26. In the present case the Kingdom of Belgium does not contest it has not complied with the Commission Decision of 4 May 1976.
27. The Kingdom of Belgium has therefore failed to fulfil its obligation under Article 93 in conjunction with Article 189 of the Treaty.

. . . . .

(5) Failing transport policy Case

European Parliament v. *Council*; Case 13/83; Judgment of 22 May 1985; [1985] ECR 1513

Facts:

See the judgment below.

The Court held:

1. By an application lodged at the Court Registry on 24 January 1983 the European Parliament brought an action under the first paragraph of Article 175 of the EEC Treaty for a declaration that the Council has infringed the EEC Treaty, in particular Article 3 (e), 61, 74, 75 and 84 thereof, by failing to introduce a common policy for transport and in particular to lay down the framework of such a policy in a binding manner and further by failing to reach a decision on 16 specified proposals submitted by the Commission in relation to transport.
2. The common transport policy is included among the activities in which the Community must engage according to Article 3 of the EEC Treaty in order to establish a common market and progressively approximate the economic policies of the Member States. It is the subject of Title IV of Part Two of the Treaty, namely the part concerned with the 'foundations of the Community'. The first article under that title, Article 74, lays down that the objectives of the Treaty are to be pursued in the transport sector 'within the framework of a common transport policy'. Article 75 (1) provides that for the purpose of implementing Article 74 the Council must lay down, on a proposal from the Commission and after consulting the Economic and Social Committee and the European Parliament:
   (a) common rules applicable to international transport to or from the territory of a Member State or passing across the territory of one or more Member States;
   (b) the conditions under which non-resident carriers may operate transport services within a Member State;
   (c) any other appropriate provisions.'
   Article 75 (2) states that the provisions referred to in (a) and (b) of paragraph 1 are to be laid down during the transitional period.

. . . . .

62. It should first be borne in mind that Article 61 (1) provides that freedom

to provide services in the field of transport is to be governed by the provisions of the Title relating to transport. Application of the principles governing freedom to provide services, as established in particular by Articles 59 and 60 of the Treaty, must therefore be achieved, according to the Treaty, by introducing a common transport policy and, more particularly, by laying down common rules applicable to international transport and the conditions under which non-resident carriers may operate transport services, the rules and conditions of which are referred to in Article 75 (1) (a) and (b) and necessarily affect freedom to provide services.

63. Accordingly, the argument of the Netherlands Government to the effect that on the expiry of the transitional period the provisions of Articles 59 and 60 are of direct application even in the transport sector cannot be accepted.

64. However, the Parliament, the Commission and the Netherlands Government have rightly contended that the obligations imposed on the Council by Article 75 (1) (a) and (b) include the introduction of freedom to provide services in relation to transport, and that the scope of that obligation is clearly defined by the Treaty. Pursuant to Articles 59 and 60 the requirements of freedom to provide services include, as the Court held in its judgment of 17 December 1981 (Case 279/80 *Webb* [1981] ECR 3305), the removal of any discrimination against the person providing services based on his nationality or the fact that he is established in a Member State other than that where the services are to be provided.

65. It follows that in that respect the Council does not have the discretion on which it may rely in other areas of the common transport policy. Since the result to be achieved is determined by the combined effect of Articles 59, 60, 61 and 75 (1) (a) and (b), the exercise of a certain measure of discretion is allowed only as regards the means employed to obtain that result, bearing in mind, as required by Article 75, those features which are special to transport.

66. In so far as the obligations laid down in Article 75 (1) (a) and (b) relate to freedom to provide services, therefore, they are sufficiently well-defined for disregard of them to be the subject of a finding of failure to act pursuant to Article 175.

67. The Council was required to extend freedom to provide services to the transport sector before the expiry of the transitional period, pursuant to Article 75 (1) (a) and (2), in so far as the extension related to international transport to or from the territory of a Member State or across the territory of one or more Member States and, within the framework of freedom to provide services in the transport sector, to lay down, pursuant to Article 75 (1) (b) and (2), the conditions under which non-resident carriers may operate transport services within a Member State. It is common ground that the necessary measures for that purpose have not yet been adopted.

68. On that point the Court must therefore hold that the Council has failed to act since it has failed to adopt measures which ought to have been adopted before the expiry of the transitional period and whose subject-matter and nature may be determined with a sufficient degree of precision.
69. The Parliament, the Commission and the Netherlands Government also refer to the legal situation which would arise if, after judgment against it, the Council still failed to act. That problem is, however, hypothetical. Article 176 requires the Council to take the measures necessary to comply with this judgment; since that provision does not prescribe a time-limit for such compliance it must be inferred that the Council has a reasonable period for that purpose. It is not necessary in the present judgment to consider what would be the consequences if the Council still fails to act.
70. Accordingly, the Court must find that in breach of the Treaty the Council has failed to ensure freedom to provide services in the sphere of international transport and to lay down the conditions under which non-resident carriers may operate transport services in a Member State.
71. The Council is at liberty to adopt, in addition to the requisite measures of liberalization, such accompanying measures as it considers necessary and to do so in the order it holds to be appropriate.

(6) Asjes (Nouvelles Frontières) Case

Ministère Public v. *Lucas Asjes and Others*; joined Cases 209–213/84; judgment of 30 April 1986, [1986] ECR 1925.

Facts:

See the judgment below.

The Court held:

1. By five judgments of 2 March 1984, received at the Court on 17 August 1984, the tribunal de police de Paris referred to the Court a question on the interpretation of certain provisions of the EEC Treaty for a preliminary ruling under Article 177 of that Treaty in order to enable it to appraise the compatibility with those provisions of the compulsory approval procedure laid down by French law for air tariffs.
2. That question was raised in several criminal proceedings against the executives of airlines and travel agencies who had been charged with infringing Articles L 330–3, R 330–9 and R 330–15 of the French Civil Aviation Code when selling air tickets by applying tariffs that had not

been submitted to the Minister for Civil Aviation for approval or were different from the approved tariffs.
3. Article L 330–3 provides that air transport may be provided only by undertakings approved by the Minister for Civil Aviation. Those undertakings must also submit their tariffs to the Minister for approval. Article R 330–9 specifies what items must be submitted when approval is sought. The second paragraph of Article R 330–9 provides that foreign undertakings are also covered by the rules. Under Article R 330–15 infringements of those rules are punishable by a prison sentence of between 10 days and one month or a fine of between FF 600 and FF 1 000 or both. A decision approving the tariff proposed by an airline therefore has the effect of rendering that tariff binding on all traders selling tickets of that company in respect of the journey specified in the application for approval.
4. When the cases came before it, the tribunal de police de Paris considered the issue of the compatibility of the system set up by the aforementioned provisions with the EEC Treaty, and in particular with Article 85 (1), in so far as in the tribunal's view the French rules made provision for concerted action between the airlines that was contrary to Article 85. The tribunal also dismissed the objection that Article 85 was not applicable to air transport by virtue of Article 84 (2) on the ground that the aim of that provision was merely to leave the organization of a common policy in that sector to be decided by the Council, without removing it from the ambit of other rules in the Treaty such as Article 85.
5. The tribunal de police de Paris thereupon decided to stay the proceedings and ask the Court for a 'ruling as to whether Articles L 330–3, R 330–9 and R 330–15 of the code de l'aviation civile are in conformity with Community law'.

. . . . .

C. Applicability of the competition rules in the Treaty to air transport

35. It should be noted that Article 74, the first article in the Title on transport, provides: 'The objectives of this Treaty shall, in matters governed by this Title, be pursued by Member States within the framework of a common transport policy.'
36. It is clear from the very wording of Article 74 that the objectives of the Treaty, including that set out in Article 3 (f), namely the institution of a system ensuring that competition in the common market is not distorted, are equally applicable to the transport sector.
37. Article 61 of the Treaty provides that freedom to provide services in the field of transport is governed not by the provisions of the chapter on services but by the provisions of the Title relating to the common transport policy. In the transport sector, therefore, the objective laid

down in Article 59 of the Treaty of abolishing during the transitional period restrictions on freedom to provide services should have been attained in the framework of the common policy provided for in Articles 74 and 75.
38. However, no other provision in the Treaty makes its application to the transport sector subject to the realization of a common transport policy.
39. As regards the competition rules in particular, it should be noted that under Article 77 aids are compatible with the Treaty 'if they meet the needs of coordination of transport or if they represent reimbursement for the discharge of certain obligations inherent in the concept of a public service'. Such a provision clearly presupposes that the Treaty competition rules, of which the provisions on State aids are part, are applicable to the transport sector whether or not a common transport policy has been established.
40. It should also be noted that where the Treaty intended to remove certain activities from the ambit of the competition rules, it made an express derogation to that effect. That was done in the case of the production of and trade in agricultural products to which, under Article 42, the competition rules apply 'only to the extent determined by the Council within the framework of Article 43 (2) and (3) and in accordance with the procedure laid down therein, account being taken of the objectives set out in Article 39'.
41. As regards transport there is no provision in the Treaty which, like Article 42, excludes the application of the competition rules or makes it subject to a decision by the Council.
42. It must therefore be concluded that the rules in the Treaty on competition, in particular Articles 85 to 90, are applicable to transport.
43. As regards air transport in particular, it should be noted that, as is clear from the actual wording of Article 84 and its position in the Treaty, that article is intended merely to define the scope of Article 74 *et seq.* as regards different modes of transport, by distinguishing between transport by rail, road and inland waterway, covered by paragraph (1), and sea and air transport, covered by paragraph (2).
44. The Court ruled in its judgment of 4 April 1974 (*supra*) that Article 84 (2) serves merely to exclude, so long as the Council has not decided otherwise, sea and air transport from the rules of Title IV of Part Two of the Treaty relating to the common transport policy.
45. It follows that air transport remains, on the same basis as the other modes of transport, subject to the general rules of the Treaty, including the competition rules.

2. Literature

P. J. Kuyper, Legal Problems of a Community transport policy; with special reference to air transport', (1985/2) LIEI 69.

Chapter Six

External relations

I. The external competences of the EEC

A. Introduction

The extent to which the European Communities can participate in the field of international relations depends in first instance on their *capacity* to enter into international legal commitments given the scope of the Treaties establishing the Communities. Whether the Communities in a given case also have the *authority* is a matter which is to be established subsequently.

As far as the capacity is concerned the Court has established in the first case dealing with this matter that the scope of the external capacity of the Communities is as wide as 'the extent of the field of objectives defined in part one of the (EEC) Treaty' (*ERTA Case* infra pp. 6, 51, 169, 245, 676.)

The authority arises not only from an express conferment by the Treaty (e.g. Article 113) but may equally flow implicitly from other provisions of the (EEC) Treaty, from the Act of Accession and from the measures adopted within the framework of those provisions by the Community Institutions' (*Kramer Case*; 3, 4, 6/76; [1976] ECR 1305)

The jurisprudence of the Court in the two cases referred to as well as *Opinion 1/76* (and *Euratom Opinion 1/78*) may be summarized as follows: Each Community's competence under the Treaties to lay down legally binding measures comprises internal action (regulations, directives, decisions) as well as external action, the latter, however, only under the condition that the external measure is necessary to achieve one of the objectives of the Treaties. 'One cannot, ... , in implementing the provisions of the Treaty, separate the category of measures internal to the Community from that of external relations'. (*ERTA Case*).

The fact that the Community has authority in a given case in a particular field does not necessarily mean that this fact excludes the Member States from laying down rules in relation to the same subject. Only 'each time the Community, with a view to implementing a common policy, envisaged by the Treaty, lays down common rules, ... , the Member States no longer have the right, ... , to contract obligations towards non-Member States affecting these rules ... This Community authority excludes the possibility of a concurrent authority on the part of the Member States' (*ERTA Case*). Phrased in a

675

negative way', ... the Community not yet having fully exercised its functions in the matter, ... , the Member States had the power to assume commitments ... (internationally). (*Kramer Case*). Whether this means that each time the Community *has* enacted common rules its external competence in the matter necessarily becomes exclusive remains to be seen. *E.g.* directives enacted on the basis of Article 100 EEC are these *per se* 'the implementation of a common policy' where these directives only serve for the 'approximation of such provisions of law (etc.) in Member States as directly affect the establishment or functioning of the Common Market' (Article 100 EEC). To the extent the Member States remain competent internally under the Directive also external competence could remain.

B. CASES

(1) ERTA Case

See pages 6, 51, 169, 245, 666.

(2) Opinion of the Court 1/76

Opinion 1/76 of 26 April 1977; see pages 23, 666.

C. LITERATURE

Hartley, 'International Agreements and the Community legal system, Some recent developments', 8 EL Rev. 1983, 383–394.
Koers, 'The European Economic Community and International Fisheries Organisations', LIEI 1984/1, 113–133.
Lachmann, 'International Legal Personality of the EC: Capacity and Competence', LIEI 1984/1, 3–23.
Leenen, 'Participation of the EEC in International Environmental Agreements', LIEI 1984/1, 93–113.
Mastellone, 'The external relations of the EEC in the field of environmental protection', (1981) ICLQ, 104–117.
Simmonds, 'The Community's Participation in the U.N. Law of the Sea Convention' in: *Essays in European Law and Integration*, David O'Keeffe (ed.), pp. 179–197.
Simmonds, 'The U.N. Convention on the Law of the Sea 1982 and the Community's Mixed Agreements Practice', in: *Mixed Agreements*, David O'Keeffe (ed.), p. 199–207.
Temple Lang, 'The Ozone Layer Convention: A new solution to the Question of Community Participation in Mixed International Agreements', 23 CML Rev. (1986), pp. 157–176.

Timmermans, Völker, (eds.) *Division of Powers between the European Communities and their Member States in the field of External Relations*, Deventer, 1980.

II. The relationship between community law and international law: the question of direct effect.

A. INTRODUCTION

At an early stage the Court of Justice was in a position to give an indication of the relationship between Community law and international treaty law. In the *Van Gend en Loos Case*, the Court observed that ' ... the Community constitutes a new legal order of international law ... ' (pp. 110, 160, 255) whereas considering the place of an international agreement (the Association Agreement with Greece) within the Community legal system the Court ruled that: 'The Athens Agreement was concluded by the Council under Article 228 and 238 ... This Agreement is therefore, in so far as concerns the Community, an act of one of the Institutions ... The provisions of the Agreement, form an intergral part of Community law'. *(Haegeman Case;* 181/73 [1974] ECR 459).

In order for a Community subject to be able to contest a Community act before a court on the basis of rights claimed under international law, the Community must not only be bound by that provision of international law but also one must consider the meaning, the spirit, the general scheme and the form of the provision and of the agreement in which it is included. See further the *Kupferberg Case* below.

B. CASES

(1) Kupferberg Case

Hauptzollamt Mainz v. *C.A. Kupferberg & Cie KG a.A.*; Case 104/81; Preliminary Ruling of 26 October 1982; [1982] ECR 3659.

Facts:

See the case below.

The Court held:

1. By order of 24 March 1981, received at the Court on 29 April 1981, the Bundesfinanzhof [Federal Finance Court] referred to the Court for a preliminary ruling under Article 177 of the EEC Treaty a number of

questions on the interpretation of Article 95 of the Treaty and the first paragraph of Article 21 of the Agreement between the European Economic Community and the Portuguese Republic which was signed at Brussels on 22 July 1972 and concluded and adopted on behalf of the Community by Regulation No 2844/72 of the Council of 19 December 1972 (Official Journal, English Special Edition 1972 (31 December), L 301, p. 165).
2. The main proceedings are between a German importer and the Hauptzollamt [Principal Customs Office] Mainz on the question of the rate of the duty known as 'monopoly equalization duty' (Monopolausgleich) which was applied on the release for free circulation, on 26 August 1976, of a consignment of port wines from Portugal.

. . . . .

6. . . . . . Hauptzollamt Mainz levied on the importation in question the sum of DM 18 103.80 per hectolitre of wine-spirit. The importer brought an action against that decision before the Finanzgericht Rheinland-Pfalz [Finance Court, Rhineland-Palatinate] which varied the decision by reducing the monopoly equalization duty on the basis of paragraph 79 (2) of the Branntweinmonopolgesetz and the first paragraph of Article 21 of the Agreement between the Community and Portugal which reads as follows:

'The Contracting Parties shall refrain from any measure or practice of an internal fiscal nature establishing, whether directly or indirectly, discrimination between the products of one Contracting Party and like products originating in the territory of the other Contracting Party.'

In doing so the Finanzgericht treated the imported port wines in the same was as it would have treated domestic liqueur wines if there had been added to the latter spirits from fruit farm cooperative distilleries produced within the aforesaid limits.
7. The Hauptzollamt Mainz appealed on a point of law to the Bundesfinanzhof which referred the following questions to the Court:
   1. Is the first paragraph of Article 21 of the Agreement between the European Economic Community and the Portuguese Republic of 22 July 1972, adopted and published by Regulation (EEC) No 2844/72 of the Council of 19 December 1972, directly applicable law and does it give rights to individual Common Market citizens? If so, does it contain a prohibition of discrimination in like terms to the first paragraph of Article 95 of the EEC Treaty and does it also apply to the importation of port wines?
   2. . . .

. . . . .

First part of the question

9. In the first place the Bundesfinanzhof wishes to know whether the German importer may rely on the said Article 21 before the German court in the proceedings which it has brought against the decision of the tax authorities.
10. In the observations which they have submitted to the Court, the Governments of the Kingdom of Denmark, the Federal Republic of Germany, the French Republic and the United Kingdom have laid the most stress on the question whether a provision which is part of one of the free-trade agreements made by the Community with the member countries of the European Free Trade Association is in principle capable of having direct effect in the Member States of the Community.
11. The Treaty establishing the Community has conferred upon the institutions the power not only of adopting measures applicable in the Community but also of making agreements with non-member countries and international organizations in accordance with the provisions of the Treaty. According to Article 228 (2) these agreements are binding on the institutions of the Community and on Member States. Consequently, it is incumbent upon the Community institutions, as well as upon the Member States, to ensure compliance with the obligations arising from such agreements.
12. The measures needed to implement the provisions of an agreement concluded by the Community are to be adopted, according to the state of Community law for the time being in the areas affected by the provisions of the agreement, either by the Community institutions or by the Member States. That is particularly true of agreements such as those concerning free trade where the obligations entered into extend to many areas of a very diverse nature.
13. In ensuring respect for commitments arising from an agreement concluded by the Community institutions the Member States fulfil an obligation not only in relation to the non-member country concerned but also and above all in relation to the Community which has assumed responsibility for the due performance of the agreement. That is why the provisions of such an agreement, as the Court has already stated in its judgment of 30 April 1974 in Case 181/73 *Haegeman* [1974] ECR 449, form an integral part of the Community legal system.
14. It follows from the Community nature of such provisions that their effect in the Community may not be allowed to vary according to whether their application is in practice the responsibility of the Community institutions or of the Member States and, in the latter case, according to the effects in the internal legal order of each Member State which the law of that State assigns to international agreements concluded by it. Therefore it is for the Court, within the framework of its jurisdiction in interpreting the provisions of agreements, to ensure their uniform application throughout the Community.

15. The governments which have submitted observations to the Court do not deny the Community nature of the provisions of agreements concluded by the Community. They contend, however, that the generally recognized criteria for determining the effects of provisions of a purely Community origin may not be applied to provisions of a free-trade agreement concluded by the Community with a non-member country.
16. In that respect the governments base their arguments in particular on the distribution of powers in regard to the external relations of the Community, the principal of reciprocity governing the application of free-trade agreements, the institutional framework established by such agreements in order to settle differences between the contracting parties and safeguard clauses allowing the parties to derogate from the agreements.
17. It is true that the effects within the Community of provisions of an agreement concluded by the Community with a non-member country may not be determined without taking account of the international origin of the provisions in question. In conformity with the principles of public international law Community institutions which have power to negotiate and conclude an agreement with a non-member country are free to agree with that country what effect the provisions of the agreement are to have in the internal legal order of the contracting parties. Only if that question has not been settled by the agreement does it fall for decision by the courts having jurisdiction in the matter, and in particular by the Court of Justice within the framework of its jurisdiction under the Treaty, in the same manner as any question of interpretation relating to the application of the agreement in the Community.
18. According to the general rules of international law there must be *bona fide* performance of every agreement. Although each contracting party is responsible for executing fully the commitments which it has undertaken it is nevertheless free to determine the legal means appropriate for attaining that end in its legal system unless the agreement, interpreted in the light of its subject-matter and purpose, itself specifies those means. Subject to that reservation the fact that the courts of one of the parties consider that certain of the stipulations in the agreement are of direct application whereas the courts of the other party do not recognize such direct application is not in itself such as to constitute a lack of reciprocity in the implementation of the agreement.
19. As the governments have emphasized, the free-trade agreements provide for joint committees responsible for the administration of the agreements and for their proper implementation. To that end they may make recommendations and, in the cases expressly provided for by the agreement in question, take decisions.
20. The mere fact that the contracting parties have established a special institutional framework for consultations and negotiations *inter se* in relation to the implementation of the agreement is not in itself sufficient to exclude all judicial application of that agreement. The fact that a court of one of the parties applies to a specific case before it a provision of the

agreement involving an unconditional and precise obligation and therefore not requiring any prior intervention on the part of the joint committee does not adversely affect the powers that the agreement confers on that committee.
21. As regards the safeguard clauses which enable the parties to derogate from certain provisions of the agreement it should be observed that they apply only in specific circumstances and as a general rule after consideration within the joint committee in the presence of both parties. Apart from specific situations which may involve their application, the existence of such clauses, which, moreover, do not affect the provisions prohibiting tax discrimination, is not sufficient in itself to affect the direct applicability which may attach to certain stipulations in the agreement.
22. It follows from all the foregoing considerations that neither the nature nor the structure of the Agreement concluded with Portugal may prevent a trader from relying on the provisions of the said Agreement before a court in the Community.
23. Nevertheless the question whether such a stipulation is unconditional and sufficiently precise to have direct effect must be considered in the context of the Agreement of which it forms part. In order to reply to the question on the direct effect of the first paragraph of Article 21 of the Agreement between the Community and Portugal it is necessary to analyse the provision in the light of both the object and purpose of the Agreement and of its context.
24. The purpose of the Agreement is to create a system of free trade in which rules restricting commerce are eliminated in respect of virtually all trade in products originating in the territory of the parties, in particular by abolishing customs duties and charges having equivalent effect and eliminating quantitative restrictions and measures having equivalent effect.
25. Seen in that context the first paragraph of Article 21 of the Agreement seeks to prevent the liberalization of the trade in goods through the abolition of customs duties and charges having equivalent effect and quantitative restrictions and measures having equivalent effect from being rendered nugatory by fiscal practices of the Contracting Parties. That would be so if the product imported of one party were taxed more heavily than the similar domestic products which it encounters on the market of the other party.
26. It appears from the foregoing that the first paragraph of Article 21 of the Agreement imposes on the Contracting Parties an unconditional rule against discrimination in matters of taxation, which is dependent only on a finding that the products affected by a particular system of taxation are of like nature, and the limits of which are the direct consequence of the purpose of the Agreement. As such this provision may be applied by a court and thus produce direct effects throughout the Community.
27. The first part of the first question should therefore be answered to the effect that the first paragraph of Article 21 of the Agreement between the

Community and Portugal is directly applicable and capable of conferring upon individual traders rights which the courts must protect.

. . . . .

(2) International Fruit Company Case III

International Fruit Company v. *Produktschap voor Groenten en Fruit*; Case 21–24/72; Preliminary ruling of 12 December 1972; [1972] ECR 1226; [1975] 2 CMLR 1.

Facts:

See the judgment below.

The Court held:

. . . . .

2. The first question invites the Court to rule whether the validity of measures adopted by the institutions of the Community also refers, within the meaning of Article 177 of the EEC Treaty, to their validity under international law.
3. The second question, which is raised should the reply to the first question be in the affirmative, asks whether Regulations Nos 459/70, 565/70 and 686/70 of the Commission – which laid down, by way of protective measures, restrictions on the importation of apples from third countries – are 'invalid as being contrary to Article XI of the General Agreement on Tariffs and Trade (GATT)', hereinafter called 'the General Agreement'.
4. According to the first paragraph of Article 177 of the EEC Treaty 'The Court of justice shall have jurisdiction to give preliminary rulings concerning ... the validity ... of acts of the institutions of the Community'.
5. Under that formulation, the jurisdiction of the Court cannot be limited by the grounds on which the validity of those measures may be contested.
6. Since such jurisdiction extends to all grounds capable of invalidating those measures, the Court is obliged to examine whether their validity may be affected by reason of the fact that they are contrary to a rule of international law.
7. Before the incompatibility of a Community measure with a provision of international law can affect the validity of that measure, the Community must first of all be bound by that provision.

8. Before invalidity can be relied upon before a national court, that provision of international law must also be capable of conferring rights on citizens of the Community which they can invoke before the courts.
9. It is therefore necessary to examine whether the General Agreement satisfies these two conditions.
10. It is clear that at the time when they concluded the Treaty establishing the European Economic Community the Member States were bound by the obligations of the General Agreement.
11. By concluding a treaty between them they could not withdraw from their obligations to third countries.
12. On the contrary, their desire to observe the undertakings of the General Agreement follows as much from the very provisions of the EEC Treaty as from the declarations made by Member States on the presentation of the Treaty to the contracting parties of the General Agreement in accordance with the obligation under Article XXIV thereof.
13. That intention was made clear in particular by Article 110 of the EEC Treaty, which seeks the adherence of the Community to the same aims as those sought by the General Agreement, as well as by the first paragraph of Article 234 which provides that the rights and obligations arising from agreements concluded before the entry into force of the Treaty, and in particular multilateral agreements concluded with the participation of Member States, are not affected by the provisions of the Treaty.
14. The Community has assumed the functions inherent in the tariff and trade policy, progressively during the transitional period and in their entirety on the expiry of that period, by virtue of Articles 111 and 113 of the Treaty.
15. By conferring those powers on the Community, the Member States showed their wish to bind it by the obligations entered into under the General Agreement.
16. Since the entry into force of the EEC Treaty and more particularly, since the setting up of the common external tariff, the transfer of powers which has occurred in the relations between Member States and the Community has been put into concrete form in different ways within the framework of the General Agreement and has been recognized by the other contracting parties.
17. In particular, since that time, the Community, acting through its own institutions, has appeared as a partner in the tariff negotiations and as a party to the agreements of all types concluded within the framework of the General Agreement, in accordance with the provisions of Article 114 of the EEC Treaty which provides that the tariff and trade agreements 'shall be concluded ... on behalf of the Community'.
18. It therefore appears that, in so far as under the EEC Treaty the Community has assumed the powers previously exercised by Member States in the area governed by the General Agreement, the provisions of that agreement have the effect of binding the Community.
19. It is also necessary to examine whether the provisions of the General Agreement confer rights on citizens of the Community on which they can

rely before the courts in contesting the validity of a Community measure.
20. For this purpose, the spirit, the general scheme and the terms of the General Agreement must be considered.
21. This agreement which, according to its preamble, is based on the principle of negotiations undertaken on the basis of 'reciprocal and mutually advantageous arrangements' is characterized by the great flexibility of its provisions, in particular those conferring the possibility of derogation, the measures to be taken when confronted with exceptional difficulties and the settlement of conflicts between the contracting parties.
22. Consequently, according to the first paragraph of Article XXII 'Each contracting party shall accord sympathetic consideration to, and shall afford adequate opportunity for consultation regarding, such representations as may be made by any other contracting party with respect to ... all matters affecting the operation of this Agreement'.
23. According to the second paragraph of the same article, 'the contracting parties' – this name designating 'the contracting parties acting jointly' as is stated in the first paragraph of Article XXV – 'may consult with one or more contracting parties on any question to which a satisfactory solution cannot be found through the consultations provided under paragraph (1)'.
24. If any contracting party should consider 'that any benefit accruing to it directly or indirectly under this Agreement is being nullified or impaired or that the attainment of any objective of the Agreement is being impeded as a result of', *inter alia*, 'the failure of another contracting party to carry out its obligations under this Agreement', Article XXIII lays down in detail the measures which the parties concerned, or the contracting parties acting jointly, may or must take in regard to such a situation.
25. Those measures include, for the settlement of conflicts, written recommendations or proposals which are to be 'given sympathetic consideration', investigations possibly followed by recommendations, consultations between or decisions of the *contracting parties*, including that of authorizing certain contracting parties to suspend the application to any others of any obligations or concessions under the General Agreement and, finally, in the event of such suspension, the power of the party concerned to withdraw from that agreement.
26. Finally, where by reason of an obligation assumed under the General Agreement or of a concession relating to a benefit, some producers suffer or are threatened with serious damage, Article XIX gives a contracting party power unilaterally to suspend the obligation and to withdraw or modify the concession, either after consulting the contracting parties jointly the failing agreement between the contracting parties concerned, or even, if the matter is urgent and on a temporary basis, without prior consultation.
27. Those factors are sufficient to show that, when examined in such a context, Article XI of the General Agreement is not capable of conferring on citizens of the Community rights which they can invoke before the courts.
28. Accordingly, the validity of Regulations Nos 459/70, 565/70 and 686/70

of the Commission cannot be affected by Article XI of the General Agreement.

C. LITERATURE

Aschenbrenner, 'The Interpretation of the Free Trade Agreements: The EC Court of Justice's Decision on Polydor and Kupferberg', *EFTA Bulletin* 2/83,14.
Bebr' Agreements concluded by the Community and their possible direct effect: from Int. Fruit Cy to Kupferberg' (1983) CML Rev., 35–75.
Buhl, 'The Third United Nations conference on the Law of the Sea', (1981) CML Rev. 553–567.
Manin, 'The European Communities and the Vienna Convention on the Law of Treaties between States and International Organizations or between International Organizations', 24 CML Rev. (1987). pp 457–481.
Schermers, 'The Direct Application of Treaties with Third States: Note concerning Polydor and Pabst Cases', (1982) CML Rev., 563–569.
Steenbergen, 'The Status of GATT in Community Law', 5 JWTL 1981, 337–344.
Völker, 'The Direct Effect of International Agreements in the Community's Legal Order', LIEI 1983/1, 131–145.

III. The common commercial policy

A. INTRODUCTION

The setting up of a customs union implies by necessity a common or at least a joint policy on which to base the level of the levies of the common tariff as well as all other measures related to the regulation of external influences of a commercial character on the internal market and its producers. As such the Common commercial policy differs from the Community agricultural and transport policies which are part of the common market because of the specific characteristics of both sectors at the time the Communities were set up. That the Common commercial policy nevertheless is not found in Part Two of the EEC Treaty (Foundations of the Community) but in Part Three (Policy of the Community) Title II (Economic Policy) indicates that the CCP was intended as an instrument to regulate internal Community activity via the (more or less liberal) access of third country producers to the Common market. The liberal character of the CCP to which the Community has pledged itself in the EEC Treaty (Articles 18 and 110) and to which it has bound itself internationally in a multitude of bilateral and multilateral agreements determine the extent to which Community producers can be protected against outside competitive pressure which protection might be required especially in periods of slow-down of economic activity. Over the past number of years the Court has been asked to deliver rulings in respect of certain types of instruments available to the Community under the CCP to check imports into (parts of) the Common market. They include anti-dumping measures and the use of the safeguard clause of Article 115 EEC In *Opinion 1/75* the Court dealt with the legal composition of the Common Commercial Policy as well as more specifically with the Common Export Policy. In *Opinion 1/78* the Court inter alia delimitated the scope of the Common Commercial Policy versus the other parts of the title on Economic Policy. In *Case 45/86* the norm to define the scope of the commercial policy power as established in *Opinion 1/75 and 1/76* was confirmed.

B. THE COMMON COMMERCIAL POLICY POWERS OF THE EC

1. Introduction

In an attempt to achieve more equal conditions internationally for exporters to the world market the OECD instituted negotiations amongst its members to set minimum conditions for export credits. In the *Opinion 1/75* (below), which the Court delivered as regards the Community's power in this matter, the basic structure of the policy and its goals were also outlined. The conclusion at which the Court arrived was that the Community's powers under Article 113 EEC are necessarily of an exclusive nature.

2. Cases

(1) Opinion of the Court (1/75)

Opinion of the Court given pursuant to Article 228 of the EEC Treaty; *Opinion 1/75* of 11 November 1975 (Understanding on a Local costs standard); [1975] ECR 1361; (1976) 1 CMLR 85.

Facts:

See the opinion below.

The Court held:

The object of this request is to obtain the opinion of the Court on the compatibility with the EEC Treaty of a draft 'Understanding on a Local Cost Standard' drawn up under the auspices of the OECD, and more particularly on the question whether the Community has the power to conclude the said Understanding and, if so, whether that power is exclusive. The draft agreement is drawn up in the following terms:

'The Standard
1. The participating governments agree not to finance or cover credit for more than 100% of the value of the goods and services exported (exported 'goods and services' including goods and services supplied by third countries). This means that the amount of local costs supported on credit terms must not exceed the payments to be received for the goods and services exported by the completion of the exporter's contractual obligations.

. . . . .

3. 'Local costs' mean expenditure for the supply of goods and services from the buyer's country. These goods and services must be necessary either for executing the exporter's contract or for completing the project of which the exporter's contract forms part.'

. . . . .

The reply to be given to the questions submitted

1. The existence of a Community power to conclude the OECD Understanding on a Local Cost Standard

Articles 112 and 113 of the Treaty must be borne in mind in formulating a reply to this question.
The first of these provisions provides that:
'...Member States shall, before the end of the transitional period, progressively harmonize the systems whereby they grant aid for exports to third countries, to the extent necessary to ensure that competition between undertakings of the Community is not distorted.'

Since there is no doubt that the grant of export credits falls within the system of aids granted by Member States for exports, it is already clear from Article 112 that the subject-matter of the standard laid down in the Understanding in question relates to a field in which the provisions of the Treaty recognize a Community power.

Furthermore, Article 113 of the Treaty lays down, in paragraphs (1) and (2), that:
'...the common commercial policy shall be base on uniform principles, particularly in regard to...export policy....'.

The field of the common commercial policy, and more particularly that of export policy, necessarily covers systems of aid for exports and more particularly measures concerning credits for the financing of local costs linked to export operations. In fact, such measures constitute an important element of commercial policy, that concept having the same content whether it is applied in the context of the international action of a State or to that of the Community.

Directives concerning credit insurance, adopted by the Council towards the end of 1970 and the beginning of 1971 expressly recognize the important role played by export credits in international trade, as a factor of commercial policy.

For these reasons the subject-matter covered by the standard contained in the Understanding in question, since it forms part not only of the sphere of the system of aids for exports laid down at Article 112 of the Treaty but also, in a more general way, of export policy and, by reason of that fact, of the sphere of the common commercial policy defined in Article 113 of the Treaty, falls within the ambit of the Community's powers.

In the course of the measures necessary to implement the principles laid down in the abovementioned provisions, particularly those covered by Article 113 of the Treaty, concerning the common commercial policy, the Community is empowered, pursuant to the powers which it possesses, not only to adopt internal rules of Community law, but also to conclude agreements with third countries pursuant to Article 113 (2) and Article 114 of the Treaty.

A commercial policy is in fact made up by the combination and interaction of internal and external measures, without priority being taken by one over the others. Sometimes agreements are concluded in execution of a policy fixed in advance, sometimes that policy is defined by the agreements themselves.

Such agreements may be outline agreements, the purpose of which is to lay down uniform principles. Such is the case with the Understanding on local costs: it does not have a specific content adapted to particular export credit transactions; it merely lays down a standard, sets out certain exceptions, provides, in exceptional circumstances, for derogations and, finally, lays down general provisions. Furthermore, the implementation of the export policy to be pursued within the framework of a common commercial policy does not necessarily find expression in the adoption of general and abstract rules of internal or Community law. The common commercial policy is above all the outcome of a progressive development based upon specific measures which may refer without distinction to 'autonomous' and external aspects of that policy and which do not necessarily presuppose, by the fact that they are linked to the field of the common commercial policy, the existence of a large body of rules, but combine gradually to form that body.

2. *The exclusive nature of the Community's powers*

The reply to this question depends, on the one hand, on the objective of the Understanding in question and, on the other hand, on the manner in which the common commercial policy is conceived in the Treaty.

At Nos I and II the Understanding itself defines the transactions to which the common standard applies, and those which, on the other hand, are excluded from its field of application because they are directed to specifically military ends or because they have been entered into with developing countries.

It is to be understood from this definition that the subject-matter of the standard, and therefore of the Understanding, is one of those measures belonging to the common commercial policy prescribed by article 113 of the Treaty.

Such a policy is conceived in that article in the context of the operation of the Common Market, for the defence of the common interests of the Community, within which the particular interests of the Member States must endeavour to adapt to each other.

Quite clearly, however, this conception is incompatible with the freedom to which the Member States could lay claim by invoking a concurrent power, so as to ensure that their own interests were separately satisfied in external relations, at the risk of compromising the effective defence of the common interests of the Community.

In fact any unilateral action on the part of the Member States would lead to disparities in the conditions for the grant of export credits, calculated to distort competition between undertakings of the various Member States in external markets. Such distortion can be eliminated only by means of a strict uniformity of credit conditions granted to undertakings in the Community, whatever their nationality.

It cannot therefore be accepted that, in a field such as that governed by the Understanding in question, which is covered by export policy and more generally by the common commercial policy, the Member States should exercise a power concurrent to that of the Community, in the Community sphere and in the international sphere. The provisions of Articles 113 and 114 concerning the conditions under which, according to the Treaty, agreements on commercial policy must be concluded show clearly that the exercise of concurrent powers by the Member States and the Community in this matter is impossible.

To accept that the contrary were true would amount to recognizing that, in relations with third countries, Member States may adopt positions which differ from those which the Community intends to adopt, and would thereby distort the institutional framework, call into question the mutual trust within the Community and prevent the latter from fulfilling its task in the defence of the common interest.

It is of little importance that the obligations and financial burdens inherent in the execution of the agreement envisaged are borne directly by the Member States. The 'internal' and 'external' measures adopted by the Community within the framework of the common commercial policy do not necessarily involve, in order to ensure their compatibility with the Treaty, a transfer to the institutions of the Community of the obligations and financial burdens which they may involve: such measures are solely concerned to substitute for the unilateral action of the Member States, in the field under consideration, a common action based upon uniform principles on behalf of the whole of the Community.

(2) Opinion of the Court (1/78)

Opinion of the Court given pursuant to Article 228 EEC; *Opinion 1/78* of 4 October 1979 (International Agreement on Natural Rubber); [1979] ECR 2909; [1979] 3 CMLR 639.

Facts:

The essential purpose of the International Agreement on Rubber is to achieve a balanced growth between the supply and demand for natural rubber with a view to stabilizing its prices around their long-term trend. The function of these principles is to guarantee stable export earnings for the exporting countries whilst ensuring reliability of supplies for the importing countries at a fair price level.

The objective thus described is to be realized by building up a buffer stock, the purpose of which is to purchase surpluses of rubber at a time when prices are declining and to sell the stocked rubber when prices are rising so as to contain the price within a margin of fluctuation determined in advance. The operations of the buffer stock are financed by means of public funds provided by the contracting parties by equal contributions from both the producer group and the consumer group.

The Court held:

IV – The subject-matter and objectives of the agreement envisaged

36. As the Council has indicated, the problem of competence which has been submitted to the Court must be examined from two aspects. The first question is whether the agreement envisaged, by reason of its subject-matter and objectives, comes within the concept of common commercial policy referred to in Article 113 of the Treaty. The second question – but only if the first question is answered in the affirmative – is whether, by reason of certain specific arrangements or special provisions of the agreement concerning matters coming within the powers of the Member States, the participation of the latter in the agreement is necessary.

. . . . .

(a) Consideration of the agreement's links with commercial policy and development problems

41. By its special machinery as much as by certain aspects of its legal structure, the International Agreement on Natural Rubber which it is

proposed to conclude stands apart from ordinary commercial and tariff agreements which are based primarily on the operation of customs duties and quantitative restrictions. The agreement in question is a more structured instrument in the form of an organization of the market on a world scale and in this way it is distinguished from classical commercial agreements.

. . . . .

44. Following the impulse given by UNCTAD to the development of this type of control it seems that it would no longer be possible to carry on any worthwhile common commercial policy if the Community were not in a position to avail itself also of more elaborate means devised with a view to furthering the development of international trade. It is therefore not possible to lay down, for Article 113 of the EEC Treaty, an interpretation the effect of which would be to restrict the common commercial policy to the use of instruments intended to have an effect only on the traditional aspects of external trade to the exclusion of more highly developed mechanisms such as appear in the agreement envisaged. A 'commercial policy' understood in that sense would be destined to become nugatory in the course of time. Although it may be thought that at the time when the Treaty was drafted liberalization of trade was the dominant idea, the Treaty nevertheless does not form a barrier to the possibility of the Community's developing a commercial policy aiming at a regulation of the world market for certain products rather than at a mere liberalization of trade.

45. Article 113 empowers the Community to formulate a commercial 'policy', based on 'uniform principles' thus showing that the question of external trade must be governed from a wide point of view and not only having regard to the administration of precise systems such as customs and quantitative restrictions. The same conclusion may be deduced from the fact that the enumeration in Article 113 of the subjects covered by commercial policy (changes in tariff rates, the conclusion of tariff and trade agreements, the achievement of uniformity in measures of liberalization, export policy and measures to protect trade) is conceived as a non-exhaustive enumeration which must not, as such, close the door to the application in a Community context of any other process intended to regulate external trade. A restrictive interpretation of the concept of common commercial policy would risk causing disturbances in intra-Community trade by reason of the disparities which would then exist in certain sectors of economic relations with non-member countries.

. . . . .

(b) The agreement's links with general economic policy

47. In its arguments the Council has raised the problem of the interrelation within the structure of the Treaty of the concepts of 'economic policy' and 'commercial policy'. In certain provisions economic policy is indeed considered primarily as a question of national interest; such is the meaning of that concept in Articles 6 and 145 which, for that reason, prescribe for the Member States nothing more than a duty to ensure co-ordination. In other provisions economic policy is envisaged as being a matter of common interest as is the case with Articles 103 to 116, which are grouped together in a title devoted to the 'economic policy' of the Community. The chapter devoted to the common commercial policy forms part of that title.
48. The considerations set out above already form to some extent an answer to the arguments relating to the distinction to be drawn between the spheres of general economic policy and those of the common commercial policy since international co-operation, inasmuch as it does not belong to commercial policy, would be confused with the domain of general economic policy. If it appears that it comes, at least in part, under the common commercial policy, as has been indicated above, it follows clearly that it could not, under the name of general economic policy, be withdrawn from the competence of the Community.

. . . . .

50. It is in the light of the same considerations that the the connexion between Article 113 and Article 116 must be determined in the context of the chapter of the Treaty devoted to the common commercial policy. Whilst those two provisions contribute to the same end inasmuch as their objective is the realization of a common policy in international economic relationships, as a basis for action the two articles are founded on different premises and consequently apply different ideas. According to Article 113 the common commercial policy is determined by the Community, independently, that is to say, acting as such, by the intervention of its own institutions; in particular, agreements entered into under that provision are, in the terms of Article 114, 'concluded...on behalf of the Community' and accordingly negotiated according to the procedures set out in those provisions and in Article 228. Article 116 on the other hand was conceived with a view to evolving common action by the Member States in international organizations of which the Community is not part; in such a situation the only appropriate means is concerted, joint action by the Member States as members of the said organizations.
51. In this case a problem relating to the demarcation of the sphere of application of Articles 113 and 114 on the one hand and 116 on the other

hand arises from the fact that the agreements on commodities are at present being negotiated within UNCTAD. The Court has already given its views on this problem in its Opinion 1/75 which itself concerned an international agreement arrived at within the framework of an international organization (the OECD). In that opinion the Court stressed that what counts with regard to the application of the Treaty is the question whether negotiations undertaken within the framework of an international organization are intended to lead to an 'undertaking entered into by entities subject to international law which has binding force'. In such a case it is the provisions of the Treaty relating to the negotiation and conclusion of agreements, in other words Articles 113, 114 and 228, which apply and not Article 116.

V – Problems raised by the financing of the agreement and by other specific provisions

52. Consideration must still be given, having regard to what has been stated above as regards correspondence between the objective and purposes of the agreement envisaged and the concept of common commercial policy, whether the detailed arrangements for financing the buffer stock, or certain specific clauses of the agreement, concerning technological assistance, research programmes, the maintenance of fair conditions of labour in the rubber industry and consultations relating to national tax policies which may have an effect on the price of rubber lead to a negation of the Community's exclusive competence.

. . . . .

55. The Court feels that a distinction should be made in this respect between the specific clauses referred to by the Council and the financial provisions which occupy a central position in the structure of the agreement and which, for that reason, raise a more fundamental difficulty as regards the demarcation between the powers of the Community and those of the Member States.
56. The Court takes the view that the fact that the agreement may cover subjects such as technological assistance, research programmes, labour conditions in the industry concerned or consultations relating to national tax policies which may have an effect on the price of rubber cannot modify the description of the agreement which must be assessed having regard to its essential objective rather than in terms of individual clauses of an altogether subsidiary or ancillary nature. This is the more true because the clauses under consideration are in fact closely connected with the objective of the agreement and the duties of the bodies which are to operate in the framework of the International Natural Rubber Organiza-

tion which it is planned to set up. The negotiation and execution of these clauses must therefore follow the system applicable to the agreement considered as a whole.

. . . . .

58. Having regard to the uncertainty which exists as regards the final solution to be adopted for this problem, the Court feels bound to have regard to two possible situations: one in which the financial burdens envisaged by the agreement would be entered in the Community budget and one in which the burdens would be directly charged to the budgets of the Member States. The Court itself is in no position, within the limits of the present proceedings, to make any choice between the two alternatives.
59. In the first case no problem would arise as regards the exclusive powers of the Community to conclude the agreement in question. As has been indicated above, the mechanism of the buffer stock has the purpose of regulating trade and from this point of view constitutes an instrument of the common commercial policy. It follows that Community financing of the charges arising would have to be regarded as a solution in conformity with the Treaty.
60. The facts of the problem would be different if the second alternative were to be preferred. It cannot in fact be denied that the financing of the buffer stock constitutes an essential feature of the scheme for regulating the market which it is proposed to set up. The extent of and the detailed arrangements for the financial undertakings which the Member States will be required to satisfy will directly condition the possibilities and the degree of efficiency of intervention by the buffer mechanism whilst the decisions to be taken as regards the level of the central reference price and the margins of fluctuation to be permitted either upwards or downwards will have immediate repercussions on the use of the financial means put at the disposal of the International Rubber Council which is to be set up and on the extent of the financial means to be put at its disposal. Furthermore sight must not be lost of the fact that the financial structure which it is proposed to set up will make necessary, as is mentioned in the documents submitted to the Court and reflecting the most recent stage of negotiations, co-ordination between the use of the specific financial means put at the disposal of the future International Rubber Council and those which it might find in the Common Fund which is to be set up. If the financing of the agreement is a matter for the Community the necessary decisions will be taken according to the appropriate Community procedures. If on the other hand the financing is to be by the Member States that will imply the participation of those States in the decision-making machinery or, at least, their agreement with regard to the arrangements for financing envisaged and consequently their participation in the agree-

ment together with the Community. The exclusive competence of the Community could not be envisaged in such a case.

. . . . .

In conclusion,

THE COURT

gives the following opinion:

1. The Community's powers relating to commercial policy within the meaning of Article 113 of the Treaty establishing the European Economic Community extend to the International Agreement on Natural Rubber which is in the course of negotiation within the United Nations Conference on Trade and Development.
2. The question of the exclusive nature of the Community's powers depends in this case on the arrangements for financing the operations of the buffer stock which it is proposed to set up under that agreement.

    If the burden of financing the stock falls upon the Community budget the Community will have exclusive powers.

    If on the other hand the charges are to be borne directly by the Member States that will imply the participation of those States in the agreement together with the Community.
3. As long as that question has not been settled by the competent Community authorities the Member States must be allowed to participate in the negotiation of the agreement.

3. Literature

Bronckers,*Selective Safeguard Measures in Multilateral Trade Relations; Issues of Protectionism in GATT, European Community and United States Law*, Deventer 1985.

Lasok/Cairns,*The Customs Law of the European Economic Community.* Deventer, 1983.

Le Lièvre/Houber,'EC versus Japan: the Community's Legal Weapons'. 22 *CMLRev.* (1985), pp. 533–561.

McGovern, *International Trade Regulation*, Exeter, 1983.

Steenbergen, De Clercq and Foqée,*Change and adjustment, external relations and industrial policy of the EC*, Deventer, 1983.

Steenbergen, 'Annotation to Case 45/86, *Commission* v. *Council.* Judgment of 26 March 1987', 29 CMLRev. (1987), pp. 731–737.

Völker (ed.), *Protectionism and the EC.*, 2nd ed., Deventer, 1987.

C. DUMPING

1. Introduction

Article VI of the General Agreement on Tariffs and Trade (GATT) is the basis for the second Anti-Dumping Code contained in the international agreements which were negotiated during the so-called Tokyo-round to implement Article VI. This article provides that:
'1. The contracting parties recognize that dumping, by which products of one country are introduced into the commerce of another country at less than the normal value of the products, is to be condemned if it causes or threatens material injury to an established industry in the territory of a contracting party...(A) product is to be considered as being (dumped) if the price of the product exported from one country to another:
(a) is less than the comparable price, in the ordinary course of trade, for the like product when destined for consumption in the exporting country'.

. . . . .

The second Anti-Dumping Code (at present by the Community enacted by Regulation No 2423/88) forms the legal basis for the application of anti-dumping duties by the parties to GATT. It also provides for the possibility for exporters to undertake, instead, to raise their export prices. Anti-dumping duties are in the Community laid down by regulation. The Court has declared admissable requests for annulment of decisions in anti-dumping proceedings (including Regulations applying a/d duties) of parties directly involved in anti-dumping procedures, with exception of requests filed by independent importers.

2. Cases

(1) FEDIOL Case

EEC Seed Crushers and Oil Processors' Federation (FEDIOL) v. *Commission of the EC;* Case 191/82; Judgment of 4 October 1983; (1983) ECR 2913.

Facts:

See the judgment below

The Court held:

. . . . .

1. By application lodged at the Court Registry on 29 July 1982 the EEC Seed Crushers' and Oil Processors' Federation (Fediol) (hereinafter referred to as 'the Federation') brought an action under the second paragraph of Article 173 of the EEC Treaty for a declaration that a communication dated 25 May 1982 by which the Commission informed the applicant pursuant to Article 5 (5) of Council Regulation No 3017/79 of 20 December 1979 on protection against dumped or subsidized imports from countries not members of the European Economic Community (Official Journal 1979, L 339, p. 1) that an anti-subsidy proceeding would not be initiated in respect of imports of soya-bean oil-cake from Brazil, was void.
2. By a document lodged on 11 October 1982 the Commission, pursuant to Article 91 of the Rules of Procedure, requested the Court to give a preliminary decision on the admissibility of the action.

. . . . .

25. It appears from a comparison of the provisions governing the successive procedural stages described above that the regulation recognizes the existence of a legitimate interest on the part of Community producers in the adoption of anti-subsidy measures and that it defines certain specific rights in their favour, namely the right to submit to the Commission all evidence which they consider appropriate, the right to see all information obtained by the Commission subject to certain exceptions, the right to be heard at their request and to have the opportunity of meeting the other parties concerned in the same proceeding, and finally the right to be informed if the Commission decides not to pursue a complaint. In the case of the proceedings being terminated on the completion of the stage of preliminary investigation provided for in Article 5 that information must comprise at least a statement of the Commission's basic conclusions and a summary of the reasons therefor as is required by Article 9 in the event of the termination of formal investigations.
26. Whilst it is true that the Commission, when exercising the powers assigned to it in Regulation No 3017/79, is under a duty to establish objectively the facts concerning the existence of subsidization practices and of injury caused thereby to Community undertakings, it is no less true that it has a very wide discretion to decide, in terms of the interests

of the Community, any measures needed to deal with the situation which it has established.

27. It is in the light of those considerations, originating in the scheme of Regulation No 3017/79 that it is necessary to decide whether complainants have the right to bring an action.

28. It seems clear, first, in that respect – and the point is not disputed by the Commission – that complainants must be acknowledged to have a right to bring an action where it is alleged that the Community authorities have disregarded rights which have been recognized specifically in the regulation, namely the right to lodge a complaint, the right, which is inherent in the aforementioned right, to have that complaint considered by the Commission with proper care and according to the procedure provided for, the right to receive information within the limits set by the regulation and finally, if the Commission decides not to proceed with the complaint, the right to receive information comprising at the least the explanations guaranteed by Article 9 (2) of the regulation.

29. Furthermore it must be acknowledged that, in the spirit of the principles which lie behind Articles 164 and 173 of the Treaty, complainants have the right to avail themselves, with regard both to the assessment of the facts and to the adoption of the protective measures provided for by the regulation, of a review by the Court appropriate to the nature of the powers reserved to the Community institutions on the subject.

30. If follows that complainants may not be refused the right to put before the Court any matters which would facilitate a review as to whether the Commission has observed the procedural guarantees granted to complainants by Regulation No 3017/79 and whether or not it has committed manifest errors in its assessment of the facts, has omitted to take into consideration any essential matters of such a nature as to give rise to a belief in the existence of subsidization or has based the reasons for its decision on considerations amounting to a misuse of powers. In that respect, the Court is required to exercise its normal powers of review over a discretion granted to a public authority, even though it has no jurisdiction to intervene in the exercise of the discretion reserved to the Community authorities by the aforementioned regulation.

31. It follows from the foregoing that the attitude adopted by the Commission is excessive inasmuch as it considers that any action brought by the complainants described in Article 5 of the regulation is, in principle, inadmissible. As has been shown above, the regulation acknowledges that undertakings and associations of undertakings injured by subsidization practices on the part of non-member countries have a legitimate interest in the initiation of protective action by the Community; it must therefore be acknowledged that they have a right of action within the framework of the legal status which the regulation confers upon them.

32. It is therefore for the applicant to put forward its submissions in the course of the subsequent proceedings and to show that they fall within the

limits of the legal protection given to it by Regulation No 3017/79 and by the general principles of the Treaty.
33. For all those reasons the application must be declared admissible and the proceedings must be allowed to continue.

(2) Allied Corporation Case

Allied Corporation, Michel Levy Morelle, Transcontinental Fertilizer Company, Kaiser Aluminium and Chemical Corporation v. Commission of the EC; Joined Cases 239 and 275/82, Judgment of 21 February 1984; [1984] ECR 1029.

Facts:

Allied Corporation of New Jersey (United States of America), Demufert S.A., a company governed by Belgian Law, having its registered office in Brussels and now in liquidation, Transcontinental Fertilizer Company, of Pennsylvania (United States of America), and Kaiser Aluminium and Chemical Corporation of Delaware (United States of America), brought an action under the second paragraph of Article 173 in which they request the Court to declare void Commission Reg. 1976/82 imposing a provisional anti-dumping duty on certain imports of certain chemical fertilizer originating in the United States of America and Reg. 2302/82 amending Reg. 1976/82 and adopted pursuant to Reg. 3017/79 on protection against dumped or subsidized imports from countries not members of the EEC, meanwhile replaced by Regulation 2423/88. The Commission initiated a proceeding in 1980 concerning imports of certain chemical fertilizer originating in the United States of America and imposed a provisional anti-dumping duty on the products in question. It accepted the undertakings given by the applicants Allied, Transcontinental and Kaiser, to increase their prices to a level eliminating the dumping margins which had been established at 6.5% in respect of the first two applicants and at 5% in respect of Kaiser. By Regulation 349/81, the Council imposed a definitive anti-dumping duty and fixed the rate of duty at 6.5% on the basis of the customs value. The 23rd recital in the preamble to that regulation states that Allied, Kaiser and Transcontinental have voluntarily undertaken to increase their prices to a level eliminating the dumping margins found and that the Commission has accepted those undertakings. Accordingly, Article 2 of that regulation exempts from anti-dumping duty fertilizer exported by certain United States undertakings, including Allied, Kaiser and Transcontinental.

Allied and Transcontinental withdrew their undertakings by letters of 7 June and 2 July 1982 respectively, whereupon the Commission adopted Reg. 1976/82 imposing a provisional anti-dumping duty on fertilizer exported by those two undertakings at the rate of 6.5% of the customs value. Following

Kaiser's withdrawal of its undertaking, by telex of 23 July 1982, the Commission adopted Regulation 2302/82 amending Regulation 1976/82 so as to confirm the levying of an anti-dumping duty of 6.5% on exports by Allied and Transcontinental and to impose a duty of 5% on exports by Kaiser. Those are the two regulations which are at issue in this case.

The Court held:

. . . . .

10. The questions of admissibility raised by the Commission must be resolved in the light of the system established by Regulation No 3017/79 and, more particularly, of the nature of the anti-dumping measures provided for by that regulation, regard being had to the provisions of the second paragraph of Article 173 of the EEC Treaty.
11. Article 13 (1) of Regulation No 3017/79 provides that 'anti-dumping or countervailing duties, whether provisional or definitive, shall be imposed by regulation'. Although it is true that, in the light of the criteria set out in the second paragraph of Article 173, such measures are, in fact, as regards their nature and their scope, of a legislative character, inasmuch as they apply to all the traders concerned, taken as a whole, the provisions may none the less be of direct and individual concern to those producers and exporters who are charged with practising dumping. It is clear from Article 2 of Regulation No 3017/79 that anti-dumping duties may be imposed only on the basis of the findings resulting from investigations concerning the production prices and export prices of undertakings which have been individually identified.
12. It is thus clear that measures imposing anti-dumping duties are liable to be of direct and individual concern to those producers and exporters who are able to establish that they were identified in the measures adopted by the Commission or the Council or were concerned by the preliminary investigations.
13. As the Commission has rightly stated, to acknowledge that undertakings which fulfil those requirements have a right of action, in accordance with the principles laid down in the second paragraph of Article 173, does not give rise to a risk of duplication of means of redress since it is possible to bring an action in the national courts only following the collection of an anti-dumping duty which is normally paid by an importer residing within the Community. There is no risk of conflicting decisions in this area since, by virtue of the mechanism of the reference for a preliminary ruling under Article 177 of the EEC Treaty, it is for the Court of Justice alone to give a final decision on the validity of the contested regulations.
14. It follows that the applications lodged by Allied, Kaiser and Transcontinental are admissable. All three applicants gave an undertaking under

Article 10 of Regulation No 3017/79, they were accordingly referred to individually in Article 2 of Regulation No 349/81 and, after withdrawing their undertakings, their individual circumstances formed the subject-matter of the two regulations contested in the applications.

15. However, the position is different in the case of Demufert, since that applicant is an importer established in one of the Member States and is not referred to in any of the measures which are contested in the applications before the Court. As such, therefore, Demufert is concerned by the effects of the contested regulations only in so far as it comes objectively within the scope of the provisions of those regulations. The uncontested fact that Demufert acted as importing agent for Allied does not alter that conclusion. In contrast to the situation considered by the Court in its judgment of 29 March 1979 in Case 113/77 (*NTN Toyo Bearing Company Ltd and Others*, [1979] ECR 1185, paragraph 9 of the decision), in the present case the existence of dumping has been established, as is stated in the 10th recital in the preamble to Regulation No 349/81, by reference to the export prices of American producers and not by reference to the retail price charged by European importers, with the result that the findings relating to the existence of dumping are not of direct concern to Demufert, whereas they are of direct concern to the producers and exports. It must be pointed out that, in so far as it was compelled to pay anti-dumping duties, it is open to the applicant to bring an action in the competent national court in the context of which it can put forward its argument against the validity of the regulations at issue.
16. If follows that the application submitted by Demufert must be declared inadmissable.

3. Literature

Van Bael/Bellis, *International Trade Law and Practice of the European Community – EEC Anti-Dumping and other Trade Protection Laws*, Bicester (UK), 1985.

Beseler/Williams, *Anti-Dumping and Anti-Subsidy Law; The European Communities*, London, 1986.

Vermulst, *Anti-Dumping Law and Practice in the United States and the European Communities: A Comparative Analysis*, Amsterdam, 1987.

D. ARTICLE 115 EEC

1. Introduction

The part of the EEC Treaty dealing with the Common Commercial Policy contains a separate safeguard clause, to remedy deflection of trade and economic difficulties caused by the execution of national measures of commercial policy. Over the past few years the Court issued several rulings concerning the various aspects of Article 115. These concerned its interpretation, its relations to Articles 9 and 30 EEC and the direct applicability of the decisions issued under this Article by the Commission and addressed to the Member States.

2. Cases

(1) Donckerwolcke Case

Donckerwolcke & Schou v. *Procureur de la République au Tribunal de Grande Instance at Lille and Directeur Général des Douanes*; Case 41/76; Preliminary ruling of 15 December 1976; (1976) ECR 1934; [1977] CMLR 535.

Facts:

Messrs. Donckerwolcke and Schou imported from Belgium into France consignments of synthetic fibres which had been imported from Syria and Lebanon into the EEC via Belgium. Customs duties and other formalities had been complied with in Belgium and therefore the goods were in free circulation. Consequently the documents supplied by the Belgian customs authorities stated the origin of the goods to be the Belgo-Luxembourg Economic Union. The French customs authorities considered the subsequent importation into France to involve false declarations of origin and thus evasion of the requirement of automatic import licenses of origin and thus evasion of the requirement of automatic import licenses to which the imports should have given rise. The applicants lodged an appeal against the heavy penalties which were impeded. The Cour d'Appel at Douai referred two questions to the Court of Justice.

The Court held:

. . . . .

10. The questions referred concern the rules applicable to products originating in third countries not yet subject to common provisions of commercial policy and which, after being put into free circulation in one Member State, are re-exported to another Member State.

11. They concern more particularly the compatibility with the Treaty of monitoring measures introduced unilaterally by the importing Member State before obtaining a derogation, pursuant to the second sentence of the first paragraph of Article 115, from the rules of free circulation within the Community.

. . . . .

17. It appears from Article 9 that, as regards free circulation of goods within the Community, products entitled to 'free circulation' are definitively and wholly assimilated to products originating in Member States.
18. The result of this assimilation is that the provisions of Article 30 concerning the elimination of quantitative restrictions and all measures having equivalent effect are applicable without distinction to products originating in the Community and to those which were put into free circulation in any one of the Member States, irrespective of the actual origin of these products.
19. Measures having an effect equivalent to quantitative restrictions prohibited by the Treaty include all trading rules enacted by Member States which are capable of hindering, directly or indirectly, actually or potentially, intra-Community trade.
20. This provision precludes the application to intra-Community trade of a national provision which requires, even purely as a formality, import licences or any other similar procedure.

. . . . .

24. However it results from the system of the Treaty that the application of the principles referred to above is conditional upon the establishment of a common commercial policy.
25. The assimilation to products originating within the Member States of goods in 'free circulation' may only take full effect if these goods are subject to the same conditions of importation both with regard to customs and commercial considerations, irrespective of the State in which they were put in free circulation.
26. Under Article 113 of the Treaty this unification should have been achieved by the expiry of the transitional period and supplanted by the establishment of a common commercial policy based on uniform principles.
27. The fact that at the expiry of the transitional period the Community commercial policy was not fully achieved is one of a number of circumstances calculated to maintain in being between the Member States

differences in commercial policy capable of bringing about deflections of trade or of causing economic difficulties in certain Member States.
28. Article 115 allows difficulties of this kind to be avoided by giving to the commission the power to authorize Member States to take protective measures particularly in the form of derogation from the principle of free circulation within the Community of products which originated in third countries and which were put into free circulation in one of the Member States.
29. Because they constitute not only an exception to the provisions of Articles 9 and 30 of the Treaty which are fundamental to the operation of the Common Market, but also an obstacle to the implementation of the common commercial policy provided for by Article 113, the derogations allowed under Article 115 must be strictly interpreted and applied.
30. It is in the light of this interpretation that the compatibility of the monitoring measures' described above with the rules concerning the free circulation of goods within the Community should be considered.
31. First of all it should be stressed with regard to the scope of such provisions, that under Article 115 limitations may only be placed on the free movement within the Community of goods enjoying the right to free circulation by virtue of measures of commercial policy adopted by the importing Member State in accordance with the Treaty.
32. As full responsibility in the matter of commercial policy was transferred to the Community by means of Article 113 (1) measures of commercial policy of a national character are only permissible after the end of the transitional period by virtue of specific authorization by the Community.
33. Within the context thus defined the Member States are not prevented from requiring from an importer a declaration concerning the actual origin of the goods in question even in the case of goods put into free circulation in another Member State and covered by a Community movement certificate.

. . . . .

3. Literature

Timmermans, 'Community Commercial Policy on Textiles: A Legal Imbroglio', in Völker (ed)., *Protectionism*, pp. 125–147.

IV. The Common Fisheries Policy

A. INTRODUCTION

According to Article 38 of the EEC Treaty, 'Agricultural Products' mentioned in that Article, include the products of fisheries, which means that

the agricultural policy foreseen in Article 3 (d) EEC should include a policy in the sphere of fisheries. There is little doubt that over the past years external events have had a major impact on the developments in the Community in the field of fisheries. The unilateral steps by third countries to extend their fishing zones to 200 miles off their coasts had a number of consequences:
– the fishing by the fleets of the Member States off the coasts of North America, Iceland, Africa etc, was now taking place in the 200 miles zones of the various coastal states,
– if the Member States of the Community did not proclaim a 200 miles zone of their own the fishing grounds of their coast outside the 12 miles zone were left unprotected,
– a European 200 miles zone made a Community fisheries policy imperative.

Subsequently the Council, in the so-called The Hague resolution of 3 November 1976, announced the following steps:
– as from 1 January 1977, Member States shall, by means of concerted action extend the limits of their fishing zones to 200 miles off their North Sea and North Atlantic coasts without prejudice to similar action being taken for the other fishing zones within their jurisdiction such as the Mediterranean,
– the exploitation of fishery resources in these zones by fishing vessels of third countries shall be governed by agreements between the Community and the third countries concerned,
– by means of appropriate agreements fishing rights shall be obtained and existing rights retained in the waters of third countries.

In Annex VI to the resolution it was furthermore laid down
– that autonomous fisheries measures by the Member States are no longer allowed,
– and that, if by 1 January 1977 the necessary common fisheries measures had not been taken, the Member States were required to take measures on the following conditions:
  : that these measures were of a temporary character only,
  : that these measures were not discriminatory in nature,
  : and that approval had been obtained from the Commission.

The Resolution, Article 102 of the Act of Accession and the implementing legislation have led to a number of proceedings before the European Court concerning the internal and external competences of the Communities in the field of fisheries.

B. CASES

(1) Commission – United Kingdom Case

Commission of the EC v. United Kingdom; Case 804/79; Judgment of 5 May 1981; [1981] ECR 1072; [1982] CMLR 543.

Facts:

On 13 November 1979 the Commission of the European Communities brought an action under Article 169 of the EEC Treaty for a declaration that, by applying in the matter of sea fisheries unilateral measures, the United Kingdom has failed to fulfil its obligations under the Treaty.

History of the dispute.

At the beginning of 1979 the Council, to which the Commission, in pursuance of Article 102 of the Act of Accession, had proposed the adoption of a series of measures for the conservation of fishery resources in the waters under the jurisdiction of the Member States, failed to adopt the necessary provisions. In the circumstances the Council adopted interim measures, one of which was applicable at the time of the bringing into force of the unilateral British measures and which is worded as follows:

. . . . .

'As regards technical measures for the conservation and surveillance of fisheries resources, Member States shall apply the same measures as they applied on 3 November 1976, and other measures taken in accordance with the procedures and criteria of Annex VI to the Council resolution of 3 November 1976'.

By a letter of 21 March 1979 the Government of the United Kingdom informed the Commission of its intention to bring into force on 1 July 1979 a series of measures for the conservation of fishery resources concerning the mesh of nets, minimum landing sizes and by-catches and sought the approval of the Commission in this matter in accordance with Annex VI to the The Hague Resolution. The measures in question were brought into force on 1 July 1979.

The criticisms made by the Commission are that measures of this type cannot be effectively adopted except for the whole of the Community, that the Council would have been in a position to adopt them in the form intended by the Treaty if the United Kingdom had not itself blocked the decision-making process in the Council and that by unilaterally adopting the measures in question the United Kingdom has encroached upon the powers which belong in their entirety, as from 1 January 1979, to the Community. According to the Commission, in the circumstances the disputed measures could therefore be adopted only with its authorization.

The Court held:

. . . . .

The state of the law at the time in question
17. The Court has had occasion to recall in former judgments and most recently in its judgment of 10 July 1980, to which reference has already been made, the elements of Community law which are applicable in this matter. The situation described in those judgments has in the meantime undergone a substantial change by reason of the fact that since the expiration on 1 January 1979 of the transitional period laid down by Article 102 of the Act of Accession, power to adopt, as part of the common fisheries policy, measures relating to the conservation of the resources of the sea has belonged fully and definitively to the Community.
18. Member States are therefore no longer entitled to exercise any power of their own in the matter of conservation measures in the waters under their jurisdiction. The adoption of such measures, with the restrictions which they imply as regards fishing activities, is a matter, as from that date, of Community law. As the Commission has rightly pointed out, the resources to which the fishermen of the Member States have an equal right of access must henceforth be subject to the rules of Community law.
19. It is in the light of this position of principle that the legal situation must be assessed. It is characterized by the fact that, in a matter in which the powers are in the hands of the Community, the Council has not adopted, within the required periods, the conservation measures referred to by Article 102 of the Act of Accession.
20. On this subject it is appropriate to stress, first of all, that the transfer to the Community of powers in this matter being total and definitive, such a failure to act could not in any case restore to the Member States the power and freedom to act unilaterally in this field.
21. It follows, as has been stated by the French Government, that in the absence of provisions adopted by the Council in accordance with the forms and procedures prescribed by the Treaty, the conservation measures as they existed at the end of the period referred to in Article 102 of the Act of Accession are maintained in the state in which they were at the time of the expiration of the transitional period laid down by that provision.
22. However, it is not possible to extend that idea to the point of making it entirely impossible for the Member States to amend the existing conservation measures in case of need owing to the development of the relevant biological and technological facts in this sphere. Such amendments would be of a limited scope only and could not involve a new conservation policy on the part of a Member State, since the power to lay down such a policy belongs henceforth to the Community institutions.
23. Having regard to the situation created by the inaction of the Council, the conditions in which such measures may be adopted must be defined by means of all the available elements of law, even though fragmentary, and by having regard, for the remainder, to the structural principles on which the Community is founded. These principles require the Community to retain in all circumstances its capacity to comply with its responsibilities,

subject to the observance of the essential balances intended by the Treaty.
24. In this respect it should be recorded first of all that at the time of the events giving rise to the dispute, the Commission had presented the proposals required by Article 102 of the Act of Accession so that the Council had before it a draft relating to the whole of the conservation measures to be adopted. Although it is true that the Council did not follow those proposals, it did at least lay down certain guide-lines, expressed in the decisions referred to above and, in particular, in that of 25 June 1979, which was applicable at the time of the events in question.
25. These decisions, which were essentially of an interim nature, adopt the Commission's proposals as regards total allowable catches (TACs) as a limit to the aggregate of fishing activities during the period in question. They moreover consolidate the technical measures for conservation and control of fishery resources in force at the relevant time. They thus reflect, on the one hand, the Council's intention to reinforce the authority of the Commission's proposals and, on the other hand, its intention to prevent the conservation measures in force from being amended by the Member States without any acknowledged need.
26. As regards any amendments which may be necessary to the existing conservation measures, the decisions which have been mentioned refer to the 'procedures and criteria' of the Hague Resolution. It may be recalled that that Resolution excludes in principle unilateral measures by the Member States and that in the absence of Community measures it admits only of measures adopted to ensure the protection of resources and in a form which avoids discrimination. Furthermore it emphasizes that such measures shall not prejudice the guide-lines to be adopted for Community policy on the conservation of resources.
27. Before adopting such measures the Member State concerned is required to seek the approval of the Commission, which must be consulted at all stages of the procedure. It should be noted that these requirements, which were originally defined during the transitional period laid down by Article 102 of the Act of Accession, must be considered henceforth in a new setting, characterized by the exclusive powers of the Community on this subject and by the full effect of the relevant rules of Community law, without prejudice to the transitional provisions of Articles 100, 101 and 103 of the Act of Accession, the application of which is however not at issue in this case.
28. According to Article 5 of the Treaty Member States are required to take all appropriate measures to facilitate the achievement of the Community's task and to abstain from any measure which might jeopardize the attainment of the objectives of the Treaty. This provision imposes on Member States special duties of action and abstention in a situation in which the Commission, in order to meet urgent needs of conservation, has submitted to the Council proposals which, although they have not been

adopted by the Council, represent the point of departure for concerted Community action.

29. Furthermore it should be remembered that in pursuance of Article 7 of the Treaty, Community fishermen must have, subject to the exceptions mentioned above, equal access to the fish stocks coming within the jurisdiction of the Member States. The Council alone has the power to determine the detailed conditions of such access in accordance with the procedures laid down by the third subparagraph of Article 43 (2) of the Treaty and Article 102 of the Act of Accession. This legal situation cannot be modified by measures adopted unilaterally by the Member States.

30. As this is a field reserved to the powers of the Community, within which Member States may henceforth act only as trustees of the common interest, a Member State cannot therefore, in the absence of appropriate action on the part of the Council, bring into force any interim conservation measures which may be required by the situation except as part of a process of collaboration with the Commission and with due regard to the general task of supervision which Article 155, in conjunction, in this case, with the Decision of 25 June 1979 and the parallel decisions, gives to the Commission.

31. Thus, in a situation characterized by the inaction of the Council and by the maintenance, in principle, of the conservation measures in force at the expiration of the period laid down in Article 102 of the Act of Accession, the Decision of 25 June 1979 and the parallel decisions, as well as the requirements inherent in the safeguard by the Community of the common interest and the integrity of its own powers, imposed upon Member States not only an obligation to undertake detailed consultations with the Commission and to seek its approval in good faith, but also a duty not to lay down national conservation measures in spite of objections, reservations or conditions which might be formulated by the Commission.

. . . . .

(2) Ireland – Commission Case

Ireland v. *Commission*; Case 325/85; Judgment of 15 December 1987 (not yet published).

Facts:

The facts are similar to the previous case except as far as mentioned in the judgment below.

The Court held:

(Referring to Case 304/79, above):

. . . . .

16. The Court thus accepted that where the Council had failed to adopt the conservation measures necessary to protect fish stocks, such measures, designed to answer urgent needs, might be agreed upon by means of a process of co-operation between the Member States and the Commission, in order to enable the Community to meet its responsibilities.
17. It is common ground that no such process of co-operation was initiated in 1981 between Ireland and the Commission in relation to the fish in question since Ireland did not respond to the Commission's invitation to adopt the measures needed to ensure compliance with its proposals. In those circumstances, and without it being necessary to rule on the legal consequences of that lack of co-operation on the part of a Member State, it must be found that the proposals unilaterally made by the Commission in relation to the fish quotas to be allocated to Ireland cannot be regarded as Community rules.
18. Moreover, as the Court has repeatedly held, Community legislation must be certain and its application foreseeable by those subject to it. That requirement of legal certainty must be observed all the more strictly in the case of rules liable to entail financial consequences, in order that those concerned may know precisely the extent of the obligations which they imposed on them.

. . . . .

C. LITERATURE

Churchill, *EEC Fisheries Law*, Dordrecht, 1987.
Leigh, *European Integration and Common Fisheries Policy*, London, 1983.
Swirds. 'The External Competence of the European Economic Community in Relation to the International fisheries Agreements', LIEI 1979/2, pp. 31–64.
Wallace, 'Special Economic Dependency and Preferential Rights in respect of Fisheries; Characterization and Articulation within the European Communities', (1984) 21 CMLRev. pp. 525–537.
Wise, *The Common Fisheries Policy of the European Community*, London, 1984.

Table of extracted Cases and Opinions – by number

Name of the Case: *Chapter with subdivision:*   *page:*

2/56 Geitling Case I   Ch. Two II A 1 a (1)   51
9/56 Meroni Case I   One IV D 2 (1)   18
                                             Two II A 3 a i (1)   73
                                             Two II C 1 (1)   91

25/59 Publication of Transport Tariffs
      Case   One IV C 2 (1)   14

13/61 Bosch Case   Two IV C 2 (1)   118

24/62 Brennwein Case   Two II A 3 c i (1)   77
25/62 Plaumann Case   Two II A 2 c i (1)   61
26/62 Van Gend en Loos Case   Two IV B 1 (1)   110
                                             Three II A 1 (1)   160
                                             Four III A 2 a i (1)   255
28–20/62 Da Costa-Schaake Case   Two IV D 1 (3)   123
33/62 Wöhrmann Case   Two II C 1 (2)   93

13/63 Refrigerators Case   Four II C 1 (1)   249
66/63 Netherlands-High Authority Case   One III A (1)   1
                                             One IV D 2 (2)   18
75/63 Hoekstra-Unger Case   Four III B 2 b (1)   393
79,82/63 Reynier and Erba case   One III A (2)   2
90,91/63 Dairy Products Case   One V B 2 (1)   34
106–107/63 Toepfer Case   Two II A 2 c i (2)   63

6/64 Costa-ENEL Case   Two IV B 1 (2)   114
                                             Two IV D 1 (1)   121
                                             Three II A 1 (2)   161
                                             Four III C 1 a (1)   406
                                             Five III B 1 (1)   573
45/64 Tax refund in Italy Case   Two V B (1)   135
56,58/64 Grundig Case   Five II A 1 b i (1)   492

711

Name of the Case:	Chapter with subdivision:	page:
	Five II A 2 d i (1)	505
	Five II A 2 h i (1)	518
15/65 Schwarze Case	Two IV B 1 (3)	115
44/65 Hessische Knapschaft Case	Four III B 2 b (2)	395
48/65 Lütticke Case I	Two V B (4)	139
56/65 LTM-MBU Case	Five II A 1 b i (2)	494
	Five II A 2 a i (1)	502
	Five II A 2 g i (2)	517
57/65 Lütticke Case II	Four III A 2 c i (1)	264
61/65 Widow Vaassen Case	Two IV E 1 (1)	128
5,7,13–24/66 Kampffmeyer Case I	Two III A 2 (1)	97
8–11/66 Cement Convention Case	One V C 3 b (1)	45
	Two II A 2 a i (1)	55
5/67 Beus Case	Two II A 3 ci (2)	79
6/68 Zuckerfabrik Watenstedt Case	One V C 1 b (1)	36
7/68 Art treasures Case I	Four III A 1 a (1)	254
	Four III A 4 a (1)	323
13/68 Salgoil Case	Four III A 3 a (1)	299
14/68 Walt Wilhelm Case	Three II B 2 (2)	167
18/68 Eridania Case I	Two II B 1 (1)	87
24/68 Statistical Levy Case	Four III A 2 b i (1)	256
31/68 Chanel Case	Two IV C 2 (2)	119
4/69 Lütticke Case III	Two III A 2 (2)	100
5/69 Völk-Vervaecke Case	Five A 2 f i (1)	514
6,11/69 French rediscount Case	Five II C 1 (1)	547
	Five IV A 1 (1)	574
7/69 Wool imports Case	Two V B (2)	137
15/69 Ugliola Case	Four III B 1 c i (1)	358
29/69 Stauder Case	Three II C 2 (1)	174
38/69 Lead and Zinc Case	One IV B (2)	10
	One V A 2 (1)	33
40/69 Turkey Tail Case	One V C 1 b (2)	38

Name of the Case:	Chapter with subdivision:	page:
	Four III A 2 d i (1)	292
45/69 Boehringer Case I	Two III B 1 (1)	108
47/69 French textile industry Case	Five II C 1 (2)	547
48/69 ICI Case	Two II A 3 c i (4)	81
77/69 Wood Case	Two V B (3)	138
9/70 Grad Case	Three III B 3 (1)	181
11/70 Handelsgesellschaft Case	Two II A 3 d i (1)	82
	Three II C 2 (2)	174
	Five V A a i (2)	625
14/70 Deutsche Bakels Case	Four III A 2 d i (2)	294
15/70 Chevalley Case	Two II B 1 (2)	88
22/70 ERTA Case	One IV B (1)	6
	Two II A 1 a (2)	51
	Three II B 2 (3)	169
	Four II B 1 (2)	245
	Five V B 1 (1)	666
	Six I B (1)	676
25/70 Köster Case	One IV D 2 (3)	18
	Five V A 5 b i (1)	629
31/70 Deutsche Getreide Case	Five V A 5 a i (1)	624
39/70 Reliable Importers Case	Three II B 2 (1)	165
40/70 Sirena Case	Five II A 1 a iii aa (1)	491
41–44/70 Int.'l Fruit Company Case I	Two II A 2 c i (3)	65
59/70 Steel subsidies Case	Two II B 1 (3)	89
62/70 Chinese Mushrooms Case	Two II A 2 c i (4)	67
78/70 Deutsche Grammophon Case	Four II B 1 (1)	244
10/71 Port de Mertert Case	Five II B 1 (1)	541
23/71 Janssen Case	Four III B 2 b (4)	397
48/71 Art Treasures Case II	Two V B (5)	140
51–54/71 International Fruit Company Case II	Four II B 1 (3)	246
93/71 Slaughtered Cow Case I	Three III C 1 (1)	195
6/72 Continental Can Case	Five II A 3 d i (1)	532
8/72 VCH Case	Five II A 1 b i (3)	496
21–24/72 Int.'l Fruit Company Case III	Two II A 3 d i (2)	84
	Six II B (2)	682

713

Name of the Case:	Chapter with subdivision:	page:
39/72 Slaughtered Cow Case II	One V C 1 b (3)	40
	Three III C 1 (2)	197
70/72 Kohlegesetz Case	Two V B (6)	142
77/72 Capolongo Case	Four III A 2 b i (2)	260
4/73 Nold Case II	Two II A 3 di (3)	85
	Three II C 2 (2)	174
5/73 Balkan Import-Export Case	Five IV A 1 (2)	578
	Five V A 1 a (1)	610
	Five V A 7 b i (2)	659
8/73 Massey-Ferguson Case	One IV B (3)	12
48/73 Heacht Case II	Five II A 2 g i (1)	516
152/73 Sotgiu Case	Four III B 1 c i (2)	360
	Four III B 1 e i (1)	383
155/73 Sacchi Case	Five II B 1 (2)	542
158/73 Kampffmeijer Case III	Five V A 6 b i (1)	639
166/73 Rheinmühlen Case	Two IV C 2 (3)	120
167/73 French maritime labour code Case	Four II A 1 (1)	242
	Four III B 1 b i (1)	356
	Five V B1 (2)	666
173/73 Italian textile industry Case	Five II V 1 (3)	550
185/73 König Case	Five V A 2 a (1)	614
2/74 Reijners Case	Four III C 1 a (2)	407
8/74 Dassonville Case	Four III A 3 a (2)	302
8/74 Casagrande Case	Four III B 1 c i (3)	361
15/74 Centrafarm-Sterling Drug Case	Four III A 4 a (2)	324
31/74 Galli Case	Five V A 6 c iii aa (1)	646
33/74 Van Binsbergen Case	Four III C 2 a (1)	434
36/74 Walrave-Koch Case	Four III C 2 a (2)	438
39/74 Costa Case	Four III B 2 b (3)	396
41/74 Van Duyn Case	Four III B 1 b i (2)	357
	Four III B 1 d i (1)	366
48/74 Charmasson Case	Five V A 3 a (1)	619
67/74 Bonsignore Case	Four III B 1 d i (2)	370
71/74 Frubo Case	Five V A 4 a (1)	622
74/74 CNTA Case	Two III A 2 (3)	102
	Five V A 7 d i (1)	665
100/74 CAM Case	Two II A 2 b i (1)	57

Name of the Case:	Chapter with subdivision:	page:
1/75 Opinion of the Court	Six III B 2 (1)	686
23/75 Rey Soda Case	Five V A 5 b i (2)	629
24/75 Petroni Case	Four III B 2 b (6)	401
36/75 Rutili Case	Four III B 1 d i (3)	372
43/75 Defrenne Case II	Five IV B 1 (1)	582
48/75 Royer Case	Four III C 1 a (3)	411
50/75 Massonet Case	Four III B 2 b (5)	399
51/75 EMI-CBS Case	Four III A 4 a (4)	334
52/75 Marketing of vegetable seed Case	One V C 2 b (1)	42
60/75 Russo Case	Five V A 6 c iii aa (2)	649
	Five V 7 a i (1)	657
104/75 De Peijper Case	Four III A 4 a (3)	329
105/75 Giuffrida Case I	Two II A 3 b i (1)	76
110/75 Mills Case	One III A (3)	4
119/75 Terrapin-Terranova Case	Four III A 4 a (5)	336
1/76 Opinion of the Court	One IV D 2 (5)	23
	Five V B 1 (3)	666
	Six I B (2)	676
26/76 Metro Case I	Five II A 2 e i (1)	506
27/76 United Brands Case	Five II A 3 a i (1)	522
33/76 Rewe Case	Four II B 1 (4)	246
41/76 Donckerwolcke Case	Six III D 2 (1)	702
45/76 Comet Case	Three III C 1 (3)	198
46/76 Bauhuis Case	Four III A 2 b i (3)	262
49/76 Überseehandel Case	Four III A 2 d i (3)	296
50/76 Amsterdam Bulb Case	Five V A 6 c i aa (1)	641
51/76 Tax deduction Case	Three III B 3 (2)	184
71/76 Thieffry Case	Four III C 1 a (4)	414
78/76 Steinike Case	Five II C 1 (4)	553
85/76 Hoffmann-La Roche (vitamins) Case	Five II A 3 b i (1)	526
	Five II A 3 c i (1)	531
101/76 Scholten Honing Case I	Two II A 2 b i (2)	59
107/76 Hoffmann-La Roche Case I	Two IV D 1 (2)	122
111/76 Van den Hazel Case	Five V A 6 c ii aa (1)	644
5/77 Tedeschi Case	One IV d 2 (4)	21
8/77 German Aliens Act Case	Four III B 1 d i (4)	374
11/77 Patrick Case	Four III C 1 a (5)	417

Name of the Case:	Chapter with subdivision:	page:
30/77 Bouchereau Case	Four III B 1 d i (5)	378
38/77 Enka Case	One V C 2 b (29)	43
	Five III A 1 (1)	571
80–81/7 Commissionaires Réunies-Ramel Case	Five V A 3 a (2)	620
82/77 Van Tiggele Case	Four III A 3 a (3)	304
85/77 Santa Anna Case	Five V A 2 a (2)	616
106/77 Simmenthal Case II	Three III C 1 (4)	200
142/77 Statens Kontrol Case	Four III A 2 c i (2)	267
149/77 Defrenne Case III	Five IV B 1 (2)	589
156/77 Belgian Railway subsidies Case	Two II C 1 (3)	94
	Five V B 1 (4)	666
1/78 Opinion of the Court	Six III B 2 (2)	690
7/78 Thompson Case	Four III D 1 (1)	467
16/78 Choquet in redriving licence Case	Four III B 1 c i (4)	363
83/78 Pigs Marketing Board-Redmond Case	Five V A 6 c i aa (2)	642
103–109/78 Beauport Case	Five V A 6 a i (1)	637
110–111/78 Van Wesemael Case	Four III C 2 a (3)	441
115/78 Knoors Case	Four III C 1 a (7)	423
120/78 Cassis de Dijon Case	Four III A 3 a (4)	306
136/78 Auer Case	Four III C 1 a (6)	420
148/78 Ratti Case	Three III B 3 (3)	186
	Four III A 4 a (6)	339
171/78 Taxation of alcohol in Denmark Case	Four III a c i (4)	274
175/78 Saunders Case	Four III B 1 c i (5)	364
209–215,218/78 Fedetab Case	Five II A 2 b i (1)	503
251/78 Denkavit Case II	Five III A 1 (2)	572
15/79 Groenveld Case	Four III A 3 a (5)	312
34/79 Obscene articles Case	Four III A 4 a (7)	339
35/79 Taxation of alcohol in Ireland Case	Four III A 2 c i (3)	272
	Three II C 2 (4)	174
44/79 Hauer Case	Five V A 7 c i (1)	660
52/79 Debauve Case	Four III C 2 a (4)	443
55/79 Taxation of Alcohol in Ireland Case	Four III A 2 c i (3)	272
62/79 Coditel Case I	Four III C 2 a (6)	448

Name of the Case:	Chapter with subdivision:	page:
92/79 Italian sulphur Case	Five IV C 1 (1)	605
98/79 Pecastaing Case	Four III B 1 d i (6)	382
129/79 Macarthys-Smith Case	Five IV B 1 (3)	592
139/79 Maizena Case	Two II A 3 c i (3)	79
145/79 Roquette Case IV	Two IV F 1 (2)	133
147/79 Hochstrass Case	Four II C 1 (2)	250
149/79 Belgian enployment in public service Case	Four III B 1 c i (2)	383
730/79 Philip Morris Case	Five II C 1 (5)	558
804/79 Commission-United Kingdom Case	Six IV B (1)	705
27/80 Fietje Case	Four III A 3 a (6)	313
36,71/80 Irish excise duty Case	Five V A 6 c iii aa (3)	651
46/80 Vinal Case	Four III A 2 c i (5)	283
53/80 Eyssen Case	Four III A 4 a (8)	345
64/80 Giuffrida Case II	Two II A 2 b i (3)	60
66/80 International Chemical Corp. Case	Two IV F 1 (1)	131
96/80 Jenkins Case	Five IV B 1 (4)	594
155/80 Oebel Case	Four II C 1 (3)	252
	Four III A 3 a (7)	316
172/80 Züchner Case	Five II A 1 a ii aa (1)	487
	Five II A 2 c i (1)	504
203/80 Casati Case	Four III D 1 (2)	469
244/80 Foglia Novello Case II	Two IV B 1 (4)	116
246/80 Broekmeulen Case	Four III C 1 a (8)	428
279/80 Webb Case	Four III C 2 a (5)	446
8/81 Becker Case	Three III B 3 (4)	188
12/81 Garland Case	Five IV B 1 (5)	597
15/81 Schul Case	Four III A 2 c i (6)	285
19/81 Burton Case	Five IV B 1 (6)	599
60/81 IBM Case	Two II A 1 a (3)	53
95/81 Commission-Italy Case	Four III A 4 a (9)	348
102/81 Nordsee Case II	Two IV E 1 (2)	129
104/81 Küpferberg Case	Six II B (1)	677
249/81 Buy Irish Case	Four III A 3 a (8)	318
238/81 CILFIT Case I	Two IV D 1 (4)	124
262/81 Coditel Case II	Four III C 2 a (7)	449
292–293/81 Lion Case	Five V A 7 b i (1)	658

Name of the Case:	Chapter with subdivision:	page:
42/82 Wine Case	Two V B (8)	144
43,63/82 VBVB-VBBB Case	Five II A 2 h i (2)	520
191/82 FEDIOL Case	Six III C 2 (1)	696
239,275/82 Allied Corporation Case	Six III C 2 (2)	699
286/82, 26/83 Luisi and Carbone Case	Four III C 2 a (8)	450
	Four III D 1 (3)	474
	Five IV A 1 (3)	582
323/82 Intermills Case	Five II C 1 (6)	563
13/83 Failing transport policy Case	Five V B 1 (5)	670
41/83 British Telecom Case	Five II B 1 (3)	544
72/83 Campus Oil Case	Four III A 4 a (10)	348
77/83 CILFIT Case II	Five A 2 a (3)	617
107/83 Klopp Case	Four III C 1 a (9)	428
193/83 Windsurfing Case	Five II A 1 b i (4)	497
229/83 Leclerc Case	Five II A 4 a (1)	537
240/83 Waste oil Case	Five IV C 1 (2)	606
293/83 Gravier Case	Four III C 2 a (9)	454
	Five IV B 1 (8)	601
1/84 Ilford Order	Two II D 1 (1)	94
41/84 Pinna Case	Four III B 2 b (7)	404
42/84 Remia Case	Five II A 2 e i (2)	508
60–61/84 Cinéthèque Case	Four III A 3 a (9)	320
142,156/84 Philip Morris-Rothmans Case	Five II A 2 e i (3)	510
152/84 Marshall Case	Three III B 3 (5)	189
	Five IV B 1 (7)	601
169/84 COFAZ Case	Two II A 2 c i (5)	69
	Five II C 1 (7)	564
175/84 Krohn Case	Two III A 2 (4)	105
205/84 German insurance Case	Four III C 2 a (10)	454
209–213/84 Asjes (Nouvelles Frontières) Case	Five II A 1 a ii aa (2)	491
	Five V B 1 (6)	672
236/84 Malt Case	Five V A 5 c i (1)	633
250/84 Eridania Case II	Five V A 1 a (2)	611
	Five V A 7 b i (3)	659
5/85 AKZO Chemie Case	One IV D 2 (6)	29

Name of the Case:	Chapter with subdivision:	page:
89,104,114,116–117,125–129/85 Woodpulp Case	Five II A 1 a i aa (1)	484
157/85 Brugnoni Case	Four III D 1 (4)	478
314/85 Foto-Frost Case	Two IV D 1 (5)	126
325/85 Ireland-Commission Case	Six IV B (2)	709
58/86 South African maize Case	Five V A 5 a i (3)	627
68/86 Hormones Case	Five III A 1 (3)	573
	Five V A 6 c iv aa (1)	654
80/86 Kolpinghuis Case	Three III B 3 (5)	193
302/86 Danish bottle Case	Five IV C 1 (3)	608
81/87 Daily Mail Case	Four III C 1 a (10)	431
226/87 Public insurance Case	Two V B (7)	143

Table of extracted Cases, Decisions and Opinions – alphabetical

Name of the Case: *Chapter with subdivision:*   *page:*

A

AKZO Chemie Case (5/85)	One IV D 2 (6)	29
Allied Corporation Case (239,275/82)	Six III C 2 (2)	699
Amsterdam Bulb Case (50/76)	Five V A 6 c i aa (1)	641
Art Treasures Case I (7/68)	Four III A 1 a (1)	254
	Four III A 4 a (1)	323
Art Treasures Case II (48/71)	Two V B (5)	140
Asjes (Nouvelles Frontières) Case (209–213/84)	Five II A 1 a ii aa (2)	491
	Five V B 1 (6)	672
Auer Case (136/78)	Four III C 1 a (6)	420

B

Balkan Import-Export Case (5/73)	Five IV A 1 (2)	578
	Five V A 1 a (1)	610
	Five V A 7 b i (2)	659
Bauhuis Case (46/76)	Four III A 2 b i (3)	262
Beauport Case (103–109/78)	Five V A 6 a i (1)	637
Becker Case (8/81)	Three III B 3 (4)	188
Belgian employment in public service Case (149/79)	Four III B 1 e i (2)	383
Belgian Fromagerie Le Ski Case	Three IV C 1 b (1)	210
Belgian Railway subsidies Case (156/77)	Two II C 1 (3)	94
	Five V B 1 (4)	666
Beus Case (5/67)	Two II A 3 c i (2)	79
Boehringer Case I (45/69)	Two III B 1 (1)	108
Bonsignore Case (67/74)	Four III B 1 d i (2)	370
Bosch Case (13/61)	Two IV C 2 (1)	118
Bouchereau Case (30/77)	Four III B 1 d i (5)	378
Brennwein Case (24/62)	Two II A 3 c i (1)	77
British Telecom Case (41/83)	Five II B 1 (3)	544
Broekmeulen Case (246/80)	Four III C 1 a (8)	428
Brugnoni Case (157/85)	Four III D 1 (4)	478
Burton Case (19/81)	Five IV B 1 (6)	599
Buy Irish Case (249/81)	Four III A 3 a (8)	318

721

Name of the Case:	Chapter with subdivision:	page:

C

CAM Case (100/74)	Two II A 2 b i (1)	57
Campus Oil Case (72/83)	Four III A 4 a (10)	348
Capolongo Case (77/72)	Four III A 2 b i (2)	260
Casagrande Case (9/94)	Four III B 1 c i (3)	361
Casati Case (203/80)	Four III D 1 (2)	469
Cassis de Dijon Case (120/78)	Four III A 3 a (4)	306
Cement Convention Case (8–11/66)	One V C 3 b (1)	45
	Two II A 2 a i (1)	55
Centrafarm-Sterling Drug Case (15/74)	Four III A 4 a (2)	324
Chanel Case (31/68)	Two IV C 2 (2)	119
Charmasson Case (48/74)	Five V A 3 a (1)	619
Chevalley Case (15/70)	Two II B 1 (2)	88
Chinese Mushrooms Case (62/70)	Two II A 2 c i (4)	67
Choquet in re driving licence Case (16/78)	Four III B 1 c i (4)	363
Christiani and Nielsen Decision	Five II A 1 c i (2)	500
CILFIT Case I (238/81)	Two IV D 1 (4)	124
CILFIT Case II (77/83)	Five A 2 a (3)	617
Cinéthèque Case (60–61/84)	Four III A 3 a (9)	320
CNTA Case (74/74)	Two III A 2 (3)	102
	Five V A 7 d i (1)	665
Coditel Case I (62/79)	Four III C 2 a (6)	448
Coditel Case II (262/81)	Four III C 2 a (7)	449
COFAZ Case (169/84)	Two II A 2 c i (5)	69
	Five II C 1 (7)	564
Comet Case (45/76)	Three III C 1 (3)	198
Commissionaires Réunies-Ramel Case (80–81/77)	Five V A 3 a (2)	620
Commission – Italy Case (95/81)	Four III A 4 a (9)	348
Commission – United Kingdom Case (804/79)	Six IV B (1)	705
Continental Can Case (6/72)	Five II A 3 d i (1)	532
Costa Case (39/74)	Four III B 2 b (3)	396
Costa – ENEL Case (6/64)	Two IV B 1 (2)	114
	Two IV D 1 (1)	121
	Three II A 1 (2)	161
	Four III C 1 a (1)	406
	Five III B 1 (1)	573

D

Da Costa-Schaake Case (28–30/62)	Two IV D 1 (3)	123
Daily Mail Case (81/87)	Four III C 1 a (10)	431

Name of the Case:	Chapter with subdivision:	page:
Dairy Products Case (90.91/63)	One V B 2 (1)	34
Danish bottle Case (302/86)	Five IV C 1 (3)	608
Dassonville Case (8/74)	Four III A 3 a (2)	302
Debauve Case (52/79)	Four III C 2 a (4)	443
Defrenne Case II (43/75)	Five IV B 1 (1)	582
Defrenne Case III (149/77)	Five IV B 1 (2)	589
Denkavit Case II (251/78)	Five III A 1 (2)	572
De Peijper Case (104/75)	Four III A 4 a (3)	329
Deutsche Bakels Case (14/70)	Four III A 2 d i (2)	294
Deutsche Getreide Case (31/70)	Five V A 5 a i (1)	624
Deutsche Grammophon Case (78/70)	Four II B 1 (1)	244
Donckerwolcke Case (41/76)	Six III D 2 (1)	702

E

EMI-CBS Case (51/75)	Four III A 4 a (4)	334
Enka Case (38/77)	One V C 2 b (2)	43
	Five III A 1 (1)	571
Eridania Case I (18/68)	Two II B 1 (1)	82
Eridania Case II (250/84)	Five V A 1 a (2)	611
	Five V A 7 b i (3)	659
ERTA Case (22/70)	One IV B (1)	6
	Two II A 1 a (2)	51
	Three II B 2 (3)	169
	Four II B 1 (2)	245
	Five V B 1 (1)	666
	Six I B (1)	676
Eyssen Case (53/80)	Four III A 4 a (8)	345

F

Failing transport policy Case (13/83)	Five V B 1 (5)	670
Fedetab Case (209–215,218/78)	Five II A 2 b i (1)	503
FEDIOL Case (191–82)	Six III C 2 (1)	696
Fietje Case (27/80)	Four III A 3 a (6)	313
Foglia Novello Case II (244/80)	Two IV B 1 (4)	116
FOTO-FROST Case (314–85)	Two IV D 1 (5)	126
French maritime labour code Case (167/73)	Four II A 1 (1)	242
	Four III B 1 b i (1)	356
	Five V B 1 (2)	666
French Ramel Case	Three IV B 2 b (1)	206

723

Name of the Case:	Chapter with subdivision:	page:
French rediscount Case (6,11/69)	Five II C 1 (1)	547
	Five IV A 1 (1)	574
French textile industry Case (47/69)	Five II C 1 (2)	547
French Vabres Case	Three IV B 2 b (2)	208
Frubo Case (71/74)	Five V A 4 a (1)	622

G

Galli Case (31/74)	Five V A 6 c iii aa (1)	646
Garland Case (12/81)	Five IV B 1 (5)	597
Geitling Case I (2/56)	Two II A 1 a (1)	51
German Aliens Act Case (8/77)	Four III B 1 d i (4)	374
German Handelsgesellschaft Case	Three IV C 2 b (1)	214
German insurance Case (205/84)	Four III C 2 a (10)	454
Giuffrida Case I (105/75)	Two II A 3 b i (1)	76
Giuffrida Case II (64/80)	Two II A 2 b i (3)	60
Grad Case (9/70)	Three III B 3 (1)	181
Gravier Case (293/83)	Four III C 2 a (9)	454
	Five IV B 1 (8)	601
Groenveld Case (15/79)	Four III A 3 a (5)	312
Grundig Case (56, 58/64)	Five II A 1 b i (1)	492
	Five II A 2 d i (1)	505
	Five II A 2 h i (1)	518

H

Handelsgesellschaft Case (11/70)	Two II A 3 d i (1)	82
	Three II C 2 (2)	174
	Five A 5 a i (2)	625
	Three II C 2 (4)	174
Hauer Case (44/79)	Five A 7 c i (1)	660
Heacht Case II (48/73)	Five II A 2 g i (1)	506
Hessische Knapschaft Case (44/65)	Four III B 2 b (2)	395
Hochstrass Case (147/79)	Four II C 1 (2)	250
Hoekstra-Unger Case (75/63)	Four III B 2 b (1)	393
Hoffmann-La Roche Case I (107/76)	Two IV D 1 (2)	122
Hoffmann-La Roche (vitamins) Case (85/76)	Five II A 3 b i (1)	526
	Five II A 3 c i (1)	531
Hormones Case (68/86)	Five III A 1 (3)	573
	Five V A 6 iv aa (1)	654

Name of the Case:	Chapter with subdivision:	page:

I

IBM Case (60/81)	Two II 1 a (3)	53
ICI Case (48/69)	Two II A 3 c i (4)	81
Ilford Order (1/84R)	Two II D 1 (1)	94
Intermills Case (323/82)	Five II C 1 (6)	563
Int.'l Chemical Corporation Case (66/80)	Two IV F 1 (1)	131
Int.'l Fruit Company Case I (41–44/70)	Two II A 2 ci (3)	65
Int.'l Fruit Company Case II (51–54/71)	Four II B 1 (3)	246
Int.'l Fruit Company Case III (21–24/72)	Two II A 3 d i (2)	84
	Six II B (2)	682
Ireland – Commission Case (325/85)	Six IV B (2)	709
Irish excise duty Case (36,71/80)	Five V A 6 c iii aa (3)	651
Italian Costa-ENEL Case	Three IV C 3 b (1)	221
Italian Frontini Case	Three IV C 3 b (2)	223
Italian Granital Case	Three IV C 3 b (4)	226
Italian ICIC Case	Three IV C 3 b (3)	225
Italian sulphur Case (92/79)	Five IV C 1 (1)	605
Italian textile industry Case (173/73)	Five II C 1 (3)	550

J

Janssen Case (23/71)	Four III B 2 b (4)	397
Jenkins Case (96/80)	Five IV B 1 (4)	594

K

Kampffmeyer Case I (5,7,13–24/66)	Two III A 2 (1)	97
Kampffmeyer Case III (158/73)	Five V A 6 b i (1)	639
Klopp Case (107/83)	Four III C 1 a (9)	428
Knoors Case (115/78)	Four III C 1 a (7)	423
Kohlegesetz Case (70/72)	Two V B (6)	142
Kolpinghuis Case (80/86)	Three III B 3 (5)	193
König Case (185/73)	Five V A 2 a (1)	614
Köster Case (25/70)	One IV D 2 (3)	18
	Five V A 5 b i (1)	629
Krohn Case II (175/84)	Two III A 2 (4)	105
Küpferberg Case (104/81)	Six II B (1)	677

725

Name of the Case:	Chapter with subdivision:	page:

L

Lead and Zinc Case (38/69)	One IV B (2)	10
	One V A 2 (1)	33
Leclerc Case (229/83)	Five II A 4 a (1)	537
Lion Case (292–293/81)	Five V A 7 b i (1)	658
LTM-MBU Case (56/65)	Five II A 1 b i (2)	494
	Five II A 2 a i (1)	502
	Five II A 2 g i (2)	517
Luisi and Carbone Case (286/82, 26/83)	Four III C 2 a (8)	450
	Four III D 1 (3)	474
	Five IV A 1 (3)	582
Lütticke Case I (48/65)	Two V B (4)	139
Lütticke Case II (57/65)	Four III A 2 c i (1)	264
Lütticke Case III (4/69)	Two III A 2 (2)	100

M

Macarthys-Smith Case (129/79)	Five IV B 1 (3)	592
Maizena Case (139/79)	Two II A 3 c i (3)	79
Malt Case (236/84)	Five V A 5 c i (1)	633
Marketing of vegetable seed Case (52/75)	One V C 2 b (1)	42
Marshall Case (152/84)	Three B 3 (5)	189
	Five IV B 1 (7)	601
Massey-Ferguson Case (8/73)	One IV B (3)	12
Massonet Case (50/75)	Four III B 2 b (5)	399
Meroni Case (9/56)	One IV D 2 (1)	18
	Two II A 3 a i (1)	73
	Two II C 1 (1)	91
Metro Case I (26/76)	Five II A 2 e i (1)	506
Mills Case (110/75)	One III A (3)	4

N

Netherlands – High Authority Case (66/63)	One III A (1)	1
	One IV D 2 (2)	18
Nold Case II (4/73)	Two II A 3 d i (3)	85
	Three II C 2 (3)	174
Nordsee Case II (102/81)	Two IV E 1 (2)	129

Name of the Case:	Chapter with subdivision:	page:

O

Obscene articles Case (34/79)	Four III A 4 a (7)	339
Oebel Case (155/80)	Four II C 1 (3)	252
	Four III A 3 a (7)	316
Opinion of the Court (1/75)	Six III B 2 (1)	686
Opinion of the Court (1/76)	One IV D 2 (5)	23
	Five V B 1 (3)	666
	Six I B (2)	676
Opinion of the Court (1/78)	Six III B 2 (2)	690

P

Patrick Case (11/77)	Four III C 1 a (5)	417
Pecastaing Case (98/79)	Four III B 1 d i (6)	382
Petroni Case (24/75)	Four III B 2 b (6)	401
Philip Morris Case (730/79)	Five II C 1 (5)	558
Philip Morris – Rothmans Case (142,156/84)	Five II A 2 e i (3)	510
Pigs Marketing Board – Redmond Case (83/78)	Five V A 6 c i aa (2)	642
Pinna Case (41/84)	Four III B 2 b (7)	404
Plaumann Case (25/62)	Two II A 2 c i (1)	61
Port de Mertert Case (10/71)	Five II B 1 (1)	541
Publication of Transport Tariffs Case (25/59)	One IV C 2 (1)	14
Public insurance Case (226/87)	Two V B (7)	143

R

Ratti Case (148/78)	Three III B 3 (3)	186
	Four III A 4 a (6)	339
Refrigerators Case (13/63)	Four II C 1 (1)	249
Reliable Importers Case (39/70)	Three II B 2 (1)	165
Remia Case (42/84)	Five II A 2 e i (2)	508
Reuter-BASF Decision	Five III A 1 c i (1)	499
Rewe Case (33/76)	Four II B 1 (4)	246
Reijners Case (2/74)	Four III C 1 a (2)	407
Reynier and Erba Case (79, 82/63)	One III A (2)	2
Rey Soda Case (22/75)	Five V A 5 b i (2)	629

Name of the Case:	Chapter with subdivision:	page:
Rheinmühlen Case (166/73)	Two IV C 2 (3)	120
Roquette Case IV (145/79)	Two IV F 1 (2)	133
Royer Case (48/75)	Four III C 1 a (3)	411
Russo Case (60/75)	Five V A 6 c iii aa (2)	649
	Five V A 7 a i (1)	657
Rutili Case (36/75)	Four III B 1 d i (3)	372

S

Sacchi Case (155/73)	Five II B 1 (2)	542
Salgoil Case (13/68)	Four III A 3 a (1)	299
Santa Anna Case (85/78)	Five V A 2 a (2)	616
Saunders Case (175/78)	Four III B 1 c i (5)	364
Scholten Honig Case I (101/76)	Two II A 2 b i (2)	59
Schul Case (15/81)	Four III A 2 c i (6)	285
Schwarze Case (15/65)	Two IV B 1 (3)	115
Simmenthal Case II	Three III C 1 (4)	200
Sirena Case (40/70)	Five II A 1 a iii aa (1)	491
Slaughtered Cow Case I (92/71)	Three III C 1 (1)	195
Slaughtered Cow Case II (39/72)	One V C 1 b (3)	40
	Three III C 1 (2)	197
Sotgiu Case (152/73)	Four III B 1 c i (2)	360
	Four III B 1 c i (1)	383
South African maize Case (58/86)	Five V A 5 a i (3)	627
Statens Kontrol Case (142/77)	Four III A 2 c i (2)	267
Statistical Levy Case (24/68)	Four III A 2 b i (1)	256
Stauder Case (29/69)	Three II C 2 (1)	174
Steel subsidies Case (59/70)	Two II B 1 (3)	89
Steinike Case (78/76)	Five II C 1 (4)	553

T

Taxation of alcohol in Denmark Case (171/80)	Four III A 2 c i (4)	274
Taxation of alcohol in Ireland Case (55/79)	Four III A 2 c i (3)	272
Tax deduction Case (51/76)	Three III B 2 (2)	184
Tax refund in Italy Case (45/64)	Two V B (1)	135
Tedeschi Case (5/77)	One IV D 2 (4)	21
Terrapin-Terranova Case (119/75)	Four III A 4 a (5)	336

Name of the Case:	Chapter with subdivision:	page:
Thieffry Case (71/76)	Four III C 1 a (4)	414
Thompson Case (7/178)	Four III D 1 (1)	467
Toepfer Case (106–107/163)	Two II A 2 c i (2)	63
Turkey Tail Case (40/69)	One V C 1 b (2)	38
	Four III A 2 d i (1)	292

U

Uberseehandel Case (49/76)	Four III A 2 d i (3)	296
Ugliola Case (15/69)	Four III B 1 c i (1)	358
United Brands Case (27/76)	Five II A 3 a i (1)	522

V

Van Binsbergen Case (33/74)	Four III C 2 a (1)	434
Van den Hazel Case (111/76)	Five V A 6 c ii aa (1)	644
Van Duyn Case (41/74)	Four III B 1 b i (2)	357
	Four III B 1 d i (1)	366
Van Gend en Loos Case (26/62)	Two IV B 1 (1)	110
	Three II A 1 (1)	160
	Four III A 2 a i (1)	255
Van Tiggele Case (82/77)	Four III A 3 a (3)	304
Van Wesemael Case (110–111/78)	Four III C 2 a (3)	441
VBVB-VBBB Case (43,63/82)	Five II A 2 h i (2)	520
VCH Case (8/72)	Five II A 1 b i (3)	496
Vinal Case (46/80)	Four III A 2 c i (5)	283
Völk-Vervaecke Case (5/69)	Five II A 2 f i (1)	514

W

Walrave-Koch Case (36/74)	Four III C 2 a (2)	438
Walt Wilhelm Case (14/68)	Three II B 2 (2)	167
Waste oil Case (240/83)	Five IV C 1 (2)	606
Webb Case (279/80)	Four III C 2 a (5)	446
Widow Vaassen Case (61/65)	Two IV E 1 (1)	128
Windsurfing Case (193/83)	Five II A 1 b i (4)	497
Wine Case (42/82R)	Two V B (8)	144
Wöhrmann Case (33/62)	Two II C 1 (2)	93
Wood Case (77/69)	Two V B (3)	138

Name of the Case:	Chapter with subdivision:	page:
Woodpulp Case (89, 104, 114, 116–117, 125–129/85)	Five II A 1 a i aa (1)	484
Wool imports Case (7/69)	Two V B (2)	137

Z

Zuckerfabrik Watenstedt Case (6/68)	One V C 1 b (1)	36
Züchner Case (172/80)	Five II A 1 a ii aa (1)	487
	Five II A 2 c i (1)	504